Albemarle: Jefferson's County

1727-1976

ALBEMARLE
Jefferson's County
1727–1976

John Hammond Moore

Published for the
ALBEMARLE COUNTY HISTORICAL SOCIETY
by the
UNIVERSITY PRESS OF VIRGINIA
Charlottesville

THE UNIVERSITY PRESS OF VIRGINIA
Copyright © 1976 by the Rector and Visitors
of the University of Virginia

First published 1976

as the Albemarle County Historical Society's
contribution to the Bicentennial

Library of Congress Cataloging in Publication Data

Moore, John Hammond.
    Albemarle, Jefferson's county, 1727–1976.

    Bibliography: p. 493.
    Includes index.
    1.   Albemarle Co., Va.—History.   I.   Albemarle
County Historical Society.   II.   Title.
F232.A3M66   975.5′482   76–13860
ISBN 0–8139–0645–8

Printed in the United States of America

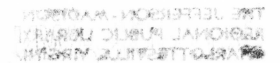

There are many persons
who even consider it to be the
garden of the United States.

—Isaac Weld (1796)

Preface

Telling local history is an awesome task, especially that of a county such as Albemarle where life has been dominated from time to time by figures important on the national scene and where an educational institution has wielded great influence. Perhaps it is both refreshing and a bit sobering to realize that for every American who knows this lovely Piedmont region as the home of Thomas Jefferson and his university, another probably views these Blue Ridge foothills only as the realm of television's John-Boy Walton. This volume is not, however, the story of Jefferson, Madison, Monroe, and other luminaries of that golden age in our nation's past, nor is it, of course, the saga of any mythical family. Instead, the focus of the tale unfolding in the following pages is the people of Albemarle County through two hundred and fifty years of their history, how they made a living, and how they coped with problems and opportunities presented by a frontier existence, wars, seasons both good and bad, and constantly changing conditions—local, state, national, even international at times. To a marked degree their experiences mirror those of millions of other Americans as they struggled to create homes in a New World, fought for independence from British rule, and tried to build a stable agricultural society which, since 1900, has become increasingly urban.

Like all local histories spanning two centuries or more, Albemarle's story is based upon official documents, newspaper files, recollections and reminiscences of various kinds, and a healthy helping of folklore which, once committed to print, inevitably has gained the imprimatur of truth. This region drained by the Rivanna and the James rivers is especially fortunate in having long been peopled by individuals with a sense of history, a love and reverence for the past, and a keen appreciation for the vital influence that past can have upon future generations. Families have retained thousands of records, some personal in nature, others shedding light upon political, social, religious, and community affairs through the years. The University of Virginia has become a depository for vast collections of manuscripts, many of them relating to the Old Dominion, some to Charlottesville, Scottsville, Greenwood, and other towns and villages dotting the local countryside. Scholars and students have delved into these materials to produce countless books, articles, dissertations, and theses describing the life of both state and county. Since 1940 the Albemarle County Historical Society has been in the forefront of efforts to preserve more and more of this regional past, and to its members go full credit for conceiving and fostering publication of this book.

As chairman of the society's History Committee, Professor Edward Younger of the University of Virginia's Corcoran Department of History directed this project. He was very ably assisted by Professor William W. Abbot, James A. Bear, Jr., Bernard P. Chamberlain, Professor Oron J. Hale, and Mrs. William B. Murphy, secretary of the committee. Thomas C. Barringer, who served as fund raiser for the project, was named to the group following the death of John M. Nalle in 1973. Professor Charles K. Woltz, while president of the society, initiated this undertaking, and his successor as president, Charles E. Moran, Jr., provided invaluable leadership. Both men served as ex-officio members of the History Committee. Professor Younger succeeded Mr. Moran as president and continued to direct the project until the book was published. All of these individuals read the manuscript and made critical comments and helpful suggestions, as did Virginius Dabney and Professors Bernard Mayo, David Alan Williams, and Francis L. Berkeley, Jr.

I would like to express my sincere appreciation to the committee members and others who assisted them for their cooperation and encouragement and to the membership of the Albemarle County Historical Society at large. Scores gave freely of their time, granted interviews, and both answered and asked provocative, stimulating questions. I also would like to thank Karen Dawley Paul for her assistance in preparation of the manuscript and the Thomas Jefferson Memorial Foundation for fellowship support.

JOHN HAMMOND MOORE

April 13, 1975

Contents

Preface   vii

Part I   Tobacco, Turmoil, and Triumph, 1727–1820   1

Chapter 1   In the Beginning   5
Chapter 2   First Settlers, First Families, First Things   16
Chapter 3   Making a Living   31
Chapter 4   Albemarle in the Revolutionary War   45
Chapter 5   Thomas Walker's Albemarle   68
Chapter 6   In the Shadow of Monticello   87

Part II   The Lean Years, 1820–1888   107

Chapter 7   That Vexatious Institution   111
Chapter 8   The University   128
Chapter 9   The World of Judith Rives   150
Chapter 10   Turnpikes, Canals, and Steam Engines   176
Chapter 11   Albemarle in the Civil War   191
Chapter 12   The Freedman's Albemarle   214
Chapter 13   Seeds of Change   239

Part III   Decades of Diversity and Innovation, 1888–1945   271

Chapter 14   Trolley Cars, Autos, Industry, and Suburbs   275
Chapter 15   An Educational Revolution   308
Chapter 16   Tom Martin's Albemarle   333
Chapter 17   Roaring Twenties, Troubled Thirties   366
Chapter 18   Albemarle in World War II   391

Part IV   An Urban City-County, 1945–1976   419

Chapter 19   Race Relations, Annexation, and Rural Change   423
Chapter 20   Bill Hildreth's Charlottesville   445
Chapter 21   Albemarle—The Lucky County   471

Appendixes   479

A   Albemarle Soldiers of the Revolutionary War   481
B   Telephone Subscribers in Charlottesville and Albemarle
      County, 1901   486
C   Albemarle County Newspapers   491

Sources for Charlottesville-Albemarle History   493
Index   497
Illustration Credits   531

Illustrations

1. Looking east from Rockfish Gap   11
2. William Anne Keppel, earl of Albemarle   11
3. Order Book, Albemarle County Court, 1744/45–1748   24
4. Transporting tobacco to market   37
5. The Barracks, 1779   59
6. Thomas Walker   63
7. Castle Hill   63
8. Jack Jouett   63
9. Banastre Tarleton   63
10. Thomas Jefferson   91
11. Monticello   91
12. Plan of Charlottesville, 1818   101
13. Edward Coles   135
14. Francis Walker Gilmer   135
15. William Holmes McGuffey   135
16. James Alexander   135
17. University of Virginia, 1856   143
18. Judith Rives   157
19. James River and Kanawha Canal   184
20. John Bowie Strange   198
21. Sarah Ann Strickler (Mrs. Robert Herndon Fife)   198
22. Flag presented to Stuart's Horse Artillery   198
23. Old Ash Lawn   225
24. First Baptist Church—Colored   225
25. David P. Powers   241
26. John E. Massey   241
27. John B. Minor   241
28. Henry Clay Marchant   241
29. Jefferson Monroe Levy   241
30. The Reverend Edgar Woods   241
31. Albemarle sawmill, ca. 1895   247
32. Edgehill School, class of 1891   251
33. Sewing class at Miller School, 1899   251
34. Greenwood School for Boys, 1897   265
35. Albemarle County Courthouse   265
36. Charlottesville's Main Street, ca. 1890   280
37. Charlottesville and Albemarle Railway employees   280
38. Streetcar at the University of Virginia   283

39. J. P. "Dry Goods" Ellington in Charlottesville's first auto   291
40. Electric ranges for Wertenbaker Apartments, 1916   291
41. Ralph W. Holsinger and friends   298
42. Dr. Paul B. Barringer and Dr. William Randolph   298
43. Martha Jefferson Hospital   306
44. University of Virginia Hospital, 1901   306
45. Edwin A. Alderman   322
46. Rotunda banquet honoring Alderman, 1905   322
47. R. T. W. Duke, Jr.   337
48. Thomas Staples Martin   337
49. Hollis Rinehart   337
50. John Armstrong Chaloner   337
51. World War I parade   348
52. Negro Odd Fellows march up Main Street, 1915   348
53. Tom Martin's law office   363
54. Paul Goodloe McIntire   371
55. Black choir on Rotunda steps during war loan drive   399
56. Veterans' housing on Copeley Hill   399
57. Alexander Archer Vandergrift   409
58. John S. Battle, Sr.   409
59. Mary Rawlings   409
60. William S. Hildreth   447
61. George R. B. Michie   447
62. Morton Frozen Foods, Crozet   458
63. University of Virginia installs fifth president.   462
64. Medical School complex   465
65. John-Boy Walton on the Hatton Ferry   468
66. A Bicentennial event: the restored Rotunda   470
67. Tally-ho!   472
68. "All my wishes end, where I hope my days will end, at
    Monticello."   477

Tables

1. Rates at Albemarle ordinaries, 1745   26
2. Albemarle County tax returns, 1782   84
3. Albemarle County population, 1820–60   115
4. Canal freight, Scottsville, 1842   186
5. Albemarle County population, 1870   215
6. Area population, 1890   238
7. City-county population, 1890–1920   276
8. Local bank assets and resources, 1921   300
9. Area industrial operations, 1922   303

10. Public education, Albemarle County, 1905   324
11. Albemarle County schools, 1910–20   328
12. Local religious membership, 1916   342
13. Growth of Charlottesville by annexation   438
14. Population growth, 1950–70   449
15. Major manufacturing firms in the Charlottesville-Albemarle
    area, 1972   454–456

Maps

1. Big Albemarle, 1744–61   7
2. Albemarle, 1780–1800   73
3. Charlottesville, ca. 1828   116–117
4. Roads and Canals, 1850   178
5. Railroads, 1900   285

   Maps 1, 2, 4, and 5 drawn by J. Middleton Freeman

Part I
Tobacco, Turmoil, and Triumph
1727–1820

THE essential fact of Albemarle life during these years is the creation of a prosperous, stable community wrested from virgin frontier. The county's early citizens were spared bloody confrontation with Indian tribes and never suffered the attacks from England's enemies that made day-to-day existence so hazardous in other colonies and in the western counties of Frederick and Augusta. But the men and women who took up the arduous task of establishing new homes, farms, and plantations in the foothills of the Blue Ridge had to contend with the loneliness of isolation, separation from loved ones, and the rigors that wilderness living imposes upon all who dare to push forward into its depths.

Most of these hardy folk came from the east, bringing with them attitudes and customs nurtured during the first century of English settlement in the Tidewater; however, in their midst—in fact, perhaps waiting to greet them—was an important Scotch-Irish minority which came down through the gaps of the mountain range forming Albemarle's western boundary. Although the easterners clearly intended to re-create a low-country society as quickly as possible and the settlers from the Valley envisioned merely an extension of the life they had known on the other side of the Blue Ridge, what emerged was somewhat different from what each group contemplated as they cleared land, created fields, and planted crops. Three basic elements brought about this change: the soil of Albemarle, its system of rivers and streams, and the tyranny of distance. Most of these early settlers came in search of new land on which to grow tobacco, and soon, dark green, broad-leafed plants were shooting up in hundreds of little clearings dotting the countryside. Since the entire economy of colonial Virginia was geared to production of this crop, even the Scotch-Irish found themselves caught up in a tobacco-slave way of life. Within a few years their hogsheads also were gliding down the James toward warehouses located at the fall line, and some even found themselves masters of a handful of black workers.

But by the 1760s it was becoming apparent to all that Albemarle's soil was not well suited to tobacco, and those distant from waterways always experienced difficulty getting their crop to market. As county residents were wrestling with these truths, they were forced to turn their attention to revolution. This they did with outspoken vigor, an attitude prompted undoubtedly by concern for a ready supply of still more new land in the west which, they thought, could solve their immediate agricultural dilemma. However, just as Albemarle's soil and terrain changed their lives, so did war. The enemy, as marauders, only appeared once, but as prisoners they came by the thousands and almost overnight nearly doubled the local population. Their presence, as well as the Revolutionary War itself, produced unusual demand for a local crop which always had been of some importance: wheat. Once dethroned, tobacco never regained its former prominence, and by the turn of the century wheat reigned supreme. This golden harvest also gave birth to better highways, ready access to markets, and commercial activity which made of Albemarle a regional crossroads. The result was an agricultural community which looked, at times, much more like Valley than Tidewater, but with two very important differences. Many of the wheat fields were within the confines of large estates, and thousands of slaves left over from the days of tobacco tilled their sprawling acres.

There is one other factor, difficult to assess but nonetheless important, that sets Albemarle apart from other Virginia counties in the Piedmont. The masters of its estates were men of unusual ability and breeding. Thomas Jefferson, by far the best known, is merely representative of this distinctive class. Many were the product of several generations of, if not wealth, better than average circumstances. Often sons of aggressive, self-made Tidewater gentry and not frontiersmen in the usual buckskin sense, they flocked to the Piedmont in the mid-1700s to develop tobacco land. They stayed on to grow wheat and discovered in Albemarle a comfortable existence which began to exert upon them a strange charm which exists for many of their descendants even today. These men were an intelligent lot, well educated for their day, who soon built great houses appropriate to their extensive lands. Few of these homes remain from pre-Revolutionary decades, and nearly all have been altered somewhat through intervening years, but structures such as Edgehill, Morven, Old Woodville, Tallwood, Edgemont, and, of course, Monticello reveal better than mere words the society they were designed to serve. However, before getting lost in a dream realm of days gone by, one should remember at all times that these founders of Albemarle were, for the most part, hardheaded, multipurpose businessmen striving for worldly success. One individual's interests (and income) frequently encompassed agriculture, medicine, surveying, land speculation, and politics, as well as the military arts, theology, and mercantile trade.

By 1820 or so these men and their offspring had created a thriving community of nearly twenty thousand souls which had a newspaper and a handful of little towns (most of them river depots) and was busy building, of all things, a university! The secret of Albemarle's success during these early decades lies, of course, in both geography and events that often took place many miles away; but most of all, credit must be given to an intelligent, adaptable leadership—men who knew a good land when they saw it and were willing to change even their livelihood to remain there.

Yet within this highly individual society, even in triumph, lay seeds of discord and trouble. A countryside of great slave estates is not calculated to attract new inhabitants searching for a land of opportunity, and even some native-born citizens may become restless and move on, as they certainly did in substantial numbers during the nineteenth century. There is, of course, great irony in this tale. Mr. Jefferson and his neighbors who had done so much to forge the American nation had created at home, in their Albemarle, a way of life which their children would be forced to defend with much rhetoric and even with their blood.

Chapter 1

In the Beginning

MUCH of Albemarle County's early story lies shrouded in mystery. Indian braves, fearless fur trappers, and frontier squatters certainly lived from time to time in this lovely, rolling countryside nestled in the shadows of the Blue Ridge Mountains. Hardy explorers and would-be planters marveled at its beauty and dreamed of its potential, but not until 1727, one hundred and twenty years after Jamestown, did someone "seat and plant" a grant on Albemarle's soil. And another seventeen years would elapse before the name "Albemarle" appeared on maps of the Old Dominion.

Captain John Smith and Thomas Jefferson both wrote about the Indians of the region. Smith learned of the Monacans and their town of Monasukapanough from natives he met in eastern Virginia in 1607. They told him the Monacans were their friends and "did dwell as they in the hilly Countries by small rivers, living upon rootes and fruits, but chiefly by hunting." [1] In his *Notes on the State of Virginia* Jefferson described how he excavated a burial mound on the south branch of the Rivanna River about two miles above its principal fork. Upon examination of skeletal remains, he concluded the site contained about a thousand bodies arranged in several levels with dirt and stone covering each layer. He found no evidence of battle wounds, nor did he think this was "a common sepulchre for a town." Jefferson remarked that when he was a youth, a party of Indians passing through the county went directly to this mound "without any instructions or inquiry, and having staid about it for some time, with expressions which were construed to be those of sorrow, they returned to the high road, which they had left about half a dozen miles to pay this visit."

According to local legend, about 1840 another party of Indians appeared seeking permission to perform memorial services at a burial mound located on the grounds of Tallwood, a Coles estate in the southern part of the county. When this request was granted, they conducted a series of dances watched with considerable interest by

[1] Smith, *The General Historie of Virginia, New England, and the Summer Isles* (2 vols.; Glasgow and New York, 1907), 1:131.

many citizens. This is apparently the last time that descendants of Albemarle's aboriginal inhabitants were seen in the county.

In this century two scholars, David I. Bushnell, Jr., and Dr. Charlton G. Holland, Jr., have shed more light upon these early residents.[2] They have established that the village of Monasukapanough was located close by Jefferson's mound, about one-half mile above the Rivanna's fork, an area visible from Route 29 North. Holland has found Indian artifacts at some sixty-three sites along rivers and streams that flow through the surrounding countryside. It is now apparent that these seventeenth-century inhabitants were the Saponi, linguistically of Sioux stock, and part of a Monacan confederacy. Sometime before 1700 they migrated to the southwest and settled for a time in North Carolina, by no means the last of Albemarle's citizens to succumb to the lure of new lands lying beyond the setting sun. It is possible that the Saponi once lived in the Tidewater and were forced out by the rise of the powerful Indian group headed by Powhatan when the first Englishmen arrived at Jamestown. If so, then they undoubtedly pushed out still earlier residents of Albemarle County, and remains found today may reflect two or more distinct native cultures. Anyway, by the time white settlers ventured into the valley of the upper James River they had no reason to fear hostile arrows or war whoops: the Indians had departed.

In a sense, much that occurred in this region before 1744 can be classified as Albemarle County's prehistory, not only Indian life but what white men did there as well. And it is equally true that what was happening in eastern Virginia and even in faraway London had profound effect upon the emerging Piedmont frontier. By the first decades of the eighteenth century, because of factors in both the Old and New Worlds, Virginians were poised for an unprecedented push to the west, the first of many which would become a continuing theme in our nation's history. The need to find new land for tobacco crops was obvious to all, the Indian threat was gone, and slave labor was becoming more plentiful. In addition, Virginians now were able to buy land directly from the crown, thus bypassing the cumbersome and frequently abused headright system. With the stage set for change, at precisely the right moment Alexander Spotswood appeared in Williamsburg as lieutenant governor and gave voice to yet another argument for expansion: colonial defense. Fearful of French activity

---

[2] See Bushnell, "Evidences of Indian Occupancy in Albemarle County, Virginia," *Smithsonian Miscellaneous Collections* 89 (1933):7–10, and Holland, "Albemarle before 1700," *Magazine of Albemarle County History* 9 (1949):5–12, hereafter cited as *MACH*.

BIG ALBEMARLE, 1744-1761

Early Albemarle included present counties of Nelson, Buckingham, Amherst, Fluvanna, Appomattox, and part of Campbell. Monasukapanough was the Indian village located near the present city of Charlottesville. Early Louisa county is shown extending into present Albemarle at upper right.

in the great Mississippi Valley, he proposed a counter wedge of British settlement which would strike at communications between the enemy's far-flung outposts stretching from Louisiana to Canada.

Although many historians see the James River as the logical path to the west, Spotswood—for personal reasons—disagreed. Instead, intrigued by the lure of mineral wealth along the Rappahannock River and irked by political opposition from powerful families who had staked out their domains near the falls of the James at Richmond, he pushed settlement to the north and south of present-day Albemarle.[3] These efforts, aided by the celebrated foray of the Knights of the Golden Horseshoe in the summer of 1716, culminated four years later in the creation of two Piedmont counties, Spotsylvania to the north and Brunswick to the south. Despite these successes, Spotswood's twelve-year reign (1710–22) was a mix of frustration and disappointment. Attempts to implement a more humane Indian policy, limit importation of slaves, and regulate large landholdings were thwarted, either by action of the king or by pressures exerted by powerful interests in the colony. In fact, as he grew older, Spotswood himself acquired several huge tracts of upland soil.

Five years after Alexander Spotswood was forced to retire, another man, an equally able administrator and possibly more skillful in negotiating the hazards and pitfalls of colonial politics, assumed the helm in Williamsburg. For over two decades William Gooch did battle with those eager to unseat him, while establishing a firm record of unusual competence. During his administration the county of Albemarle came into being.

Along the moving frontier, counties constantly were being formed and subdivided to provide badly needed centers of local government. Even the whims of a man like Spotswood could not stem for long the restless tide of humanity as Virginians moved westward from the coast and still other pioneers filtered into the Shenandoah Valley from Pennsylvania and Maryland, some of them occasionally spilling over into tiny isolated enclaves hidden in the coves and recesses of the eastern slopes of the Blue Ridge. The latter group included families bearing names such as Woods and Wallace and perhaps Jameson, Kinkead, and Stockton, all early residents of western Albemarle. Dur-

---

[3] Two of the most helpful sources on early county life are William Minor Dabney, "Jefferson's Albemarle: History of Albemarle County, Virginia, 1727–1819" (Ph.D. diss., University of Virginia, 1951), and Charles Wilder Watts, "Colonial Albemarle: The Social and Economic History of a Piedmont Virginia County, 1727–1775" (M.A. thesis, University of Virginia, 1948). Watts has a sixty-nine page appendix of Albemarle land patents to 1774.

ing his first year in office, 1728, the new governor established a huge county west of Richmond by cutting off part of Henrico, bestowing upon this creation his own name, Goochland. In 1744 Albemarle was formed from that county. At its inception it encompassed much of the James River valley above the fall line—not only present-day Albemarle but the counties of Fluvanna, Buckingham, Nelson, Amherst, much of Appomattox, and part of Campbell. In 1761 the county's lands south of the James and west of a line from the mouth of the Rockfish River northwest to the Blue Ridge were subdivided so as to form more new counties. Perhaps to compensate for this loss, at the same time a western portion of Louisa County (part of Fredericksville Parish) was added to Albemarle. Thus three sides of the county's familiar wedge-shaped boundaries were established. Sixteen years later, in 1777, a final change occurred when Fluvanna was formed out of the southeastern sector. As those who have studied early Albemarle note, there is an uncanny rhythm in this sequence of eighteenth-century subdivisions in 1728, 1744, 1761, and 1777. Every sixteen years or so migration pressures prompted colonial leaders to carve out new local jurisdictions, new county seats more accessible to a citizenry traveling by horse or on foot. With the separation of the Fluvanna area in the midst of the Revolutionary War, this process came to an end, and the boundaries of present-day Albemarle were established.

The county that emerged had an area of approximately 750 square miles, a figure decreased somewhat in recent decades by the growth and expansion of the city of Charlottesville. About half of the county, now the sixth largest in the state, lies in the Piedmont section, and half in what is sometimes called the Middle Virginia region. The elevation varies from 400 feet above sea level in the eastern part to 3,161 feet in the west. A soil survey conducted in 1902 revealed eighteen types within Albemarle. Of these soils, Cecil clay, varying in color from brown to reddish or dark brown and found in abundance in the Crozet-White Hall area, is considered best for general farming. Soapstone and slate quarries are common in southwestern communities, and copper, lead, zinc, and pyrite also have been mined from time to time in small quantities. Shaped somewhat like a trapezoid, Albemarle is bounded on the southeast by Louisa and Fluvanna counties and the James River, on the southwest by Nelson County, on the west by the Augusta County line along the crest of the Blue Ridge Mountains, and on the north by Greene and Orange counties.

In the southeastern section are the first "peaks" the settlers encountered as they traveled inland from the sea. Named by them the

Southwest Mountains, this range runs parallel to the more lofty Blue Ridge twenty-five miles to the west and, as Charles Wilder Watts comments in his excellent study of early Albemarle, perhaps should be called merely "hills." This range is unbroken except for passage of the Rivanna and Hardware rivers; yet there are a number of low passes or sags which enabled early settlers to travel to and fro with ease. In the southwestern part of the county lie the more massive Ragged Mountains pierced by the Rockfish and Hardware, and the entire area—mountains, hills, and lowlands—is honeycombed by innumerable small creeks, most of which empty into either the Hardware or the Rivanna. These two rivers, both tributaries of the James, transect the entire county and drain the southern and northern parts respectively. Though today many of these streams appear small and inconsequential, during Albemarle's first century they were busy avenues of commerce and trade; in fact, their waters (sometimes too swift, sometimes virtually nonexistent) were the lifeblood of this growing frontier community and the means by which precious hogsheads of tobacco got to market. Along their banks rose innumerable small mills that ground corn and wheat and helped fashion lumber out of the plentiful timber.

The most important of these streams was the Rivanna, which joined the James at Point of Fork and provided a waterway from The Shallows where the village of Milton appeared all the way to Richmond.[4] Yet, although double canoes, bateaux, and various types of small, horse-drawn boats would ply these waters and the Rivanna certainly lured settlers to eastern Albemarle, transport on that tributary always was capricious, unpredictable, in fact, unreliable. Storms and floods wrecked locks as fast as a struggling canal company erected them, millers failed to keep dams in good repair, and the river that flowed past Thomas Jefferson's boyhood home never quite fulfilled the hopes and dreams of those living along its banks. Residents of what is now southern Albemarle were more fortunate, for they had the broad James almost at their doorsteps. And, in time, rude pathways became roads cutting through the forest to various landings and ferry sites, some of them growing into little river towns of considerable importance, notably Howardsville, Warren, and Scottsville.

According to Rev. Edgar Woods, pioneer chronicler of Albemarle, many local place-names date from the beginning of white settlement

---

[4] See Thomas Jefferson Wertenbaker, "The Rivanna," *MACH* 14 (1945): 1–8.

1. Looking east from Rockfish Gap

2. William Anne Keppel, earl of Albemarle

and were handed down by word of mouth until incorporated in maps and records. Who bestowed them or why they did so is often unknown. Sometimes geographical features or the presence of animals were determining factors. On other occasions an original settler gave his name to a region; however, since eighteenth-century families were large and moved frequently, this custom produced both repetition and confusion. In 1900, Woods recounted the origins of some of the more common place-names.

The Southwest Mountain on which the first lands were entered was originally called the Chestnut Mountains. It was also spoken of as the Little Mountain. Particular portions had local names, for the most part taken from owners or first settlers, as Peter's, Carter's, Lively's, Sugar Loaf, Monticello. Green Mountain no doubt derived its name from the color of its luxuriant vegetation. The Blue Ridge bore that name from the first planting of the country. The early inhabitants called it also the Blue Ledge and the Blue Mountain. Sometimes it was designated as the Great Mountain, in opposition to the Little Mountain, and occasionally the South Mountain, in opposition to the North Mountain on the west side of the Valley. Buck's Elbow and Pasture Fence—at first Smith's Pasture Fence—Mountain have always been so called. Brown's Gap and Brown's Cove were named from the family that largely settled the land in that region. Turk's Gap was first called Jameson's, and Jarman's bore the name of Woods'—all from families who lived nearby. Rockfish Gap has always had that name, acquiring it from the river which rises in part at its base. Pigeon Top was once called Jameson's Mountain and may have obtained its later name from a roost of that bird. Fox's Mountain took its name from a family that lived on it, and High Top from its lofty peak. Currant's and Webb's Mountains were named from persons who possessed the adjoining lands, and Buck Mountain and the creek of the same name from the abundance of deer that roamed the forests. Piney Mountain was first called Poindexter's from the man who entered the land at its foot. Yellow Mountain at one time went by the name of Epperson's. Castle Rock was so denominated from its huge towering form, Chalk Mountain from the light-colored rocks which face its crest, and Heard's, Appleberry's, Fan's, Gay's, Dudley's, from primitive settlers in their vicinity. In early times the mountains north of Moorman's River and south of Mechum's were called Ragged, from their disordered appearance, and not from the garments of their inhabitants as has sometimes been suggested.

The Hardware River has always borne that name. Rivanna was in use from the first, according to the fashion then in vogue of honoring Queen Anne with the names of rivers recently discovered. In the earliest patents and deeds it was more frequently called the north fork of the James, as the James above the Rivanna passed under the name of the South Fork, or more euphuistically, the Fluvanna. In some instances the Rivanna was simply termed the North River and the Fluvanna the South. The crossing of the Rivanna at the Free Bridge was known at the beginning of the century as Moore's Ford, or Lewis' Ferry, according to the stage of the water, and its north fork was sometimes called, down to a quite recent date, the Little River. Red Bud was first named Key's Mill Creek or Swamp. In early days swamp seemed to be interchangeable with creek, no doubt from the rubbish of logs and leaves which for ages had obstructed the channels of the smaller streams. Priddy's, Buck Mountain, and Rocky Creeks and Jacob's and Piney Runs had those designations from the beginning. The names of Meadow and Ivy Creeks obtained from the earliest times. Moorman's River was named from Thomas Moorman, one of the earliest patentees on its banks, and Mechum's from a George Mechum, who was an owner of land near its head. The north fork of Mechum's was called Stockton's Creek and its south fork, now regarded as the main stream, Stockton's Mill Creek, from a numerous family occupying its margins. The middle fork was always termed Virgin Spring Branch. Union Run was first named Mountain Falls Creek; afterwards, from being a favorite feeding place of the wagoners who brought their produce to Milton, it acquired the name of Camping Branch. Carroll's Creek was the original title of that stream. Limestone was first called Plum Tree Branch, then Scales' Creek, and finally its present name, from washing the only vein of limestone in the county. Buck Island Creek was so designated from the beginning. It is a mistake to write it Buckeyeland, as if derived from the deer-eyed tree. The name was taken from an island in the Rivanna opposite its mouth, and, as in the case of so many objects of natural scenery, was suggested by the great numbers of deer found everywhere in the country. There were two other tributaries of the Rivanna below Milton in early times, though their names are never heard at present, Henderson's and Miller's Branches. Moore's Creek has been so called from the first. The same is true of Biscuit Run; but the names of its branches, Plum Orchard on the east and Cow Branch on the west, have slipped from the memory of men. A small prong of Moore's above Biscuit Run once had the name of Edge's Creek; it is forgotten now.

There were three Beaverdams in the county, one running into Mechunk, another into Lynch's River, and the third into Eppes' Creek. Besides Ivy Creek that passes the depot of that name, there is another which empties into Rockfish. An affluent of Priddy's Creek and one of Ballenger's were both called Wolf Trap. Wolf Pit was a branch of Beaver Creek, and a cavity on the west side of Southwest Mountain had the same name. Piney Mountain was the designation, not only of the present mountain of that name, but also of Lewis' Mountain near the University and of an eminence near Afton. A branch of the lower Rockfish was called Buck Island, besides the stream so named that flows into the Rivanna. A Turkey Run empties into Priddy's Creek, and another of the same name enters the Hardware. There were three Round Top Mountains, one in the Buck Mountain region, another not far from Batesville, and another near the University.

White Hall was an election precinct under the successive names of Glenn's Store, William Maupin's Store, Maupin's Tavern, Miller's Tavern, Shumate's Tavern, till at length the present name was established about 1835. For a long time Batesville went by the name of Oliver's Store. Mechum's Depot was anciently known as Jarman's Mill, and afterwards as Walker's Mill. Ivy Depot was formerly Woodville. The name of Glendower at first was Scott's Mill, then Dyer's, and then Dawson's. Woodbrige was for many years denominated McGehee's Old Field. Besides Stony Point on the Barboursville Road, there was a Stony Point not far from Scottsville. Free Union formerly went by the name of Nixville and is still so spoken of by the older citizens. Petersburg is the appellation of a hamlet on Priddy's Creek between the Southern Railroad and the Barboursville Road. Cartersburg is a straggling collection of houses on the hill south of the Rio Bridge. Brownton and Lemon Hill stand for places not far from Glendower.

As already intimated, the former denizens of the forest were frequently alluded to in the names by which objects were distinguished. When the county was first occupied, game of every kind abounded. Traces of the buffalo still remained. A trail is said to have run from Rockfish River to the Gap of that name. It is also reported that the old Richard Woods Road closely followed a buffalo trail. A tract of land belonging to the Webb entry, sold in 1769 to Isaac Davis and lying on the north fork of the Rivanna, is described as adjoining Buffalo Meadow. A branch of Buck Mountain Creek was called Elk Run. Deer were exceedingly plentiful. A tradition, which descended from one of the first settlers near the Blue Ridge, states, that by stepping from his door almost any morning, he was able to shoot a deer. From this circumstance it arose that the word "Buck" so frequently forms part of the names of the county. Lick Run was a branch of Beaverdam in its northern part. Bears were found, not only as they still are in the deep ravines of the Blue Ridge, but also in every neighborhood. Near the Rich Cove were Bear Creek and Red Bear Hollow. Benjamin Brown devised to his son Bezaleel the "Bear Cornfield." In a deed of 1789, conveying land north of Stony Point, one of the lines passed by "the Bear Spring on the road." [5]

Woods notes that wolves, beaver, turkeys, ducks, and even fish also have been memorialized by various landmarks scattered throughout the county. Although one may question his confident assertion that certain mountains and streams always bore their present names, the absence of lyrical Indian words within Albemarle's boundaries reinforces the belief that the native inhabitants had departed when the

[5] Woods, *Albemarle County in Virginia* (Charlottesville, 1901), pp. 19–23.

first white settlers appeared. With no aboriginals in residence the frontiersman obviously had no way of learning what the Indian had called the hills, streams, and rivers which dot the countryside. Thus, much as Woods describes, in a haphazard, unplanned, often obscure fashion, names familiar to all twentieth-century residents of Albemarle County emerged.

There is, however, little mystery concerning the name of the county itself, although as Thomas Cary Johnson has observed, the word *Albemarle* has a rather bizarre history.[6] Named for the colony's official governor in England, William Anne Keppel, earl of Albemarle, thus perpetuating the traditional practice of honoring statesmen and royal personages, Albemarle nevertheless is, in many ways, a unique designation for a Virginia county. It is, as Johnson has written, nothing more than the Englishing of the name of the county of Aumale in northwestern Normandy. A count of Aumale (one Odo or Eudes) crossed the Channel in 1066 with William the Conqueror, reputedly his uncle. After the Battle of Hastings the counts of Aumale for a time held lands in England as the lords of Holderness and Skipsea. One of these lords eventually became the earl of Aumale (or Albemarle, as the English pronounced it). In the late thirteenth century this noble line died out and the title lapsed, but it was revived by Charles II in 1660 in order to reward a professional soldier who had helped him gain the throne of England. This man, General George Monck, as duke of Albemarle and one of the Carolina proprietors, gave his name to Albemarle Sound in North Carolina.

In 1688, upon the death of this duke's heir, the title once more fell vacant; but in the 1690s it was granted to a charming Dutchman named Arnold Joost van Keppel who had accompanied William of Orange to England. Although Arnold, earl of Albemarle, returned to his homeland after William's death, he was able to pass his English estates and title to his son, William Anne Keppel, the second earl of Albemarle. William, a man of considerable ability, distinguished himself during the reigns of George I and George II in the realms of diplomacy, warfare, and society and was governor of Virginia from 1737 until his death in 1754. Although he traveled widely throughout Europe, this mid-eighteenth-century courtier never visited either the colony he governed or the county that honored his name. One can merely conjecture as to what might have happened if he had; it is most unlikely that the Right Honourable the Earl of Albemarle, accustomed to the pleasures of London and Paris, would have tarried long in this rude but growing outpost of the British Empire.

[6] Johnson, "How Albemarle Got Its Name," *MACH* 16 (1958):20–24.

Chapter 2

First Settlers, First Families, First Things

Establishing a successful community in the wilderness is indeed an awesome undertaking. Problems abound on every hand—poor communications, shortages of sorely needed materials, isolation, unknown soil and weather conditions, wild animals, and, at times, hostile natives, but the first Virginians who settled in Albemarle knew from the experiences of their fathers and grandfathers that the odds were in their favor. Land was wealth, and new land produced bountiful crops of tobacco, wheat, and corn. The chief implement of early local agriculture was the axe. Areas that demonstrated natural fertility by hardwood growth were cleared, perhaps in a crude fashion by burning and girding the trees, and the soil was turned with a small, bull-nosed plow and loosened with a primitive spike-tooth harrow. Then hills for tobacco plants could be created with a hoe. After three annual crops of tobacco, these "fields" then grew wheat for a year or so before being abandoned and allowed to revert to pine forest. Corn usually was produced on low ground or bottomland thought unsuitable for tobacco.

Although tobacco was not colonial Albemarle's only crop from the first, it was the one that dominated the dreams of most of these pioneers; and despite later controversy about what that "weed" was doing to the soil, for over a century it remained a potent factor in Albemarle's economy. Reformers could present proof of their arguments, landowners might complain bitterly of erosion and depletion of their once-rich acres; but given the promise of good market conditions, as late as the 1850s Albemarle County continued to produce a substantial annual harvest of tobacco. These first settlers knew from the experience of others that, properly cured and shipped off to England, tobacco would buy them still more land, slaves, and some of the luxuries their cousins of the Tidewater enjoyed. Even those hardy pioneers who arrived quietly through the back door of the Shenandoah Valley must have been beguiled by the world developing about them, the last gasp of a way of life which had produced such lordly mansions as Westover and Carter's Grove. Yet, even though a few well-to-do families with large landholdings tended to dominate this new county's political and social life well into the nineteenth century, Piedmont never became Tidewater.

The differences, though subtle at times, created a somewhat more democratic society. Of paramount importance was the fact that upland tobacco, which usually was too coarse, never produced great wealth. Within three or four decades Thomas Jefferson and his neighbors were searching for new crops to rejuvenate their troubled agricultural economy. In fact, they proclaimed loudly and with much truth that the rude plant not only failed to provide a sound income, it actually was ruining their fields. In the absence of great fortunes there were no Westovers, no vast gangs of slaves numbering in the hundreds. Although difficult to prove today, it would appear that the local mansion houses that arose between 1780 and 1850 were paid for, not by agricultural produce alone, but with income derived from the sale of lands outside of Albemarle, shrewd investment in stores, canals, turnpikes, and railroads, and perhaps the loan of money to neighbors at exorbitant rates of interest.

In addition to some frustration and disappointment arising from an uncertain tobacco culture, two other factors had incalculable effect upon the development of early Albemarle: the fall line of the James River to the east and the Shenandoah Valley to the west. Once a settler left the falls of the James behind, he severed many of his direct ties to England. Residence over one hundred miles from the seat of colonial government in Williamsburg diminished somewhat the appeal of royal trappings and the power of princely proclamations. Piedmont settlers became more interdependent, capable of solving problems common to all, and relied less and less upon assistance from London or even Williamsburg, neither of which seemed to understand the challenges presented by frontier life. To the west, only a few miles over the Blue Ridge, a society was emerging which bore little resemblance to that found in the steaming lowland peninsulas washed by the York and lower James.

Frontiersmen of English stock usually just girded large trees and left them to die while ploughing lightly around them, let their stock roam wild, made no use of animal manure, and practiced only rudimentary crop rotation. The Germans of the Valley, in contrast, cleared their fields of all trees and stumps, ploughed deep to arrest erosion, housed their cattle in great barns, used manure as fertilizer, and practiced a precise scheme of crop rotation. Writing in 1939, Richard H. Shryock pointed to these and other basic conflicts between British and German farmers in colonial Virginia.[1] In his opinion many early English settlers were not farmers, but town folk who

---

[1] Shryock, "British versus German Traditions in Colonial Agriculture," *Mississippi Valley Historical Review* 26 (1939):39–54.

saw this colony as a chance to get land. The Old Dominion was, in his words, "a back-to-the farm" movement for thousands who often had little, if any familiarity with the soil. To a great extent, he adds, merchants, not the farmers themselves, directed the development of this emerging economy, always looking for quick return—first it was tobacco; then, in later decades throughout much of the South, cotton. To any settler coming from the east, the basis of such an economy was slave labor. The Valley people, on the other hand, were farmers of long tradition, not city dwellers, and they were accustomed to doing their own work, with the help of sons, relatives, and hired hands. They came to stay, develop the best farms they could with their own hands, and harbored no thoughts of quickly raping a rich land and in a generation or so moving still farther west. No overseer, indentured servant, or slave with little interest in this precious undertaking was permitted to desecrate their fields.

Although Albemarle, for the most part, was settled by men dedicated to the get-rich-quick, single-crop outlook, their cautious Valley neighbors must have exerted considerable influence, especially as tobacco became less and less profitable. By 1820, the close of the first period of county history, we can discern quite clearly a compromise of man with his environment. The dream of transplanting the Tidewater to the rolling Piedmont has been abandoned. Instead, local farmers are turning to a diversified agriculture much more like that of the Shenandoah Valley than the Tidewater, but aided on every hand by a substantial number of slaves left over from the days when tobacco seemed so all-important.

Of course, some men would not compromise. They are the sons of Albemarle who pursued the dream west to Kentucky or south to Alabama where they could once more plant tobacco or develop vast fields of cotton. This is no attempt to portray the tobacco experiment as a failure. Far from it. Those broad green leaves were the backbone of eighteenth-century Albemarle, the very reason for the birth of the county, and for many years proved to be a marketable staple which, if it did not furnish silver and satin in lavish abundance, gave the young community a more than adequate return on its investment in time and labor. Those green leaves also had one other result of tremendous importance in the following decades: despite subsequent changes in agriculture, they bestowed upon the region the pattern of master-slave relationships so common throughout the rest of the South.

The men who pioneered this attempt to extend the Tidewater to the foothills of the Blue Ridge Mountains are an interesting lot, especially those who after 1744, as Albemarle's "founding fathers," organized and nurtured local government. Between 1722 and 1726 three grants of land were made which lay, at least in part, within what is now Albemarle County, but these tracts never were properly developed; that is, the would-be owners failed to clear at least one acre of land in each section, build a cabin, and pay annual quitrents. In 1727 George Hoomes, Jr., received 3,100 acres near the Chestnut (Southwest) Mountains, and Nicholas Meriwether, whose descendants would include numerous distinguished citizens, obtained a huge grant of 13,762 acres in the same region. Two years later George Nicholas of Williamsburg acquired 2,600 acres on the left bank of the James in southern Albemarle. This trio proceeded to "seat and plant" these lands as the law required, and within a few years others took up patents nearby, including Thomas Carr, John Carter, Francis Eppes, Allen Howard, Charles Hudson, and Charles Lewis.

Of these nine individuals, all but Hoomes already had established themselves as substantial property owners and community leaders elsewhere. John Carter, son of wealthy Robert Carter of the Northern Neck, was secretary of the colony of Virginia. Some of these men were colonels in the militia, and several were described as "gentlemen"; these first landowners were not the underprivileged of Tidewater society. Yet, though they were the first owners of Albemarle soil, they were not necessarily the county's first settlers. As was the custom, they dispatched overseers and slaves to clear and cultivate new quarters for some years before moving themselves and their families to the Piedmont. By 1735 men employed by George Nicholas, who established the first recorded settlement within Albemarle's present boundaries, had cleared eighty-six acres of land near Warren, built six houses, cut 6,400 fence rails, set up a hand mill, planted peach and apple trees, and turned loose thirty-five head of cattle. At about the same time Thomas Meriwether had eleven slaves, two horses, a plow and other farm implements, eighteen head of cattle, and over a hundred hogs, sows, and pigs on his Totier Creek property. Soon the overseers and slaves of John Carter, William Stith, Colonel Richard Randolph, Peter Jefferson, and others were developing similar holdings.

It is possible that the first man to occupy land awarded to him by colonial officials was Benjamin Thurman, who was living in the Southwest Mountains area in 1732. Michael Woods, a pioneer who arrived via the Shenandoah Valley, apparently resided in Albemarle County for several years before acquiring title to his tract of land in 1737. Peter Jefferson appeared in the same year; his famous son once remarked that his father was the third or fourth settler in his neighborhood. About one-tenth of the county's early settlers came from the west through Woods's Gap and, like Woods himself, did not immediately acquire land from the crown. Some of these hardy folk followed his example; others chose to lease land from more affluent citizens, although this practice was not widespread. Watts has found only seven such contracts between 1752 and 1767. The average size of these tracts was 160 acres; the rent was approximately three shillings per acre per year, and the leases usually were for a ten-year period. Jefferson, however, represents the more typical pattern of settlement —men who came from the east or northeast armed with legal papers to prove their right to hundreds, even thousands, of acres of virgin soil.

Regardless of who has the honor of being the first citizen of the county, by 1744, the year Albemarle was created, much of the land within its present boundaries had been patented. Some of those acres were given in additional grants to the original nine, but there also were a substantial number of small patents of 400 acres or so. Those receiving land units of that size or less during the first decade, 1727–37, individuals one can probably classify as small farmers, included Robert Adams, Charles Caffry, John Cannon, Howard Cash, Christopher Clark, William Coursey, William Craddock, Timothy Dalton, James Defaux (or DeFoe), Daniel Desoin (or Designs), Hugh Dohorty, Bartholomew Durrett, Forest Green, Arthur Hopkins, Patrick Howland, Thomas James, Charles Jordan, Alexander Mackilligott, Nicholas Meriwether, Jr., Mathew Mills, John Minor, Charles Moreman, Anthony Pouncey, Henry Runalds, Ambrose Joshua Smith, James Stuart, Roger Thompson, Roger Thompson, Jr., Thomas Tulloch, William Verdeman, William Wallace, John Waller, Jr., David Watts, and Archibald Wood. One should keep in mind, however, that some of these men acquired more land in succeeding decades and that a handful may never have settled in Albemarle at all.[2]

Watts estimates that it cost these prospective landowners about £8 to patent a 400-acre farm. This sum includes surveying and patent fees and incidentals such as trips to Williamsburg to tidy up legal details. Watts has compiled an exhaustive list of Albemarle County patents from 1722 to 1774 which reveals how very quickly Virginians acquired title to local soil. After 1744, although several hundred

[2] Watts, pp. 112–23.

patents were issued, only a handful exceeded 1,000 acres. Most were for a few hundred acres, and the smallest was the 3-acre patent by which Peter Jefferson, John Harvie, and four of their friends gained possession of a group of islands in the Rivanna River. S. Edward Ayres, another student of early Albemarle, notes that 46 of 191 patents issued between 1727 and 1745 were for more than 1,000 acres, and 6 exceeded 5,000 acres. The average size was 831 acres. But, for the years 1727 to 1755 as a whole, the average was only 470 acres, reflecting a dramatic decrease in the size of individual patents shortly after Albemarle separated from Goochland.[3]

Although most of these pioneers acquired land on which they planned to grow tobacco and eventually settle, there were a few speculators. Charles Lynch, whose family would give their name to Lynchburg, patented two tracts of 400 acres in 1733. He settled on one and within three years sold the other for a handsome profit, thus avoiding the necessity of improving the land as required by statute. During the next two decades Lynch, who probably began life in the New World as an indentured servant but eventually acquired the rank of gentleman, patented and sold fourteen more plots of similar size and, by keen foresight, realized a profit of over 300 percent on each transaction. However, such speculative activity seems to have been rare within the county. Even in this instance relatively small units of land were involved. Although considerable buying and selling of property occurred, for the most part Albemarle farmers acquired their holdings directly from the crown. As a result, large estates remained intact or even increased in size, providing the economic basis for a resident landowning class which, in turn, furnished both political and social leadership for years to come. The masters of these expanding domains often participated in land speculation on a grand scale elsewhere, especially in western Virginia and Kentucky. And, with the tobacco market frequently in turmoil during colonial decades, revenue from the sale of those lands provided very welcome income.

By 1744 the estates and farms of western Goochland—complete with slaves, overseers, small fields of tobacco, wheat, and corn, cabins, and occasionally a more pretentious frame structure—had a total population of four or five thousand, and the stage was set for creation of a new center of local government. On the fourth day of Septem-

---

[3] See Ayres, "Albemarle County, Virginia, 1744–1770: An Economic, Political, and Social Analysis" (M.A. thesis, University of Virginia, 1968), another work containing valuable insights into colonial life.

ber in the eighteenth year of the reign of His Majesty George II, the General Assembly meeting in Williamsburg passed an act providing for the division of Goochland County.

I   Whereas divers inconveniences attend the upper inhabitants of Goochland County, by reason of their great distance from the courthouse, and other places, usually appointed for public meetings:

II   *Be it therefore enacted, by the Lieutenant Governor, Council, and Burgesses, of this present General Assembly, and it is hereby enacted, by the authority of the same.* That from and immediately after the last day of December next, the said county of Goochland be divided, by a line, to be run from the point of the fork of the James River, north, thirty degrees, east to Louisa county line; and from the said point of the fork, a direct course to Brook's mill; and from thence, the same course continued, to Appommatox river: And that part of the said county which lies below the line, be erected into one distinct county, and retain the name of Goochland; and all that other part thereof, above the said line, be one other distinct county, and called by the name of the county of Albemarle. And, for the due administration of justice.

III   *Be it further enacted, by the authority aforesaid.* That after the said last day of December, a court for the said county of Albemarle, be constantly held, by the justices thereof, on the fourth Thursday in every month, in such manner, as by the laws of this colony is provided, and shall be, by their commission, directed. . . .[4]

On February 28, 1745, one month later than the date specified by this act, a small group of citizens gathered near the present town of Scottsville to inaugurate county government. Those present included Thomas Ballou, William Cabell, Joshua Fry, Allen Howard, Peter Jefferson, and Joseph Thompson. Since succeeding sessions of the county court convened at Totier, a plantation owned by Mrs. Edward Scott, this meeting probably occurred at the same place. By a commission of peace dated January 2, 1745, Howard and Cabell were empowered to administer the proper oaths to Fry and Jefferson, who swore in the others. Charles Lynch, James Daniel, and Edwin Hickman, also named in the commission but not present, later assumed their duties as justices. Then, in quick order, other key positions were filled: Joseph Thompson, sheriff; Patrick Napier and Carleton Harper, undersheriffs; Joshua Fry, surveyor of lands; and Edmund Gray, king's prosecutor. This first session, which appears to have been brief, concluded with an order to the new sheriff "to give publick n[otice] to all persons that have a mind to undertake the Buildings

[4] W. W. Hening, comp., *The Statutes at Large* . . . (Richmond, 1810–23), 5:266–69.

[of] the Prison, Court House & Stocks &c., in Albemarle County [that] they make their proposals to the Court that will be held in th[e] County in April next." [5]

Of the six magistrates present at this meeting, five were large land-owners, men of wealth and prominence. Little is known concerning Ballou; however, this family name reappears from time to time in Albemarle history. Thompson, the first sheriff, also remains somewhat obscure, although one of his sons added to his father's lands and distinguished himself during the Revolutionary War. Enough is known of the others to prove conclusively that this group was by no means a representative cross section of the community.

Joshua Fry was perhaps the most interesting and undoubtedly the best educated. Born in England, he probably matriculated at Oxford in 1718 and within a decade was teaching at the grammar school of the College of William and Mary. In 1729 he became master of that school and later served briefly as professor of mathematics. Sometime in the 1730s Fry married a well-to-do widow, gave up the academic world, and, in the words of a contemporary, "retired . . . to the back settlements [western Goochland] in order to raise up a fortune for his family." During the years after 1745 Fry was busy surveying lands in Albemarle and adjacent counties; then, when the French and Indian War erupted, he went west as colonel of Virginia's regiment with young George Washington as his lieutenant. Upon his death in 1754 near Cumberland, Maryland, the man who would lead our nation's forces during the Revolutionary War, the squire of Mount Vernon, assumed his first command.

Peter Jefferson, one of Albemarle's first settlers, was Fry's close friend and the man with whom he published a celebrated map of Virginia in 1751. He was born near Richmond, and although his father died in somewhat reduced circumstances, for two or three generations the Jeffersons had been prominent members of the colonial gentry. Peter, a huge, ambitious man, married Jane Randolph, member of a powerful, well-known Virginia family, and served in Goochland as both magistrate and sheriff. He inherited some two thousand acres of land from his father and by the time of his death in 1757 had increased his holdings at least tenfold. This pioneer had become, in the words of Dumas Malone, "a man of substantial property, though it would be an exaggeration to call him a land baron." [6] Although

[5] Mary Rawlings, ed., "Albemarle County Court, Order Book, 1744/45," *MACH* 5 (1945):8–9.
[6] Malone, *Jefferson the Virginian* (Boston, 1948), p. 31.

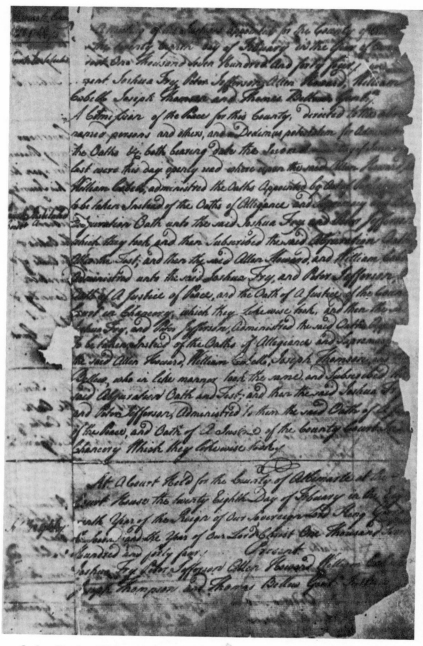

3. Order Book, Albemarle County Court, 1744/45–1748, page [1]

Peter Jefferson is now remembered because of the exploits of his tall, red-haired son, the father was a forceful, dynamic personality in his own right, an individual of considerable ability whether dealing with local government matters, military affairs, or land surveys. When he died he left a substantial library which compared favorably with any found throughout the Piedmont.

Allen Howard, like Jefferson one of Albemarle's first settlers, came from obscure origins. Since his ears were cropped and slit, he probably possessed an exciting, unsavory past, perhaps having spent some time in prison. Although Howard first acquired only a small tract of land, within a few years he was able to enlarge his holdings, become a major in the local militia (third in rank behind Fry and Jefferson), and assume the title of gentleman, mutilated ears notwithstanding. His estate was at the mouth of the Rockfish River where the town of Howardsville later developed. There in 1744 he began construction of a "great house" called West Cote, today known as Summer Hill. By the time of his death in 1761 Howard's will, recorded in Goochland County, not Albemarle, reveals that he was master of six large plantations along the James.

William Cabell was one of the most versatile of colonial planters. English-born and educated at the Royal College of Surgeons in London, he arrived in the New World while in service in the British navy. Impressed by what he saw during a brief visit to Virginia, Cabell returned to England, resigned his position, and emigrated. He lived briefly in Williamsburg but soon moved to Richmond, where he married a local girl. Together they joined other pioneers in upper Goochland, eventually settling at Warminster in 1741. This site, named for Cabell's birthplace, became the center of the doctor's far-flung activities. Located several miles up the James River from Howardsville, in what is now Nelson County, Warminster has since disappeared. As a surgeon Cabell maintained there a private hospital where he dispensed medicine and wooden legs. A man of practical mind, Cabell frequently offered his services on a "no cure—no pay" basis, and the same employee who turned out peg legs also could fashion a free coffin when necessary. But the doctor by no means limited himself to curing the ill, repairing the maimed, and burying deceased patients. He was also an Indian fighter, surveyor, political leader, and owner of a warehouse, store, and tavern.

These founding fathers—Fry, Howard, Jefferson, and Cabell—from time to time represented Albemarle in the House of Burgesses at Williamsburg. And this unusual foursome experienced yet another common bond by no means unique in frontier Albemarle: they were unashamedly ambitious, men "on the make." Teacher, ex-criminal, surveyor-planter, doctor-merchant, each was determined to acquire as quickly as possible more land, more wealth. Involvement in local and colonial affairs was one path to their goal.

By some odd twist of fate, the county's first order book, covering the years from 1745 to 1748, is the only one remaining from pre-Revolutionary decades. Ably edited by Mary Rawlings, known to many as the author of *The Albemarle of Other Days*, it presents a clear picture of the businesslike manner in which these original justices went about the task of creating a functioning local government. At the March 1745 session (Fry, Cabell, Jefferson, and Ballou present) the rates for liquor, beer, and meals at ordinaries were established for the coming year (see table 1). At the same time the justices appointed James DeFoe, Charles Lynch, and John Woody as surveyors of specific roads to be built throughout the county. In each instance all male tithables (blacks over fifteen years of age and whites eighteen or more) residing along these proposed roads were ordered to help out. Entries authorizing the construction of "a high way from Number 12 to Number 18," "a high way from Number 18 to the County line," or "a high way from the late Secretary's ford to Number 12," are extremely common during these early years. It appears that energetic citizens such as Defoe, Lynch, and Woody saw the need

Table 1. Rates at Albemarle ordinaries, 1745

Commodity	Price
West India Rum by the Gallon	Ten Shillings
New England Rum by the Gallon	Eighteen pence
Whiskey by the Gallon	Eighteen pence
Peach Brandy by the Gallon	Ten Shillings
Maideira Wine by the Quart	Two Shillings and Six
Virginia Cask Beer by the Quart	Seven Pence half peny
English Bottle Beer by the Quart	One Shilling
English Strong Beer by the Quart	Eighteen pence
French Brandy by the Gallon	Twenty Shillings
Good Virginia Cyder by the Quart	Six pence
For a Diet	Twelve pence
For a Servant's Diet	Six pence
For one night Lodging	Seven pence half peny
Indian Corn by the Gall	Four pence
And so proportionately for a Greater or less Quantity	

SOURCE: Rawlings, "Albemarle County Court, Order Book, 1744/45," *MACH* 5 (1945):9.

for a road from their farm to some stream, river, or ford and sought county approval for an undertaking, which was granted with alacrity by the justices. Though the results were crude by modern standards, they did provide a rudimentary framework for communication and better access to markets. Also at the March 1745 session, Peter Jefferson was named a lieutenant colonel and Allen Howard a major in the local militia.

In May 1745 Fry and Cabell contracted to purchase weights and scales to be used as standards for the county, and Samuel Scott proposed to build a courthouse, prison, stocks, and pillory "as good and according to the same Dimensions as those now in Goochland County, on condition he may Build them on his own Land." One month later Scott posted a £500 bond with a promise to complete construction within two years. In July, Daniel Scott received permission to operate a ferry "from the Court House Landing to the opposite side" and posted bond in the sum of ten thousand pounds of tobacco for the right to operate for one year an ordinary with "good, wholesome, and Cleanly Lodging and Diet for Travellers and Stablage &c. for Horses." Although the original meeting of county officials on Scott property may have been a chance happening, it is apparent that this family was making the most of the opportunity presented. In short order they were creating a center of economic activity which could not help benefiting those living on the banks of the James. Though this first nucleus of county government failed to develop into a village of any immediate consequence, all this activity may have troubled the thoughts of Peter Jefferson, Thomas Walker, and others who resided some twenty miles away.

These justices had to deal with cases of adultery, mistreatment of indentured servants, minor civil disputes, and debt cases, but their principal concern remained roads. Petitions flowed in from all parts of the huge county seeking better transportation, better means of communication with the outside world. Within a few months gangs of workers were becoming almost professional road builders as they were shifted from one project to another. The existence of these crews is clear evidence that not every male tithable was eager and willing to do his part and that the justices, ever mindful of local pressures, were reluctant to ruffle the sensitivities of gentlemen who thought such work demeaning.

Despite keen interest in roads, the most obvious avenues of commerce were the James and Rivanna rivers. The latter was navigable for about eight months of each year, beginning in November; and even during dry summer months, given an occasional shower, small boats could make their way downstream to the James, though it was obstructed by rocks and generally proved difficult and hazardous to navigation. And there often were man-made obstacles to be encountered on all streams and rivers—stone hedges designed to catch fish and numerous mill dams, although the General Assembly usually acted promptly to have these destroyed or means found to circumvent them. When conditions were propitious, boats could proceed swiftly from Milton to Richmond, a distance of eighty miles.

The first highway, which predates the organization of Albemarle, was the so-called River Road authorized to be constructed in 1731 from Goochland Courthouse along the north bank of the James and the Fluvanna to the mouth of the Rockfish River. The next was the Mountain Ridge Road, which followed the watershed between the South Anna and the James to Secretary's Ford at the Rivanna water gap. By 1745 this highway had been extended through the center of present-day Albemarle to Woods's (now Jarman's) Gap and renamed the Three Notched Road, often called Three Chopt. At the same time other roads were being built southward, the principal one being the Barboursville Road which ran along the base of the Southwest Mountains to Lynch's Ferry and joined Three Notched near the present site of Charlottesville. This vital link connected to the main highway through Orange and Louisa counties and provided access to trade centers on the South Anna and the Rappahannock. It was this framework of the River, Three Notched, and Barboursville roads which men such as DeFoe, Lynch, and Woody sought to expand to fit their immediate needs and those of other citizens as well.

These pioneer years of "big" Albemarle, 1745 to 1761, must have been both exhilarating and frustrating. There was the excitement of creating a new life in the wilderness, but distances were so great, travel so time-consuming, problems so many. County officials soon were permitted to convene every three months, not monthly as originally stipulated by law. Also, with boundaries being altered frequently, the first settlers undoubtedly found it difficult to develop any sense of county loyalty. Yet, however ponderous and ill-defined, a community slowly was taking shape. Parishes and vestries were formed, merchants and mills appeared, schools were started for the young, and a fledgling legal fraternity pleaded cases. Rare was the gentleman who had a single profession. He was almost without exception a multipurpose individual. Whether businessman, surveyor, soldier, minister of the gospel, barrister, or doctor, he was first and foremost a planter. Even the more numerous although less affluent tilling small farms frequently augmented their incomes by operating a ferry, running an ill-smelling ordinary, or practicing some trade or craft part-time. Of course, such jacks-of-many-trades are typical of any frontier settlement far from markets with too much land, too few people.

Although very few churches or meetinghouses existed in Albemarle before 1761, the vestry, men charged with administering parish affairs, had civil powers as well as religious duties. They were responsible for poor relief and the care of orphans and the mentally deficient. Chosen by the freeholders whenever a new parish was established (which usually coincided with a change in county boundaries), they often were wealthy citizens. Once elected, a vestry became a self-perpetuating body free to select new members whenever vacancies occurred. This system was somewhat undemocratic, but since alterations in political units were frequent, so was creation of new vestries, at least along the moving Piedmont frontier. Those attending the first meeting of the vestry of St. Anne's Parish in 1742, the sole religious unit within Albemarle until 1761, were Thomas Meriwether, Ambrose Joshua Smith, Robert Lewis, and Abraham Venable. Others who subsequently joined this select group, all representatives of the landed gentry, included Henry Fry, John Harvie, Thomas Jefferson, Nicholas Lewis, John Meriwether, Nicholas Meriwether, John Walker, and Thomas Walker.[7]

With the division of "big" Albemarle in 1761, the county which emerged was of a more manageable size and gained another parish, Fredericksville. The simultaneous decision to move the seat of government from the banks of the James to a central location provided a practical, accessible nucleus for local life. The site chosen was just west of the Rivanna water gap through the Southwest Mountains on the main road leading west to the Blue Ridge. A thousand-acre tract was acquired from Colonel Richard Randolph and conveyed in trust to Dr. Thomas Walker to be sold for the benefit of the county. On December 23, 1762, the General Assembly established there a new town to be called Charlottesville in honor of the young queen of George III, Charlotte Sophia of Mecklenburg-Strelitz. The act of incorporation stipulated that fifty acres (the original expanse of the town) would be laid off in streets and lots. This property sold rapidly, and within three years only nine lots remained in the possession of public authorities. A frame courthouse, pillory, stocks, and whipping post soon appeared, but no details of these early structures remain.

Many early citizens of the county must have shaken their heads

[7] Watts, p. 88.

in disbelief at the decision to establish this town, a far-sighted move indeed (perhaps too much so). In an age when water transport was crucial, the new community, located on a small creek running into the Rivanna, had no direct connections to Richmond and the outside world. As a result, in the heyday of canal traffic—as well as during the first decades of railway travel—Charlottesville remained a small, rural county seat almost untouched by improvements and changes in transportation. Yet obscurity often has its merits. More pretentious Virginia towns and cities reverberated to the sound of gunfire and fell before the onslaught of invading armies, but Charlottesville emerged unscathed from two cataclysmic wars, and in the twentieth century the advantages of a centrally located seat of local administration are obvious to all.

It should be noted that division of Albemarle in 1761 was not accomplished without some outcry and turmoil. Property held in common by "big" Albemarle seems to have been treated in a rather cavalier fashion by community leaders of "new" Albemarle. Despite orders from colonial officials that a public sale be held, the wardens of St. Anne's Parish quietly assumed title to glebe lands within present-day Albemarle which belonged, at least in part, to residents of Amherst and Buckingham counties. The weights and scales purchased by Fry and Cabell were another source of irritation. Former county residents insisted that they be reimbursed for their share of the original cost. Eventually, all of these complaints were aired in Williamsburg, and the General Assembly instructed Albemarle to make a fair settlement of outstanding accounts. The last of these directives came late in 1764 when the justices of Albemarle received orders to grant residents of Amherst and Buckingham a reasonable proportion of 6,027 pounds of tobacco credited for public levy three years earlier.

Chapter 3

Making a Living

THROUGHOUT the eighteenth century, every resident of Albemarle County depended directly or indirectly upon agriculture for his livelihood. There were, of course, mills, ordinaries, stores, a handful of professional folk, an occasional craftsman, and even some manufacturing of both clothing and crude iron; but slave, overseer, indentured servant, landowners great and small, everyone in the final analysis drew his income from the soil. And, looking ahead, it might be noted that agriculture remained the county's economic base for decades to come. Only within the memory of thousands of present-day citizens has the produce of field and orchard relinquished its long-held position of top priority in local life.

The prime crop of early Albemarle, but by no means the only one, was tobacco. Cultivation involved a series of easily learned manual operations that could be performed readily by blacks under proper supervision. In the spring after the danger of frost had passed, a seedbed, 20 by 100 feet, was laid out. Wood was burned on it to destroy weeds and insects, and then the minute tobacco seeds were sown. As soon as the young plants were tall enough, usually about the first of May, they were transplanted into the fields during the first rainy weather and set out in hillocks three or four feet apart. About a month later (or when the plants were a foot high) they were topped and the lower leaves and suckers cut off. About twice a week until the crop matured, the plants were cleaned of worms and weeds. After six weeks, when the leaves attained full growth and began to turn brownish, plants were cut down as they ripened and piled into heaps.

Writing in his diary on August 28, 1750, Rev. Robert Rose, the first rector of St. Anne's Parish and a man who had considerable influence upon early Albemarle, described how one neighbor carried out this harvesting process.

. . . a serene Morning, busie cutting down Tobo which by Thomas Merrill is managed as follows. When it is cut down it must be turned carefully & often till it falls, then laid in heaps till it is so as without pain you can endure your Hand in it (then after the Top is taken off and put in heaps to heat likewise). Spread it abroad thin on trees . . . if You

fear Rain let it Lye till next day and when the Dew is off turn it . . .
then when the dew falls in the Evening bring it in and scaffold it. Let it
stand till it be cured red then house it at nights as in case; coop it and
let it lye till it sweats greatly which will be from 3 days to 6, according
to the heat of the weather. Then let it hang Singly so that the leaves
Stick not together. By these Means Tobo may be Stemd fourteen days
after it is cut. N. B. When it is sweated aneough it will be Nutmeg
Colour. Tobo ought not be handled Wett either with Rain or dew. Should
it by Rain get yellow, it must hang without or within door till it is cured
of the red Colour & then coop it as before.[1]

After "tobo" achieved that nutmeg color, as Rose relates, slaves
stripped the leaves and packed them into hogsheads that weighed
800 to 1,000 pounds when filled. All tobacco destined for export had
to be sent to official warehouses, in colonial days located at or below
the fall line. There the tobacco was inspected, and if it was of good
quality, the hogshead was branded with a hot iron and a certificate
issued to the owner. This certificate was negotiable and, in effect,
became circulating currency. In 1779, for example, a student could
attend the College of William and Mary for 1,000 pounds of tobacco
per year.

Getting that heavy hogshead to a warehouse on the James, Rappahannock, or Pamunkey and on its way to market in England often
was no small achievement, especially if its owner lived in isolated
parts of Albemarle far from reliable waterways. Usually a hogshead
was rolled—that is, dragged by oxen—to the nearest creek or river,
then placed precariously in a shallow canoe and floated downstream.
Although most local tobacco went down the James, good prices at
such ports as Fredericksburg could induce a planter to attempt an
overland route. In the closing decades of the century, as roads improved, more and more planters rolled their hogsheads all the way
to a warehouse or transported them by means of a wagon maintained
by Charlottesville merchants for that purpose.

In 1789 this transport problem was eased considerably by the establishment of two inspection stations within the county—one at Milton
at the head of navigation on the Rivanna only six miles from
Charlottesville and the other at the mouth of Ballenger's Creek on
the James about five miles above the site of the original courthouse.
A few years later a third official warehouse was constructed on the
property of Thomas Mann Randolph just across the river from Milton. Erected as a convenience for planters on the Rivanna's north

[1] Rose's diary is quoted with the permission of Colonial Williamsburg, Inc.
A microfilm copy of the diary is available at the University of Virginia Library.

bank, North Milton had a short life because of declining interest in tobacco, and Randolph soon converted this facility into private storage space.

While Albemarle still was largely wilderness, the Reverend Mr. Rose, who lived on the Tye River, devised an ingenious method for overcoming some of the handicaps posed by poor transportation. Rose concluded that two canoes lashed together were better than one bobbing along alone, and soon scores of these pontoonlike craft were taking tobacco down the Rivanna and the James. Once they deposited their heavy cargo at the warehouses, the light canoes were separated and poled or paddled back upstream. Rose's intriguing diary makes no specific mention of this contribution to Albemarle's colonial economy, but on March 14, 1749, he commented that his "people" at Roseisle, his home on the Tye, "were making a Canoe—being the 3d—for carrying Down Tobo." Two days later Rose remarked that his brother, an overseer, and a joiner accompanied a canoe to the mouth of the Tye "to see the Nature of the Navigation." Rose may well have been describing an innovative experiment here, referring to lashed-together canoes as a single craft. At any rate, subsequent chroniclers of Albemarle credit this pioneer rector, who seems to have given as much attention to his farms and worldly goods as to the welfare of souls entrusted to his care, with offering a solution to one of the most perplexing problems faced by the Piedmont frontiersman.

In general, Albemarle citizens who produced large quantities of tobacco and Indian corn were called "planters"; those specializing in small grains, "farmers." Yet, since tobacco was the principal money crop and often was needed to pay parish and county levies, even small farmers grew some tobacco, although in 1752 individuals living in the county received permission to pay such taxes in cash if they wished to do so. Those who did not produce even a hogshead of tobacco had some difficulty marketing their crop. If fortunate they might persuade a planter to take their produce to a warehouse. They also could sell to middlemen who collected small crops or forego export and dispose of their leaves within the county for local consumption. In any case, whatever method was selected, the return on their crop was diminished, for transport to a warehouse was costly, and neither middleman nor storekeeper paid top prices.

Planters in time cursed tobacco because it was destroying their soil; yet the great staple was uniquely suited to the needs of Albemarle during the county's formative years. New land was easily acquired; labor was relatively expensive, but certainly more readily available than capital. In fact, the Piedmont planter calculated production, not in how many pounds of tobacco he could grow per acre, but by how many pounds were produced annually per field hand. The only implements needed were an axe, a plow, a hoe, and perhaps a harrow. The crop grew fast, could be packed and transported by water with relative ease, was nearly indestructible once cured, and—most important—was much in demand and could yield high profits. Since tobacco took so much nitrogen and potash from the soil, cultivation was tied closely to clearing of the land. According to Avery Craven, the second crop on a new field was usually the best.[2] Then, after the third or fourth year planters substituted corn and wheat or let their land revert to forest and sought out new acres. In Craven's opinion this one-crop mentality could produce destructive habits. Planters often ignored their stock, demonstrated little interest in the use of manure as fertilizer, and sacrificed everything for "tobo."

Colonial landowners estimated they needed 50 acres for each field hand and at least twenty slaves before hiring an overseer. Thus the smallest economic unit for conventional plantation agriculture complete with overseer and slaves was approximately 1,000 acres, considerably larger than the holdings of nearly all Albemarle residents in the mid-eighteenth century. Ayres concludes that in the 1760s 25 percent of local white males held less than 100 acres and owned no slaves. The majority (57 percent), aided by a handful of blacks, tilled 100 to 400 acres of land. The upper middle class (13 percent) —prosperous farmers, professional men, and part-time merchants— had perhaps five to twenty slaves working some 400 to 1,000 acres, and the gentry (5 percent), men controlling still larger estates and more slaves, were the only individuals turning out hogsheads of tobacco in the traditional manner.

Tobacco flourished best in rich bottomlands, and as Craven comments, although the Piedmont possessed some excellent soil, its river valleys were narrow and upland areas usually produced inferior tobacco. Also, of paramount importance, just as Albemarle was growing in population, so was the rest of Virginia. With that growth came unprecedented demand for food. Even before the Revolutionary War rents in the colony often were being quoted in wheat, not tobacco, and the Old Dominion—in contrast to some parts of the empire—was approaching a state of near self-sufficiency. For example, at about the time "big" Albemarle disappeared in 1761, each white

[2] Craven, *Soil Exhaustion as a Factor in the Agricultural History of Virginia and Maryland, 1606–1860* (Urbana, Ill., 1926), pp. 33–34.

person in the West Indies was receiving annually £20 of exported goods from the mother country; each white Virginian, £1. So, although tobacco gave Albemarle its beginning and long held a strange fascination for the planters and farmers of the region, while bestowing upon them a certain social prestige, the future lay instead with wheat, corn, and other once despised "small grains."

In addition to the great staple grown for export and foodstuffs largely consumed locally or within the colony itself—corn, wheat, barley, rye—one other crop, hemp, was destined for the English market. There was much to be said in favor of its cultivation, and Albemarle appears to have produced a substantial amount in colonial days. The government paid a bounty, and it required little attention during summer months when field hands were busy with tobacco and corn, did little damage to the soil, and sometimes could bring even greater profits than tobacco. There were disadvantages, too. The nearest inspection stations were at Fredericksburg and Manchester, and though Albemarle hemp was of satisfactory quality, the soil of the Valley and western Virginia was much better suited to its production. In 1772 the tobacco-hemp inspection system was extended to flour, but not until roads and highways improved could county farmers raise wheat on a truly commercial scale.

Another marketable commodity, one which found its way from Albemarle's hills and mountain slopes to faraway China, while actually not a cultivated crop and certainly of marginal economic importance, was ginseng. "Sang" roots, possessing reputed sexual powers of great renown, were carefully packed in small kegs and shipped along with hogsheads of tobacco to London. From there they went via India to eager Chinese customers. Just how much "sang" was shipped in colonial days is not clear, but in November 1770 Dr. Thomas Walker's London factor reported that, although three hogsheads of tobacco (two of them marked "GWR 12 & 13") landed safely and sold well, another hogshead of tobacco and "a moiety of 3 casks of Gensang" were lost when a ship was "cast away in the Channell." This agent consoled Walker with the comment that ginseng was not much in demand at the moment, adding he had failed to make any profit on similar transactions with Indian shippers in 1769.

Nearly every landowner grew tobacco, wheat, Indian corn, barley, and oats and kept cows, sheep, pigs, and chickens. What they sold each year depended, naturally enough, upon their own needs and the scope of their operations. Only the gentry professed much interest in vegetables, although entries in Thomas Jefferson's *Garden Book* reveal that he was growing peas (his favorite vegetable), asparagus, celery, onions, radishes, broccoli, cauliflower, and cucumbers as early as 1767. Philip Mazzei experimented with viniculture at Colle on the eve of the Revolution and brought a small colony of Italian migrants to Albemarle to work for him; however, as soon as hostilities erupted Mazzei returned to Europe as Virginia's spokesman, and the promising vineyards were abandoned. Some of his employees joined the local militia and the Continental Army, hired out as gardeners on nearby estates, or became independent farmers specializing, of course, in the skills they knew best. Some of their descendants are citizens of Albemarle today. The Gianniny family, for example, probably came to the region to work for Mazzei. According to Woods, in 1784 Anthony Gianniny bought land on Buck Island Creek and eight years later sought permission to build a mill on that stream. In 1807 another man by the same name, undoubtedly a son, was licensed to perform marriages as a Baptist clergyman.

Many planters, among them Jefferson's father, built water mills to produce flour for their plantations. The first of which we have record was located on Pretty's (Priddy's) Creek in 1742, but by that date others no doubt were scattered along rivers and streams throughout the county. The year after Peter Jefferson's death his mill at Shadwell earned a net profit of £41, a handsome sum considering that construction of an ordinary house cost less than half that amount. This income came from fees paid by small farmers who used the mill to grind their wheat and corn. Some millowners accepted part of the flour as payment, a practice obviously not followed by the Jefferson family.

Charles Watts, who has analyzed records of Shadwell in the mid-1700s, concludes it was a very profitable operation. Admittedly, a frontier farm or plantation produced little during the first few years; but if Jefferson had patented the property, rather than buying it from William Randolph in 1741, the original cost of those 400 acres would have been about £8. The place was worked by a few slaves (the current price of a good field hand was about £30 and it cost perhaps one-fifth that sum to maintain him each year) and an overseer who received one-seventh of the principal crops as his pay. In 1760 Shadwell showed an annual net profit in tobacco sales alone of £17; that is, nearly all operating costs (maintenance of slaves, property, payment of quitrents, etc.) were charged against the return realized from those hogsheads of the "great staple" shipped to England. However, this farm was only a small part of the Jefferson lands and much more than tobacco was grown and sold. The total estate

4. Transporting tobacco to market. (From William Tatham, *An Historical and Practical Essay on the Culture and Commerce of Tobacco*, London, 1800)

showed a net profit of £188 (again in tobacco sales) which, according to Watts, represents a return of about 16 percent on Peter Jefferson's original investment in land and slaves. To this must be added, of course, income from the mill and sums realized from the sale of grain and other produce.

Though this one accounting gives a rather inadequate picture of overall plantation economy, it reveals that when tobacco brought good prices, Albemarle's eighteenth-century elite did very well, for most members of the privileged class had still other sources of income. These included fees earned as surveyors, doctors, or lawyers, payment for service in the militia and local and colonial governments, and — above all else — very lucrative speculation in lands lying outside of Albemarle's boundaries.

Surveying was both necessary and profitable. Often first on the scene, a surveyor was able to pick out choice tracts for himself and his friends. Joshua Fry, Peter Jefferson, Thomas Turpin, William Cabell, and Thomas Walker were Albemarle's pioneer surveyors. Fry, the county's first official surveyor, averaged one hundred surveys during each of the years from 1744 to 1748. At the rate of £3 per assignment, this gave him an annual income of at least £300, less a salary for his assistant, Turpin, and travel and attendant expenses.

Cabell and Walker, both doctors, were equally important members of this frontier society. Because of great distances, most families relied upon their own ingenuity and home remedies when anyone became sick, but one of these two men usually was called in cases of serious illness. Bleeding and purging were popular cures, along with cordials, pills, blisters, drops, powders, plasters, sweats, and emetics. Cabell frequently advised use of "Turlington's Basalm," "Bateman's Drops," "Stoughton's Bitters," and "Anderson's Pills." Rhubarb was a favorite all-round remedy for multitudinous complaints. Cabell imported some medicinal items and conducted his own apothecary shop where he mixed scores of compounds. He charged £1 to £5 per house visit, depending upon distance traveled. This sum undoubtedly was in Virginia paper currency, not sterling. Walker, on the other hand, charged his good friend Peter Jefferson only eight shillings for a house call and fifteen shillings for "a visit and attendance." Since Dr. Cabell operated on a "no cure–no pay" basis, his fees were not necessarily excessive. He also, when necessary, amputated legs and arms at his Swan Creek surgery. Nevertheless, such medical care was much too expensive for Albemarle's poor or middling classes. But they may very well have been better off without a doctor's attention, since there is little evidence that the doctors of that day could do much more than the patients could do for themselves.

Early lawyers of Albemarle include William Battersby, Edmund Gray, John Harvie, Thomas Jefferson, Gideon Marr, James Meredith, and Clement Reed. Fees, not large, were regulated by law; but through constant application, one could make a good living. In 1767, for example, young Tom Jefferson received for his services about £43 in cash and was owed £250, making a total income from his practice—providing he could collect those outstanding debts—of nearly £300.

A planter also might be engaged in trade as a merchant and own (but rarely operate) an ordinary. Several early citizens, among them David Lewis, Jr., Robert Lewis, Thomas Meriwether, Thomas Walker, and Richard Woods bought and sold various goods. Although they did not maintain stores in the usual sense, they frequently referred to themselves as merchants. They were joined by an important group of local factors representing prestigious Glasgow firms. Finding the Tidewater controlled by London, these enterprising Scots followed migration into the backcountry and established stores at convenient spots throughout the Piedmont. At their places of business they bought farm products, usually in exchange for imported goods or slaves, and sold to planters and farmers on credit terms of nine months or more. It was the duty of these factors to handle area business and see that their employers always held a proper mortgage for money due them. The activities of these merchants, both local and imported, appear to have been widespread and lucrative. In 1762 David Lewis, Jr., had 155 accounts due him totaling nearly £500.

Albemarle's colonial ordinaries, although ostensibly controlled by the county court, appear to have been rather dismal, often filthy affairs far removed from romantic pictures we have today of cosy rural inns complete with jovial host and voluptuous serving maids. If the justices themselves occasionally had been forced to seek meals or lodgings in them, perhaps conditions would have improved in short order. Constant complaints indicate these public facilities left much to be desired; whenever possible, travelers preferred to spend the night in private homes. The usual meal consisted of eggs, bacon, and hoecake washed down with either peach brandy or whiskey, both of local origin. Beds often were crawling with bugs and vermin. Both Peter Jefferson and William Cabell owned taverns, although these structures were not within present-day Albemarle nor were they operated by these gentlemen. However, at least three tavern keepers were doing business within the county in the 1760s: Daniel Scott near the old courthouse on the James, Joel Terrell on Three Notched Road just west of Charlottesville, and William Michie on the Buck Mountain Road in the northern part of the county.

The only industrial enterprise appearing before the Revolution was a short-lived and ill-fated attempt to manufacture iron. In 1768 three men from Baltimore County, Maryland, bought land in South Garden among mountains thought to contain substantial quantities of ore. Two of the trio quickly abandoned the project, but John Wilkerson persisted, gained the attention of Thomas Walker, William Cabell, Alexander Trent, and Edward Carter, and on December 28, 1770, founded the Albemarle Iron Works. Wilkerson, as manager, held a one-third share and was to invest £1,000; the others, £500, entitling each of them to a one-sixth share. Woods reports that three furnaces were built, but within a few years Wilkerson was charged with inefficiency and the undertaking collapsed.

There are intriguing hints of yet another industry, perhaps cottage type, within the county. Writing to a British merchant on January 24, 1770, William Nelson, father of General Thomas Nelson, bragged of how self-sufficient American colonials had become. "I now wear," he wrote, "a good suit of cloth of my son's wool, manufactured as well as my shirts, in Albemarle, my shoes, hose, Buckles, Wigg & hat, etc., of our own country, and these we improve every year in Quality as well as Quantity." [3]

One of the most successful of Albemarle's early citizens, a gentleman whose name appears as pioneer county justice, member of the General Assembly, planter, surgeon, merchant, investor, and professional man, was Dr. William Cabell. For nearly four decades before his death in 1774 he seems to have taken a personal interest in practically every step which helped transform a wilderness into a frontier settlement of plantations and farms. In 1753, when he turned over his surveying duties to his son, Cabell held 20,000 acres of very choice land. The best of this he gave to his children; the rest he sold for high prices and reinvested in still more land. This ambitious gentleman, smitten with Virginia as a young naval surgeon in the service of George I, found his multi-faceted career on the American frontier extremely rewarding. While his is certainly no rags-to-riches tale, it is apparent that this tall, spare figure with keen, alert mind made the very most of every opportunity. His various roles as healer

[3] *William and Mary Quarterly* 7 (1898):26.

to the sick, surveyor, businessman, politician, and land speculator gave him an enormous circle of contacts and friends throughout central Virginia. Probably no citizen of early Albemarle was so widely respected — respect which was well deserved.

However, for every William Cabell there were hundreds of independent small farmers about whom we know little and several thousand slaves about whom we know even less. Most of these farmers tediously tended crops year in and year out and sometimes supplemented their income by means of various skills, just as their "betters" did. Yet at least one tinker, weaver, blacksmith, and haberdasher and several carpenters were living in Albemarle County from 1745 to 1763. According to Ayres, these craftsmen were moderately prosperous since they bought and sold tracts of land of 250 acres or more, but artisans and technicians of this sort were rare. Most Piedmont settlers out of necessity were do-it-yourself types, and demand for such skills remained limited. The frequency with which tools are mentioned among the possessions of deceased persons indicates that nearly every household harbored a general repairman who could do some carpentry, lay brick, or tan leather and a good woman who could spin, card wool, and turn her hand at making clothes. Although there are no colonial records detailing how many of these individuals actually owned land, tax lists of 1782 indicate 87 percent of Albemarle's free white males over twenty-one held some property, an extremely high figure which undoubtedly had not changed appreciably during the war years.

There appear to have been about two thousand slaves in "big" Albemarle at mid-century, and although both white and black populations increased rapidly during the next two decades, the latter probably constituted only 40 percent of the total population of present-day Albemarle at the end of the colonial period. Since many farmers owned only one or two blacks, we can assume most of them existed pretty much as members of the family, not unlike indentured servants, working in the household or at their master's side in the fields. Few estates, if any, boasted more than fifty slaves, and rarely were these workers to be found in great numbers; instead, in groups of eight or ten they toiled away on isolated quarters under the watchful eyes of a lonely, bored overseer. Although free Negroes were rare indeed, their presence cannot be discounted entirely since several Albemarle blacks served in the Revolutionary War, and presumably they had to be free before they could enlist. The majority of local slaves were found on the estates and farms of eastern and southern Albemarle, the region dominated largely by tobacco culture.

Meanwhile, in western regions now known as the White Hall and Samuel Miller districts and an area of few slaves, several individuals began to acquire or add to their landholdings. During the years from 1744 to 1761, the days of "big" Albemarle, members of the Woods family, David Stockton, Dennis Doyle, and Benjamin Brown (both Sr. and Jr.) arose to positions of local prominence. All of these men bequeathed their names to rivers, streams, mountain coves, and other geographical features of that region. Benjamin Brown the elder first gained title to property "on the Great Mountains" in 1747 and, in time, became master of several thousand acres. However, William Robertson, who patented 6,190 acres in the Buck Mountain Creek area in 1739, and David Mills, holder of an equally impressive patent in the same vicinity after 1748, probably were western Albemarle's largest landowners during those decades.

Others who patented lands in the region that would generally become known for its small farms, wheat fields, and an absence of blacks, at least compared to the tobacco-growing estates to the east, included Richard Blalock, William Burrus, William Carr, Christopher Curtis, John Dickey, Samuel Garlick, David Goss, Robert Harris, John Jemirson (or Jameson), Thomas Joplin, David Kinkead, Thomas Lankford, William Little, William McCord, Robert Mackneely, Daniel Maupin, John Mayfield, John Moran, William Morris, John Mullins, Mathew Mullins, Alexander Patton, Joseph Phillips, John Rogers, John Snow, Joel Terrell, James Warren, and William Whiteside. Three small patents of special interest are those of Rebecca Bunch (1741) on Ivy Creek, the first woman to gain direct title to the soil of Albemarle; John Braham, who acquired 176 acres "in the North Garden" five years later; and Jeremiah White, who got 125 acres "in the South Garden" in 1756. According to Watts, these are among the earliest references to these adjoining communities lying southwest of Charlottesville, although Woods indicates Robert Lewis obtained a huge patent of 4,030 acres "in the North Garden" in 1736. Lewis, who married Jane, daughter of Nicholas Meriwether, acquired some 16,000 acres in various parts of Albemarle during his lifetime and made his home, not on his North Garden lands, but at Belvoir near Cismont.

Until 1760, thanks to high prices for tobacco, both small and large landowners, those with one slave and those with fifty, were doing well, but a decline in prices in ensuing years caused some economic reverses. Also, at about the same time, as frontier farms developed into enterprises more commercial in nature, the number of slaves

increased. Ayres notes that inventories of estates reveal that during
the years 1748 to 1752, only 29 percent of deceased individuals with
property owned slaves (average 2.7), but for the years 1764 to 1770
Albemarle records show that 61 percent of those bequeathing property to their heirs owned, on the average, 9.7 slaves. Possession of
black labor increased the value of a man's personal property faster
than anything else; hence the desire to become master of at least a
handful of sturdy field hands. One local farmer wrote a creditor in
1765, "I had rather sell anything [but] the negroes . . . as it would
hurt the estate very much to take the negroes out of the crop and
sell them." And slaves gave a master not only the essential for
economic advancement but social prestige as well.

Thus it appears that during the days of Goochland and "big"
Albemarle an individual of ability and moderate means could move
to the Piedmont and, through diligent, hard work, improve both his
economic and social status. Some men of only second rank in the
east easily advanced into the circles of the elite, ambitious individuals such as Allen Howard and Charles Lynch. After 1760 there are
indications that younger sons of wealthy Tidewater planters began
to migrate into Albemarle, bringing with them slaves, economic resources, and social status. Division of the county, in effect tripling
the number of local offices and seats to be had in the House of
Burgesses, may have induced some of these well-to-do youths to
move westward. Names such as Lewis, Meriwether, Walker, and
Carter appear on the lists of Albemarle County justices, replacing
Ballou, Hickman, and other pioneers. Edward Carter, son of Secretary John Carter, took up his father's lands about that date and in
1766 defeated Henry Fry, son of "the noble Fry," for a seat in the
General Assembly, clear evidence of the winds of change.

Despite widespread ownership of land throughout the community,
as Albemarle's colonial decades came to a close a small elite, the
privileged 5 percent, obviously ruled the county. They lived on the
largest estates with the most slaves, often held still more land in
neighboring counties, controlled key positions in local government,
represented their fellow citizens (and their own special interests)
at Williamsburg, and gave orders whenever muster day was held.
Yet this was no idle, pleasure-seeking aristocracy. These men took
their civic duties seriously and, because of bonds created by frontier
surroundings, paid less attention to the niceties of a more conventional class structure found in the Tidewater. Many of them, only
one or two generations removed from meager surroundings, could

both appreciate and understand the yearnings of the ambitious, sturdy young farmers who comprised the bulk of the county's population.

As Albemarle turned the corner into the troubled decade of the 1770s, ominous clouds appeared on the horizon. The obvious trend to large, commercial estates tilled by slave labor created substantial uneasiness among small farmers. More and more of them looked to the west for new opportunities, new (and cheaper) lands, especially in the fabulous region beyond the mountains known as Kentucky where virgin soil yielded up bumper crops which could be sent swiftly to market down the broad rivers of the Mississippi-Ohio basin. In addition, tobacco was becoming less and less profitable. Many big planters found their indebtedness to British merchants increasing year by year. According to Thomas Jefferson, the shift from tobacco to wheat was beginning even before colony and mother country became embroiled in acrid debate. The implications of these developments—a society of extensive landholdings which seemed to limit the economic potential of the less affluent and general disenchantment with the great staple upon which Albemarle's economy rested—are profound indeed. Added to this general malaise, touching to some degree every local household, was fear of what the future held. Although slave, indentured servant, and small farmer probably paid little heed to the transatlantic controversy concerning taxation, rights of Parliament, and the prerogatives of colonial assemblies, they could not help but know from conversations of the gentry that all was not right with their world: a crisis was at hand.

Chapter 4

Albemarle in
the Revolutionary War

ALBEMARLE's experiences during the Revolutionary War were both typical and not so typical of those encountered by scores of isolated backcountry communities far from the sea. Opposition to the British, in the beginning, was extremely strong, although during the long, eight-year conflict patriot ardor ebbed and flowed considerably under the weight of boredom and enemy successes. Charlottesville, site of one minor skirmish in 1781, was occupied briefly by His Majesty's dragoons; but, for the most part, this war was a faraway thing to the north or south. What was unique about those frightful years was the number of state and national leaders the county provided and the presence of thousands of enemy prisoners on Albemarle soil.

Even as we approach the bicentennial of our independence, historians still disagree on causes of the rupture between colony and mother country, but clearly the roots of disagreement lie in Britain's victory over the French in 1763, debts created by that conflict, and British efforts to make Americans share increasing costs of government and defense as they tried to organize what is often called their first empire. Mingled with these basic ingredients for discord is one fact of paramount importance: the unprecedented growth of the thirteen colonies, which by 1775 had a population nearly one-half that of Great Britain itself. And within that population, lest we forget, were fifth- and sixth-generation Americans who no longer thought of themselves primarily as Englishmen and thousands who had no British blood whatsoever in their veins. But perhaps the crux of the matter for key citizens of the Old Dominion was a growing realization that the new imperial policy emanating from London between 1763 and 1776 constituted a direct threat to that colony's ruling class.[1] Since that elite group both controlled and led a relatively homogeneous society, it is not surprising that public opinion was easily marshaled for the patriot cause. It is also possible that anti-British sentiment may have run especially high in Albemarle

---

[1] Thad W. Tate, "The Coming of the Revolution in Virginia: Britain's Challenge to Virginia's Ruling Class," *William and Mary Quarterly*, 3d ser., 19 (1962):323–43.

because so many citizens—both well-to-do and less affluent—looked eagerly to new lands in the west which, if London had its way, would be closed to them. All Virginians were stirred by the Townshend Acts of the late 1760s, customs duties on paint, glass, paper, and tea; and in 1772, when royal authorities proposed taking citizens of Rhode Island accused of attacking a British sloop to England for trial, the House of Burgesses created a standing Committee of Correspondence, the first colonywide committee to be organized. It was Dabney Carr of Albemarle County, Thomas Jefferson's brother-in-law, who introduced the resolution establishing this body; and although Carr succumbed to fever a short time later, his action reveals that Albemarle's leaders, more than four years before independence, were deeply concerned.

Two years later, at the urging of Thomas Jefferson and John Walker, local members of the House of Burgesses, citizens of the county gathered at "the new church on the Hardware" on Saturday, July 23, for a day of prayer and a sermon by Rev. Charles Clay, rector of St. Anne's Parish. Meeting at the courthouse on July 26 (election day), a group of angry freeholders, aroused both by ominous news from Massachusetts and what Jefferson and Walker told them, issued this fiery salvo:

Resolved, That the inhabitants of the Several States of *British America* are subject to the laws which they adopted at their settlement, and to such others as have been made by their respective legislatures, duly constituted and appointed with their own consent. That no other Legislature whatsoever can rightfully exercise authority over them; and that these privileges they hold as the common rights of mankind, confirmed by the political Constitutions they have respectively assumed, and also by several Charters of compact with the Crown.

Resolved, That these their natural and legal rights have in frequent instances been invaded by the Parliament of *Great Britain*, and particularly that they were so by an Act lately passed to take away the trade of the inhabitants of the town of *Boston*, in the Province of *Massachusetts Bay;* that all such assumptions of unlawful power are dangerous to the rights of the *British* Empire in general, and should be considered as its common cause, and that we will ever be ready to join with our fellow-subjects in every part of the same, in executing all those rightful powers which *God* has given us, for re-establishing and guarantying such their constitutional rights, when, where, and by whomsoever invaded.

It is the opinion of this meeting, that the most eligible means of effecting these purposes, will be to put an immediate stop to all imports from *Great Britain*, (cotton, osnabrigs, stripped duffil, medicines, gunpowder, lead, books and printed paper, the necessary tools and implements of the handicraft arts and manufactures excepted, for a limited term) and to all exports thereto, after the first day of *October*, which shall be in the year of our Lord, 1775; and immediately to discontinue all commercial intercourse with every part of the *British* Empire which shall not in like manner break off their commerce with *Great Britain*.

It is the opinion of this meeting, that we immediately cease to import all commodities from every part of the world which are subjected by the *British* Parliament to the payment of duties in America.

It is the opinion of this meeting, that these measures should be pursued until a repeal be obtained of the Act for blocking up the harbour of *Boston;* of the Acts prohibiting or restraining internal manufactures in *America;* of the Acts imposing on any commodities duties to be paid in *America;* and of the Act laying restrictions on the *American* trade; and that on such repeal it will be reasonable to grant our brethren of *Great Britain* such privileges in commerce as may amply compensate their fraternal assistance, past and present.

Resolved, However, that this meeting do submit these their opinions to the Convention of Deputies from the several counties of this Colony, and appointed to be held at *Williamsburg* on the first day of *August* next, and also to the general Congress from the several *American* States, when and wheresoever held; and that they will concur in these or any other measures which such Convention or such Congress shall adopt as most expedient for the *American* good; and we do appoint *Thomas Jefferson* and *John Walker* our Deputies to act for this county in said Convention and instruct them to conform themselves to these our Resolutions and Opinions.[2]

These words, drafted by Jefferson and outspoken indeed, are an emotional appeal to both natural, God-given rights and to all of the American "states," as well as other parts of the British Empire, for cooperative action against the policies of London.

Angered when the House of Burgesses agreed with Albemarle and denounced the closing of the port of Boston, the governor, John Murray, earl of Dunmore, dissolved the Assembly. Ousted from their meeting place, members moved to the Raleigh Tavern's genial surroundings and proceeded to call for "a general Congress of Deputies from the several *American* States." The result was the first Continental Congress, which met in Philadelphia on September 5, 1774. Neither of Albemarle's representatives to Williamsburg was present, but Jefferson composed a paper which was widely circulated there and had considerable influence. Although *A Summary View of the Rights of British America* was considered by many to be too radical, it nevertheless reflected the opinions at that time of both the author and many of his neighbors.

[2] *American Archives*, 4th ser., 1 (Washington, D.C., 1837):638.

Deterioration of transatlantic relations caused many citizens of the Old Dominion to take most seriously these warning words from Albemarle; however, it was Patrick Henry who, at Richmond's St. John's Church, gave voice to the rising cry for action. And, at the same moment, a young firebrand, no less emotional than Henry, emerged on the local scene. His name was George Gilmer. Son of a Scottish physician who migrated to Williamsburg, in 1771 young Gilmer married Lucy, daughter of Thomas Walker, settled in Albemarle, began to practice medicine, and soon was in the forefront of agitation which eventually led to war. He is a prime example of the leadership that the gentry of the county provided for the patriot cause.[3]

Late in 1774, after the formation of the Continental Association in Philadelphia, Albemarle citizens elected a general committee and regional subcommittees to enforce resolutions urging restrictions on trade with Britain. Some confusion exists concerning membership of the county's central committee. On June 1, 1775, Purdie's *Virginia Gazette* listed these gentlemen: John Walker (chairman), John Coles, Isaac Davies, George Gilmer, John Henderson, Jun., Charles Lewis, Nicholas Lewis, John Marks, James Quarles, David Rodes, and William Sims. However, in his record book Jefferson recorded his own name (noting proudly that he received the most votes) and added to the above list the names of James Hopkins, Thomas Napier, Thomas Walker, and John Ware, but omitted that of John Marks. Since Jefferson's entry (dated November 8, 1774) cites fifteen individuals in all with the votes each received, it would appear these men actually were elected but for various reasons did not serve on the committee and that the eleven gentlemen listed by Purdie composed the body which, as royal authority collapsed, became a quasi-legal government of sorts. In fact, this committee came to represent stability and order, making the transition from colony to state relatively smooth at the local level.

Jefferson's records also indicate that obeying regulations of this group presented some complications and irritations, even for dedicated patriots. He was somewhat embarrassed by an order to London for a pair of "sash windows . . . with a parcel of spare glass to mend with." Jefferson requested these materials in June 1774, and they were shipped before he could cancel the order. When he discovered that these goods would arrive at a Virginia port and be

[3] See Mary M. Sullivan, "The Association in Virginia, 1774–1776" (M.A. thesis, University of Virginia, 1963).

subject to action by the state committee, the squire of Monticello wrote Archibald Cary and Benjamin Waller in Williamsburg to explain what had happened. He agreed that the windows and glass should be placed at their disposal and, according to established policy, be reshipped, handed over to the Association, or sold for benefit of the citizens of Boston.

While the semilegal Albemarle committee struggled with similar problems presented by importation of British goods and tried to coordinate its activities with those of other counties throughout Virginia, military action against royal authority became a distinct possibility. Alarmed by the ringing phrases of Patrick Henry and signs of increasing unrest, on the night of April 20–21, 1775, Dunmore removed military supplies stored in the magazine at Williamsburg to a British vessel. Colonial leaders had placed an impromptu guard of local citizens about the building to avert just what happened; but, bored and tired, the men had gone home. This matériel included fifteen half barrels of powder and all arms bearing the king's mark, guns which Dunmore emphasized were not purchased at the colony's expense. At the same time the governor stressed that the magazine was "a very insecure Depository" and promised to return both powder and other public stores as soon as the structure was repaired. Unfortunately, just as word of this action spread throughout the colony, Virginians learned of Lexington and Concord where shots had been fired and blood shed and of equally alarming British plans to extend acts aimed at New England to all thirteen colonies.

George Gilmer, a leading member of the local committee and a first lieutenant in the Albemarle Volunteers, called for an immediate march upon Williamsburg. He and other high-ranking officers (Charles Lewis and John Marks) wrote Colonel George Washington telling him of their intentions. Washington replied he had assurances the "powder affair" could be settled amicably, adding that an expedition seemed unnecessary. By the time his letter reached Charlottesville, eighteen local citizens already had set out. According to Woods, these individuals accompanied Gilmer, Lewis, and Marks: David Allen, Flavy Frazier, Edward Garland, John Henderson, William Johnson, Charles L. Lewis, William T. Lewis, Reuben Lindsay, John Lowry, John Martin, Thomas Martin, Jr., James Quarles, Fred William Wills, Isaac Wood, and William Wood. On the way, however, these men met Patrick Henry, who expressed an optimistic view of the situation, noting royal authorities had agreed to pay for the powder seized; so Albemarle's patriots turned around and came home.

By mid-May the furor over the governor's action had subsided, and he and his family were back in the palace once more, but this state of normalcy proved to be brief. Soon after the Burgesses convened in special session on May 24 they learned that Dunmore, claiming he feared civil disorders and attacks upon his family, had fled to the security of the British man-of-war *Fowey* anchored in the York River. Although Virginia lawmakers thought this action precipitious and asked his lordship to return, Dunmore had cause for alarm. Several patriots, among them Richard Bland, had suggested he be hanged.

On June 10, a Saturday, the Burgesses wrote Dunmore citing their specific grievances, but the governor, in reply, put full blame for the impasse upon the Burgesses themselves. They, he said, had aroused the populace, placed guards about the magazine without his knowledge, and assembled men to repel the king's forces coming to protect him. He insisted he be reinstated in his full powers, law and order restored, all independent companies disarmed, and arms stolen in May returned to the government. Dunmore accused the lawmakers "by your own example and by every means in your power" of establishing a spirit of persecution against all "who differ from the multitude in public opinion, or are attached from principles and duty to the service of their King and government." It is apparent that, as tempers rose, the House first talked on an elevated plane of constitutional rights while the governor stressed his irritation at local developments. Not surprisingly, the Burgesses answered in kind.

During the remainder of June 1775 Burgesses and governor bickered back and forth, the legislators recalling happy days under Botetourt and accusing Dunmore of misrepresenting facts of Virginia life to London and disturbing the local scene by intemperate actions. On June 23 the House urged the governor to come to Williamsburg to sign various bills. It was time to harvest crops; and, they insisted, they had to return to their homes at once. Dunmore refused to go to the capital; the Burgesses refused to meet him aboard his vessel in the York River. The following day the House adjourned. Attempts to reconvene in October 1775 and March and May 1776 failed to produce a quorum. For all practical purposes, after 168 years royal government in the Old Dominion had ceased to exist.

While this stalemate was developing in the Tidewater, events were moving swiftly toward a climax in Albemarle. Early in June, Lieutenant Gilmer, who seems to have been the county's Sam Adams, once more exhorted his men to act. For Gilmer, at least, the "powder affair" was far from over. They must choose, he said, between free-

dom and becoming "voluntary and abject slaves to a wicked Administration. . . . My God, soldiers, let me beg you to look on
this matter with a serious eye, and make yourself masters of every
art of war with the quickest dispatch." [4] Two weeks later at a muster
held on June 17 Gilmer reiterated his call for a display of force
against Dunmore, who "in a clandestine manner" had seized powder
placed in the magazine for the defense of Virginia by "good" Lord
Botetourt.

From these circumstances, Gent'n, can there be any rashness in con-
jecturing the designs of our enemies? Does it require any penetration to
discover their Diabolical plan? Is it not self-evident that they want to
deprive us of the means of self-defence, hoping thereby to make easy con-
quest of us; this clearly appears their design, and are not these provoca-
tions sufficient, Gent'n, to redouble the flame of opposition in us; are we
not daily receiving the shocks of some outrageous wrong? Do we not
suffer matters to pass unchecked and unobserved? Our country cries aloud
for us to let fall our Just indignation on the head of every apostate to
the Grand American Cause. The man who can reflect on all our publick
injuries, and not rouze up every spark of defensive courage in his constitution, must be deemed a timid, contemptible mortal. When, Gent'n, we
cannot attain redress by reasonable and constitutional means, let our resistance be made with fortitude and undaunted resolution. Should we be
distressed with the horrors of civil war (which cup of bitterness God in
his wisdom forever pass from us), but should it be unavoidable, I say
let us not behold it in such a fatal view as to be terrified at the event.
Let us look [at] the Justness of our cause and up to Him who holds victory and justness in His hands, to crown our undertaking with the success it deserves, and let us determine to make a glorious exit in the field
rather than bow our necks to the yoke of Tyranny and Infamy.

Swayed by this appeal, the men voted to march on Williamsburg
a second time. Two volunteers, John Coles and David Rodes, dis-
sented and were summarily drummed out of the company. On July
11 twenty-seven Albemarle patriots, led by Gilmer, set out for the
capital. There they joined contingents from other counties encamped
at Waller's Grove and remained ready to counter any moves made
by Dunmore. Just how and when they might act was far from clear,
and although records indicate the local group was a spirited lot and
provided considerable leadership—Gilmer said his men were applauded "everywhere for their earnestness"—this ill-organized little

[4] "Papers, Military and Political, 1775–1778, of George Gilmer, M.D., of
'Pen Park,' Albemarle County, Va.," *Miscellaneous Papers of the Virginia
Historical Society* 6 (Richmond, 1887):79–89.

army soon became disorderly. Even Gilmer admitted in a letter to Jefferson that the 250-man force was a confused, inactive rabble. "We appear rather invited to feast than fight," he observed tartly.

Yet, while privately disheartened, publicly this patriot's zeal remained unabated. While in Williamsburg, Gilmer, under protest, paid a bill due James and Donald Webster, druggists and chemists of London, charges which he claimed were "extravagant beyond all bounds."

The people of Great Britain are to such a degree corrupted that Gold is the only medium thro' w'ch they'l admit any reasoning. . . . Our Governour had abdicated; taken off Numbers of our Slaves, and intended to raise the whole body into rebellion, but he is disappointed in all his hellish schemes; he, it is said, expects Troops, but we are prepared to make them scamper by the Lexington March. I am down with a chosen Detachment of Riflemen to salute any that may be rash enough to Land in this Colony. We wish Union and peace on Constitutional principles, but will not yield or surrender one jot of our Natural or acquired rights, and I remain a declared enemy to all the Sons of Corruption.

Not surprisingly, this hastily gathered band of volunteers soon became a source of embarrassment to the Old Dominion's civil authorities, and on July 28 the Committee of Safety officially asked the men to disband and return quietly to their homes. At the same time they transformed these independent companies into "minute men," a decision which Lieutenant Gilmer resisted strenuously. A few weeks later, addressing Albemarle citizens, he commented caustically upon what had happened to his once proud company. "Out of near three hundred Volunteers there are how many Minute Men? So few that I am afraid to name them. . . . We were once all fire, now most of us are become inanimate and indifferent."

This view was, of course, somewhat extreme. What this fiery young officer and thousands of other patriots were learning in those confused months of 1775 was the hard lesson that if thirteen colonies were sincere in their wish to become a nation, they must develop, as quickly as possible, national policies and national programs. Local and state views for the good of all would have to yield to larger considerations.

During the next few years Albemarle experienced war only in a peripheral fashion. Late in November 1775 the county committee expressed concern over distress being encountered by some Virginians living in coastal communities. They were, it was said, being driven from their homes by those loyal to George III. Albemarle's leaders urged local citizens to aid those so harassed in every way possible, even furnishing them with accommodations, homes, and lands—suggestions which, despite patriotic overtones, sound like an open invitation to settle permanently in the Piedmont.

In October 1776 three petitions from local dissenters, similar to many penned throughout Virginia by disgruntled Baptists, Methodists, and Presbyterians, as well as some Anglicans who believed strongly in religious freedom, were dispatched to Williamsburg.[5] These individuals, alarmed by fears that the Church of England might regain its privileged status, expressed their opposition in clear, firm language. The first of these, dated October 22 and bearing the signatures of sixty-nine residents of Albemarle, Amherst, and Buckingham counties, promised all-out aid and assistance to a "Common Wealth" based upon religious freedom, but noted "that they solemnly declare that the same motive, namely liberty, that exerted them to venture life & fortune opposing the measures adopted by the King of [sic] Parliament, will still Determine them to bleed at every vain [sic] before they will submit to any form of Government that may be subversive of these Religious Privileges that are a natural Right, and that stand nearer every man of Principal [sic], than even life itself." Two more petitions, similar in intent but less vehement in tone, followed in November. Signers included George Gilmer, George Divers, Philip Mazzei, Jacob Moon, Thomas and David Garth, Edward Carter, and several members of the Lewis family. Occasionally the same individuals signed more than one of these appeals.

Another resolution, nonreligious in nature, somewhat puzzling, and composed with a mixture of singular and plural pronouns, appears in the papers of George Gilmer. This is the so-called Albemarle Declaration dated April 21, 1779, which bears over two hundred names and firmly renounces all ties to George III and his heirs and successors. The document concludes with this binding oath: "I will be faithful & bear true allegiance to the commonwealth of Virginia as a free & independent state, & . . . . I will not at any [time] do or cause to be done, any matter or thing that will be prejudicial or injurious to the freedom & independence thereof as declared by congress & also . . . we will discover & make known to some one justice of the peace for the said state all treasons or traitorous conspiracies which we know or hereafter shall know to be formed against this or any of the united States of America. So help me God." [6] Why virtually every male voter on the home front felt

[5] See *Virginia Magazine of History and Biography* 18 (1910):140–43, 255–58, 262.

[6] *Miscellaneous Papers of the Virginia Historical Society*, p. 134.

compelled to append his signature or mark to this statement so late in the conflict is not clear. Perhaps the frustrating campaigns in the North, indications that the war was moving southward, a flagging spirit in frontier Albemarle, or . . . just perhaps . . . evidence of "treasons or traitorous conspiracies" convinced Gilmer and others that this step was necessary. Also, it is quite possible that the arrival a few months before of several thousand enemy prisoners taken at Saratoga may have prompted special concern and resulted in this reaffirmation of faith in the patriot cause.

During these hectic years other men marched away to do battle at such far-flung sites as Quebec, Long Island, Saratoga, Germantown, Brandywine, Trenton, Monmouth, Charleston, Guilford Courthouse, Camden, Savannah, and Yorktown. Woods lists 152 individuals who either enlisted in the county during the war or, as veterans, lived there after hostilities ceased (see Appendix A). Some served in the state militia for only a brief time; others saw extended duty in the Continental ranks up and down the Atlantic Coast. Among those who became officers were four Thompsons and three each bearing the well-known names of Lewis, Meriwether, and Nicholas. The most common names among enlisted men were Maupin and Goolsby; three of the latter gave their lives in behalf of the struggle for independence.

In the ranks of Albemarle's Revolutionary warriors, interestingly, were at least five black men: Johnson Smith, David Barnett, Stephen Bowles, Sherard Goings, and Shadrack Battles.[7]

Little is known concerning Smith, a seaman, or Barnett, who apparently deserted after four month's service in 1777. Bowles joined the Fourth Virginia Regiment for two years in February 1776—his pay was 6⅔ dollars per month—and died in September 1777. Both

[7] Luther P. Jackson, "Virginia Negro Soldiers and Seamen in the American Revolution," *Journal of Negro History* 27 (1942):247–87. Some confusion exists concerning the spelling of these names. National Archives records, cited in the text, indicate Shadrack Battles (not Battle) and Sherard (not Sherwood) Goings are correct. According to established policies, only free blacks could enlist; but, under pressure of events, slaves often were pressed into service and as a reward for valor sometimes won their freedom. Also, early in the conflict masters occasionally sent slaves as substitutes when called for duty; however, by 1779 these practices had ceased. Many blacks fought for the British, and at least 14,000 left with them when the war ended. Officially, at least, Virginia refused to act against any slave found guilty of treason. In 1781 Governor Thomas Jefferson agreed with two judges that a slave could not commit treason—"not being admitted to the Privilege of a Citizen [he] owes the State No Allegiance."

Goings and Battles served with distinction, lived on into the nineteenth century, and applied for pensions. As a result, extensive records exist concerning their Revolutionary War careers. From 1828 until his death nine years later, Goings received $96 per year. A veteran of Germantown, Monmouth, and the seige of New York City, this ex-private testified in the late 1820s that his property consisted of "two indifferent horses, one 14 or 15 years old—the other 4 or 5, a small pony, about two hundred acres of land situated on one of the spears of the Blue Ridge, and it is poor, mountain land, not productive, about thirty or forty acres of this track is cleared, one cow." A day laborer disabled by age, he sought assistance for himself, his wife Susannah, and their two children, aged "about 10 or 12." After his death Susannah received a widow's pension.

Battles, who was a member of Gilmer's Volunteers but did not march to Williamsburg, enlisted as a private in Captain James Franklin's Tenth Virginia Regiment in 1777 and served throughout the war, seeing action at Brandywine, Germantown, Monmouth, and Savannah. A carpenter by trade, he enlisted in Amherst County and received an honorable discharge at Augusta, Georgia. Brought to court on a litter in October 1820 so he could make formal request of aid, Battles noted with pride that he was the "right hand man" of Clough Shelton, who succeeded Franklin as captain of his regiment. During the war, records rarely made reference to race, and it is only through pension requests that one can discern such information. Thus, in this fashion, "col." (for colored) has been inserted in papers relating to Private Battles, an addition which inspired one chronicler of Albemarle's past to promote him to "colonel." Although this promotion is both posthumous and incorrect, it does give Battles some small claim to being the first black officer in American history.

At first, enthusiasm for the struggle for independence made any draft of manpower unnecessary, but in May 1777 the General Assembly enacted a law both encouraging enlistments and establishing a draft for the first time. Specific provisions of this and subsequent drafts changed from time to time, but in general unmarried men were selected by lottery to fill county quotas for the Continental forces. It is apparent, however, that these regulations were highly unpopular and difficult to administer, and Jefferson, for one, opposed them. Those affected often were already in the state militia or working in war installations, and their departure could cause considerable confusion. This was especially true during the last years of the war in Albemarle, 1780–81. As governor, Jefferson had extensive correspondence with officials at the Barracks near Charlottesville, which held enemy prisoners and also became a significant quartermaster depot, concerning the status of men working there.[8] As in all wars, the basic problem was the same: how to balance the supply of fighting men equitably between national and local needs and, at the same time, maintain production of badly needed foodstuffs and military supplies.

On the home front there is little evidence of injustice done in the name of patriotism. There were, of course, a few Tories within the county. John Tidderdale, Robert Bain, and Francis Jerdone (owner of Farmington) do not appear to have fought for the enemy, but they were pro-British and, as a consequence, their lands were confiscated temporarily. In the Old Dominion as a whole loyalty to the crown was confined largely to the merchant class, especially Scottish factors living in the Tidewater. Wallace Brown estimates that 56 percent of Virginia's Tories were found in five communities: Norfolk, Portsmouth, Gosport, Williamsburg, and Petersburg.[9] He notes that although royal sentiment was weak in Virginia, more than half of those loyal to the king served in His Majesty's forces, among them many individuals who dealt profitably with the quartermaster departments. Virginia's Anglican clergymen, on the other hand, generally cast their lot with the colonials. One-third of them became active patriots, and only nine filed for compensation from the crown after the war ended.

Why was Tory sentiment so weak? Brown places considerable blame upon Lord Dunmore, especially his proclamation freeing slaves, which only united opposition against an already unpopular administration. In addition, Brown credits chronic indebtedness to British creditors [10] and the lack of British military successes in the area. But, he concludes, as does Thad Tate, colonial Virginia was a very homogeneous society. Once the leaders of that society, the "big" planter class, decided for independence, the die was cast.

During the late 1770s the county's economy changed somewhat to meet the demands of war which increased diversification of crops even more and probably hastened the demise of tobacco culture, a trend which became obvious to all a decade later. This desire for

[8] John McBride, "The Virginia Executive and Exemptions from Military Duty, 1780–1782," paper prepared for Professor W. W. Abbot, University of Virginia, 1972.

[9] Brown, *The King's Friends* (Providence, 1965), pp. 181–86.

[10] For an opposing view, see Emory Evans, "Planter Indebtedness and the Coming of the Revolution in Virginia," *William and Mary Quarterly*, 3d ser., 19 (1962):511–33.

self-sufficiency was fed both by patriotic zeal and practical necessity. Addressing local citizens concerning wartime shortages, George
Gilmer boasted that Americans could provide many items once obtained from Britain. They could make their own clothes, for example;
and although many talked much of a need for salt, one could get
along without it. And, according to this physician-patriot, resulting
dietary changes might actually bring unexpected benefits, for Americans suffered greatly from their consumption of great amounts of
meat. "It may, with truth be declared, that more Americans are
destroyed by the disorders brought on from an inactive life and an
over-indulgence in animal food than from any other cause." Blacks,
he noted, compared to whites, were the healthiest members of the
community: "Where they are kindly used and plentifully fed with
good hoe-cake and milk, they live as long, look as well, and get as
many children. To our existence neither flesh nor salt are absolutely
necessary."

From these remarks (just when they were uttered is not known)
it would appear that many animals were being slaughtered to feed
colonial soldiers, thus creating a substantial shortage of meat on
local tables and some criticism of government policies. As for making
one's own clothes from native materials, scores of Albemarle citizens
had been doing just that for years. In addition to supplying farm
produce, during the war years the county manufactured harnesses
and wagons and, when shot was scarce, contributed lead from windows for military use.

However, the most direct impact of the conflict upon the Albemarle scene was the presence of enemy prisoners of war, at first only
a few, then thousands. In April 1776 a handful of individuals, probably Tories, were transported from Richmond and placed under the
charge of the local militia. Two months later fifteen Highlanders
joined them. Some of these men were put in jail, but most were
paroled within the town limits. In August 1777 a quartet of Tidewater Tories escaped and picked up four slaves as they made their
way toward Richmond. They were later recaptured but were not returned to Charlottesville.

Of much greater importance are the British and German prisoners
taken at Saratoga in October 1777. These men, some four thousand
in all, were first quartered in Massachusetts. Since food was scarce
in New England and winters long, in October 1778 Congress decided
to move them to Virginia. Colonel John Harvie, a member of that
body, offered his land on Ivy Creek about four miles west of Charlottesville as a campsite. Consequently, in the midst of an unusually

severe winter, the prisoners marched 628 miles to Albemarle County, arriving early in January 1779. Unfortunately, new quarters were not ready; and for a time there was considerable grumbling, especially among officers who complained of poor food and inadequate liquor, only peach brandy being readily available.

The prisoners set to work constructing huts and sealing them against the cruel weather, and two months later, when a move was afoot to relocate the men once more, Thomas Jefferson dispatched a thoughtful but glowing picture of idyllic scenes to be found at the Barracks to Governor Patrick Henry.[11] He emphasized that provisions for the prisoners were available; if they had not been provided, then the commissaries obviously were at fault. The men were surrounded, he said, by scores of mills churning out grain and flour with "5 or 6 round about Charlottesville" alone. Ever mindful of both economic and cultural opportunities this unprecedented influx of Europeans brought to his native county, Jefferson also stressed the healthful atmosphere. "The barracks occupy the top and brow of a very high hill (you have been untruly told they were at the bottom). They are free from fog, have four springs which seem plentiful, one within 20 yds. of the picket, 2 within 50 yards, and another within 250 and they propose to sink wells within the picquet. Of 4000 people it would be expected according to ordinary calculations that one should die every day. Yet in the space of nearly 3 months there have been but 4 deaths among them. 2 infants under three weeks old, two others by apoplexy. The officers tell me, the troops were never before so healthy since they were embodied." Jefferson conceded that some prisoners experienced true hardship at first, but now the officers were comfortably housed throughout the county. Some had leased quarters which they were improving at considerable personal expense, and they were stocking their new homes with grain and provisions of all kinds. The soldiers, he noted, had made their environs "delightful." The Barracks was surrounded by hundreds of separate gardens and small pens filled with poultry. Baron von Riedesel, the highest-ranking German officer, had spent some £200 for seed which he distributed to his troops. The men also had built numerous structures in addition to those provided for them by Congress. In view of all these facts, Jefferson cautioned Governor Henry that moving the men elsewhere—either within or outside of the state—made no sense whatsoever.

[11] Julian P. Boyd, ed., *The Papers of Thomas Jefferson* (19 vols.; Princeton, N.J., 1950—), 2:237–45.

5. The Barracks, 1779

Although this appraisal may have been a bit too optimistic, it is true that Virginia could house and feed these troops in the midst of war more easily than any other state; and it is equally true that as the officers and men became accustomed to their surroundings, they discovered incarceration in the shadows of the Blue Ridge Mountains was not so wretched an existence as first supposed. Major General William Phillips, the British commander, established himself at Blenheim, the seat of Colonel Edward Carter. Baron von Riedesel and his family set up housekeeping at Colle, once Philip Mazzei's estate. At the outset officers were permitted to live within fifty miles of the camp where their men were quartered (a handful of them being on duty at all times); later their movements were restricted somewhat. The troops were guarded by six hundred volunteers from nearby counties, young men apprehensive of being drafted into the Continental forces and eager to enlist for a year's duty close to home.

By the late spring of 1779 the center of all this activity had taken on the appearance of a small town which suddenly ranked as a major concentration of population within Virginia. It had a commissary store, a coffeehouse, and a theater. John Hawkins, an enterprising local citizen, built four houses of entertainment equipped with billiard tables, an undertaking inaugurated without permission from the authorities. When called to account for his actions, Hawkins stoutly maintained he ran clean, orderly establishments. This answer somehow avoided the thrust of the question, and though it was perhaps true, local peach brandy did cause considerable disorder at times, and some citizens suspected the prisoners were sleeping with black women. But on the whole this experiment worked remarkably well. The troops were relatively content, in many instances preferring life in Albemarle to campaign duty; and although the outnumbered populace feared insurrection, none ever occurred.

On the other hand, escapes were numerous, perhaps with the connivance of guards if the prisoners seemed intent upon settling in the New World and expressed no desire to fight again under the British flag. Of the 4,000 men who arrived in Albemarle in January 1779, fewer than 3,000 remained in May 1780 (about equally divided between British and German forces). When they were marched away at the end of the year because of enemy incursions, their numbers had shrunk to 2,000, of whom fewer than 800 were British. Neither death nor exchange accounts for this dramatic decrease. Some of the British certainly joined up with Cornwallis; but the Germans, for the most part, had little heart for this foreign expedition and by the hundreds fled westward across the mountains into surrounding counties of the Shenandoah Valley to be welcomed in their native tongue by their former compatriots. There they took wives, raised families, and became, through the vagaries of war, American citizens.

It is most difficult to say how many Hessians, if any, remained within Albemarle. Apparently no prisoner lists exist today, and early state census records of the 1780s do not reveal substantial evidence of German households in the county. The widely held belief that the very prolific Shiflett family (also spelled Shifflet, Shifflett, Shifflette, and perhaps Shiplett as well) is of Hessian origin may be true; however, Thomas Shiflett, 5 feet 10 inches tall, a twenty-one-year-old Louisa County planter, served in the Virginia militia during the French and Indian War long before any mercenaries appeared on American soil. In 1785 only one Shiflett family resided in Albemarle, although there were five such households in nearby Orange County. A quarter of a century later seven families by that name lived in Albemarle (one in St. Anne's Parish, six in Fredericksville). By 1930 over 270 Shiflett children were enrolled in county schools, sometimes filling nearly all of the seats in some of the little one-room schoolhouses scattered along the eastern slope of the Blue Ridge Mountains.

This "friendly invasion" of Albemarle soil with all of its unique aspects—unusual economic and cultural benefits for local citizens and unintended migration to the American frontier—has been ably described by numerous participants, among them the Riedesels, a British officer named Thomas Anburey, and several unidentified Hessians. In general, high-ranking officers seem to have been welcome at the homes of local gentry, free to use their libraries, drink their wine, and carry on animated nonpolitical conversations. However, limits to this hospitality (even in Virginia) did exist. A man named Watson reportedly beat up a British officer quartered in his home because of what he thought was undue attention paid to his wife.

In June 1779 a Hessian officer living at Staunton told a Brunswick relative that community had only thirty houses and there was "hardly a gentleman living within forty miles." [12] The enlisted men's barracks, he noted, now had vegetable gardens, a large church, wells, taverns, and a theater and attracted interested visitors from a radius

[12] Ray W. Pettengill, *Letters from America, 1776–1779* (Boston, 1924), pp. 147–52. For a good, brief summary of the story of the Germans in America, see M. H. Volm, *The Hessian Prisoners in the American War of Independence and their Life in Captivity* (Charlottesville, 1937).

of sixty miles. Some of the English had erected covered walkways, and their "comedy house" presented plays twice weekly complete with three sets of scenery and a curtain displaying a harlequin pointing with a wooden sword to these words: "Who would have expected to see this here?" For the plays, "the officers lend the actors the necessary articles of clothing; drummers are transformed into queens and beauties. Very good pieces are performed which, because of their satirical additions, do not always please the Americans, wherefore they are forbidden by their superiors to attend these comedies." It was this officer's opinion that both British and German prisoners often constructed buildings "out of spite" because conditions were so "incredibly bad" when they first arrived. At the time this man wrote no stockade surrounded the burgeoning town, but he said there were occasional threats that barriers would be erected. This writer enclosed with his words an unusual gift for his German correspondent —a pipeful of genuine Virginia tobacco which, he cautioned was "extraordinarily strong."

The Riedesels, who associated freely with Jefferson, his wife, and other local gentry, complained loudly of weather conditions which frightened them, especially extreme heat and high winds. The baron succumbed to sunstroke on one occasion, and the baroness expressed fear that Colle might be wrecked during a storm. However, it is not German views but those of Anburey which have been widely quoted by scores of historians. His two volumes, *Travels through the Interior Parts of America*, first appeared in 1789 under the patronage of several members of the royal family. While his seventy-nine letters are certainly readable (one reason he has been so frequently cited), one-half of them were copied from printed sources such as the *Annual Register*. Anburey was a prisoner in Charlottesville, true, but one must weigh carefully what he has to say. His account of life in America is, in the opinion of one scholar, essentially correct even if not truly authentic.[13]

Anburey's letters actually add little to what other visitors have said about conditions in the colonial South—great stretches of forest interspersed by occasional clearings and a few frame structures, hard-driving overseers and lazy, drink-sodden masters, and, of course, thousands of black slaves. His own host, according to Anburey, began each day with a julep of rum and sugar, then rode about his plantation for a few hours before sitting down to a huge

---

[13] Whitfield J. Bell, Jr., "Thomas Anburey's 'Travels in America': A Note on Eighteenth-Century Plagiarism," *Papers of the Bibliographical Society of America* 37 (1942):23–36.

6. Thomas Walker

7. Castle Hill

8. Jack Jouett

9. Banastre Tarleton

breakfast of cold meat, hominy, toast, and cider. A noon toddy was
followed by dinner at 2 P.M., after which the master retired for
several hours before uncorking the bottle once more. "During all
this he is neither drunk nor sober, but in a state of stupefaction,"
writes Anburey, who appears to have been awed by this daily display.

Though this picture is perhaps exaggerated, some of this man's
comments on the local scene have the ring of truth. As he and his
men were packing to leave, this officer noted that many were unhappy to depart and expressed regret over money they had expended
to improve their living conditions. John Harvie, owner of the land
on which the Barracks was located, was, he observed shrewdly, the
only individual who would benefit. The prisoners by their own sweat
and toil had cleared an area six miles in circumference around their
little town. Because of enemy activity in eastern Virginia, British
troops were sent to Fort Frederick, Maryland, in October 1780, followed some months later by the Germans. Although a few prisoners
were seen in the county during the final stages of the conflict, no
new encampment similar to the Barracks appeared.

Albemarle's final and much more dramatic experience with war
occurred in the late spring of 1781. A hectic, three-week period witnessed arrival and departure of the state government, storage and
removal of great quantities of military stores, and invasion by the
enemy. Out of these events has arisen much folklore, legend, and
some acrimony. The legislature, under pressure of British successes,
quit Richmond on May 10 and agreed to reconvene at Charlottesville
two weeks later; however, not until May 28 was a quorum present.
For the next six days the General Assembly met amid impromptu
surroundings. Senators probably gathered at the courthouse. Delegates, we know, assembled at John Jouett's Swan Tavern located
just across the street. Partitions and doors had to be removed to
provide temporary quarters (no hall in town was large enough),
and more than a year later Jouett still was trying to get compensation for damage done to his property.

Military supplies followed the government to the Piedmont, although Governor Jefferson discouraged any concentration of matériel at Charlottesville. As a result, these goods were divided among
a variety of sites—Point of Fork, Henderson's Warehouse on the
Rivanna where Milton would soon appear, the old county courthouse,
Scott's Landing on the James, and Charlottesville—and many wagon
loads were stranded somewhere along the way from Richmond. The
presence of war supplies, a few prisoners, and a beleagured state

government which the British feared might levy new taxes and draft more manpower in hopes of reviving a faltering war effort prompted Lieutenant General Charles Cornwallis to dispatch one of his best cavalry commanders to this troubled scene. Colonel Banastre Tarleton, with 180 dragoons and 70 mounted cavalry, left his base of operations near Hanover on June 3, entering the county's northeast corner via Louisa Courthouse. When this force stopped to rest at Cuckoo Tavern late on the evening of the third, John Jouett's strapping son Jack—6 feet 4 inches tall, 220 pounds, a dead shot, and an expert rider—happened to be nearby. Sensing the great danger inherent in this surprise raid, Jouett jumped upon his horse ("the best and fleetest of foot of any nag in seven counties") and plunged into the wilderness bound for Charlottesville.[14]

Jouett and Tarleton both left Cuckoo Tavern at about 10 P.M., but the latter took a longer route along the principal highway and lost some time destroying several wagons loaded with supplies and stopping at Thomas Walker's Castle Hill estate. Arriving there at about 4 A.M. on June 4, he surprised the doctor and several members of the Assembly who were his guests in their beds. In his report of this campaign, Tarleton says he remained only half an hour, but legend says he may have tarried a bit longer and let crucial moments slip through his fingers. Meanwhile, Jouett, some three hours ahead of the British, raced into Charlottesville, dispatched a messenger to Monticello to warn Jefferson and several other legislators housed there, and himself informed those residing in Charlottesville to flee at once.

Instead, in the midst of this crisis the Assembly chose to meet briefly and then departed for Staunton. Jefferson, his family, and their guests had a rather leisurely breakfast and left just as enemy troops were approaching. A small force of perhaps two hundred soldiers also retreated after putting up scattered resistance on the banks of the Rivanna. Thanks to Jouett, Tarleton failed to capture most members of the legislature, although young Daniel Boone was among those rounded up; however, the British were able to seize valuable stores, release a few prisoners, and destroy irreplacable county records. According to Tarleton's report to his superiors, items laid waste included 1,000 new firelocks manufactured in Fredericksburg, 400 barrels of gunpowder, several hogsheads of tobacco, and "some continental clothing and accoutrements." On June 5 this mo-

---

[14] For a detailed summary of published works relating to this affair, see John Cook Wyllie, "Writings about Jack Jouett and Tarleton's Raid on Charlottesville in 1781," *MACH* 17 (1959):49-56.

bile force, accompanied by some slaves and about twenty ex-prisoners (men Tarleton says were captured at Saratoga), departed for Point of Fork to join up with the other enemy troops. If the intent of Cornwallis was to panic and immobilize the government of Virginia, the raid was a rousing success. On the other hand, if he hoped to capture Henry, Jefferson, and other rebel leaders and smash resistance to the crown in Albemarle, then this foray into the Piedmont was a failure.

This incursion, naturally enough, gave the Assembly a bad scare and created embarrassment for Jefferson. Although considerable confusion still exists concerning what happened, several facts are evident. From the moment the state government left Richmond it was in flight and had almost ceased to function. Also, Jefferson's second one-year term as governor expired on June 2, leaving the ineffective legislature leaderless. Nevertheless, it is most difficult to explain why Virginia's lawmakers disregarded various warnings of impending danger and why, even when informed by Jouett that the enemy was at hand, they reacted in such a casual manner. Jefferson's reluctance to store matériel in Charlottesville is evidence of fears that just what happened might well occur. One could also ask why colonial troops, almost equal in number to the invading force, offered so little resistance.

As soon as the General Assembly convened at Staunton attempts were made to censure Jefferson for his role in this affair, and years later, when he became embroiled in national politics, details of Tarleton's raid were exploited to the fullest by his opponents. The most confused individual in the midst of the confusion reigning on the morning of June 4, 1781, may have been Jack Jouett. It must have seemed to him that his breakneck race through the darkness had been in vain. Eight days later both houses of the legislature lavished great praise upon this giant of a man and voted to give him an elegant sword and a brace of pistols. Jouett finally got the pistols in 1783, the sword in 1803.

For all practical purposes, with this raid Albemarle's involvement in the War for Independence came to an end. In October 1781 Cornwallis surrendered at Yorktown, and two years later a treaty of peace was concluded in Paris. However, two events which occurred during these years of strife should be noted in passing, one on the local scene, the other hundreds of miles to the west. In 1777, citing the much-used argument that the courthouse was too far away, residents of the southeastern part of Albemarle petitioned for creation of a new county. As a result, on June 30 of that year Fluvanna County came into existence and Albemarle assumed its present boundaries. A year later George Rogers Clark, born near Charlottesville in 1752, backed by Henry, Jefferson, and others, led a small force of rugged frontiersmen into first Kaskaskia and then Vincennes, thus securing the vast Old Northwest for Virginia and for the United States as well. Although this stalwart, red-haired son of Albemarle was by that time more Kentuckian than Virginian (his family moved away from the county when he was only five years of age and he lived most of his adult life west of the Appalachians), local citizens could take considerable pride in his exploits, and today Clark is remembered in Charlottesville by an imposing monument and an elementary school named in his honor.

The Revolutionary War brought many benefits to the county other than freedom from British rule. Anburey in 1779 described Charlottesville as merely "a courthouse, one tavern, and about a dozen houses." A few years later the marquis de Chastellux thought it "a rising little town," and the 1780s would see the beginning of several other communities nearby. War and the victories of Clark had moved the American frontier far to the west. Albemarle County no longer could be considered part of that nebulous line of scattered settlement; it was becoming, in fact, an established community which, in time, would serve as a center of business and commercial activity. Its final boundaries were established, and Albemarle's citizens faced a bright, if uncertain, future in a new republic which had been created in large part by individuals they knew personally—men such as Thomas Jefferson, George Rogers Clark, George Gilmer, and Shadrack Battles. Each in his own way fulfilled roles vital to the winning of independence, whether politician, frontier fighter, home front organizer, or common foot soldier.

Chapter 5

Thomas Walker's Albemarle

ALTHOUGH eighteenth-century Albemarle was the home of many
distinguished citizens, one man, more than any other, left
an indelible imprint upon the county's early history. For over
half a century, whether tending to the sick, exploring the far slopes
of the Appalachians and beyond, establishing the town of Charlottesville, speaking up for the welfare of the Piedmont in the House of
Burgesses, supplying the Virginians fighting with Braddock, negotiating with Indian chiefs, or pursuing his special interests in scientific
agriculture, religion, and commerce, Thomas Walker was a force
to be reckoned with.[1] From the moment he appeared in western
Goochland County in the early 1740s until his death in 1794, just
four months short of his eightieth birthday, Walker was personally
involved in every step which transformed the region he came to love
from frontier settlement to established community.

Left fatherless at an early age, Walker grew up in the household
of his uncle, Dr. George Gilmer of Williamsburg (father of George
Gilmer, the patriot). He studied medicine under the senior Gilmer
and may have practiced in Fredericksburg for a short time. Just
when Walker came to Albemarle is not known, but in 1741 he married Mildred Thornton Meriwether, widow of Nicholas Meriwether,
and acquired use of a vast estate, part of which was Castle Hill
where he later made his home. Actually, contrary to local legend,
Walker did not gain title to those 15,000 acres through marriage.
Meriwether heirs, not Mrs. Walker, owned the property until 1780,
although her husband certainly treated the estate as if it were his
long before he actually had possession of it. This attitude, typical of
a man who was one of colonial Albemarle's most ambitious land
speculators, has bequeathed to present-day residents an outstanding
example of pre-Revolutionary architecture. For, about 1765, Walker
constructed on Meriwether lands a rather spacious, clapboard home,
which, though altered somewhat through the past two centuries and
now overshadowed by an imposing brick mansion added in 1824,

---

[1] For a summary of this man's remarkable life, see Natalie Disbrow,
"Thomas Walker, Man of Affairs" (M.A. thesis, University of Virginia, 1940).

still retains the defiant air of a sturdy, no-nonsense homestead set down in the wilderness. Most of the seats of his associates, structures long since consumed by flames and forgotten or remembered only by stark historical roadside markers, probably were not unlike this original portion of Castle Hill.

Interestingly, "old" Castle Hill faces toward the mountains, perhaps a conscious reflection of its creator's preoccupation with what lay beyond the Blue Ridge. In March 1750 Walker led an extensive four-month expedition for the Loyal Land Company into southwestern Virginia and the Tennessee-Kentucky region. His remarkable journal, now in the Library of Congress, details his adventures (including helping a pioneer raise his house and carving "T. W." on innumerable trees); describes his association with the "Duncards," a German sect which fascinated him; lists game shot—"18 Buffaloes, 8 Elks, 53 Bears, 20 Deer, 4 Wild Geese, about 130 Turkeys, besides Small Game . . . we might have killed three times as much Meat, if we had wanted it"—and contains several caustic comments regarding those who dam up streams. While still in Albemarle on his way west with five companions, Walker noted the Rockfish was "a pretty river" which easily could transport tobacco, "but it has lately been stopped by a Mill Dam near its Mouth to the prejudice of the upper Inhabitants, who would at their own expence clear & make it navigable, were they permitted." The following day he visited the Tye River and spent the night at the home of Rev. Robert Rose. The Tye, he observed, still was open; "but how long the Avarice of Millers will permit it to be so, I know not." On July 16 Rose returned Walker's visit, spending the night and recording in his diary that his host had just completed "His Ramble on the branches of Missisippi on the 13th." According to some sources, the traditional Walker luck was at a low ebb at that time, and the good doctor was searching for new opportunities to exploit.

Thomas Walker never lost interest in the west and may have lived in southwestern Virginia for a time; yet his construction of Castle Hill and deep involvement in affairs of town, county, and colony indicate that, like many of his neighbors who first thought of Albemarle as merely a temporary residence, by the 1760s he considered the Piedmont as "home." During these same years Walker served as guardian to the children of Peter Jefferson and in the 1770s was a member of the state executive council which guided the Old Dominion's destiny during the war years. Why Thomas Walker and hundreds of other individuals decided to remain in Albemarle in the late eighteenth century while others pushed ever westward is, of course, a key question in American life not easily answered two centuries later. Personal considerations undoubtedly caused some to stay, others to pack up and move on. But growth of the county's population during Walker's lifetime, a substantial increase in commercial activity, accessibility to more and more of the amenities once enjoyed only in the Tidewater, and, above all else, after 1775 the exhilarating sensation of being part of an important center in the leading state of a vibrant, new nation must have weighed heavily whenever local families gathered to debate the pros and cons of migration. That some, in the closing years of the century, would abandon tobacco, long the foundation stone of their livelihood, rather than seek out new lands is clear evidence that the lure of Albemarle's lovely rolling countryside is by no means a twentieth-century phenomenon.

Although living conditions in the county were rather crude and primitive in the mid-1700s, most households were self-sustaining to a remarkable degree, and all basic necessities (with the exception of iron and salt) could be raised or produced on the place. This was true of both small farm and plantation. Food among lower classes consisted mainly of meat, bread, and milk, supplemented occasionally with vegetables and wild fruits. They rarely used sugar—coffee and tea, never. Peaches abounded, and both folklore and reports of travelers indicate brandy made from them was the community's principal liquor. In fact, this noble fruit would remain a mainstay of those with a yen for spirits almost to the present. One gracious lady recalls that at the turn of the century a favorite uncle always began each day with a "cream toddy," and another remembers fondly "mountain dew" supplied to her family during the dark days of Prohibition (1920–33). They both maintain that peach brandy was the principal ingredient of these very potent potions. According to Charles Watts, few inventories of property from 1727 to 1775, less than 5 percent, mention stills. "Apparently," he writes, "this article was too expensive for ordinary folks." However, by the end of the century more and more households seem to have considered such apparatus necessary for comfortable day-to-day living. Clothes, except for hats and shoes, were largely homemade, and shoes usually were worn only in winter months. Almost every family owned a spinning wheel, but few possessed looms; thread or yarn could be spun at home, and cloth could be woven at the house of a more affluent neighbor who owned suitable equipment.

Though farmer and planter were equally self-sufficient, the latter could afford to buy some luxuries. His food, basically the same as that of lesser folk, was seasoned with sugar and spices. He drank coffee, tea, chocolate, and fine wines. His family's clothes were made of linen, broadcloth, chintz, woolens, and calico, and they possessed watches and buckles made of silver, gold sleeve buttons, satin shoes, and silk purses. To illustrate differences between classes, Watts examines two individuals living in the county in the mid-1700s—one a farmer, the other a well-to-do planter.[2]

In 1753, Richard Hammack was living on his 150-acre farm on the west side of Southwest Mountain at Hammack's Gap. His house was probably the typical log cabin of the day with peaked roof and buttressed at one end by a huge stone chimney. Chinks between the logs were filled with mud or moss plastered over with clay. One room downstairs served as living quarters, and a small attic above was used for storage.

Furnishings for the room downstairs were few and simple but completely adequate for the family needs. There was a bedstead and mattress covered with a hide and blanket, probably a crude table and a few homemade chairs (too simple to be mentioned in the inventory), an old chest with a lock, a Bible, shoemaker's tools with thread and tanned leather, and a pair of money scales.

Very likely, at one end of the room was a large fireplace with deep jambs and a long crane, where all the meals for the family were cooked. Here were most of the accessories for cooking such as an iron pot, a frying pan, and a skillet. Two jugs, a churn, two buckets, and a funnel were nearby. On the shelf overhead were a dish, a pewter basin, a plate, and six spoons. Over the fireplace, Hammack probably hung his most cherished possession—his gun.

Outside, probably under a lean-to attached to the house, Hammack kept his tools and farm implements. Here were his bellows, anvil, and vice, a whipsaw, turning tools, carpenter's tools, cooper's tools, and a brass rule. His plow and gear were here, too, along with hoes, an ax, and other implements. For weighing his tobacco he had a steelyard, and a saddle and bridle for his horse. In the barnyard were 3 head of cattle, 4 hogs, a small heifer, and a horse.

Watts notes that some small farmers fared better than Hammack, some worse; but, on the whole, they possessed the same essentials. He indicates items not found in an inventory of this frontiersman's possessions but common to others of his class include looking glasses, iron candlesticks, razors and hones, powder horns, and bullet molds. Theirs was not a comfortable existence and required much effort on the part of all members of the family, but it was adequate for the times, and it was self-sufficient.

[2] Watts, pp. 71–75.

Across the Southwest Mountains from Hammack lived John Harvie, a prominent planter born in Scotland in 1706. By the early 1740s he had settled in Albemarle on a 2,500-acre plot adjoining land owned by Peter Jefferson. He was admitted to the local bar in 1747, soon acquired the title of colonel, and counted among his friends Thomas Walker, Joshua Fry, and other members of the emerging gentry. His home, Belmont, was also built of wood, but it was much larger than that rude cabin in Hammack's Gap. It was a story-and-a-half structure and contained nine rooms, space which the colonel and his lady (Martha Gaines) certainly needed since they produced nine children.[3] Belmont had dormer windows, was clapboarded on the outside, and had wings at each end, a structure not unlike the old portion of Castle Hill.

Surrounding the mansion house were very probably numerous outbuildings, causing the whole place to resemble a small village. Most plantation establishments included, besides the main house, a kitchen, meat house, dairy, stables, barns, mills, and numerous Negro cabins. Harvie possessed 14 slaves to work his plantation.

The furniture in Harvie's house was of walnut and cherry and indicated some special artistry or careful workmanship in its design. There were, for example, arm chairs, desks, book cases, and chests of drawers. His beds were covered with foreign and domestic counterpanes, quilts, and Dutch blankets. Crown linen table cloths, brass candlesticks, fine silverware, and china dishes graced his table. A riding chair was ever ready to carry him to visit his friends; or, if he preferred to remain at home, there was backgammon or reading to be had from an extensive library.

Watts emphasizes that this man was by no means the wealthiest planter in Albemarle at the time of his death in 1767, but his estate illustrates well the difference between mountain cabin and plantation home. Among items not cited in the Belmont inventory but often found in similar households are leather- and damask-covered chairs, safes, spinets, hairteen window curtains, clocks, and writing paper.

Although Harvie's Belmont and Hammack's rude cabin have long since disappeared, at least two homes remain which serve as examples of late eighteenth-century, middle-class architecture. Both are less imposing than Castle Hill and undoubtedly have been added to and altered somewhat. One is Mount Walla located on a high bluff above Scottsville, originally the home of John Scott, who operated a

[3] For details of Harvie's life, see Mary Foy Hester, "The Public Career of John Harvie" (M.A. thesis, University of Virginia, 1938). A nineteenth-century structure, long owned by the Ficklin family, not Harvie's Belmont, gave its name to much of present-day Charlottesville.

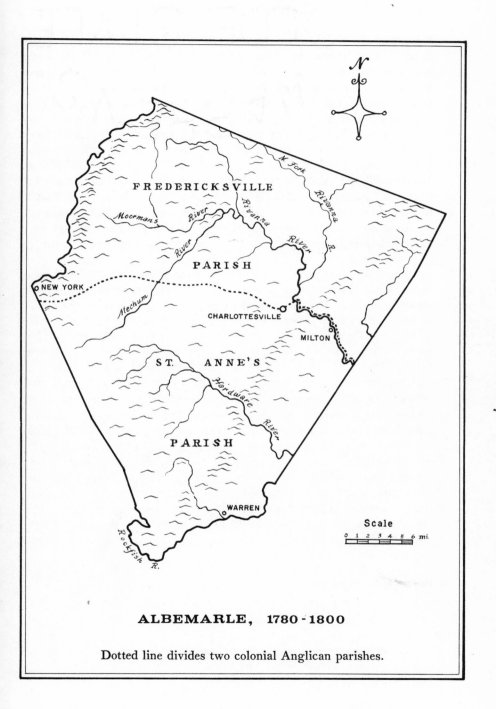

ALBEMARLE, 1780 - 1800

Dotted line divides two colonial Anglican parishes.

ferry and other businesses in the village below. In the nineteenth century this house, now elegantly restored, was owned by Peter Jefferson, a grandnephew of the squire of Monticello. The other structure, known as the Butler-Norris house, sits securely on the south side of Charlottesville's historic Court Square at 410 East Jefferson Street. According to the research of Margaret Fowler Clark and others, Edward Butler purchased this site from Samuel Woods sometime before 1779 and soon after that date erected the brick house which now is the home of a real estate firm.[4] In 1808 Edward Butler sold the property to John Kelly for $550 (a sum much too high for land alone), and he eventually gave the house and land to his son-in-law, Opie Norris, who held title until 1860, thus bequeathing to what is undoubtedly the oldest house within the original town of Charlottesville and perhaps the community's first brick home its present name.

Living in Albemarle along with Richard Hammack, John Harvie, John Scott, Edward Butler, and Thomas Walker were hundreds of individuals who left no record of property at the time they took leave of this earthly world because they had none. Yet it was their sweat and toil which made the machinery of colonial life work. They were the black slaves and indentured servants found in many households. How they fared day to day is pretty much a matter of conjecture, but we can assume, human nature being what it is, that their existence was tedious and humdrum, bounded by seasons and crops, and subject to the caprice of the head of the family they served and intertwined with his status in the community. A handful of blacks were able to win their freedom, usually upon the death of a kindly or guilt-ridden master, and a few indentured whites established themselves as artisans and independent farmers, although it is unlikely that many in the late eighteenth century enjoyed the economic success similar individuals achieved in earlier decades. And, as Albemarle became less and less of a frontier community, the poorest class were apt to become pioneers once more, perhaps somewhere beyond the crest of the Blue Ridge.

This society, influenced strongly by an English background and life in the Tidewater, was one of class distinctions clearly drawn, with deference shown to those of wealth; from earliest times, with

[4] Mrs. Clark, aided in this undertaking by Mary Shoemaker and William Allen, has documented her research in an article in her possession entitled "Who Built 410 East Jefferson Street?"

the proper political and social credentials, one could expect to be addressed as "gentleman" or "esquire." This was an agrarian aristocracy, based, not entirely upon birth, but upon how much land one held and how many slaves tilled those acres, though those of good family naturally possessed inherent advantages if they had the ability to use their status intelligently to gain more land and political power as well. The large estates developing in Albemarle in the late 1700s provided certain families with the means to tighten their control of county life, and their preeminence in local affairs soon was recognized.[5]

Devereux Jarratt, a youth of lower-class origins who came to the county at mid-century to teach school, expressed the prevailing attitude toward these aristocrats, both self-made and born. The "gentle folk" were, he observed, a sort of superior order of beings. "For my part, I was quite shy of them, and kept off at a humble distance. . . . Such ideas of the difference between gentle and simple were, I believe, universal among all of my rank and age." [6] This young man lived first at the home of Jacob Moon, overseer for a Surry County resident. Later, Jarratt boarded and taught in other local households which, in his opinion, were "rough and uncivilized." There was no minister or any public worship to be found. "The Sabbath day was usually spent in *sporting:* and whether *this* was right or wrong, I believe no one questioned." But apparently Jarratt did, and at his last residence he encountered a mistress fascinated by the "New Light" revival. This association changed Jarratt's life and led him shortly from the classroom to the pulpit.

Among these "gentle folk" whom Jarratt held in awe, visiting back and forth among their equals seems to have been the principal form of entertainment. Because of great distances, journeys usually were made on horseback, and a visit often lasted overnight or several days. The Reverend Robert Rose, who traveled frequently to visit his parishioners, conduct religious services, and keep an eye on his developing plantations, usually encountered several friends wherever he stopped for the night. Other recreations included dancing, read-

[5] The Coles family, which emerges in the nineteenth century as the county's greatest concentration of wealth, is an example of shrewd management and careful attention to detail sometimes absent in other local families. Some Coles heirs credit an infusion of Quaker stock through marriage for this practical frame of mind.

[6] Devereux Jarratt, *Life of Rev. Devereux Jarratt, Rector of Bath Parish, Dinwiddie County, Virginia* (Baltimore, 1806), pp. 14–28.

ing, and sometimes fishing. According to his diary, Rose went fishing on numerous occasions with indifferent success, although on one outing he "catched above 5 Doz of Carp."

Middle-class individuals seem to have been addicted to gambling in many forms, especially horse racing and cockfighting. Anburey described a "quarter race" which he thought peculiar to the frontier. Nearly every ordinary had a track cleared for this purpose—two paths about six or eight yards apart on which two horses ran a quarter of a mile in a matched, straight-line encounter, probably the outgrowth of much bragging over drafts of ale or too many peach brandies. This sport, he commented, was a great favorite among middling and lower-class folk of the frontier but was ridiculed by those living in more settled parts of the Old Dominion.

En route to Monticello in 1782, the marquis de Chastellux stopped at an isolated ordinary which, to his surprise, was overflowing with people.

As soon as I alighted I inquired what might be the reason of this numerous assembly in such a deserted spot, and learned that it was a cock fight. This diversion is much in fashion in Virginia, where English customs are more in evidence than in the rest of America. While my horses were feeding, I had an opportunity of seeing a fight. The stakes were very considerable; the money of the parties was deposited in the hands of one of the principal persons, and I took pleasure in pointing out to them that it was chiefly French money. While the bettors urged the cocks on to battle, a child of fifteen, who was near me, leaped for joy and cried, "Oh, it is a charming diversion." [7]

The lower elements, in addition to engaging in sports enjoyed by the middle class, had a pastime peculiarly their own, one in which their "betters" (for very obvious reasons) declined to participate. It was called "boxing," but seems to have been a sort of wrestling bout matching contestants who agreed beforehand whether all the pleasures of such a contest (biting and gouging of eyes, for example) would be allowed. Once rules were established and perhaps adhered to, the adversaries went at it, urged on by the cries and shrieks of their backers.

Isaac Weld, a young Irishman who, accompanied by a servant, visited the Piedmont in May 1796, found both cockfighting and "boxing" still in vogue. These activities, he observed with some ir-

[7] Marquis de Chastellux, *Travels in North America in the Years 1780, 1781, and 1782,* ed. Howard C. Rice, Jr. (2 vols.; Chapel Hill, N.C., 1963), 2:386–87.

ritation, almost invariably took place at taverns and made traveling decidedly unpleasant. He was especially distressed by eye gouging. "Whenever these people come to blows, they fight just like wild beasts, biting, kicking, and endeavouring to tear out each other's eyes with their nails." [8] Weld was even more shocked by emasculation that could result from these rough and tumble free-for-alls. Apparently, on rare occasions, unfortunate participants emerged with more than their eyesight impaired.

Unseemly behavior of this sort should not overshadow advancements in other realms of community life during Thomas Walker's lifetime. Before the Revolution the Anglican church was the established faith and consequently by far the largest and most influential religious body in the county. Even before 1775, however, Presbyterians, Quakers, and Baptists settled there and organized congregations, despite the fact that they had to pay taxes to support a state religion. As Albemarle was evolving two Anglican parishes appeared. The first was St. Anne's (1742) which for sixteen years encompassed the entire county. With the addition of western Louisa in 1761, part of Fredericksville Parish, organized in 1742, came within Albemarle's new boundaries. The dividing line was the Rivanna River to Secretary's Ford and Three Notched Road from there to the Blue Ridge.

Fredericksville was always a rather compact unit. At the outset, St. Anne's, a huge enclave, was served spasmodically by a Goochland rector who made frequent use of lay readers. From 1746 until his death five years later, Robert Rose—inventor, fisherman, planter, chronicler—ministered to the needs of the parish. Closely associated with the frontier gentry and executor of numerous large estates (including that of former governor Spotswood), Rose traveled widely and preached frequently, although his diary indicates little, if any, religious zeal. These jaunts usually end with this benediction: "Got Home Where thanks to God found my Family in Health." Rose christened children,[9] performed marriages, buried the dead, and read the Bible and classics; but as noted earlier, this man's prime interests were tobacco and his plantations on the Tye . . . or at least they appear to have concerned him fully as much as his ecclesiastical responsibilities. His successor, John Ramsay, proved to be even more worldly and, at his death in 1767, was under investigation for neglect of his duties and committing fornication and adultery. Charles Clay,

[8] Weld, *Travels through the States of North America* (2 vols.; London, 1799), 1:191–92.

[9] This diary entry of April 16, 1750, is especially puzzling: "Christned Jno Marrs Child, cut off two of Her fingers."

a relative of Henry Clay, served the parish from 1769 until 1784 when it was disestablished, not to be revived until forty-five years later.

Before 1750 the only church within present-day Albemarle was a "Mountain Chappel" located on the lands of William Randolph near Three Notched Road, but as a result of the efforts of Rose, more were built, and by 1772 there were at least four structures. These included one located in what is now Fluvanna County, Ballenger's Church near Boiling Springs, and Forge Church on the Hardware below Carter's Bridge. The so-called Garden Church near North Garden originally was a wooden structure situated near the cross-roads of that community. Shortly before the Revolution work was begun on a more commodious brick building a short distance away; however, it never was completed as an Episcopal house of worship. Throughout much of the nineteenth century this church was used by all denominations in the area, and from 1892 to 1922 it was a public school. Since that time it has been a private home and, as such, is the only building with even remote ties to Albemarle's early religious life, all of the other structures having disappeared.

Like St. Anne's, Fredericksville had only three rectors before the Revolution, the most prominent being James Maury, who served from 1754 until his death in 1770. Sometime in the 1760s a church was built near Belvoir and another (the "middle" church) appeared on the Buck Mountain Road. Until that time the faithful gathered in private homes or at the Louisa Courthouse, just as St. Anne's parishioners often used the Albemarle Courthouse for religious purposes well into the nineteenth century.

Scotch-Irish families who arrived on the local scene even before the birth of Albemarle provided the nucleus for Presbyterian congregations. In 1747 pioneers living at Ivy and Mountain Plains secured the services of Rev. Samuel Black and requested him "to administer ye ordinance of ye gospel." Black, along with others, preached in the county until his death in 1770. In 1769 William Irvin became pastor of the Cove Church near Covesville, and a year later Samuel Leake accepted a call to the D. S. (Ivy) Church.[10] Numerically speaking, Presbyterians were a distinct minority compared to Anglicans, perhaps 7 percent of all the families in the county, and appear to have been small landowners who did not play a prominent role in local affairs.

---

[10] Woods interprets "D. S." as the initials of David Stockton; but since these same initials appear as the designation for meetinghouses throughout Virginia, they probably can be translated as "Dissenter."

Quakers and Baptists were even less numerous; however, the Quakers had an organized "meeting" within Albemarle as early as 1749 and, unlike the Presbyterians, included in their ranks some well-to-do citizens. Sober and industrious, they voiced firm and frequent opposition to the established church. Each year their records, headed by the words "Friends Suffering," reaffirmed disdain for sums they had to pay for "Priests' wages" and "Church rates so-called." Baptists appeared only on the eve of the Revolution, some of them apparently being former Presbyterians. In 1773 forty-eight Baptists organized a congregation at the Lewis Meeting House near where the university now stands, but they failed to secure a minister and were of little consequence until some years later. However, this group continued to gather faithfully on the first Saturday of each month.

Until the Revolution the Anglican church, supported by public levies, was an important factor in community life, and each parish had both religious and civil power. Vestrymen, usually wealthy citizens who often viewed their duties as an important step on the path to political success, were charged with care of the poor, orphans, and mentally deficient. After disestablishment these civil functions were assumed by overseers of the poor, again men of well-to-do background.

Religious life in the days of Thomas Walker centered in the countryside, not the town, and Charlottesville did not have a church within its confines until 1826. To some extent this situation was a reflection of the disarray Anglicans experienced during the early decades of independence and a general agnosticism prevalent among intellectuals which, at times, bordered upon atheism. These developments did not result in a decline in religious expression by all classes of society; in fact, some churches benefited from turmoil rampant within what had been a state-supported institution, turmoil created in part by suspicion that many Anglican clergy were pro-British during the war. And the same charge was leveled at some Methodist preachers who, until 1785, remained ostensibly within the Anglican fold.

For many Albemarle citizens their churches continued to be a focus of social activity, not only for formal services whenever a minister could be found, but for funerals, weddings, christenings, and such, although, because of distances, these functions often were performed in private homes. Some individuals evangelized actively among the black population, especially Baptists and Methodists. Presbyterians, more inclined to be masters of a few slaves, provided galleries for them in their churches but disciplined severely any pastor who sought to "teach" their "people." Albemarle Baptists, also somewhat less hostile to slavery than Methodists, were puritanical to the point of austerity. On the eve of the Revolution two leading members were obliged to confess to the sin of traveling on the Sabbath, and each had to pay a hogshead of tobacco as repentance. At the same time members discussed what action should be taken against "a Brother or Sister who was seemingly superfluous in apparell or anything Else And Rather Delt, or Contracted in Stoores or Elsewhere more than what their income or labour would Discharge Annually." They concluded that anyone seeing a good Baptist in such a fallen state "should Caution them in Love to refrain from the very appearance of the Above said Evils." [11]

Local Baptists apparently did not frown upon the use of alcohol per se, although in their eyes drunkenness was a sin and they excommunicated one Richard Woodfork because of excessive tippling. In the 1770s they also had to deal with Sarah Johnson, a newcomer to the community accused of fornication with her former employer in Goochland County. Sarah, a free spirit of independent mind who neither denied the charge nor exhibited any sign of repentance, was excluded from fellowship. A black brother received similar treatment when accused by a Negro woman of "attempting her chastity (or something of that kind)." On the other hand, Ann Gardner got off with only a stern reprimand for taking "her Child or Children to the Methodist minister and having them Springkled as they call Infant Baptism." Footwashing, not common in the county, was discouraged by leading Baptists, who thought it merely a form of entertainment, not religion. In the first decade of the new century they also were distressed by the "jerks," an emotional display prevalent at revival gatherings. During the late 1700s blacks frequently outnumbered whites in Baptist congregations, and as late as 1810 both races were being admitted to membership on equal footing, although white brethren appear to have led and regulated church affairs at all times.

Methodists, who tended to absorb local Quakers once they embarked on an independent course, established their first church, Mt. Moriah, near White Hall in 1788 and five years later obtained a resident pastor, Athanasius Thomas. Their work in evangelizing slaves was outstanding, and most of the county's early Methodists wore the antislavery mantle long associated with the Quakers. They probably were fully as puritanical in spirit and outlook as the Bap-

[11] W. M. Dabney, p. 176.

tists, their chief rival in the religious reawakening which swept the Piedmont soon after the turn of the century.

Two prominent Jewish families lived in early Albemarle. One was that of Michael Israel, a landowner of the 1750s active in the militia. He or his brother probably gave his name to Israel's Mountain and Israel's Gap. A few decades later Isaiah Isaac moved into the county, and in the early 1800s one of his sons, David, became a well-known Charlottesville merchant.

During the last half of the eighteenth century education of the young was considered a function of the family, and free citizens endeavored to provide enough training, either entirely within the household or with outside help, to enable their children to read and write. Some knowledge of fundamental arithmetic was the next most important attainment. More affluent parents, not satisfied with merely the "three R's," often employed tutors. Very few individuals had the resources or the incentive to seek out higher education. If they did, they usually went to William and Mary, Princeton, or one of the new church academies spawned by disestablishment during the revolutionary period such as Hampden-Sydney.

The minimum goal apparently was widely achieved, for between 1727 and 1745 86 percent of the local landowners were able to sign deeds and other legal papers. Philip Mazzei, who came to the county in 1774, was favorably impressed by the literacy of his neighbors. He once remarked that he had never known anyone who could not read and write. This statement is a bit extreme since Mazzei once signed a petition to the Virginia legislature featuring several X marks for signatures; yet his comments on local life, such as this one, do have some significance: "In the homes of all those who work in the fields, or who practice some mechanical trade, one finds books, inkwells, and writing paper. Not infrequently they also know arithmetic." [12] A large number of inventories found in colonial records do include books, though not quite in the profusion Mazzei indicates. Watts found that about 57 percent mentioned books of some sort—usually the Bible, a prayer book, and the Psalter. Some well-to-do planters had several hundred volumes on their shelves; yet Nicholas Meriwether, the second of that name in Albemarle and scion of a leading family, owned books valued at only ten shillings. Charles Irving, a merchant in the southern part of the county, stocked these items for his customers: *The Spectator, Don Quixote, Tom Brown, Johnson's*

[12] Ibid., p. 106.

Dictionary, various histories and encyclopedias, and the works of such men as Pope, Addison, Rabelais, Euclid, Cicero, Swift, and Milton. Professional books, of course, were not available locally, and Thomas Walker, John Harvie, and others of their class ordered whatever volumes they needed from England.

Education, beyond what a parent could impart to his child, had to be paid for, and not everyone could afford such a luxury even if they considered it highly desirable. Devereux Jarratt, the youth who thought the "gentle folk" a race apart, came to the Piedmont about 1750 under unusual circumstances. His first employer, an overseer, prevailed upon Jarratt to teach less well-to-do children on a fee basis, but this scheme proved unprofitable. Jarratt collected only £9 the first year and £7 the second. Consequently, he departed and accepted at £15 per annum a more conventional post as tutor to a planter family. These folk wanted their children educated, especially their sons, and generally hired young men like Jarratt or helped support a neighbor's tutor on a cooperative basis. They also sought out visitors skilled in music, fencing, dancing, and other social arts. In 1769 Thomas Walker paid for dancing lessons for Mildred Meriwether, Milly and Sally Syme, John Hamilton, and James Madison, all of whom were relatives or neighbors. It cost the doctor about £2 for each girl, £1 for each boy. Whether males learned how to dance more readily or merely got fewer lessons is not clear; but, in general, education of females, not deemed of much importance, cost much less than that of their brothers. Martha Jefferson's classes, as a rule, cost only £1 a year.

Schools operated by colonial Anglican and Presbyterian ministers were both a source of additional income and a means of properly indoctrinating young minds in the wonders of the true faith. James Maury maintained a classical school at his home under the Southwest Mountains, and Samuel Black did the same near Mechum's River. Maury's classroom is probably the most famous of these parson's schools (which, of course, flourished after the Revolution as well) since it was there that Nicholas Cabell, Thomas Jefferson, John Taylor of Caroline, Dabney Carr, and others of note received early training. Their parents paid £20 per year, including board, not an excessive sum.

It appears that, almost from the outset, Albemarle had a handful of private schools designed to fill a variety of specific needs. The offspring of both farmer and planter learned to read and write at the knees of their parents or those of a local minister or hired tutor; however, the aims of various families differed greatly. For some the rudiments were enough; for others, especially sons destined to run plantations and assume greater responsibilities, the classics and a smattering of social niceties also were required. Thus differences of social status, religion, and sex as well were further accentuated in the classroom itself.

It is difficult to say just how many individuals were living in Thomas Walker's Albemarle during some decades of his lifetime. Colonial population statistics tend to be a rather hit-or-miss affair, but the first federal census (1790) reveals there were 12,585 people in the county. This total included 6,835 whites and 5,750 blacks, 171 of them free. Ten years later the population had increased to 16,439 (8,796 whites, 7,436 slaves, and 207 free blacks). Looking ahead, during the next seven decades, 1800–1870, county population, compared to growth of the nation as a whole, remained relatively stationary, and although Albemarle never recorded a decline from census to census, in 1870 it had only 27,544 citizens. Also, from 1810 to 1880 blacks slightly outnumbered whites, and since the number of free Negroes remained inconsequential (only 606 in 1860), this means the often deplored institution of slavery remained in excellent health in Albemarle and more than kept pace with county population growth as a whole.

The most common family names found in a state census of Albemarle households conducted in 1784 are Brown, Maupin (often spelled Maupine), and Wood or Woods, each being represented by a dozen or so families. There were about half as many citizens bearing names such as Gentry, Harris, and Wingfield, but only one Shiflett and two Via families. In 1810 Wood or Woods (thirty-two households) was by far the most common name in the county, followed by Brown, Harris, and Thomas, perhaps half as many families having those names. Other names prevalent in that era include Sprouse, Wingfield, Hammer (or Hamner), Via, Carr, and Shiflett.

Pertinent details of federal head counts for Virginia before 1810 have been lost, but one very revealing record of early Albemarle remains: a state property tax list compiled in 1782.[13] In colonial days the government levied three kinds of taxes—a poll tax, an export tax on tobacco, and certain excise taxes. Occasionally, in times of stress, land taxes (usually soon repealed) also were imposed. Reacting to a sharp reduction in trade during the Revolution, state officials began to look for new sources of revenue. During the war they increased

[13] Lester J. Cappon, ed., "Personal Property Tax List of Albemarle County, 1782," *MACH* 5 (1945):47–73.

the poll tax and placed levies on marriage and ordinary licenses, law processes, and carriages and, after Yorktown, placed a more sweeping tax on personal property. This levy, £1 for every £100 valuation, also included a tax of ten shillings on free male citizens over twenty-one years of age and on all slaves; two shillings on every horse, mare, colt, and mule; threepence per head on "nett cattle"; five shillings per wheel for coaches, chariots, phaetons, four-wheeled chaises, stage wagons used for riding carriages, chairs, and two-wheeled chaises; £50 for each billiard table; and £5 for an ordinary license.

Early in 1782 Albemarle magistrates forwarded the results of their survey to Richmond (see table 2). Of course, hidden within these statistics are indications of who controlled the most land and owned the greatest number of slaves. The winner, in fact it was no contest

Table 2. Albemarle County tax returns, 1782

Item	Rate	Tax
928 whites	at 10s. each	£ 464. – .–
4,409 blacks	at 10s. each	2,204.10.–
9,882 cattle	at 3d. each	123.10.6
3,160 horses	at 2s. each	316. – .–
38 wheels	at 5s. each	9.10.–
		£3,117.10.6

SOURCE: Cappon, "Personal Property Tax List of Albemarle County, 1782," *MACH* 5 (1945):47–73.

whatsover, was Edward Carter, Esq., who, possessed of 237 slaves, 198 cattle, 62 horses, mules, and colts, and 4 wheels, paid a tax of £128.13.6. Carter was the only individual in the county whose returns exceeded £100. In the £50-to-£100 category were Thomas Jefferson and the estate of Robert Carter Nicholas. Jefferson paid about £70 on 129 slaves, 106 cattle, 23 horses, and 6 wheels. The Nicholas heirs paid slightly less (£65) on 120 slaves, 65 cattle, 29 horses (no wheels). Dr. Thomas Walker appears to have been the fourth wealthiest citizen in Albemarle in 1782 with 86 slaves, 93 cattle, 22 horses, and 2 wheels. His tax was £47.

Four citizens—Key Martin, Charles B. J. Lewis, Robert Nelson, Esq., and John Coles, Esq.—paid taxes of £30 to £40. Margarett Merewether (or Meriwether), Thomas Mann Randolph, John Walker, John Scott, and the estate of John Fry paid taxes totaling between £20 and £30. Forty-six other individuals were assessed in excess of £10, among them George Gilmer (29 slaves, 32 cattle, 9 horses) who was busy developing his Pen Park estate which would give its name to Park Road, now Park Street. George Nicholas, Esq., who paid only £11, was the proud owner of 8 wheels, the greatest number in the county—which may indicate he was involved in transport or perhaps reflects ownership of all carriages and vehicles used by the wealthy Nicholas family.

No one admitted to having a billiard table in his possession; and, according to these returns, strangely, no citizen conceded that he held a license to operate an ordinary. Such omissions raise questions concerning the accuracy of these figures and make one wonder what happened to the biliiard tables John Hawkins provided for the enjoyment of Hessian and British prisoners only a few years before. However, considering that a billiard table was assessed at a whopping £50 and an ordinary license at £5, it is easy to understand why some individuals simply "forgot" to mention such items when the magistrate came to call.

Nevertheless, this 1782 list provides invaluable insight into how Albemarle citizens were living during these years and reveals that a substantial number of them were living very well indeed. This aura of well-being, aided substantially by the transition from tobacco to wheat as the county's principal crop, the growth in population, and the satisfaction of no longer being rough frontier, ushers in what might be called a golden age. The words of Isaac Weld, the young man from Dublin who made a pilgrimage to Monticello in 1796, reflect the good life which he saw on all sides. At the same time, while full of praise, Weld tempered his observations with a note of caution. Despite much erosion and hundreds of acres laid waste by tobacco, he found more people living in Albemarle than in counties near Richmond. He thought the climate good, less oppressive than in the Tidewater, and the populace, in general, "healthy-looking." "There are many persons," he wrote, "who even consider it to be the garden of the United States."

The female part of the peasantry in particular is totally different from that of the low country. Instead of the pale, sickly, debilitated beings, whom you meet with there, you find amongst these mountains many a one who would be a fit subject to be painted for a Lavinia. It is really delightful to behold the groups of females, assembled here, at times, to gather the cheeries and other fruits which grow in the greatest abundance in the neighborhood of almost every habitation. Their shapes and complexions are charming; and the carelessness of their dress, which consist of little more, in common, than a simple bodice and petticoat, makes them appear even still more engaging.

The common people in this neighborhood appeared to be of a more frank and open disposition, more inclined to hospitality, and to live more contentedly on what they possessed, than the people of the same class in any other part of the United States I passed through. From being able, however, to procure the necessaries of life upon easy terms, they are rather of an indolent habit, and inclined to dissipation. Intoxication is very prevalent, and it is scarcely possible to meet a man who does not begin the day with taking one, two, or more drams as soon as he rises. Brandy is the liquor which they principally use, and having the greatest abundance of peaches, they make it at a very trifling expense. There is hardly a house to be found with two rooms in it, but where the inhabitants have a still. The females do not fall into the habit of intoxication like the men, but in other respects they are equally disposed to pleasure, and their morals are in like manner relaxed.[14]

If, as his fourscore years came to a close, Thomas Walker sensed that his beloved county was enjoying relatively good times and was, in fact, on the threshold of a truly bountiful era, he indeed was correct. During the next two or three decades it would be, for all practical purposes, the fountainhead of political life in the new republic. Three giants closely associated with the hills of Albemarle would direct its course from 1801 to 1825, and their friends and neighbors, naturally enough, basked in this reflected glory. Yet, when we say that a society embarks upon a golden age, one must remember this implies a time of growth before and less pleasant years to follow. Such would be Albemarle's fate. And, despite the perceptive observations of that young Irishmen delighted with the "careless" dress of local females, the snake in the garden was, of course, neither drink nor "relaxed" morals but that troublesome, frustrating, many-headed hydra bequeathed to the county by its tobacco years—the institution of slavery.

[14] Weld, pp. 205–6. He also described the unfinished state of Monticello where he tarried for several days as Jefferson's guest and predicted that viniculture, still being tried by some landowners, would not develop into a true industry for many years to come. Despite his relatively pleasant sojourn in the Piedmont, Weld returned to Europe "without entertaining the slightest wish" to revisit America, and didn't.

Chapter 6

In the Shadow of Monticello

N O MYSTERY exists as to the identity of Albemarle's most
famous son. His presence is still very strong in the county
today, and his deeds and good works in behalf of his community, state, and nation are known to every Virginian, most Americans, and many citizens of the world as well. Yet, for much of his
adult life, as patriot, diplomat, and chief executive, Thomas Jefferson lived outside the boundaries of his native Albemarle and, consequently, for months on end was absorbed by both national and
international affairs. Although this "apostle of Americanism" (as
one of his biographers, Gilbert Chinard, calls him) always retained
keen interest in Albemarle and returned to his "little mountain" as
frequently as possible, only in the last decade or so of an event-filled
life, as patriarch and elder statesman free of national woes and
triumphs, could he turn his full attention to the rolling countryside
he loved.[1] The most important product of those years was, of course,
creation of the University of Virginia, which in our own century has
come to have a profound influence upon the well-being of both
Charlottesville and Albemarle. In fact, with the decline of agriculture
in recent years, that institution has emerged as a key element in the
economic life of the entire community. One is hard put to imagine
what the county would be like today had not Jefferson prevailed and
almost by his own hands built brick by brick his lovely "academical
village."

Nevertheless, even though the remarkable Mr. Jefferson often
was off in Philadelphia, Paris, New York, or Washington, as holder
of high political office and master of substantial acres he still exerted
considerable influence in Albemarle. His role as president and leader
of a new political party gave him, for nearly two decades, the power
to appoint young men to key government posts, and this fact undoubtedly was not lost upon many of his neighbors who otherwise

---

[1] In addition to Chinard's work, *Thomas Jefferson, the Apostle of Americanism* (Boston, 1939), see Dumas Malone's multivolume *Jefferson and His Time*
(Boston, 1948—), Bernard Mayo's *Jefferson Himself* (Boston, 1942), and
Merrill D. Peterson's *The Jefferson Image in the American Mind* (New York,
1960).

might have pulled up stakes and joined the movement to Kentucky, Tennessee, Alabama, and other burgeoning frontiers. Their "frontier" was in truth the task of building a functioning republic free of the restraining hands of archaic Federalists. For example, Isaac Coles became private secretary to Jefferson during his second administration, and his brother, Edward, served James Madison in the same capacity. Another of these local young men (also once Jefferson's private secretary) won immortality when he forsook quill and paper and headed an expedition into the vast western wilderness which lay far beyond the last outpost of American settlement. His name was Meriwether Lewis, and at his side was William Clark (brother of George Rogers Clark), who, although not born in Albemarle, had obvious ties to the county.

It should be emphasized that local citizens clearly were for federalism as such. In 1788 when the Constitution was being debated in the state ratifying convention, Albemarle's delegates (the Nicholas brothers, George and Wilson Cary) lined up solidly in favor of adoption, thus joining the majority formed by the Tidewater and western Virginia counties. One does not have to search far for the reason. The county was served by navigable waterways, and as better roads developed, residents were aware of their community's commercial potential, an advantage not enjoyed by most Piedmont counties, whose inhabitants, as a result, opposed adoption. As political parties crystallized a decade later, with very few exceptions Jefferson could count upon the allegiance of Albemarle voters. Those still in the Federalist fold included the Carters of Blenheim and the John Nicholas family of Charlottesville.

The average Albemarle citizen, not eager to become a trailblazer through the Rockies or a civil servant in Washington, probably was influenced much more by Jefferson's interest in scientific agriculture; for, like the squire of Monticello, he, too, was a farmer. Throughout much of the late eighteenth century everyone was aware of what tobacco was doing to Virginia's soil. Travelers frequently commented upon the ravaged, despoiled landscape, often filled with abandoned fields in eastern counties and in the Piedmont badly eroded by gullies and washouts; but, as noted earlier, despite the havoc tobacco was creating, year after year until the Revolution it continued to be the principal cash crop. Virginia's entire economy was geared to its production, the supply of new land seemed inexhaustible, and it was a crop both white and black knew how to grow with relative ease.

The war, however, created an unprecedented demand for wheat, always an important product of Albemarle's fields, and during the last two decades of the 1700s more and more local farmers abandoned tobacco. William Minor Dabney, although unable to say precisely when this shift occurred, thinks it may have happened between 1790 and 1795.[2] Jefferson, like many other large planters, gave up tobacco during these years but returned to it later when prices rose. Dabney credits Robert Gamble, a Richmond merchant, with convincing Wilson Cary Nicholas to turn to wheat. Thomas Mann Randolph also was won over in the early 1790s and soon converted his famous father-in-law to the cause. "The small farmer often followed the example of their wealthier neighbors; and, at this time, since roads were better and wagons more plentiful, they converted mainly to wheat growing. Travelers found that in 1796 the shift away from tobacco was almost complete."[3]

Wheat, like tobacco, presented problems. Weevils, wildly fluctuating prices, and poor growing weather could bring disaster; but in general the expanding fields of grain bestowed a measure of prosperity upon Albemarle County. They also stimulated construction of flour mills, demand for highway improvements, and jobs for scores of wagoners, and soon Charlottesville citizens were passing ordinances prohibiting these hardy folk from camping overnight in Court Square, a popular site close by several taverns. Wheat contributed immeasurably to the growth of several villages—shipment depots such as Milton and Warren, and, in time, Scottsville, which emerged as an incorporated community in 1818. Transport of wheat and flour over the Blue Ridge from the Valley gave birth to a short-lived little boom town, a wagoners' stop of sorts, New York (or Little York), on the eastern side of Rockfish Gap.

Conversion to wheat in the 1790s was only one phase of a soil improvement program inaugurated by Nicholas, Randolph, and Jefferson, an undertaking tinged with desperation because upon its success could well depend the future of their county. These three men experimented with various systems of crop rotation.[4] Though their plans differed slightly, each aimed to restore and maintain the fertility of his lands through judicious planting of three basic crops: wheat, corn, and rye. They also began to apply both animal and vegetable manures freely, and other farmers, both great and small, as Dabney indicates, soon followed their example.

Thomas Mann Randolph went one step further and attacked the

---

[2] Dabney, pp. 84–87. Of course, loss of British markets as a result of the Revolutionary War had considerable impact upon local agriculture.

[3] Ibid., p. 87.   [4] See ibid., pp. 99–101, for details.

very serious problem of soil erosion by perfecting a hillside plow.[5]
Although his scheme of contour plowing proved its effectiveness
when Edgehill's fields alone withstood the onslaught of a heavy
rainstorm which lashed the county in 1810, few farmers were won
over. Many found his system much too intricate to duplicate and too
expensive to implement; others thought the proposed cure worse than
the evil they were attempting to eradicate. For the most part, Albemarle landowners continued to plant corn rows across their hillsides,
which sometimes slowed the ravages of erosion.

Out of these experiments in crop rotation, emphasis upon the use
of fertilizer, and better care of the soil emerged a county agricultural
society. Organized in 1817 with Thomas Jefferson among its leading
spirits and encompassing some thirty planters from a five-county
area, the Agricultural Society of Albemarle would have considerable
influence during ensuing years. Within a few months members were
discussing ambitious plans to establish nurseries for orchards and
fruit gardens and a factory to produce "implements of husbandry."
They even tried to obtain an Andalusian stallion for the county to
improve the quality of local horseflesh. This project received a
gracious nod from the Spanish monarch and had the blessing of
several illustrious individuals, but after four frustrating years ended
in failure.[6]

Despite this disappointment, for a decade or so this agricultural
society was among the best-known in America. Men such as Thomas
Mann Randolph, Peter Minor, Joseph C. Cabell, General John H.
Cocke, James Barbour, Dabney Minor, and Benjamin Colman turned
out scores of informative papers which, soon after being read to members, were reproduced in the *American Farmer*, published in Baltimore by John S. Skinner. He apparently was introduced to the work
of these local innovators by Dr. Thomas G. Watkins, a Maryland-
born physician who lived for a time at Glenmore near Milton.
Skinner tried without success to obtain something from the pen of
Jefferson, who, although he helped establish this society, never attended a meeting or wrote a paper to be read before its members. In
1820 Skinner visited Monticello where he enjoyed the conversation,
but not the cuisine. Jefferson served up millet, which his guest

---

[5] William H. Gaines, Jr., "Thomas Mann Randolph, Piedmont Plowman,"
MACH 11 (1951):37–43.

[6] See Lucretia Ramsey Bishko, "A Spanish Stallion for Albemarle," *Virginia
Magazine of History and Biography* 76 (1968):146–80; and, by the same
author, "The Agricultural Society of Albemarle and John S. Skinner: An
Enduring Friendship," *MACH* 31 (1973):76–111.

10. Portrait of Thomas Jefferson by Bass Otis

11. Monticello, a nineteenth-century view, signed by Pierson

thought perhaps "very palatable to *Philosophers*—to a Socrates, or a Jefferson—but rather dry for common folks!!" [7]

One would assume these new wonders of scientific agriculture (millet excluded) soon were disseminated throughout the hills of Albemarle, and perhaps, as William Dabney and others indicate, they were. Whether this seed scattered from on high took root is quite another matter. As everyone knows, farmers can be a cantankerous lot, especially if new notions are urged upon them "for their own good" by their betters. Conceding that both fellow planters and small farmers greatly admired Jefferson and may have followed his lead in affairs both political and agricultural, one is struck by the obvious truth that all the citizens of Albemarle County were doing as they faced increasing competition from new frontier farmlands in the Mississippi Valley was coming to grips with the harsh realities of their rural world. Attending an agricultural society meeting and reading the learned pamphlets carefully produced by its genteel members were unnecessary. For practical solutions to many aspects of their dilemma, they had to look no farther than the rich farms lying just across the crest of the Blue Ridge. For every farmer who learned about fertilizer and crop rotation from the gentry, ten undoubtedly got the same invaluable information face-to-face from a husky wagoner who stopped to rest his horses or oxen while transporting a load of wheat from Augusta County to the banks of the James. In essence, transition to wheat, dictated by what tobacco was doing to local fields, like every fundamental change in the life of any community had innumerable unexpected results. Huge hogsheads of tobacco could glide silently downstream with little or no influence upon the surrounding countryside, but with the rumble of wheels and the snap of the wagoner's whip came conversation with "outsiders," new ideas, new roads, new commercial facilities, and new communities as well.

In 1797 when Jedidiah Morse, Yankee preacher and father of American geography, published the first edition of his *American Gazetteer*, he could find only three small towns worthy of note within Albemarle's boundaries. He described Charlottesville, the "capital," as lying on the post road between Richmond and Danville, Kentucky. It contained, he said, about forty-five houses, a courthouse, and a gaol. Warren, also a "post town," lay 10 miles from Warminster, 21 miles from Charlottesville, and 326 miles from Philadelphia. Milton,

[7] Bishko, *MACH* 31 (1973):87.

situated on the southern side of the Rivanna, was about half the size of Charlottesville and had a tobacco inspection warehouse.

Thirteen years later in 1810 the last edition of Morse's compendium appeared with new population statistics for the county and listed four towns, all with post offices – Charlottesville, Warren, Milton, and New York. The county seat and Milton apparently had about the same number of houses as before, but (according to Morse) Charlottesville now possessed an academy; and, interestingly, both Warren and New York were described as being 178 and 167 miles, respectively, from the new capital city of Washington. As for the academy, in 1810 it had no students, teachers, or buildings and existed only on paper; but under Jefferson's shrewd management "Albemarle Academy" would soon be transformed into Central College, the institution which, in turn, gave birth to the University of Virginia.

In 1816 Christopher Daniel Ebeling, a professor of Greek and history in Hamburg with an inordinate interest in the New World, published the final volume of his *Geography and History of America: the United States of North America*. Although Ebeling never visited Virginia, he read and researched widely, and his comments on Albemarle circa 1815 contain several fascinating observations. Charlottesville, he said, had about three hundred inhabitants.

Here is the courthouse, where both the district courts and those of the county are held. There are also a prison, a post office and an academy. The inhabitants trade in grain and other products of the vicinity which are sent to Richmond by water, where they are traded for European and West Indian wares. . . .

MILTON . . . a little village situated in recent years on the south-west side of the Rivanna, which is navigable from here on, containing about twenty-five houses, a post office, a public tobacco warehouse, a tobacco display (of which there are several in this county) besides a grain display. There is here in general a repository of local products which are traded in the same way as at Charlottesville.

NEW YORK, a village springing up at Rockfish Gap, as well as WARREN, in the southern corner at the James River. The former lies on Rockfish Mountain itself and consists of miserable block houses, among which is a taproom and a general store from which local products are sent to Milton and Richmond. These are bartered for foreign wares that result in lucrative sales in the mountains. The farms in the mountains are according to the local fashion rather fertile and yield eight to twelve bushels of wheat per acre. From here on westwards tobacco culture completely discontinues. Warren has a post office.

MONTICELLO, country residence of the former President of the United States, Thos. Jefferson, on the leveled point of a mountain in the Southwest Mountains, whose high situation affords a magnificent view of the eastern lowlands and toward the Blue Ridge. Not far from here the Rivanna breaks forth from the series of mountains. The dwelling house is attractive and beautifully built, however not yet completed. The gardens and other rural buildings are well planned. The five thousand acres which belong to the estate, however, are divided into leased farms that are well taken care of and yield chiefly wheat. The famous proprietor lives here, after the happy completion of his active years, in rural peace and dedicated to the sciences, for which a considerable and well-selected library provides him ample assistance.[8]

The next federal census (1820), in addition to listing the county's 19,747 inhabitants—8,715 white and 11,032 black (373 free)—contained extremely revealing details on mills and factories. This information, compiled for each parish by assistant marshals, was set down in a chatty dialogue style so foreign to government reports of subsequent decades.

John Price has a tan Yard, which cost five hundred Dollars, containing fifteen Vats, taning five hundred hides per annum, which cost two thousand Dollars, making four thousand pounds of Leather, which is sold at thirty Cents per pound. In which establishment are employed two hands, the wages of which are two hundred and fifty Dollars per an.

John Dickerson has a Tobacco Factory, which cost eighty-five Dollars, working one screw,[9] presing from ten to twelve thousand pounds of Tobacco per an. which cost from three to six Dollars per hundred, and is sold at from eighteen to twenty-five Cents per pound. In which establishment is employed one hand, whose wages is one hundred Dollars per an. Contingent expences five Dollars per annum.

Brightberry Brown has a Saw Mill which cost three hundred Dollars, runing one saw, sawing thirty thousand feet of plank per An. which is sold at six shillings per hundred feet. In which establishment is employed One hand, contingent expences five Dollars per Annum.

John H. Craven has a merchant Mill, which cost six thousand Dollars, runing two pair of burr stones grinding fifteen thousand bushels of wheat per An. which cost from three to twelve Shillings per bushel, making three thousand barrels of flour, which is sold at from four to twelve Dollars per barrel. In which establishment are employed two hands,

[8] John Lancaster Riordan, "Albemarle in 1815: Notes of Christopher Daniel Ebeling," *MACH* 12 (1952):39–45.

[9] "Screws" or presses were used in making plug and twist tobacco to be sold locally.

whose wages are two hundred and fifty Dollars per An. contingent expences are one hundred Dollars per An.[10]

In all, there were forty-eight mills, factories, and manufacturing
establishments within the county, more than two-thirds of them in
Fredericksville Parish, which included returns for the Charlottesville community. Most had only one or two employees, but a few
had six or seven workers. Some establishments carried on several
trades. Flour (or "merchant") mills often went hand in hand with
sawmills, both, of course, utilizing waterpower. Occasionally these
multipurpose establishments also had wool-carding machines, and
there was at least one for cotton which processed about a thousand
pounds each year. In 1820 Albemarle had seventeen sawmills, twelve
flour mills, ten tanneries, seven tobacco manufacturing plants, four
carding machines, two distilleries, a printing office, a hatter's shop,
and a carriage shop.

These sawmills produced nearly 900,000 feet of lumber each year,
although most of these operations appear to have been small, part-
time affairs with only one employee. The flour mills ground 126,000
bushels of wheat annually. At least one local miller thought everyone
should grind his own wheat. In 1820 Joseph Bishop inserted a notice
in the *Central Gazette* stating he had operated his mill for sixteen
years and often had ground for others "toll free." "During this time
I had to rebuild the mill—I have again rebuilt it and will not grind
on any terms whatsoever—Every person who has anything to grind,
may have a mill at small expense—it wants no bed stone, only a
runner, a crank, and small frame—will go by either wind or water." [11]
Despite this protest, others continued to grind for a fee, either charging a fixed sum to produce flour or retaining for their own purposes
a part of each shipment of grain received. Virginia law required that
both flour and tobacco destined for export from the state be inspected. In 1819 the county court was authorized to appoint flour
and tobacco inspectors to serve at Milton, Moore's Ford, and Scottsville, all centers of commercial activity.

The county's nine tobacco screws processed 189,500 pounds of

[10] For Fredericksville Parish returns, see Newton B. Jones, "A List of
Manufactures in Fredericksville Parish, Albemarle County, Virginia, in 1820,"
MACH 10 (1950):20–27. Those for St. Anne's Parish can be found with
population statistics for the county on microfilm at the University of Virginia
Library. Although officially disestablished, the parish obviously retained con-
siderable regional importance.

[11] Newton B. Jones, "Charlottesville and Albemarle County, Virginia, 1819–
1860" (Ph.D. diss., University of Virginia, 1950), p. 99.

tobacco in 1820. These operations must have been extremely lucrative since the original investment was considerably less than that needed for mills, perhaps one-fourth as much. Elijah Brown's single screw cost only $150 and turned out 30,000 pounds of tobacco annually. Brown employed two men and five boys who received wages totaling $390. He had, according to the census summary, "contingent expences" of $5 per year. In 1820 Brown advertised that he was prepared to fill orders from some distance away, and should his cigars and chewing tobacco prove unsatisfactory, the products could be returned at his expense.

The annual output of Albemarle's tanneries was valued at $15,650. Joseph Bishop's twenty-five vats, located near Vinegar Hill, produced 18,000 pounds of leather per year. John L. O'Neal, the carriage maker, turned out about a dozen four-wheeled carriages and six or seven "Giggs" every twelve months. Lumber, leather, and iron cost him $700 to $800, and he sold his annual output for $3,000 to $3,800. O'Neal employed seven men who received wages totaling $1,300. Andrew McKee, the hatter, worked two kettles with the aid of four assistants. His raw materials cost $700 per year, and his hats sold for $4 each. McKee paid his employees a total of $1,000 per annum. The two distilleries, one operated by the Rivanna Mills near Charlottesville and the other located in Warren, produced about 6,700 gallons of whiskey each year, which sold locally for fifty to eighty cents per gallon. One small sawmill was owned by a woman, Mrs. Susanna Humphreys. The printing office was, of course, that of the *Central Gazette* which began publication in January 1820. Owned by C. P. and J. H. McKennie, the presses cost $1,500 and printed 21,000 copies yearly. The McKennies also did job work valued at $1,500 annually. Not surprisingly, each of their four employees received rather handsome wages, about $250 per annum.

The Rivanna Mills, representing a total investment of $10,000 and employing six to nine men, was by far the most extensive operation within Albemarle County, turning out flour, lumber, and whiskey and carding wool.

Rivanna Mills employed by Richard and James Duke, which cost eight thousand Dollars runing two pair of burr stones, grinding thirteen thousand bushels of wheat per An. which cost from three to twelve Shillings per bushel, making twentysix hundred barrels [of] flour, which is sold at from four to twelve Dollars per barrel. In which establishment are employed from two to five hands, whose wages are five hundred Dollars per Annum. Contingent expences One hundred Dollars per an.

Also one saw Mill, which cost five hundred Dollars runing one saw, sawing fifty thousand feet of plank per An. which is sold at six shillings per hundred feet. In which establishment One hand is employed, whose wages is one hundred and fifty Dollars per An. Contingent expences thirty Dollars per An.

Also One distillery, which cost one thousand Dollars, working three stills, distilling two thousand bushels of grain per An. which cost from three to six Shillings per bushel making four thousand gallons of whiskey, which is sold from fifty to eighty Cents per Gallon. In which establishment are employed two hands whose wages are four hundred Dollars per An. Contingent expences fifteen Dollars per Annum.

Also One Carding Machine, which cost five hundred Dollars, carding from two to three thousand pounds of wool per An. (at eight Cents per pound). In which establishment One hand is employed, whose wages is one hundred Dollars per An. Contingent expences twenty Dollars per An.[12]

Not covered by this survey of manufacturing are taverns, hotels, stores, and other public places of considerable economic and social significance in any rural setting. Those who went to Charlottesville on business or on court day frequently gathered in taverns. In 1819 Captain G. W. Kinsolving was operating the Central Hotel in the block bounded today by Main, East Fifth, East Fourth, and Market streets. A more convenient rendezvous for many was Jesse Davenport's Swan Tavern on Court Square. It was so popular that early in January 1822 the harassed owner published this sad notice in the *Central Gazette.*

It was the misfortune of the subscriber to have taken a stand, which from its conveniency to the Court-House, and from its rooted habits, for houses have habits, too, was the open and convenient resort of the idle and noisy. He has long known, that this was an annoyance to travellers and his friends, and he has attempted to remove it. But he has found that the crowd will gather, whilst the attraction remains, and to root out the evil forever, he has nailed up his Bar-Room. To his friends, to travellers, to the public, he promises in their *rooms* the best of liquors—he promises his ardent assiduity to please, and a calm and quiet house. To those who have patronized his Bar-Room exclusively, he returns his thanks for their punctuality of attendance, and kindly begs them to remember the hearth by which they so often reposed, is without a fire.[13]

The Eagle Tavern, also on Court Square, was taken over by a new owner in that same year, refurbished, and opened to welcome those

[12] N. B. Jones, "A List of Manufactures," *MACH* 10 (1950):25–26.

[13] N. B. Jones, "Charlottesville and Albemarle," pp. 94–95. It is obvious, of course, that the columns of the *Gazette* provide rich detail on Charlottesville life which is lacking for earlier decades.

who could no longer warm themselves at the cold hearth of the historic Swan. The 1820s would see considerable hotel construction in the community, no doubt in anticipation of the needs of university students and their families.

Unfortunately, little information exists concerning taverns and private houses of entertainment scattered throughout the county. In 1820 thirteen annual tavern licenses were issued by the local court, and six individuals received permission to operate private houses of entertainment. Among those securing tavern licenses were Nathaniel Burnley of Stony Point, William Brown of Warren, Meredith W. D. Jones, whose facility was entered in court records as being "at Michie's Place," and William D. Fitch of Milton. Benjamin Hardin operated a country inn, the Albemarle Hotel, nine miles west of Charlottesville on the road to Staunton.

By the second decade of the nineteenth century travelers, merchants, and farmers had access to several new canals and roadways. The Rivanna was cleared up to Moore's Ford near Charlottesville by 1812, a project which sounded the death knell of Milton; however, the final illness was a prolonged affair. The locks of that waterway filled slowly, often froze over in winter, management seemed capricious and irresponsible, and, most important of all, tolls were high. As a result, many farmers continued to transport their produce to Milton by land, although some of these problems eventually were ironed out and charges reduced somewhat. Commerce in the lower end of the county depended heavily upon the broad but shallow waters of the James. There for many decades a bitter feud existed between the Scott family and Wilson Cary Nicholas, with the Howards occasionally joining the fray. Debate was over where tobacco and wheat warehouses, centers of commercial activity, would be located. Nicholas won a temporary victory in 1789 with establishment of Warren upon his lands, but the decision in 1817 to locate the eastern terminus of the proposed Rockfish Gap Turnpike at Scottsville represented the final triumph of his rivals. In the late 1700s another and much more important canal company, the James River and Kanawha, was formed to clear out major obstructions to travel on those waterways, and Albemarle citizens invested heavily in its stock; however, until 1820 when this facility was taken over by the commonwealth, the results were rather disappointing.

During these same years several highways were added to the original framework of the River, Three Notched, and Barboursville roads. The most important were those connecting Brown's Gap and Turk's Gap to Three Notched (roughly Route 250), the turnpike

from Rockfish Gap to Scottsville, and the road from Charlottesville
to Lynchburg. Like canals, they often proved unsatisfactory, especially in winter. With luck, Thomas Jefferson found he could travel
from Monticello to Richmond in twelve hours by sulky, and in the
1790s it usually took him ten days to return home from Philadelphia.
A balloon ascent of 1793 presented, he thought, high hopes for the
future. "The security of the thing appeared so great," Jefferson wrote
to his daughter Martha, "that everyone is wishing for a baloon to
travel in—I wish for one sincerely, as instead of 10 days, I should be
within 5 hours of home." [14]

At this time the county had very few bridges, only short ones
spanning the Hardware and other smaller streams, and one usually
had to ford rivers or pay ferry charges, four cents for man or horse.
Mail delivery was a private affair until 1791, but whether public or
private, service seems to have been extremely unreliable. Even after
it boasted of a postmaster Charlottesville sometimes received no mail
for three weeks or more, and in 1814 a man in Lexington, Kentucky,
asked a local resident to write him via Washington: "letters from
Washington City reach us in Eight days . . . your letter was up-
wards of 30 days from Char." [15]

The typical store of village and country stocked a wide range of
commodities, including groceries, dry goods, hardware, and whiskey.
More specialized services available in Charlottesville in the early
1820s were those of three tailors, several milliners, a jeweler, a cabi-
netmaker, a chairmaker, two bookbinders, a gunsmith, and several
metal workers, in addition to the hatter and carriage maker already
cited as manufacturers. Postmaster John Winn's all-purpose store
stocked clover seed, osnaburgs, domestic cottons, and a small supply
of British and Indian dry goods. His "groceries" included Java and
green coffee and Antigua and Jamaica rum. Winn also had shoes
for sale. Items carried by other merchants included straw bonnets,
figured silk handkerchiefs, silk and kid gloves, cotton hose, hairnet
caps, sheeting, shirt material, bedticking, Spanish cigars, parasols,
"prime" new herring, salt, gin, cordials, sugar, soap, crockery, glass-
ware, and books.

The tailors, who made frequent trips to larger centers such as
Richmond, Washington, and Petersburg to consult fashion trends,
seem to have done a flourishing business. Several millinery shops
furnished bonnets, silk for dresses, dress trimmings, infants' apparel,
and some ready-to-wear items. A Mrs. Miller arrived from Baltimore

[14] W. M. Dabney, pp. 154–55.   [15] Ibid., p. 158.

in 1820 and opened an establishment on Court Square, stating that "should she meet with the encouragement this growing town promises, she will make this place her permanent residence." After a buying trip to Philadelphia and Baltimore, this lady exhibited her new merchandise in a house belonging to William Watson, the local jailer. Within a few months Mrs. Miller was gone, apparently not having received the "encouragement" she thought her efforts merited. However, her place soon was taken by others eager to cater to female whim.

The cause of much of this commercial activity is no secret. Construction of the new university proved an unusual source of income for merchant and farmer alike. Expenditures connected with the building of Central College, which in 1819 became the University of Virginia, helped Albemarle ride out with relative ease the economic panic which that year wrought havoc in so many American communities. From the day in 1817 when Mr. Jefferson, on his way from Monticello to stake off the site of Pavilion VII (the first structure of Central College), asked his overseer to get a ball of twine at David Isaac's Main Street store, more and more funds found their way into local pockets. Although many of the skilled workmen came from Philadelphia, numerous Albemarle citizens supplied the materials they used and also furnished housing, clothing, and food for the labor force involved in this exciting undertaking. John M. Perry, whose land was purchased as the site for the new institution, held the contract for the brickwork on Pavilion V, and James Dinsmore, a Charlottesville landowner who had worked for Jefferson previously, did the woodwork. Both men also helped construct other buildings. Perry provided brick for the Rotunda and the famous serpentine walls and sold lumber, more brick, flour, and cornmeal to the proctor and others.

A Philadelphia contractor, Richard Ware, bought lumber locally and paid Albemarle residents with wagons $5 a day to haul materials. He also hired some slaves as laborers for specific periods. Though no local merchant had a monopoly on supplying clothing and food, James Leitch and the firm of Wolfe and Raphael appear to have conducted a flourishing business. They and others furnished osnaburg, leather, and whiskey in substantial quantities. In 1823 William Huntington billed the proctor $12 for "whiskey for the laborers last year." One of Leitch's bills totaled $151.64, but from this sum was deducted $125, the amount due on the third installment of his personal pledge to Central College.

The prospect of an institution of higher learning, in turn, spawned

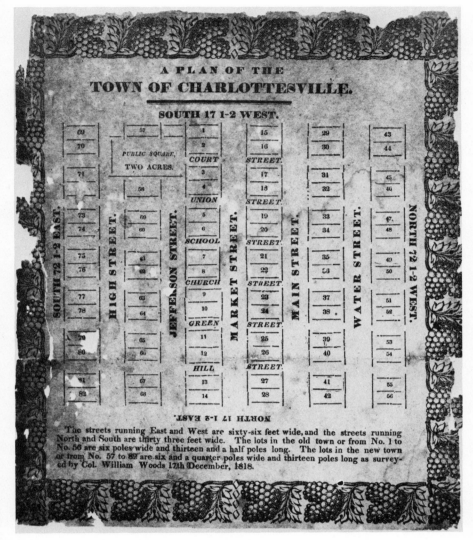

12. Plan of the town of Charlottesville, 1818

several private academies. Thanks to authorization in 1818 to use money from the State Literary Fund to educate indigents, poor children occasionally were able to attend these schools at the expense of the commonwealth. Jefferson handpicked Gerard E. Stack to head Charlottesville Academy, designed to prepare boys for the university. Stack's classes opened in May 1819 in what had been the Female Academy but closed fifteen months later. Although Stack arrived highly recommended, his school soon was in deep trouble and lost the support of Jefferson and other influential citizens. Stack departed saying he always found his pupils "docile, obedient, and affectionate." Docility and affection perhaps are not traits to be developed in the classroom, for it is apparent this man was no disciplinarian, and his academy was often the scene of rampant disorder. This school offered a classical curriculum of Greek, Latin, French, mathematics, geography, belles lettres, and ancient history. At the same time, Richard Woods was conducting an elementary school seemingly intended more for those wishing to enter the business world. Woods, who returned unexpectedly from an expedition to the West, taught orthography, reading, chirography, common arithmetic, bookkeeping, and English grammar.

On the day in 1820 that Stack quit, George Carr, a former student and an assistant at Charlottesville Academy, opened a classical grammar school at what is now 611 East Main Street. Tuition for a five-month session was $20, while board, lodging, and washing for the same period cost $50. In general, these preparatory schools led rather brief lives, at least under the same management. After a year or so schoolmasters often turned to other occupations or, as the university developed, found themselves at odds with faculty personalities and sought greener pastures elsewhere. However, the need for preparation for university entrance was real, and just as Carr followed Stack, others appeared to take up the challenge.

For those who could not afford boarding schools or wished their children to remain at home, several classrooms existed throughout the county. In 1820 William Bowen was teaching in the Ivy Creek community, but two years later he moved to Mount Ed near Batesville where he proposed to accept eight to ten boarders. Bowen also notified the public that he possessed a set of surveying instruments and "would engage in that business if required." Joseph Mills operated a private seminary ten miles north of Charlottesville, and a third country teacher, William L. Wilkerson, held classes two miles west of John A. Michie's tavern on the Buck Mountain Road.

Several women also instructed small groups of young ladies in their homes.

At the county seat itself parents could send their daughters to Charlottesville Female Academy, an institution which proved much more stable throughout the 1820s than many of its male counterparts. This was truly a community project which came into being in 1819 when twenty or thirty fathers, "having many daughters and wishing them well educated," purchased a building to house the school. Although this structure soon was taken over by Headmaster Stack and his unruly charges, the female institution reopened at the corner of High and Third streets under the able leadership of Mrs. M. P. George. Classes offered were divided into two groups: the first encompassing "the English language, grammatically, Sacred, Ancient, and Modern Geography, History, Astronomy, use of Globes, Drawing of Maps, and Composition"; the second, reading, writing, English grammar, and arithmetic. French and music could be taken in addition to these studies. The charge for fuel, washing, and board was $60 per session; each young lady was required to furnish her own bed and bed linen. There were two sessions per year, with a vacation at the end of each session. After four years Mrs. George, who earlier had been in charge of the Fredericksburg Female Academy, departed to conduct a private school in Scottsville, the little river town which was emerging as Charlottesville's chief economic rival within the county.

Two less prestigious female institutions, one at the foot of Vinegar Hill and the other at the top, also were operating in the early 1820s. A Mrs. Spencer conducted classes for girls under twelve years of age near the base "opposite Mr. Bishop's tannery." Tuition was $8 for five months' instruction in spelling, reading, and writing. At the crest, Rebecca Estes offered slightly more advanced classes for young ladies.

In addition to formal classroom instruction, from time to time local citizens could attend crash courses presented by itinerant scholars. In 1820 a Dr. Horwitz delivered a fifteen-day seminar on the Hebrew language. Before his arrival, Horwitz had given a similar series of lectures in Richmond, Norfolk, Lynchburg, and Staunton. He was warmly endorsed by several prominent individuals, one of whom published a statement in the *Central Gazette* urging all to attend because Charlottesville must become the "Athens of Virginia." Additional opportunities of this sort included classes conducted by Rogers and Wyatt, who in 1821 taught geography by the projection of maps. Each student was supervised as he drew seven maps, and upon completion of the course, he was supposed to be able to draft a map of any region in the world. Although this claim may have been a bit exaggerated, the method used was highly praised, and Rogers returned a year later to offer three successive three-week courses in the mysteries of his special art.

New educational facilities, an agricultural society, and a thriving economy were, however, not the only sources of local gossip during these years. On an otherwise dull winter's day in February 1819, those lounging about Court Square were treated to an amazing confrontation between two well-known citizens, one armed with a riding whip, the other with a knife, in fact, several knives! [16] No one who witnessed this frontier-type skirmish between Jefferson's grandson, Thomas Jefferson Randolph, and Randolph's brother-in-law, Charles L. Bankhead, was sure who struck the first blow, but little doubt existed concerning the root of the trouble. The two men once had been close friends and apparently were on relatively good terms after the repercussions of this fracas subsided, but a short time before the quarrel occurred, Bankhead, a handsome man "given to drink," had dispatched "a very insulting letter" to Randolph's wife, Jane. According to the Randolphs, Bankhead advanced, knife drawn, and their kinsman defended himself with a whip until he stumbled and fell. Bankhead suffered a gash on his head, but Randolph was severely cut before those nearby could separate the two men. Informed of what had occurred, the squire of Monticello, seventy-six years of age, sped down the mountainside on horseback in the dark of night to find his beloved grandson lying on a pile of blankets in a counting room. He wanted to take the young man back to Monticello by litter, but doctors said he could not be moved.

Within a month Randolph was up and about, and all of the family, except Anne, Bankhead's devoted wife, maintained that her husband was at fault. Although a trial was scheduled, none ever took place. Bankhead and his family left Albemarle for a time, but within a few years they were back at their former home, Carleton. Following Anne's death her children were cared for by the Randolphs at Tufton, and Bankhead apparently visited them whenever he wished, the old antagonisms of that February day having vanished. He died suddenly of "a fit" in the summer of 1833 after a prolonged siege of drinking. Randolph, however, carried to his grave the scars of the altercation

[16] See Joseph C. Vance, "Knives, Whips, and Randolphs on the Court House Lawn," *MACH* 15 (1956):28–35.

which briefly split the county into pro-Randolph and anti-Randolph factions.

The year 1820, or thereabouts, was a major turning point in the life of Albemarle County. Construction of a university and birth of an active agricultural society represent developments of considerable import. At the same time, the individual most responsible for both clearly was in his declining years. Mr. Jefferson was nearly eighty, although still very alert and surprisingly active, and it was obvious to all that his brilliant age was drawing to a close. His Albemarle now had approximately 20,000 people living within its borders, but during the next five decades they would watch as thousands of their sons, daughters, and cousins packed up and moved to other areas and other states, especially new lands opening up in the South and West. As a result, the population remained relatively static, not declining but increasing at a very slow rate indeed, inching its way upward to 27,554 in 1870.

No longer was Albemarle exclusively an agricultural community. Although produce of farm and plantation would continue to be of prime importance for a century or more, a growing minority of merchants, shopkeepers, teachers, millowners, and manufacturers were less concerned with crops, weather, and seasons than many of their neighbors. Also, an element of specialization was becoming apparent to all. The days of the aggressive plantation pioneer whose annual earnings might be derived from almost anything—sermons, medicine, surveying, politics, land speculation, and, of course, agriculture —were over.

The year 1820 represents, then, both an end and a beginning. In microcosm, Jefferson's lovely Albemarle mirrors trends apparent on the national scene: the waning of the once-powerful Virginia dynasty, the pervasive influence of an industrial revolution, and more and more specialization in American life. This was also the year in which the master of Monticello thought he heard "a firebell in the night," a direct reference to the rising tide of controversy surrounding the very institution upon which so much of Albemarle's economic well-being was based. In retrospect, many county residents must have looked back wistfully to these years, a rich, warm summer full of promise and contentment. Untroubled by scattered clouds on the northern horizon, they busied themselves building their "Athens of Virginia," unmindful that all too soon that distant haze would build up into a threatening thunderhead streaked with lightning.

Part II
The Lean Years, 1820-1888

For Albemarle and its people these were not especially happy times. War and Reconstruction, with all of the drama and controversy they entail, are only part of the story, the tip of the iceberg. The county's problems were merely those of the Old Dominion and much of the seaboard South in miniature. The very things that had created the region and bestowed considerable prosperity upon it in the eighteenth century became troublesome liabilities in the nineteenth. Slavery, an effective and cheap form of labor in an expanding tobacco economy, was somewhat of a burden to settled, more diversified agriculture. True, Albemarle's farmers made slavery work for them under these changed conditions, but at considerable sacrifice in efficiency and productivity. And, of course, after 1820 the system itself faced mounting criticism. Agriculture, the lifeblood of the county, had to contend not only with worn-out fields and problems presented by black servitude, it also faced mounting competition from new lands beyond the mountains. The frontier that gave birth to Albemarle quickly moved on and continued to lure millions ever westward, both new immigrants from the Old World and hundreds of native sons and daughters as well.

No longer did men like Peter Jefferson, Thomas Walker, and George Gilmer appear, provide able leadership, and contribute their great talents to the well-being of Albemarle; instead, sturdy young men of their ilk and many of their own descendants sought residence elsewhere. Their frontier might be the West or Southwest, the industrial and commercial North, or perhaps growing cities of the South. Two of three boys born to William Cabell Rives (thus Walker's great-grandsons) were, for example, living in New York City in 1860, and the third was an engineer in Richmond.

The problems of Albemarle—a rural, agricultural world in an age which witnessed the beginnings of urban industrialization—were complicated both by internal divisions and failure to develop a meaningful system of basic education. While these flaws are evident in many contemporary communities within and without the Old Dominion, some unity of purpose and a few elementary classrooms might have mitigated considerably the effects of these troubled decades. It is quite possible that basic schooling could have discovered native talent which was wasted and stemmed, in part, the outflow of migration; and if the "little wars" between Charlottesville, Scottsville, Howwardsville, Milton, and so on could have been avoided, the entire region would have been somewhat more prosperous. In retrospect it appears that, at least in the years between 1820 and 1860, moving county government to a more central site was a serious error. Although Charlottesville possessed certain admitted advantages, had the county focused its attention upon use and development of the James, a superb natural waterway, considerable coin would have been saved and much heartache avoided. In passing it might be noted that on the state level, transfer of government from Tidewater to fall line fostered similar discord. Richmond fought and thwarted Norfolk just as Charlottesville did battle with its river town competitors. Both won, but at tremendous cost. Had the Old Dominion (even merely the area east of the Blue Ridge) and the county each been somewhat more united, their leaders could have spoken with more authority, and (who's to say) though the disasters of the 1860s probably were inevitable, some vital decisions of preceding decades might have been made differently and produced different results.

However, one should not belabor the dark shadow of war and its aftermath, out-migration of thousands of native-born, and the ups and downs of a troubled rural scene. There were bright spots—establishment of a flourishing university, improvements in transportation, steady growth of two small commercial centers, and some truly good years. The 1850s, aided by rail lines, new fertilizers, and momentary demand for Albemarle's "first love," tobacco, were a generally prosperous era. And this period of 1820 to 1888 concluded on a hopeful note. By 1888 the turmoil of secession and war had abated considerably, a Democrat sat in the White House, and Charlottesville had thrown off the cocoon of town government and become a full-fledged metropolis.

Yet, although overall population rose markedly in the 1870s (27,544 to 32,618), in-migration and natural growth did not quite offset the black exodus which began during the following decade. Nearly all of these newcomers were hardworking white citizens, some of them from out-of-state and a few possessed of considerable wealth. Riding this crest of better times, in tune with Henry Grady's siren song of a "New South," residents in 1888 published a formidable handbook listing fourteen reasons why "settlers" should consider Albemarle as their new home. Among these were an unequaled climate with "a minimum of fatal diseases," cheap land centrally located, a diversity of soils and minerals, good natural springs, abundant woodlands, fine educational facilities, and (perhaps most important of all) low taxes, "less than one per cent. per annum."

Although agriculture remained supreme and dominated this publication, Charlottesville was offering "extra inducements to manufacturers who wish to locate," and real estate ads appear with great frequency. J. Massie Smith had a Shadwell factory for sale, W. G. Merrick of Glendower (agent for the James River Valley Migration Society) was seeking "intending settlers," and two large sections of house lots in or near the city of Charlottesville were being offered by R. H. Fife and the firm of Payne and Massie. J. W. Dolin, proprietor of the Virginia Piedmont Real Estate Agency ("office near the city post office"), was publisher of *Dolin's Land Register* which offered for sale not only local property but farms near Williamsburg, Manassas, and even a 4,400-acre spread in the Texas Panhandle country. One of Dolin's prize estates was Belle View, a 365-acre farm two miles from Charlottesville. It was well-supplied with water, had a twelve-room dwelling complete with outbuildings, a 16-acre orchard, and about 100 acres of woodland. Price: $6,500.

A new wave of settlement was underway, but these folk came by train, not by wagon or on foot, and they often spoke with a northern tongue. The lean years were over. Men who once fought for the Old Dominion's soil and cursed the land as they sweated in trenches carved from it now were buying up acre after acre from those who had fought valiantly to defend it. Thomas Jefferson's county was even toying with the idea of becoming a center of mills and factories, not farms. Change, that hallmark of restless American life, was coming to Albemarle.

Chapter 7

That Vexatious Institution

B
Y THE TIME Albemarle came into existence in 1744, slavery was well established in Virginia, and slaves were among the county's earliest settlers. Yet in colonial decades white indentured labor also was widespread, and the practice of hiring slaves from their owners for a year to perform specific duties increased markedly in the mid-nineteenth century as industrial outlets expanded and the innate abilities of certain black workers was recognized. Local slave census rolls of those years are so confusing that it is virtually impossible to tell precisely how many Negroes a master of a substantial estate owned. He was using his slaves and those belonging to others, and at the same time a few of his blacks might be working at a local mill or in the fields of his neighbors and relatives.

Development and growth of this sometimes troublesome but obviously profitable [1] form of labor gave rise to considerable controversy long before abolition per se became a matter of national concern. Numerous Virginians, Jefferson and Madison among them, wrestled with slavery during the Revolution and the decades which followed, at times proposing various schemes for gradual emancipation; relocation of freed blacks in western lands, Africa, and the West Indies; or halfway measures which would give ex-slaves a twilight sort of freedom enjoying some, but not all, of the privileges of citizenship. Of course, how Virginia, the wealthiest and most important state in the new American nation, handled this perplexing issue was crucial, for it would chart the course followed by the rest of the South. And it seems unnecessary to point out that the dilemma between 1780 and 1820 was real indeed, although at the outset slavery was not a southern problem alone since masters and slaves were found in all thirteen states.

How this situation came about and how attitudes toward race, color, and involuntary servitude which are a vital part of this whole question developed has been intricately detailed by Winthrop Jordan

---

[1] Whether slavery actually was profitable has been the subject of prolonged debate, but its wide acceptance and vitality as an institution indicate—more clearly than columns of figures—that it was.

in his remarkable study, *White over Black: American Attitudes toward the Negro, 1550–1812*. It is his opinion that in the early 1600s black workers arriving in Virginia may or may not have been treated in the same fashion as white indentured servants. The evidence, according to Jordan, simply does not provide a definite answer. What is certain, however, is that by the mid-seventeenth century black slavery had gained legal approval and, as the demand for cheap tobacco labor mounted, more and more slave ships dumped their human cargo at wharves located in the Tidewater. Apparently no one gave much thought to the implications involved, at least not enough to reverse this trend of events. The slave-master relationship simply became an accepted way of life and a century later was planted in Albemarle along with tobacco seed, the Anglican church, and British law.

While the Old Dominion remained a colony, a dependency of Great Britain, citizens troubled by slavery (and some were) could do little to alter what was happening. In fact, colonial status provided a convenient, ready response: slavery was forced upon us by London and is being perpetuated despite our protests. With independence, Virginians and other Americans as well found themselves saddled with both this vexatious institution and an embarrassing arsenal of high-flown rhetoric which would haunt them and their descendants to the present day: "We hold these truths to be self-evident, that all men are created equal, that they are endowed by their Creator with certain unalienable Rights, that among these are Life, Liberty, and the pursuit of Happiness." One could argue that a slave was property, not a man, or that Jefferson's ringing phrases were merely a wartime expediency lacking the force of law; but as debate increased, these tortuous interpretations satisfied only a minority in a republic based upon the principle of rule by the majority.

To their horror Jefferson and other founding fathers discovered that by preaching revolution, they had unleashed a tiger in their midst. At home Quakers, Methodists, and slaves themselves could and did utilize their words and their example to advocate emancipation and freedom. Abroad the citizens of France and black Santo Domingo put into action, with devastating consequences, the very ideas they had espoused with such fervor. Jordan devotes an entire chapter to the troubled mind of the squire of Monticello as he recoiled from the effects of this whirlwind. Once uncaged the tiger of liberty seemed to know no bounds. He roamed at will. Events in Paris, the West Indies, and especially Richmond's Gabriel insurrection plot of 1800 summarily ended two decades of reflective contemplation about how to eradicate slavery from American life. The

answer, clear and strong, from Albemarle, Virginia, and other regions
where slavery was entrenched was that the institution would not (or
could not) be abolished or phased out through some intricate form
of gradualism, at least not now.

The experiences of the master of Monticello reflect clearly what
had happened. Soon after writing the Declaration of Independence,
Thomas Jefferson composed an intricate plan for very gradual emancipation of Virginia's slaves and their removal from the state. This
scheme was never submitted to the legislature. The Old Dominion,
he apparently thought, was not yet ready for such a proposal. Also
there were both political and personal considerations. He could not
afford to take an unpopular stand or to lose the labor of his own
slaves. By the time Jefferson became president he had shelved any
ideas he once may have harbored of becoming an advocate of emancipation, and near the close of his life he wrote that he had ceased
to think about the matter entirely "because [it is] not to be a work
of my day." [2]

In 1806 Virginia, which for twenty-four years officially had encouraged manumission, passed a law requiring any slave freed by a
master to leave the Old Dominion within twelve months or face the
possibility of being seized and sold into servitude once more. "On its
face," writes Jordan, "not a remarkable measure, in fact it was the
key step in the key state and more than any event marked the re-
versal of the tide which had set in so strongly at the Revolution. It
was the step onto the slippery slope which led to Appomattox and
beyond." [3] This law created a dilemma for masters willing to free
their slaves. For, in addition to espousing liberty and freedom for
all, the founding fathers gave each state considerable power to regulate its own affairs. This meant any commonwealth could limit im-
migration by free blacks and many did. By special act of the General
Assembly it was possible for an ex-slave to stay in Virginia, and in
1827 five freedmen granted their new status by the last will and
testament of Thomas Jefferson were permitted to do so. Nine years
later state authorities conferred this power upon county courts, and
though there was a momentary increase in the number of free blacks
living in Albemarle during the 1830s (404 to 602), their ranks remained virtually unchanged after that decade.

[2] Paul L. Ford, ed., *The Writings of Thomas Jefferson* (10 vols.; New
York, 1892–99), 10:362. These words are found in a letter written to William
Short on Jan. 18, 1826, concerning possible conversion of slaves into serfs.

[3] Jordan, *White over Black* (Chapel Hill, N.C., 1968), p. 574.

Quite frankly, Mr. Jefferson's county was confronted with a painful, seemingly insoluble situation. Most residents did not like slavery. (A statement not subject to debate since blacks were in the majority.) Some whites did not like what the institution was doing to them as masters and to their society or what it was doing to those suppressed by it. Until the 1830s much of this local criticism had its roots in moral arguments. Generations imbued with concepts inherent in the American Revolution felt slavery was innately "wrong," but once fanatical outsiders launched their stern abolitionist crusade, those living within Virginia who continued to criticize tended to stress the economics of slavery, especially during hard years. As Patricia Hickin shows in her study of antislavery sentiment in the Old Dominion from 1831 to 1861, this attitude waxed and waned depending upon farm income.[4]

There are several aspects of nineteenth-century slavery, some abhorrent in today's intellectual climate and others subject to considerable interpretation, which should be mentioned nevertheless. The slave was a good investment, but an owner did not merely invest in slave labor; he speculated in it as well. Money laid on the auction block brought higher returns than dollars invested in canal stocks or deposited in the capricious, short-lived banks of those times. The price of slaves continued to rise year after year, and breeding of slave offspring made this speculation even more attractive. Also it is obvious that the slave was very much an integral part of the day-to-day life of Albemarle. Large farms, large families, and substantial homes made his labor a virtual necessity. Unlike those living in most parts of the Northeast, county farmers and mistresses of expanding households did not have access to a ready supply of immigrant stock to help them till fields, do household chores, and care for young children. As a result, even university professors who came to Charlottesville from such hotbeds of antislavery sentiment as Ohio soon succumbed to local ways and became masters themselves.

By the 1830s neither emancipation nor colonization seemed feasible. Just as Albemarle's colonial pioneers could not stem the rise of slavery, even if they wanted to do so, their descendants could not eradicate it, whatever their views might be. The system, a fait accompli, was at one and the same time vexatious, troublesome, profitable, and extremely useful. Educating the slave to any degree would give him "bad ideas" and breed still more Gabriels, but keeping him

[4] See her "Anti-Slavery in Virginia, 1831–1861" (Ph.D. diss., University of Virginia, 1968).

in complete ignorance was out of the question since that would limit
his value as a worker. So, like hundreds of other communities, Albemarle skidded along on the knife edge of disaster, hoping for some
miraculous cure for the cancer in its bosom but, under increasing
pressure from northern abolitionists, putting up an uneasy defense
of what some, in time, would maintain was "a positive good." This,
then, is the background against which we must view slavery in Albemarle County during the last tempestuous decades of its existence.

Perhaps the best way to begin is to look at population statistics
for those years (see table 3). The white and black populations in-

Table 3. Albemarle County population, 1820–60

	Total	White	Black [a]	Free
1820	19,747	8,715	11,032	373
1830	22,618	10,455	12,163	404
1840	22,924	10,513	12,411	602
1850	25,800	11,875	13,925	587
1860	26,625	12,103	14,522	606

SOURCE: Compiled from manuscript returns, Fourth-Eighth
Census, National Archives, Washington, D.C.
[a] Some confusion exists concerning precise totals for these
years. On some occasions "free" Negroes appear to have been
included in the totals for all blacks; at other times they were
not. Note: Here free are included.

creased very slowly, reflecting substantial outward migration of both.
Though the number of free Negroes nearly doubled during these
decades, they constituted less than 3 percent of the total population.
Since early census returns often yield little extraneous information,
it is difficult to say just where such individuals lived within the
county; but in 1810 less than one-third of these freemen resided in
incorporated communities. Forty years later only 184 of 587 were
found in Charlottesville and Scottsville, indicating that tales of numerous little enclaves of free blacks throughout the countryside are
true and that in contrast to what most scholars of slavery have written, those released from the fetters of servitude (at least in Albemarle) did not congregate in towns. According to legend, one of
these centers, known as the Free State and said to have been in existence even before the Revolutionary War, was located near the Carr
family estate of Dunlora, a few miles north of Charlottesville.[5] Census

[5] W. M. Dabney, p. 130.

Legend

○ *Existing Buildings*

1 Two houses built by Mrs. Tracy Zigler
2 Norris' Blacksmith Shop
3 David Fowler ~ Cabinet Maker
4 John Thompkins ~ Carriage Maker
5 Origin unknown ~ Later General Store
6 O'Neal Residence
7 Mr. Schroff ~ Tinner
8 Store built in 1781
9 John Benson ~ Residence & Business
10 Charles Day ~ Tailor
11 Nancy West ~ Residence & Business
12 John R. Jones ~ Mercantile
13 James Leitch ~ 1770
14 Lyman Peck ~ Deputy Sheriff
15 Mercantile Store
16 Mrs. Grant ~ Dry Goods Store
17 Jesse Scott ~ Fiddler
18 Old Barracks owned by David Issacs
19 Issac Raphael ~ Residence & Business
20 Store & House owned by Nancy West
21 Joshua Grady ~ Blacksmith
22 Wm. Summerson ~ Carpentry Shop
23 David Wolf ~ Grocery Store
24 Matthew Casey ~ House & Tenement
25 Mr. Thomas' Residence
26 Market House
27 Presbyterian Church built 1828
28 Daniel Keith ~ Constable

29 Peter Lott Residence ~ before 1815
30 James Monroe ~ 1790 ~ later Old Stone Tavern
31 Store ~ Fleming & Boyd
32 David Fowler Res. ~ built by Joel Tewell before 1773
33 John Yeangain ~ 1811 ~ Fine Liquors
34 Lewis Leschot ~ Swiss Jeweler
35 Public Library ~ founded by Harper & Southall
36 Storehouse by James Leitch
○ 37 No. 0 ~ Mercantile with Slave Auction Block
38 Eagle Tavern ~ circa 1791
39 Post Office and Stores
○ 40 Court House and Stone Jail
41 Mercantile Stores by John Kelly
42 John Cochran Residence
43 McKee's Row: (left to right)
   Thomas Wayt ~ Shop & Residence
   Andrew McKee ~ Shop & Residence
   Thos. Wells & Geo. Toole Res. & Shop
   Branham & Bibb ~ Dry Goods, Grocery
   Jno. Simpson ~ Residence & Store
   Samuel Leitch ~ Residence & Store
   Printing Shop

A
View of
Charlottesville, Virginia
circa 1828

Information based on "Early Charlottesville Recollections
of James Alexander, edited by Mary Rawlings, and
"Wood's History of Albemarle County"

44 Opie Norris Residence ~ 1816
45 V.W. Southall Residence ~ post 1829
46 Col. John R. Jones Residence ~ 1814
47 Christ Episcopal Church ~ 1824-26
48 Cornelius Schenk Residence ~ 1792
49 Hardin Davis ~ Postmaster
50 J. A. & Davis Residence ~ 1826
51 Valentine W. Southall Residence
52 Dr. Thos. Jameson Residence ~ 1806

53 "Swan Tavern" c1773, owned by John Jouett
54 Mrs. Milly Jones Residence
55 The Rev. Francis Bowman Residence
56 William Watson ~ Jailor
57 John Kelly Residence
58 Dr. Ragland's Widow

returns of 1820 indicate that 54 free blacks also were living near or on the lands of Robert Carter. One can merely surmise what effect these "free states" had, but as abolition agitation increased, it is safe to assume they were scrutinized carefully and often by both slave and master.

During those years a feeble effort was made to return some blacks to Africa (with their own consent, of course). The Albemarle Auxiliary Colonization Society, branch of a national organization, frequently solicited funds to speed Negroes on their way. Editorials appearing in the *Virginia Advocate* stressed the group's humanitarian objective but at the same time expressed fear that blacks soon would "fill up the Southern States." Editors estimated that within a century the nation would have sixty million Negroes living within its borders, most of them below the Mason-Dixon line. In 1830 a group of local ladies staged a fair at which items were sold and proceeds donated to promote this illusive goal of African colonization.[6]

John Adam Kasson, a young Vermont-born tutor who later emerged on the national political scene, lived with the Isaac White family at Keelona near Carter's Bridge in the early 1840s.[7] In letters to his family he noted that Albemarle's blacks, at least household help, always were called "servants," not slaves. On one occasion he described a black wedding performed by a Negro parson who read the Episcopal service. Kasson himself was not present, but he told of the traditional festivities complete with feasting, laughter, and conviviality. "The servants often have feasts among themselves when the table is in truth furnished with greater variety than you will find at most country evening visits amongst the middle class in our State. But this is principally confined to the house servants. They are all moving around at a wonderful rate during their Christmas holidays."

A few weeks later Kasson became deeply enmeshed in a controversy involving the subject which cast a dark shadow over Albemarle and the rest of the nation during those decades: abolition. Although antislavery in sentiment, he never was a radical emancipationist; however, a chance remark made while dining at the home of George Rives that he could only admire the spirit of any "servant" who tried to be free troubled his host. Rives later sought out Kasson and asked him to urge his own tutor, also a Northerner, to have less intercourse with blacks. This young man was holding regular Sunday

[6] N. B. Jones, "Charlottesville and Albemarle," p. 135.

[7] See Edward Younger, "A Yankee Reports on Virginia, 1842–1843: Letters of John Adam Kasson," *Virginia Magazine of History and Biography* 56 (1948):408–30.

services and Rives feared a plot of some sort might be afoot. Kasson ridiculed the idea but did discuss the matter with his fellow tutor. They both thought the affair ended; yet within a few days Rives dismissed the youth, replacing him with another Vermont student, a personal friend of Kasson's. Later Kasson viewed the episode as an attempt to frighten both young men, who were less than twenty-one years of age, or perhaps an effort to provoke an incident which might counterbalance in the public mind a sensational runaway case that recently had stirred considerable interest throughout Virginia.

Census records of 1850, the first giving a detailed picture of the 104 free black households within the county, present some surprises. Several individuals owned real estate valued from $500 to $2,500. The wealthiest was Nancy Isaacs, a sixty-eight-year-old mulatto who lived with her son, Tucker Isaacs, a painter. She held title to land worth $7,000, a substantial sum for those years. Most of these free blacks were farmers, although some, like Isaacs, practiced trades; others lived in white households as servants. Also, under circumstances far from clear, a number of these homes headed by freedmen contained white citizens. Whether they were boarders, common-law spouses, or merely friends is anyone's guess. The most common surnames among these free families were Tyree, Goings, Scott, Kennie (or Kenny), and Battle (or Battles).

Similar statistics gathered ten years later are even more impressive. One hundred and fifty-eight households included free Negroes (110 of them being headed by blacks). They owned real estate worth $25,410 and personal property valued at $20,650. S. Barnett and his family of six had a net worth of $10,300; Jane West, who lived alone, $14,600. As before, most of these free blacks were engaged in agriculture or worked as domestics, although this time numerous females gave their occupation as "washwoman" or "seamstress." And a handful of whites of both sexes continued to reside among these folk.

There were, of course, several means by which these lucky few gained their privileged status in a slave society. Most of them, simply by working at night and on Sundays, saved up enough money to buy their freedom. If a master agreed, it was possible to make payments on an installment plan scheme. Others were granted freedom upon the death of their owner, and still others won it because of unique ability or as the result of exceptional conduct, such as an act of bravery in behalf of the family they served or during time of war. According to Kenneth Stampp,[8] slaves often comported themselves

---

[8] See his *Peculiar Institution* (New York, 1956), pp. 92–100.

in such a way as to enhance their chances for freedom—that is, malingering to decrease their worth or, on the other hand, proving extremely attentive to an elderly master or mistress with hope or promise of freedom when that individual died. Of course, such machinations only were available to house servants whom their owners knew personally. Field hands on great estates were merely a list of anonymous names, sturdy black bodies with little or no contact with those owning their labor.

Free blacks who were respected members of the community were accorded some of the social niceties granted any citizen, sometimes being addressed as "Mr." and "Mrs.," not merely by their first names. When Susannah Goings, widow of Sherard Goings, applied for a pension in the 1840s, Albemarle County officials writing to Washington in her behalf praised "Mrs. Goings" as "a very estimable colored woman." Christopher McPhearson, a free mulatto who became a successful storekeeper and once aided in thwarting a slave uprising in Fluvanna County, served for some years as a clerk in the Charlottesville law office of William Waller Hening. Hening and others referred to him as "Mr. M'Pherson." [9] However, those caught up in this third track of a biracial society—free and perhaps mulatto as well—led difficult lives. They were resented by many whites, especially as the abolition fury increased, and offenses that would have been overlooked if committed by others often got them into trouble with local authorities. They frequently were charged with illegal gambling, excessive drinking, disturbing the Sabbath in some fashion, as well as robbery and stabbing.[10]

It is virtually impossible to establish what relations were like between free blacks and whites, or all Negroes and whites for that matter. Lafayette, who visited America in 1824–25, reportedly was shocked by the widening gulf between the races, recalling how men of various hues had eaten, fought, and died together during the Revolution. Yet it is obvious that close personal friendship could exist between slave and master, and as noted, a few Albemarle whites lived by choice in the homes of free blacks.

The actions of Edward Coles, the young man who was secretary to President Madison, present a unique chapter in the history of slavery in the county.[11] In 1808, barely twenty-one, he inherited a farm

[9] W. M. Dabney, pp. 129–30.   [10] Ibid., pp. 131–32.
[11] See Elizabeth Langhorne, "Edward Coles, Thomas Jefferson, and the Rights of Man," *Virginia Cavalcade* 23 (1973):30–37, and E. B. Washburn, *Sketch of Edward Coles, Second Governor of Illinois and the Slavery Struggle of 1823–4* (Chicago, 1882).

and some twenty slaves, nine of them children, from his father, master of Enniscorthy. Strongly imbued with abolitionist spirit, he announced to the dismay of his relatives that he was going to set his slaves free. To evade the law of 1806 he planned to retain these blacks as farm laborers, not record any official papers, and instead grant his former slaves legal freedom upon his death. However, Coles soon realized that local sentiment would not condone such a devious plan; the only course was for both him and his slaves to leave their native county and take up residence on free soil. While contemplating this step, he was offered the position with Madison which he eventually accepted, delaying his scheme of manumission for a time.

During the next few years Coles discussed his views on slavery with both Madison and Jefferson, once even urging the latter "to put into practice those hallowed principles contained in that renowned Declaration, of which you were the principal author." Jefferson demurred, saying he was much too old to lead any such campaign. Benjamin Franklin, Coles replied, was more advanced in years when he assumed the heavy responsibilities of being a founding father. Jefferson did approach several younger men and suggested that they cooperate with Coles by forming a "phalanx" to eradicate slavery. But no "phalanx" appeared, and it was soon obvious that if Edward Coles wanted to be Albemarle County's pioneer abolitionist, he would have to act alone. In 1819 he did just that, taking his slaves to Edwardsville, Illinois, where he set them up as free farmers on free soil.

Brave as this decision was, Coles possessed numerous advantages denied most Albemarle slave owners, however much they might deplore the institution of slavery. A well-to-do young man with powerful connections in high places, he had no immediate family responsibilities and was free to carve out a career wherever he wished. Coles obtained a lucrative post as registrar of lands in Edwardsville and within two years became governor of Illinois. In this capacity he led antislavery forces in a crucial and successful referendum fight which stymied for all time efforts to expand slavery to that state. A decade later he moved to Philadelphia and married. One of his sons when twenty-one (the same age his father had been when he announced his determination to become an active abolitionist) came to Albemarle County, bought a farm, and became a master of slaves. Two years later, an officer in Confederate gray, young Coles was killed in the battle of Roanoke Island.

The great majority of Albemarle blacks were not fortunate enough to have as master an Edward Coles who would transport them to Illinois or an owner who, upon his deathbed, granted them their freedom. Called merely "Sam" or "Suzy," slaves they were born and slaves they would die. How they lived in the interim is subject to much conjecture. One would like to believe that in the county of Mr. Jefferson, of all places, the master-slave relationship was embued with a special kind of enlightenment, and perhaps it was. But, as with the question of how Virginia's first black residents of the early 1600s fared, no available evidence provides a definite answer.

Everyone is familiar with tales of benevolent masters and happy, devoted slaves, some of whom stayed on the place after 1865, and also with stories of runaways, slave families split asunder, and mistreatment of Negroes, even torture and death. Each of these glimpses into the mysterious realm of slavery contains elements of truth, and all of these aspects of this vexatious institution are evident in Albemarle. This ad concerning a runaway appeared in the *Central Gazette* on May 27, 1820.

100 Dollars Reward

Runaway from the subscriber residing in Albemarle County, near Charlottesville, Virginia—a Negro Man, by Name

Winston.

Twenty-two years of age—five feet seven or eight inches high— of a bright yellow complexion—well made—apt to smile when spoken to—well clothed—the particulars are not recollected. He eloped from me on the twenty-first inst. I have every reason to believe he is endeavouring to get to some of the Northern States, as I understand he has obtained free papers. He will, in all probability, call himself by the name of

Shank.

He is a first-rate House Joiner and will, probably, try to get employment in that line of business—I will give the above reward of

One Hundred Dollars

To any person who will deliver the said fellow to me or

Fifty Dollars

If secured in any jail in the United States, so that I can get him again.

John M. Perry.[12]

Perry undoubtedly wanted this slave to return to work on construction at the university, but Winston apparently was more interested in freedom than helping to build the "Athens of Virginia." In many

[12] Quoted in N. B. Jones, "Charlottesville and Albemarle," pp. 57–58.

ways, this runaway is typical of most—young, male, mulatto, intelligent, and obviously agile as well. Some such individuals were aided in their efforts, not necessarily to go north but west, perhaps with promises of better working conditions or eventual freedom. In 1822 William Langley was apprehended and bound over for trial on charges of attempting to entice local slaves to accompany him to western lands.

Using files of the *Central Gazette* for 1820–22 as a guide, Newton Jones has established that local slaves usually were sold under three conditions: by provisions of the will of a deceased person, to pay debts when put up as security in connection with some business transaction, or simply in the course of everyday economic life—to reduce one's complement of black labor or to obtain money. Owners sometimes placed restrictions on these sales. In 1820 Thomas Jefferson Randolph offered for sale or hire a "first-rate female cook, regularly bred to the business, young and has two children—Likewise a very excellent plain Cook, who is a first-rate Seamstress, Dairy-Maid, and Washerwoman," but he stipulated that neither was to leave Albemarle County.[13] Other masters and mistresses stated that slaves to be sold could not be transported to states such as Georgia and Louisiana without their specific permission. Albemarle had no central auction site. Sales usually took place at gathering places such as the county courthouse or country taverns.

The practice of hiring out slaves for one year was very common, and the columns of the *Central Gazette* indicate cooks and female servants were much in demand in the 1820s. This custom led to abuses both by those who hired such labor and by slaves themselves. Prospective employers were cautioned that blacks must be returned on time, in good condition, and properly clothed. Ambitious Negroes sometimes contracted their services without obtaining an owner's permission. In 1822 Hugh Chisolm warned local residents not to employ "Louis and Stepheny" on their own account and threatened that "those offending may expect to be dealt with according to the law." [14]

The county's 10,659 slaves constituted 54 percent of the population in 1820. There were approximately 1,052 heads of families who owned blacks and 660 who did not. Jones emphasizes that slave owning per se is not an accurate index of wealth. Economically those without slaves and those with a handful hardly were distinguishable from each other. Twenty-nine citizens owned more than 40 slaves; and, of these, only four had more than 100. As Jones notes, it is impossible

[13] Ibid., p. 54.   [14] Ibid., p. 57.

to know precisely how many slaves some masters owned. Pages of the 1820 census are torn and difficult to decipher. Blacks occasionally are listed under the name of an overseer, while others may have been hired out to work for neighbors or relatives of their masters and mistresses. Dabney Minor, Hugh Nelson, Mrs. Robert Carter, and Thomas Jefferson appear to have had 100 or so slaves in 1820. A decade later John Harris, who lived at Viewmont and was the county's wealthiest citizen, had 159 slaves. The Minors, Carters, and Nelson still had over 100 slaves, as did Tucker Coles. Others who were masters of 70 or more blacks included John Coles, John Craven, James Henderson, Mann Page, Thomas Jefferson Randolph, and John Rodes.

Despite the views of some that there were too many blacks in Albemarle and that diversified agriculture did not require such an abundance of slave labor, their ranks continued to grow during the next three decades, just about keeping pace with those of the free sector. In 1860 50 citizens owned 40 or more slaves, but the greatest increase was in the number of individuals who owned only one Negro, from 180 in 1820 to 289 forty years later. The agricultural population schedules of 1850 reveal that, of 943 farmers in the county, 734 (roughly 78 percent) were slaveholders. A slightly smaller number, 695 (about 74 percent) held title to their lands.

These figures reflect both general farm prosperity and the realization that slavery, with all of its inherent problems, was not incompatible with either diversified agriculture or incipient industrialization. One did not have to grow staples such as tobacco, cotton, or rice to utilize their labor efficiently. Also, it is apparent slavery was not a dying institution in Albemarle County on the eve of the Civil War; in fact, it was alive and flourishing and demonstrated no signs of debility or ill health whatsoever. There are in these statistics, however, indications that many of these local slaves may have been well treated, especially compared to those found on extensive plantations of the Deep South. A substantial number of masters, nearly half, owned fewer than five blacks. These workers—whether house servants, field hands, or a bit of both serving as general all-purpose labor—were virtually members of the family. Daily face-to-face contact must have mitigated some of the abuses said to have occurred under overseers and created, at times, strong bonds of common interest between slave and master.

Well treated or not, by the 1850s the slave had become the central issue in national politics. According to Jones, it is impossible to say how Albemarle citizens reacted in this crisis. Newspaper files (Charlottesville now had two weeklies) are woefully incomplete, but one publication, the *Review*, sternly opposed secession until faced with the inevitable in 1861. Owners continued to debate the merits of how to manage their workers. William W. Gilmer, writing in the *Southern Planter* in April 1852, said young servants should be taught to respect their master and mistress.[15] Gilmer, who owned nineteen slaves housed in two structures, had these words of advice: "Talk to them, take notice of them; it gives them confidence and adds greatly to their value." He felt that, for every owner who was too strict, one hundred erred by being too lenient. A slave, he cautioned, may become restive and wander at night if not given sufficient work to do each day. Yet, blacks should not be driven too hard. A great deal of whipping, he said, was unnecessary. It was sufficient that a slave knew he would be disciplined if orders were disobeyed. "Kindness when sick, and at all times when they deserve it, or will *permit* it, is the great thing. . . . Never scold or threaten."

Ebenezer Boyden, a Vermont native and a graduate of Virginia Theological Seminary, came to Albemarle in 1839, apparently from Ohio. Rector of Grace Church, Cismont, for many years, he conducted a school for young ladies at his home, Holly Fork, and in 1860 published a strong defense of slavery. His *Epidemic of the Nineteenth Century* compared northern attacks on the institution to the witchcraft craze of earlier times. Although he justified slavery on biblical grounds, this clergyman considered it to be really only a form of temporary guardianship. The poor everywhere were faced with a constant struggle to provide for their families, but the slave went about his daily labor and left to his master the responsibility of his wife and children. Boyden said he had often heard a slave owner state that the task of the master was harder than that of the slave. Actually, the Reverend Mr. Boyden did not need to listen to what others said concerning the arduous responsibilities of being a master; he himself owned one slave, a seventeen-year-old female, and hired the services of four additional blacks. Census records reveal he had a large family (eight children), so these workers undoubtedly helped out in the household and at the school. Despite his Yankee birth and clerical garb, this man's analysis of slavery hardly can be considered free of bias.

In the same year that Boyden's pamphlet appeared, the death of a slave belonging to Eugene Garth created a major controversy between James Alexander, editor of the *Jeffersonian Republican*, and

[15] Ibid., pp. 165–66.

Green Peyton and J. C. Southall of the *Review*.[16] Alexander, for many years the community's leading newspaperman and author of *Recollections* which tell us much about early Charlottesville, was born in Boston in 1804 and came to Albemarle County when twenty-four years of age.[17] Though circumstances surrounding this tragedy are unclear, Garth's overseer was acquitted of murder charges by a local jury. Alexander endorsed this decision and accused the *Review* of furnishing ammunition for abolitionists by "parading before the public the blemishes of our social system and the incidental evils of our peculiar institution." He said the editors painted a picture of injustice contrary to actual sentiment prevalent in Albemarle. "We believe that there is as much kindness and humanity shown by the master to his slave in this county as in any other slaveholding community, and as is shown toward any other laboring class. . . . Self-interest as well as humanity prompt the master to treat the slave with as much humanity as is consistent with his proper subordination."

The *Review* countered that the *Jeffersonian Republican* was a slanderer trying to hide the blemishes of slavery. Its editors maintained that "when slavery becomes a hypocrisy, when slavery is to be carried on in the dark, when it cannot stand *in the light*, when it sulks and cries 'Oh, there comes a Northern man!,' then we are against slavery!" At the same time they maintained that Albemarle had "nothing to be ashamed of" and intimated they were attacking an instance of immediate injustice, not the entire system. This fracas appears to have been more of a clash between rival journalists than disagreement over a substantive issue. All concerned really favored the institution of slavery, but that public debate could occur in the county in 1860 on the eve of war is not without significance.

How a slave spent his leisure hours was, of course, regulated by both state law and local custom. In 1851 Charlottesville became somewhat independent of the county and thus was able to enact ordinances in its own right, although there are indications it had been doing so for many years.[18] Early town records, though often fragmentary, reveal racial controls common in wartime to all parts of a nervous South.

[16] See ibid., pp. 167–68, for an account of this affair.

[17] See Mary Rawlings, ed., *Early Charlottesville: Recollections of James Alexander, 1828–1874* (Charlottesville, 1942).

[18] See Margaret Fowler Clark, "Random Selections from the Charlottesville Council Minute Book," *MACH* 18 (1960):47–51.

June 13, 1863. Ordered that no negroes, or negroes living in the Corporation be permitted to leave the premises of their masters after 9 O'clock P.M. without a written permit.

Ordered that a nightly patrol be established under the direction of the Sergeant, from among the Citizens, and all to be so arranged as to names and times he shall serve, so that each one may not be called out to Serve said Patrol more than once in 2 weeks.

January 7, 1864. Be it ordained that the ordinance of December 19, 1846, regarding games be altered and amended so as to read as follows: That any person found playing bandy, or baseball or football in the street or alleys within the Corporation shall be subject to a fine of Two dollars for each such offence if a free person, or a minor then parent or guardian of them, but if a slave he shall receive any number of lashes not exceeding five.

January 5, 1865. Ordered that no negroes free or colored [19] be allowed to gather on the platform of the Railroad Depot at the time of arrival and departure of trains.

Ordered that smoking shall not be allowed on the street by any slave or free person [of color] under penalty of 10 stripes for a slave and $10. fine for free colored persons.

A few months later, with the "stillness" at Appomattox, slavery was dead. The vexatious institution—deplored, attacked, reviled, tolerated, and defended—was no more. In its wake appeared an unclear situation fraught with confusion for both black and white, tempestuous decades which would leave their imprint upon Albemarle and all of America to the present day no less than the institution of slavery itself.

[19] Probably should read "slave."

Chapter 8

The University

S OME of the circumstances surrounding the creation of the University of Virginia, an event of supreme importance in the history of Albemarle County, have already been alluded to—plans for an academy which, within a few years, became Central College, neither of which ever had students or faculty. Other developments, both within and without the county, favored establishment of an institution of higher learning in the Piedmont. The Old Dominion's population, like that of the nation, was moving westward. The College of William and Mary, Jefferson's alma mater, did not follow the state government to Richmond in 1780 and, instead, languished in the Tidewater. Jefferson once advised Francis Walker Gilmer, the young man who later helped recruit the first faculty for the new university, not to accept either the presidency or a professorship there: "A more complete cul de sac could not be proposed to you." [1] And in 1820 he acknowledged with regret that Virginia had no satisfactory college or university and urged his grandson, Francis Eppes, to enroll at Columbia College (the University of South Carolina) where Thomas Cooper presided. Other young Virginians, in increasing numbers, were going to Princeton in New Jersey and similar northern seats of learning, a situation which, after the heat of the Missouri controversy, Jefferson found intolerable. "Five hundred of our sons," he complained, "[are] imbibing opinions and principles in discord with those of our own country. This canker is eating on the vitals of our existence, and if not arrested at once, will be beyond remedy." [2] These words stand in stark contrast to some uttered by a much younger Jefferson half a century earlier.

Also, during the decade after he left the White House, this elder statesman's influence in national affairs was, quite naturally, on the wane. Rapport with his successor, Madison, was good, but some coolness existed between the squire of Monticello and the administration of Monroe. Thus it was inevitable that his agile mind would turn to local matters and to one specific need which always had fascinated

[1] Nathan Schachner, *Thomas Jefferson: A Biography* (New York, 1951), p. 958.
[2] Ibid., p. 979.

him: public education. At first, Jefferson projected a comprehensive scheme with elementary schools offering separate classes for laborers and those planning professional careers. After completing these courses, the latter would proceed to regional "colleges" (really high schools) and from there to a new, state-supported university. Although the preponderance of both college and university students would come from well-to-do homes, he proposed that some poor but able young men attend both levels at state expense.

One of Jefferson's most able assistants on the local scene was Alexander Garrett, county officeholder, trustee of Albemarle Academy, proctor of Central College, and bursar of the University of Virginia from 1819 to 1850. Garrett Street is named in his honor. Jefferson's lieutenant in the General Assembly was Joseph Carrington Cabell. Grandson of the good doctor who founded Warminster on the James and sometimes offered his professional services to patients on a "no cure—no pay" basis, he was, like Jefferson, a William and Mary alumnus. Nevertheless, as legislator, visitor, and rector, he labored for more than three decades in behalf of the University of Virginia. And at times the road was rough indeed. In 1818 Virginia's lawmakers nearly scrapped the entire educational program, but Cabell was able to salvage the provision for a new university. As a result, Jefferson turned his energies to making certain that this would be Central College, incorporated two years earlier and already in the first stages of construction.

On August 1–4 of that year, despite ill health, he met with the Rockfish Gap Commission, a group of citizens appointed to select the site for the university. The three locations in contention were Washington College at Lexington, Staunton, and Central College at Charlottesville. Jefferson arrived at the crest of the Blue Ridge armed to the teeth with documents, statistics, plans for buildings, even a set of rules for governing the student body. For four days these materials flowed from his portfolio, including a remarkable survey which demonstrated that Charlottesville was the geographical and population center of the Old Dominion. This survey was entirely in keeping with a concept which the leading men of Albemarle and Charlottesville seem to have embraced with considerable enthusiasm in the early 1800s—*Central Gazette*, Central College, etc. They were convinced, by some sort of pre–Chamber of Commerce mentality, that their community actually was a crossroads of commercial activity destined for greatness, a center with considerable promise; and to no one's great surprise, Mr. Jefferson had his way, the commission voting 16 to 5 in favor of Central College. In January 1819 the General

Assembly concurred, and the University of Virginia was a reality
. . . on paper.

Impressive as this performance was at Rockfish Gap, many Virginians did not accept the decision reached there as final. During the
next six years proponents of the Charlottesville site had to fight hard
and often to beat back efforts either to thwart plans for the university
or to scrap them completely. Prime adversaries were loyal William
and Mary alumni, Presbyterian clergymen alarmed by views of
Jefferson which they thought atheistic, and citizens of western counties who, unlike the twenty-one men who gathered at Rockfish Gap,
did not believe Charlottesville really was the center of the state's population or, even if it was, would be for long.

Jefferson was the architect of the university buildings and of the
overall design of the entire "academical village," but making these
dreams which sprang so readily from his mind come true presented
additional problems, not the least being the isolation of Charlottesville
which, at times, did not seem to be centrally located at all. Distance
from major cities made it difficult both to secure competent crafts-
men and to ascertain fair prices for wages, materials, and work being
done.[3] As early as August 1817 Jefferson was uttering weary complaints of troubles that would plague him almost to the grave. He
discovered, for example, not only did bricklayers charge different
prices in various parts of the nation, but they sometimes made their
own brick and sometimes they did not. (Those living in the Charlottesville area did.) When one finally arrived at an agreement with
bricklayers, carpenters, plasterers, and stonecutters, adequate living
quarters had to be found for them. And added to these problems was
the distinct possibility those engaged neither could or would live up
to the terms agreed upon. "It is small wonder in view of the many
disagreements over prices, complaints such as those of Coffee and
Percival, workmen who fled from debtors' prison, undertakers who
confessed their lack of knowledge about the work they proposed to
do, the employment of a potential murderer, and the many minute
details of housing, clothing, feeding, and even buying workmen that
Jefferson should have a somewhat jaundiced outlook on workmen as
early as the end of 1823, when he said, 'I always fear settlements left
to workmen however honest; because on that subject they have a
special code of morality of their own.' " [4]

[3] See William B. O'Neal, "The Workmen at the University of Virginia, 1817–
1826, with Notes and Documents," *MACH* 17 (1959):5–48.
[4] Ibid., p. 16.

Certainly the two workmen possessing the most exotic personal codes were Michele and Giacomo Raggi, stonecutters summoned from Italy in 1819.[5] Almost from the moment they signed contracts at Leghorn to work in Charlottesville for three years they were a source of "vast embarrassment" to both Jefferson and university authorities. Four days after their arrival, they announced they could not fashion either Corinthian or Ionic capitals out of the stone at their disposal. There followed a series of unexpected bills created by their trip across the Atlantic. The brothers seem to have changed boardinghouses with alarming frequency and, within a few weeks, requested that $150 be sent to each of their wives. Just as suddenly they decided it would be best if they returned to Italy and worked there on columns destined for the university. These proposals and requests were followed by still more, and by September 1820 Jefferson had had enough of the Raggis. On September 5 he told General John Hartwell Cocke, of Bremo, a man also intimately involved in development of the university, "the sooner the Raggis can go, the better for us, and most agreeable to them." Seventy-two hours later Michele did just that. He fled to Washington but dispatched frequent complaints that "this stone of yours . . . ruined my stomach along with the sheep . . . sent me to eat, for the mere sight of the said food turned my stomach." By the end of the year, Michele, beleaguered innards and all, was in Gibraltar, still demanding money for work which, according to Jefferson, he did not do. Now that Michele was safely out of the county, however, Jefferson could speak of him as "a good man and a good workman, but very hypocondriac."

Giacomo apparently returned home early in 1822 but was back again later in the same year with more counterproposals and, like his brother, armed with demands for more money. Eventually it became obvious that this stonecutter could not execute the work desired for the Rotunda in either the Old World or the New; yet this did not stop him from coming once more to Charlottesville in 1825 for a last, unsuccessful attempt to be reimbursed for services not rendered. Jefferson was so chagrined by this entire fiasco that in the midst of it in 1821, he felt compelled to issue a carefully phrased explanation to the State Literary Fund, the body providing some of the funds being used to construct the university. After describing difficulties encountered with local stone, he told how at much less cost arrangements had been made to have the capitals executed in Italy. Referring spe-

[5] See William B. O'Neal, "Michele and Giacomo Raggi at the University of Virginia: with Notes and Documents," *MACH* 18 (1960):5–31.

cifically to Giacomo, he noted, "We arrested the work here therefore, and compromised with our Artist at the expence of his past wages, his board and passage hither, amounting to $1390.56. These are the only instances of false expence which have occurred within our kno[w]le[d]ge." [6] "Arresting" the work of the brothers Raggi does not appear to have been a formidable task. Fortunately for both Jefferson and the university few, if any, other workmen proved to be as troublesome, unproductive, and, at the same time, demanding.

To get underway and function properly any institution of higher learning needs money, buildings, teachers, and students; and from the outset the University of Virginia seems to have been blest with a goodly share of these basic ingredients.[7] Unlike most American universities, Jefferson's brainchild was not the outgrowth of some little academy possessing both alumni and experience. Instead, by March 1825 it was a ready-made, full-blown institution complete with nearly all of the trappings of any seat of learning yet self-consciously trying to maintain a delicate (and difficult) balance between considerable innovation and instant tradition.

Thomas Jefferson and his Albemarle friends had raised $40,000 for Central College, and the Old Dominion was rather generous in its support, underwriting some construction costs, promising an annual appropriation of $15,000, and also paying tuition and board for thirty-one "state" students, one from each senatorial district. Erection of buildings, despite innumerable delays and incompetent workmen such as the Raggi brothers, proceeded apace. By 1825 approximately $350,000 had been expended, and the beautiful original complex was nearly complete. Some decorative features such as columns for the Rotunda were lacking, but students and faculty could be housed in reasonable comfort and classes held.

At first Jefferson tried to lure well-known professors from Harvard and other established universities. Rebuffed in this effort and unwilling either to settle for second-rate men or employ theologians (standard practice in those decades), he dispatched Francis Walker Gilmer to England in search of properly trained individuals. Gilmer,

[6] Ibid., p. 27.

[7] Standard source on the university's early years is P. A. Bruce's centennial history, *History of the University of Virginia, 1819–1919* (5 vols.; New York, 1920–22). For a brief, lively, perceptive account, see T. P. Abernethy's *Historical Sketch of the University of Virginia* (Richmond, 1948). Another publication by a one-time university librarian also reveals many details of that institution's formative years—John S. Patton, *Jefferson, Cabell, and the University of Virginia* (New York, 1906).

a distinguished Richmond lawyer and youngest son of George Gilmer of Pen Park, spent five months abroad in 1824 interviewing and talking with a number of prospective professors, most of them of British birth. As a result, five of the original faculty members came from the Old World.

They were George Long (ancient languages), George Blaetterman (modern languages), Charles Bonnycastle (natural philosophy), Thomas Hewitt Key (mathematics), and Robley Dunglison (anatomy and medicine). These men, all hired in Great Britain, were the only professors present when classes got underway. Soon they were joined by John Patton Emmet (natural history and chemistry), who was born in Dublin but educated in America, and George Tucker (moral philosophy), a former congressman with Virginia ties born in Bermuda who was elected as first chairman of the faculty. Francis Walker Gilmer was named professor of law but never lectured because of ill health. Following his death in 1826, John Tayloe Lomax, a well-known Richmond lawyer, succeeded to that post, although Jefferson and others tried unsuccessfully to secure the services of William Wirt, Gilmer's famous brother-in-law.

Each of these professors received $1,000 per year, a pavilion in which to live, the right to use as firewood limbs which dropped from trees on university grounds (but not to saw or cut them off), and tuition fees paid by students attending his lectures. Two of these imported scholars returned home within a few years; yet Gilmer seems to have performed his difficult recruiting task in admirable fashion, and Jefferson reportedly was extremely pleased with the results, although one of these men (Blaetterman) proved a source of constant embarrassment because of his irascible temper. Not everyone approved of these "foreigners." Newspapers of New England and Pennyslvania considered their employment "the greatest insult the American people have ever received. . . . Mr. Jefferson might as well have sent to England for brick to build his taverns and dormitories." "Gilmer," they snorted, "could have fully discharged his mission, with half the trouble and expense, by a short trip to New England . . . or by a still shorter one to Pennsylvania." [8]

Classes began on March 7, 1825, with sixty-eight students, opening day having been delayed about a month pending arrival of three of the European professors. Local young gentlemen enrolled included Thomas Barclay, Robert Hill Carter, John A. G. Davis, John Bol-

[8] Quoted from the *Central Gazette* (Dec. 25, 1825) in William Robert Woods, "Gessner Harrison: The Early Life and Teaching of an Albemarle Classicist," *MACH* 19 (1961):22.

ling Garrett, William Farley Gray, Miles L. Greetham, William H. Meriwether, James R. Miller, Thomas Miller, Thomas H. Nelson, Calvin L. Perry, Charles Peyton, Benjamin F. Randolph, James Randolph, William A. W. Spottswood, Charles Thomas, Robert W. Thomas, and William Wertenbaker.

Despite Jefferson's meticulous attention to detail, some problems remained. For one, there were few, if any, textbooks. The enthusiasm of Gessner Harrison, a pioneer student from Harrisonburg who would, within a few years, be a faculty member himself, soon began to wane. A sober youth destined to become a distinguished classical scholar, Harrison wrote to his father, "I would be well contented were it not that we have paid money for which we are not at present receiving any adequate return." His brother, Edward, voiced similar reactions, but much more bluntly: "So far I am very disappointed in my expectations as to the advantages we would have here, and I confess if the money had not been paid in advance I should have been home by this time." [9]

Lack of texts was a minor inconvenience which, in due course, was easily alleviated. Of much greater importance was the organization of the university itself which seems to have possessed serious flaws that only decades of both turmoil and hard experience could eradicate. The institution was controlled by a board of visitors appointed by the governor. They chose one member as chairman or rector, a post held first by Jefferson and then by Madison. This group appointed the faculty, who, in turn, selected one of the professors as chairman. Upon his shoulders fell the task of running the university from day to day. This man, of course, wore two hats. He was both teacher and administrator and, more important, in times of crisis, arbitrator in disputes between student and teacher and dispenser of justice. His was a difficult role even when university life was tranquil, and during the first two decades, 1825–45, it was anything but that. In addition, to insure discipline Jefferson proposed a board of student "censors" appointed by the faculty, an innovation which floundered hopelessly within a very few months. Also, he devised a handful of basic rules for daily conduct. No student could keep a servant, horse, dog, or weapon; however, in 1825 dueling was the only cause for expulsion. Although simple, direct, and eminently practical, this scheme of administration did not work very well. When immediate issues arose, the chain of command from governor to rector to chairman was ponderous and slow; and once it became

[9] Ibid., pp. 25–26.

13. Edward Coles   14. Francis Walker Gilmer

15. William Holmes McGuffey   16. James Alexander

apparent that these first students could not or would not govern themselves, issues were immediate indeed!

Bernhard Karl, duke of Saxe-Weimar-Eisenach, arrived in Charlottesville on the evening of November 25, 1825, found "lodgings in a rather mediocre inn," and the following morning walked out to view Mr. Jefferson's university. He was not entirely pleased with what he saw.

The institution was opened last March only and already it numbers more than 130 students. Reportedly, however, a certain spirit of insubordination has already made itself felt, and several students who were the ring leaders have been dismissed. The buildings are all of rather recent construction and yet already several appear dilapidated; others appear fated for similar deterioration since the principal material used for their building was lumber.[10] The interior of the library [Rotunda] is as yet incomplete; however, judging from present appearances, it promises to be very beautiful. The dome is designed after the Pantheon in Rome, reduced to half size. This space is intended for public academic occasions; we were told, however, that loud talking in the building would give such an echo that a speaker's voice would be unintelligible. Underneath the Rotunda there are three elliptic halls the use of which has not yet been decided upon. The colonnades in front of this building, so we are told, are going to be very beautiful; the capitals for the columns were made in Italy and supposedly have already arrived here. By the way, the ten pavilions which stand to the right and left of the library are by no means of equal design, but rather each is in a different style; thus there is no unity of the whole, and it is neither a pretty nor a grand sight. Similarly, the garden walls of the corner buildings are set in serpentine lines. The affect is odd but not good. The whole, by the way, has been constructed according to a plan by Mr. Jefferson, whose favorite avocation it is. He is the rector of this university, to which the state of Virginia is reported to have contributed considerable sums. We stopped a gentleman whom we happened to meet and asked him for some information, which he most courteously gave. He was a Mr. Donaldson [Robley I. Dunglison], Professor of Medicine, a native Englishman who, with three other European professors, had come from England last spring. He showed us the library, still very meager and provisionally put up in a lecture room. It contains several works of German literature, among them a set of Kotzebue's *Almanac of Dramatic Plays*. We were told that a large quantity of books is on the way from Europe. The University is situated on a hill in a very healthy location, with a beautiful view from this height of the Blue Ridge Mountains.[11]

[10] The writer obviously refers here to the interior of the pavilions or to some of the smaller outbuildings since brick was used extensively elsewhere.

[11] Francis H. Heller, "Monticello and the University of Virginia, 1825: A German Prince's Travel Notes," *MACH* 7 (1947):31–32.

That evening the prince and a traveling companion were to be dinner guests at Monticello; but, unable to hire a carriage, they again had to walk, making their way along several paths and over a "crudely hewn tree trunk without balustrade" which served as a footbridge over Moore's Creek. They found the meal already in progress but appear to have thoroughly enjoyed the well-known hospitality of a host who insisted they spend the night. Reflecting upon their quarters and a trip back to town in the dark, they readily agreed. The next day they took the stage to Richmond and continued their leisurely ramble throughout the United States.

Many will disagree—and rightfully so—with the duke's impressions of the University of Virginia during its first months. Jefferson's striking architectural design is now recognized as one of the most beautiful and effective groups of buildings found anywhere in America. Moreover, some of his educational concepts and goals such as freedom to choose courses of study, emphasis upon practical pursuits, and training of youth for public leadership have exerted widespread influence. And within five years the library had some eight thousand volumes, the equal of any institution of higher learning in the nation except Harvard. The University of Virginia was indeed the crowning achievement in the creative career of a great statesman and humanist.

The fledgling university which this European nobleman viewed with a too critical eye was divided into eight schools, each headed by a professor: ancient languages, modern languages, mathematics, natural philosophy, natural history, anatomy and medicine, moral philosophy, and law. Under Jefferson's original plan no degrees were to be given. Also, at least at its inception, he did not consider the school of anatomy and medicine to be a professional school as such. A student came, studied whatever he wanted to for as long as he wished, provided he had sufficient preparation for the discipline involved; however, to be fully enrolled he had to attend at least three classes. Upon successful completion of the basic courses in any school, he was granted a certificate. This scheme, although altered somewhat from time to time, continued throughout the nineteenth century, and most "graduates" of those years received only certificates.

For some twelve months after that opening day Thomas Jefferson was able to stroll the "Grounds" of his university, chat with students and faculty, and reflect upon the success of his last great venture. However, these were not especially happy months. The first major crisis occurred in October 1825 when the student censor plan collapsed and, as the duke related, a disorderly riot ensued. Two professors submitted their resignations, the visitors hurriedly convened, and Jefferson, aged and ill, broke down when trying to speak. Touched deeply by this unusual display of emotion, the students curtailed their protest, the professors agreed to remain, and Jefferson, as rector, gave the faculty the right to administer discipline.

The result was an extremely rigid life—up at dawn, to bed by 9 P.M., classes six days a week, gambling, liquor, and tobacco forbidden, no parties without special permission, and spending money deposited with the proctor and doled out as he saw fit. But, most irksome of all was the requirement that students wear dull gray uniforms of Oxford broadcloth purchased "at a price not exceeding six dollars per yard." Pantaloons and waistcoat could be white or brown linen during summer months. Boots were prohibited. With this gay costume students were compelled to wear a plain black neck cloth in winter, white in summer, and a small hat, "round and black." The faculty's answer to the troubles of October 1825 also included proposals for a "Court of the University" similar to and concurrent with the Albemarle County court. They suggested that offenders might be lodged in the local jail until suitable quarters were available, but Virginia's legislators, apparently convinced one court per county was enough, never gave approval, and this idea died stillborn.

Rigid discipline worked no better than virtually none at all. Riots and turmoil continued from time to time, convincing a few of the visitors that what the university really needed was a full-time president. Like the suggestion to put erring students behind bars, resolutions to this effect received little support. In May 1830 Gessner Harrison, now a faculty member, exchanged blows with a student whose conduct he had criticized as "profane" and "vulgar." Nine years later, as chairman of the faculty and responsible for discipline, he was horsewhipped by two youths who obviously resented his firm control. Although a crowd of one hundred watched, only two or three young men tried to aid Harrison. When released, he reprimanded the pair again, and they, in turn, snapped their whips anew. The most tragic result of this rampant insubordination was the murder of Professor J. A. G. Davis on November 12, 1840, by a masked student.

Despite subsequent investigations, it is far from clear why this tragedy occurred. Two nights earlier the university had celebrated news of the election of William Henry Harrison amid wild uproar, and the evening of the twelfth marked the fourth anniversary of a serious student rebellion. However, neither politics nor a sense of history seems to have inspired a sixteen-year-old youth from Georgia and a seventeen-year-old South Carolinian to launch a two-man riot which ended in death. The strangely dressed pair evidently fired shots at or near the doorways of several pavilions as they roamed about the lawn shortly after the supper hour. No one joined them, although several students watched in an unconcerned fashion. Davis, who left his study to investigate, ran head-on into Joseph E. Semmes, the boy from Georgia. Semmes, who apparently bore no animosity toward Davis, fired point blank, wounding the professor in the stomach. Although Davis rallied and appeared to be recovering, two days later he died. His bereaved family insisted Semmes should not be prosecuted; however, he was arraigned, but later forfeited bail rather than face trial. Rumors persist that this ill-fated youth eventually committed suicide. His companion, William Kinkaid, was in and out of the university during these years. Early in 1843 two of his professors reported he was "doing but little good" in moral philosophy and law, and the faculty admonished him to repair his ways at once.

In 1840, the year that Davis was murdered, one of the original professors, George Blaetterman, was dismissed for publicly whipping his wife. Blaetterman, who had a violent temper and often argued heatedly with students during lectures, was a trial for both his pupils and the visitors. Many youths, dismayed by his outbursts, fled to a school near the university for private instruction in French, and the visitors often discussed but never instituted a tutorship to rescue all students from his wrath. Nevertheless, it is apparent that scores heaved sighs of relief when they learned that Frau Blaetterman had been humiliated publicly, not privately, and hence clear grounds for dismissal existed.

One would like to believe these shocking developments—murder of one professor and public whipping both by and to other faculty members—were the climax of these disorders; but, in fact, this state of affairs continued for several more years. Two somewhat unrelated events appear to have provided a solution to these perplexing problems of discipline: creation of an honor code for examinations and abandonment of uniforms. On June 1, 1841, as chairman of the faculty, Henry St. George Tucker, who succeeded Davis as professor of law, proposed this resolution which was adopted: "The Faculty will refuse to confer a degree, or to allow distinction in every case in which they shall be satisfied, that the student has, at any examination or distinction, attempted to commit a fraud upon the Committee in any way or to any extent whatever." [12] This rule, undoubtedly

[12] Faculty Minutes, 5:295, University of Virginia Library.

prompted by fraud which had occurred, applied to any student who either gave or got assistance. Within a year, in response to this action by the professors, students developed an honor code of their own. During these same months faculty members, who were spending long hours trying valiantly to punish students who refused to wear their uniforms (especially when they went out on the town for some clandestine revel), finally gave up the fight. This decision to abandon gray broadcloth was merely a temporary measure on a year-to-year basis, but in 1845 it became permanent. Demise of the hated uniform removed an obvious source of student irritation, and the honor code soon made its influence felt in many realms of university life, much in the manner that Jefferson had hoped his censors would function.

Most historians, with a casual "boys-will-be-boys" shrug, have placed blame for these two decades of unrest upon hotheaded young blades, restless southern youths full of fire and imbued with a reckless spirit born of plantation surroundings. Not so. The causes are much more complex. As noted, the chairman of the faculty who dispensed justice also was a teacher. If Gessner Harrison may be taken as an example, tact was not always with these individuals. Squaring off with a student blow for blow or censuring those who have just whipped you before an approving mob is not calculated to foster good student-faculty relations. And the European instructors appear to have advocated even more rigid rule than men of American birth such as Harrison. The student body, drawn almost entirely from the Southeast, represented very diverse backgrounds. Many came from homes where liquor flowed freely and tobacco grew in profusion, yet both were verboten at the university. During these first sessions some students in their early teens and others in their twenties arrived in various stages of preparation for study to be confronted by a faculty which took its work very seriously, for this was the age when American institutions of higher learning were shedding swaddling clothes and becoming something more than merely glorified high schools. These years, the 1830s and 1840s, also were a period of widespread social unrest which had profound effect upon many campuses throughout the nation. In truth, numerous schools not frequented by southern hotheads were experiencing similar difficulties and for much the same reasons—rampant social change mixed with cries for reform, more demanding curriculums, rigid, uncompromising discipline, and, at times, tactless professors and irresponsible students.

Yet these first decades of university life were not dominated completely by either tumultuous riots or stern, repressive rule. Most of

the early students were Virginians, two-thirds of them nineteen years
of age or less. The little library available to them grew slowly; and,
to borrow a volume, one needed specific permission from a professor.
As a result, many purchased books of their own, perhaps at the
University Book Store, opened in March 1825 and Albemarle's oldest
business establishment still in existence in the 1970s. Originally this
was a branch of a Boston firm (Cummings and Hilliard), but William Wertenbaker, a pioneer student, took over the store in 1831 and
also became postmaster for the university community, a position he
held for over thirty years. The students' most frequent choice in reading matter was the works of Lord Byron, who was, according to
Thomas Perkins Abernethy, "by far" the most popular author among
students of that day. Jefferson had set aside a room in the Rotunda
for religious services, and in 1832, at student suggestion, a chaplain
was engaged. Within two years he became a permanent fixture, re-
futing, to some extent, charges of atheism hurled so frequently at
the university. Through some oversight the faculty failed to outlaw
cockfighting, marbles, and fisticuffs (or "knuckles," as such pre-
arranged encounters were then called), and students enjoyed these
as well as other diversions of their own invention. "There were, for
instance, the 'dyke' and the 'calathump.' When a student 'dyked'
himself to go calling on a young lady, if he was discovered in the act
by his fellow-students, they would converge upon him with horns and
whistles, and other noise-making machinery. They would conduct
him pell-mell to the Rotunda where they would call upon him for a
speech, but he was never permitted to speak. Then they dogged his
steps to the door of the home where he was calling, compelled him to
run the gauntlet, and finally shoved or kicked him into the entrance.
Any similar noise-making procession, minus the 'swain,' was a
'calathump.' " [13]

Presumably it was a "calathump" that Professor Davis was attempting to suppress when he was fatally wounded outside of Pavilion X in 1840. Other social outlets included the Jefferson Society
(1825), Temperance Society (1830), and Washington Society
(1835). In 1852 Delta Kappa Epsilon, the first Greek letter fraternity, made its appearance, although for many years the literary
societies (the temperance group being considered one of them) were
much more important. Six years later the University Young Men's
Christian Association was formed, the first in the nation, and on the
eve of the Civil War a cricket club enjoyed a brief moment of

[13] Abernethy, p. 16.

popularity. By 1860 the YMCA had 162 members. Each Sabbath day 50 of them taught Sunday schools held at the university, in Charlottesville, and throughout the county. One youth went to the Ragged Mountains and another to the poorhouse to lead religious services. On Sunday evenings there was a class for black youngsters and one during the day for Negro adults. As a result of this religious awakening, many students became church members, twenty-seven entering the Episcopal fold on one occasion. Four professors conducted Bible classes at the university, and efforts of the young law professor, John B. Minor, and William Holmes McGuffey, remembered today chiefly for his *Readers* used by millions of American young people, elicited special praise from numerous newspapers and journals. McGuffey, who joined the faculty in 1845, was the first clergyman on the university staff. Although this professor came to Virginia from Ohio where he had been closely associated with Lyman Beecher and others prominent in the abolition crusade, within five years, like other faculty members, McGuffey was master of a few blacks. The 1850 census reveals that virtually all of the professors had slaves in their households or owned laborers employed elsewhere, from John Staige Davis with two to Addison Maupin who had a dozen.

Bible study, Sunday schools, and religious zeal on the part of many students did much to erase unpleasant local memories of riots, gunplay, horsewhipping, and murder. Gone were the days, said the *Review* in 1860, of town-gown brawls and the times when surly, armed youths thronged Courthouse Square and signs "hung uneasily over our merchants' doors." Students now were treated as gentlemen and responded by affording "an example of good behavior that we believe is unsurpassed." These editors noted that the university's high scholastic standards were generally recognized, "we suppose even in the North." They added with satisfaction that the University of Virginia had no superior in the entire nation, being "the pride and ornament of Southern educational institutions . . . the crown and glory of the Slave States." [14]

Though academic excellence is most difficult to weigh and evaluate, much of this praise was based upon sound statistics: soaring enrollment and substantial economic benefit to the community. In 1850 the university had 350 students and 11 professors, who, according to census estimates, were spending $22,000 annually in the community. During the 1856–57 session the student population, augmented in part by an exodus of southern youths from northern schools, swelled

[14] N. B. Jones, "Charlottesville and Albemarle," p. 140.

17. University of Virginia, 1856

to 645, a peak not surpassed in the remainder of the nineteenth century. This made the University of Virginia the nation's third largest institution of higher learning, exceeded in size only by Harvard and Schenectady's Union College. If spending kept pace, and it undoubtedly did since it was probably the most expensive American university of that era, this means that perhaps $50,000 was pouring into local pockets each year. And, as in the beginning, some of these funds came from construction of buildings. To meet demands of a much larger student body several halls and dormitories were added to Mr. Jefferson's "academical village." The most notable of these were an enormous extension grafted onto the Rotunda, a rather ungainly edifice consumed by flames in 1895, and Dawson's Row, six dormitories stretching along the south end of the grounds from a parsonage housing the university chaplain to Monroe Hill. It was here that for decades "state" students resided. Some of the money to pay for these improvements, which included illuminating a few buildings with gas, came from tuition fees, which after 1850 went to the university, not the professors. Since larger enrollments obviously increased their income, they objected strenuously but in vain to this change. At the same time their salaries were raised to $3,000. Nevertheless, Harrison, for one, resigned in 1859 to establish an academy in order to support his growing brood of seven sons and three daughters.

During these thirty-five years of growth, minor changes occurred in the conferring of degrees and in the organization of various schools. In 1828 the School of Medicine began awarding degrees, and three years later the faculty established a master's degree, a very stiff program permitting no electives and requiring superior performance in six schools (all except law and medicine). In 1840 the law school was authorized to grant degrees, and eight years later a liberal arts diploma was instituted. The latter, however, was widely viewed as a mere consolation prize for those who aimed for a master's degree and missed. As a result, the great mass of students continued to prefer the original elective program outlined by Jefferson and departed from Charlottesville content with their highly prized certificates. As Abernethy notes, by 1856 the university had conferred only ninety-eight masters' degrees, and by 1860 only forty students had received liberal arts diplomas. In 1851 the law school became a department consisting of two schools—one encompassing common and statute law and the other, constitutional and international law, equity, evidence, and the law merchant. Five years later ancient languages was divided into two distinct schools of Latin and Greek, and to give more prominence to the study of past civilizations, a new school of history and literature was created.

Although Jefferson and those following in his wake made mistakes, it is apparent his university, despite riots, ridiculous rules, and questionable behavior by both students and faculty, was doing much for both Albemarle and the South. Its graduates went forth to become teachers, lawyers, and doctors and quite literally raised standards of living and learning in scores of states. The University of Virginia, as Jefferson had hoped it would do, was training ever-increasing numbers for leadership throughout the South. Alumni were serving conspicuously as state judges, legislators, and governors, and as U.S. senators and representatives. Moreover, Mr. Jefferson's elective system, scorned and ridiculed by many, fitted the needs of an essentially rural society extremely well. It dovetailed perfectly with the desires and the requirements of the type of young men who came to Charlottesville—some ill prepared for university study, others seeking only a smattering of refinement to enable them to run a plantation or a business, and still others who had to have in-depth study in preparation for professional careers. "No early American save Mr. Jefferson would have dared," according to Abernethy, "to house a University in Roman temples, employ a majority of foreign professors, and exclude the clergy and all its theologians. His ideal of education, fitted to the needs of the individual student, with a maximum of self-determination, was equally radical in his day." [15]

Just as rumors of a university had inspired a spate of preparatory schools, a functioning institution of higher learning fostered growth and development of numerous academies, frequently staffed by University of Virginia graduates. Census statistics of 1840 indicate that the county had one university with 247 students, eighteen academies or grammar schools with 400 pupils, and twenty-one primary or common schools with a total enrollment of 386—96 of these students being educated at public expense. Schools seem to have been scattered throughout the region in a very uneven manner. Fredericksville Parish (which usually contains census data for Charlottesville) had thirteen academy–grammar schools with 297 students and three primary–common schools with 47 pupils, all of them public charges. St. Anne's had five academies or grammar schools with 103 students and eighteen primary–common schools with 339 enrolled (49 at public expense). This preponderance of elementary classrooms in

<hr>

[15] Abernethy, p. 45.

the latter parish appears to be reflected in the number of whites over twenty-six years of age who could not read and write—204 in St. Anne's, 534 in Fredericksville. Also there is evidence here of two distinctly different attitudes toward education of the poor. In Fredericksville all common school students were paupers; in St. Anne's, approximately one out of seven was being educated by means of the public purse.

Ten years later, in 1850, census takers found only seven academies in Albemarle County (three for boys and four for girls), with 13 teachers and 115 students. This decline in preparatory education may be an illusion, however, since there were forty "public schools" with 40 teachers and 550 pupils. Federal authorities reported that 1,110 whites attended various Albemarle County schools (including the university) at mid-century. No free blacks were enrolled, although a few were attending classes in some Virginia counties. Seven hundred and twenty-five free residents could not read and write. Only three of them were manumitted Negroes, indicating somewhat more zeal on the part of blacks than whites for the basic rudiments of learning. State officials painted a much more optimistic picture of Albemarle education in 1850. They reported there were eighty-eight in existence (apparently counting scores of little country classrooms disregarded by census takers) and claimed that 702 of the community's 1,366 poor children were enrolled during the year. Virginia's school commissioners also heaped lavish praise upon these schools, noting that indigent parents were expressing increasing interest in education and emphasizing that the progress of local students was not only satisfying but "in some cases, indeed, highly gratifying." [16]

The widely used term *academy* designated a type of secondary school which had evolved from the earlier classical school. The *Review* editors used it interchangeably with *high school* when they described four Albemarle schools conducted by university alumni in 1860. These were Brookland School at Greenwood operated by Rev. William Dinwiddie; Brookhill School, six miles from Charlottesville, where Dr. Charles Minor was assisted by several university graduates; Dr. Gessner Harrison's Locust Valley Academy near Greenwood; and Bloomfield Academy at Ivy, operated by W. LeRoy Broun and W. Willoughby Tubbs. According to this survey, 326 pupils attended these schools during the 1859–60 session, and there were an estimated 50 students enrolled at academies in the town of Charlottesville. In 1857–58, for example, Bloomfield had 63 pupils, 36 of

[16] N. B. Jones, "Charlottesville and Albemarle," p. 143.

them from the Old Dominion and the remainder from eight other southern states. The curriculum included Latin, Greek, German, French, Spanish, arithmetic, algebra, geometry, calculus, civil and mechanical engineering, natural philosophy, astronomy, and chemistry. The charge for board and tuition increased from $200 in 1854 to $280 in 1860.[17]

More publicized than these academies preparing young men for college or university were the female academies or institutes. The Piedmont Institute opened in 1853 under the direction of two English sisters, Ann and Jane Leaton. The former, in 1858, was principal. She, her sister, and Betty Lewis taught English, a Miss Rees taught beginning French, and A. von Fischerz was instructor in senior French, German, painting and drawing. G. Lanza, an assistant instructor at the university, taught Latin, Spanish, and Italian; and Charles T. Frey was in charge of music. In 1857–58 sixty students were enrolled. The "prospectus" for that session, printed in Philadelphia, indicates that board for ten months was $140.[18] Most classes cost an additional $20 to $30, but piano lessons were $44 and private vocal lessons, $66. There was a small additional charge for pew rent at church. Pupils were expected to attend evening prayers regularly, and each was cautioned to come equipped with a half dozen table napkins, marked and numbered, to have every article of clothing distinctly labeled, and also to bring overshoes. All communication and packages were sent to the principal, not directly to students themselves. Young ladies could shop once a week, accompanied by a teacher, and their access to the opposite sex was extremely limited, at least in theory: "It being of first importance that young ladies of the School have their attention undivided, it is an object of especial care with the Principal, that those who live with her form as few acquaintances as possible. The Pupils therefore, receive company only on Friday evening, and are not allowed to receive attention from gentlemen, such as walking with them, &c. &c." This school was located at the corner of Seventh and East Market streets, a structure which in recent decades became the Children's Home. In 1865 Principal Leaton married Rev. R. K. Meade, who for thirty-three years was rector of Christ Episcopal Church. She died in 1890, and the institute closed fifteen years later.

Albemarle Female Institute, originally owned by Baptists, in 1860

---

[17] Ibid., p. 145.
[18] See Jennie Thornley Grayson, "Piedmont Institute Catalogue, 1857–1858," *MACH* 2 (1942):9–18.

was under the direction of John Hart, a University of Virginia graduate. As was true at his alma mater, students could get a diploma of sorts upon completion of basic courses, but to become a "graduate," one had to satisfy requirements in all seven schools. There also were preparatory and juvenile departments. Tuition was slightly higher than at Piedmont Institute ($160), and students had to provide not only napkins but towels as well. During 1860 this school moved to new quarters described as being "400 yards from the depot."

There were at least two similar female academies in the county. One, the famous Edgehill School, had been established by Mrs. Jane Nicholas Randolph, wife of Colonel Thomas J. Randolph. Piedmont Female Academy at Stony Point was operated by James W. Goss, a relatively wealthy man who in 1860 had assets in excess of $100,000 and was master of twenty-five slaves. Goss, with the aid of two assistants, offered traditional instruction, plus classes in harp, melodeon, guitar, painting, and embroidery. He advertised that there would be a conveyance waiting at the Cobham depot on the Virginia Central line each day during the first week of September to meet incoming students.

Smaller, less expensive schools for both boys and girls existed in a number of private homes throughout Albemarle. In 1860 James H. Lewis, who lived near Cobham, announced plans to open a school for girls, and in that same year John R. Woods and M. L. Anderson of Ivy inserted a notice in the *Review* stating that they had employed an instructor to prepare their sons for the university and would share his services for $210 per year per pupil. Some of these classrooms, many offering only primary subjects, undoubtedly make up in part the total of eighty-eight schools cited by state authorities. Although they played an important role in these decades, more notable was the growing tendency toward centralized secondary education. With a staff of several teachers, perhaps three to ten and sometimes including part-time help by university personnel, these academies offered instruction which had been available only at the college level three or four decades earlier.

It is apparent that, for the most part, these academies, institutes, and especially the University of Virginia, served the needs of only the well-to-do. Most residents of Albemarle continued to garner a bit of reading, writing, and "figures" from their parents just as their forefathers had done for generations; or, if lucky, when not needed on the farm, they might receive a few weeks of classroom instruction at an old-field school. It is impossible to say whether these various institutions had any effect upon illiteracy within the county. What census records there are indicate they did not. Since many students enrolled at these grammar schools, academies, institutes, and the university came from homes located outside of Albemarle County, it is quite possible that the percentage of local young people attending classes in this "Athens of Virginia" in 1860 was no greater than it had been in 1820. Education had become a minor local industry, true, but excessive costs prevented hundreds of area young people from enjoying its benefits. Despite the good intentions of Thomas Jefferson, public education, both for Albemarle and most of the nation, remained an elusive goal.

Chapter 9

The World of Judith Rives

HOSTESS to presidents and former presidents, crowned heads of Europe, the Rothschilds, Henry Clay, Daniel Webster, and numerous other figures prominent upon the national and international scene, Judith Rives, granddaughter of Thomas Walker, led a life far different from that of her pioneer ancestor who went about the western wilderness carving "T. W." on trees while looking for lands to exploit. Even the handsome structure which she and her husband, William Cabell Rives, added to Castle Hill about 1824 is symbolic of this young lady's interests . . . and perhaps those of Albemarle as well. No longer does that comfortable, clapboarded pre-Revolutionary home face the challenge of the brooding mountains; instead, proudly flaunting Flemish bond brick and stout white columns, it gazes majestically toward the south. It is very easy to imagine the Rives family happily making their way up the handsome boxwood drive as they returned from a session of the U.S. Congress or an extended sojurn in Europe, but most difficult to picture the good Doctor Walker astride a trusty horse coming home from attending a sick patient, conferring with a business associate, or exploring the wondrous world beyond the Blue Ridge. What met the eye after the 1820s was a typical mansion of the upper South whose cultured occupants had no frontier zeal whatsoever. Their interests lay in the metropolitan centers of two continents, although, naturally enough, they looked forward with great pleasure to the days they could spend at this rural retreat, their home.

Here Judith Walker was born in March 1802. When she was only five, her parents and a brother died suddenly, and she and a sister, Jane, were bundled off to their maternal grandmother in Yorktown, Mrs. Hugh Nelson. This lady quickly moved to Richmond to give her young charges the opportunities that city presented for education and refinement. Shortly after the War of 1812, Jane married Dr. Mann Page and set up housekeeping at Castle Hill. During these years Judith was a frequent guest and also was feted at neighboring estates such as Farmington. She remarked in autobiographical reminiscences composed for her grandchildren in 1861: "It was laughingly said by malicious people, that whenever Mr. Jefferson had any distinguished visitors of the bonvivant character, he always had them invited to Farmington, as furnishing a higher specimen of Virginia good cheer than they found at Monticello." [1] It was at Farmington, home of George Divers who was married to one of Thomas Walker's eight daughters and thus uncle to Judith, that she met a young lawyer, a twenty-seven-year-old member of the House of Delegates. Judith Walker describes William C. Rives as "a small man . . . with fair complexion, chestnut hair, blue eyes, and handsome features." Rives was ready to marry at once, but his bride-to-be kept him waiting until her seventeenth birthday in 1819. Shortly before their wedding the Walker estate was divided by lot between the two girls—Judith getting Castle Hill and a considerable tract of land; Jane, the remaining portion. Each got about 3,800 acres; Jane, slightly more.

During these decades the Rives, Page, and Nelson families represented perhaps the greatest concentration of wealth in the county, a preeminence which soon would be challenged by numerous Coles heirs who were building a handful of gracious homes in the Green Mountain area—Enniscorthy, Old Woodville, Tallwood, and Estouteville. Not until 1850 do census returns give some indication of real estate owned by local citizens. In that year 31 individuals held land worth $25,000 or more. Almost without exception these were farmers, masters of a substantial number of slaves. Tucker Coles, age sixty-eight, led the list with 121 blacks and property valued at $92,000. Fifty-eight citizens had land worth from $15,000 to $25,000, 201 were in the $5,000-to-$15,000 class, and 629 owned land appraised at less than $5,000. As has been noted, ownership of slaves per se is no indication of great wealth. Twenty citizens owning 50 or more blacks held lands worth less than $25,000, among them Daniel Scott, George Rives, Andrew Stevenson, and Tucker Coles, Jr.

A decade later federal census takers added estimates of personal property to those of landed wealth. In that year 107 Albemarle citizens owned personal property (largely slaves) and lands valued in excess of $50,000. This wealth appears to have been spread about equally throughout the county, with sixty-seven of these individuals residing in Fredericksville Parish and fifty in St. Anne's. Though most members of this well-to-do class were farmers, their ranks also

---

[1] See John H. Moore, "Judith Rives of Castle Hill," *Virginia Cavalcade* 13 (1964):30–40. Additional excerpts from her autobiography and letters are cited throughout this chapter.

included several merchants and attorneys, a bank president, a judge, a physician, two university professors, and numerous females controlling substantial estates. The wealthiest was William P. Farish, age sixty-three (no occupation cited), with resources valued at $309,760, including 131 slaves. The various branches of the Coles family owned real and personal property worth more than $800,000; the Rives clan was second with land, slaves, and property valued at approximately $641,000. William Cabell Rives, who owned 77 slaves and held real estate and personal goods worth $165,000, was by no means the wealthiest member of that family. In summary, in 1860 12,709 free inhabitants owned real estate worth $11,112,279, and personal property valued at $16,124,021, making Albemarle the fourth richest county in the Old Dominion. This overall total of $27.2 million was exceeded slightly by returns from Fauquier and Norfolk; Henrico (including Richmond) led the state with personal wealth of $57 million.

In the early 1820s Albemarle's most famous citizen spent a few days at Castle Hill en route to visit James Madison. According to Judith Rives, "Mr. Jefferson was far advanced in life at this period, but his manners were pleasing, his voice and general conversation very attractive, his eye bright, and his tall figure had lost none of his uprightness. With his back turned, and especially on horseback, no one would have suspected nearly eighty years had passed over such a form." A short time later Judith and William Rives visited Jefferson at Monticello, which they found "much desecrated." Judith felt "the passion for architecture which distinguished its owner" was the root of this evil. In 1823 Castle Hill was host to James Madison, then on his way to Charlottesville to discuss plans for opening of the university. Writing in the summer of 1861, Mrs. Rives mourned the passing of such men, the well-known Virginia dynasty, and looked with horror upon what was transpiring throughout the nation.

People had not then forgotten the days of Washington and Madison; the levelling system, leading inevitably to something far below the *mediocrity* which has been since the distinguishing characteristic of our age, was as little in favor as downright atheism is in the present day, and would have been thought almost as impious. Nobody believed the doctrine that "all men were born free and equal," though it was repeated every Fourth of July, nor that even if born free and equal, they could ever remain so. A *rail-splitter* might have been deemed a useful citizen, but he could never have aspired to the Presidency. A cabinet composed of hucksters and printers' devils would have justly been laughed to scorn. It has been left to modern wisdom to break down all the barriers raised by the great

Creator, and since there is no rail-way method of attaining real excellence in anything, to be content with mediocrity, or something less.

By the time the mistress of Castle Hill wrote these distraught phrases she had had considerable experience in both national and international affairs. Her husband served at times in the House of Representatives and the U.S. Senate and twice was minister to France, informally filling a similar post in London as well. This family's tenure in Paris is unique. There from 1829 to 1832 and again two decades later, 1849 to 1852, they were thus able to witness the coming to power of "Citizen King" Louis Philippe and the strategy which transformed President Louis Napoleon into Emperor Napoleon III. One daughter, Amélie Louise, was born during the first sojourn and had as godmother the queen of France for whom she was named.

Members of the Rives family were not the only citizens of Albemarle consorting with European heads of state; so was Sallie Coles Stevenson. "Charming Sallie," sister of Edward "the abolitionist," was a tall, dark-haired beauty some thirteen years older than Judith Rives. A favorite of "Cousin Dolley" Madison, she was courted by many adoring swains but in 1816 married Andrew Stevenson, a Richmond widower born in Culpeper. Stevenson's political career soon took them to Washington, and in 1827 he became speaker of the House of Representatives. Suave, handsome, a devout Jacksonian, Stevenson in 1836 was named minister to the Court of St. James's, a post which, because of domestic political turmoil, had been vacant for four years.

The Stevensons remained in England until 1841, and their experiences are described in intimate detail in numerous letters that Sallie wrote to Virginia relatives.[2] One incident early in 1838 brought lasting fame to her native Albemarle. Upon returning from a visit to France, Mrs. Stevenson discovered three barrels containing hams and apples had arrived from America. At the suggestion of her husband she sent two dozen of the best yellow-skinned fruit to young Queen Victoria. These apples, later to be known as Albemarle Pippins,[3] created a sensation and for decades were shipped each year to British monarchs, who permitted them to enter the realm duty-free. Many came from an estate near the crest of the Blue Ridge which acquired the title of "Royal Orchard," now the summer retreat of the Scott

[2] See Edward Boykin's *Victoria, Albert, and Mrs. Stevenson* (New York, 1957).
[3] Atcheson L. Hench, "The Name 'Albemarle Pippin,'" *MACH* 14 (1955):21–25.

family of Richmond resplendent with twentieth-century baronial ramparts. Interestingly, the letter which describes how a basket of local fruit was dispatched to Britain's sovereign treats the incident in a rather offhand manner; instead, Sallie Stevenson was much more eager to tell many brothers and sisters of her wonderful tour of Versailles and Paris, noting with pride how she was kissed "most effcy as the French do upon both sides of my face" by Napoleon's youngest sister, Caroline, the former queen of Naples.

However, in these years before the Civil War few Albemarle housewives were being kissed by ex-queens, sending baskets of apples to reigning monarchs, or watching proudly as titled nobility served as godparents to their offspring. Theirs was a rural, work-a-day world of hard seasons, one following fast on the heels of another, occasional outings to Charlottesville or perhaps Richmond, and an unending sequence of weddings, births, and funerals. Even the mistresses of great estates led boring, monotonous lives much of the time. They worked long hours attending to the needs of large families and often had to consult with overseers and minister to slaves, especially when their husbands were off in Richmond or Washington.

Caroline Morrill, a tutor from Bangor, Maine, who came to live with the Maury family at Piedmont in 1860 and spent two years behind the Confederate lines, had considerable praise for the diligence of local women in both peace and war. By candlelight she and her mistress knitted socks for soldiers, Miss Morrill's going to local Yankee prisoners and those of Mrs. Maury (who could turn out one sock in four hours) to the Confederates. This young lady, who later made her way through enemy lines to her home, commented that when she arrived in Albemarle the county could boast of only one cookstove and a single sewing machine. According to Joseph Vance, the Randolph women of an earlier era were contemptuous of local society and in their letters frequently expressed a desire for city life or even a house in the village of Charlottesville free from farm surroundings and their incessant demands.[4] Dances held at local taverns in the 1820s they found crude and preferred instead to hold "a grand *kick-up* of a *family fancy* ball," an evening at home with music and gossip attended only by close friends and relatives. Thomas Mann Randolph's term as governor presented little relief since his daughters soon discovered that their father (and they as well) had to enter-

[4] Vance, "Thomas Jefferson Randolph" (Ph.D. diss., University of Virginia, 1957), pp. 145–77.

tain scores of backwoods politicos and their dull wives and boring offspring.

In contrast to previous decades, much of local social activity centered about a new church or meetinghouse. Before the consecration of Christ Episcopal Church in 1826 the village of Charlottesville had no religious structure, and various denominations—Methodist, Baptist, Presbyterian, and Episcopalian—held services on successive Sundays at the county courthouse. Within a short time Presbyterians of the community erected a church of their own, and other sects soon followed these examples. At first there was some effort to build a single church, but these plans soon evaporated. By mid-century the county had forty-five churches which could accommodate fourteen thousand souls. These included thirteen Methodist houses of worship, twelve Baptist, eight Presbyterian, six "Free" Baptist, five Episcopal, and one Universalist.[5] The average value of these structures was $1,000, although Presbyterians and especially Episcopalians seem to have lavished somewhat more money on their buildings. Ten years later the number of churches had declined to forty-three, but the estimated value of each had more than doubled.

In addition to the religious realm, other social outlets of previous times continued important—court day; visiting neighbors, friends, and relatives; gathering at a local tavern for repasts which might feature gambling, cockfighting, brawling, and horse racing; perhaps a day or so of fishing and hunting now and then—and as town ordinances of the 1860s indicate, youngsters were playing bandy (a type of field hockey) and some forms of football and baseball. R. T. W. Duke, Jr., comments in his reminiscences that in the days immediately before the Civil War he and his playmates enjoyed "chinning" or "chumney" (a precursor of baseball), hide and seek, marbles, tops, and occasionally a rock battle between rival gangs, although these forays were a bit dangerous and frowned upon by their elders.

During the 1820s, thanks to creation of the university and improvements in transportation, some sporting activities became more organized. Each autumn race meets were sponsored by the Birdwood Jockey Club, and residents also could patronize the lotteries frequently advertised in the local press. In 1828 the club staged a three-day affair. On the first day there was a two-mile heat—entrance fee,

[5] Census returns for Albemarle County (1850), National Archives, Washington, D.C.

$10; the purse, $100. Winnings rose to $250 on the second day. The final day featured one-mile heats, the winner of the best three out of five being awarded the balance of the funds, "supposed to be one hundred and twenty dollars." [6] In 1821 Henry Gantt of North Garden won $40,000 in a Maryland lottery, and some years later "a gentleman near Scottsville" received $3,500 for one-half of a ticket purchased in the Grand State Lottery of Virginia. In the 1830s the town of Charlottesville conducted its own lottery in order to raise funds for paving village streets.

There also were library, debating, Bible, and theatrical societies to cater to special interests, although associations of this sort seem to have led rather brief lives, appearing with much fanfare, quietly disappearing, and then reforming with surprising frequency. The Albemarle Literary Society's catalog of April 1823 (really a printed sheet) lists some 250 titles, many of them multivolume works such as John Marshall's *Life of Washington*. Four months later a library room opened, and the following year the society was incorporated by act of the General Assembly. In January 1829 the Charlottesville Debating Society was born. Its purpose, according to President Jefferson Clark, was to add to each member's store of knowledge and prepare him to be a public servant, a role which obviously required some forensic ability. The Albemarle Bible Society, formed the previous year, had as its goal furnishing a Bible to every white county home not possessing one. To determine how many were needed, two agents were named for four "battalion areas" throughout the county and one for Charlottesville. Members promised sincere efforts to secure subscriptions "without note or comment." The Bibles, they emphasized, would be distributed without charge.[7] In 1820 a commercial troupe of actors nipped in the bud local plans to produce *Clementina*. The visitors' performances at the Swan Tavern, which included both traditional Shakespeare and homespun merriment, were so well received that the company remained for three weeks instead of one. Seven years later the Charlottesville Thespian Society produced Goldsmith's *She Stoops to Conquer*, but it is not clear how long this group was in existence.

In addition to court and muster days, there were two other events which both youngsters and older folk looked forward to with keen anticipation—Washington's Birthday and the Fourth of July. In 1822 the birth of our first chief executive was marked by a dinner

---

[6] N. B. Jones, "Charlottesville and Albemarle," p. 131.
[7] Ibid., pp. 136–37.

18. Judith Rives

and ball at the Eagle Tavern. Six years later, in commemoration of February 22, John Keller exhibited a plum cake some eight to ten feet in circumference topped with a candy pyramid. In 1820 the Fourth was celebrated at a dinner held near the university. After a reading of the Declaration of Independence, thirteen toasts were offered in unison. Thomas J. Maury, president of the gathering, led off with these words: "Thomas Jefferson—may his setting sun be as serene and tranquil, as his Meredian has been splendid and glorious." After these symbolic toasts came eighteen voluntary (and perhaps exhuberant) salutations; yet the editors of the *Central Gazette* noted with pride, "harmony and good order prevailed—nothing occurred to mar the pleasure of the day.[8] Two years later an even grander Fourth featured patriotic fireworks, a balloon ascension, barbecue, speeches, and dance. If the pyrotechnics went off as planned, the effect must have been awesome indeed. They included "a pigeon, which will take its flight to a distance of 200 feet and return and illuminate the Tree of Liberty." The whole thing ended in a fiery representation of the Washington Monument.[9]

Even such spectaculars as these—huge plum cakes, thirty-one toasts, and pigeons of fire—were overshadowed by the visits of Lafayette to Albemarle County in November 1824 and August 1825. On the first occasion the general and his entourage were met at the Fluvanna line by the Albemarle Lafayette Guards. Following an address by William Cabell Rives, then a member of Congress, and a reply by the guest of honor, the dignitaries assembled at Mrs. Boyd's tavern for refreshments. Then the procession of carriages and horsemen set out for Monticello. "It seems," commented one observer, "that thousands of Freemen had sprung from the hills, and woods and mountains to hail the arrival and shout the welcome of our country's friend." The emotional reunion of two elderly comrades—Lafayette and Jefferson—brought tears to the eyes of many who watched the scene. The following day Lafayette, Jefferson, and Madison (urgent business forced President Monroe to return to Washington) were honored at a reception at the Central Hotel and a three-hour dinner in the unfinished Rotunda at the university. A few days later the local Lafayette Guards escorted the visitors to Gordonsville as hundreds watched them depart. "Ever and anon were discernable from the neighboring farm-houses the fair daughters of

[8] Ibid., p. 125.
[9] Ibid. It is unclear what Washington monument is referred to here. Baltimore's memorial was erected in 1829, and the cornerstone of the towering obelisk in our nation's capital was laid in 1848.

the mountains, waving their white 'kerchiefs." In August 1825 the general was feted at another lengthy dinner held in the Rotunda. At that time he was given honorary membership in the Jefferson Society and taken on a tour of the university's pavilions. Among those present were William B. Preston, former president Monroe, and William Wirt, son-in-law of George Gilmer and U.S. attorney general under both Monroe and John Quincy Adams.

Young and old of that decade could learn to dance under the tutorship of several instructors. Thomas W. Vaughan held classes at the Central Hotel and also offered private lessons at home to ladies during the day and to gentlemen at night. Under certain conditions Vaughan proposed mixed dancing at this school. "He will instruct young ladies only, for the first two days of each dance until the evening of each day; then he will instruct young gentlemen only, till the close of each evening. On the third and last day of each dance, Mr. Vaughan proposes (with the consent of the parents and patrons) to unite the two schools together for the purpose of practising some fashionable dances which cannot be perfected without. At which time he hopes from strict and unremitted attention to give the most approved satisfaction to all those interested." [10] Tuition was $15 for six dances, each dance consisting of three daily instruction periods. Before taking charge of the Midway Hotel, J. A. Xaupi held dancing classes at the Eagle Hotel. Ladies were respectfully invited to attend these "practising balls," and gentlemen were advised to secure tickets at the bar. After June 1829, Xaupi's classes moved to the Midway. He also taught children ($12 per quarter) and invited adults to attend cotillions held every Friday evening.

A Mrs. Spencer who came to Albemarle from New York State in the 1820s offered pianoforte lessons, Samuel O. Hendren taught sacred music in a Main Street room, and J. H. Hoffman maintained classes in the Jefferson Hotel where he taught students to play various musical instruments. Hoffman, the most enterprising of the three, also repaired pianos "on the shortest notice" and offered to go regularly to any county home to give musical instruction.

By mid-century Charlottesville had 1,890 residents—922 white, 968 black (128 free). Scottsville, which because of canal traffic for a time challenged the county seat's dominance of Albemarle's commercial and business life, was about one-third as large, with 666 inhabitants—404 white, 262 black (56 free). A most important con-

[10] *Central Gazette* (March 25, 1820), quoted in N. B. Jones, "Charlottesville and Albemarle," p. 132. Virtually all of the material in the remainder of this chapter comes from this dissertation unless otherwise indicated.

tribution to organized social life in Albemarle was construction in the 1850s of the Charlottesville Town Hall, which stood at what is now 350 Park Street.[11] Completed in December 1852, it seated some eight hundred people and soon was host to a variety of concerts, lectures, church fairs, and even university functions. In 1853 Ole Bull, a celebrated Norwegian violinist, appeared, and in his troupe was a young singing prodigy, Adelina Patti, who seven years later returned as a star in her own right. Only seventeen, Spanish-born of Italian parents, she was so radiant that university students in the audience "nearly went wild." Six years later, on invitation of that institution's literary societies, C. P. Baldwin of Richmond gave a series of lectures to "immense audiences" on these topics: "Old Fogies," "Woman's Rights," and "The Battle of Life."

Local music instructors now were holding their classes in co-operation with various Charlottesville schools. C. T. Frey in 1857 presented his pupils in concert at Piedmont Female Institute, and in the same year J. M. Deens conducted singing classes at Albemarle Female Institute. E. Teltow, instructor in violin, guitar, flute, clarinet, and cornet, was leader of the Cornet Band which serenaded editors of the *Review* on September 7, 1860. This was probably the same group which won high praise for its performance at the university's alumni dinner held two months earlier in conjunction with graduation exercises, or finals as they were called. The *Review* editors stirred up a local hornet's nest by commenting that women and children with the best seats at that function talked so much and so loudly that others could not hear speakers. Man should pay due deference to woman, who, these journalists stoutly maintained, should return the same respect—"The shallow sentiment about the matter is that man ought to break his neck if he goes into the presence of a woman: we despise the man who makes such a fool of himself and we despise the woman whom it gratifies." Within a few days their offices were deluged with letters, some flippant, others caustic, and a few of approval and support.

In the 1820s the county court, composed of justices of the peace (magistrates) named by the governor, remained the mainspring of local government, although this body's importance as a court of law appears to have been declining somewhat. This was a self-perpetuating group since appointment to fill vacancies was made upon recommendation of the presiding justices themselves. Regular

[11] Margaret Fowler Clark, "Charlottesville's Cultural History Echoes through the Old Levy Opera House," *Daily Progress* (April 8, 1973).

meetings were held on the first Monday of each month and quarterly sessions in March, June, August, and November at which time a grand jury was empaneled to inquire "into the breaches of the penal laws and to make presentments of the offenders." The justices also nominated or appointed virtually all county officials. It was customary for a senior justice who had not held the office of sheriff to be nominated for a two-year term. Though three names usually were submitted to the governor, the man who headed the list always won out. The coroner, escheator, and militia officers also were nominated by the court and appointed by the governor. The justices, however, named their clerk, commissioner of revenue, Commonwealth's attorney, surveyors, and constable. Overseers of the poor, the only local officials selected by the voters, served three-year terms. As noted earlier, the county court appointed tobacco and flour inspectors, licensed taverns and public houses, and established annual rates for food, drink, and lodgings.

Another responsibility of the magistrates was maintenance of the courthouse, jail, whipping post, stocks, and pillory. Apparently the latter were not used very frequently. In March 1820 bids were received to repair these facilities, and two years later when David Reynolds was sentenced to receive twenty stripes for theft of some tobacco, the editors of the *Central Gazette* expressed shock and amazement, stating categorically that it was, to their knowledge, the first time such punishment had been inflicted upon a local white man. In addition to the county court, a circuit court held semiannual sessions in Albemarle. Its jurisdiction was somewhat broader, and it heard cases on appeal from the county court. As a result, the local justices began to lose some of their influence as a law court, although, of course, their appointive powers were unimpaired.

According to the research of Daniel Smith, a "transformation" occurred in county leadership during the half century or so following the Revolution, reflected principally in the composition of that body.[12] Several developments appear to have brought about this change. The work load of the courts increased so much that service became more burden than venerable honor. As a result, many well-to-do citizens found it a less attractive place to begin political careers and shifted their interests to state and national governments or new states and territories in the West where other opportunities existed, areas gen-

[12] See Smith's "Changing Patterns of Local Leadership: Justices of the Peace in Albemarle County, Virginia, 1760–1820" (M.A. thesis, University of Virginia, 1973). This work contains tables listing all of the justices for those years.

erally closed to all but a select few before 1776. By the turn of the century the court, enlarged and often subject to public criticism for failure to permit voter participation in county government, was composed largely of moderately prosperous folk—merchants, small farmers, and professional people. Although a few descendants of the original gentry still exerted some influence in local matters, it was not as members of the county court. There may have been a measure of democracy in all this, but probably not much because until the mid-1800s the court continued to fill all vacancies by appointment and those named, unlike the gentry of the previous century, tended to serve for much longer periods, twenty or thirty years or more.

It is far from clear how the town of Charlottesville was governed during the early 1800s. Records are fragmentary and imprecise. In 1801 the General Assembly authorized the annual election of five trustees by freeholders, housekeepers, and free white male inhabitants who had lived in Charlottesville for more than twelve months. This act gave the trustees power to open streets and alleys in accordance with the original plans of the town, keep them in good repair, settle boundary disputes among landowners, erect a market house, impose limited taxes on tithables and real property (not to exceed a total sum of $200), appoint a tax collector, remove nuisances and obstructions to travel within the town, and hire a town clerk. At monthly meetings the trustees could enact bylaws, rules, and ordinances to implement these powers.

In March 1821 the *Central Gazette* published "Ordinances" of the town, but whether these represent all such enactments or merely new ones is not clear. They include a fine of $1.50 for wagoners who camped on the public square overnight and prohibited Sunday sale of "goods, wares, merchandise, spirits, or wine" within the town under penalty of a $10 fine; however, this ban did not apply to tavern keepers or to other citizens if they felt an emergency existed at the time of the transaction. Another Sabbath regulation provided that goods brought to town for sale on that day could be confiscated, one half to go to the informer and one half to the town itself. Other ordinances of that date dealt with stud horses and public shows within the town limits.

From time to time the town fathers had to contend with minor riots, rabid dogs, faulty building construction, and unsanitary conditions. In August 1820 several young men insulted a large number of citizens "in the grossest manner" and broke windows in private homes and at the newspaper offices. The next morning John B. Preston, Warner Lewis, and Charles Selden were arrested and charged with being the principal culprits. The editors of the *Central Gazette*, furious over damage done to their property, said this was by no means an isolated incident and urged the trustees to implement a nightly patrol of the town. Two years later a dog, presumed to be mad, ravaged the community, biting numerous other dogs and several owners as well. In days when rabies vaccine was unknown, a general slaughter of animals thought to be contaminated ensued. The trustees ordered all dogs confined for thirty days and authorized citizens to shoot on sight any found in the streets. A local housewife, Mrs. Ann Brockman, came to the aid of humans who had suffered during this rampage, offering use of her miraculous, poison-extracting "Mad-stone" to all comers for only $5 per application.

At mid-century significant changes occurred in both county and town government. In essence, voters in both areas gained more power, and the town of Charlottesville became a separate entity free from most county controls. The new state constitution of 1851 left the county court with its old judicial powers intact, but henceforth magistrates were to be elected by all eligible voters, not appointed by the governor. Each county was divided into districts with four magistrates chosen from each area. Within a short time Albemarle had ten such districts, approximately equal in size and population. Eight years later twenty election precincts were scattered throughout the county as follows: Courthouse, Lindsay's Turnout, Everettsville, Stony Point, Earlysville, Blackwell's, Free Union, White Hall, Woodville, Batesville, Hillsboro, Cross Roads, Covesville, Porter's, Warren, Wingfield's, Milton, Scottsville, Monticello House, and Howardsville. In addition to magistrates, voters now elected the clerk of court, surveyors, Commonwealth's attorney, and revenue commissioners. Some individuals deplored these innovations, noting that pressure from the rich and employers could influence how electors marked their ballots; but for the most part, these democratic changes seemed to have enjoyed general approval.

By an act of the General Assembly in March 1851, a mayor, four aldermen, and a town sergeant were authorized to assume all powers and duties formerly held and exercised by Albemarle's magistrates and sheriff within the limits of Charlottesville. The sergeant had jurisdiction one mile beyond the town's borders, and he and other officials continued to use the county jail for prisoners and the county clerk's office for the processing of legal papers. Although an election was supposed to be held in February 1852, none was, and for two years state legislators proceeded to add more amendments to the town charter. In 1853, for example, Charlottesville was granted permission to assess free blacks over the age of sixteen (male and female) the same taxes levied upon all white males over twenty-one. In general, however, except for an occasional increase in both boundaries and the number of aldermen and changes in the electorate that occurred during Reconstruction, this mayor-council form of town government continued until Charlottesville became a city in 1888. Also, until that date town residents were exempt from county taxes for the upkeep of roads and maintenance of the indigent only if they kept their streets in good repair and provided adequately for the poor living within the corporate limits.

On February 25, 1854, Charlottesville held its first mayoral election. Drury Wood, who received seventy-five votes, was the winner. R. T. W. Duke, John B. Dodd, Andrew J. Brown, and William M. Keblinger were chosen as aldermen, each having received slightly fewer votes than Wood. Seven months later Wood quit the post and was succeeded briefly by Duke and then Dodd. The council voted to present the town's first mayor with "properly engraved" silver plate worth $250; however, successors came and went so frequently that Wood was the only man so honored. Dodd won election as mayor in his own right in February 1855 but soon quit and was replaced by Wood. A year later Wood resigned once more and was succeeded by Eugene Davis; however this gentleman was soundly trounced at the polls (48 to 6) in February 1858. As this game of musical chairs continued, the council wisely decided to call those replacing the elected mayor merely "acting mayor" or "senior alderman," titles assumed by Thomas W. Savage, a staunch Republican businessman who later served as mayor under federal rule, 1868–70.

During the 1850s this young corporation's principal concerns were fires and improvement of streets and sidewalks. On March 2, 1855, the council offered a $300 reward for the apprehension and conviction of arsonists said to be terrorizing the community. At the same session members authorized a special election to determine if voters would agree to spend $1,000 for a fire engine and firehouse. Four days later a conflagration occurred at the home of R. T. W. Duke, a pioneer council member, and Duke was summarily fined $2.50 "on account of his chimney taking fire." Within two weeks voters agreed to buy that fire engine, and in July construction began on a new building to house the imposing machine to be purchased shortly in New York City.

Getting rid of muddy streets and hazardous walkways probably presented far more headaches than fires. In 1851 the General Assembly outlined provisions encouraging taxpayers to underwrite part of the cost of paving streets near their homes. During the following decade this act was altered somewhat, and in 1859 by a vote of nearly six to one (clear proof of local sentiment) Charlottesville freeholders agreed to levy taxes not exceeding $3,000 and to borrow up to $5,000 for general improvements throughout the town. First priority was given to grading and macadamizing Main Street, although a committee appointed to study the problem suggested that paving of sidewalks begin simultaneously.

And a problem there certainly was! In an editorial entitled "Art and Nature in Town," the *Review* on June 22, 1860, rhapsodized over the spectacular sights to be seen. "We have in our midst one of the wildest and most romantic chasms in the mountains of Virginia. Indeed Charlottesville combines to a greater degree than any village we know the diverse attractions of city and country." Describing in glowing detail perils and vistas to be encountered as one walked along a ravine carrying water from the Vinegar Hill area to Wills's Ice Pond in what is now the 200 block of Preston Avenue, the editors continued.

Like the traveler over some Alpine pass, the danger will add to the vividness of his feelings. The best time to go is on your way to evening service at the Episcopal Church—when the moon is overspread by some black cloud. One inch to the right will break both legs, and if the torrent is up, sweep you romantically under the planks and under the fence—"down to the endless seas."

We do not know who designed this. It is greatly superior to the Serpentine in London, or those artificial cascades in the *Bois de Boulogne*. It was a good thought, to have a real ravine amid the hum of a city, and when after a rain the water comes thundering down, the view is sublime. . . . It was left to the genius of an inland town in Virginia to develop the idea of a civic ravine—a mountain gorge amid the populous haunts and the confined air of a busy municipality.

Judith Rives, who had seen the Serpentine, Bois de Boulogne, and all the attractions European capitals had to offer, probably was not much interested in this unsightly gash marring the Charlottesville landscape, but there was one aspect of Albemarle life (and an extremely important one) which held some fascination for her: agriculture. Mistress of a large estate and wife to a man in the forefront of the revival of field and livestock, she undoubtedly followed closely the experiments and innovations of these years. For three decades after its creation in 1817 the Albemarle Agricultural Society exerted substantial influence through its members, the wealthiest farmers in a five-county area. Though vital but routine matters such as crop rotation, contour plowing, selective breeding, and utilization of better fertilizers were not especially intriguing (except to those directly involved), the annual county fair inaugurated in 1825 attracted widespread attention. Preparations for this event began weeks, even months, before the gala opening day.

On October 6, 1828, the committee on arrangements met and nominated judges for seven categories: horses, cattle, swine, sheep, agricultural implements, domestic manufactures of woolen and woolen and cotton goods, and domestic manufactures of cotton goods or goods made of flax or flax and cotton. A marshal appointed for each group was charged with assembling displays and given a handsome blue sash as his badge of office. Three days later, on the first day of the fair, members of the society gathered at the Eagle Tavern for "refreshments," grouped themselves into committees, and proceeded to the fair grounds. That year George M. Woods's Selim won top honors as the stallion "best calculated to improve the breed of horses," and Diana, owned by Richard D. Sims, carried off first prize as the best brood mare. Thomas J. Randolph's bay (by Monticello) was judged the best two-year-old colt. Other awards went to J. Harper's ram and Seth Burnley's ewes, Hugh Nelson's bull, and John H. Craven's cow. (Craven, who lived at Gilmer's Pen Park, received $6.) No oxen were exhibited that year, and no prizes were given for swine or agricultural implements. Colonel John Thom of Culpeper took top honors for the best pieces of flannel, carpeting, linen shirting, and linen and cotton shirting. Major James Clarke received first prize for wool and cotton material designed for ladies' and children's dresses. Craven, owner of the county's best cow, displayed the "best and most complete suit of clothes entirely home made," with second honors going to James Duke, and third to Garland Garth. Mrs. Frank Carr's counterpane of wool and cotton and Mrs. T. W. Meriwether's woolen knit hose caught the judges' eyes, as well as a cheese displayed by Mrs. James Clarke, although no "cheese" category seemed to exist. Mrs. Meriwether received $2; Mrs. Clarke, $5.

These fairs continued until the 1840s when the society ceased to function. By that date members apparently felt they had achieved some of their avowed goals, and a state fair held in Richmond by the Virginia State Agricultural Society replaced, in part, the local version. Nevertheless, county entrants continued to reap more than their share of blue ribbons. In 1853 a Cleveland bay imported by William Cabell Rives was named best among two-year-old colts and fillies at the state fair. The judges commented that "the introduction of so perfect a specimen of one of the highly valued races of Great Britain may well be regarded as a public benefaction and entitles this distinguished member of our Society to its thanks." Red Rover, a bull owned by Rives, won another prize in the class of Shorthorns and Herefords, and the former minister to France also walked off with two blue ribbons for imported sheep. One of these animals, an Oxford Down named Duke of Marlborough, received a $20 prize as "the best buck in any breed." Other local farmers who promoted selective breeding and frequently won top honors at Richmond fairs included Slaughter W. Ficklin of Belmont, John R. Woods of Holkham, and William Garth of Midway.

In Albemarle, Hole and Corner Club No. 1 succeeded the defunct society as a round table for agricultural discussion and innovation. Organized in 1843, the club's members decided to conduct a series of carefully monitored experiments and report on results obtained, a technique which, they claimed, would work wonders if implemented statewide by similar clubs. In 1850 they tried a relatively new fertilizing agent, Peruvian guano. At a meeting held at Birdwood, Peter Meriwether told of greatly increased yields when guano was applied to his oats, adding that William C. Rives had achieved similar results with wheat.

The principal crops of Albemarle at mid-century continued to be tobacco and cereal grains such as wheat, Indian corn, and oats. Extensive records found in the census of 1850 reveal how many farms were being operated. Newton Jones, selecting a dozen individuals, details the value of real estate, farm machinery, and livestock, number of slaves owned, and crops produced during the year ending June 30, 1850. William C. Rives, Peyton S. Coles, and William Garth each were masters of substantial acres valued at about $50,000; however, their holdings varied greatly in size—Rives, 3,000 acres, Coles, 2,000, and Garth, 1,000. Each had livestock worth about $3,000 and farm machinery estimated to be worth from $600 to $1,000. Rives had fifty-four slaves; Coles, eighty-three; and Garth, fifty-two. These men produced a substantial amount of wheat and corn, along with some oats and hay. Garth was the only member of this well-to-do trio growing tobacco (30,000 pounds), and while he and Coles harvested a few bushels of Irish and sweet potatoes for market sale, Rives did not. Each man's estate also produced some wool and butter. Garth estimated his "home manufactures" were worth $200; Rives and Coles reported "none."

The operations of three less affluent farmers with less extensive holdings—Slaughter W. Ficklin, James T. Early, and William W.

Gilmer—present a similar picture. Each owned 1,000 acres or less and had fewer slaves. Strangely, Gilmer, with the smallest farm (380 acres), had the most slaves (twenty-two). He also had live-stock valued at $3,000 and raised more wheat and corn than Rives. Early was the only one growing tobacco in 1850; none of them re-ported any "home manufactures." Shepherd Moore and Robert Harmer each farmed 200 to 300 acres with the aid of six to eight slaves. They owned farm machinery worth $60 and livestock valued at about $500. Both raised similar crops on a much smaller scale. Moore said he produced "home manufactures" valued at $10; Harmer, $40. Two other farmers, William C. Reynolds and Richard Pleasants, had much smaller farms worked without slave labor. Pleasants thought his 45 acres worth $100. His only produce included corn, oats, livestock, forty pounds of butter, and "home manufactures" worth $30. Reynolds was master of 11 acres of land worth $80. In 1850 he grew small quantities of corn, oats, and potatoes and pro-duced some wool, butter, and "home manufactures."

At the bottom of the scale were two farmers who also owned no slaves and whose land had no value whatsoever. Henderson Goings, a free black, farmed 150 acres (perhaps mountain land inherited from his Revolutionary War ancestor) on which he grew wheat, corn, oats, and potatoes. Daniel Reg had 45 acres which produced corn, oats, and potatoes and a relatively large amount of butter (350 pounds). Each man had a few animals and reported "home manu-factures" worth $15 to $20.

While these profiles tend to support the general picture one has of nineteenth-century agriculture in Albemarle County, it is obvious that grains dominated the local scene; and in contrast to what might be supposed, smaller farmers do not appear to have grown "a little bit of this and that," at least not for sale commercially. Instead, they produced smaller quantities of fewer crops than those planted by their well-to-do neighbors. Caught up in an endless cycle of poverty, they could not afford the equipment, seed, or fertilizer needed to undertake such ventures even if they wished to do so.

Yet the lure of tobacco remained strong, and Hole and Corner Club members continued to debate from time to time the best method of cultivation. There was a dramatic upsurge in tobacco production during the 1850s, the result of improved market conditions, com-mercial fertilizers, rail and canal transport, and better growing seasons. The county's tobacco yield rose from 1,456,000 pounds in 1850 (down somewhat from 1840) to 5,429,395 pounds in 1860. This renewed interest in Albemarle's "first love," almost a mania in the southern part of the county near Scottsville, is an extremely interesting phenomenon. According to Ann Stauffenberg, prices rose as much as 40 percent during the 1850s, and for a brief period Albemarle became a major producer, the fourth most important county in the Old Dominion.[13] This was, however, no "rags-to-riches" cycle. Farmers with land, slaves, and money in 1850 took full advantage of higher prices, guano, and the James River Canal and increased their wealth substantially on the eve of war.

The same decade witnessed an increase in production of beef cattle. A number of well-to-do farmers apparently added to their income by purchasing cattle in western Virginia, Kentucky, and Tennessee in late fall, fattening them throughout the winter and early spring on local grain, and then driving them to Richmond, Washington, and Baltimore for sale. In 1850 the *Southern Planter* cited thirty-one local landowners who bought and sold 1,296 cattle in this fashion and estimated Albemarle residents had driven some 2,000 head to market that year alone.[14]

Throughout these years glowing pictures of an abundant, verdant Albemarle County are to be found in various newspapers and agricultural journals—waving fields of grain, well-tended crops and sleek animals, intelligent, hard-working farm folk. The editor of the *Southern Planter* in July 1860 issued this summary of his visit to the foothills of the Blue Ridge: "The more we saw of the country, the more we were pleased, and the more we felt it to be excusable for Virginians to be proud of the Old Dominion—having within her borders the elements of wealth, prosperity, and greatness. We proved to our heartfelt satisfaction the justice of her claim to unlimited hospitality, and kindness to the stranger within her gates."

Hospitality and kindness are very commendable attributes indeed, but they do little to augment agricultural production. More important, the haunting suspicion remains that some of this praise for Albemarle's rich, rolling lands was a not-so-subtle defense of the local labor system. Comparison of agricultural census returns for 1840 and 1850 reveal virtually no change in the number of animals on county farms. In fact, while sheep and swine populations were stable, horses and mules declined from 5,765 to 5,002; cattle, from 14,819

[13] See Ann Lenore Stauffenberg, "Albemarle County, Virginia, 1850–1870: An Economic Survey Based on the U.S. Census" (M.A. thesis, University of Virginia, 1973).

[14] It is intriguing to note that this publication interviewed thirty-one individuals in Albemarle, the same number who in 1850 had wealth in excess of $25,000.

to 12,331, despite reputed imports from the West. Yet this was the ten-year period in which the local population grew fastest during the decades from 1820 to 1860, from 22,924 to 25,800, and one would expect more farm households (if truly prosperous) to have more farm animals.

The sad truth is, most of the benefits of this seeming agricultural prosperity were limited to a few, the descendants of the gentry who controlled large estates and many slaves, a hundred or so individuals prominent at meetings of the Albemarle Agricultural Society and its successor, Hole and Corner Club No. 1. Isaac White, employer of that young Yankee tutor, John Adam Kasson, and the man who inherited part of Farmington from George Divers (including the mansion house), sold that famous landmark to John Carter Coles in 1840 and settled down at Keelona a short distance from Redlands, the traditional Carter home.[15] Although White hobnobbed with Albemarle's richest farmers, he was not a member of that select inner circle; and as Kasson related in letters to his father, in February 1843 even Isaac White, obviously a well-to-do man, because of hard times was contemplating going to Missouri. Three years later White sold Keelona and took up residence in Lewis County, Virginia. That a gentleman of White's means found it necessary to move west is stark commentary upon the state of affairs. And it should be noted that White departed at a time when, from all outward indications, Albemarle had solved many of its agricultural problems. This example undoubtedly was repeated hundreds of times during these decades as numerous families, many less affluent than the Whites, packed up their household belongings, said goodbye to friends, neighbors, and relatives, and left the land they loved. A nine-page appendix which Edgar Woods added to his *Albemarle County* published in 1901 lists some four hundred "Emigrants from Albemarle to Other States." It is, of course, by no means a complete accounting of this tremendous flow of outward migration. In particular, this list does not include the name of Isaac White or anyone else who departed for what, in 1863, became West Virginia. Perhaps Woods, like many citizens of the Old Dominion, even in the opening decade of the twentieth century still was irked by creation of the Mountaineer State amid confusing, wartime circumstances.

When Judith Rives and her growing family returned from their last overseas sojourn in 1853, they found the little stores of Charlottesville far different from the grand emporiums of Paris, London,

---

[15] See Younger, "A Yankee Reports on Virginia," pp. 408–30.

and New York; but the county seat certainly was much more of a marketplace than it had been three or four decades earlier. Railroad lines, which reached that community in 1850, created keen competition among wholesale outlets located in Richmond, Alexandria, Baltimore, and Philadelphia and brought many new products directly to eager customers. Jones and Wiant, for example, invited local housewives to stop by their store and use a "family" sewing machine for a day or so, "though a few minutes will be sufficient," they boasted, to convince anyone of its worth. At the Oyster Depot on Main Street, Thomas H. Duke was serving fresh Norfolk seafood received daily from the coast.

In 1857 Thomas Cogan, a "Practical Gas Fitter," announced he would furnish and install gas fixtures, and several visionaries dreamed of lighting town streets with this new medium that recently had made its appearance in Charlottesville. Gas lighting soon was available to homes and offices in a restricted area, many of the lamps and much of the coal oil being supplied by Frederick M. Wills. Wills, an extremely enterprising businessman, also was local agent for German Cologne, stationery, and various drugs, although he faced stiff competition in the pharmaceutical field. (The Review's editors said his shelves contained "medicine enough to kill the county!") Burke Archer and Company claimed they could supply physicians who had been securing medical supplies from Richmond and some northern cities with drugs "equally as cheap and reliable as they can be bought anywhere." This company also advertised certain toiletries prepared on the premises—"Glycerine Lotion for Chapped Hands" and "Kisalik Bouquet," a perfume which they jauntily challenged the entire world to excel. Tobacco was not yet found at drugstore counters, but a notice by C. L. Thompson concerning the "nicotine habit" reveals, not surprisingly, that it was well established in Albemarle: "Crops may fail, commerce stagnate, wars devastate the country, *banks suspend specie payment, and wives fret and scold*, yet our people will chew and spit, smoke and puff, snuff and sneeze in spite of these disasters. By calling at the sign of the Wild Indian, you can procure, at the lowest possible rates, the very best quality of these indispensable articles to soothe your sorrows and drive dull care away."

J. Huff maintained a newsstand with an assortment of periodicals and daily and weekly publications. Meerschaum pipes, walking canes, "segars," perfume, soap, nuts, raisins, jellies, and preserves were stocked by Fred Hartnagle in 1860, although earlier this gentleman seems to have been merely a confectioner. In 1857 he offered cakes and candies fresh daily and, upon order, would supply ice cream for special functions. Andrew Mannoni, a rival, proclaimed in December 1860 that his newly refitted shop on the public square was "Headquarters for Santa Claus." He had, he said, "every delicacy for parties," French confections, toys, and fireworks. Whiskey, now sold more often by the quart than the gallon, could be obtained from W. D. Perry: "Let the World Say What They Can, for selling fine Liquors—Perry's the Man!"

Groceries, ready-made clothing, dry goods, boots, shoes, carpet-bags, and trunks were available at a variety of outlets, and Charlottesville had at least two jewelry stores in 1860, one owned by J. W. Lipop and the other by Edward Benner. Lipop boasted he had a Geneva-born watchmaker on his staff, and Benner offered for sale an assortment of sterling and plate items, among them coffee urns, pitchers, and cake baskets. As in the 1820s the millinery trade seems to have been marked by rapid turnover in personnel as one lady after another unabashedly proclaimed her "unequalled" skills, opened up a shop, and then within a few months sold out and moved on.

In 1859 the county had four banks, although it is difficult to evaluate their influence upon local business activity. The Farmers' Bank of Virginia opened a branch in Charlottesville in 1840, and shortly after that date the Monticello Bank appeared, perhaps the first exploitation of a name which would endear itself to so many tourist-minded businessmen of the twentieth century. In 1850 Charlottesville's pioneer banking institution erected a new building, forty-four feet square, clear evidence of its success. The other two banks in the county were located in Scottsville and Howardsville. The Albemarle Insurance Company sold life, fire, and marine insurance and also carried on some banking functions, often accepting funds for deposit. In 1859 this company moved into a new building at the corner of Main and Bank streets. At that time the directors boasted they had paid out $80,000 in claims over a four-year period and had cash assets of $372,311.90.

Another new service, one which many viewed as a mixed blessing at best, was the telegraph. The line from Charlottesville to Lynchburg, the last gap between New York and New Orleans, was completed in April 1860. Two months later the *Review* proclaimed this wonder a "failure." One of its editors had gone to the Constitutional Union Convention in Baltimore which nominated John Bell for the presidency. This information had been telegraphed from that city at 2:30 P.M. but did not reach Charlottesville until 11 o'clock that evening. The telegraph companies, these editors complained, "take your money and send their dispatches at their convenience. If several towns intervene lightning is passed by the express mail train—and sometimes, no doubt, follows the freight. . . . We have post-offices and telegraph wires in Virginia; but they are like bills of a circus; when it comes to the performance, most of the fine things are coolly omitted." There was also a telegraph line from Charlottesville to Scottsville which apparently offered similar service. Residents of that thriving little river town protested that the agent at the county seat often waited two or three days to relay messages received at his office.

In 1860 Charlottesville's leading hostelries were Smith's Central Hotel located east of the present Chesapeake and Ohio Station and the Farish House on the Court Square site of the old Eagle Tavern. With the coming of the railroad and greatly increased enrollment at the university, these two public houses and others such as the Monticello House and Delevan House did a thriving business, and several advertised themselves as "summer retreats" as well.

There was little change in manufacturing within Albemarle between 1820 and 1860. Hats, carriages, cotton and woolen goods, tobacco products, and some farm implements were produced locally as they had been four decades earlier. Sawmills and flour and grist mills still dotted the countryside, and production of the latter exceeded in value that of all other industries combined. Milling of corn and wheat from the county's extensive fields continued to be Albemarle's major industry; yet one small complex, which at mid-century was producing lumber, flour, plaster, and cotton and woolen goods, was destined to become, in time, an important factor in the local economy. In the early 1850s John Adams Marchant gained control of the Charlottesville Factory, as it was called. Within a short time he offered, when customers furnished three-fourths of a pound of washed and picked wool for each yard of cloth, to turn out white jeans for twenty-one cents a yard and colored jeans for twenty-four cents per yard. The success of this venture, essentially production of slave clothing, encouraged Marchant to enter other textile fields, and during the war years he produced uniforms for the Confederate forces. In 1864 Marchant bought up the company stock, dissolved the parent concern, and sold out to his son, Henry Clay Marchant, a veteran crippled by a minié ball. It was this young man who would create, through hard work and in trying times, the Charlottesville Woolen Mills.[16]

Early in 1861, as the hostilities which young Marchant experi-

---

[16] See Harry E. Poindexter, "Henry Clay Marchant and the Foundation of the Charlottesville Woolen Mills, 1865–1882," *MACH* 14 (1955):26–48.

enced loomed so ominously on the horizon, Judith Walker Rives wrote to her son, Alfred, describing his father's recent adventures in the nation's capital. She recounted how Rives, respected as an elder statesman and once thought of by some as a possible presidential nominee, suffered a brusque confrontation with Secretary of State William Seward when he tried to air his moderate views at a Washington dinner party. Seward apparently departed in a huff, "puffed up with grand ideas of his consequence, now that he is 'dressed in a little brief authority.' " Judith Rives said her husband still hoped for a national conference to settle matters but added that he reluctantly had agreed to represent Charlottesville at a state convention to be held in Richmond. Mr. Rives, she concluded, was very disturbed by the erratic course events seemed to be taking.

Several weeks later she wrote this comment on the national scene to Alfred's wife:

Poor old Abe is in a tight place, it will be impossible for him to please either his friends or foes. His foreign appointments, however, are some of them very good. Papa approves highly of Mr. Adams and Mr. Dayton. . . .[17] So far, I don't see that anybody is hurt, and really if people would go to work and mind their business, it would be difficult notwithstanding all the hammering and tinkering of the politicians for them to ruin the country, which they seem bent upon. . . . I "rayther" think Virginia will be apt to stand still, being somewhat conservative, rather lazy, and more disposed to keep old fashions than set up new ones. Unless something new turns up I don't see much excuse for further fuss at present.

But, as we all know, the "fuss" continued and grew even worse, and a few months later the mistress of Castle Hill closed her autobiography on this tragic note:

I have lived to see the proudest nation on earth humbled to dust . . . to see my beloved country bathed in tears and drenched with blood . . . to find myself separated as by an impassable gulf from seventeen of my loved children and grandchildren . . . almost a childless mother with living children, orphans with living parents! [18]

Let drop the curtain!

Although the war that ensued was an extremely traumatic experience for both Albemarle and the nation, Judith Rives, in proper Victorian fashion, was being somewhat overly dramatic. Life did not

---

[17] Charles Francis Adams was named minister to England; William Lewis Dayton, to France, the post held twice by Rives.

[18] Mrs. Rives refers here to the fact that three of her five children were living in Boston and New York.

end in the summer of 1861 for either her or her beloved country. She lived on until January 1882, a respected and revered reminder of an earlier and perhaps more gracious era, but one would be hard put to say that the changes she witnessed during those two decades were any greater than what passed before her eyes during the first half of the nineteenth century. In her three score and twenty she saw the United States stretch its arms to the Pacific as it grew in wealth and power, aided immeasurably by the foresight of Thomas Jefferson and the explorations of Meriwether Lewis and William Clark. And, on the local scene, she watched her Albemarle become a relatively prosperous rural community complete with railroads, better highways, telegraph lines, a university, and more and more of the comforts of everyday life common to urban centers throughout the nation. By way of contrast, it is interesting to compare Thomas Walker's reaction to war in 1775 with that of his granddaughter in 1861. Both were about sixty years of age at the time; but where one saw opportunity, the other saw disaster. Of course, to a large degree, each was right.

Chapter 10

Turnpikes, Canals, and Steam Engines

ALBEMARLE'S struggle to create and maintain vital avenues of commerce, whether by water or land, is as old as the history of the county itself. However, during the first half of the nineteenth century special efforts were made to improve turnpikes and canals, build bridges, and lure railroad tracks to the Piedmont. The purpose of these often substantial expenditures, in most instances, was not simply to foster better means of communication within Albemarle but to provide a network serving a much larger area. Yet county leaders, like their counterparts in hundreds of other American communities of that era, were engaging in a very dangerous game. Improvements in transport, while highly desirable, might merely enable goods and people to pass through a town, city, or county; and if a region did not grow and generate substantial economic activity of its own, it faced the risk of becoming only a way station en route to larger, more prosperous centers.

Today many view these decades, 1820–60, as a knock-down, drag-out fight between canals and railroads, with turnpike advocates watching from the sidelines ready to join up forces with the winner, which was, of course, the railroad. This picture is somewhat distorted on several counts. There was no valid reason that all three modes of travel could not function simultaneously and complement each other, as they still do in some parts of our nation today. Even at mid-century it was by no means certain that rail lines would prevail over canal and turnpike, and as we have seen in our own time, the steam engine's victory, once thought so complete, was considerably less than that. Yet there is no denying that for some sixty or seventy years following the Civil War railroad barons dominated many aspects of American life and even the outcome of that conflict itself was dictated, in large measure, by control of railroad tracks.

Perhaps two other aspects of this unfolding transportation picture should be noted. Albemarle's failure to become a canal or rail center of vital importance before 1860 actually was a blessing in disguise since it saved the county from ravages of war experienced by nearby communities; and, second, much of this construction between 1820 and 1860, as far as the Old Dominion was concerned, had political as well as economic implications. Not only were Norfolk and other coastal cities dreaming of tapping the wealth of the burgeoning midwestern heartland and funneling those riches through their wharves, Virginia was trying valiantly to hold a sprawling, diverse commonwealth together. Although these schemes did not achieve their major objectives, Albemarle, caught somewhere in the middle, benefited greatly.

In pre-railroad days the answer to local problems seemed to be more and better turnpikes and increased utilization of natural waterways such as the Rivanna and the James. In the early 1820s Albemarle was served, as it had been for several decades, by two major east-west, north-south roads. One was Three Notched, leading from Richmond to the Valley and forming the main street of the village of Charlottesville. This well-known thoroughfare crossed the Rivanna at Secretary's Ford and the Blue Ridge at Jarman's Gap, although west of Mechum's River one could choose from a variety of roads leading to other passes through the mountains—Rockfish, Turk's, and Brown's gaps. A north-south road connected Lynchburg and Alexandria by way of Gordonsville, utilizing a small section of Three Notched in the vicinity of Charlottesville.

The first important addition to these highways came in the summer of 1827 with completion of the Staunton, or Rockfish Gap, Turnpike. Although authorized in 1818, the same year Scottsville was incorporated as a town, it took some six years to collect funds, secure contractors, and get work underway. This road, bisecting the southwestern quarter of the county, ran from Scottsville to Rockfish Gap. It followed roughly what is now Route 20 to Keene and two county roads (712 and 692) to Route 250 just east of the crest of the Blue Ridge. Claudius Crozet, principal engineer of the commonwealth who later would have an Albemarle community named in his honor, was not happy with the results. After several inspection trips he reported that the builders too frequently had used soft bottomland instead of hard, nearby ridges and that, at times, descent down hills and mountains along the way was much too rapid. Crozet thought the section from the Green Mountains to Scottsville good, and despite some criticism, he maintained that if "miry" places were made firm with broken stone, this turnpike could become one of the finest in the entire state. There were five tollgates. One was located at Garland's Store, about a mile southeast of North Garden; and, in

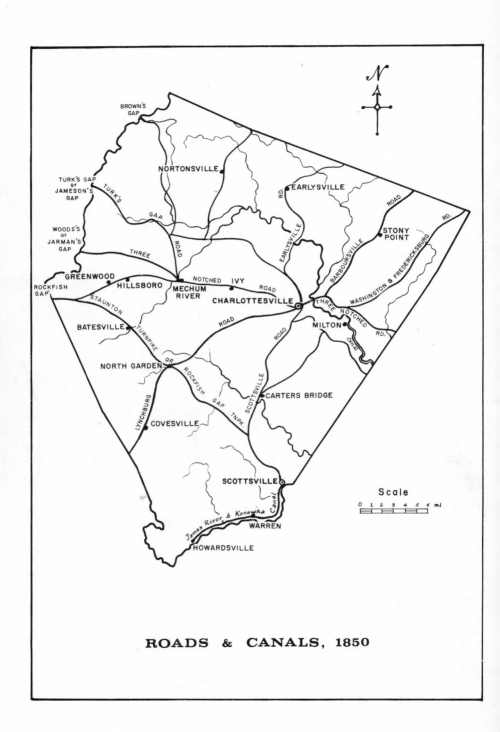

ROADS & CANALS, 1850

1831, a wagon hauling wheat through its gates was charged $2.76 for six trips, or forty-six cents per trip.[1]

Despite "miry" places and toll charges, Valley farmers discovered, to the distress of Charlottesville merchants and to the joy of their elated competitors in Scottsville, that this shortcut to the waters of the James was of substantial benefit to them, and its opening marks the beginning of a lengthy trade war, at times rather spirited, between these two communities, one the county seat and the other, for all practical purposes, also once the focus of local government, if only for a decade or so. In 1821 as many as 130 wagons per week were rolling through Charlottesville with flour and wheat bound for the Richmond market. As their rumble and the accompanying jangle of coin decreased, the citizens of central and northern Albemarle bestirred themselves, giving support to a number of schemes designed to thwart the machinations of the upstart Scotts and their neighbors.

In 1826, as the Staunton–James River Turnpike neared completion, William H. Meriwether petitioned the General Assembly for permission to build a toll bridge across the Rivanna. It was to be located above the juncture of Moore's Creek, approximately where Three Notched crossed the river. Early in January 1827 legislators gave their approval, stipulating that the structure must be at least fourteen feet wide with well-braced handrails on each side. If, upon completion, his bridge was satisfactory in all respects, Meriwether could collect four cents for every person, mule, horse, or work ox that crossed and six and one-half cents per wheel for wagons and carriages. Sheep, hogs, goats, and lambs cost owners twelve and one-half cents per score. Since the Rivanna could still be forded easily throughout much of the year, the Assembly added that if this situation changed as a result of improvements made in navigation, such as deepening the channel, Meriwether was to reduce his tolls by one-fourth.

A year later Virginia lawmakers passed an act incorporating "a company to construct a turnpike road from the Rivanna river near Charlottesville to intersect with the Staunton and Scottsville turnpike road." [2] Books were opened in Charlottesville, Milton, and Little

---

[1] For details concerning this turnpike, see N. B. Jones, "Charlottesville and Albemarle," pp. 63–64 and Robert L. Goldstone, "Historical Geography of Scottsville, Virginia" (M.A. thesis, University of Virginia, 1953), pp. 33–34. This important highway went by various names: Staunton Turnpike, Staunton–James River Turnpike, and Rockfish Gap Turnpike.

[2] N. B. Jones, "Charlottesville and Albemarle," p. 68.

York to receive stock subscriptions to the amount of $15,000. The aim of this enterprise, the Rivanna and Rockfish Gap Turnpike Company, was twofold: to win back valuable Valley trade and to improve a substantial section of Three Notched. Its backers also planned to construct a bridge 169 feet long over Mechum's River. In time, tollgates were erected; and for some three decades, fees were collected from all who passed. According to Woods, "The first gate west of town was immediately opposite the large oak tree on Jesse Lewis's place, under which General Washington is said once to have lunched, and which was blown down by a violent storm in September, 1869; its keeper was Patrick Quinn. In 1857 the road was purchased by the county for fifteen hundred dollars, John Wood, Jr., being appointed to receive the purchase money for distribution among the stockholders." [3]

Even before Quinn began collecting tolls or bridges spanned Mechum's River and the Rivanna, considerable agitation was afoot for immediate improvements in various waterways serving the county. The so-called Rivanna Canal never functioned satisfactorily, principally because locks circumventing milldams were maintained in a haphazard manner, if at all. This meant customers often had to unload their merchandise and carry or roll it around these obstructions to another boat waiting downstream. John Craven noted in 1820 that a vessel loaded with his tobacco sank when a bank of the canal caved in on top of it, and in 1822 his men had to roll five hundred barrels of flour around a milldam because the lock was not functioning.

Three years later, as Scottsville's dreams were becoming a reality, the editors of the *Central Gazette* pointed with alarm to "examples of active enterprise which have occurred around us" and expressed surprise that "no active and energetic attempts have been made to effect an object [so] desirable" of improvement as river transport. "We must be up and doing, or we shall be left at a sightless distance behind those whom it is in our power to surpass." In 1826 members of the Albemarle Agricultural Society urged the General Assembly to turn its attention to the noble Rivanna, an essential highway of commerce for Albemarle and Fluvanna, which, they said, also could offer Nelson, Augusta, and Rockingham counties to the west and Louisa, Orange, and Madison to the east "their most eligible communication with the great central market of the State." [4]

[3] Edgar Woods, p. 70.
[4] N. B. Jones, "Charlottesville and Albemarle," pp. 69–70.

Though perhaps the society overstated its case somewhat, there is little doubt that an unobstructed Rivanna could have brought benefits to a substantial area; but before any construction began, advocates of such a venture had to make some basic decisions: how wide should locks be and what depth of water was desirable? These two factors would determine, of course, the size of boats to be used. About the same time that he was inspecting the new turnpike from Scottsville to Staunton, Crozet also surveyed the connecting waterways from the juncture of Ivy Creek and South Fork to Columbia where the Rivanna flowed into the James. He found the situation deplorable but outlined a plan for immediate action. At a cost of $132,500 he thought new dams, locks, and canals could make these streams navigable for steamboats from Moore's Ford, near the present Free Bridge, to Columbia; or for about half as much ($68,500), the thirty-seven-mile stretch could accommodate bateaux.

On March 2, 1827, the General Assembly authorized formation of the Rivanna Navigation Company and granted it permission to open a channel two feet deep and twenty-five feet wide from Moore's Creek to Point of Fork at Columbia. This company could charge four and one-half cents per ton per mile on all goods except plaster of Paris, which passed free. As soon as one-half of the stock was subscribed ($50,000), construction would get underway; and the legislators stipulated work must begin in two years and be completed within five. Stockholders, at their discretion, could improve either branch of the Rivanna. The General Assembly also devised an elaborate scheme (one which time proved was usually unsuccessful) for settling disputes between the company and millowners who had dams across the river. In April 1829 Martin Dawson, the man whose bequest built the university's Dawson's Row in the 1850s, as president of the Rivanna Navigation Company advertised that bids for work would be received. However, construction did not get underway until the following year, somewhat after the date specified by state authorities. And as for the five-year limit on completion, that was disregarded entirely.

During that same decade citizens of eastern Albemarle, Louisa, and Fluvanna counties obtained permission to extend the Rockfish Gap Turnpike eastward to Boyd's Tavern, essentially another improvement of venerable old Three Notched. Despite various meetings and proposals, nothing came of these plans. An attempt by ambitious little Scottsville to construct a turnpike to Rock Springs in Nelson County and from there to the headwaters of the Rockfish River met a similar fate. Earlier the General Assembly granted special powers to the county courts of Albemarle, Nelson, and Amherst to undertake development of a more direct route from Charlottesville to Lynchburg. This new thoroughfare was to be built by surveyors and "the hands through whose precincts it shall pass," or by workmen paid by county levy. At first Amherst County was reluctant either to contribute labor or tax its citizens, but eventually the road was built. In general, this highway, present Route 29 to Lynchburg, took advantage of country roads already in existence, although it cut new ground by striking west of Dudley's Mountain to Cross Roads.

Efforts to improve land and water routes reached a climax at a convention on internal improvements held at Charlottesville in July 1828. Ironically the principal issue discussed, with former president Madison presiding, was improvement of the James, a goal in which Charlottesville, to say the least, had rather limited interest. Nevertheless, that this matter was of vital concern to many is evident by the membership of this body—representatives from fifty-nine counties and six cities, among them John Marshall of Richmond. Hugh Nelson and Thomas Walker Gilmer were the delegates from Albemarle. As was custom, this assemblage drew up a memorial seeking extensive improvements on that waterway, but little came of this request for some years.

During the 1820s stagecoach lines serving Albemarle increased markedly.[5] In 1820 S. P. Beleu (or Ballou) operated a hack between Charlottesville and Richmond. He made a round trip each week, departing from Charlottesville on Wednesday morning and from Richmond at noon on Saturday. One-way fare was $5. This service came to an abrupt halt when half of a $50 note sent by Opie Norris to a Richmond merchant was discovered on Beleu's person. He was promptly arrested, convicted of robbing the mails, and dispatched to Richmond (a one-way trip) for a term in the state penitentiary. Others soon took over the route and improved service substantially. These mail contractors included Porter, Belden and Company for a time, followed by Farish, Ficklin and Company (William P. Farish and Slaughter W. Ficklin). Nevertheless, late in 1825 the duke of Saxe-Weimar-Eisenach reported he boarded "a fairly good stage coach" for Richmond at noon but only got as far as Boyd's Tavern that day. By 1828 coaches made three round trips per week. In the summer one could leave Charlottesville at 3 A.M. and arrive in the state capital at 8 P.M. that evening. In that same year the

[5] Ibid., p. 76.

"Accommodation Mail Line" was taking passengers from Charlottesville to Alexandria twice each week. The return trip could be made in a coach leaving Alexandria at 2 P.M. on Thursday and arriving at Albemarle's county seat two days later. One-way fare was $9. The same line made two round trips weekly to Lynchburg via Amherst and Nelson counties. One coach left Charlottesville at 8 A.M. on Monday, reaching Lynchburg thirty hours later. In 1829 weekly trips from Lynchburg to Washington by way of Charlottesville were added to the schedule. The fare from Charlottesville to Washington was $8, slightly less than what had been charged for a ticket to Alexandria a year earlier.

Despite plans to accommodate either steamboats or bateaux on the waters of the Rivanna and construction of various roads and bridges in eastern and central Albemarle, Scottsville continued to prosper, some thought at the expense of Charlottesville. In 1827, the year the turnpike to Staunton began operation, $2,085.69 in tolls was collected, and a decade later it was estimated that produce valued at more than $500,000 was being transported over the highway annually. With the opening of the James River and Kanawha Canal to Richmond in 1840, both land and water traffic through Scottsville increased even more. During the first year canal authorities collected $30,000 on freight shipped between there and Richmond, almost all of it passing over the Staunton road as well. A traveler reported in May 1845 that he saw at least fifty heavy wagons on that thoroughfare, an average of more than one per mile. During one week in October of that same year some fourteen hundred barrels of flour were inspected at Scottsville, while a large quantity destined for consumption within the state went down the canal to Richmond without being inspected.

Although nearly the entire 43½-mile stretch of the roadway to Staunton was covered with gravel from time to time, rains and heavy traffic often made that vital link to Scottsville impassable. As a result, in some seasons considerable Valley freight was diverted to the macadamized highway from Staunton to Winchester en route to the Baltimore market. To remedy this situation, in 1847 the Rockfish Gap Turnpike Company was reorganized, and its headquarters moved from Staunton to Scottsville. Under new management plans were made to eliminate excessive grades and improve the roadbed with either planks or macadam. Crozet recommended the latter, but once more his advice was ignored as stockholders voted for planks. While these improvements were underway, traffic continued to flow,

19. Last days of the James River and Kanawha Canal. Note railroad ties
stacked and ready for laying tracks.

and in May 1850 a correspondent of the *Southern Planter* counted
some seventy mountain wagons in Scottsville. By 1852, however, only
ten miles, roughly one-quarter of the road, had been covered with
wood; and eight years later, on the eve of war, construction was
still going on. After 1853 rail competition began to cut deeply into
revenues and, of course, dampened stockholder enthusiasm for additional outlays. For the year ending September 30, 1860, tolls collected amounted to $293.45; repairs for the same period cost $805.85.
This turnpike staggered along through the war years with little or
no maintenance, and in 1866 the section lying within Albemarle
simply reverted to the county to be treated like any other county
road, despite its colorful, exciting past.

When the James River and Kanawha Canal began operation in
December 1840, it extended from Richmond to Lynchburg, a distance of 147½ miles. It was fifty feet wide at the waterline (thirty
feet at bottom) and five feet deep. The towpath along the side was
twelve feet wide. Lock 23 lay a short distance west of Scottsville, and
the lockkeeper's house, still in existence, is now a private dwelling.
A canal basin, used to service boats, was located within the town;

and at one time vessels also were constructed at a boatyard on the northern edge of the basin. Freight was loaded at this point, and tolls assessed at a gauge dock built in 1846. During that decade passenger or packet boats departed daily at 11 A.M. for both Lynchburg and Richmond, reaching the latter at 8 P.M.

The principal effect of this waterway was to furnish easy, safe, and unobstructed communication to the east and west, for the canal remained in operation during floods and in times of low water. "The new system of navigation," management boasted after the first year, "has already been signally successful in the reduction of the price of transportation. . . . It has ranged below one cent per ton per mile for agricultural products and heavy goods." [6] Naturally enough, the canal also brought substantial prosperity to the southern end of Albemarle. A petition seeking a branch bank (January 14, 1842) estimated the Scottsville community had some one thousand souls, together with twenty-one stores, "twenty-four mechanics' shops of various kinds," three taverns, a tobacco factory, and four churches. Canal transport eastward was conducted by nine freight boats and two packets. Produce and freight valued at over $1 million was being shipped annually, and according to this petition, merchandise valued at $255,000 was sold in the town each year. The petitioners estimated that the community annually contributed some twenty-five thousand tons of freight to canal traffic (see table 4).

As we know, these efforts eventually paid off, and Scottsville got a bank of its very own. This is not surprising since the little village set in that dramatic horseshoe bend of the James had become a transshipping point of considerable importance, but sadly, the foundations of this prosperity were fragile indeed and this river town's moment of glory was brief. For all of the wringing of hands which occurred some twenty miles to the north, Charlottesville's merchant class really had little to fear. Without Valley freight Scottsville was no challenge at all, and as noted, the "mud" turnpike (the term critics used to describe the Staunton road) was, for much of each year, virtually useless. And as rail lines crept through the Albemarle countryside in the 1840s and 1850s, Scottsville's economic hopes dwindled. Although the canal also pushed westward, despite efforts to reach Covington, Buchanan remained the terminus, and dreams of the James joining the Kanawha never materialized. In 1853 the canal recorded its greatest gross revenue, $293,512, of which

[6] Goldstone, p. 39.

Table 4. Canal freight, Scottsville, 1842

Commodity	Amount
Flour	50,000 barrels
Tobacco	1,000 hogsheads
Wheat	60,000 bushels
Corn and meal	10,000 bushels
Oats	10,000 bushels
Clover seed	1,000 bushels
Flax seed	500 bushels
Provender of various kinds	500,000 pounds
Butter	100,000 pounds
Bacon, pork, and lard	250,000 pounds
Apples	1,000 barrels
Whiskey	500 barrels
Wool, venison, etc.	50,000 pounds
Pig iron and castings	500 tons
Bar iron	100 tons
Lumber (value)	$15,000
Merchandise sold	$255,000
Contribution of tonnage to James River Canal	25,000 tons

SOURCE: Goldstone, "Historical Geography of Scottsville, Virginia" (M.A. thesis, University of Virginia, 1953), pp. 40–41.

$173,368 was net profit. As a result of reduced rates to meet rail competition, tonnage continued to increase until 1860, although profits declined somewhat.

War and use of rail lines limited canal traffic considerably during the next four years, and in March 1865 Union troops wrecked the canal almost beyond repair, destroying virtually all of the facilities located in and around Scottsville. However, the waterway was rehabilitated and, despite floods and competition of railroads, limped along until the early 1880s, when, upon completion of a rail link between Richmond and Clifton Forge, this once busy avenue of business and trade was drained, ending commercial river transport along the banks of the James west of Richmond. While historians of Scottsville tend to attribute that community's decline to the Civil War (and it certainly had a devastating effect), it is apparent that citizens of the ambitious town had little control over their own destiny. That macadam road leading north from Staunton, steam engines puffing their way into Charlottesville, and rugged mountains west of Buchanan which resisted all efforts to push them aside would have dashed Scottsville's hopes of economic growth even if Phil Sheridan's men had never wreaked havoc upon that community.[7]

Construction of a railroad, discussed as early as the mid-1830s by some farsighted leaders of both Charlottesville and Scottsville, revolutionized the life of much of Albemarle twenty years later. The county seat first sought a line to Richmond, while Scottsville looked toward Staunton, but neither project received serious support at that time. Just as rail competition stirred the James River Canal to greater efforts, it had a similar effect upon the lethargic Rivanna Navigation Company, which at mid-century suddenly launched an unprecedented flurry of spending activity. In addition, stage lines slashed fares in an attempt to retain passengers. Although the Rivanna's management invested over $200,000 in new locks and dams between 1851 and 1857 (compared to $152,456.07 for the years before 1851), its story is all too reminiscent of that of the James River–Kanawha enterprise. By 1857 horse-drawn boats of "50 tons burden" could reach a point five miles below Milton, and it was estimated that at a cost of $60,000 a channel for similar vessels could be dug all the way up to Charlottesville. In May 1860 the river still was not navigable at Shadwell for much smaller horse-drawn craft, and it is most unlikely that even boats of this size ever were seen north of Milton. In short, Charlottesville's dream of becoming a river port never was realized, despite petitions, conventions, various plans for improving the Rivanna, and considerable expenditure of funds. The Rivanna Navigation Company, born amid fond hopes and rosy predictions of success, at length died a peaceful and generally unlamented death, as did hundreds of other canal projects launched throughout the eastern United States with similar fanfare. Yet, according to Woods, Albemarle's infatuation with water transport, like its longstanding love affair with tobacco, continued to defy reality and lingered on. In the final decades of the nineteenth century, he writes, still another attempt was made to exploit the Rivanna. Dams were built near Milton and Shadwell, but both soon were washed out by floodwaters, and "the whole matter" was finally dropped.[8]

[7] Two recent works have examined closely the growth and development of the Scottsville community. See Virginia Moore's delightful "informal" history which encompasses more than two centuries of local life, *Scottsville on the James* (Charlottesville, 1969), and Karl Hess, "Four Decades of Social Change: Scottsville, Virginia, 1820–1860" (M.A. thesis, University of Virginia, 1973).

[8] Edgar Woods, p. 85.

These spasmodic efforts which continued for nearly a century appear, in retrospect, to have been completely unnecessary. Much of the county had easy access to the waters of the James and the canal developed along its banks, each decade brought improvements in land transport, and after the 1830s prospects of rail communication brightened with each passing year. This was, in truth, an exercise in frustration. If all of the money dumped into the waters of the Rivanna had been used to macadamize old Three Notched or construct a turnpike south to Scottsville (admittedly a proposal abhorrent to Charlottesville merchants), county residents would have been much better served. Instead, this will-o'-the-wisp drained off both coin and energy that a rural community could ill afford to squander.

The first rail line to inch its way into Albemarle County was that of the Louisa Railroad Company, better known as the Virginia Central and now part of the Chesapeake and Ohio. In the late 1840s, aided by the sturdy muscles of several hundred Irish immigrants, tracks started west from Gordonsville; and by August 14, 1848, a fourteen-mile stretch was open to Cobham Depot. Within five months another seven miles had been added. By November 1850 trains were steaming into Charlottesville on schedule, and much of the grading required was completed as far as Woodville, eight miles to the west.[9] The first station agents were A. J. Bell at Cobham, E. J. Timberlake at Shadwell, and James Minor at the county seat. By October 1852 trains could go as far as Mechum's River, and the Woodville agent reported receiving three times as much Valley freight as Charlottesville handled the previous year. Two years later the first train cautiously made its way over temporary tracks, up one side of the Blue Ridge and down the other, and the Piedmont and Valley were joined.

Meanwhile the Blue Ridge Railroad Company, an organization financed entirely by the commonwealth, was busy burrowing through mountain rock. On April 13, 1858, appropriately the anniversary of Thomas Jefferson's birth, the first Virginia Central train made its way through four tunnels and emerged triumphantly into the Valley. These engineering marvels, constructed largely under the direction of Claudius Crozet, represented years of careful planning and extremely hard work.

By April 1860 east-west "Mail" trains carrying first- and second-class passengers traveled along this line each day. Accommodations

[9] For details of rail construction during these years, see N. B. Jones, "Charlottesville and Albemarle," pp. 172–78.

for both classes were identical, but at fueling points those in first class could watch in elegant leisure as second-class customers helped load wood. The westbound flyer from Gordonsville arrived in Charlottesville at 8:45 A.M. and departed five minutes later. The train from Staunton was due at 11:45 A.M. and left at noon. Freight trains went east on Monday, Wednesday, and Friday; west, on Tuesday, Thursday, and Saturday. After 1852 Charlottesville also was served by the Orange and Alexandria line, utilizing Virginia Central tracks as far as Gordonsville. In 1855 this company commenced work on tracks linking Charlottesville and Lynchburg, and four years later executives said trains soon would be moving along its entire length. Scottsville, as noted earlier, had to wait some twenty more years before the first steam engine appeared there. The economic benefits of these railroads to much of Albemarle are almost too numerous to mention. Above all else, they provided a reliable, constant, all-weather means of communication with the rest of the Old Dominion and most parts of the nation. No longer did one have to worry about rains, floods, mud, or snow; and for all practical purposes, Charlottesville had triumphed over its rival on the banks of the James, just as rail had bested water.

Hidden deep within this exciting drama of railroad building is a social phenomenon on the local scene, difficult to evaluate but nonetheless very intriguing. For the first time in its long history, except for that brief confrontation with Hessian and British prisoners during the Revolutionary War, Albemarle (and especially Charlottesville) came face to face with a substantial foreign element. The 1850 census indicates the county seat then had 1,890 residents; Scottsville, 666. Suddenly injected into the midst of a people overwhelmingly of native birth were nearly 300 Irish railroad workers, undoubtedly a boisterous group, overwhelmingly Catholic, hard-drinking, probably scornful of regional customs and traditions, and many of them attractive, hell-for-leather bachelors. In that year, out of a total population of 25,000, slightly more than 50 percent black, only 213 county residents had been born in states other than Virginia and 363 in foreign countries. Of that number, 289 were Irish. Some of these workmen boarded in various homes, but more than half (179) appear to have been living in huge, dormitorylike structures—94 at one address and 54 at another. By 1860 most of these individuals had followed the railroad tracks west, but by no means all of them. In that year Albemarle still had 102 sons of the "old sod" within its borders, more than double the number of immigrants from any other country. However, war decimated this incipient Gaelic colony, and by 1870 the

Irish element was insignificant, giving way to German-born residents who always clung tenaciously to second place among the county's tiny immigrant population during these mid-nineteenth-century decades.

Despite this interesting but short-lived Irish invasion, Albemarle entered the Civil War with a population overwhelmingly of native birth, American and Virginian to boot. In 1860, in addition to those 102 Irishmen, there were 51 Germans, 28 Englishmen, 9 Welshmen, and a handful of individuals from such countries as Austria, France, Italy, and Persia. The only states represented by more than 30 former citizens were Maryland (38), New York (36), and Pennsylvania (31). The import of these figures is, of course, crystal clear. Outward migration during the first half of the nineteenth century was considerable and in no way was balanced by any counterflow of humanity. And, as civil strife loomed, Albemarle had little reason to fear subversive activity within its bosom from whites of northern or foreign birth. Yet there always were some slaves not content with their lot, and according to Woods, a certain uneasiness crept through the countryside in the late 1850s.[10] A man named Rood was arraigned in 1859 but subsequently acquitted of "conspiring against the southern people and endangering the safety and perpetuity of the Union," and wild rumors of black revolt, both planned and thwarted, circulated freely. Patrols made the rounds of various neighborhoods with greater frequency and new vigilance. One sedate matron was charged with permitting her slave "to hire himself out according to his own pleasure," an indictment which in normal times would have been thought ridiculous. Sadly, the times were not normal, and the telegraph, the daily "Mail" train, and all of the other innovations which Albemarle embraced so enthusiastically brought in their wake not only commerce but ideas as well. As a result, despite considerable evidence that its population was extremely homogeneous, on the eve of war the county seems to have been swept by the same fears and hopes that engulfed much of a nervous South. That "fuss" so deplored by Judith Rives was about to overwhelm Albemarle and its people with all of its fury.

[10] Edgar Woods, p. 116.

Chapter 11

Albemarle in the Civil War

HE experiences of the citizens of Albemarle during the tragic four-year conflict which almost split the American nation asunder are strongly reminiscent of those of their grandparents eight decades earlier during another traumatic conflict. As in the 1770s, county residents appear to have been generally united in a cause they thought right, and hundreds of their sons marched away to do battle; but again, on the local scene, home front activity loomed much larger than actual warfare. Some individuals raised badly needed foodstuffs, others cared for sick and wounded, and numerous facilities were converted to wartime needs. Benjamin H. Magruder, a member of the House of Delegates from Albemarle (1857–65), was instrumental, for example, in getting state authorities to take over the production of salt, a vital commodity in the midst of war. Face-to-face confrontation with the enemy was rare, and as a result, today Albemarle's highways boast far fewer of those familiar black and silver Civil War markers than can be found in other parts of the Old Dominion.

To a great extent, geography, as in the days of the Revolution, protected the county from the ravages of invasion, at least until the last years of the conflict. Instead, Albemarle was inundated from time to time by hundreds of wounded evacuated from battlefields to the north and scores of refugees from areas overrun by the enemy. On occasions, these incursions proved almost as disruptive as actual invasion might have been. University authorities were especially incensed by what they considered to be rather high-handed usurpation of their buildings and grounds by both military and civilian personnel. Most of the fighting within Virginia involved efforts by the North to reach the Confederate capital at Richmond and counterdrives by southern armies to relieve this pressure or threaten Washington itself. In the east, the principal routes of the invader were either directly overland or by sea and river. To the west, Confederate defenders, notably Stonewall Jackson, repeatedly used the Valley to frustrate the carefully laid plans of Yankee generals. Albemarle, lying at the base of this huge triangle of Valley, Richmond, and Washington and not yet a prime rail center, had little reason to fear enemy activity until Phil Sheridan scorched the Valley late in 1864 and a few months later launched his successful drive from the west. Then the county lay directly (and virtually defenseless) in his path.

The political furor that preceded the outbreak of hostilities, naturally enough, was felt strongly throughout Albemarle. Voters of the 1850s appear to have been about equally divided between Democrat and Whig loyalties, with Whigs somewhat more potent much of the time. In 1856, for example, James Buchanan (Democrat) carried the county by only 62 votes, but three years later that party's nominee for governor received 931 votes compared to 1,303 for the Whig nominee. In 1860, as far as Albemarle was concerned, the race for the White House was between John Bell, the Constitutional Union standard-bearer who enjoyed Whig support, and John C. Breckinridge, Buchanan's vice-president and spokesman for the southern wing of the Democratic party. Shelton Leake, a Democrat and the county's man in the House of Representatives, alarmed as he watched his party split apart, at first suggested that a special state convention should choose between Stephen A. Douglas of Illinois (presidential candidate of the northern Democrats) and Breckinridge; but, after the North-South rupture became complete, he campaigned vigorously for Breckinridge, the proud Kentuckian who eventually became a Confederate general and a member of the Davis cabinet. A visit to Albemarle by William L. Yancey, "prince of the Fire Eaters," in October 1860 aroused considerable animosity in some circles. The fiery words of this Alabama agitator, the real power behind the candidacy of Breckinridge, depicted the horrors Albemarle would experience under the administration of Abraham Lincoln, the Republican leader, and brought prompt rebuttal from the editors of the Charlottesville *Review*, Green Peyton and J. C. Southall. This weekly favored fighting the man from Illinois within the Union, even if he won. Domination by the North was not permanent, they vowed; and, there were vast differences, they added, between mere political irritation and the imaginary tyranny so eloquently described by Yancey. In a special edition published on election eve, voters were forcefully reminded that a vote for Breckinridge was actually a vote for secession.

Judged by this yardstick, Albemarle County did not favor secession.[1] Bell carried virtually every precinct, capturing 1,317 votes. Breckinridge was second with 1,056. The only polling places where the vice-president prevailed were Earlysville, North Garden, Porter's,

---

[1] See N. B. Jones, "Charlottesville and Albemarle," pp. 212–16, for an account of this election and its impact upon the local scene.

Wingfield's, and Batesville, where he ran especially strong and outdrew Bell, 113 to 31. Bell carried Charlottesville 337 to 240 and Scottsville 173 to 71. Douglas received 97 votes, 45 of them in Charlottesville and 19 in Howardsville, where he displayed unusual strength. In Albemarle the tempestuous presidential election of 1860 was not a four-way affair. No one voted for the winner, "Honest Abe"; yet he did receive nearly 2,000 votes from Old Dominion residents living in Norfolk, communities near Washington, and western counties. Returns from the state as a whole reflect the same pattern found in Albemarle, although Bell carried Virginia by a razor-thin margin, only 322 votes.

Although no one in Albemarle voted for Lincoln, this does not mean he failed to enjoy a smattering of support. Writing several decades later, R. T. W. Duke, Jr., only seven years of age in 1860, recalled those tempestuous days: "My father had been a Whig up to the days of the Know Nothings. Then he became a Democrat and voted for Breckinridge and Lane. I had a United States flag with their names on it, and also a severe combat with the Norris boys who were Bell and Everett men and had a flag with their names on it. Lincoln's name was never mentioned, but was ridiculed. Outside of the Town Hall (Levy Opera House now) was an ingenious caricature representing him splitting rails. I recall the voting. One man, old [T. W.] Savage, I believe, wanted to vote for Lincoln's election, but the clerks wouldn't cry his vote." [2] According to Duke, no Republican tickets had been printed in Albemarle, and no one knew who the electors were. When voting, one wrote his name on the back of a ticket listing a party's electors. This was handed to a clerk who "cried out" the vote for all to hear while someone else wrote down the essential information. Savage, he noted, was "hooted in fine style as he left the Court House."

On December 21, 1860, the *Review* expressed the belief that the victorious Republicans would yield to southern demands if "only a little time and a decent opportunity is afforded them." Rather than be sacrificed to the caprice of South Carolina and men like Yancey, the editors felt border states should stand firm. This same view was echoed by William C. Rives, the county's elder statesman. After listing various southern grievances in a letter to the *Review*, Rives maintained it still was possible for the South to gain assurances that its

[2] Quoted, with permission, from Judge Duke's diaries in the possession of Miss Helen Duke, Charlottesville. Some excerpts have been printed in *MACH:* see volume 3 (1943):33–55, and volume 22 (1964):157–58.

interests would be protected. "If these securities be demanded with calm and dignified but inflexible firmness—not with bluster and denunciation—I cannot doubt," he wrote, "that they will be yielded by a large majority, if not by all, of our co-states."

But, as we know, despite great exertions upon his part, these last-ditch hopes of the master of Castle Hill were doomed to disappointment. In January 1861 he met in Washington with former president John Tyler and others at a national Peace Convention which attempted to find grounds for compromise. Ominously, this group included no spokesman from seven states already out of the Union. These men, described by Bruce Catton as "distinguished Americans, but elderly, a little tired, and shopworn," [3] accomplished nothing. A month later Rives reluctantly agreed to represent his community at yet another so-called Peace Convention, this one a statewide conclave in Richmond. There he continued efforts to find some way out of the dilemma facing his county, state, and nation; but with Lincoln's call for troops following the fall of Fort Sumter, there was no way out. On April 17, 1861, by a wide margin, the men in Richmond simply repealed Virginia's ratification of the U.S. Constitution, making the Old Dominion an independent state once more and free to join the southern Confederacy. They based their action upon a claim that when forming the Union in the 1780s, Virginians had reserved the right to withdraw if policies of the federal government ever endangered their freedoms. They now were exercising that right. The Richmond convention stipulated that this decision was to be submitted to the voters, and on May 25, by a majority of nearly six to one, the electorate concurred.

This actually was an after-the-fact decision which meant little since war was already in progress and Virginia, for all practical purposes, was divided into Union and Confederate sectors; yet one gets the impression that Albemarle, like William Cabell Rives, did not embark down this new path without some misgivings. As Virginius Dabney notes in *Virginia: The New Dominion*, slavery actually was the root of the trouble and Virginia certainly was not about to risk everything for the sole purpose of preserving "a discredited institution." "In the final analysis," he writes, "Virginia simply was driven against her will to seek independence." [4] President Abraham Lincoln's appeal to Virginia for troops to suppress rebellion in sister states to the south was asking too much.

[3] Catton, *The Coming Fury* (Garden City, N.Y., 1961), p. 23.
[4] Garden City, N.Y., 1971, p. 299.

Yet, even if Albemarle's enthusiasm for the Confederate cause was tempered by sober realities, extreme secessionist fervor was evident in some parts of the community. Young people, especially the university's student body, were caught up in a heady wave of excitement long before any shells exploded over Charleston Harbor. In the fall of 1860 only seven of about six hundred students came from "free" states, and in October, by a vote of 33 to 6 members of the Washington Society decided the South should secede if Lincoln was elected. A few days later the Jefferson Society agreed. Following Abe Lincoln's victory at the polls, the faculty lifted a long-standing ban on student military companies; and within a short time, the harsh sounds of drill commands were heard throughout the grounds as the Sons of Liberty and the Southern Guards prepared for war.

On the night of February 25, 1861, a group of students decided to erect a Confederate flag atop the Rotunda. According to R. C. M. Page, one of the ringleaders, this was an attempt to beat to the punch some residents of Dawson's Row who were having an expensive silk banner made by local ladies and planned to unfurl it within a few days. To erect this flag, a hastily contrived standard, these youths had to break into the building by removing a door panel and make their way to the roof. The chairman of the faculty, not amused, issued an order the next day that if the flag was removed at once by those who installed it, there would be no punishment, and it quickly disappeared. Writing in *Corks and Curls* in 1890, Page agreed that such conduct was "utterly reprehensible." [5]

On the evening of April 17, seven weeks later, 140 members of the Sons of Liberty and the Southern Guards, fired with excitement, boarded an Orange and Alexandria train bound for Manassas Junction. With them were two local militia companies dressed in colorful, even elaborate, uniforms, the Monticello Guard and the Albemarle Rifles. Many of these tunics and trousers had been fashioned in Charlottesville's Town Hall, which, according to R. T. W. Duke, Jr., for a time became "a gigantic tailor shop & every tailor in town was there cutting out gray uniforms whilst the ladies basted them & sewing women sewed them up." Although some of the university students later joined units in their native counties or states, by mid-June many of the men making this journey were part of the Nineteenth Virginia Regiment, Albemarle's major contribution to the military arm of the

[5] See his account of this incident reproduced in *MACH* 22 (1964):14–16. This special Civil War issue contains fifteen articles relating to the local scene, 1861–65.

Confederacy.[6] This regiment was composed of ten companies in all, each averaging about eighty-three men. Its members, actually from three counties (Albemarle, Nelson, and Amherst), included units from five local communities which supplied the bulk of this man-power—Charlottesville, Scottsville, Howardsville, Stony Point, and Hillsboro. Most of these men were in their early twenties, more than half of them farm-born, although two Charlottesville companies were composed almost exclusively of laborers, carpenters, mechanics, machinists, and a handful of students, teachers, and lawyers.

That original group which set out in the darkness of April 17 has a unique place in the annals of American military history. Those young men hardly could have wished for a more romantic introduction to warfare, cloaked as their venture was in intrigue, deception, and secrecy. Several days earlier, while Virginia's leaders debated secession, a youthful captain from Staunton, John D. Imboden, foreseeing that war was inevitable, convinced the governor that it would be possible to transport several military units by rail on a mission of extreme importance.[7] What Imboden had in mind was seizure of the vital federal arsenal at Harper's Ferry. On the morning of April 18 those young men from Albemarle, tired, sleepless, and their finery somewhat rumpled, steamed into Manassas Junction, where they joined other excited Virginians and soon were off on the Manassas Gap line toward Strasburg. To deceive federal officials, authorities in Richmond telegraphed that the train was bound for the Portsmouth Navy Yard. A short distance from Manassas the cars ground to an abrupt halt when a Unionist in the engine crew discovered the true destination. Imboden rushed forward and, with the aid of his revolver, persuaded the man that the journey should be continued at once. Although the federal detachment at Harper's Ferry destroyed considerable matériel before fleeing in the face of this attacking force, the mission was generally successful; and the captain from Staunton proved his point, one which was not lost upon leaders of either the North or the South: with a minimum of tactical planning, men could be moved easily by rail behind the lines in time of war.

During the months between that exciting foray to Harper's Ferry and the first Battle of Manassas (or Bull Run) in mid-July 1861, these men and others from Albemarle underwent intensive training,

[6] Herbert A. Thomas, Jr., "The 19th Virginia Regiment, 1861–1865," *MACH* 25 (1967):5–35.

[7] George Edgar Turner, *Victory Rode the Rails: The Strategic Importance of the Railroads in the Civil War* (Indianapolis, 1953), pp. 15–18.

although for many war was still something of a grand adventure. The Howardsville Grays, for example, remained at home for several weeks engaging in drill, military exercises, and sports. In early May they moved to the outskirts of Charlottesville, where officers and men of various companies mingled together amid white tents and in a congenial, relaxed atmosphere which one observer thought "presented the spectacle of a holiday picnic party, or the brilliancy and gayety of a bazaar or agricultural fair." [8] Songs at night and patriotic speeches during the day eased nerves and increased enthusiasm. Although the familiar gray frock coat became standard uniform, equipment varied greatly from unit to unit, some tents, clothing, and knapsacks being supplied by enthusiastic Charlottesville ladies.

On June 1, 1861, these companies were officially designated as the Nineteenth Virginia under the command of Colonel Philip St. George Cocke. Cocke, a West Point graduate and wealthy Powhatan County planter, actually had very little to do with his men, the task of command falling instead upon the able shoulders of Lieutenant Colonel John Bowie Strange. Cocke, whom one contemporary described as "evidently oblivious to his surroundings, the expression of his eye not normal," committed suicide in December 1861. Strange, a graduate of Virginia Military Institute and founder of Albemarle Military Academy, proved to be a very able leader until mortally wounded during the Antietam campaign at Boonsboro, Maryland, in September 1862. His mantle was assumed by Colonel Henry Gantt, who led the regiment throughout the remainder of the war.

By the second week of June 1861, ready or not, the men of the Nineteenth either were at Manassas Junction or were preparing to leave for that vital northern Virginia rail center. Joseph A. Higginbotham recorded in his diary that as his unit departed from Charlottesville, the men were "all in fine spirits hooping and hullowing on there way and waving their hats and hankerchiefs." [9] Within a short time the Albemarle detachment was quartered at Camp Strange near Centreville, where training and surveillance increased markedly. Strange, who often tested the alertness of his sentries, once was rebuffed as he tried to enter camp late at night and found himself temporarily under arrest. Eventually, however, his identity was established by a guard detail which obviously enjoyed this altercation, and Lieutenant Colonel Strange was permitted to go to bed.

One of the Nineteenth's proudest possessions was its regimental

[8] Thomas, p. 9.
[9] Ibid., p. 10. The spelling is Higginbotham's.

20. John Bowie Strange

21. Sarah Ann Strickler (Mrs. Robert Herndon Fife)

22. From the ladies of Charlottesville to Stuart's Horse Artillery. The flag is now hanging in Charles Town, West Virginia.

band. Soon after the "invasion" of Harper's Ferry, the Charlottesville Silver Cornet Band enlisted for twelve months and quickly won fame as one of the finest musical units in the Army of Northern Virginia. It consisted of eleven musicians, led by Band Master G. A. Teltow who played first cornet. On one occasion, Teltow, full of applejack, stormed into Strange's tent, complained bitterly of low pay, and climaxed this diatribe by calling his commanding officer "a louse." The following morning First Cornetist Teltow awoke in the guardhouse.

At Centreville, new recruits found themselves sleeping on the bare ground under planks leaned against fences which provided little protection from early summer rains. One youth was sent home after he shot and mangled his hand "acidently by himself." At the Battle of First Manassas the Nineteenth received its baptism of fire and captured a few Federal prisoners, including a baggy-trousered New York Zouave, but, because of the defensive position it was assigned to protect, suffered little. One man, George Thompson, a private in Company I, was killed instantly when struck by a stray bullet, the unit's first casualty, and several other young men discovered actual warfare to be much less appealing than they had supposed. George A. Hundley, an officer, noted in reminiscences written years later that the antics of one tall soldier artfully dodging shells caused him to "part" with a breakfast "swallowed so eagerly a short while before." [10]

After this excitement the regiment went into camp near Centreville once more, establishing a pattern of summer campaigns and winter quarters which continued for four long, hard years. Their camp, at first merely a collection of tents, soon grew into log cabins and even some clapboarded structures surrounded by picket posts and breastworks. Negroes helping to construct these fortifications, one youth noted, "are paid the same as Privates $11 per month." Some men spent their idle hours at ball games, gambling, wrestling "at $15 a side," or drinking whiskey. Others read, played chess, and attended evening worship services. Each company was divided into mess units of about eight men, and discipline seems to have been good at all times. Sickness, the bane of all armies, appeared in the form of mumps, measles, whooping cough, typhoid fever, and "yaller jaundice." In February 1862, a bitterly cold month, most enlistments expired; and despite numerous incentives, only 140 men of the Nineteenth agreed to remain. One sergeant observed tartly that more

[10] Ibid., p. 13.

would have stayed except "for their being mistreated." [11] Yet within a few weeks the vacant places were filled, and the regiment regained much of its former strength.

Early in March these men, both veterans and raw recruits, suddenly packed up and headed south to Orange Courthouse and from there went to Richmond where they boarded vessels bound for Yorktown. On May 3 they were in the thick of the Battle of Williamsburg, and in one sharp exchange charged Federal positions and captured some two hundred enemy troops and several heavy guns. After Williamsburg the Nineteenth performed well on numerous now-famous battlefields, among them Seven Pines, Gaines Mill, Boonsboro, Antietam, and Gettysburg, where some 60 percent of those who fought were wounded or killed. According to Herbert Thomas, "The Battle of Gettysburg was both the high point and the low point of the 19th Virginia's career. All their previous battles were only preludes to this, their largest engagement. The casualty figures attest not only to the overwhelming fire of the Federals, but also to the courage of the regiment. The men retreated only when it became suicidal to move forward; they were soundly defeated. From this point onward, the 19th Virginia saw little action." [12]

In his assessment of the Nineteenth, Thomas maintains that these soldiers of Albemarle fought well when called upon to do so and established a record of solid achievement. Both spirit and discipline were generally good, despite one execution for desertion en route to Gettysburg, very short rations at times (the men once found a cat to be inedible even after boiling it for two days), and all the discomforts and frustrations inherent in both war and defeat. He credits much of this success to John Bowie Strange, the man who for some fifteen months provided sound, sensible leadership and established an esprit de corps which kept the regiment together throughout most of the years of war after his tragic death.

The Nineteenth spent the final months of the conflict in trenches near Chester Station, about halfway between Richmond and Petersburg. Weakened by casualties and disease, they watched as Grant's forces waited only about 150 yards away. Where the opposing lines disappeared into woods, pickets and sentries often exchanged words and even coffee or tobacco. Now and then a quick foray produced a prisoner or so, but relations between the two armies remained reasonably friendly. Settled camp life produced a church, a Masonic lodge, and time for furloughs and sports. In March 1865 the remain-

[11] Ibid., p. 19. [12] Ibid., p. 31.

ing men, weak and tired, began the withdrawal toward Appomattox. On April 6 they halted on a hill overlooking Sayler's Creek and prepared to parch some corn. Before they could eat this crude meal the enemy appeared, and all twenty-nine men surrendered. The exciting experiment launched so jauntily in the festive camps on the outskirts of Charlottesville in the spring of 1861 thus came to its sad end.

In Albemarle the effects of the Civil War, while felt in every household from the mountain coves of the Blue Ridge to the banks of the James, were most evident in the community of Charlottesville and at the nearby university. Enrollment dwindled as scores of young men left for the front; but each autumn, despite fears that classes would not be held, fifty or sixty students—some very young and others maimed veterans—gathered for lectures. Among those attending the 1861–62 session was Robert E. Lee, Jr., who formed yet another student military company and, before the school year closed, departed to enlist. Some of the professors also donned uniforms or summered in Confederate gray between terms. In the spring of 1864 a disabled veteran enrolled at the university lured seven excited fifteen-year-olds off to Spotsylvania Courthouse where they campaigned for a week or so before returning to their studies. The appearance of Sheridan's army in March 1865 closed the university for a few days, but classes soon were resumed. One student even was granted special permission to complete a Latin exam "interrupted by the approach of the enemy."

In contrast to most southern institutions of learning, the University of Virginia continued to function in a relatively normal manner. Classes met, lectures were given, examinations were held, and the faculty and students carried on as best they could amid numerous disruptions and distractions. At times, as hundreds of wounded and civilian refugees filled buildings and classrooms and often treated university property in a rather cavalier fashion, it seemed that the institution might suffer somewhat more from thoughtless actions by its friends than from any depredation by the enemy. Yet Mr. Jefferson's school survived mainly because of the firm dedication of a few stalwart educators such as John Barbee Minor, William Holmes McGuffey, and Socrates Maupin. They realized that regardless of their individual views concerning secession, win or lose, the South would need trained leaders when peace came. It was their duty, as they saw it, to nurture and stimulate that leadership. In the fall of 1865 that faith was rewarded when 258 students appeared, less than half the number enrolled five years earlier, but nevertheless a most gratifying indication that the University of Virginia had withstood the upheaval of war and remained a vigorous, stable seat of learning.

While the university struggled along through these very difficult years, citizens from all walks of life did whatever they could to aid the Confederate cause. Men too old for service organized home guard units. Women became temporary nurses, rolled bandages, spun wool, and made uniforms and other badly needed military equipment. When gray dye was no longer available for frock coats and trousers, they resorted to butternut juice. County authorities tackled such problems as procuring salt, preventing the spread of smallpox, and rounding up provisions, horses, forage, and blankets. They sometimes drafted family servants (at $3 per day) to help build fortifications, and many able-bodied males were pressed into similar service by the state. Families of indigent soldiers in the Charlottesville area were objects of special concern. Local officials supplied these households with firewood and often paid their rent as well. The few industries located in the community also turned their attention to the demands of war, the woolen mills producing cloth for uniforms and blankets and a Shadwell rail facility becoming a major engine repair shop.

A letter appearing in the Lynchburg *Daily Republican* on April 25, 1862, described still more home front activity. According to the local correspondent ("Monticello"), a scrap metal drive was enjoying huge success. All of Charlottesville's five churches had agreed to contribute their bells, estimated to weigh some three thousand pounds, and scores of individuals had donated "hand-bells, fire fenders, candlesticks, preserving kettles, boilers, curtain rings, &c—one lady sending in her engraved card-plates." [13] Another artillery company was to leave for Richmond within a few days. "I have understood that two other artillery companies have recently been formed in the county," this reporter boasted, "which would make twenty volunteer companies from Albemarle, Va, 5 artillery, 2 cavalry, 2 rifle, and 11 infantry." He also told of local sales of condemned government horses, "some bringing over $150 each." Put to pasture in rolling Piedmont fields, these limping nags soon would be "fat, sleek, and young again."

However, despite these far-flung efforts—collecting scrap metal, raising military companies, and providing a great variety of war matériel from forage to blankets—Albemarle's prominence as a medical center was by far its most important contribution to the welfare of the Confederacy, especially during the first two years of the war.

[13] This letter is reproduced in *MACH*, 10 (1950):28–30. Since the town's church bells tolled in mourning for Stonewall Jackson a year later, it would appear they never actually were melted into cannon.

Designated as the Charlottesville General Hospital, this facility seems to have grown in a rather unplanned fashion within hours of the first encounter at Bull Run. With hundreds of wounded men flowing into Manassas, Culpeper, and other communities to the north, trainloads of soldiers in need of immediate attention arrived at the local depot, and those disabled in battle soon were filling up the Rotunda, classrooms, hotels, boarding schools, even private homes, the courthouse, and the Town Hall.[14]

By late August 1861 the Richmond *Examiner* stated that the Charlottesville community was now "a vast hospital for the sick and wounded of our army." This semiweekly had high praise for the manner in which hundreds of local citizens opened their homes to receive soldiers and were helping them on the road to recovery. Ten months later, following fighting near Port Republic in the Valley, the university once more was host to nearly fourteen hundred wounded. However, neither army officers nor university officials were completely happy with these impromptu arrangements. The faculty feared their institution might be converted completely to medical needs, thus ending all classroom activity; and according to some reports, mortality rates were higher among wounded treated there and in various private homes than among soldiers consigned to tents under military care.

Even before this "invasion" of wounded from Port Republic, several permanent hospital centers had developed. These included Delevan, located near the present Southern Railway station, Midway on Ridge Street, and Monticello House on Market Street. The Delevan building had been a hotel, boys' boarding school, and briefly a barracks for troops. Long wooden buildings were built on both sides of the structure to care for the wounded as they arrived from the front. This structure was sometimes called "Mudwall" since the original building was surrounded by a wall of clay. Midway, also a veteran of hotel and boarding school days, was, in time, replaced by the familiar Midway School of more recent decades. The Monticello House, part of which was known as the Old Stone Tavern, was destroyed by fire in 1862; although it was filled with soldiers, no lives were lost.

According to records in the National Archives, approximately 22,700 individuals were admitted to these various facilities, both permanent and temporary, in 1861–65. An analysis by Chalmers Gemmill of 124 selected cases during the first year of the war indicates that

[14] See Chalmers L. Gemmill, "The Charlottesville General Hospital, 1861–1865," *MACH* 22 (1964):91–160.

only about 10 percent were suffering from wounds; instead, pneumonia, measles, rheumatism, and especially typhoid fever exacted a heavy toll. During the entire conflict the Charlottesville General Hospital admitted 5,391 soldiers with gunshot wounds. Of these, 270 later died. The university's medical school faculty, as well as various students and many town and county residents, helped care for this continuing wave of patients, and Thomas Harris Brown of Brown's Cove reportedly outfitted many disabled veterans with artificial limbs while they convalesced at his farm, now known as the Headquarters.

Letters written by soldiers are full of high praise for the treatment they received. R. W. Barnwell, Jr., a South Carolinian, commented in August 1861 that his ward in the Midway Hospital was neatly outfitted with furniture, dressing gowns, slippers, and "even a vase of flowers." Fresh mountain butter and rich milk were readily available, but Barnwell conceded that flannel undershirts, socks, drawers, and brandy (badly needed to combat typhoid fever, he added) were in short supply. Judge R. T. W. Duke, Jr., a small boy in the 1860s, later recalled visits to these hospitals.

I went to them very often with my mother. Nurses were very scarce & the ladies in the town each in turn helped to nurse. My mother had her regular turn and occasionally I went with her. She always carried some delicacy and went from couch to couch a very "ministratering angel." I remember seeing her wipe the death sweat from a handsome young fellow, who murmured "Mother" and gazed at her with dim eyes as he died. I recall car-loads of wounded unloaded and figures of men, desparate-wounded carried on stretchers into the wards from the cars. I remember seeing a great heap of arms and legs outside a ward soon after Second Manassas and was fearfully shocked at the indifferent way in which a severed leg or arm was tossed on the heap by the surgeon.

We were hard pressed for Hospitals early in the War. At one time I remember seeing the Chapel . . . and the old Public Hall . . . of the University filled with wounded men lying on pallets on the floor. Some of the wounded "Canvalesced" at Morea. . . . One was a Texan by whom I saw the first cigarettes made. He used the tender inside of the corn shuck instead of paper & I took great pride in getting the shuck for him and cutting it into proper length.[15]

Joseph Jones, a Georgia-born expert on diseases and a major in the Confederate surgeon general's department, toured the local hospitals in September 1863 and after a week's visit departed "highly pleased" with both the facilities and treatment he found there. His overall

[15] Ibid., p. 158.

summary, completed after the war ended, reveals that between July 1861 and February 1865 the Charlottesville General Hospital admitted 21,540 cases. Many of the soldiers were suffering from typhoid, malaria, diarrhea, dysentery, pneumonia, and measles, although two-thirds were victims of gunshot wounds (5,337) and "other diseases" (9,764). Only 5.2 percent (1,123) died; in other words, there was one death in every 19.2 cases during months which encompass virtually the entire war.[16]

It is apparent that though Charlottesville General Hospital was the center of all this wartime medical activity, the wounded (including occasional Yankee prisoners) sometimes were lodged in other structures such as Scottsville's Baptist Church, and those recovering from both battle injury and disease were housed in numerous private homes throughout the county, among them Morea and the Headquarters. Chalmers Gemmill bemoans the fact that historians have paid little attention to this very important contribution of Albemarle citizens to the Confederacy and notes that it is remembered today by no memorial marker in either the town or the university. Admittedly, it was a diverse, almost indefinable operation lacking clear geographical boundaries and ministering to a constantly changing volume of patients, at times thousands, sometimes a mere handful, depending upon the vagaries of warfare. Most of the buildings used have since disappeared. The Charlottesville General Hospital's true memorial lies instead in the satisfaction of a community enterprise accomplished despite innumerable difficulties and in the sincere thanks of hundreds of boys in gray who were nursed back to health amid pleasant surroundings, whether housed briefly in public structures such as the Rotunda or in private homes.

Military operations within Albemarle County, as noted, were extremely limited. Thousands of troops, boys from Tennessee, Alabama, and other states, passed through the community from time to time, but the sound of gunfire was rare indeed. In the late spring of 1862 Stonewall Jackson and his men appeared in the western fringes of the county on several occasions as they maneuvered to outsmart superior enemy forces during the renowned Valley Campaign. Early in May they slipped down through Brown's Gap to Mechum's River where they clambered aboard Virginia Central cars bound for Staun-

[16] James O. Breeden, "Insights into the Medical Statistics of the Charlottesville General Hospital, 1861–1865," *MACH* 30 (1972):43–59. Statistics gathered by Jones and quoted by Breeden differ slightly from those of Gemmill since they cover a somewhat briefer period.

ton and the Battle of McDowell on May 8. A month later, following further successes at Cross Keys and Port Republic, these now celebrated troops rested at Brown's Gap for a week or so before again marching to Mechum's River and boarding another train, this time heading east to Richmond, where they helped halt McClellan's push toward the Confederate capital.[17]

Then, nearly two years later, on February 29, 1864, a minor skirmish occurred a few miles north of Charlottesville at Rio Hill. According to James O. Moore, this was the "nearest approach to a Civil War battle in Albemarle County." [18] Confederate and Union records tell conflicting stories; but, in essence, Brigadier General George A. Custer, the man famed for his yellow locks and later demise at Little Big Horn, was sent south through Culpeper and Madison with some fifteen hundred men. His goal was twofold: to destroy the railway bridge over the Rivanna at Charlottesville and to create a diversion while a stronger Union force swept toward Richmond in another lightning raid. At about 8:15 A.M. on the morning of the twenty-ninth, blue-clad troops encountered Confederate pickets near Stanardsville, alerting the defenders that the enemy was advancing.

For reasons far from clear, a small southern detachment in winter quarters located in the woods near the Rio Mills on the Charlottesville-Earlysville road received only an hour's warning. These men, four batteries of Major General Jeb Stuart's Horse Artillery Battalion, were under the temporary command of Captain Marcellus N. Moorman. The Confederates immediately evacuated their log cabins and took up positions below the wooden bridge crossing the South Fork of the Rivanna at that point. Custer's men reached the area at about 1:30 P.M., wreaked considerable damage upon the abandoned camp, and destroyed the bridge and the nearby mill, but then retreated without reaching either Charlottesville or its vital railway span.

Moorman reported that Union troops became confused and in one exchange fired upon each other. Custer said he withdrew because he thought Major General Jubal Early's infantry were nearby. Alfred R. Waud, a well-known artist and the only northern civilian to accompany the invaders, told a somewhat different tale in *Harper's Weekly*

[17] During these marches Jackson's army used a well-known turnpike established by the General Assembly in 1800, the so-called Brown's Gap Road, which was closed in the 1930s by creation of the Shenandoah National Park. Subsequent efforts to reopen this highway as a tourist attraction have failed.

[18] See Moore, "Custer's Raid into Albemarle County: The Skirmish at Rio Hill, February 29, 1864," *Virginia Magazine of History and Biography* 79 (1971):338–48.

(March 26, 1864). He described how the Union forces left Rapidan soon after midnight, seizing both men and horses to prevent bushwacking and assure secrecy as they advanced. At Stanardsville, he said, the whole town turned out "as if it were a show got up for their amusement. The men were exceedingly disgusted when they found they had to accompany the column as temporary prisoners." Waud, whose account was illustrated by several drawings, claimed that as soon as fighting developed, "train after train came up from Gordonsville with troops." He told readers of *Harper's* that the Yankees had only "two little guns" and, since they were being shelled "in a random way by the enemy's artillery," were forced to withdraw.

In any case, this raid, deep within enemy-held territory, was only partially successful. One Yankee was wounded, and the Confederates lost two men, seven horses, and two mules. That evening Moorman's troops slept some four miles south of Charlottesville on the Scottsville Road, but they returned to their quarters the following day. It would appear that neither army garnered much glory from this very brief encounter. Both Custer and Moorman received faulty intelligence during these crucial hours. The Confederate captain should have been told of Union movements much sooner than he was, and Custer's fears of Early's men were completely unfounded. The only force between his troops and Charlottesville was that scattered group of Confederates, greatly outnumbered, which watched from the woods as men in blue destroyed numerous facilities in and around Rio Mills; however, one must remember that these invaders were operating some fifty or sixty miles behind enemy lines, hence the need for great caution.

Within hours "Monticello" dispatched exciting accounts of "The Raid upon Charlottesville" to the Lynchburg *Republican*.[19] He reported that numerous slaves were carried off by the Yankees, "some of whom have since returned home again," and added that the "ruthless invaders" burned some fences in the Earlysville area en route to and from the battle site.

The citizens of Charlottesville and vicinity were not wanting in their efforts to meet and check the invader. All the stores were closed and their occupants armed themselves and marched to face the foe—boys, old men, Aldermen of the town, the Methodist clergymen, farmers from the country, were all animated with the same spirit; there was no unnecessary excitement or panic. While fears were entertained that the foe would come to town, yet all had determined to resist or die in the attempt. Official

[19] See John R. Brown, "The Battle of Rio Hill," *MACH* 22 (1964):23–33.

information had been given that the invaders had taken the encampment near Rio, and were marching slowly to town, the roar of cannons and the bursting of shells were heard, and the lurid blaze of burning buildings were seen by our citizens, and no man with his heart in the right place, and with proper respect for himself would taunt a whole community with being panic-striken or unduly excited.

Decades later R. T. W. Duke, Jr., recalled that he and a black friend named Caesar heard the boom of gunfire while playing in a hayloft. Within a short time Charlottesville residents became convinced that the men of Stuart's Horse Artillery had saved their community from the enemy, and considering the confusion evident on both sides on that leap-year day, perhaps they did. A group of local ladies raised $500 and presented the unit with a handsome battle flag inscribed "Our Brave Defenders." That banner, four feet by six feet, now is displayed in Charles Town, West Virginia.

A year later, almost to the day, George Armstrong Custer was back in Albemarle once more, but this time he was conducting no mere hit-and-run raid. The Federal noose was tightening about Lee's army as four years of warfare drew to a close. On March 2, 1865, General Philip H. Sheridan, the scourge of the Valley, decisively defeated Jubal Early's men near Waynesboro; and on the same day, the vanguard of his substantial force, led by Custer, second in command, swept down through Rockfish Gap, easily overrunning Brooksville and Greenwood Depot. At 4 P.M. on the third Custer entered Charlottesville, where he was met by Mayor Christopher Fowler and several prominent citizens who delivered up the keys to important public buildings.

About an hour before Custer appeared, Professors John B. Minor and Socrates Maupin, standing near the entrance to the university and prominently displaying a white flag of truce, watched nervously as the first enemy units came into view. Minor later noted in his diary what happened: "10 or 15 men approached at a gallop with their pistols in rest. The residue of the column dragging its slow length through the mud. We announced to these men, who were accompanied by a dirty-looking lieutenant, that no defense of Charlottesville was contemplated, that the town was evacuated, and that we requested protection for the University, and for the town." [20] These men replied that Custer would be along shortly, "put spurs to their horses, and rode as fast as the deep mud would permit them towards town,—we feared to plunder."

[20] Anne Freudenberg and John Casteen, eds., "John B. Minor's Civil War Diary," *MACH* 22 (1964):45-55.

The forty-eight-hour occupation which followed seems to have gone off rather smoothly, at least in Charlottesville. Guards were posted at the university, all public buildings, and many private homes. Some violence and plunder (as feared) certainly occurred, but a century later it is most difficult to sort out fact from rumor. There is little doubt that many country estates suffered considerable damage as the Yankees made their way from the slopes of the Blue Ridge to Albemarle's county seat and from there to Scottsville and neighboring river communities. Food was seized, storehouses and homes broken into, horses taken, and slaves by the hundreds joined the triumphant army. Professor Minor was especially distressed by the loss of his boy, Henry—"poor misguided creatures . . . I lament it more on his account than my own."

Sarah Ann Strickler, a nineteen-year-old student from Madison County enrolled at Albemarle Female Institute on East Jefferson Street, has left us a very graphic account of her reaction to these tempestuous days.[21] A devout Confederate partisan ("Oh! if I were only a boy, to fight them—it chafes me sorely to have to submit to their insolence"), she nevertheless found flames leaping up from stores being destroyed at the local depot "beautiful" and was thoroughly intrigued by the momentous events transpiring about her.

                                                                March 3rd
. . . They have burned part of the iron bridge, & the cotton factory there. The conflagration was magnificent, sublime, it illuminated the whole canopy of heaven, with a lurid glare. The band is now playing "no one to love," at the camp opposite us—it is pouring down rain—the men are cutting down trees, & calling to each other. The rogues say that they came here from Waynesboro. Of course no one is thinking of school, nor has been for some time.

                                                                March 4th
The Vandals did not move last night, as some of them expected. The hills & valleys are black with them; we are completely encircled. It has stopped raining, & the wind is blowing briskly. Here come about 2000 right through our yard. One is riding up to the window, I am going to speak to him . . . I said to him, "Yankee what are you going to do with these dismounted men"; "tear up the railroad," he replied. "If you live in Richmond you can go with us, we'll be there in a few days." I told him never, that if they fought 10,000,000 of years they could not conquer us. He rode away, and some of them actually waved their hats at us—Mollie and I were so incensed, that with one impulse we clenched our fists & shook them at them; we could do nothing else. . . . They have set fire

[21] Anne Freudenberg, ed., "Sheridan's Raid: An Account by Sarah A. G. Strickler," *MACH* 22 (1964):57–66.

to the other part of the iron bridge; it looks beautiful, at this distance, like a burning city in miniature. Some of our men set fire to the Rivanna bridge on the Barboursville road yesterday, but the Yankees put it out today & are going over it foraging. The camp fires look like so many beaming stars. The moon is shining brightly & it is a lovely night—the band is playing on the hill opposite; it is so sweet, like a chorus of birds, and the camp fires look like they are dancing to the musick; they are playing "old folks at home."

March 5th

Enemy are still here. I heard the bugle sounding "reveille" this morning. The band has been playing "Dixie," although it is Sunday. . . . Our guard has certainly been informed of our opinions on the war, we give to them on all occasions. The Yankees have taken several of our citizens prisoner. Two of "the crew" came through our yard today with two of our battle flags, which they had captured; when they saw us standing on the porch, they rode up close to the steps, holding up the flags & smiling trumphantly; it was so low of them. We know nothing that goes on in town.

March 6th

The barbarians commenced moving this morning about 7 o'clock; there is a rumor afloat that Gen. Longstreet was not far from here. Some of them went towards Scottsville. "Siemandel" [an Indiana soldier assigned to guard Albemarle Female Institute] did not leave, until all of the army had gotten out of sight. He amused himself yesterday by reading Schiller; just think, that ignorant dutchman can read Schiller & I cannot. Two of our maids went off with their brethren, taking two of my dresses & several skirts, together with things from other girls.

Two years later this young lady, who was severely censured by some local residents for shaking her fist at the enemy, married a Confederate veteran, Robert Herndon Fife. They settled down at Oak Lawn on the edge of Charlottesville where they raised nine children, and in time, "Sally" Fife taught herself to read Schiller every bit as well as that "ignorant dutchman."

There are, of course, numerous other accounts of these hectic days in Albemarle County history, such as official battle reports and recollections of various citizens; however, they differ only in minor detail from these on-the-spot diaries written by professor and schoolgirl.[22]

---

[22] For Sheridan's report, see *The War of the Rebellion: A Compilation of the Official Records of the Union and Confederate Armies* (Washington, D.C., 1880–1901), ser. 1, vol. 46, Pt. 1, pp. 474–81; and, on the local scene, Margaret Fowler Clark, "Facts Relating to the Surrender of Charlottesville, March 3, 1865," *MACH* 17 (1959):67–73.

It appears that Mayor Fowler may have met the enemy at Wood's Crossing some distance west of town, not in Charlottesville. Fowler's son stated many years later that Custer readily acceded to requests that the town and university be spared, emphasizing, "Now there must be no sniping at my troops." Apparently only interested in a few days' rest, he added wearily as he glanced at an aide, "I would damn well like to sleep between a pair of white sheets." This unorthodox general's wish was realized; but, whether he slept at Piedmont, the Maury family residence near Observatory Mountain, or at the Farm on East Jefferson Street, home of Captain Tom Farish, is not entirely clear.

According to letters written by the Maurys soon after the Yankees left, Custer certainly was at their home during at least part of the occupation; but since Piedmont was a mile or so from town, it is possible the general moved to a more central site as his army prepared to depart. Anyway, his presence failed to protect that historic mansion from severe damage on Sunday at the hands of "those drunken ruffians," as Nannie Maury (later Mrs. Matthew Fontaine Maury) called them in a letter to her future husband written on March 15.

After leaving Charlottesville, enemy forces marched south to the James where they wrecked the canal in the Scottsville area and put the torch to numerous subsidiary facilities such as warehouses, stores, and factories. Their advance slowed momentarily by high water, Sheridan and Custer established headquarters at Cliffside, now the home of Virginia Moore, author of *Scottsville on the James*. On March 10 the Union army moved eastward toward Columbia en route to Richmond, and Federal occupation of Albemarle came to an end.

During these weeks William Cabell Rives tried valiantly through face-to-face conferences with General Lee and various Confederate senators to construct a peace resolution which could be approved by the Confederate Congress and perhaps would stop the fighting. These unofficial efforts (Rives had been a member of the Confederate House of Representatives for a time) got nowhere. The lawmakers concluded that even if passed, this action would have little effect upon President Jefferson Davis. In mid-March they adjourned for the last time amid acrid debate with their chief executive. Within a month Grant and Lee met in the living room of a farmhouse in Appomattox Courthouse, and the agony of war was over.

Although this conflict cast a dark, uncertain shadow over both county and nation, today there are remarkably few reminders of the Civil War within Albemarle. Those who fought or experienced the travail of deprivation at home have long since passed on. Stonewall Jackson still rides Little Sorrel jauntily across the rich, green lawn of a park near the courthouse, and nearby stands a monument to the Confederate dead guarded by two cannon. Within the courthouse there is a marker honoring John Bowie Strange, and a statue of Robert E. Lee, one of many gifts to Charlottesville by its great benefactor, Paul Goodloe McIntire, has been erected in another city park. The Rotunda at the university bears two bronze tablets listing over five hundred alumni who died wearing Confederate gray, and a short distance away in the University of Virginia Cemetery lie the bodies of twelve hundred southern dead: "Fate denied them victory but clothed them with glorious immortality."

Missing, however, is any memorial to Charlottesville's most prominent Civil War campaigner, John Singleton Mosby.[23] Perhaps this is no oversight since Mosby, a controversial figure in his youth, was equally so during the war and in decades of peace which followed. The famed Gray Ghost of the Confederacy was born in Powhatan County, but his family moved to Albemarle a few years later and settled at Tudor Grove, a farm located on the old Lynchburg Road not far from Charlottesville. Young Mosby attended local private schools and at the age of sixteen enrolled at the University of Virginia. There he did well enough in languages but flunked mathematics. In March 1853, during his third year of study, he was arrested for shooting a fellow student, convicted, and spent seven months in the local jail until pardoned by the governor. While it appears that George R. Turpin, the youth wounded in this affair, provoked the attack and little doubt existed as to Mosby's guilt, only after many entreaties from his family, friends, and fellow students would state authorities consent to his release. Mosby's health, always frail, was a prime factor as they weighed these appeals. Within a few months he began the study of law in the offices of William J. Robertson, the man who had been prosecuting attorney in his case, was admitted to the bar, and in the late 1850s practiced law in Howardsville and Bristol.

During the war this intrepid campaigner's dashing exploits in northern Virginia were a constant thorn in the side of the Union and, on occasions, irked officials of the Confederate government as well. A report in August 1863 that Mosby and his men realized "thirty odd

[23] See Virgil Carrington Jones, "Ranger Mosby in Albemarle," *MACH* 5 (1945):36–45; William M. E. Rachal, ed., "Petitions concerning the Pardon of John S. Mosby in 1853," *MACH* 9 (1949):13–41; and "Colonel John Mosby," *MACH* 22 (1964):79–84.

thousand dollars" from the sale in Charlottesville of "Yankee plunder" brought demands for prompt investigation from both General Lee and the Confederate Secretary of War. With peace Mosby settled in Warrenton, supported Ulysses S. Grant and the Republican party in 1872, and was rewarded with a post as consul at Hong Kong. Upon his return this indefatigable little man held several civil service positions and rounded out his days as a resident of Washington, D.C. Stern to the last, in 1896, while visiting Charlottesville, Mosby was severely injured when kicked in the face by a horse. Taken apparently unconscious to the university infirmary, an intern bent over the inert form and asked his name. "None of your damned business," the wartime raider snapped in reply. "He's conscious all right," remarked a surgeon as he removed his coat and began to prepare to operate. During the first decade of the twentieth century, when the excesses of college football became something of a national scandal, Mosby jumped into the fray. The sport, he told the university's board of visitors, was "only a polite term for prize fighting," and so-called college athletes were merely "professional mercenaries . . . hired to advertise colleges." Mosby died in Washington in May 1916, a little more than a year after his alma mater, which he had left rather precipitously over half a century before, honored him with a special bronze medal and an embossed address. All was forgiven—shooting a fellow student, allegedly profiting from wartime plunder, going over to the Republican party, and criticizing university athletics.

Unlike John S. Mosby, few residents of Albemarle sought posts with the federal government or embraced the hated black Republicans. Numbed by the catastrophe which overwhelmed them in the spring of 1865, many turned to agriculture, the true basis of the county's well-being, while others tried to reconstruct some elements of the economic life they had known. Yet they found themselves in a strange, strange world, an existence without slavery, filled with innumerable social dislocations, and fraught with unanswered questions on every hand.

Chapter 12

The Freedman's Albemarle

LIFE in Jefferson's county during the decade following Appomattox, despite current research arising from unprecedented interest in the role of blacks in America's past, remains something of an enigma. Whites, stunned by defeat with all its doleful ramifications, have left us few contemporary records. Charlottesville's *Tri-Weekly Chronicle*, the only local newspaper whose files are still in existence, was ultraconservative in outlook and usually contemptuous of any action taken by Negroes, the Freedmen's Bureau, and other federal authorities. As for blacks themselves, who outnumbered whites in the county by some twenty-five hundred, they were much too busy experiencing their newfound freedom to write diaries, even if able to do so. In an era of hard times and innumerable dislocations, the prime goal of all citizens, regardless of color, was simply to make a living as best they could. Nevertheless, little doubt remains that the most important citizen of Albemarle during these years was the freedman. His prominence did not arise from wealth or political power but came merely as a result of his presence. Like the slave he had been, but even more so, he was the center of considerable controversy, and the outcome of debate raging at all levels from country store to national Capitol would determine not only his future but that of his county as well.

In 1870, five years after the war's end, Albemarle had 27,544 people within its borders, 14,994 of them black and 12,550, white (see table 5). This population included 5,276 families housed in 5,131 dwellings. Only 209 individuals were foreign born, and about twice as many (412) had migrated to the county from other states. Nearly half of these non-Virginians came from New York, Pennsylvania, and Maryland. The town of Charlottesville consisted of 166 families living in 160 homes—total population, which undoubtedly included some residents of the surrounding countryside, 2,838. The county seat now lay within Charlottesville District, one of five such geographical units which replaced the old parishes. Grouped around this central district in a clockwise fashion, Rivanna and Scottsville districts encompassed the eastern half of Albemarle; Samuel Miller

Table 5. Albemarle County population, 1870

	Total	Native	Foreign	White	Black
Charlottesville District	7,145	7,008	137	2,899	4,246
Charlottesville	2,838	2,748	90	1,365	1,473
Rivanna District	4,697	4,683	14	1,988	2,709
Scottsville District	5,994	5,964	30	2,609	3,385
Scottsville	388	382	6	252	136
Howardsville	83	83	0	56	27
Samuel Miller District	4,959	4,933	26	2,738	2,221
White Hall District	4,749	4,747	2	2,316	2,433

SOURCE: *Ninth Census: The Statistics of the Population of the United States* (Washington, D.C., 1872), 1:278.

and White Hall, the western half. (Ivy District, located west of Charlottesville, was created in 1875.)

For a very few years these divisions were called, in the New England manner, townships, but in 1874 they became magisterial districts ruled by a supervisor and equipped with various officials such as assessor, clerk, and overseers of roads and the poor. (As late as 1900, however, several perverse census ennumerators continued to use the term *township*.) A board of supervisors, composed of all individuals holding that title, was created by the Constitution of 1870 and soon emerged as the central authority in Albemarle. In time, the duties of the several lesser officials within each township, or district, were concentrated in a single treasurer, assessor, clerk, and so on who served the entire county. Charlottesville received a new town charter in 1871, but its local government remained essentially unchanged, consisting of a mayor, six aldermen, and other town officials; however, during succeeding years, as population grew, the state legislature granted these men more and more power over loans, bond issues, and taxes.

In 1870 942 students were attending local schools, 809 of them white, 133 black. White males outnumbered females, although this ratio was reversed among blacks. The community had 9,834 residents over the age of ten who were unable to read, and slightly more (10,504) could not write. Virtually all of these individuals were Negroes recently released from the bonds of slavery. Some sixty churches served the religious needs of whites, although in 1869 only three were ministering to blacks. At that date there were fifty clergymen in Albemarle, half of them Baptist. Of the sixty-three religious groups, twenty were Methodist, seventeen Baptist (white), three

Baptist (black), eight "union" (Methodist and Baptist, but open to all congregations for worship services), six Presbyterian, six Episcopalian, and three Christian. During the next few years several new churches appeared. Lutherans dedicated a chapel on the outskirts of Charlottesville in 1871. Black Baptists, who purchased old "Mudwall" in 1868, sixteen years later replaced that famous old school-hotel-hospital with a large structure appropriately named the First Colored Baptist Church of Charlottesville. Roman Catholics, as others had done before them, continued to hold services in the Town Hall until January 1880, when they dedicated their own church.

Despite the ravages of war Albemarle still contained a large group of well-to-do citizens in 1870. Eighty-nine individuals had real and personal property worth from $25,000 to $50,000; thirty-three were in the $50,000-to-$100,000 category; and four controlled estates valued at more than $100,000. This privileged foursome included Mary A. Harper, the English-born mistress of Farmington ($144,000), Samuel Moon, a merchant-farmer ($190,000), Peyton S. Coles ($150,-000), and T. S. Coles ($106,560). The census taker seems to have experienced some difficulties with the Coles family. John S. Coles insisted he was worth only $50,261 (this official noted the figure should be at least $150,000), and T. S. Coles reported his total belatedly under protest. Nevertheless, in that year the various branches of that wealthy clan were worth nearly $500,000 in all, compared to $800,000 ten years earlier. This decline of 30 to 40 percent, largely due to loss of slaves, is reflected in many large households, although one individual, W. H. Southall, a farmer with seven servants, was worth considerably more than he had been in 1860. Some citizens, among them T. S. Coles and T. J. Randolph, Jr., emerged from the war with their personal wealth virtually unchanged. House servant staffs on large estates appear to have been cut in half following the war; yet they remained formidable by present standards. T. L. Farish, for example, had nine, W. J. Robertson, six, and C. D. Everett, seven (including two gardeners).

Viewing Albemarle in a slightly different but intriguing fashion, Ann Lenore Stauffenberg has discovered that some local residents, while they certainly lost money in the tumultuous 1860s, still were slightly better off in 1870 than they had been in 1850.[1] Much of this economic well-being she attributes to the tobacco boom before the war. Tracing the careers of 420 individuals through two decades, Miss Stauffenberg found that, of twenty-five citizens who fared es-

[1] Stauffenberg, pp. 81–89.

pecially well, nine were farmers; six, merchants; six, skilled crafts-men; and four, professional folk. By 1870 a few were making money by the sale of town real estate, an enterprise not universally admired. Mrs. Benjamin C. Flannagan, daughter of Walker Timberlake and wife of a wealthy local banker, was given exclusive control of her paternal inheritance because Timberlake disapproved of his son-in-law's involvement in "speculation and business of hazard."

A small group of new freedmen also were possessed of some wealth, although on a much smaller scale, of course, than that of their white counterparts. In 1870 only fifty-six blacks in the county owned real estate,[2] sixteen of whom had total resources of $1,000 or more. Most were tradesmen—carpenters, shoemakers, musicians, and hotelkeepers. The most affluent was William H. Brown ($10,300), a thirty-two-year-old restaurant owner, followed closely by two members of the musical Scott family without whom no ball or dance was complete. Despite freedom, the decade of the 1860s does not appear to have been especially kind to local blacks. Ownership of real estate may have doubled during those years, but the census taken on the eve of war reveals nearly as much wealth in the hands of a few hundred free Negroes as all of their brethren had ten years later.

Many residents of Charlottesville continued to list their occupation as farmer; and, in truth, in the 1870s that community seems to have been almost an appendage of several large estates, despite rumors of traffic in town property. W. W. Waddell, who became a youthful resident in 1874 when his father accepted a position as editor of the *Chronicle*, in 1940 told members of the Albemarle County Historical Society of his recollections of those days.

The area covered by Charlottesville in 1875 was practically from West High to the top of Beck's Hill to East High where it turns to the River Road and from there across to the Chesapeake & Ohio Depot, up the C. & O. Railroad via Garrett Street to the Junction and back by the Gas House to Beck's Hill.

There were a few streets like Park, Ridge, and First running off from the main body of the town.

The town was surrounded by about half a dozen large farms. On the northeast the Sinclair Estate ran up to High Street and down to the river, the section now known as Locust Grove. On the east Captain Tom Farish's farm came up close to High Street. On the southeast and south the Brennan Estate and Mr. Slaughter Ficklin's farm ran to the C. & O. Depot. On the southwest was the Fife Estate which is now covered by

[2] Ibid., p. 65.

Fifeville and ran up to the Southern Railroad. The Colonel T. L. Preston and Andrew J. Craven farms were on the northwest and north and extended to the old line of the Southern Railroad. This section is now Preston Heights and Rose Hill.

You were on country roads when you left East High Street, crossed the C. & O. Railroad, or left the foot of Beck's Hill, which after all were not much worse than the town streets. In bad weather sometimes four horses were necessary to pull a carriage up Vinegar Hill and to the University.

The principal residential streets were Park, High Street, Ridge, and First Streets, but none of these had been closely built up. East High Street from Park had only three houses on it, the homes of the McIntires, Captain Micajah Woods, and C. D. Fishburne. On the other side were no buildings at all. Park Street had only eight houses on one side and seven on the other. High Street from Park west to the Episcopal Church had only three houses on the south side and nine on the north side.

There were no houses on streets north of High Street except two on North Second Street which were the Presbyterian Manse and J. W. Lipop home, and on North First Street eight houses, five on one side of the street and three on the other.

Ridge Street was built up in about the same proportions. Jefferson and Market Streets had only a few residences on them.

There were still a few stores and barrooms on the Square. I recall Mr. Allan Bacon had a grocery. John Mannoni had a bar, and Mr. John Saunders had a barroom in connection with a boarding house called the Saunders House.

Main Street of today bears no resemblance to the street of 1875. The old bank building is about the only building which remains on it as it was in 1875. The mercantile business was entirely unlike it is today. The stores confined themselves strictly to their own lines. You could enter a store with your eyes blindfolded and recognize it from the odor of its drugs, leather, or molasses.

Water Street had very few buildings of any kind on it. I presume it got its name from the fact that there were several springs on it. One I recall was located back of the old Methodist Church and flowed under Main Street and down Preston. A plank sidewalk covered it down Preston Avenue and water could be seen through the cracks. This stream flowed into Wills ice pond, which at that time covered the block upon which the Piedmont Candy Company stands.

Another spring in Water Street was located near where the Sea Food Grill stands and ran down towards the C. & O. freight depot.

There were several springs in Beck's Hill and Preston Avenue, the water from which was used by washerwomen of the locality.[3]

[3] Waddell, "Charlottesville in 1875," *MACH* 2 (1942):5–6.

By the time young Waddell and his family settled in Charlottesville the tumult of Reconstruction was over, at least as far as Albemarle was concerned. The Reverend Edgar Woods, who lived through those years, wrote in 1901 that "affairs moved with tolerable smoothness until the early part of 1869"[4] and, even then, described only a few weeks of political turmoil before a statewide election. By July of that year, Woods added with a sigh of relief, "the State and county were rescued from negro control. Things gradually returned into their proper channels."[5] More recent students of life in Albemarle during that decade, notably William E. Webb and Joseph C. Vance, see somewhat more happening, but the broad outlines of the picture sketched by Woods remains unchanged.[6] Largely because of its isolation far from disruption of actual warfare and failure of so-called outside agitators to be much interested in such a rural community, the county emerged from Virginia's rather brief Reconstruction era (1865–70) virtually unscathed. True, tense moments occurred, but most of the familiar earmarks of that troubled time (race riots, hooded night riders, and bloodshed) are missing.

While Albemarle and the nation were adjusting to the first days of peace, news came of the assassination of Abraham Lincoln, an event which was "viewed with general satisfaction" by many residents of Charlottesville.[7] James Alexander, a leading newsman in the community who lost his only two sons in the war, was so elated that he jumped up and down repeating the cry of John Wilkes Booth, "Sic Semper Tyrannis!" In May the first of a series of military commanders appeared, Lieutenant Colonel Franklin A. Stratton, a Pennsylvanian. He found the area already garrisoned and wrote to his superiors from Charlottesville: "Not many disorders have come to my notice throughout the country, but there is much need of a military post at this place to preserve order and to protect the citizens from small bands of mauraders and robbers investing various localities between here and the Blue Ridge."[8]

At about the same time Robert G. H. Kean, formerly head of the

[4] Edgar Woods, p. 119.   [5] Ibid., p. 122.
[6] See Webb, "Charlottesville and Albemarle County, 1865–1900" (Ph.D. diss., University of Virginia, 1965), and Vance, "The Negro in the Reconstruction of Albemarle County, Virginia" (M.A. thesis, University of Virginia, 1953). Two chapters of the latter work have been published: "Race Relations in Albemarle during Reconstruction," MACH 13 (1953):28–45, and "Freedmen's Schools in Albemarle during Reconstruction," Virginia Magazine of History and Biography 61 (1953):430–38.
[7] Webb, p. 1.   [8] Ibid., pp. 2–3.

Confederate Bureau of War, returned to Edgehill. He noted in his diary that the Negroes on some farms had quit in a body, eager to see Richmond, Washington, and other metropolitan centers. Some ex-masters tried to retain their best workers; others simply acquiesed and hired new ones. The fixed wage in Albemarle was $5 per month (specie) for a first-class man, $3 for a first-class woman. These hands were to be fed, but not clothed,

and those who remain on the plantation enjoy the privileges of gardens, fowls, etc., which they used to enjoy as slaves. The planters here (Edgehill) have fixed November 15 as the end of their year of labor, and contract till that time. The great scarcity of provisions throughout Virginia greatly facilitates the reorganization. The negroes must get prompt employment or starve. There is little to eat in the country and less currency. Hence wages are low and subsistence dear. Many however are idling about. They cannot by the harshest usage be kept from collecting at the garrisoned towns, whence (as in Richmond) they are arrested, put in barracks and hired out by the provost marshal without consulting their wishes as to employer and price.[9]

In June 1866 Stratton was replaced by Captain William L. Tidball, who served both as military commander and district supervisor of the Bureau of Freedmen, Refugees, and Abandoned Lands. This agency, generally known as the Freedmen's Bureau, was created by Congress during the final months of the war to care for free Negroes but soon wielded considerable political influence as well. Tidball, who remained for a year, seems to have been generally popular and quite effective. Rumors in March 1867 that he might leave even won him endorsement from the *Chronicle:* "No officer could have conducted himself with more fairness, kindness, and tact than he has exhibited in the difficult position he has occupied here. . . . He has been truly a mediator and peacemaker between the blacks and whites." [10] Tidball was followed by Lieutenant A. F. Higgs and Higgs, in turn, by a Lieutenant Town. Because Albemarle proved stable and quiet, federal authorities obviously concluded that the area was in need of no special attention, for officers of less and less rank assumed what could be an odious responsibility.

According to Vance, Reconstruction on the local scene can be divided into two distinct periods. The first, which he terms "Native Reconstruction," ended in the spring of 1867 when Congress took a

[9] Edward Younger, ed., *Inside the Confederate Government: The Diary of Robert Garlick Hill Kean* (New York, 1957), pp. 207–8.
[10] Webb, p. 3.

much more active interest in southern affairs; the second, widely known as "Congressional Reconstruction," came to a close in mid-1869 when conservative Virginians regained control of their state and local governments. During the first two years the black man was actually more a "free slave" than a "freedman." Emancipation gave him freedom of movement, but this meant little since the old land-owning class continued securely in power. A wage and sharecropping system simply replaced the slave-master relationship, and to eat, the ex-slave had to work, often on the same farm or estate where he lived before 1865 and for his old master. In addition, federal officials, eager to minimize their own headaches, were quick to impress upon blacks that freedom did not mean idleness. Vance, who has examined Freedmen's Bureau records for Albemarle closely, notes that during the first two years, the major source of friction was disputes when an employer failed to make satisfactory payment for labor or a black did not fulfill the terms of his contract. There also were numerous complaints of petty thievery by ex-slaves. He believes that race relations were best among those who had known each other for a generation or so, worst between the freedmen and less affluent whites who knew nothing of the former master-slave relationship and feared the black man as an economic competitor.

Addressing the graduating class at the University of Virginia in 1866, Alexander H. H. Stuart cautioned students that they must care "for the unfortunate and dependent race that has been cast loose amongst us."

Let us remember that no blame attaches to the Negro. They were our nurses in childhood, the companions of our sports in boyhood, and our humble and faithful servants through life. Without any agency on their part, the ties that bound them to us have been rudely broken. Let us extend to them a helping hand in the hour of their destitution. We can give them employment. ·. . . Thousands who, in the first intoxication of freedom, wandered from their homes, have returned to seek shelter and protection from their former masters. They should be received kindly . . . and we should spare no pains to improve their conditions and qualify them . . . for usefulness in our community.[11]

The political fury of Congressional Reconstruction (1867–69) strained this commendable spirit of noblesse oblige, but it never perished completely. Rarely did Albemarle whites criticize the Negro per se; instead, they directed their anger toward carpetbaggers, scalawags, and certain black leaders.

[11] Vance, "Race Relations in Albemarle," pp. 29–30.

The first months of peace, understandably, were marked by considerable confusion, and during those weeks local federal authorities sometimes were maligned or referred to contemptuously as "agents of the Meddling Bureau"; however, thanks to considerable tact, men such as Tidball soon won general approval. Yet, to some extent, these same individuals often contributed to this confusion. A provost marshal commented early in 1866: "The plain fact that freedmen are free and not subject to them cannot be realized by the whites, and they are constantly using and carrying into effect their illogical maxim and argument, 'if the freedmen whom I employ, support, and pay, will not do as I tell [them], if [they] on my sboulding "sauce" me, am I not justified in having recourse to physical power?' "[12]

Several weeks later this official told one white resident in clear, precise language: "You will have little difficulty in determining your official duty toward freedmen, by keeping in mind one fact, that they are entitled to all of the civil rights of citizens." However, on some occasions farmers were informed they were responsible for freedmen "belonging" to them. David Goodman, who lived four miles north of Charlottesville, once was ordered to take some ex-slaves back to his farm or provide transportation so they could join their friends elsewhere. Thus whites, on one hand, were reminded that blacks were free, independent citizens; on the other, they were told to attend to the immediate needs of those who "belonged" to them. Blacks themselves contributed to this atmosphere of uncertainty which could produce harsh words and even bodily harm. They were, as one Bureau official noted, much "addicted to thieving . . . opening smokehouses and stealing therefrom." But in their defense he pointed out that whites quickly attributed all crime, great and small, to "the Yankee Soldier or the Nigger."[13] In addition, the ex-slave was inclined to think "incivility and perfect independence, if not impudence" toward his new employer constituted freedom. By the end of 1866 relations between the races seem to have achieved some sort of equilibrium which would only be disturbed in the future by political campaigns. Whites began to accept and appreciate the true status of their "free slaves" and, in dire need of their labor, accommodated themselves to the new way of life decreed by Appomattox. Blacks, in turn, had learned the hard lesson that freedom had inherent responsibilities as well as advantages.

With one notable exception—the Yankee schoolmarms who tried to educate the freedmen—Albemarle's white minority got along well

[12] Ibid., p. 30.   [13] Ibid., p. 31.

with federal authorities quartered in their midst between 1865 and 1867. A Lieutenant Joyes, who represented the Bureau during the first six months of 1866, merely marked time while awaiting discharge from the army and did not take his duties seriously. His successor, Captain Tidball, more than made up for this negligence, demonstrating genuine concern for both black and white. No detail was too unimportant for his personal attention. He once complained to superiors that the "meat" ration given a blind man included too much "Rappanock [sic] herring," and the gentleman had considerable trouble with the bones. Tidball also told a black woman living near what had been Delevan Hospital that she must take better care of her hogs: "Ned Willis complains that your hogs are destroying his garden. This must be avoided. You must pen up your hogs, at least at night. He can watch his garden in the day time." [14] On another occasion the captain informed a hard-pressed white farmer that he would postpone calling in one of his field hands until after crops were harvested.

Despite Tidball's resolute concern, some matters which contributed to racial tension were beyond his control. Soon after he arrived in Albemarle, the local courts reinstated the old practice of whipping those convicted of petty crimes. Although to prove impartiality the authorities whipped one white man (very lightly, it is said), blacks naturally resented this reversion to prewar custom, and Tidball intervened. However, the judges ignored his commands and continued to sentence offenders as before. On August 10, 1866, two days after Tidball won the support of higher authorities on this matter, a local court ordered additional whippings for still more blacks, including an old woman and a boy of twelve. The captain renewed his campaign, and these sentences were not carried out; nevertheless, he was immediately faced with yet another subterfuge, "whipping by consent." Tidball told Bureau officials precisely how whites were carrying out this insidious scheme: "A few days since a colored girl in her teens took six ears of corn from a white man's field. She was caught in the act and brought before a magistrate, who told her that he must send her on for trial, and that if she could not give bail, she would have to go to jail until the November term of the county court. When, if convicted she would be undoubtedly whipped. After which the complaintant proposed that if she would take the whipping then, and from him, he would drop the prosecution. The girl consented. Whipping by agreement will become common." [15] Tidball was wrong;

---

[14] Ibid., p. 33.   [15] Ibid., pp. 34–35.

it did not. And, by the end of 1866 he could report considerable improvement in local affairs.

Yankee soldiers who lived with black women and fights among Negroes themselves caused both Joyes and Tidball innumerable headaches. Probably the greatest cause of turmoil in black households was a Virginia law which stipulated that adults living together on February 26, 1866, were to be considered legally married. Although eminently practical and direct, this enactment sometimes defied reasonable application. Preston and Mary White had different local masters before 1861 but were allowed to live together as man and wife. Then Preston was sent to the Gordonsville area where he took himself a new "wife." When Sheridan came to Albemarle, Mary set out in search of Preston, and eventually this trio appeared before Tidball seeking his advice. Preston wanted to keep both women, by each of whom he had three children. When told he could not, he chose Mary. She claimed him by prior possession; her rival, on the basis of the new law. Each woman was willing to accept the children of the other if they could keep Preston. This was all too much for Captain Tidball, who referred the matter to his superiors.

Tidball and others were especially alarmed by the high rate of domestic desertion among blacks. In the fall of 1866 he predicted that soon the poorhouse would not hold all of the abandoned wives and children to be found in the county. Negroes themselves realized how serious the situation had become, and according to the captain, "among certain of them" there was "considerable ill feeling resulting from the abandonment of wives and the seduction of married women." While it would be absurd to expect ex-slaves to embrace immediately established codes of social behavior with which they were unfamiliar, failure of so many to do so constituted a major problem for all residents of Albemarle in the late 1860s, whether they were white, black, or U.S. officials.

With the beginning of Congressional Reconstruction nearly all of these irritants—petty thievery, disputes over labor contracts, desertion of new families by black men, misunderstandings concerning the true nature of freedom, and "meddling" by federal officials—were overshadowed by activity in the political realm. Conventions and meetings at the local and state level, battles over voter registration, and considerable behind-the-scenes maneuvering all the way from Albemarle's courthouse to the highest offices in Washington dominated life in the county from 1867 to 1869. In essence, Radical Republicans, in firm control of Congress after the mid-term election of 1866, reaffirmed military rule throughout the South and insisted the

23. Old Ash Lawn

24. First Baptist Church—Colored. (From *Daily Progress Magazine*, 1906, by Albert E. Walker)

"free slave" must become a free man with all rights of citizenship firmly secured by new state constitutions.

The effects of these measures soon were felt in Albemarle. Several county and town officials were removed because of the test oath required of ex-Confederates. Concerning one individual, the *Chronicle* commented on March 28: "Captain C. C. Wertenbaker lately turned out of the University Post Office because of his inability to take the oath . . . is going to open a tobacco shop. He is a good fellow, was a gallant soldier, and has lost his occupation. Men in his position have peculiar claims upon the community." Voter registration in succeeding weeks confirmed the worst fears of the conservatives. Totals within the county were 2,488 blacks and 2,166 whites, although if rural Negroes had been better organized this disparity could have been even greater.

The initial reaction to this new Reconstruction program was an unsuccessful attempt by whites to demonstrate to blacks that they were being "used" by "outsiders" and that their only true friends were former masters with whom their economic destiny was closely intertwined. However, these whites had little to offer which rivaled the thrill of active participation in politics, and Radical spokesmen, many of local origin, soon gained the upper hand. During these months, as Vance notes, the *Chronicle* did a complete about-face in its attitude toward blacks.[16] In April 1867 they were praised as "unusually intelligent." By June, as Negroes rebuffed suggestions which, for the most part, would give control of political affairs to whites, this triweekly lamented the fact that while "intelligent colored men are inclined to be reasonable . . . the mass, we fear, will not be satisfied with any offers we make them—no matter what they are." Eight weeks later the *Chronicle* despaired of any cooperation whatsoever. "We have come pretty much to the conclusion that we have made enough overtures to the colored people for the present, and until they are met in a more hearty manner, we are inclined to leave them to manage their affairs." This meant, of course, abandoning the field to the Radicals.

The first large assembly in which Albemarle blacks participated was a gathering held at the old Delevan Hospital on April 24, 1867. This meeting, initiated by whites, featured speeches by T. J. Randolph, Jr., and three blacks representing different points of view. Randolph and Ossian Johnson, a local Negro who gained his freedom before the Civil War, stressed the advantages of supporting educated,

[16] Vance, "The Negro in the Reconstruction of Albemarle," pp. 17–18.

experienced white leaders. Fairfax Taylor, who also had bought his way out of slavery, presented with much fervor the Radical argument. According to the *Chronicle*, he even demanded the right to serve on juries and to attend the university and "became more offensive to the whites present." [17] Nicholas Richmond, a free-born Baptist preacher, and another local black gave support to a middle-ground approach. They eschewed direct confrontation with whites and stressed that the Negro must work for his own improvement. Mollified somewhat by these moderate voices, whites in the audience agreed to subscribe to the so-called Petersburg Resolution which called for equal school facilities and equal political and legal rights for both races.

Whatever harmony existed at the close of this important gathering at old "Mudwall" was short-lived. Johnson, the pro-white, soon dropped from the political arena, and Preacher Richmond within months felt the scorn of fellow blacks. On November 12, 1867, the *Chronicle* reported that when he arose to read a hymn in his church, almost the entire congregation marched out. By that date the majority of Albemarle's freedmen, and especially those living in the Charlottesville community, were supporters of Fairfax Taylor, the man who dared to demand jury duty and access to the lecture halls of the University of Virginia.

During the summer months of 1867 conservative elements in Virginia's Republican party tried to foster a spirit of cooperation, advocating as a minimum goal acceptance of the Congressional Reconstruction Acts; however, the radical wing beat back this assault. This drove many of the losers into the ranks of an emerging Conservative party. One notable exception was Judge Alexander Rives, who chose (at times) to remain within the Radical fold, despite his party's advocacy of equal legal rights and free schools, planks which most whites found unacceptable. In September, Rives was nominated by the Radical Republicans to be a delegate to an anticipated constitutional convention to be held in Richmond. The other county nominee was James Taylor, son of Fairfax, despite his father's strange declaration that he, for one, would not vote for his offspring. In jest the *Chronicle* (October 3, 1867) suggested Republicans should have bestowed this honor upon a man named Kelly, evidently the town moron. "Mr. Kelly is illiterate; but so is Mr. Taylor: he is black, but Mr. Taylor is brown, he is no speaker, but neither is Mr. Taylor. Dress up Aleck Kelly, part his black hair, and board him for a month

[17] Ibid., p. 19.

at the Ballard house, and he will know as much as Taylor, if not more."

At a biracial meeting held on October 7 Conservatives named rival nominees, William H. Southall, brother of the *Chronicle*'s editor, and Judge Rives. Southall, a so-called floater who would represent a three-county area, previously had been placed on the ballot by residents of Louisa and Augusta. Rives, by this date, had jumped to the Conservative party, and his place on the ticket was taken by C. L. Thompson, a white Radical. Thomas W. Savage, a native Virginian and a highly respected local merchant, also sought a convention seat.

The results of balloting held on October 22 demonstrate how unified blacks were. Only 300 of those registered did not vote, while nearly 1,000 whites failed to go to the polls. Ninety-seven whites voted for the convention; 29 Negroes opposed it. The convention was approved by a huge majority, nearly 900 votes, and Thompson and Taylor easily won the right to speak for Albemarle. However, largely because of support received outside of the county, Southall was elected as a floater. Several hundred blacks, elated by success, gathered in Charlottesville to celebrate. Thompson, the principal speaker, told them that, though elected by their votes, he considered himself a representative of no race. Actually, once they got to Richmond, Albemarle's delegates voted strictly along party lines and did not figure prominently in the proceedings. The *Chronicle*, thoroughly dejected, could only wail in defeat: "This is the 'Union as is.' How long, O Lord, How Long!" [18] This publication now tried to unify whites by promoting racial animosity. Rather than "Mr." or "Gentleman," the black leader became "a reverend, backsliding, carpetbagging, fire eating, clovenhoofed, weasel-nosed, wood stealing, church bilking, soup house lunch grabbing, league shrieking nigger missionary!" [19] The editor also began a blatant appeal to white pocketbooks: "The amount collected from the negroes in Charlottesville for corporation taxes in the past 3 years has been the enormous sum of $89!!! The whole amount of the levy last year in the corporation was $2300, of which the negroes paid $40. . . . We suspect the tax-payers of Charlottesville will be very much surprised to learn that half of the expense of the Radical Convention recently held in the Town Hall, came out of their own pockets. We have it from no less reliable authority than his honor the Mayor." [20]

This personage was T. W. Savage, unsuccessful aspirant to the

[18] Vance, "Race Relations in Albemarle," p. 31. [19] Ibid., p. 36.
[20] Ibid.

constitutional convention, who was named to that post by federal authorities in April 1868. Contemptuously referred to by the *Chronicle* as "Lord Mayor and Military Dictator of the Town of Charlottesville" and later described incorrectly as a "black" by many historians, Savage had been a resident of Charlottesville since the 1820s. Owner of slaves in 1840, he somehow was converted to abolition, yet on the eve of the Civil War appeared to enjoy the esteem of his fellow citizens. He was a ranking member of the town council, served for a time as acting mayor, and, according to the census of 1860, was "commissioner of revenue." Savage was, as young Duke noted, the gentleman who tried in vain to vote for Abraham Lincoln. He seems to have been a relatively prosperous storekeeper and was honored with a glowing obituary when he died in 1876 at the age of seventy-three. Nevertheless, association with the military government won Savage the undying scorn of some local whites, despite the fact that he had experience in town affairs and was well qualified for the post he held for two years.[21] Perhaps it is unnecessary to point out that it was the *Jeffersonian Republican*, not the *Chronicle*, which spoke kindly of Savage when he expired a few years later.

Meanwhile, by mid-1868 delegates in Richmond had finished their work, and political leaders began preparing for the creation of a new state government; however, military authorities, unsympathetic to a Radical measure which sought to bar ex-Confederates from the ballot box, continued to postpone the election for nearly a year. This delay enabled A. H. H. Stuart, the man from Staunton who urged University of Virginia graduates to care for their ex-slaves, to step forward with a proposal which eventually won widespread support: Conservatives would grant suffrage to blacks if the Radicals would concede the same right to ex-Confederates. Eventually, soon after taking office, President Grant agreed that Virginians could vote separately on ratification of their new constitution and acceptance of what had come to be known as the "iron clad" oath and other disfranchising clauses. The result was a realigning of native white strength behind the gubernatorial nomination of Gilbert C. Walker, a New York–born carpetbagger, now a resident of Norfolk. Walker, who campaigned as a moderate Republican, was opposed by yet another carpetbagger, H. H. Wells, the incumbent governor under military rule and an outspoken Radical, the Conservative candidate having withdrawn in favor of Walker. Some white Virginians, still

[21] See Peter Bacque, "Was Mayor Savage Black?" *Daily Progress* (Aug. 31, 1974).

suspicious of the new constitution and of any Republican, however moderate his views, were converted to Walker's side when Professor John B. Minor prepared a paper for Stuart which backed his efforts for compromise.

Albemarle blacks, like most in the state, not grasping the full significance of white strategy, went ahead with plans to support the Radical ticket. As political fury mounted in the late spring of 1869, the *Chronicle* and local Conservatives pursued a contradictory course, but one which would prove successful. While attacking blacks as ignorant, at the same time they openly courted those known to be somewhat disenchanted with the Radicals. They were feted at barbecues and extended numerous courtesies not common only a few months before. Vance and others are unable to explain why several hundred Negro voters eventually climbed on the Walker bandwagon, but the answer probably lies in disagreements within the black community and in ties which some had with their former masters. After all, Walker was a Republican and certainly, they concluded, would look after their interests.

In the election held on July 6 Walker received 2,911 votes in Albemarle; Wells, 2,220. This same margin of about 700 ballots carried the rest of the moderate slate to victory. Only twenty-five voters opposed the constitution, and the test oath and disfranchising clauses were rejected, again by about 700 votes. Throughout the state as a whole, Walker won by 18,000 votes, and his supporters elected substantial majorities in both houses of the General Assembly and five of nine congressmen. To those living outside of the Old Dominion this looked like a victory for the moderate wing of the Republican party and a rebuke to the Radicals, but in effect it was a triumph of native whites marching a bit self-consciously under the Republican banner, intent upon ridding their beloved commonwealth of carpetbag-Negro rule. And that is just what they did; for within a few months the new legislature was sworn in, and in January 1870 Congress readmitted Virginia to full-fledged membership in the Union. The political "reconstruction" of Albemarle and Virginia was over. As Rev. Edgar Woods observed, things were gradually returning "into their proper channels."

Yet, as we all know from experience, "things" never actually return fully to their old ways, especially after so profound an upheaval as that which convulsed Albemarle during the years from 1860 to 1870. In no realm is this more apparent than in public education. The Freedmen's schools established in the county faced considerable opposition, but the seed of learning, once planted, was never snuffed out, and in time these institutions and their successors gained recognition as a permanent contribution of Reconstruction years. While hopes of the freedmen for immediate social and political equality were doomed to disappointment, these classrooms, often desperately in need of public funds, nevertheless continued to function. And, at the same time, their presence fostered grudging acceptance of similar schools for less affluent whites as well. Thus, by a strange twist of fate, the death of slavery, an institution which Thomas Jefferson often deplored, brought into being a program of basic education even more sweeping than the one he once proposed, a development which undoubtedly would have had his wholehearted approval.

Freedmen's schools were launched in the fall of 1865 with the arrival in Charlottesville of a Yankee schoolmarm, Anna Gardner.[22] These schools were financed mainly by the New England Freedmen's Aid Society with some assistance from local citizens of both races. Miss Gardner, fifty years old and member of the seventh generation of a Nantucket family, possessed impeccable abolitionist credentials. At the age of twenty-five she was instrumental in organizing the first antislavery meeting held on her native island. She subsequently became an avid admirer of William Lloyd Garrison and, with the coming of the war, followed in the wake of Union armies teaching ex-slaves how to read and write. Miss Gardner, who was in the Carolinas for two years before coming to Albemarle, was a lady of tireless energy and real ability and had a sincere regard for the freedman's welfare. She viewed the former master class with proper abolitionist disdain, "those alien and hostile people . . . primitive in appearance and habits." Throughout her five-year sojourn in Charlottesville, she doubted the good intentions of most local whites toward blacks and, once her school was established at "Mudwall," feared "those subtle, slippery Virginians" would resort to some legal chicanery to close it down. To her the University of Virginia was a place of special wickedness. She constantly deplored its "baleful shadow" over her classrooms and daily expressed fears they might be attacked during a noisy undergraduate calathump, "the terror of the place."

Reports of Captain William Tidball (1866–67) indicate Miss Gardner's misgivings were somewhat exaggerated. Influential whites, he said, agreed that immediate education of ex-slaves was "a great necessity," but he conceded widespread suspicion of public schools

22 For detailed information concerning the freedmen's schools, see the Vance thesis, pp. 78–93.

existed. "I have met with no manifest opposition to the education of the children of freedmen, but the encouragement is by no means zealous. The common school system of education is almost wholly unknown to these people, and they regard it with jealousy, as they do all innovations upon their established usages."

In the same report Tidball pointed directly to the major source of local irritation. Whites, he emphasized, resented "the social and political doctrines taught by Miss Gardner and her colleagues." And, as political passions mounted during the late 1860s, so did resentment. No doubt exists that such doctrines were being taught since Miss Gardner, in an exchange of letters with the *Chronicle*'s editor, even boasted of doing so. Early in 1867 she wrote J. C. Southall requesting a donation of printed diplomas for her projected teacher training institution, Jefferson School. After two years in Charlottesville her appeal begins with these revealing words: "Not knowing any Southerner personally . . . ." Southall replied that he indeed was interested in the Negro's welfare but feared Miss Gardner was more "political missionary" than teacher. If wrong, he added that he would gladly supply the materials requested free of charge. Within forty-eight hours Southall received this answer.

Mr. J. C. Southall, I teach *IN SCHOOL* and *OUT*, so far as my political influence extends, the fundamental principles of "politics" and "sociology" apply, viz.—"Whatever you would that men should do to you, do ye even so unto them."

Yours in behalf of truth and justice,
Anna Gardner.

This determined Yankee spinster first set up classes in "Mudwall," old Delevan Hospital. By November 1865, assisted by R. A. Musgrove, a local white who already was operating a tuition school for 32 blacks, the institution had 90 pupils. In this free school special emphasis was placed upon arithmetic and training of the more able as teachers. By April 1866 three more instructors had been added to cope with an enrollment of 241. Although Lieutenant Joyes, the rather casual Freedmen's Bureau representative of those months, mentions other free schools in rural communities throughout the county, these, if ever established, enjoyed brief lives; for as soon as Captain Tidball arrived, he consulted with the magistrates of various Albemarle districts and urged that more classes be opened for freedmen. Specifically, he suggested schools be established in Batesville, Boyd's Tavern, Brown's Cove, Carter's Bridge, Cobham, Covesville, Earlysville, Free Union, Garland's, Greenwood Depot, Keswick, Mechum's

River, Millington, Moorman's River, South Garden, Owensville, Scottsville, Warren, and Yancey's Mill. At that time this entire area was being served by two tuition schools for blacks.

When the Bureau took no action to implement these very ambitious proposals, local Negroes tried to recruit teachers themselves. By the fall of 1866 Tidball noted they had found three but could not pay them. One was Lindsay Smith, a freedman, who devoted part of his time to instructing thirty-three students in the African Church near Carter's Bridge. Another was Mrs. J. W. Pleasants, a "white lady," who proposed to furnish a room and teach for $10 a month. The third was a "white gent" for whom blacks would build a log school. Apparently a few rural classrooms did appear, supported solely by freedmen. Tidball commented in the spring of 1867 that several were functioning but gave no pertinent details.

In March 1867 the Charlottesville schools for freedmen had four teachers and 280 pupils, 100 of them over sixteen years of age. All studied writing and arithmetic, 40 were "in alphabet," 60 "read easy lessons," none were yet "in higher branches," and 30 had been free before the war. A year later eight day schools were operating within the county, four of them in Charlottesville. In addition there were six Sabbath schools and two night schools located in Charlottesville and Scottsville. By 1869 enough students had completed elementary work to justify a graded system. Two of the Charlottesville schools became primaries, both taught by freedmen, one of whom (judged by reports he submitted) was almost illiterate. Each school had some 60 students and held classes six hours a day, eighteen days per month. Above these was the intermediate Lincoln School, taught by Philenae Caskie of Boston. It had an enrollment of 50, 27 of them males. Jefferson School, presided over by Miss Gardner, was the capstone of this system. This institution was designed to train teachers. It also had 50 students, with girls slightly outnumbering boys. To mark the dedication of this school Miss Gardner composed a lengthy ode, part of which went as follows:

> Six years ago—on this ground
>   We dedicate to-day—
> Hundreds of human souls were bound
>   In abject slavery.
>
> Then Knowledge, Education, rolled
>   The heavy stone away
> From buried mind—where wealth untold
>   Folded in darkness lay.

Fetters no longer chattles bind;
But still the task remains
To sever shackles from the mind—
And climb to lofty plains.[23]

During 1869 the Bureau became more generous with funds, allocating $800 for repairs to the Charlottesville school and $500 for construction of a new one in Scottsville. Several more classrooms appeared in 1870. Among these were a primary school and a Sabbath school near Glendower and another collection of mixed grades at Mount Pleasant. Vance notes that during that year Scottsville blacks complained that their Negro teacher was incompetent and suggested the names of several local whites ready to assume the position. Freedmen in that region, he adds, seem to have been rather well off since they owned two school buildings valued at $2,400.

With only seven black schools operating in the county in 1870 the system fell far short of Captain Tidball's goal announced four years earlier; and, as a result, probably only one-fourth of potential students actually ever attended classes. Theoretically, following adoption of the new state constitution with its specific provisions for free public schools, Yankee schoolmarms and northern financial support were no longer needed. In fact, the first schools under the Walker administration were mere token affairs. With the departure of Miss Gardner and her colleagues for colder climes, the Negro schools of Albemarle declined for a time, but within a decade the teachers they trained, aided by the dedication of State Superintendent W. H. Ruffner, created a reasonably adequate system. Ruffner, by the way, received substantial assistance from Professor John B. Minor in drafting the original bill which established the state's public school system. The two men met at Minor's home, Pavilion X on the Lawn at the University of Virginia, in April 1870 and spent four days pouring over legal and technical details. Although the General Assembly later amended their proposals somewhat, in large measure the design of the Old Dominion's first system of free, public education was fashioned during these discussions.[24]

In 1888 D. P. Powers, the man who spearheaded this experiment in public classrooms on the local scene, published a brief summary of his efforts.

[23] Gardner, *Harvest Gleanings* (New York, 1881), p. 173.
[24] Walter Javan Fraser, "William Henry Ruffner: A Liberal in the Old and New South" (Ph.D. diss., University of Tennessee, 1970), pp. 307–8.

The public school system was organized in Albemarle County by D. P. Powers, County Superintendent, during the winter of 1870–'71. Fifty-seven schools, 38 for whites and 19 for colored, were opened with an enrollment of 2,268, and an average attendance of 1,443 pupils. The cost was $9,258.15. The average length of the term was 4.52 months, and the value of school property then owned by the county was only $114.62.

In 1875 the number of schools had increased to 90, of which 57 were for whites and 33 for colored. The enrollment was 4,036, and the average attendance 2,136 pupils. The total cost was $21,061.70, and the average length of the term was 6.68 months. In 1880 there were 101 schools in operation, 62 for whites and 39 for colored. Enrollment 4,155, and the average attendance 2,539 pupils. The total cost was $21,958.11, the average length of the term being but six months. In 1885 there were 124 schools open, 77 for whites and 47 for colored, for which there was expended $26,215.13. The enrollment was 5,228, and the average attendance was 3,169. The average length of the term was 6.32 months.

During the session just closed, 1887–'88, 81 schools for whites and 50 for colored, making a total of 131, were in operation. The enrollment was 5,541, and the average attendance was 3,207. Although the schools in several places were severely interfered with by measles, the average length of the term was 6.1 months. $27,165.34 was expended for the work, $17,682.34 by the State, $9,483 by the county.

The county now owns between sixty and seventy good school houses, and others are now in preparation for building. The value of the property has increased from $114.62 in 1871 to $25,000.

In the city of Charlottesville and the town of Scottsville there are good graded schools, and in the country districts there are a number of schools employing two teachers.

The average pay per month of male teachers is $34.50, while females receive on an average $27.50.[25]

Although the determined New England ladies who invaded Albemarle during Reconstruction certainly had few admirers among whites, they must have won grudging approval in some circles. This report by Superintendent Powers indicates they did their job well indeed. They charted the course that Negro education took in succeeding years, especially in teacher training; and as Captain Tidball emphasized, their work, aided by a handful of local whites, was absolutely essential to the well-being of the county, 1865–70. More important, growth of black public schools mitigated, to some extent,

[25] *Albemarle County (Virginia): A Handbook* (Charlottesville, 1888), pp. 64–65. Compared to census totals cited earlier, enrollment figures given by Powers for 1870–71 appear somewhat exaggerated, although his estimates for later years are substantiated by federal statistics.

abhorrence of free public schools in general. Despite the protests of J. C. Southall, if blacks were to be citizens, they needed much more than just reading, writing, and basic arithmetic. The years which followed demonstrated that the freedmen of Albemarle, like those in most parts of the nation, North and South, would not really become full-fledged citizens, not yet. But those classes started by Anna Gardner, that hardheaded product of a stern New England background, continued to function, a vital contribution of Reconstruction to Albemarle—perhaps, in view of their influence upon both races, the single most important result of those often disturbing years.

Largely because most whites living within the county long had favored some scheme of emancipation, little hostility existed toward the freedman as such. Slavery had been a profitable but very troublesome institution. Now it was gone. Opposition arose, however, when free blacks and federal authorities tried to create a new society in which the Negro would have an equal voice. Yet, despite this protest, often accompanied by angry words and much demagoguery on both sides, there was little serious racial friction. Disputes over how to replace slavery with free labor dominated the years from 1865 to 1867; politics, the remainder of Reconstruction.

During the 1870s Conservatives and Radicals (aided by many black voters) continued to do battle at each election held in the county. The two forces appear to have been evenly matched, with the former usually winning out, but not always. With the role of the freedman generally agreed upon, economic matters came to the fore: hard times in agriculture, the growth and power of railroad interests, and, of special concern to many, settlement of Virginia's prewar debt. Debate between Funders, those favoring payment of that debt in full, and Readjusters, less conservative elements seeking some repudiation to compensate for wartime losses, became so heated in the late 1870s that all other questions, especially that of the black voter, receded into the background.

Yet feelings still remained taut on election day. Grant's sweeping national triumph over Horace Greeley, Charles O'Conor, Thomas Hendricks, and Victoria Claflin Woodhull in 1872 was marked by a courthouse "jollification" which nearly ended in a riot when a white man allegedly struck a black celebrant. A mob quickly gathered, stones were hurled, pistols drawn; and except for prompt action by town authorities, bloodshed might have ensued. Greeley, by the way, carried Albemarle County by a scant sixteen votes, 2,455 to 2,439. Four years later county residents endorsed Democrat Tilden by a margin of 500 votes, but even if Republican Hayes had been victorious, he could not have been accorded a much warmer welcome than he received when he toured Charlottesville, Monticello, and the university on September 25, 1877. W. W. Waddell, whose mother had attended school with Mrs. Hayes, was forced to entertain the president's son. "I had been chinquapin hunting and had my pockets full of them. He had never seen any and the thing I recall most clearly about the visit is that my mother insisted I give him all my chinquapins. I later gathered and sent a large box of them to the White House." [26]

Actually, as we know now, settlement of the hotly contested Hayes-Tilden election ended Reconstruction throughout the entire South and cleared the way, in time, for effective elimination of the black man from politics. Nevertheless, until the opening years of this century the Republicans, supported largely by Negro ballots, were a force to be reckoned with in Albemarle County. In any national election they usually fell five hundred to a thousand or more votes short of victory, but until 1904 they could rally up to 40 percent of the electorate to their standard-bearer. The state constitution of 1902 ended these battles as the city-county vote dwindled from over 5,000 in the 1890s to less than half that number. And, with one-party control assured, apathy cut still deeper into election returns. From 1872 to the Eisenhower years the Democrats emerged triumphant in every presidential canvass held in the county and city, although they experienced some difficulty in 1880 because of a Greenback-Readjuster defection. Eight years later Benjamin Harrison ran surprisingly strong against Grover Cleveland, clear evidence of local disenchantment with the policies and programs of his first administration. These protests, a reflection of hard times on Albemarle's farms, did not help the Populists in the 1890s. Instead, local voters went solidly for Democratic nominees and continued to do so for many decades which followed.

Yet for a brief moment the freedman had exerted some control over life in Albemarle, his native county, where his race slightly outnumbered whites. In 1880, with an increase in total population to 32,618, the margin of black over white became razor thin—16,569 to 15,959. During the next ten years, six decades of white minority status came to an end, both in the county and in the new city of Charlottesville, a separate, independent entity after 1888.

In the 1880s the overall white population rose from 15,959 to 18,252, while that of blacks declined from 16,659 to 14,126 (see table

26 Waddell, p. 8.

Table 6. Area population, 1890

	Total	White	Black	Japanese
City-County	32,379	18,252	14,126	1
City	5,591	3,062	2,528	1

SOURCE: *Compendium of the Eleventh Census: 1890* (Washington, D.C., 1892), Pt. 1, pp. 512, 577.

6). Here, of course, is evidence of the beginning of a Negro exodus from the South and to growing urban areas within the state such as Hampton Roads. For the first and only time since federal census taking began, Jefferson's city-county community recorded a decline in population: 239 fewer residents than in 1880. This substantial inflow of whites and events on the state and national scenes doomed all hopes of the blacks for continued, meaningful participation in social and political life. If a few chinquapins, surrendered however reluctantly to the son of a Republican president, helped to hasten this process, most white residents of Albemarle County, with the exception perhaps of young Waddell, would have considered that small gift worthwhile indeed.

Chapter 13

Seeds of Change

I N THE 1870s and 1880s Albemarle's citizens struggled with three major questions, all economic in nature, whose solutions presumably would aid their troubled agricultural world. These were readjustment of the state's prewar debt, improvements in transportation, and diversification of agriculture. Though both causes and cures for the county's problems actually lay far beyond its borders and residents often could exert little, if any, control over the drift of events, nevertheless they took stands, voted in elections, and voiced their views for all to hear. The outcome, symbolized in part by creation of the city of Charlottesville in 1888, is clear evidence of substantial change in an era which, in retrospect, often appears almost changeless; yet by the time the county seat abandoned its swaddling clothes, one can see outlines of the twentieth-century community which would evolve. The town that Thomas Walker laid out more than a century before was destined to become a major trading center of the Piedmont complete with financial institutions, more and more mercantile outlets, some industry, and a growing and increasingly important fraternity of real estate agents. The surrounding farmlands, tied no longer to a one-crop mentality of either wheat or tobacco, would be turned over to viniculture, orchards, sheep, beef cattle, and dairying, although, one might add, the greatest gains often seemed to accrue when those acres were turned over from one owner to another.

In short, Albemarle, while paying lip service to its southern heritage, as a result of the spread of national rail lines, the influx of both ideas and people, and, above all else, the demands of the local economy, was becoming more and more like some rural sections of the Northeast. With the county still overwhelmingly agricultural even at the turn of the century, like scores of communities in New York, Pennsylvania, and Maryland before them, residents learned the hard lesson that basic crops they once had grown in profusion could not compete with the wealth of the vast Mississippi Valley; instead, they had to turn to other means of livelihood. These included not only varied agricultural pursuits and jobs in commerce and industry, but increasing reliance upon education, both public and private, long an element of some consequence on the local scene.

The debt question of the 1870s pitted the Conservatives against a group of more liberal, sometimes reform-minded folk, some of them old Radical Republicans, who in 1879 achieved formal organization as Readjusters. Although few voters could comprehend all of the intricacies of this controversy, most knew that payment of interest on the debt was imperiling their infant system of public education. General William Mahone, the colorful, irascible, elegantly tailored hero of the Crater, rode to power on this issue and created a short-lived political machine which eventually gave him a seat in the U.S. Senate and considerable influence in national Republican party circles. However, long before "Billy" Mahone discovered the magic of readjusterism, a one-time Baptist preacher from Albemarle, Parson John Massey, was in the thick of this battle.[1] Massey, having forsaken theological pursuits in 1862 because of ill health, had settled down at Monroe's Highland Tract, which he greatly enlarged and renamed Ash Lawn. There he farmed and conducted missionary work among local blacks. According to some sources, Massey's retreat from pulpit to plow was prompted, not by health, but impending financial difficulties with fellow Baptists. Outraged by the Funding Act of 1871 which gave payment of the debt precedence over allocations for schools, roads, and other public services, Massey made an unsuccessful bid for a seat in the General Assembly, vowing at the time that he was a staunch Conservative. Although he was defeated, it soon became apparent he had ignited a crusade which was attracting support among many voters, especially residents of the far Southwest and the Valley where he was well-known, as well as members of the lower and middle classes, white and black, who were vitally interested in the new classrooms their children were attending.

In 1873 a second campaign for the House of Delegates was successful, and there, as "father of the Readjuster movement," Massey's fight against the money power was uncompromising. Although the popularity of his cause was increasing, his initial antifunding legislation went down to defeat by two votes. Realizing that grass roots organization was essential to victory, Massey, James Michie, and other Albemarle residents in September 1875 launched the "New Light" movement which, in time, became readjusterism. In that same year the parson was returned to the legislature as an independent and

[1] See Richard B. Doss, "Parson John E. Massey, Relentless Readjuster," *MACH* 11 (1951):5–18.

25. David P. Powers

26. John E. Massey

27. John B. Minor

28. Henry Clay Marchant

29. Jefferson Monroe Levy

30. The Reverend Edgar Woods

continued his fight, and even though he and his friends eventually did what they set out to do, when they won control of the governor's mansion in 1881, paving the way for repeal of the Funding Act passed ten years earlier, Mahone, not Massey, was leading this unprecedented revolt. Refusing to be an obsequious subordinate to the general and thwarted in attempts to secure high office, Massey already had split with the calculating little man from Petersburg who had stolen his mantle.

As research of James T. Moore reveals, readjusterism was an uneasy alliance of both Republicans and Democrats, most of them yeoman farmers, blacks, and members of a rising middle class, all hit hard by the economic disasters of the 1870s.[2] Although their leaders included some political opportunists, what the rank and file had in common for a time was a firm conviction that the conservative government in Richmond was wasting tax dollars, paying exorbitant interest on the state debt, and diverting financial support from public services, especially the young system of public education. Charlottesville's weekly press and local financial leaders were solidly Funder and howled in protest, but as the movement gathered momentum, Albemarle voters joined this unprecedented upheaval of Virginia politics. Once in power, however, this unusual coalition across racial and party lines began to fall apart. Some Readjusters were alienated by Senator Mahone's close alliance with Republicans on the national scene; others, by the new prominence Negroes were enjoying within the state. In 1881, for example, more than a dozen blacks won seats in the General Assembly, and Governor William Cameron appointed Negroes to school board posts in both Richmond and Petersburg. In essence, the debt question was what held the Readjusters together. With that matter apparently settled, substantial differences came to the fore—disagreements over race, poll tax reform, regulation of railroads, leadership, patronage, and so on—and in 1883 a revived and somewhat sobered Democratic party emerged triumphant, backed once more by the voters of Albemarle County.

In the field of transportation the most significant development within Albemarle was extension and consolidation of rail facilities, final abandonment of illusive and persistent dreams of canalboats plying the waters of the Rivanna, and some improvement of public roads. Although rail lines serving the county experienced several name changes during these years, by 1868 the Virginia Central had

[2] See Moore's *Two Paths to the New South: Funders, Readjusters, and the Virginia Debt, 1870–1883* (Lexington, Ky., 1974), pp. 83–92.

evolved into the Chesapeake and Ohio, crossing the county as it does today from Afton Mountain to Gordonsville. At the outset of this period, the Orange and Alexandria, which after a tortured history would become the Southern Railway, still had no tracks between Gordonsville and Charlottesville. In addition to numerous inconveniences such as a ban by the C. & O. on all local traffic not originated by its own agents and fears that line might summarily terminate any existing lease, the cost of shipping goods between Charlottesville and points to the north was increased substantially. The *Jeffersonian Republican* (February 13, 1878) estimated that three-fifths of all freight charges from Baltimore to Charlottesville were accrued in the final twenty-four miles over C. & O. tracks.[3] Thus it is not surprising that in the late 1870s the Charlottesville and Rapidan Railway Company was organized for the sole purpose of constructing a direct link to Orange. After numerous delays work got underway in 1879, and in January 1881 the first passenger train steamed into Charlottesville over the new tracks. The throttlehold long held by the C. & O. was broken.

Several additional rail lines were chartered, but only one actually appeared. These included proposals to connect Charlottesville with, among other places, the university, Farmville, Scottsville, Stanardsville, and Fredericksburg. The Richmond and Allegheny Railroad, closely paralleling and successor to the James River and Kanawha Canal, did connect the river towns from Scottsville to Howardsville by rail in the early 1880s as it made its way westward toward the mountains. Even before construction of the Rapidan line, Charlottesville had established itself as a rail center of some importance in the state, a goal which eluded it in prewar years. In 1870, for example, the C. & O. reported that 47,602 passengers arrived and departed from its Charlottesville station in a twelve-month period, a figure higher than recorded by its facilities in Richmond, Staunton, or Gordonsville, and in 1884 only Richmond and Newport News shipped more freight on that same railroad.[4]

Annual totals such as these in freight and passenger traffic prompted both major railroads to locate repair shops in Charlottesville, bringing some industry and a few hundred new citizens to the community. Although local residents certainly appreciated the improved service and economic advantages the railroads bestowed upon Albemarle, this appreciation did not stiffle criticism. Random protests concerning the lack of waiting rooms or stations with platforms too

[3] Webb, p. 97.   [4] Ibid., pp. 100–101.

high were voiced, but excessive freight rates proved to be especially infuriating in a time of rural depression. In 1885 B. H. Magruder complained to the state railroad commissioner that the C. & O. charged twenty-nine cents per hundred pounds to transport sumac (used in tanning) from Charlottesville to Richmond but only fourteen cents per hundred to ship wheat. "If your office has not the power to have the abuse corrected," he added, "I hope and trust the coming legislature . . . will confer the requisite authority upon it." [5] Of course, here are the roots of the Granger-Alliance-Populist protest of those decades which, so long as these movements did not chart separate political courses and threaten the sometimes delicate balance between Democrats and their rivals, merited some support from Albemarle farmers.

While area residents might grumble about high freight rates and the absence of waiting rooms, a *New York Times* reporter who in 1883 traveled to the mountains of Bath County where he bought spring chickens for $2 per dozen and butter for sixteen cents a pound, found much, much more to criticize. [6] To begin with, there were no parlor cars south of Washington, although one could get a berth on night trains. Smoking cars usually were packed with black railroad employees and men of both races who opened bottles with their teeth. Trains invariably were several hours late, "nice-looking folk" traveled with barefooted offspring, and yet, to this visitor's astonishment, Virginians who never had been outside of the state considered their railroads and stagecoaches "the perfection of modern progress." This anonymous writer rose to the peak of his eloquence as he described Charlottesville junction, a low wooden structure some distance west of town.

Dust lies half a foot thick in the roads, and the only sign of civilization is a row of darkies with little stands loaded with fried chicken, home-made and home-sick cakes, "cone" bread, buttermilk, and fruit. The thermometer is only 110° in the shade, but must be somewhere near 212° in the sun. After you have scraped off the outer coating of dust, a bit of fried chicken tastes very good. It combines the flavors of fowl, onion, snuff, darky, and lard; and nowhere can a greater variety of tastes be suited for a smaller amount of money. When you buy a glass of butter-milk and the darky wipes off a piece of ice with his handkerchief and drops it in the glass, you—well, your sensations will be various, but you will probably be thirsty enough to drink the buttermilk.

[5] Ibid., p. 103.   [6] *New York Times* (Sept. 10, 1883).

Sometime later the train stopped at Afton for a twenty-minute, "catch-as-catch-can" dinner. The meal consisted of more chicken, tough mutton, and fresh vegetables. The seat at the head of the table was reserved for the "captain" (conductor) who got the best of everything.

Apparently having learned nothing during decades of frustration, much like the Bourbons of France who bestowed their name upon the resurgent conservative leadership of the postwar South, in the 1870s and 1880s many local citizens waxed eloquent once more concerning the potential of the Rivanna's waters. As late as 1878 the *Jeffersonian Republican* asserted that "while railroads are superior for light classes of freight and those requiring rapid transportation, where water transportation could be used it is much cheaper." [7] This may be true, but it overlooks the tremendous cost which might be involved in providing locks and dams required. In 1870 the General Assembly chartered another Rivanna Navigation Company and eight years later even granted it permission to use convict labor in proposed construction work. Yet, as before, little happened, and with the demise of the James River and Kanawha Canal in 1881 no reason for building a feeder waterway remained.

According to frequent editorials of these years, county highways left much to be desired. As W. W. Waddell noted, they "after all were not much worse than the town streets." Some major repair work was begun in 1876, and three years later Judge John L. Cochran persuaded the board of supervisors to levy $3,000 for a general road fund. With this support, he undertook "permanent" improvement of all main thoroughfares within a radius of four miles of Charlottesville. Even before this work was completed, the *Southern Planter* lavished considerable praise upon the project. Previously, it said, "vehicles, cavaliers, and pedestrians were obliged, if they could go at all, to make an arduous and mournful passage. . . . But all this has changed now as far as the immediate vicinity of Charlottesville is concerned. Her approaches are no longer reproaches. . . . This has brought Judge Cochran as near to immortality as he could desire." [8] In June 1884 the supervisors decided to extend similar efforts to 150 miles of county roads. For purposes of construction and maintenance Albemarle was divided into four areas: Scottsville to North Garden, North Garden to Covesville, the university to Afton, and Charlottesville to Nortonsville. Each of these regions was assigned a

---

[7] Webb, p. 104.   [8] Ibid., p. 109.

squad of fifteen workmen. While truly permanent improvements and all-weather highways would not appear until well into the twentieth century, a much more systematic approach to highway problems is evident in these decisions. At long last Albemarle officialdom concluded that requiring all males between sixteen and sixty, with the exception of ministers of the Gospel, to work on roads near their homes for a few days each year was an inadequate method of maintenance, little better than none at all.

Streets and roads within the town of Charlottesville were kept in reasonably good repair by a street commissioner, a position long held by C. L. Fowler. Fowler and his crew took their duties seriously and with good reason; for as long as they did their work well, by state law citizens of a town were exempt from paying taxes or furnishing labor for the upkeep of county highways. Even before the war gaslights appeared on the principal thoroughfares of the community, but as late as the mid-1870s some streets lay in darkness each night. Seeking to correct this situation, in January 1876 the *Jeffersonian Republican* unleashed a stinging attack: "It is a great annoyance to anyone whose business requires his attendance in other parts of town to have to be incommoded with lanterns or to take mud and slush to the destruction of clothing and more frequently temper. . . . Providence more gracious than our city fathers has kindly lent us the moon to lighten our way through the Egyptian darkness." [9] Within a few weeks the council ordered lamps to be erected on Church Street south of Main. Victory at hand, this editor commented somewhat apologetically on February 16: "Gentlemen. We didn't say it. We take our hats off to you. Who cares for the moon? We don't want it—never did." [10]

Not everyone was so easily satisfied. Whether in private or public hands, the local gasworks seem to have had a checkered career at best. [11] Records are scanty, but it appears that about 1855 the Charlottesville and University Gas Light Company built its first plant near Schenck's Branch, then outside of the town limits. In 1867 this private concern was sold and reorganized; and though it was profitable to its new owners, service was unpredictable and the product nearly twice as expensive as that available in centers such as New York and Philadelphia. In 1876, for $20,000, the town became sole owner; but despite the *Jeffersonian Republican's* minor victory of that year, prob-

[9] Ibid., p. 111.   [10] Ibid.

[11] See Elmer C. Crowell, "A Financial Analysis of Charlottesville's Gas Works, Charlottesville, Virginia" (M.S. thesis, University of Virginia, 1933).

31. Albemarle sawmill, ca. 1895

lems persisted. In 1880 W. O. Watson, local C. & O. agent, told the company's superintendent in very clear language what he thought of the municipal gasworks: "Your infernal old gas machine is giving about as much light as a small size candle. If it isn't fixed by tomorrow night somebody will be hurt and don't you forget it." [12]

In 1888, when Charlottesville became a city, its leaders considered construction of an electric plant, but Edison's magic bulb was not in general use locally until 1901. Fully a decade before the town entered the gas business, the state legislature authorized construction of a municipal waterworks. It was not until February 1885, however, when yet another law increased the amount that could be borrowed and permitted the university to share both costs and benefits of the project, that work actually began. With sale of $70,000 in bonds, pipe-laying and trenching got underway and was complete by mid-July. Soon water was flowing to the town and university from the reservoir situated in the Ragged Mountains between Round Top and Newcomb's Mountain. To pay for this luxury citizens faced a substantial increase in the tax rate (from sixty cents to ninety-six cents per $100), but most were more than willing to pay for a service which provided clean drinking water and reduced the hazard of fires. At the same time, after several years of delay, the town council agreed to furnish equipment needed by the Charlottesville Hook, Hose, and Ladder Company, a voluntary group organized in 1881. Once ac-

[12] Ibid., p. 20.

tivated, members were excused from jury duty, and officers authorized to arrest and fine anyone who interfered with their work while they were fighting a conflagration.

On January 2, 1878, less than two years after Alexander Graham Bell perfected his telephone, the *Jeffersonian Republican* announced a demonstration of that wonder would be held in the Town Hall the following evening. "Wires will be stretched from the telegraph line to the hall and music will be transmitted from some point on the Chesapeake and Ohio Railroad so as to be distinctly heard and recognized all over the hall." This event apparently was a success, for within a few months the management of the Charlottesville Woolen Mills installed the first telephone system in the community. To satisfy public curiosity, a *Jeffersonian* reporter visited the Main Street office building where the company recently had opened a sample display room for visiting merchants. To his amazement he discovered that when a Colonel Peagram who managed this facility "wishes to communicate with the mills he springs a signal button which is attached to the instrument and that strikes an electric bell at the mills. . . . Then Colonel Peagram adjusts his instrument and every word over the line is heard distinctly by him." [13]

Widespread use of the telephone was, however, many years in the future. The General Assembly chartered the Albemarle Telephone and Telegraph Company in 1887, but although its backers included the cream of local society, nothing came of this effort. In 1890 the city council gave W. A. Lankford and William Pitcher permission to operate a telephone exchange, but these gentlemen could not secure enough subscribers to proceed with their plans. Undaunted, Lankford persisted and five years later opened a small central office at the corner of Fourth and Main streets with T. Frank Kelley as manager. Within a few months he had sixty-six customers and for their benefit circulated these instructions: "Anyone wishing to talk through the phone will press button on the left of bell box and turn handle on the right. Don't wait to be answered by a ring but immediately after ringing take down the receiver. . . . When through talking be careful in hanging up the receiver and see that the hook is pulled out as soon as the receiver is hung up properly. Ring your bell to let the operator know you are through with the phone for the present." [14]

Lankford's persistence was not rewarded with success. With the organization of the Albemarle Telephone Company in 1897 (J. Edwin Wood, president, J. F. Harlan, vice president), he faced an aggres-

[13] Webb, pp. 112–13.   [14] Ibid., p. 235.

sive concern which soon overwhelmed his pioneer effort. One of Wood's earliest customers, perhaps the first, was the Charlottesville Hardware Company, and within weeks he secured permission to bury wires under certain conditions. By 1899 Wood and Harlan had extended their lines to Batesville, the Miller School (an institution for indigent children launched in 1877), and Crozet; and, with over five hundred telephones in operation, they had completely outdistanced all rivals (see Appendix B).

These improvements—better rail service, better roads, and arrival of the telephone—had their impact upon Albemarle's farm folk, but of still greater importance were changes taking place upon farms themselves. For the most part, these were not true innovations, merely shifts in emphasis as wheat and tobacco tended to give way to fruit orchards, vineyards, and herds of sheep and beef and dairy cattle. Because of unsettled labor conditions, the years 1865–70 were marked by a substantial number of land transfers; and even at that date, many purchasers were former residents of northern states, especially New York, Pennsylvania, and Maryland, as well as a few immigrants from overseas. Some of these individuals, notably those of Irish origin, appear to have settled for a brief time in New York City. A few Englishmen first tried their luck in such far-flung outposts as Australia, India, and Jamaica before making their way to the hills of Albemarle. Yet, despite land sales and inward migration, there actually were fewer farms in the county in 1870 than in 1860, 824 compared to 935. But during the next decade the number more than doubled. Of 2,099 individual units in 1880, 1,584 were cultivated by their owners, 162 rented for a fixed amount, and 353 operated on a sharecropping basis. In that year, while less than a thousand residents were non-Virginians, the "foreign-born" element included 119 Englishmen, 77 Germans, some 60 to 70 former citizens of New York, Pennsylvania, and Maryland, 42 South Carolinians, and 34 Irishmen.

Far from being viewed as carpetbaggers (a term hardly applicable to those from the Palmetto State and most individuals from overseas), these folk were welcomed with open arms, possibly because some were well-to-do and exerted a very beneficial influence upon local agriculture. William Hotopp, German-born and formerly a resident of Hudson City, New York, in 1866 purchased Gilmer's Pen Park and began planting extensive vineyards. Other Germans followed in his wake, and soon local farmers were taking renewed interest in an undertaking begun by Philip Mazzei a century earlier but terminated by revolution. Most looked upon viniculture as an adjunct to general farming which during some seasons proved quite profitable. In 1873 a large group of farmers formed the Monticello Wine Company, assuring them of at least a home market and encouraging others to plant vineyards. A decade later that company purchased nearly five hundred thousand pounds of grapes at prices ranging from two to four cents per pound, and Hotopp bought an equal amount for processing at his cellars. In an ad published in 1888 Oscar Reierson, secretary of the Monticello Wine Company, stressed that his product was neither cheap nor equal to the renowned vintages of European hillsides.

This company does not claim *cheapness*. It offers, at figures so reasonable as to be accessible to all, *well-matured, pure fermented grape wines*. Imported wine, of similar good quality, would cost double the price. It does not claim to produce the equals of the *Grand Vins* of Europe. Taking price and character into consideration, it does claim a quality at half the price of that imported, when of similar character. The white wines are *Delaware*, Sautern Nature; *Dry Catawba, sui generis* (see Longfellow's poem); while the red wines are *Norton's Virginia*, Burgundy character; *Cythiana*, first class among the red wines at the Vienna Exposition of 1876; *Clinton*, aged, a superior claret; *Extra Claret*, superior character; *Ives Seedling*, ruby colored claret; *Virginia Claret*, sound, plain table wine; pure grape brandy, three summers old.[15]

In addition to grapes, farmers increased their production of apples and peaches. For some, small orchards were simply an essential part of any well-balanced, completely equipped farm, but this enterprise became much more of a commercial venture for those living in the shadow of the Blue Ridge. In 1879, for example, J. F. Wayland shipped thousands of those highly prized Albemarle Pippins to Liverpool via the Allen Line out of Baltimore, and J. W. Porter sold seven hundred crates of apples in northern markets. To furnish young trees several nurseries appeared, one of the best-known operated by John Dollins of Greenwood. Cherries and strawberries also were grown for city customers, some farmers planting cherry trees along fences where they took up little space and did well. In 1888 Miller School had a huge strawberry bed four years old which was said to produce five thousand quarts per acre.

While nearly all farmers raised more livestock than before the war, it was the large and specialized herds of a few individuals that won the county an outstanding reputation for fine cattle. Slaughter W. Ficklin, probably the most famous breeder, with his

[15] *Albemarle County Handbook*, p. 122.

32. Edgehill School, class of 1891

33. Sewing class at Miller School, 1899

son, William, operated Belmont, located on the outskirts of Charlottesville. In 1866 he imported four Norman-Percheron stallions and
two mares and ever after was attempting to perfect this strain and
urging others to do the same. His favorite breed of cattle was Short-
horn, which he claimed best suited to local conditions. This gentleman also raised hogs, mostly of the Berkshire variety, and some
sheep.

Few landowners had interests as varied as Ficklin, but several became specialists in particular fields. Captain R. J. Hancock's Ellerslie
on the eastern slope of Carter's Mountain boasted some forty thoroughbred race horses in 1878, the most famous of these being Eolus,
holder of numerous track records. Another prominent horseman was
R. H. Fife, owner of Robin Adair. A decade later the *Albemarle
County Handbook* hailed Ellerslie as an example of "What Albemarle Can Do." This laudatory sketch noted that John O. Harris had
purchased that farm in 1841, and his wife, a great admirer of William Wallace, Knight of Ellerslie, bestowed the new name upon it.

Captain R. J. Hancock married a daughter of Mr. John O. Harris, and
at the close of the war took charge of the place. Then the stock, fencing,
and agricultural implements were not in the best condition—for Sheridan
had passed through the country. Additions have been made to the place
until now it comprises 1,800 acres of land, a merchant mill, excellent
barns, stables, &c. Every field and paddock is supplied with an abundance
of pure water, while there is not an acre of marsh land upon the tract. In
spite of the vicissitudes of war and other pestilences, the farm for forty-
seven years has made its own corn and provender, not a dollar's worth of
either being purchased in that period.

After several paragraphs praising Eolus (son of Leamington and
Fanny Washington) and telling of his success at Pimlico and other
tracks, this account concluded with a general description of the
estate and Hancock's plans for the future.

No more race horses will be trained, and the stock business at Ellerslie
will be confined hereafter to breeding and to annual sales of yearlings.
The stud consists of three stallions and twenty-five brood mares.

There is also on the farm a splendid herd of Shorthorns, of the best
blood and milking families, which were collected by Mr. Lewis F. Allen,
editor of the *American Herd Book*, (an uncle, by the by, of President
Cleveland); pure Cotswolds and Berkshires; in fact, everything is thoroughbred except work horses, even to setter dogs, Maltese cats and game
chickens.

If nothing else, here is sound evidence that love of cockfighting among some Albemarle residents has a long and glorious history.

Missing from this intriguing publication designed to lure settlers to Albemarle (strangely) is any reference to the master of the county's most famous estate and (not so strangely) comment upon the many problems faced by all farmers during these harsh decades. Five years after the death of Jefferson, Monticello was purchased from his daughter, Martha, for $7,000 by James Barclay, an eccentric Charlottesville chemist, druggist, and preacher. In 1836 Uriah P. Levy, descendant of an indentured servant, an inmate of Britain's Dartmoor Prison during the War of 1812, and frequently in hot water throughout a tempestuous career in the U.S. Navy, bought the property, now reduced to only 218 acres, from Barclay for $2,700. Both he and an appropriately named nephew who acquired Monticello in 1879 spent substantial sums on repairs and upkeep and also bought back huge tracts once part of its sprawling acres. Both gentlemen treated that famous landmark as a summer retreat, preferring to maintain legal and official residence in Manhattan. Both also from time to time harbored thoughts of placing the estate in the hands of the United States government in trust for all Americans. Jefferson Monroe Levy was especially kind to tourists, and any distinguished guest who came to Charlottesville or the university for over half a century was assured of a gracious welcome.

Although Jeffersonian scholars and architectural purists might scoff at some of the alterations made by this family, in general they tried as best they could to restore the estate to its former grandeur; but more important, for nearly one hundred years Monticello was in the hands of men who recognized it as a vital part of America's heritage. Every Fourth of July, Jefferson Levy, a bachelor who served three terms in Congress as a representative from New York, staged a grand fireworks display. He was extremely considerate of Jefferson's many descendants living in Albemarle, despite some misunderstanding as to the ownership and care of the graveyard. One of them recalls visiting Monticello with an aunt at the turn of the century who tipped a black woman at the gate ten cents so she would not ring a bell and alert Levy that they were en route to the final resting place of their distinguished ancestor. In 1913 the Randolphs, Taylors, Keans, Shacklefords, and other descendants formed the Monticello Graveyard Association which began holding annual meetings and continues to administer the graveyard today under the name of the Monticello Association. In December 1923 Jefferson Levy sold

Monticello to the Thomas Jefferson Memorial Foundation for $500,000, and this body commenced restoration of the estate, in time making it a mecca for thousands of tourists from all parts of the world. In recent years the foundation has given substantial sums of money to Jefferson's university in support of endowed chairs and in the form of fellowships for students in history, government, and architecture. The Levys, in effect caretakers of Monticello for eighty-seven years, performed a tremendous service for Albemarle and America.[16]

One of the best sources of information on county life during the last decades of the nineteenth century is Green Peyton's comprehensive map of Albemarle published in 1875. Peyton not only cites agricultural and population statistics but also details geographical features, roads, railroads, towns, and villages, crossroads stores, even rural homes with the names of their owners. This survey includes scores of little communities which have since disappeared; yet at that date what is now western Albemarle's most important trading center, Crozet, was still known as Wayland's, merely a railroad siding bearing the name of a prominent fruit grower and shipper. Although never incorporated as a town, in the late 1870s this growing village took the name of the famed railway engineer, Claudius Crozet, and, in time, became a center of peach and apple production, one of the most important in the Old Dominion.

The basic problem confronting the vast majority of Albemarle's farmers at the time Peyton was drawing up his map (and in the next two decades) can be summed up simply enough: costs continued to rise while income declined. They owned neither race horses nor sleek herds of purebred livestock; instead, they continued to raise corn, wheat, tobacco, and an assortment of scrawny animals much as their fathers and grandfathers had done, hoping each season would bring renewed demand for their produce. The nub of the matter was, of course, that the products of other regions, notably tobacco from Kentucky and grain from the burgeoning Midwest and Far West, as well as bumper crops from Canada and new lands overseas, were usurping markets once theirs. The result was gradual emulation of well-to-do landowners with somewhat more reliance upon peaches,

[16] See Donovan Fitzpatrick and Saul Saphire, *Navy Maverick: Uriah Phillips Levy* (Garden City, N.Y., 1963), and George Green Shackleford, ed., *Collected Papers to Commemorate Fifty Years of the Monticello Association of the Descendants of Thomas Jefferson* (Princeton, N.J., 1965), pp. 3–26.

apples, grapes, and dairy cattle, but these undertakings cost money, and farmers often were reluctant to change established modes of operation. Yet the agrarian protests which shook the national fabric from 1870 to 1900 do not seem to have had much effect in Albemarle. Local residents were sympathetic to efforts of the Grange to curb excesses of railroad barons in the 1870s, but few actually joined that organization. The Farmers' Alliance of the 1880s, more of a home-grown product, enjoyed success as long as it was essentially non-political and limited its program to setting up cooperatives selling fertilizers, seed, and farm implements at wholesale prices. When it became Populism in the 1890s support melted away. Most rural voters, alarmed by what they saw happening in North Carolina where that party gained power and fearful that if it was triumphant in the Old Dominion, this might mean resurgence of Republican-black rule in yet another guise, preferred the security of the Democratic fold. In 1892 when James G. Field, state attorney general under two governors, a highly respected citizen, and master of what is now Logon near Gordonsville, ran for vice-president on the Populist ticket, he received only sixteen votes in Albemarle.

Census statistics for these years help to explain, to some extent, why outside protest movements exerted little appeal, for even in 1880 local farmers were doing relatively well. Their buildings and lands were worth $6,015,736, making Albemarle the fourth richest county in Virginia, exceeded only by Augusta, Fauquier, and Loudoun. Perhaps of greater importance, no leader like Parson John Massey appeared to harness the frustration and despair which must have been present in scores of households from the banks of the James to the crest of the Blue Ridge during these years.

While the most notable change in education was establishment of functioning free public schools for both races, private schools continued to operate with indifferent success. At the close of the war buildings and grounds at the University of Virginia were run-down and neglected, scientific apparatus depleted, students poor, and the treasury empty. Hard work and sobriety were central to university life in the postwar years. Rival state universities and newly emerging land grant institutions throughout the South attracted scores of students who once would have enrolled at Charlottesville. Moreover, while sister schools in the North waxed fat from new industrial wealth, the university struggled along in poverty. Although approximately half of the students were non-Virginians, enrollment in the 1870s slipped from 447 to 375. Peak enrollment of prewar years was not equaled until the early 1900s. Not until well into the twentieth century did it seem that the University of Virginia was overcoming the shock and devastation of the war years.

One student of the 1880s, a future president of the United States, Woodrow Wilson, wrote revealing letters concerning university life. As a stepping-stone to a public career, Wilson attended the law school from September 1879 to December 1880. He complained bitterly of how hard he and most of his associates had to work: "Study is made a serious business and the loafer is the exception. Everyone has the highest regard for culture and scholarship." [17] He conceded the instruction was excellent, the facilities attractive, and the atmosphere cosmopolitan. He gained prominence as an orator, revised the constitution of the Jefferson Literary Society, and was elected its president. He also published two essays in the *University Virginia Magazine*, one on John Bright, the other on Gladstone—essays which suggested his own ambition to become a great leader.

Still Wilson chafed at the long hours of study and yearned for greater social bonds similar to those he had known as an undergraduate among southern friends at Princeton. He no doubt missed the camaraderie fostered by undergraduate classes there, freshmen, sophomore, etc., for University of Virginia students were not organized into neat, distinct classes. As they had for generations, they came, chose a course of study, and proceeded more or less at their own pace. This program permitted considerable individual freedom (this Wilson admitted), but at the same time, it created a milieu which he found confusing. University life certainly was not so rowdy or exciting as it had been in previous decades; instead, there was a continuing round of lectures and debates, enlivened by campus politics from time to time and outings in town. And, as Wilson noted, there were celebrations marking Jefferson's birthday and the end of the school year. Some students complained about food served at boardinghouses, protested regulations which discouraged them from eating at their private clubs, and yearned for a sidewalk which would enable them to avoid mud and potholes whenever they strolled into the town of Charlottesville.

Although Wilson had his moments of frustration at the university, he nevertheless sharpened his appetite and qualifications for public leadership. His most intimate friend was Richard Heath Dabney, later chairman of the history department and dean of the graduate

[17] Arthur S. Link, ed., *The Papers of Woodrow Wilson* (12 vols.; Princeton, N.J., 1966—), 1:582.

school. The teacher who most impressed him was John B. Minor, the influential law professor, who was launching scores of young men into careers throughout the South and other parts of the country— men who, as Jefferson had expected, would play distinguished public roles in state and nation. As during prewar years, the University of Virginia continued to train students whose numbers were conspicuous in the U.S. Senate and House, state legislatures and governors' mansions, the judiciary, medicine (especially the army and navy medical corps), the ministry, and education, notably private academies.

Soon after Wilson left Charlottesville, in 1882 conservative students and faculty for a time feared they were being overwhelmed by change. Like an unexpected seasonal storm sweeping down from the coves of the Blue Ridge, a new board of visitors appointed by William E. Cameron, the Readjuster governor, dismissed all of the key administrators—librarian, proctor, bursar, and boardinghouse keepers—and replaced them with individuals thought to be more responsive to both their dictates and the needs of higher education.[18] Despite howls of protest from some undergraduates, faculty, alumni, and townspeople, within a very few months these men also had revamped the curriculum, authorized new degrees and construction of a Gothic chapel, laid the foundations of a modern graduate school, regularized payment of faculty salaries, cut expenses somewhat, put carpenters and painters to work repairing years of neglect, and settled a vexatious dispute with the trustees of Miller School. All of this was accomplished with such dispatch that editors of the *University Virginia Magazine* lamented there really was no cause for "virtuous indignation." Actually, these Readjusters seem to have accomplished the impossible. Though winning few converts to their political cause, they soon became heroes to those once hostile to them, and in 1884 a Democrat-controlled General Assembly even increased the state's annual appropriation to the university and authorized an additional $40,000 for construction of a new reservoir being built in the hills west of Charlottesville. When replaced in 1886, the board left behind a surplus of over $13,000 and a much more efficiently run institution. As James Moore notes, "The University, a citadel of the state's traditionalist elite, had felt the invigorating touch of new men with new ideas." [19]

[18] James T. Moore, "The University and the Readjusters," *Virginia Magazine of History and Biography* 88 (1970):93–94.

[19] Ibid., p. 101.

In the mid-1870s private school enrollment continued high, 1,345 students attending various academies in 1875.[20] By the end of that decade, however, these institutions, both primary and secondary, had fallen upon hard times and by 1885 had only 304 pupils. Though some were day schools, nearly all served either boys or girls, not both sexes. Many were small affairs operated in private homes with several families sharing the expense of hiring and maintaining a teacher. Piedmont Female Institute, Albemarle Female Institute, and Edgehill School, all founded before the war, continued to uphold their reputations for excellence throughout these years. Total costs for boarding students were $280 to $300 for a ten-month session. Albemarle Female Institute, which eventually became Rawlings Institute and in 1910 St. Anne's School, inaugurated a somber, dark gray worsted uniform in 1875; and, several schools, Edgehill among them, began to hold summer sessions in an effort to boost sagging income. About 1890 the Randolph family, which owned Edgehill farm and operated the school, one of the South's most prestigious throughout the nineteenth century, built a small Gothic chapel designed to serve both students and the local community.[21] After some forty years of weekly services, weddings, and funerals, in 1930 the structure was deconsecrated and eventually sold by the Episcopal Diocese to an individual who intended to convert it into a private residence; however, these plans were not carried out and the structure eventually was torn down. The school, successor to one by the same name begun by Mrs. Thomas Jefferson Randolph in 1829, closed shortly before the turn of the century.

One of the most successful boys' schools of these years was Charlottesville Institute, better known as "Major Jones's School." Founded in 1857 and reopened after the war by Major Horace W. Jones, it was under his personal direction until 1876 when he left to teach in Hanover County. Located first in the vicinity of the present McGuffey School and later at the corner of Seventh and Market streets, "Major Jones's" continued to prepare young men for university education until about 1900.

As research of Harold Mopsik on Charlottesville's academies makes clear, most led very short lives and depended almost entirely

---

[20] For a complete survey of private education on the local scene, see Harold Mopsik, "A History of Private Secondary Education in Charlottesville" (M.S. thesis, University of Virginia, 1936).

[21] See two articles by Olivia Taylor, "The Edgehill School," *Annual Report of the Monticello Association* (1967), pp. 17–33, and "The Edgehill Memorial Chapel," *Annual Report of the Monticello Association* (1969), pp. 15–19.

upon the energies of a single individual. Pantops Academy (1879–1906), a Presbyterian school for boys, was established on a well-known estate some two miles east of town by Rev. Edgar Woods, pioneer county historian. Its primary goal, like that of Charlottesville Institute, was to prepare young men for college and university. By 1886 John R. Sampson was principal, with Woods serving as his associate. In time, this school had as many as seven instructors and an average enrollment of seventy pupils, many of them from out-of-state and some from foreign countries. Suddenly, when apparently at the crest of its popularity, Sampson announced in 1906 that, "for reasons connected with his family," he was closing the school.

Obviously, if private classrooms were to continue in the face of rising costs and increasing reliance upon public education, they had to tie their fortunes to something more than the energies, abilities, and whims of a few individuals, regardless of how great their skills might be. Miller Manual Labor School, established in Batesville in the 1870s as a result of a most unusual bequest, was not only under the aegis of a self-perpetuating board, it also marked a unique departure in education in Albemarle. Here, not the offspring of the well-to-do, but indigent young people would be taught.

Samuel Miller, second illegitimate son of a poor widow, was born in a small cabin near Batesville in 1792.[22] Despite abject poverty the mother insisted that her two boys get as much education as possible, and, it is said, she sometimes followed Samuel and his elder brother, John, down the mountainside with a switch on mornings when they approached learning with juvenile reluctance. In 1814 John went to work in a Lynchburg retail store, later becoming a partner in a grocery business. After a few years as a teacher, Samuel joined him and began his remarkable career as a businessman. John died in 1841, leaving his entire estate ($100,000) to his brother who, within two decades, by trading in agricultural commodities and shrewd investment, had amassed a considerable fortune. In 1859 Samuel, who never married, wrote a complex will providing bequests to aid poor children in both Lynchburg and his native Albemarle. Before he died a decade later Miller added a proviso designed to create an agricultural school at the University of Virginia.

This generous gift of $100,000, the largest the university had received up to that time, does not appear to have been utilized quite in the spirit intended, since it was used to endow a professorship in the biology department; nevertheless, this sum helped to create the first

[22] See Bernard Chamberlain, "Samuel Miller, 1792–1869: Albemarle Philanthropist," *MACH* 27–28 (1970):119–27.

agricultural experiment station in the nation and established a custom of placing such funds in the hands of alumni trustees free from
state control. During the decade or so that followed, perhaps inspired by Miller, several other individuals also gave substantial gifts
to the University of Virginia.[23] These included an observatory and
telescope from Leander J. McCormick of Chicago, over $100,000
from W. W. Corcoran, a Washington financier, to aid the study of
chemistry, natural history, geology, and history (the latter department when it evolved being named in his honor), and some $70,000
from Lewis Brooks, a Rochester, New York, manufacturer, to build
a museum of natural history. In 1881 William H. Vanderbilt donated
$25,000 to the university, but the most impressive bequest of these
years was some $400,000 given by Arthur W. Austin of Milton,
Massachusetts, when he died in 1884.

The Austin money, consisting of railroad stocks, bonds, and land,
came to the University of Virginia by a most bizarre route. The
donor, apparently a stern Democrat with no ties to the South or the
Old Dominion, was turned out of his post as a port collector when the
Republicans won in 1860. Always an admirer of Thomas Jefferson,
his writings, and his political theories, he directed that the interest
on his estate should belong to one of his daughters, Mary, as long as
she lived, then the entire sum was to go to the University of Virginia.
In 1901, seventeen years after her father's death, happily married,
well-to-do, and tired of family bickering over the bequest, Mary
agreed to settle for $5,000 per year, permitting the university to as-
sume control of an inheritance which, by that date, probably exceeded $500,000.

The bulk of Samuel Miller's estate, $1 million earmarked for the
benefit of Albemarle's indigent young people, was the object of
several lawsuits filed by purported relatives; but finally, in August
1877 the Miller Manual Labor School was incorporated by the General Assembly. According to terms of the will, Miller's money was
held in trust by the State Board of Education, with the local county
court empowered to meet expenses incurred by the institution and
appoint several citizens to employ teachers, visit the school quarterly,
and report to the court concerning its welfare. School trustees of
various districts in Albemarle, one of which now appropriately bore
the name of Samuel Miller, were to nominate deserving pupils. Once

[23] See Priscilla Lundin De Prospo, "Patterns of Charitable Giving to the
University of Virginia, 1818–1915" (M.A. thesis, University of Virginia,
1973).

enrolled, they were clothed, fed, taught, and cared for at the expense of the school. Thirty-three boys were admitted to the first session in October 1878. Six years later Professor Francis H. Smith of the University of Virginia, one of the visitors named by the court, argued successfully that since Miller had wished to aid "poor orphans and other white children of Albemarle County," girls should be admitted as well.

By 1888 the Miller School had 242 pupils and facilities and grounds valued at about $360,000. Although most of the students were boys, girls seem to have been more dedicated scholars. During that session, for example, 22 boys withdrew, but only 3 girls. The course of study included a primary department and a secondary division which offered basic courses in Latin, German, mathematics, various sciences, practical mechanics, and farm training. Some youngsters also studied bookkeeping, telegraphy, bee culture, printing, typewriting, and dressmaking. The imposing central structure was completed in 1883 at a cost of $140,000, but it was the machine shop, though smaller, which undoubtedly most impressed both student and guest. This building, in which mechanical arts were taught, supplied steam for the laundry, heat for buildings, and housed five engines which helped to light ("by Edison's incandescent electric") the entire campus! Thus, while most Charlottesville and Albemarle households continued to turn gas jets up and down and trim lamp wicks, thanks to the generosity of a thoughtful local boy who made good, scores of the county's poorest children basked in the glory of electric lights.

The impact of national industrial and business growth from 1865 to 1890 was felt in Albemarle, but commercial enterprises hardly supplanted agriculture as the prime source of economic activity. With few exceptions, much like the county's private school teachers, owners and managers came and went with great frequency as a result of hard times, disastrous conflagrations, inept administration of affairs, or lack of demand for services and products offered. Both Hotopp's wine company and the Charlottesville Woolen Mills proved stable, despite fires in the early 1880s. The latter, because of the shrewd leadership of Henry Clay Marchant, built a firm corporate structure which in the half century which followed was a bulwark of Charlottesville business life. Specializing in cloth for uniforms in the early twentieth century, these mills were supplying 90 percent of the nation's military schools (including West Point), city employees in Philadelphia, Chicago, and numerous other municipalities, and thousands of railway workers. By 1930 company officials claimed they could travel from coast to coast on railroads whose crewmen were outfitted with their cloth.[24]

The Rio Mills, burned by Custer in 1864, were rebuilt under the direction of W. R. Burnley and F. M. Wills. In addition to manufacturing flour and meal, they ran a circular sawmill processing up to six thousand feet of lumber per day. These new owners suffered heavy flood damage in September 1870 but soon were back in operation. During the early postwar years the Charlottesville Milling and Manufacturing Company enjoyed a brief career, turning out not only flour and cornmeal but also plaster and fertilizer. This enterprise, one of many owned by B. C. Flannagan, appears to have closed down soon after 1870. On the other hand, the Monticello Cigar Factory organized by C. C. Wertenbaker, the university postmaster forced out by the Radicals, seems to have prospered and, in the mid-1870s, employed ten or more laborers.

The leading wagon and carriage builders of that era were Wingfield and Utz and L. W. Cox. In 1884 Cox had a large staff of experienced workmen and three showrooms full of buggies, wagons, carriages, road carts, and other vehicles and was selling his wares not only in Albemarle but in neighboring counties as well. Some interest in mining is evident, especially in iron ore, slate, and coal; however, soapstone quarried at Alberene proved the most profitable and enduring of these enterprises. Since this stone found in the North Garden area was nonporous, acid resistant, and fireproof, it was much in demand for use in fireplaces, laundry tubs, laboratory sinks, and bathroom fixtures. Local sandstone, by the way, was used in construction of both the Brooks Museum and the university chapel.

Comparison of Charlottesville business directories published in 1870 and 1885 reveal a substantial increase in local outlets and specialization.[25] In the 1880s Estes and Perley both sold furniture; Treiber and Gillespie, stoves; Jefferies, Thomas, Matthews, and Ambroselli, confectionaries; Balthis and Keller (which by the turn of the century became Keller and George), jewelry. Housewives could buy sewing machines from J. E. Jarman, clothes and dry goods at several emporiums, among them those of Patterson, Marshall, Kaufman, Leterman, T. T. and J. B. Woods, and M. B. Heller. The largest and perhaps most successful store of those years was owned by E. M. Antrim. Immediately after the war he purveyed not only silks, woolens, and cotton but groceries and hardware as well; however by the 1880s he dealt only in dry goods. H. P. Edwards

[24] Poindexter, p. 48.   [25] Webb, pp. 84–85.

operated a retail grocery store, while Flannagan, Reierson, and Frizell sold foodstuffs to both retail and wholesale customers. At the Excelsior Shops one could purchase pictures and have photographs made. Geiger's drugstore featured perfumes and cosmetics, and Lew Wood furnished the community with guns, knives, and toys.

Several hotels served travelers and those seeking room and board. In the mid-1870s the Central Hotel near the Chesapeake and Ohio depot was managed by James Page, while W. J. Parrott owned and operated the Farish House, now an annex of the Monticello Hotel. Guests usually were accommodated on the American plan (a fixed fee covering all costs), but in 1872 E. M. and E. H. Leftwich introduced the European plan at a house located at the corner of Main and Court streets. This meant, they emphasized in the *Weekly Chronicle*, "you call for what you want and pay for what you get." Two popular barrooms of that decade were presided over by John Mannoni and John Saunders, the latter operating a boardinghouse as well. In the 1880s Eisenmann's Saloon became a favorite haunt of university undergraduates, and there, according to one student of those years, they "frequently caroused until early dawn.[26] In addition to the *Chronicle*, which underwent frequent changes in ownership and management and vacillated between weekly and triweekly editions, area residents could also read the *Jeffersonian Republican*, successor to the prewar weekly of the same name. In 1873 the *Republican* absorbed a short-lived competitor, the *Piedmont* (or *Charlottesville*) *Intelligencer*. It, in turn, was absorbed by the *Daily Progress* in the 1890s, although the *Chronicle* continued to turn out weekly and daily editions until 1925. Scottsville, which, like the county seat, saw numerous editors come and go during the first half of the nineteenth century, was served by the *Register*, 1859–72, and the *Courier*, 1872–1906 (see Appendix C).

Immediately following the war no less than four banks were incorporated in Charlottesville (Farmers and Merchants, Citizens National, Charlottesville National, and Virginia Loan and Trust Company), but by 1877 all of them had disappeared, cut down by the panic of 1873 and hard times which ensued. They were succeeded by the People's Bank (1875), B. H. Brennan and Company (1878), and the Bank of Albemarle (1882). People's, which would become a major force in the community in the twentieth century, and the Bank of Albemarle were able to weather the stormy 1880s, but Brennan

[26] James P. C. Southall, "Reminiscences of Charlottesville in the 1880's," *MACH* 4 (1945):26.

and Company closed its doors in 1884. Another casualty of these difficult decades was the Albemarle Insurance Company. This enterprise, one more in which B. C. Flannagan was involved, appeared to be extremely prosperous but in April 1877 suddenly collapsed. "The practice of paying high interest rates on deposits," its management said, apparently with no humor intended, "has been a huge mistake."

To promote business and industry, Charlottesville's leading citizens established a board of trade late in 1872. Members, who paid an annual fee of $2, attended monthly meetings at which various committees reported on local affairs. The most active were those on manufacturing, trade and transportation, accounts, general improvements, cooperation, and immigration. Though this body enjoyed only a brief life and never measured up to expectations, it did perform valuable spadework for similar organizations which would follow.

Aftermath of war, hard times and good, improvements in transportation, growth of free public education, all affected Albemarle social life during these late nineteenth-century years. Both veterans and local ladies formed associations dedicated to remembering the dead and caring for their orphans. The most active military unit was the Monticello Guard, composed largely of ex-Confederates, at least during the decade following the war. They marched down Charlottesville's main street once each month (also on Jefferson's birthday), usually climaxing these outings with a hearty meal at a local restaurant. This company also held target practice near Cochran's Mill each year, an event watched by wives, sweethearts, and relatives, and frequently traveled to Richmond to participate in the state fair. Commanded by Captain Micajah Woods, thirty-five local men, accompanied by the Third Regimental Band, took part in the Yorktown Centennial of 1881, an extravaganza which, because of extreme heat, excessive drink, and failure to provide proper facilities for the huge crowd gathered there, was a near disaster. In April 1884, with "General" James G. Field presiding, a county veterans association was formed.[27] This group, precursor of a national organization and patterned after one in Richmond, opened membership to many more individuals than could join the guard, as well as those too old to participate in drills and target practice. Even men who had not worn Confederate gray were welcome on an honorary basis. The original officers were R. T. W. Duke (commandant), J. C. Culin, R. P.

[27] Webb, p. 145. The highest rank ever held by Field was major. The title of general, like many which emerged after Appomattox, was purely honorary.

34. Greenwood School for Boys, 1897

35. Albemarle County Courthouse

Mason, Bennett Taylor, C. C. Wertenbaker, William Fretwell, T. A. Ware, and W. C. N. Randolph.

Parades by local militiamen and veterans drew much applause, but watching people one knew march down the street hardly compared with the mystery and glamour of wild animals, acrobats, and clowns "when the circus came to town." Various shows, among them groups owned by Thayer, Robinson, Coles, Sells, and Barnett, played to very appreciative audiences during these years. James L. Thayer, in keeping with circus tradition for hyperbole, claimed in 1870 that his performances were so fun-filled that even "consumptives and dyspeptics" among the spectators would be cured.[28]

As Charlottesville grew, so did suggestions for a fair or exposition. Though nothing came of these proposals, Scottsville in 1883 launched the James River Valley Fair, three days of horse racing, games, music, agricultural exhibits, and speechmaking which soon became an annual event attracting hundreds of visitors to that little town. Among the early organizers of this community enterprise were J. C. Hill, W. G. Merrick, M. L. Van Doren, and J. S. Andrews. Charlottesville's Town Hall continued to be a center of both professional and amateur entertainment, although considerable evidence exists that the building was hardly suitable for such gatherings. According to Richard E. Waddell, "No opera house at all would have been an improvement over the Town Hall." [29] However, in 1887 Jefferson M. Levy, the New Yorker who was refurbishing Monticello, purchased the old building and did an even more extensive job than that going on a few miles away. The Levy Opera House, more recently Parkview Apartments and still standing at the corner of Park and High streets, opened a year later, but could seat only five hundred people. In 1896 William Hotopp erected Jefferson Auditorium on Main Street near the present Albemarle Hotel. Both this more spacious facility and the Levy Opera House were host to traveling theatrical companies and local groups until the early years of the twentieth century when other theaters, some showing motion pictures, appeared. The auditorium was destroyed by fire in November 1907, and five years later the Levy was converted to Jefferson School for Boys.

University athletics, especially baseball and football, attracted

[28] Ibid., p. 149.
[29] Waddell, "Theatre in Charlottesville, 1886–1912: The Levy Opera House and the Jefferson Auditorium" (M.A. thesis, University of Virginia, 1972), p. 8.

scores of interested spectators; and on occasions, local residents watched or participated in fox hunts, horse shows, crew races, and cricket matches. Though cricket proved no rival to baseball, in 1874 Gordonsville and Charlottesville teams, composed largely of British émigrés, met on a field owned by S. W. Ficklin, Charlottesville emerging victorious. Two of the best-known social groups of these years were the Camp Armistead Hunting Club and the Albemarle Jockey Club. Each fall members of the hunting club (originally called the Deer Hunting Club) journeyed to their grounds west of Staunton where, aided by a large pack of dogs, they held a week-long outing which usually resulted in a generous supply of venison and smaller game on local tables. The jockey club held races each spring and fall, often on the farm of J. A. Harris, which had several hurdles, a steeplechase track, and facilities for shorter, matched races. Another organization with both social and political overtones was the Cool Spring Barbecue Club, which met for many years on the grounds of Sunnyside, home of R. T. W. Duke, the group's first president and one of Albemarle's most distinguished Confederate veterans.

In addition to five Masonic lodges, both county and town residents had an increasing number of fraternal and social organizations vying for their attention. Several farm clubs were especially active, among them the Southside, Keswick, and Belmont associations. The Southside Club sponsored the fair held in Scottsville, while Keswick farmers held monthly meetings similar to those once staged by the Albemarle Agricultural Society. In contrast, the Belmont group seemed more interested in a lavish annual banquet complete with distinguished guests. One of the most unusual of these rural clubs was the Albemarle Ploughing Society, established in 1878, which staged daylong ploughing contests culminating with a bountiful meal, usually at the Central Hotel.

However, as in past decades for most citizens social activity centered around church and home, although visiting and entertaining were curtailed somewhat by hard times. A local lady born in the 1880s recalls: "We certainly spent a lot of time with friends and relatives, yes, often enjoying a huge dinner at about two in the afternoon, but rarely stayed overnight. Fearful of being a burden, you know." In 1870 the county had sixty-seven religious organizations with fifty-six structures seating 19,050 persons and owning property worth $156,300. By denomination, reflecting a substantial group of Negro congregations, these included twenty-three Baptist groups, twenty-one Methodist, eight Episcopal, seven Presbyterian, three

Christian, and one Lutheran. As noted earlier, Roman Catholics consecrated their own church in 1880, and in 1882 Jews laid the cornerstone of their synagogue, Temple Beth-Israel. All Protestant groups cooperated in supporting the Albemarle Colportage and Sunday School Association designed to carry on religious work throughout the county. The Reverend Charles H. Ross, who headed this organization during the 1870s, appears to have been an extremely conscientious, dedicated worker. For reasons not clear, the university's YMCA was disbanded in 1874, only to be revived a decade later by Rev. George Petrie, a prominent Presbyterian pastor.

During the late nineteenth century Albemarle was the scene of at least one lynching. On Wednesday, March 8, 1882, young R. T. W. Duke, Jr., wrote in his diary: "Our client old Jno. O. Massie & wife were murdered last night at Buckeyeland—Brained with an axe. Object presumed to be robbery. A more quiet, inoffensive old couple never lived. God bring the wretches to light." The Rhodes family which lived nearby was blamed for the tragedy, but Jim Rhodes, the prime culprit, immediately fled to Tennessee; however, some months later he got into trouble there and the authorities returned him to Albemarle. At 1 A.M. on a Sunday morning (October 1, 1882) a mob overwhelmed the Monticello Guard surrounding the jail and hanged Rhodes from a tree alongside the road leading to the Free Bridge. Duke and two of his friends pleaded with the group, but to no avail. "I left before they hung him," he noted in his diary. "It was a beautiful, moonlight night, but a horrible & dispicable & disgraceful act." [30] A month later Leroy Rhodes, his brother, was sentenced to eleven years in prison for his part in the crime.

Incorporation of Charlottesville as a city clearly was a very important event on the local scene. In February 1888, close on the heels of a mass meeting urging such action, the General Assembly granted a municipal charter. During the next four months, until July 1 when incorporation took effect, the groundwork was laid for a government consisting of a mayor, ten councilmen, and various subsidiary officials. Separation of town and county presented innumerable difficulties, the most obvious being how to divide facilities long held in common. The charter itself solved some of these problems—responsibility for county debt, ownership and use of the courthouse, jail, and clerk's office, and access to the privileges of Miller School—but many details were left to local discretion. At a series of meetings the town council struggled with matters both great and small, among them

[30] For the full details of this incident, see Vera Via, "Looking Backward," *Daily Progress* (April 22, 1954).

creation of city wards and whether hogs would be allowed to live in the city. The answer to the latter question was in the affirmative, although town fathers reserved the right to ban porkers if they ever became a nuisance.

Charlottesville's first mayor was R. F. Harris. The council members included T. W. Bailey, C. H. Barnes, John L. Cochran, C. D. Fishburne, W. O. Fry, Moses Leterman, W. C. Payne, R. C. Vandergrift, J. L. Walters, and S. B. Woods. R. T. W. Duke, Jr., was judge of the corporation court; S. J. Dudley, sheriff; W. T. Jones, treasurer; and John W. Davis, Commonwealth's attorney. At the same date, John M. White was serving as the judge of the county court, and Louis T. Hanckel was chairman of the board of supervisors. Other board members were W. H. Harris, R. J. Leckie, N. C. McGhee, Henry M. Magruder, and C. H. Parrott. Lucian M. Watts was sheriff; A. J. Farish, treasurer; Micajah Woods, Commonwealth's attorney; J. Snowden Wood, county clerk; and D. P. Powers, superintendent of schools. R. W. Duke served as clerk of both city and county courts.

These men were pioneers, no less than Joshua Fry, Peter Jefferson, and their friends who gathered at Mrs. Scott's plantation on that bleak February day in 1745 to found Albemarle. They were embarking upon an uncharted course, that of separate city-county government, and many local residents, especially those living in the county, must have harbored grave forebodings as they watched the county seat, in effect, divorce itself from the soil which had created it. Henceforth, for better or worse, Albemarle would be divided into two factions, rural and urban, with the lines of demarcation clearly drawn. At times relations between city and county would become rather tense, especially whenever Charlottesville expanded and annexed still more property. But, as Albemarle became more urban, less rural, and perhaps even suburban, differences between city and county were mitigated somewhat by demands of twentieth-century life. Nevertheless, the year 1888 marks a dramatic turning point in local history, a much clearer one than that which delineates other eras in the development of Albemarle from rough frontier to settled community. With incorporation of Charlottesville as a city Jefferson's county had come of age, albeit an event which the master of Monticello might well have viewed as a mixed blessing at best.

Part III
Decades of Diversity and Innovation, 1888–1945

THE six decades between 1888 and 1945 were a time of tremendous change in the Charlottesville-Albemarle community, as they were in all of America. Three wars, an educational revolution at every level from primary grades to graduate study, and the advent of motion pictures, automobiles, and electric lights had their impact; yet, running through all of these innovations is one consistent theme: urbanization. Charlottesville's population, thanks to annexation and the attractions of city life, was about equal to that of the county by the end of World War II, each having approximately twenty-five thousand residents. This growth means, of course, that, much more than in previous eras, the story of Albemarle becomes a chronicle of events and decisions occurring at the county seat, not what happened in the villages and on the farms dotting Albemarle County's rolling countryside.

Development of hard-surface, all-weather roads enabled farmers to get their produce to market more easily, but it also caused the demise of little country stores in Hillsboro, Porter's, Nortonsville, Mount Fair, and Milton. These general emporiums, usually post offices as well, were hard hit by the birth of Rural Free Delivery service and the growth of mail-order houses such as Sears Roebuck and Company. With their passing went much of the regional community life that had characterized rural Albemarle for generations. Churches and schools consolidated with others nearby, trains roared through instead of stopping regularly as they once had done, and some villages not only languished but disappeared completely. By the end of this period only two towns, Crozet, with its rich, annual harvest of fruit, and Scottsville, a trading center for southern Albemarle, had much commercial importance. Almost every other activity— banking, manufacturing, distribution of goods and services, even social life to a great extent—was concentrated in Charlottesville.

These years also witnessed an influx of well-to-do, even rich "outsiders," many of them of Yankee lineage, who bought up old estates and created new ones. Even before 1888 men of comfortable means, often with blood ties to Virginia, had been settling in Albemarle, lured by a slower, genteel pace of life, low taxes, lovely scenery, and the heady prospect of riding to the hounds and playing lord of the manor. By 1945 their numbers had increased, and the Greenwood, Ivy, Keswick, and Green Mountain areas had many part-time residents. Some of these individuals maintained homes in New England, Florida, and abroad and came to Albemarle only for a few months each year. Some, except for hiring a retinue of servants, had little impact on the area and looked upon their Virginia homes much as they might view Newport or Bar Harbor. Others, such as the Murray Boococks, John Armstrong Chaloner, and Ella Gordon Smith, became community leaders and shared their wealth and talents with both their neighbors and the university. Whatever their degree of community involvement, the presence of this coterie of money meant that scores of historic landmarks were carefully preserved, and in turn those well-manicured acres attracted more wealthy people, thus creating a constant market for both county and city property.

Development of a resort of sorts had considerable effect upon the city fathers of Charlottesville. During the first three decades of this era, caught up in the throes of Henry Grady's New South, they were determined to lure heavy industry to their town. As booster-minded as any Chamber of Commerce devotee anywhere in America, they lost no opportunity to trumpet the glories of their community and tell of the hearty welcome awaiting both worker and industrialist in Albemarle. However, their campaign never bore fruit. The county had no single crop such as tobacco or cotton waiting to be processed, nor did it possess any large supply of cheap labor. With the onset of the depression years, this urge to industrialize had reached its peak, and Charlottesville's bankers and commercial leaders saw that their future lay, not in factories and smokestacks, but with small, clean industries, growth of the university, real estate transactions, and tourism, the last aided immeasurably by good roads and a resurgent interest in Albemarle's first son, Thomas Jefferson. In October 1934, for example, when complaints from Keswick residents persuaded a Pennsylvania carpet manufacturer ready to provide fifteen hundred jobs not to set up shop there, Charlottesville's business community said nothing, despite the boon a $1.5 million payroll would have been during the depths of the depression. A decade earlier the city would have been ecstatic with joy at such news.

Except for the early 1890s and the 1930s—and perhaps much of the 1920s in rural areas—these were times of general prosperity. Even the Great Depression seems to have been relatively kind to both Charlottesville and Albemarle. Construction of Skyline Drive, buildings at the university, roads, and other federal projects mitigated its effects considerably. University enrollment held up well enough, even increasing a bit. Farmers, accustomed to living off the land in good times and bad, did just that. City dwellers tightened their belts, did without some luxuries, and got by. Ironically, Charlottesville's first answer to the economic slowdown was a proposal to build a municipal golf course, an undertaking which, though it would create jobs, did not win the immediate endorsement of federal and state authorities.

In some ways, changes during these sixty years were perhaps not so great as they might at first appear. At the end of World War II agriculture, long the county's economic base, was still of considerable importance. A rubber plant had come to Scottsville, but in general the business life of Albemarle continued to flow in familiar, established channels. Real estate was booming, the university was on the threshold of a period of unprecedented growth, and the commercial enterprise of Charlottesville, having taken under its wing many operations once scattered throughout the county, was much enhanced but not radically altered. By 1945 Thomas Walker's town no longer saw itself as a potential rival of bustling Roanoke or a small Upper South Atlanta, but rather as a pleasant, well-balanced university community, a crossroads of tourism, the county seat of historic Albemarle, and, above all else, "a nice place to live."

Chapter 14

Trolley Cars, Autos, Industry, and Suburbs

THE wonders wrought by Alexander Graham Bell, Thomas A. Edison, and Henry Ford that transformed American life during the late nineteenth and early twentieth centuries were enjoyed, for the most part, by city residents, not those living in the county. This fact, more than any other, accounts for substantial growth of Charlottesville and its environs and a decline in county population between 1890 and 1920. Annexation of 1,676 acres of rural land in 1916 by the city, increasing its size more than threefold from 782 to 2,458 acres, provides only a partial explanation. As these federal census totals indicate, better schools with longer terms, better roads, better paying and more interesting jobs, access to electricity, telephones, and numerous other modern conveniences lured hundreds from farm to city. Although Charlottesville registered substantial growth during the years from 1910 to 1920, the area population increased by a mere 57 souls, and the number of Negroes in both city and county continued to decline (see table 7). In 1920 Charlottesville was 27.6 percent black; Albemarle, 29.1 percent. Ten years later, despite an overall population growth of some 5,500, the city was 26.8 percent black; the county, 23.1 percent. Some local Negroes obviously were moving into town, but many more were boarding trains bound for Washington, New York, and other northern centers.

Though no single factor was responsible for city growth, the essential problem was that American technology was creating an urban world, and if not part of it, one felt he was somehow backward, isolated, perhaps even deprived. Textbooks, newspapers, magazines, vaudeville, and movies, even educators, politicians, and civic leaders, unwittingly at times, nurtured this contrast between city slicker and rural rube. As Albemarle's younger generations attended one-room schools in growing numbers, they became increasingly aware of the gulf between county and city, a distance which could not be measured in mere miles but rather in attitudes and divergent ways of life. In contrast to many American communities, Albemarle had pockets of well-to-do residents scattered throughout the county, estates in such regions as Greenwood, Ivy, Keswick, and the Green Mountain area which, whether owned by Yankees or native Vir-

Table 7. City-county population, 1890–1920

	1890	1900	1910	1920
Charlottesville	5,591	6,449	6,765	10,688
Albemarle County	26,788	28,473	29,871	26,005
Total	32,379	34,922	36,636	36,693

SOURCE: *Thirteenth Census of the United States, Abstract* (Washington, D.C., 1913), p. 50; *Fourteenth Census of the United States* (Washington, D.C., 1921), 1:647.

ginians, quickly acquired some of the trappings of city living, only accentuating these differences. Their owners undoubtedly were the first in their community to have modern interior plumbing, electric lights, telephones, and shiny new automobiles. Although the Rives family of Castle Hill and the glamorous Langhornes of Mirador long had lived more comfortably than most of their immediate neighbors, these folk soon realized that city cousins of even modest means now were able to acquire some of those niceties, luxuries which in an urban setting were becoming commonplace necessities.

One of the first of these wonders, something no Rives, Coles, or Langhorne could take to his rural home, was the streetcar. Whether horse-drawn or electric, it quickly altered the pattern of Charlottesville's growth, made suburban development possible, and tied to the city diverse little settlements such as the university section which for decades had been essentially county communities. On April 13, 1887, the *Jeffersonian Republican* proudly announced that the town (soon to be a city) was to have its own "street railway." The General Assembly had chartered the Charlottesville and University Railway Company on March 30, and already enough stock had been sold to assure that construction could get underway.

Mr. A. D. Payne has been elected President and Mr. R. P. Valentine, General Manager. Messrs. W. O. Watson, C. D. Fishburne, C. P. Benson, H. D. Porter, Dr. H. T. Nelson, George Perkins, J. M. Murphy, and others are stockholders. Work on the road begins in a short while. This is a much needed improvement and will add greatly to the comfort of our town. It will greatly appreciate the value of much of the outlying property of the town, bringing it in direct connection, as it were, with the center and business portion of the town. . . .

Our citizens should do all in their power to make this enterprise a success. Not that money for its construction is asked, for that, as we understand, has already been put up. What is needed, is that our people shall patronize the road, and in this way render practical assistance. The fare will be five cents. Let us all make up our minds that we will send the new street railway off with a boom. It is to our interest to do it.[1]

This horse-drawn affair extended from the Chesapeake and Ohio Terminal up to Anderson's Corner at the university. Each of four bobtailed cars (so called because the driver sat on a small platform in the front) was enclosed, heated by a small stove in winter, and had seats along the side. Ventilation in colder months was provided by a raised roof with small windows and gusts that entered whenever passengers got on or off through the rear door. Oil lamps lit the interior at night. Two horses or mules hauled the cars along the tracks, and the operator braked the vehicle with a huge, gooseneck handle on a vertical staff attached to his platform. This line, like the electric one that succeeded it, consisted of a double track with turnouts every half mile or so enabling cars to meet and pass each other. A car cost about $750; horses, $125 each. This railway often used mules since they could be fed cheaply, actually supplied more power, and stood heat and cold better than horses. An extra animal was kept at the foot of Vinegar Hill, steeper than today, to help cars up that slope. The mule or horse, unharnessed at the top, dutifully returned to the bottom without human guidance to await the next car.

This railway had a very propitious beginning, and only two months after it opened the *Jeffersonian Republican* said it was "very much pleased." About seven hundred people rode the cars each day, and real estate in regions served by the line already had increased in value. A year later that weekly was still enthusiastic, but soon mule, horse, and bobtailed car faced a formidable foe. In 1890 Captain T. O. Troy, a retired railroad man, secured a franchise for an electrical system, similar to one pioneered in Richmond. Although electric lines had advantages such as speed, they were more expensive; while horsecars tended to serve areas already settled, their rivals, often owned by real estate developers, usually struck out into virgin territory where customers might (or might not) follow.

In addition to the cars serving Main Street, other short-lived lines appeared during the 1890s.[2] One, also horse-powered, connected the Belmont section to downtown. Another, a steam-propelled system, chugged along Cherry Avenue from the Southern Railway station

[1] See Edward M. Donohue, "From Horse Cars to Busses in Charlottesville, 1887–1935," *MACH* 12 (1952):1–10.
[2] Interview, Jefferson Randolph Kean, Arlington, Va. (May 15, 1974). Also, see his "Early Street Railways and the Development of Charlottesville," *MACH* 33 (1975).

to Fry's Spring. At the end of the line was the new Albemarle
Hotel, a 100-room creation of the Jefferson Land Company (sometimes known as the Jefferson Park Company and the Hotel and
Land Improvement Company), said to be situated in "one of the
most attractive watering places in Virginia." Erected in 1892, three
years later the structure was sold to Troy and his associates for
$12,750 and renamed the Jefferson Park Hotel. The original pro-
prietor, by the way, was the father of a famous twentieth-century
mystery writer, Willard Huntington Wright, who died in 1939 at
the age of fifty-one. Wright, better known as S. S. Van Dine, was
the creator of Philo Vance and other sleuths. His family moved away
from Charlottesville when young Wright was six years old, soon
after the hotel changed hands.

The steam railway to Fry's Spring was often called the Belt Line
because of the route it served along the edge of town or the Dummy
Line as the result of an engine disguised as a passenger car, presumably a concession to horses which might be frightened by any
belching behemoth. Yet another horse line served residents of Ridge
Street for a few years; however, none of these trolley companies
lasted very long or ever became an integral part of Charlottesville's
electric transit network. Plans to extend horse service to the woolen
mills apparently never were carried out.

For four more years these horse and steam systems prospered.
Then, early in 1894, the university's *College Topics* boasted that
Charlottesville soon would have electric cars. The new line, it was
rumored, was going right up to the Rotunda; students no longer
would have to climb the hill from the post office to the university.
Fare would be the same as before, five cents. The two lines among
Main Street paralleled each other for some two years, finally merging
in July 1896. At that time, horses and mules disappeared, and R. P.
Valentine, chief stockholder of the original system, became a member of the board of directors of the new line, the Charlottesville City
and Suburban Railway Company.

At first, backers of the new transportation network proposed an
elaborate scheme encompassing nearly every major thoroughfare
within the corporate limits—Lynchburg Road, Main, South, First,
Market, Fourth, Seventh, Tenth, and Ridge streets—but they soon
modified these plans considerably.[3] Since the original proposal specifically mentions plans for a "horse or electric company," it appears
they may have had in mind a combination of animal and electric

[3] See *Code of the City of Charlottesville* (Charlottesville, 1909), pp. 297–98.

power with horses and mules utilized on subsidiary streets much as they already were.

The *Daily Progress* on January 12, 1895, greeted the new electric system in glowing terms: "The electric street cars began running on time this morning. Their hum as they passed through the streets had a very business-like sound. It is only necessary for wide awake citizens of Charlottesville to close their eyes in order to imagine they are in one of our metropolitan cities." In warm weather these cars were open with running boards along the sides and seats extending the full width; in winter, they were closed, somewhat like the horse variety. However, the interior design of Charlottesville's trolleys changed frequently since nearly all of the cars were secondhand, often being purchased from transit systems in cities such as Philadelphia. Each car had a device which rang a bell if the operator exceeded ten miles per hour. Cars ran every twenty minutes between the university and downtown from 6:40 A.M. to 8 A.M. and after 8 P.M. in the evening. During the business day a ten-minute schedule was maintained, and on Sundays the twenty-minute schedule was in operation. A city ordinance decreed that all cars were to be disinfected with formaldehyde each week.

Even before merger and the demise of horsecars, the electric line was extending its operations toward Fry's Spring. Cars on that route left West Main Street at the old Lynchburg Road, passed under the C. & O. tracks, and then entered a corner of the university grounds, passing by the infirmary and Dawson's Row and continuing along "a well laid-out avenue," the creation of the Jefferson Land Company. Eventually the electric trolley took passengers to the hotel at Fry's Spring, just as the old Belt Line had done, and in the 1890s amusement facilities were built to attract still more riders. This recreation center included a dance pavilion and theater. Admission to the latter was only the five-cent fare paid to ride the railway; however, this regulation was not strenuously enforced, and nearby residents who walked to the Spring were able to enjoy all the pleasures provided. A park known as Wonderland and developed by the Leterman family had a menagerie of animals and birds, swings, slides, a merry-go-round, a roller-skating rink, and facilities for "boxball." Wonderland only existed as a separate facility from 1907 to 1909, when some of its attractions were taken over by the railway. It was here that many Charlottesville residents saw their first moving pictures, at the outset projected upon a bed sheet in the open air. Since the machine had no means of rewinding the reels, the film simply tumbled out into a burlap bag to be rewound later by hand.

36. Charlottesville's Main Street, ca. 1890

37. Charlottesville and Albemarle Railway employees erecting pole

Fry's Spring became such a focal point of local life that one wag quipped, "Charlottesville is divided into two parts: Charlottesville proper and Fry's Spring improper." In 1905 the Albemarle Horse Show Association, organized five years earlier, developed grounds there and for more than a decade held shows each summer that attracted hundreds of spectators and scores of trolley riders as well. In 1905, for example, more than twelve thousand attended a two-day affair climaxed with a huge german at the armory with music provided by the Stonewall Brigade Band of Staunton. These shows were part of an annual series which included similar meets in Warrenton, Orange, and other Piedmont communities. In 1917 the local association moved to grounds near the Charlottesville Country Club where fairs and circuses also often appeared, and its Fry's Spring assets were purchased by the People's National Bank.

According to the *Electric Railway Journal* of October 17, 1914, the hotel, never a money-maker, eventually was dismantled, and the lumber and materials were used to build six cottages and enclose and heat the dance pavilion. This structure, tastefully decorated with national flags and college banners, featured "handsomely framed photographs supplied by the General Electric Company [to] remind visitors of the many domestic applications of electricity." Spires and turrets from the hotel were used to embellish the amusement park, playgrounds, and picnic areas nearby. Although the hotel proved to be a liability, Fry's Spring continued to be an extremely popular rendezvous for church groups, schoolchildren, and individuals of all ages. During the World War I era music for dancing was provided two evenings a week by George Colgan's five-piece orchestra. At other times one could waltz, glide, and turkey trot to the melodious sounds of a Welte electric organ, although "the cheek and other improper dances" were forbidden. Mable Apple Talley, a native of Charlottesville, says life would have been extremely dull without the "Spring." Nursemaids took their charges there frequently, and on Sunday afternoons hundreds gathered to eat, talk, see, and be seen. "There was," Mrs. Talley emphasizes, "really nothing else to do in this town on weekends except go to Fry's Spring!" In 1921 G. Russell Dettor purchased the property and developed a "beach club" which, although the trolley disappeared in the 1930s, continued to be a center of local social life for decades.

Of course, the spring itself was what originally attracted people, not dancing, moving pictures, trolley rides, horse shows, or wild animals. As early as the 1850s residents were drinking the waters, and by the 1890s their powers had been properly analyzed by local experts and pronounced truly miraculous. "If you are suffering from Gall Stones, Rheumatism, Kidney or Bladder trouble, or general disabilities, try drinking the water from Fry's Spring for a week or ten days and note improvement. It has helped others, and it will help you, it being the third strongest of its nature in the world." [4]

There was some talk of extending the electric railway deeper into university grounds in 1901, but the faculty, by a vote of 16 to 4, said no, and that ended westerly expansion for five years. Yet in other ways the Charlottesville City and Suburban Railway continued to grow. In 1900 it purchased the local electric and gas company organized in 1888, an effort to secure additional revenue from sources other than transportation. At the same time the line bought the Consolidated Ice and Electric Company and the Jefferson Park Company, giving it control of the resort hotel located there. However, this proliferation of activities did not bring prosperity. Throughout the years leading up to World War I the line continued to lose money, principally because of heavy fixed charges and burdensome taxation by both local and state governments, each of which seemed to consider trolley lines fair game.

On November 10, 1903, the railway was sold at public auction and reorganized as the Charlottesville and Albemarle Railway Company. Actually, the line did not change hands and emerged with the same officers and board of directors as before: Channing M. Bolton, president; E. L. Carroll, secretary and treasurer; R. R. Case, superintendent. The board included Bolton, L. T. Hanckel, H. M. Lewis, H. C. Marchant, F. A. Massie, J. B. Moon, R. P. Valentine, and C. H. Walker. The line had 3.4 miles of track and four closed cars and one which was open, and vehicles now were permitted to go twelve miles per hour. Three years later *College Topics* said plans were afoot to extend the railway up Rugby Road to Lambeth Field; however, not until 1912 were tracks laid as far west as Madison Hall. By that date the line had ten cars, which were painted brilliant university colors by an enterprising new general manager, J. L. Livers, who urged both students and townspeople to "ride the orange and blue trolley into town or out to Fry's Spring." Livers also served as vice-president for several Baltimore industrialists who took over the railway company from local owners in 1912.

Finally, in March 1914 tracks were built out Rugby Road to the C. & O. overpass, where cars revolved on a turntable and headed

---

[4] Quoted in the *Daily Progress* (Jan. 19, 1956). Much of the material in this chapter comes from the files of this newspaper.

38. Streetcar at the University of Virginia

back into town. From that point a gasoline omnibus—harbinger of the demise of the trolley throughout the nation—conveyed passengers along Rugby Road out to Preston Heights. The company owned considerable property in that area and said it planned to construct a handsome country club there to attract home buyers. This extension increased track mileage to 3.52, the highest point ever reached. The previous year, in another attempt to increase income, the railway consolidated with the Redland Power Corporation which owned an electric plant and considerable real estate. Also, in 1913 plans to extend an "interurban railway" from Charlottesville to Alberene were discussed. At that point the line could connect with the C. & O. tracks to Warren; however, no such facility ever appeared.

Livers, who never missed an opportunity to promote his suburban system, personally wrote ads encouraging citizens to buy stock in the "C. & A. Railway," published a vest-pocket booklet with time-tables and data on power and electricity for customers, and in 1915 thwarted attempts to institute jitneys in Charlottesville. The jitney (irregular buslike service by private car) could not compete with his trolley, especially when Livers maintained his faster summer schedule throughout the winter months and the city council required jitney operators to furnish a $1,000 bond and maintain regular schedules over definite routes.

During World War I and throughout the early twenties those orange and blue cars carried thousands of passengers and bestowed upon their owners a reasonable income. By 1922 traffic had increased to 1.5 million people annually, and profits to $7,500. But within three years fewer and fewer people were riding streetcars, and the company cut its staff from thirty-nine to eighteen. In July 1923 the Charlottesville and Albemarle Railway was absorbed by the Virginia-Western Power Company. Two years later its interests were sold to the National Public Service Company, which soon became the Virginia Public Service Company with headquarters in the old C. & A. facilities near Midway School. By 1933 the urban railway still was operating seven cars but was over $6,000 in debt. Nevertheless, the trolley hung on until 1935, much longer than in many communities of comparable size, when the owners were granted permission to substitute bus service. As an era ended on the night of May 30, 1935, curio seekers nearly stripped cars making their final runs. They tore off straps, parts of seats, and signs as souvenirs, despite the presence of Police Chief Maurice F. Greaver, who had ridden on the city's first electric trolley over a half century before. Most of the conductors became bus drivers as the clang of the trolley was silenced forever. The tracks, the Rugby Road turntable, a few mementos, and memories of those delightful outings to Fry's Spring were all that remained of this great venture; and during World War II some of the tracks and the turntable ended up on scrap piles destined for service once more.

While the streetcar, whether horse or electric, utilitarian green or bright orange and blue, closed or open, was transforming the life of Charlottesville, the major rail lines of Albemarle County continued to grow, usually by merger or lease, not by construction of new tracks as in the mid-nineteenth century. The train was, of course, a vital means of communication, a highway of commerce and industry, and would continue to be so for many years, despite competition from auto, bus, and truck. In 1890 the Chesapeake and Ohio acquired the Richmond and Allegheny, which since the early 1880s had run along the edge of the old James River and Kanawha Canal on Albemarle's southern boundary. When the Alberene Railway Company completed 11.1 miles of track between Warren and Alberene in 1898, it too was leased by the C. & O.

A decade earlier, in April 1886, the Virginia Midland Company

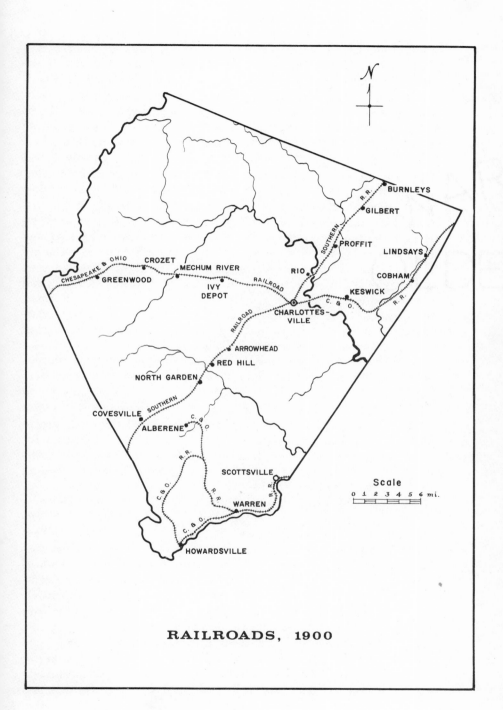

N

BURNLEYS
GILBERT
PROFFIT
LINDSAYS
CHESAPEAKE & OHIO
CROZET
MECHUM RIVER
RIO
COBHAM
GREENWOOD
RAILROAD
KESWICK
IVY
DEPOT
SOUTHERN
C. & O.
R.R.
CHARLOTTES-
VILLE
RAILROAD
ARROWHEAD
RED HILL
NORTH GARDEN
COVESVILLE
SOUTHERN
ALBERENE
C. & O.
R. R.
C. & O.
SCOTTSVILLE
R.R.
R. R.
WARREN
C. & O.
HOWARDSVILLE

Scale
0 1 2 3 4 5 6 mi.

RAILROADS, 1900

connecting Charlottesville with Lynchburg and Alexandria was leased to the Richmond and Danville, a venerable line which experienced amazing growth as various manipulators played with both stocks and assets. Forbidden by law to acquire nonconnecting, subsidiary railroads, its owners created the Richmond and West Point Terminal Company which could. Then, once the latter had served its purpose, they decided to abandon this new company; however, in a comic-opera finish, it turned out that the Terminal Company had powerful friends in high financial circles, and child ended up owning parent. By 1890 it was one of the nation's largest rail systems. Two years later the whole enterprise crumbled, and a decade of speculation, mismanagement, and fraud was laid bare. Reorganized by Drexel-Morgan interests as the Southern Railway, that company began operating the vital south-north line through Albemarle County in June 1894 and four years later purchased outright what had been the Orange and Alexandria, Washington City, Virginia Midland, and Great Southern, Richmond and Danville, and so on. In a legal sense, the Charlottesville and Rapidan continued a separate existence during these tumultuous times, but it eventually ended up as an integral part of the emerging Southern Railway empire.

In 1897 the Southern moved its Charlottesville shops to Monroe near Lynchburg, a hard economic blow since local employees were earning some $100,000 a year, nearly all of which eventually found its way into the pockets of area merchants. Proposals to connect both Scottsville and Farmville to Charlottesville by rail continued to be bantered about from time to time. Most of the enthusiasm for these projects was centered, however, in those two towns, not Charlottesville, and no sound financial backing ever materialized. And neither did the railway tracks.

By 1920, with railroads at the peak of their power and efficiency, the Southern alone had sixteen passenger trains arriving and departing from Charlottesville's Union Station each day. Eight of these (four going south, four north) provided express service between Washington and Atlanta, connecting with trains to such points as New York, Philadelphia, Baltimore, Birmingham, and New Orleans. Luxury travel on these through trains was relatively inexpensive. Parlor car fare between Charlottesville and Washington cost an extra seventy-five cents, from Charlottesville to New Orleans, $2.63. Eight other trains, some of them making local stops, had more limited runs between either Washington and Charlottesville or Charlottesville and Danville. Every day at least two Southern Railway passenger trains stopped at Proffit, Red Hill, North Garden, and

Covesville. If flagged, they would pick up residents of Arrowhead, Watts, Burnleys, Gilbert, and Rio. Thirteen Chesapeake and Ohio passenger trains were serving Albemarle at that time. Both express and local, six were westbound to Cincinnati, Louisville, and points in West Virginia; seven, eastbound for Richmond and Norfolk. One could also travel by the C. & O. to such communities as Clifton Forge, Gordonsville, Orange, and Washington. And, for some years after 1890 Norfolk and Western passenger trains arrived and left from local depots; however, this service appears to have ceased shortly before World War I.

Though trolleys and trains were improving, little could be said for streets, roads, and highways. During the late nineteenth century both state and local governments invested the road commissioners of each magisterial district with more power but failed to clothe that authority with what was really needed: money. The *Daily Progress* in 1894 asserted that Albemarle "is better off in most everything than her county roads." Two years later the *Progress* complained that "the roads on the north side of the Hardware with one or two exceptions have not been worked since 1894 except in the old way." The "old way" evidently was routine, slapdash patchwork, much as had been going on for decades. In January 1899 the daily claimed "it cannot be denied that our highways are almost impassable in winter. This accounts for much in the reduction of the value of farms." The editor frequently proposed a bond issue to provide funds for highways, but two hundred people attending a Good Roads Convention held in Charlottesville three months later favored instead an increase in the road levy from eight to eighteen cents per $100 worth of property. This, they maintained, would furnish an annual subsidy of some $27,000, with $10,000 earmarked for yearly maintenance and $17,000 for permanent improvements. These citizens also suggested that the county hire a full-time road engineer and outlined plans to hold quarterly meetings to discuss the condition of Albemarle's highways. In July 1919 the *Progress* was still grumbling and asking embarrassing questions to boot. A reporter who surveyed over two hundred miles of county roads had seen only one work crew (all fourteen years of age or under). "What," the *Progress* asked, "becomes of our taxes? Where are they spent?" One rural resident said he had not seen a road gang working in his community for three years.

The growth of Charlottesville forced city fathers to open new streets and give constant attention to old ones. During the fiscal year ending July 1, 1895, more than $9,000 was spent on thirty miles of city streets, and a month later the council voted to grade, curb, and macadamize Main Street. The following year East Market from Fifth to Eleventh streets received similar treatment; but, as in the county, results proved disappointing. On February 3, 1896, the *Progress* spoke bluntly: "Main Street has been the subject of general conversation in the city today. Its condition for a newly macadamized thoroughfare is simply awful. Although the work has been well done, seven-eighths of the citizens of Charlottesville are now agreed it was a mistake not to pave it and the many thousand dollars spent in macadamizing it were not well spent."

Within two decades city streets had improved somewhat, although county roads, for the most part, seemed to defy the best intentions of those trying to maintain them. By 1920 the city had one mile of concrete paving, two miles of brick-surfaced streets, and eight miles of macadam, despite the clearly expressed skepticism of the *Progress* concerning such roads. Since the city boasted it had forty-six miles of streets and alleys, this means less than one-fourth were paved in any manner whatsoever. The *University of Virginia Record* of October 1922 conceded Albemarle indeed had been "backward" in road construction but predicted radical improvements within two years. At that time the county had two state-maintained highways. One was Three Notched Road (soon to become Route 250) connecting Richmond and Staunton, and the other was the road from Charlottesville to Lynchburg via Covesville (Route 29). State crews had applied a hard, all-weather surface to only one section, that west from Charlottesville which linked up with the Valley Pike. This at least assured county residents of a reliable connection over the mountain to an important north-south road, and early automobile guides rate the highway from Charlottesville to Staunton as "good." Other parts of the state system—from Charlottesville eastward into Louisa County via Cobham and south to Lynchburg—had been macadamized in past years but were less dependable.[5]

In 1920 the county adopted a road system which permitted use of some state funds, and the following year voters approved a $900,000 bond issue for highway construction. The Scottsville road was the first to be rebuilt under this new program. By 1922 the county had seventy-three miles of macadam and concrete, and nearly all necessary bridges had been completed. Within twenty years nearly every-

[5] Some early auto guides recommended the route to Richmond via Boyd's Tavern and Zion's Crossroads; others favored the route through Keswick, Cobham, and Waldrop to Ashland and then south to the state capital.

thing sought by the Good Roads advocates of the 1890s had become a reality or would shortly. The prime mover in this drama was, of course, the automobile; but other factors also helped produce larger construction crews, trained engineers, and more and more money for Albemarle's highways. City and county could no longer pursue a haphazard scheme of street and road maintenance, patching and fixing up only what had to be done to get by. Real estate development, industry, agriculture, commerce, even an incipient tourist trade were all becoming dependent upon the gasoline engine; and without reliable, all-weather streets and highways, both Albemarle and Charlottesville would be left behind.

Basic to these developments was a change in public attitude toward roads and the costs involved. State authorities had concluded that Virginia must have better roads and that only with state money and at state direction would a practical transportation network evolve. In 1906 the State Highway Commission was created with William M. Thornton, dean of the university's engineering school, as an initial member. It had a budget of $16,000, most of which went for staff salaries. The state also directed counties to increase their road levy to forty cents per $100 of property. In 1916 the national government passed the first act providing federal funds for highway construction, a law designed to foster a nationwide network, and two years later the General Assembly approved creation of a state road system. Nowhere is this changing view of roads and costs more clearly demonstrated than in Albemarle itself. In 1899 residents spurned calls for a bond issue, suggesting instead that a ten-cent increase in the property levy would provide them with adequate highways. Two decades later they approved, admittedly with an eye toward state and federal funds, $900,000 in bonds! In the early 1920s the county still had very few good roads, but help was on the way. After decades of editorials deploring the condition of local highways and a desultory program of maintenance and repair, Albemarle at last was beginning to dig its way out of the mud.

Virginia's first automobile, a kerosene-powered device, appeared in Norfolk in 1899; within a decade, horseless carriages became a common sight in both Charlottesville and Albemarle. The community's pioneer automobile, at least the first officially registered in Richmond, was owned by J. P. "Dry Goods" Ellington, so called because of a pretentious sign over his West Main Street emporium. In 1906, with only 500 automobiles in the Old Dominion, Ellington was the proud possessor of number 494. A year later he shared local honors with Henry B. Sparks, a tinkering mechanic, welder, and bicycle repairman. In 1909 they were joined by Charles S. Apple, Dr. W. W. Moss, Dr. Hugh T. Nelson, Jr., A. D. Payne, and Dr. Charles C. Tennant. After that date auto ownership increased steadily, and during the years between 1910 and 1920 the number of vehicles within Virginia rose from 2,705 to 145,340. By 1922 the county of Albemarle alone had 1,833 touring cars and 363 trucks, one vehicle for approximately every seventeen persons.

In 1909 the Charlottesville city code paid scant heed to this new mode of transportation. No bicycle or auto could exceed eight miles per hour within the corporate limits, and operators were supposed to sound a bell, horn, gong, or whistle at every street crossing. Vehicles without springs could proceed no faster than a walk, and coasting down Vinegar Hill in any contrivance, whether it be wagon, bicycle, automobile, or sled, was strictly forbidden. Storage within the city of more than ten gallons of gasoline, benzine, or naphtha was also prohibited, a regulation which, if actually enforced, certainly would have curtailed use of the auto. State law of that era limited speeds to eight miles per hour in towns, on all curves or bends, and where there was "a gathering of horses or persons"; elsewhere the maximum allowed was twenty. If a horse became frightened, an auto driver was required to stop and give animal and owner sufficient time and room to pass; if requested to do so, any male driver had to climb down out of his vehicle and lead the horse past the offending monster. By 1932, a little more than two decades later, the Charlottesville code devoted an entire chapter, some thirty-eight pages, to "Vehicles and Traffic."

Of all the community's early gasoline contraptions, one of the best-known and best loved was Tootsie, a single-cylinder, four-cycle Gale which Charles Apple, a jeweler, watchmaker, and optician, purchased from Henry Sparks. The engine, located amidships under the seat, was carefully ministered to by Apple each Sabbath, much to the distress of his churchgoing wife. In the morning he took the thing apart and cleaned it; in the afternoon, following dinner and a nap, as his daughter Mable Talley recalls, "Papa put Tootsie back together again." On cold winter mornings the whole family turned out, poured hot water over the engine, and then pushed Tootsie down the hill, praying that the auto would start so Papa could drive to work. These scenes—weekend repair and tune-up sessions, hot water sloshed over cold engines, and pushing reluctant mechanical wonders—soon were duplicated in scores of local households. Usually, as soon as anyone got behind the wheel of his new car, he headed straight for Beck's Hill at the western end of High Street. Any automobile

39. J. P. "Dry Goods" Ellington in Charlottesville's first auto

40. Electric ranges for Wertenbaker Apartments, 1916. Offices of Charlottesville and Albemarle Railway in background

that could make it up that slope in high was considered to be a fine piece of machinery.

Sparks and Apple, men of obvious mechanical bent, on one occasion developed a puncture-proof tire. Their plan was to fill the tube with glue, not air. The results, however, proved disappointing; and after an initial run only succeeded in making a sticky mess of much of Ridge and Main streets, the invention was abandoned. Chic Moran, a neighbor of the Apples, recalls Tootsie fondly and says that for many years her carcass still could be seen and admired in a field near what is now Dunova Court. Moran began driving an auto when only ten years old, but had to cease two years later when apprehended. Soon after his fourteenth birthday he climbed behind the wheel once more with the sheriff at his side. They circled a downtown block; and the test over, the sheriff pronounced him competent to resume driving with a legal license.

Although any pioneer automobile owner could make minor repairs, very shortly livery stables and hardware stores were beginning to cater to the needs of "Dry Goods" Ellington, Sparks, Apple, young Chic Moran, and a growing coterie of proud but often harassed drivers. By 1911 the Charlottesville Hardware Company, agent for EMF, Mitchell, and Buick, was selling Michelin inner tubes, gas, oil, and grease. The Irving-Way-Hill funeral home and livery stable was retailing the Chalmers, and A. D. Payne, owner of another livery stable turned garage, was offering automobiles for hire. At establishments such as these one procured gas, usually filling up a large can and pouring the contents through cheesecloth (to remove any impurities) into his own tank. Gas stations and true service stations did not develop until the 1920s.

Despite the appearance of Tootsie and similar wonders given names like those once borne by the reliable steeds they replaced, the use of the auto, at least until the decade following World War I, was severely limited by weather conditions, miserable roads, haphazard repair and service facilities, relatively high costs, and the reluctance of some local residents to learn new ways. Countless tales are told of old-timers who tried to treat this newfangled mode of transportation much like its predecessor, saying "giddap" and "whoa, there" as they chugged along. Others, though willing to put their hand to wheel or tiller, frequently had considerable difficulty shifting gears or even bringing the demon to rest once they got started. Sam Gault, a Scottsville resident and proud owner of that community's third car, once drove out to Fairview to call on Senator Tom Martin's brother, John.[6] To the astonishment of his would-be host, Gault rounded the circular drive again and again, yelling a few words each time and eventually driving back on the highway. Sometime later he appeared on foot, sheepishly explaining he didn't know how to stop but eventually had run out of gas.

Scottsville's first car, a stunning, bright red Maxwell, appeared in 1910, the property of Dr. L. R. Stinson. The town's second car, a Chalmers, was owned by Captain John L. Pitts. As elsewhere, the auto had profound effects. Blacksmith shops and livery stables disappeared or became garages, and in 1907 a new bridge spanned the James, wiping out the venerable ferry that for decades had served thousands of Albemarle residents and was, in fact, the original reason for the birth of that community two centuries before.

Perhaps the most irritating problem facing any pioneer auto owner (after he finally cranked up and got underway) was how to get from here to there. Roads were not numbered in the present fashion until the mid-1920s, and once out of his own immediate neighborhood, any driver was forced to rely upon printed guides that told him to cross the trolley tracks, proceed 2.6 miles and turn left at Smith's store, go another 1.8 miles past the cemetery and the school, cross an iron bridge and two railroad tracks, and then turn left by the blacksmith's shop. All too often the guide also informed travelers that, at this point, "the good dirt and gravel road ends." The 1908 edition of *The Automobile Blue Book* tells a wary tourist how to make his way across Albemarle on old Three Notched en route from Staunton to Richmond. After leaving the Beverley Hotel in Staunton and passing through Brand, Fishersville, Waynesboro, and Basic City, one arrived at the crest of the Blue Ridge.

Miles
15.1	Summit, Rock Fish Gap, Blue Ridge Mountains; 1500 feet elevation; C. & O. tunnel underneath; beautiful view.
15.5	SPRING. (Delicious water.)
16.4	AFTON. Cross bridge over C. & O. RR.
16.5	Hotel Afton (summer resort).
17.0	Take left fork with wires.
18.9	Just after passing large brick house (on left) take left fork with wires; do not cross small bridge.
19.2	Keep right with wires; pass road on left.
19.8	Pass church on left. Entrance on right to Mr. Owsley's estate, "Tiverton."

[6] Virginia Moore, pp. 117–18.

Miles

21.1	Jog left around house in middle of road.
21.3	Cross bridge over Stockton Fork Cross Roads.
21.4	Pass estate of Mr. C. I. Langhorn, "Meridoff" [C. D. Langhorne, Mirador].
22.0	Pass estate of Mr. Graham Harris, "Seven Oaks."
23.7	Pass road on left.
23.9	HILLSBURY [Hillsboro].
25.2	Cross macadam road (leads from CROZET to Miller's School).
25.4	BROWNSVILLE. Take left fork with wires.
28.2	MECHUMS. (Station C. & O. RR.) Take sharp right with wires; pass under RR. bridge.
28.4	Turn 90° right with wires over wooden bridge over Mechums River.
28.5	Pass estate ("Oakland") on right.
30.1	Pass road on left.
31.1	IVY. Cross bridge over RR.
31.6	Pass road on left.
31.8	Cross bridge over Ivy Creek.
32.6	Small ford—branch Ivy Creek.
33.0	Pass road on right.
33.4	Cross RR to
34.8	WOODS STATION. Pass estate "Ednana" [Ednam Hall] on right.
35.5	Cross RR.
35.7	Stone road.
36.4	Cross RR.
37.4	UNIVERSITY OF VIRGINIA.
37.5	Cross under RR.
38.0	Cross RR. by station into
38.4	CHARLOTTESVILLE. (Hotel Gleason.) H. B. Sparks, 410 W. Main St., auto repairing. Turn left, follow trolley to 5th St.; turn left two blocks to West Jefferson St.; turn right to Colonial Hotel. Go straight out in front of hotel—Court House on left.
38.5	Turn right about two blocks on old Richmond-Parkersburg Pike; stone was covered up when pike was abandoned.
38.6	Turn left, then right, down long hill.
39.6	Cross iron bridge over Rivanna River.
39.7	Turn right up hill; leave river.
42.5	"Hunter's Hill" on left.
42.8	Small ford.
42.9	SHADWELL. (Station.) Cross bridge over RR.
44.0	Take left fork; follow wires.
45.1	Take right fork with wires; large white residence on left; this

is the old "Three Chopt Road" to Richmond. Marquis de Lafayette is said to have laid out this road, and to have blazed the trees.[7] Wilder country. The left fork goes to Keswick, Gordonsville, and Louisa Court House.

46.2	House on right.
46.3	Small ford.
47.1	Small ford.
47.9	Pass road on left, Shepard's [Shepherd's] Store.
48.6	BOYD'S TAVERN.
48.7	Take left fork with wires.

From this point, following similar detailed directions and passing wagon shops, schoolhouses, and sawmills, but no garages, a driver, if fortunate, covered the remaining seventy or so miles to Richmond. Near Goochland Courthouse he had to choose between a condemned bridge over Beaver Dam Creek and detouring through the state prison farm to use a better span located there. He also had to endure various stretches of corduroy (logs laid side by side) and several broken culverts. In the vicinity of East Leake the highway was said to be "badly washed and not worked." In addition to Goochland and East Leake, he passed through Trice's Store, Driggsville, Moccassin Gap, Shannon Hill, Gum Springs, Sandy Hook, Issequena, Sabot, and Manakin. Ten miles east of the state capital he found himself once more on a macadam surface, according to this guide the first encountered since leaving the outskirts of Staunton.

Two years later, in June 1910, Albemarle recorded its first auto fatality when a black child named Willard Mosely was struck and killed near Covesville by an auto driven by Goulay Martin. Mosely was driving a cow along the highway, and Martin claimed he slowed down to four miles per hour as he passed the animal but failed to see Mosely, who, he said, "dove" under his wheels. And soon auto theft, then called "auto rustling," was becoming more and more common; one vehicle disappeared from Carr's Hill when a guest of Edwin A. Alderman, president of the University of Virginia, parked it there for the night.

With the auto came the airplane as well. Although university students talked of building an "aeroplane," the first craft to perform locally appeared in April 1912, part of the general Easter's Week festivities. A pioneer named Beckwith Havens demonstrated his Curtis biplane at Lambeth Field before hundreds of goggle-eyed

[7] Obviously not true since old Three Chopt (or Notched) existed long before Lafayette ever saw either America or Albemarle.

spectators, many of whom came to town on excursion trains. Admission to the grounds was fifty cents. Havens made two twelve-minute flights to much applause. Seven years later, in December 1919, another stunt flyer came to Charlottesville to entertain court day throngs and found himself the victim of what must have been the community's (and perhaps the state's) first skyjacking. A few days later the culprit was apprehended in Baltimore and subsequently returned to Charlottesville for arraignment.

As Charlottesville became a city eager to adopt city ways, real estate developers, with an eye on the rapid growth of Roanoke and cities of the Carolinas and Georgia, continued efforts to attract industry. What they had in mind was sale of factory sites, low-cost housing for workers, and more substantial properties for management, giving their community a solid industrial base. In the early 1890s one of the most prestigious exponents of these development schemes, the Charlottesville Land Company, published an attractive sixteen-page brochure telling of the wonders of the community. Its officers and directors included a cross section of railroad men, politicians, educators, and bankers. Tom Martin, soon to become a U.S. senator, headed the company; Judge John M. White was secretary; Commonwealth's Attorney Micajah Woods served as vice-president and general manager; and Frank A. Massie was treasurer. The brochure (printed in New York City, not Charlottesville) featured pictures of the university, Miller School, several small factories, and various lovely homes. Stock with $100 par value was selling for half that amount per share; one could even purchase it on the installment plan, at only $3 per month. This bid for investment dollars concluded: "Virginia today is as new a field to the capitalist as the West was twenty-five years ago. Charlottesville, its central city, now has what many new places give promise of in years to come. It is blessed with great natural advantages and all the facilities a business man could desire, and standing as it does at the gateway to the New South, it is rapidly becoming an industrial center." Yet in those years of depression Martin, White, Woods, Massie, and others bent upon industrializing their new city had very limited success. Charlottesville might be the "gateway to the New South," but it could not really compete with rivals located there. Albemarle had no single staple such as tobacco or cotton in profusion waiting to be processed or a ready supply of cheap labor, at least not one so plentiful as found elsewhere.

In 1889 the Charlottesville Industrial and Land Improvement Company induced James A. Armstrong and his associates of Utica,

New York, to locate a knitting mill on its Rose Hill tract just north of the city limits. Within a year some one hundred employees, most of them women living in double cottages provided by the mill, were turning out 140 cotton underwear garments a day. This concern experienced difficulties in the mid-1890s, suspending operations for a time, but eventually was able to resume full production. Several other manufacturing companies appeared during these years; yet none employed many workers or functioned long enough to have much impact. The Charlottesville Woolen Mills continued to prosper despite hard times, supplying outfits for Philadelphia's postmen, uniforms for guards at the Chicago World's Fair, and, as usual, cloth for numerous military schools throughout the nation. The Monticello Wine Company also enjoyed good years. By the late 1890s its white wine had become so popular that New York grapes were being used to supplement local production and meet rising demand. Hotopp's Wine Cellar, although it employed only a handful of workers, remained prosperous (at least until the owner's death in 1898) and also had to import grapes during some seasons.

Upon the death of Mayor R. F. Harris in 1893, his agricultural implement company was operated and managed by his son Charles P. Harris. In 1895 this concern was advertising Oliver chilled plows, South Bend plows, spring-tooth harrows, grain drills, hand and power feed cutters, assorted hardware, and Longman's and Martinez's paints and offered to do all kinds of general repair work. The Rio Mills changed hands several times in the early 1890s, eventually becoming the Charlottesville Milling and Manufacturing Company. Under the management of William Thacker, this venerable concern promised to pay highest prices for wheat. Similar mills, Chewning's at Milton and one owned by R. J. Hancock on the Hardware, were destroyed by fire in 1897. In June 1912 the Rio mill met a similar fate. During these years the Alberene Soapstone Company increased the number of its employees from 70 to 200, indicating a substantial rise in production. This expansion came despite serious labor unrest in 1892. Sixty workmen quit in a body demanding shorter hours and dismissal of a new superintendent. Apparently there was no violence, although a constable was stationed at the plant for several weeks.

Two new business operations appeared in Charlottesville, both the result of demand for such services, not because of any effort expended by community leaders. A steam laundry opened in 1886, an ice plant in 1889, and soon others followed. The first laundry, under the management of Messrs. Eakins and Hillbish, advertised in the *Weekly Chronicle* on October 15, 1886: "Improved machinery

41. Ralph W. Holsinger and friends in early auto in front of Pitzer's Pool and Billiard Parlor. Albemarle Horse Show poster in window, August 3–4, 1904

42. Dr. Paul B. Barringer and Dr. William Randolph at the Corner, ca. 1900

and able-bodied help enable us to do the most satisfactory work—
lace Curtains, Dresses of Delicate Fabrics, Shirts, Collars, Cuffs a
Specialty." Six years later the Hercules Company purchased a lot
from A. D. Payne near the Virginia Midland junction and erected
another ice plant. Before the end of the century the Citizens Ice and
Manufacturing Company also was serving the community.

Several old-time general emporiums, among them that of E. M.
Antrim, disappeared. Johnson and Cator were successors to Antrim,
and in 1893 Harry Alexander George, who as a sixteen-year-old boy
had gone to work for Samuel Keller, purchased a half interest in
his jewelry business, establishing the well-known firm of Keller and
George. In 1898 the sons of Simon Leterman, Moses, Phil, Jake,
and Ben, who long had been presiding over separate facilities, purchased a Main Street lot from their father and combined their interests, creating the biggest department store Charlottesville had
yet seen. The gala opening was attended by some ten thousand wide-
eyed folk who, impressed as they were by the goods on display,
emerged fascinated by the electric cash system, "the little boxes running up and down and around." [8] However, Leterman's grand emporium lasted only about a decade, although a store owned by
members of the family continued in operation after that date. In
November 1916, portent of things to come, McCrory's opened the
first chain ten-cent store in Charlottesville. Within three years it was
joined by the Cooperative Drug Store, another chain operation.

In addition to the Albemarle Hotel at Fry's Spring, later the Jefferson Park, the Gleason Hotel was built in 1896 on West Main near
the railway junction. Owned by M. S. Gleason, this hostelry boasted
some forty rooms, less than half the number then found at the
Spring, but in 1911 it was refurbished and enlarged. In 1892 J. H.
Lindsay, who owned and edited a journal in Basic City known as the
Advance, moved over the mountains to Charlottesville and began
publication of a daily newspaper, the *Progress*. For about a year the
Advance continued to appear, but then it became the new daily's
weekly edition for rural readers. In 1894 Lindsay absorbed the
Jeffersonian Republican; the rival *Weekly Chronicle* continued in
operation until the 1920s.

Growth of the county's two principal banks cannot be called
spectacular during these decades, but People's National and the
Bank of Albemarle both weathered the crisis of 1893, no small feat
in itself. In 1895 People's purchased a Main Street lot from the
Letermans and erected new quarters costing, including land,

[8] *Daily Progress* (Aug. 31, 1899).

$11,609.67. With the deaths of Cashier B. C. Flannagan in 1896 and Teller L. R. Snead three years later, People's lost employees who had been with the bank almost from its inception. After Flannagan's death, Judge John White, president since 1894, became actively engaged in management, and within a short time he and his friends had purchased a controlling interest from Flannagan's heirs. At his direction, in 1896 People's began closing its doors at noon on Saturdays, a decision which precipitated a minor crisis since that was shopping day for many rural folk. Eventually the bank had to hire another teller, one who only received deposits but did not pay out money. Three years later People's began requiring all customers to fill out deposit slips when transacting business.

By the 1920s Albemarle had a total of seven banks, four in Charlottesville (People's being the only one still operating under its original name) and one each in Scottsville, Crozet, and Esmont. During the years immediately before World War I, People's absorbed the Jefferson National and found a formidable rival in the new Charlottesville National, organized in 1914 by Hollis Rinehart, partner in a very successful construction firm. In May 1917 People's opened a new $100,000 home at Third and Main streets; however, that classical structure soon was dwarfed by—wonder of wonders— the National's eight-story skyscraper complete with polished bronze doors. Table 8 shows the assets and resources of all local banks at the end of the business year in 1921.

In March 1895 W. J. Keller, Moses Leterman, M. C. Thomas, T. J. Wills, and Edwin Wood led a movement to establish a cham-

Table 8. Local bank assets and resources, 1921

Bank	Capital stock	Loans and discounts	Total resources	Surplus and undivided profits
Charlottesville National	$ 400,000	$1,974,701.18	$ 3,345,531.77	$181,672.93
People's National	370,000	3,800,207.35	5,166,449.23	286,037.38
Farmers and Merchants National	100,000	324,231.67	596,390.19	14,849.11
Commerce National	100,000	165,323.40	205,907.26	9,527.50
Bank of Crozet	50,000	258,873.99	304,472.05	16,210.14
Esmont National	25,000	49,228.86	149,377.26	10,863.24
Scottsville National	25,000	338,448.24	474,432.77	64,214.00
Total	$1,070,000	$6,911,014.69	$10,242,560.53	$583,374.30

SOURCE: *University of Virginia Record, Extension Series 7* (Oct. 1922):46.

ber of commerce, an organization which some citizens felt was not really needed; however, that body quickly demonstrated its worth by soliciting funds for the university after the Rotunda fire, helping to obtain summer teaching institutes for the community, seeking better rail service, and attracting several regional conventions to Charlottesville. Reorganized in 1920 under the auspices of the national association of chambers, the local body then had 410 members, a full-time secretary (F. E. LaBaume), and was attempting to serve the needs of both city and county as a whole.

According to the census of 1900, Charlottesville had 79 manufacturing establishments in which $827,234 was invested. The owners employed 487 wage earners who got $153,857 annually, used materials worth $387,857, and produced goods valued at $858,144. This summary must have included many very small operations such as Sieburg & Company, which turned out ginger ale, lemon soda, and similar beverages at 603 East Main, and perhaps Mrs. J. D. Via's hair tonic dispensary at 329 North Fourth Street. This wonder-working potion cost $1.00 per bottle, but those citing advertisements such as this one appearing in a directory of local business and professional men published in 1901 could obtain the same quantity for fifty cents: "FOUND AT LAST—A sure remedy for diseases of the scalp, such as falling out of the hair, itching sensation, and removes all dandruff . . . enlivens and beautifies the hair, thus rendering a youthful appearance, and last and best of all WILL RESTORE HAIR ON BALD HEADS."

By the early 1920s the Albemarle business-industrial scene had changed somewhat; but despite the growth of service companies such as creameries, ice companies, and bottling works (some inspired by Prohibition), and the birth of firms processing agricultural products and publishing lawbooks, those with the largest payrolls were the Charlottesville Woolen Mills and two concerns turning out lumber products. The community's hopes of becoming a manufacturing center had not been realized, a development of considerable import in later decades when city fathers and real estate agents would, in fact, take considerable pride in the absence of truly large factories with smoke, grime, labor unrest, and other attendant problems. King Lumber Company, founded by W. W. King in 1899, had 300 workers in 1922, an annual payroll of $400,000, and was turning out goods worth $1,000,000. In that year King Lumber received one of its largest contracts, an order worth $300,000 for materials to be used in construction of the university's new gymnasium. The venerable woolen mills and the Charlottesville Lumber Company, originally organized by L. W. Graves in 1890, each had some 150 employees and annual production worth $500,000. However, other enterprises, although employing fewer workers, often represented much greater capital investment; for example, the Charlottesville and Albemarle Railway Company ($622,700), Eston Updike Brickyard ($300,000), Michie Publishing Company ($300,000), and H. E. Young and Company ($900,000), a tanning concern incorporated in 1916.

In all, in August 1922, $3,484,000 was invested in twenty-four local companies. These concerns employed 1,202 individuals, had an annual payroll slightly in excess of $1,000,000, and produced goods worth almost $4,000,000, a figure which nearly equaled the value of all crops grown on Albemarle's farms. Writing in the *University of Virginia Record* of October 1922, C. F. Whitmore presented a summary of industrial operations which includes four concerns manufacturing ice cream, butter, and dairy products, nine processing lumber, fruit, grain, and quarried stone, two publishing houses (Michie and Surber-Arundale), two soft-drink plants, the well-known woolen mills, the trolley company, a huge tannery, and two metal manufacturers (see table 9).

The only local industry, if one can call it such, experiencing a boom during these years was real estate. Development companies abounded as farmland on the outskirts of Charlottesville was purchased, cut up into house lots, and sold at handsome profits. Estates once owned by such well-known names as Fife, Preston, Ficklin, Farish, Sinclair, Brennan, and Rosser disappeared. There was nothing especially new about this trend. A few individuals had been doing just that for decades, and scores of equally hopeful entrepreneurs would follow in their wake. However, to be successful, developers soon had to offer much more than before—reliable, hard-surfaced roads and access to schools, trolley lines, sewerage, water, electricity, and telephones; and, before the era closed, even recreational facilities such as golf clubs were being proposed to lure prospective customers.

At first, these real estate magnates seem to have been most interested in land lying in eastern and southern sections of Charlottesville and its environs. In June 1887 the *Weekly Chronicle* reported that twenty lots in the Fife property near the C. & O. depot had sold for $600 per acre and that land east of the town, once owned by the Farish and Brennan families, was much in demand. Among the most prominent of these operations before 1900 was the Charlottesville Industrial and Land Improvement Company, a brainchild of S. E. Craven and others, which developed the Rose Hill section added to the city in 1889, and the Charlottesville Land Company, which sub-

Table 9. Area industrial operations, 1922

Industry	Date founded [a]	Capital investment	Annual product	Number of persons employed	Annual payroll
Albemarle Creamery Co.	1908	$ 150,000	$ 150,000	7	$ 10,000
Brown Milling Co.	1904	36,000	169,770	17	21,841
Charlottesville and Albemarle Railway Co.	1903	622,700	234,000	55	65,000
Charlottesville Woolen Mills	1867	300,000	500,000	150	140,000
Charlottesville Lumber Co.	1890	30,000	500,000	150	67,800
Charlottesville Ice Co.	1901	65,000	200,000	40	41,024
Coca-Cola Bottling Works	1919	100,000	84,000	7	38,160
Dery Silk Mills	1893	150,000	50,000	65	40,000
Electric Fuseguard Co.	1914	50,000	50,000	75	
Eston Updike Brickyard	1909	300,000	12,000	16	5,850
Graves Monumental Co.	1913	8,000	20,000	2	
King Lumber Co.	1899	100,000	1,000,000	300	400,000
Locust Pin Factory	1914			15	
Lovegrove Milling and Feed Co.	1908	11,700	100,000	7	8,500
Michie Publishing Co.	1899	300,000		80	
Monticello Dairy Inc.	1919	16,000	150,000	18	17,000
Pepsi-Cola Bottling Works	1921	70,000	87,875	18	17,613
Rothwell Apple Storage Co.	1916	100,000		40	8,000
Surber-Arundale Co., Inc.	1920	125,000	100,000	25	24,000
Walker Iron Works	1922	5,000	40,000	7	10,000
Wheat Sheet Metal Works	1919	6,000	23,464	10	6,640
Yancey Ice Company	1913	20,000	25,000	20	7,000
H. E. Young & Co., Inc.	1916	900,000	400,000	75	60,000
T. S. Herbert, Crozet	1922	25,000	40,000	15	12,000
Total		$3,484,400	$3,936,110	1,202	$1,000,428

SOURCE: *University of Virginia Record, Extension Series* 7 (Oct. 1922):33.
[a] Dates of founding or organization have been added to this table. Although some businesses were in operation earlier, the date given for each one represents either that of official incorporation or when current name was acquired. The soapstone industry of Alberene is not included in Whitmore's survey because the bulk of that operation was transferred to Schuyler in Nelson County on the eve of World War I.

divided the sprawling acres that became Belmont, perhaps the largest development scheme of the late nineteenth century. Also, as noted earlier, the Jefferson Land Company pioneered suburban growth in the Fry's Spring area.

After 1900, thanks to expansion of both the university and the street railway system, developers generally turned their attention to northern and western fringes of Charlottesville. Soon, Rugby Hills (a creation of John E. Shepherd), the old Rosser property on Rugby Road, Redland Land Corporation's Meadowbrook Hills, and several well-known smaller subdivisions such as University Place, carved out by Edwin A. Alderman, W. A. Lambeth, and W. M. Lile, were filling up with new homes. Also, fraternity houses were springing up along Rugby Road, Alpha Tau Omega and Pi Kappa Alpha both appearing in the summer of 1915. After 1920, with most of the choice property in or near the city of Charlottesville already converted to business or residential purposes, developers were forced to look farther afield. And, with better roads and widespread use of the automobile, they began to eye famous county landmarks such as Farmington, dreaming of the potential possessed by those lovely rolling acres.

In short, at the beginning of this period from 1890 to 1920 housing development in Charlottesville was tied very closely to the needs of less affluent residents who often had to walk to work in mills or downtown business establishments. At the turn of the century railroad employees usually lived in Fifeville or Belmont, businessmen and merchants favored Ridge Street, most doctors and lawyers resided on Park or High streets, and professors and others associated with the university clustered around Jefferson's Lawn. The electric streetcar with its five-cent fare altered this pattern somewhat, and the automobile made possible even greater suburban growth, in fact inaugurating a spillover onto county lands which, in contrast to previous decades, might not in the foreseeable future be annexed to the city. Comfortable old neighborhoods were breaking up, and instead of buying home sites either with or destined to have city services, well-to-do citizens, egged on by real estate salesmen, were looking toward county property where, if they bought, they soon would demand similar urban services.

In the 1890s, as eastern and southern sections of Charlottesville filled up with new homes, many feared the municipal water supply would become exhausted. Attempts to install meters to prevent waste met with general disapproval; not until March 1910 were meters at length authorized. In 1897 the city council proposed to borrow $35,000 to overhaul the entire waterworks, but by 100 votes, the citizens said no. Realizing the urgency of the situation, the council got approval in March 1898 to erect a less expensive emergency pumping station near Maury's Mills to force water from Reservoir Creek into the city's principal ten-inch pipe. The university area, especially hard hit by rising demand for water in eastern suburbs during these years, often found pressure inadequate. In 1892 university authorities received permission to lay a new pipe of their own to the reservoir; however, eager for a still greater supply, they also shared the cost of the new pumping station ($12,000) and received a proportionate increase of city water in return. In 1905 the community finally got a new waterworks which, by 1920, included over one hundred fire hydrants, as well as twenty-three that were private.

In 1895 an extensive sewerage system was installed throughout the city, an innovation long advocated but delayed in deference to street repairs. This undertaking was marred by a cave-in which killed four workmen and a brief strike of all laborers in April of that year. Despite this construction, many homes within the corporate limits continued to be served by privies, and the city code of 1909 was very specific concerning their location and maintenance. No outhouse could be built within ten feet of a street or a property line, unless a neighbor agreed. Each privy was to be cleaned out every two weeks during the months from April to October, once a month during the remainder of the year. City residents also were supposed to clean and lime their basements each May.

The Charlottesville Hook, Hose, and Ladder Company, with some forty members, provided the city with reasonably adequate fire protection during the closing years of the nineteenth century; but as the Rotunda conflagration in 1895 demonstrated, it could not cope with large disasters. Insurance maps reveal that in 1920 the fire department had approximately the same number of dedicated volunteers, with three paid members on duty at all times. They had at their disposal one motorized hook and ladder, two horse-drawn engines, and two horse-drawn hook and ladder systems, one being held in reserve.

After 1888 the Charlottesville and University of Virginia Electric Light and Gas Company provided electric lighting for business establishments, public buildings, and some private homes. Until the turn of the century, however, city fathers, much to the distress of the *Daily Progress*, resisted all efforts to replace gas jets on Charlottesville's streets with electric bulbs. On December 14, 1895, the *Progress* blasted the council for yet another refusal to "keep up with

43. Martha Jefferson Hospital

44. University of Virginia Hospital, 1901

times": "It is probably not departing from facts when we say that Charlottesville is the poorest lighted city in America. Although the advance appliances for lighting have been in existence for many years, we have delayed in adopting them so long and have been so indifferent to the matter as to lay ourselves open to the charge that we prefer darkness to light. True we have slowly advanced from kerosene but we seem to have stopped there and said 'Eureka.' " In 1901 the city council finally relented and agreed to light some Charlottesville streets with electricity supplied by the street railway company at a cost of $50 per light per year. Twelve months later the councilors protested the annual bill of $4,200 and talked fretfully of establishing a municipal electrical plant, but did nothing.

As noted earlier, in September 1900 the trolley line absorbed the pioneer gas and light company and, in time, acquired still other local private utilities. At length, in 1926, ownership of all of these properties—trolley cars, tracks, barns, electric plants, and so on— passed into the hands of the Virginia Public Service Company. Thus, although the street railway system never was an extremely profitable venture for either investors or owners, it had profound effects, expanding urban and suburban growth and, at the same time, concentrating numerous essential services under a single, unified management.

These three decades from 1890 to 1920 saw failure, frustration, and success. Charlottesville's hopes of becoming an industrial wonder of the New South were thwarted by factors beyond its control. Yet at the close of this era the community was a growing business, financial, and distribution center for several Piedmont counties. It could boast of a relatively stable economy, a superb trolley system, adequate rail service, and substantial urban growth. The local "industry" with the most potential and one which someday would prove to be of extreme importance to both Charlottesville and Albemarle was generally overlooked in the race for more mills, more factories, and more suburbs. That was, of course, education.

Chapter 15

An Educational Revolution

THE decades from 1890 to 1920 witnessed a true revolution in education in Albemarle County at all levels from primary grades to postgraduate study, a development which surely would have had the wholehearted approval of the master of Monticello. Although numerous individuals aided this movement for more effective basic education and expansion of university facilities, two men, both North Carolina-born, tower over all others: Paul B. Barringer and Edwin A. Alderman. In a strange way, their careers complemented each other, and it was Barringer who, as former chairman of the faculty, in 1904 invited Alderman, a man he had known personally for many years, to consider becoming the University of Virginia's first president. As educational reformers their goals differed somewhat. Barringer, a doctor who came to Charlottesville in 1889, was primarily interested in building a better medical school complete with a functioning hospital and modern research facilities serving the needs of the local community, even those of the entire state. Alderman, a tireless missionary in the cause of popular education, led a crusade to revitalize southern higher education in general, but he was ever mindful of spadework needed at lower levels. Each, in his own way, did much to strip the University of Virginia of the exclusiveness which had characterized that institution for generations and make both hospital and lecture hall accessible to thousands who long merely admired "the" university from afar.

Both men also were keenly aware of the South's "Negro problem" of those years and, at some personal risk but with consummate tact, spoke out firmly in behalf of black education. They also met on occasions with Booker T. Washington and other leaders of both races striving to improve the plight of the Negro as Jim Crow legislation increased. Speaking at Montgomery, Alabama, in May 1900, Barringer affirmed the current belief that the black man was doomed to extinction and would, like the Tasmanian native, someday disappear because of the toll taken by typhoid, tuberculosis, and other diseases. Yet, until that time, he had to be educated; and according to Barringer (reinforcing the well-known views of Washington), this education had to be industrial and agricultural in nature with a smattering of cultural courses thrown in. Neither pure liberal arts nor all handicrafts, in his opinion, was the answer. The present system of industrial education, in his opinion, gave too much industry and too little education. Five months later, following a scrupulous public relations campaign, Alderman, then president of Tulane, introduced Booker T. Washington to a racially mixed New Orleans audience.

In a sense, as educational reformer, Barringer had the easier task. Any Virginian, regardless of schooling, could appreciate instantly the advantages of better medical services, and his work undoubtedly did much to break down long-standing town-gown barriers. To take advantage of Alderman's pioneer efforts one still had to read books, attend classes, study hard, and prepare for university admission or enroll in teacher institutes. By 1920, although both of these gentlemen continued to exert considerable influence on the local scene, their battles were over. Barringer, who left Charlottesville for a few years soon after Alderman arrived, was in retirement following a brief, tumultuous term as president of Virginia Polytechnic Institute at Blacksburg. Yet, until he died in 1941 at the age of eighty-four, he was deeply involved in a myriad of activities ranging from composition of a homecoming pageant in 1922, "The Light of Albemarle," to heading up the local Red Cross chapter. Alderman, president of the university until his death in 1931, clearly was Albemarle's "first citizen"; but troubled by ill health after a bout with tuberculosis in 1912–14, he assailed fewer and fewer ramparts and was content to watch from the sidelines as the momentum of past decades enabled his beloved institution to grow and prosper.

Paul Brandon Barringer, born in Concord, North Carolina, in 1857, was related to many of the leading families of that state.[1] He attended the University of Virginia in the 1870s and, after advanced medical study in New York City and Europe, practiced briefly in Charlotte before becoming resident physician at nearby Davidson College. There he instituted a preparatory school for medical students but constantly felt need of hospital facilities where young men could gain practical, firsthand knowledge. An invitation in 1889 to become professor of physiology and surgery at his alma mater provided just the opportunity he had been looking for. At that time the

[1] See Paul B. Barringer, *The Natural Bent* (Chapel Hill, N.C., 1949). This work, supplemented with a brief chapter by his daughter, Anna, covers Barringer's career to 1889. Also, see Anna Barringer's delightful recollections of life in Charlottesville as a young woman: "Pleasant It Is to Remember These Things," *MACH* 27–28 (1970): 5–116.

university had 482 students in all schools and a faculty of 21 professors and 10 instructors. The medical school had 104 students, 4
professors, 2 demonstrators, and 2 part-time instructors, both of them
local physicians. Although that school boasted of a cottage hospital,
in reality Piedmont Hospital was a small building of four rooms built
by charitable ladies for the poor of Charlottesville and the surrounding area. Located "down by the gas tanks" a mile from the university,
it was better known as the "pesthouse" and generally shunned by
many who feared young "medics" would merely experiment on them.

Under Barringer's direction new courses were instituted, faculty
were added, and the two-year medical course was increased to four
years in 1898. Three years earlier an outpatient clinic, now so much
a vital part of the Albemarle scene, opened and in its first twelve
months ministered to 1,200 patients. In that same year, 1895, on
October 27, the Rotunda and an ungainly public hall grafted onto it
were swept by fire, destroying the library, numerous classrooms, and
some very valuable equipment. This conflagration, which began in
the Annex, apparently the result of faulty electric wiring, was a
spectacular affair witnessed by hundreds. Scores of students formed
water brigades, while others carried books, laboratory materials, and
Alexander Galt's famous statue of Jefferson to safety. Dynamite and
a shift of wind saved nearby pavilions; yet despite all these efforts,
the Rotunda was reduced to a mere shell. Charlottesville had no fire
engine at that time, only hose and ladder crews, and an appeal for
help went out to Staunton, Lynchburg, and Richmond, but it arrived
too late to be of any assistance.[2] Within a few years the Rotunda was
rebuilt under the direction of New York architect Stanford White,
who, despite the urging of the faculty, dispensed with much of Jefferson's interior design; however, that remarkable structure now has
been renovated in accordance with the plans of its creator.

In June 1896 Barringer became chairman of the faculty, a position
he held until 1903. For the doctor these were busy, difficult years.
In addition to teaching responsibilities, administrative duties, and
spearheading plans to restore the Rotunda and construct the impressive trio of buildings that enclose the southern end of Jefferson's
Lawn, Barringer had to preside over the growth of an expanding
university which by 1903 had 711 students—299 in liberal arts, 58 in
engineering, 190 in law, and 164 in medicine. Not until 1899 did the
board of visitors at last allocate $9,200 for construction of a hospital;

[2] See Frederick Doveton Nichols, "A Day to Remember: The Burning of
the Rotunda, 1895," *MACH* 17 (1959):57–65.

by that date the clinic, somewhat enlarged, was serving 12,000 patients annually. This sum, of course, would not go far, and the visitors suggested that Barringer, during his vacation, go forth and solicit additional money wherever he could find it. According to Anna Barringer, his daughter, one donor, upon reflection, withdrew a subscription of $1,000, fearful she was contributing to a "pesthouse on university grounds." But another lady, Nancy Langhorne Shaw, later Lady Astor and long Greenwood's outspoken representative in the House of Commons, gave $600 which enabled Barringer to commence excavation. The site, nothing but a water-filled hole for nearly two years, soon was dubbed "Barringer's Frog Pond." However, in April 1901 the central administrative structure of the hospital was completed, and during the next three years wings were added to provide facilities for both white and black patients. Also in 1901 a training school for nurses was established. By the end of 1904 the essential core of "Dr. Paul's monument" was finished and already had admitted 657 patients.

The rise of the University of Virginia Hospital meant the end of private sanitariums operated by various Charlottesville physicians. One of the best known at the turn of the century was that of Dr. Edward May Magruder, who built a small but complete little hospital at 100 West Jefferson Street in 1899. Within a short time Magruder joined the University Hospital staff and later headed Martha Jefferson Hospital. Meanwhile, his growing family moved into the rooms which once had housed patients, although he continued to maintain an office in his home throughout his long career.

The fifteen years during which Barringer was both professor and faculty chairman witnessed other changes almost as momentous as the birth of a functioning hospital. Various undergraduate schools were divided or reorganized to adjust to changing needs; the engineering school, hard hit by the Rotunda fire, was rejuvenated with benefactions of the Rouss family and construction of new quarters; and degree requirements were altered. Charles B. Rouss, son of a Valley farmer who became a Manhattan merchant prince, first gave funds for a hall named in his honor. Then, in 1903 his son Peter endowed chairs in civil and mechanical engineering. In the 1890s, by the will of John Witt Randall, a Harvard-trained physician who spent his life in scientific research, the university received $20,000 earmarked for a dormitory to be named in honor of the donor and his wife. Randall Hall, long known as the nurses' residence, is now the home of the Corcoran Department of History.

Other bequests were received during the Barringer years; yet problems remained. The law faculty sought unsuccessfully to extend its course of study from two to three years. The general undergraduate program became so encumbered with hurdles that at the turn of the century, those preparing for professional careers tended to go elsewhere and enrollment actually declined for a few years. And the debate with Miller School, seemingly resolved in the 1880s, continued to simmer. University authorities, unwilling to set up a true agricultural school, tended to stress biological sciences related to the art of agriculture, but the trustees of Miller School in June 1899 informed the visitors of their displeasure. Under pressure the board agreed that lectures supported by Samuel Miller's money henceforth would be restricted to the basic principles of agriculture.

In these final years of the nineteenth century the University of Virginia faculty (at least some members) became reconciled to two facts of modern academic life: college athletics and female students, although the board of visitors, staunchly conservative and backed by equally conservative alumni, stymied all steps leading to coeducation. The athletic program, aided immeasurably by construction of Fayerweather Hall gymnasium in 1893, encompassed baseball, football, tennis, track, cricket, lacrosse, and golf, with at least one of these sports, baseball, being carried on in modern intercollegiate fashion under the eyes of a full-time coach; Murray M. McGuire was the first individual to hold such a position. With dedication of Lambeth Field in 1901, named for William A. Lambeth, pioneer instructor in physical culture, both students and townspeople had a superb natural setting, albeit beside a railway track, for the sporting events that were becoming more and more an integral part of undergraduate life.

As athletic activity was beginning to have some impact, university students decided to discard the traditional Confederate colors of silver gray and cardinal red, despite some faculty opposition. Apparently they thought gray a rather drab, unsuitable color for their uniforms, but those at a mass meeting held in 1888 were unable to offer a substitute until a student suddenly pulled a large blue and orange silk handkerchief from the neck of Allen Potts. Waving it in the air, he shouted, "How will this do?" And do it did, as those present promptly agreed to adopt the bright colors of an item which Potts had purchased at Oxford University the previous summer "with a lot of boating clothes." [3]

Not all innovations were accepted so readily. In May 1893 the faculty, reacting to winds of change, agreed by an unrecorded vote

[3] Bruce, 4:325–26.

of about 8 to 3 to admit women to Mr. Jefferson's university. This decision, it turned out, did not represent the sentiments of all professors, and some of them petitioned the board of visitors to delay action for one year. Faced with conflicting resolutions, the visitors tossed the ball back to the faculty, who in May 1894 rebuffed a committee report advocating coeducation, 17 to 6. The majority noted in a letter to board members that "the freed intercourse of university life results in influencing the character of women away from those excellencies which make them a refining power in their homes and in society. Inevitably they become familiar, boisterous, bold in manner, often rudely aggressive, and ambitiously competitive with men, thus producing, in general, a type of womanhood from which we devoutly pray to be spared. Extreme evil consequences have not always been prevented, even by a watchful supervision like that of an oriental harem." [4] The university must not, they added, succumb to "outside agitators who hold change to be progress, nor be bullied into a false position by the insensate clamor of a noisy majority of the public thereby breaking irrevocably with and condemning its honorable past." Having in hand the report they wanted, the visitors "rescinded" the faculty's earlier decision, terming it "unsatisfactory and useless."

One lone member of the board, Camm Patteson, suggested that when funds were available "an adequate annex" for women under the tutelage of "a prudent and discreet matron" be built at least two miles from the university. No other member supported his proposal. The following year University of Virginia students dedicated their yearbook, *Corks and Curls*, to "Southern Womanhood, ever the inspiration and support of Southern chivalry . . . with pride in her patriotism, reverence for her beauty, love for her matchless tenderness, and trust in her unfading truth." Perhaps this tribute atoned in part for any insult suffered at the hands of the faculty and visitors. As far as professor and student of that era were concerned, woman's place was, not in their classrooms, but at home and high on a pedestal as well.

Unlike Barringer, Edwin A. Alderman was from rather modest surroundings, and his rise to regional, even national prominence came as a result of oratorical ability and years of hard work as an educator at almost every level—grade school, college, and university. He was, in the words of his biographer, Dumas Malone, "of the New South, rather than the Old; he looked forward, not backward." [5]

[4] Faculty Minutes, University of Virginia, 13:416.
[5] Malone, *Edwin A. Alderman* (New York, 1940), p. 11.

Alderman was born in Wilmington, North Carolina, in May 1861, son of a timber inspector. He had an austere, Presbyterian upbringing which, after 1874, included weekly sermons by Rev. Joseph R. Wilson, father of Woodrow Wilson. Although Alderman later said he studied his catechism with the future president, Malone dismisses this tale as most unlikely. Thomas Woodrow Wilson was five years his senior, and if Alderman saw him at all, it was during vacations when Wilson visited his family. Alderman, who would become a crusader for public education, attended local private schools and graduated from the University of North Carolina in 1882. Because of his innate speaking ability, most of his classmates expected Alderman to study law or theology; but instead, he became a teacher in Goldsboro's new graded school, soon assuming the post of superintendent. Within a few years lectures in behalf of teacher institutes won him a position with the State Board of Education and, in 1891, appointment as professor of history at the new college for white women being formed at Greensboro. Two years later he joined the faculty of his alma mater at Chapel Hill and in 1896, at only thirty-four years of age, became president of that institution. Success there and as president of Tulane University from 1900 to 1903 made Alderman a prime candidate to head the University of Virginia when, after eighty years of faculty rule, Jefferson's venerable school went searching for its first president.

At his inaugural, as he assumed what he liked to call "the mantle of Jefferson," Edwin Alderman stressed four steps the university should take at once: establish a school to coordinate educational forces within the Old Dominion; develop a school complementary to that of law and embracing economics, politics, science, sociology, and history; reinforce practical studies such as engineering and business; and create a "nobly planned" school of English writing. Of these goals, only departments of education and commerce actually came into being under his aegis, although considerable growth and development is evident within the framework he sketched at that time. The most notable omission from this list, Malone notes, is any reference to the School of Medicine, which continued to flourish during the Alderman years. "The new president's program," his biographer continues, "strongly implied the greater participation of the University than hitherto in the progressive life of the state and nation." [6]

Alderman's most immediate problem was money. He had inherited an endowment drive known as the Thomas Jefferson Memorial Fund,

[6] Ibid., pp. 201–2.

and aided by Carnegie, Rockefeller, and other philanthropists, he soon was able to announce that the $1,000,000 goal had been achieved. These funds, most of them from the Northeast, created the Curry Memorial School of Education complete with two professorships, both of which, it turned out, went to North Carolina natives, William Henry Heck and Bruce R. Payne. Within a year of his inaugural, Alderman also could boast of an increased annual appropriation from the state (up from $50,000 to $75,000), as well as $85,000 for improvements and equipment and $450,000 for development of public schools. However, in general, especially in the 1920s, Alderman's expectations of General Assembly largess were not realized; or at least, as he was fond of pointing out, states such as North Carolina and Texas were doing much, much more for their universities than Virginia.

Despite the illness that overwhelmed him in 1912, this man ushered in a decade of substantial progress and change in university life. Buildings and statues appeared almost as if by magic, among them Madison Hall, the Commons or Refectory, and the president's home (the last two designed by Stanford White, who had guided reconstruction of the Rotunda and building of Cabell, Rouss and Cocke halls), Minor Hall, Peabody Hall, and statues of Jefferson, Washington, and Homer. The Lawn, the heart of the university, was rounded out in finished form, much as it appears today. Although the new president doubled faculty ranks during his first ten years, the student body increased less than 50 percent and at no time in that decade exceeded 1,000. Most undergraduates continued to come from private schools located in the Southeast, yet by 1914 products of Virginia's new public schools were more in evidence than ever before.

The law school, second only to the college in size and probably the most prestigious department of the university, appears to have been in serious danger of being discredited because of its archaic two-year course; but expansion to three years in 1909 and new quarters with a much larger library two years later averted this disaster. Despite Alderman's inaugural appeal, the engineering school continued relatively small for many years. (One local wit quipped after the Rotunda fire that it actually consisted of three persons—a professor, an instructor, and a student.) In part this situation resulted from the university's location far from industrial centers of the nation and fear of duplicating work being offered at VPI in Blacksburg. It was the medical school which, in the opinion of Malone, won Alderman's heart. The program begun under Barringer was greatly expanded, and in 1912 and again a decade later, Alderman thwarted attempts to consolidate all medical training within the Old Dominion in Richmond. It is quite possible that he saw good health as an integral part of his crusade for better public education, for one without the other was meaningless.

Although President Alderman maintained that his new education school should be a professional department like law and medicine, the small staff spent most of its time in the field working in Virginia's growing public school system, creating summer institutes which in 1907 began granting formal credit for classes completed, a new departure in southern education, and developing extension work which was limited by neither philosophical content nor geographical boundaries. These summer institutes or schools were not new to Charlottesville and Albemarle. As early as 1880 the university had held such classes, attended in that year by 465 teachers. What was new, however, was more formal organization and greatly expanded course offerings, a reflection of the growing vigor of public classrooms throughout the state. And, beginning in 1912, lecturers from nearly every department and school of the university went forth to tell audiences from Georgia to Pennsylvania about their specialties. On these tours professors spoke not only in Washington, Richmond, and Atlanta but in smaller communities such as Earlysville, Buckingham Courthouse, and Charlottesville itself. Much of this work was directed by Charles G. Maphis, generally known as "the high school visitor," who succeeded Bruce R. Payne when he became president of Peabody Teachers College in 1911. Five years later F. M. Alexander assumed a position as assistant director to coordinate these far-flung activities.

Under the personal direction of "Tony," as students called him, the president instituted a monthly "college hour" in January 1908. These gatherings held in Cabell Hall featured songs, speeches, and cheers and were an attempt to unify a growing, changing university community. They were, in fact, a sort of academic rally designed to stir up enthusiasm and impart information, if not actual knowledge. These sessions were, in some degree, an answer to an outburst of criticism which occurred the previous year. The leader of that movement was Morgan Poitiaux Robinson, a Richmond youth who had been injured playing football in the 1890s.[7] After several years of recuperation, he returned to Charlottesville, received his bachelor's

[7] See John H. Moore, "Morgan Poitiaux Robinson and the Association for the Preservation of the Traditions of the University of Virginia," *Virginia Magazine of History and Biography* 75 (1967):466–72.

degree in 1905, and commenced work on a prestigious M.A. To his distress, Robinson discovered that as Alderman's university adjusted its course program to national trends, he and some of his friends were caught up in a frightful dilemma. In the future an M.A. would require only one year, not three as in the past. Thus some students could enroll and finish a master's degree in a single session while Robinson continued to struggle on under the old system. At the same time, classical languages were losing their privileged status in the undergraduate curriculum, a departure which rankled many alumni and some professors as well.

Robinson's Association for the Preservation of the Traditions of the University of Virginia was a short-lived affair, but its gripes were real indeed. In addition to changed degree requirements, the fifteen or so members were disturbed by the appearance of caps and gowns at commencement for the first time ("rented" and "ill-smelling," they claimed), construction of a presidential mansion, public posting of student grades, conversion of two of the pavilions to faculty purposes (offices for Alderman and the Colonnade Club), and a sudden increase of administrative bureaucrats, some of whom were not even tipping their hats to students as they passed. As one wit commented in the jargon of the day, the University of Virginia seemed to be going to the "damnation bow-wows!"

In March 1907 this association staged a mass meeting at Madison Hall where all these protests, as well as a few more for good measure, were publicly aired. Several prominent faculty members who attended, especially James M. Page and Richard Heath Dabney, were furious and charged the students had "gone off half-cocked." W. H. Echols took a more sanguine view. The university was "a stout old school" which had weathered change in the past. "The digestive apparatus of the university should handle all of the new professors; and, with a good stiff drink, it would handle Alderman, too!"

Upon this note, Edwin A. Alderman himself arose and agreed wholeheartedly that he had come to Charlottesville to be assimilated. He apologized if he had not tipped his hat frequently enough, but the truth was he had worn out seven derbies during the past two years. As for the Rotunda and serpentine walls, they were perfectly safe, and professors would continue to live on the Lawn. Even if enrollment soared to five thousand, faculty would reside there as in the past. Yes, the professors would remain in their pavilions and the beautiful curving walls would stay "until the millennium and would be removed over my dead body!"

Concerning posting of grades, caps and gowns ("Tony" had a flair for ceremony and liked ritual), and the new M.A. degrees, Alderman was much less specific. He pledged, however, that not only would the university's high standards be maintained, there soon would be entrance requirements equal to those of Harvard, Yale, and Columbia. Turning on the famous and often irresistible Alderman charm, he expressed sincere regret that he was neither Virginia-born nor an alumnus. Perhaps the association members should have done a bit more homework, but there really was no cause for alarm. All who felt concern for the future of the University of Virginia should remember, he said, that the institution actually was the "life work" of many professors and administrators. The student body could rely upon such individuals to respect, preserve, and uphold its best traditions.

More serious than this brief flurry was the persistent charge of academics that Edwin Alderman was merely an "educator," not a scholar. Although he edited and wrote a bit from time to time, this man never was a scholar in the true sense; and as Malone comments, "there is no indication that he ever wanted to be." [8] Troubled little by these barbs, Alderman continued his educational crusade, speaking to scores of groups throughout the nation until he was struck down by tuberculosis. Even before his departure for Saranac Lake, New York, late in 1912 to regain his health, a movement was afoot once more to admit women to the University of Virginia. In time, this attack, spearheaded by Mrs. Mary Cooke Branch Munford, nearly won approval of the Virginia Senate, but the proposal always faced stern opposition from university alumni and many students and professors and apparently had only halfhearted support from Alderman himself. He thought a coordinate college like Radcliffe the best solution yet, at the same time, deplored any scattering of public funds as wasteful and undesirable. If such an institution were created, he clearly wanted it under the control of his board of visitors. The compromise reached in 1919 pleased no one. Women were admitted to graduate and professional schools at the university under certain conditions, and these rules, little changed, remained in force for half a century. Meanwhile, the College of William and Mary became coed and henceforth a more serious rival for state appropriations. Thus Alderman's fears of further dispersal of the Old Dominion's educational activities and resources were fully realized.

In 1919, as "Tony" took stock of an institution which was completing its first one hundred years (war delayed the official celebration

[8] Malone, p. 243.

until two years later), he had many reasons to take pride in what had been accomplished under his leadership. Enrollment, after a momentary slump in 1917–18, surged past 1,500. Yet he was far from satisfied. No important structures had been built since 1915, when the Cobb Chemical Laboratory opened and another wing was added to the hospital. Virginia's high school graduates were enrolling in greater numbers, but the state's annual appropriation remained, in his opinion, rather niggardly, at least compared to support being enjoyed by some other southern state universities. Specifically, Alderman wanted a new gymnasium, many more dormitories, better quarters for the burgeoning engineering school (now next to law in numbers), and increased laboratory facilities for the medical school. He also was painfully aware that faculty salaries remained low, the maximum being about $4,500, and that professors frequently had to teach throughout the entire year. Because of ill health, the president left Charlottesville during the summer months, an annual departure not unnoticed by his colleagues. His answer to some of these dilemmas was increased pressure upon the General Assembly, launching of a $3 million Centennial Fund Drive, and renewed efforts to gain more money from philanthropic sources.

As we shall see, perhaps because Edwin A. Alderman was now nearly sixty years old, clearly not a well man, or perhaps because he dared to dream too boldly, he was only partially successful in achieving these goals. In fifteen years he had taken the University of Virginia into the mainstream of both state and national life, shattering for all time its splendid isolation and some of its traditions as well. Yet, if a few traditions died (just as Robinson and his friends had feared), more were born to take their place. After all, even in an atmosphere where traditions seem to sprout at will, they must have both creation and creator. Note, for example, the spontaneous fashion in which the university acquired its "traditional" colors of orange and blue. In the 1950s, years after "Tony" had passed from the scene and during another era when hallowed ways seemed beset by change, a dean once defined the University of Virginia's traditions for a group of disturbed students in this manner: "They're the way we did it last year, as well as we can remember." Edwin A. Alderman, possessed of a superb wit, certainly would have enjoyed this reply.

All these developments at the University of Virginia had some influence in Charlottesville and throughout Albemarle County, notably Barringer's free clinic, the increased medical facilities, and the work of the new professors of education; but for most households, far more important was the growth and expansion of public school classrooms. In 1886 Charlottesville's white graded school moved from its original quarters on Garrett Street to Midway House at the top of Vinegar Hill. For a few years Henry C. Brock also conducted a private high school at the same location. Three years later, as a result of incorporation as a city, Charlottesville got its own school board, although the county superintendent continued to exert control until 1892. The original board members were John L. Cochran, H. M. Gleason, Rev. H. M. Hope, and Moses Kaufman, representing each of the four wards with one member elected at large by the city council.[9] In 1893 membership was increased to eight and in 1906 to twelve, two and then three individuals being chosen from each ward. With complete independence from county control, Howe P. Cochran served briefly as superintendent of city schools, followed by Frank A. Massie, who continued to hold that post until after the turn of the century.

By the summer of 1890, with plans afoot for a public high school, the board gave considerable thought to how this new institution would be conducted. They decided that both boys and girls should be admitted but "study in different rooms." Subjects offered would include Latin, French, history, mathematics, natural philosophy, and chemistry. City students would be charged $3 per month, unless they or their parents paid annual taxes on local property valued at $1,000 or more. J. W. Tinsley, principal during the first session, 1890–91, received $80 per month; his assistant, $65. In the first year of operation the two-year high school had 30 pupils and 2 teachers, while the lower six grades had an enrollment of 503 and 6 teachers. Two years later the 6–2 plan was expanded to the more familiar 8–4 scheme of today, and in 1894 Charlottesville High School awarded its first diploma to a graduating class of one: Nettie M. Godwin. A year later three more graduates, all girls, received diplomas: Nellie Arundale, Mabel P. Ferguson, and Bessie Yager.

Launching of the high school, though certainly commendable, resulted in serious overcrowding of Midway, and in March 1893 board members passed three resolutions aimed at correcting this situation, at the same time advocating better facilities for black students at Jefferson School located at Commerce and Fourth streets.

1. Midway School which was erected for a hotel is too small for the number of schools. If added to would increase the evils. The old building should be torn down and a new one erected.

[9] Webb, pp. 243–44.

2. In view of the rapid increase in the city's school population the new building should be adequate to house not less than 800 and should be constructed so additions could be made.

3. Jefferson School building is scarcely fit for school purposes. Another should be added without delay.[10]

The following month, as result of a special election, the city council issued $25,000 in bonds to finance construction of a new school for white students. Although Peebles and Carpenter, the architects, and Vandergrift and Son, contractors, apparently went to work at once, the well-known Midway Building was not ready when classes opened in October 1893; and for a month or so, pupils gathered in makeshift fashion at the old Garrett Street location. Once installed in the new structure, however, both teachers and students took full advantage of the new facilities. Soon the high school had four full-time teachers: J. W. Lane, J. W. Donner, Annie Caldwell, and Emma Moser; and the four-year curriculum, according to the *Daily Progress* of August 29, 1895, fully prepared any graduate "for the University of Virginia or for business." By that date, if not earlier, a football team had developed traditional rivalries with other regional high schools, practicing at first on a field near the home of Principal Lane, the man whose name would be immortalized by the imposing twentieth-century structure at the intersection of Preston Avenue and McIntire Road, long the community's only white high school.

For four consecutive years, beginning in 1895, Charlottesville was host to one of several summer institutes held for teachers throughout the state. The Peabody Fund provided most of the support for these "schools of method," although both city and county made contributions. Since teachers were permitted to substitute attendance for state-required examinations, enrollment was high, 250 to 400 individuals each year. These sessions, similar to those Alderman had organized in North Carolina, featured lecturers from the university and local school systems, as well as from other parts of the Old Dominion. E. C. Glass, superintendent of Lynchburg's schools, who, like Lane, would give his name to a prominent city high school, directed this program from 1895 to 1899.

Though county public schools of these years did not undergo such radical changes as those in the city, they increased in number; and of course, teachers could take advantage of the institutes being conducted in Charlottesville. City and county together had a total of 132 schools in 1891. It appears, however, that *classes* would be a better

[10] Ibid., pp. 245–46.

45. Edwin A. Alderman

46. Rotunda banquet honoring Alderman, 1905

term, since in the genre of those decades, this is what the word *school* actually meant, a group of students taught by one teacher. Four years later the county alone had 132 schools (or classes), in addition to 20 being operated within the city. This growth is especially significant when one realizes that the total school-age population remained almost static, about 11,300. And 15 more county classrooms appeared before 1900, nearly all of them, like their predecessors, one-room, one-teacher affairs. Yet there were exceptions. In 1890 the Scottsville school for whites had four classes and four teachers, while the Ivy school (white) had two teachers, as did black schools at Scottsville, Ivy Creek, and Piney Grove. By the mid-nineties the Scottsville school for black children had three classes and three teachers, and North Garden (white) and Forest (black) had two classes presided over by two teachers.

L. A. Michie, apparently a Readjuster appointee, retired as county superintendent in 1886 after four years and was succeeded by D. P. Powers, who had held that position from 1870 to 1882. Upon the death of Powers in 1894, I. R. Barksdale became superintendent. Barksdale, in turn, was followed by P. W. Nelson, who served until 1905. Nelson's appointment was strongly opposed by Commonwealth's Attorney Micajah Woods, who urged state officials to name instead Eldridge Turner of Howardsville, "a vigorous, active, intelligent gentleman . . . a tower of strength in the Democratic organization of this section." [11]

In 1906 Frank Massie, a former city superintendent, published a large map of Albemarle resplendent with various statistics including those for public education in 1905. At that time Midway Graded School had twenty-nine teachers and twenty-six "schools"; Jefferson Graded School, eight teachers and eight "schools." Of the potential city enrollment (1,298 white and 1,003 black), only 1,132 whites and 597 blacks actually attended during the nine-month session. Annual expenditures of $18,149.82 included $8,900 in city funds, $4,339.40 from the state government, and $4,910.42 from "other" sources.

In 1905, $39,046.90 was spent on education in Albemarle County, more than half coming from the state and the county and the various districts each contributing about $8,000. Massie's compilations (see table 10) show that, proportionally, rural blacks were attending classes in far greater numbers than their city relatives, and the vast majority of Charlottesville's white children had admirable attendance records. On the other hand, only about 50 percent of the county's

[11] Ibid., pp. 250–51.

Table 10. Public education, Albemarle County, 1905

District	Teachers		Schools		Pupils	
	white	black	white	black	white	black
Charlottesville	5	7	5	7	906	609
Rivanna	18	13	18	13	1,052	948
Samuel Miller	21	7	21	7	1,307	692
White Hall	21	5	21	5	1,047	347
Scottsville	26	15	26	15	1,182 [a]	1,017
Ivy	11	12	11	12	253	207
Total school population					5,747	3,820
Enrollment, taught six months					2,862	2,757

SOURCE: Massie map, 1906.

[a] This figure seems in error as printed and has been adjusted.

white children actually were in classrooms that year. Although some absent youngsters (166 white and 406 black in Charlottesville, 2,885 white and 1,083 black in the county) may have been enrolled in private institutions, locally and elsewhere, one is faced with the in-evitable conclusion that the educational revolution was far from complete. About half of Charlottesville's young black people and hundreds of both races in the county apparently were not being edu-cated, despite a proliferation of classrooms and teacher institutes. Also, as Massie makes clear, the city session lasted nine months each year; the county, six; and the one-room, one-teacher classroom was common throughout Albemarle. Nevertheless, it is equally apparent that public education had made great strides in little more than three decades. These little classrooms, supervised by a harassed, over-worked, underpaid teacher, who probably cut wood, stoked the stove, hauled water, and frequently ministered to the ills of her charges, were no longer thought of as "pauper schools." Public education had won substantial, if incomplete, public acceptance.

By 1920 city and county had a combined population of 36,693, re-flecting rather slow growth during the past four decades; for in 1880, before the incorporation of Charlottesville, the community could boast of 32,618 souls. However, the makeup of this population, still over-whelmingly native-born, had changed somewhat as a result of white in-migration and an exodus of blacks, first to cities within the South, then to northern centers. Albemarle in 1920 had 18,239 native-born whites and 7,569 blacks; Charlottesville, 7,635 native whites, 197 foreign-born whites, and 2,947 blacks. Negroes, slightly in the majority in 1880, now comprised less than 30 percent of the local population—29.1 percent in the county, 27.6 percent in the city. Despite some advancements in public education, 11.3 percent of all males and 9.3 percent of all females over the age of twenty-one living in the city-county area remained illiterate.

The most notable changes in public education in the county from 1905 to 1920 were the appearance of high schools, the elimination of some one-room buildings as consolidation began to take effect, and a considerable increase in allocation of funds for school needs in general, up from $39,046.90 in 1905 to $134,733.05 in 1920.[12] Yet, during the years from 1910 to 1920, many other Virginia counties posted a much better record, and Albemarle was not keeping pace with trends statewide. Teacher salaries remained well below the mean throughout the Old Dominion, the average in Albemarle being $211.86 in 1910 and $410 in 1920. One principal, and only one, received the magnificent sum of $1,500 per year. All county high schools, as well as a few others, now were holding nine-month sessions. One-room white schools, staffed by admittedly inexperienced personnel, held seven-month terms, and similar black schools were open only six months. County Superintendent A. L. Bennett, writing in the *University of Virginia Record*, could hardly suppress his anger: "This practice is indefensible and should be abandoned. All tax payers have the same rate of taxation, and all should have the advantage of the same school term. If there must be a shorter term in some schools than in others, the short term should be in the high school, because there the teachers have fewer pupils and classes. The grade teachers in the high schools have only one or two grades, whereas, the one-room teacher has to try to teach five. The people of the county should demand that justice be done in this matter." [13]

Bennett also was disturbed by the attendance rate of those enrolled in county schools, about 42 percent in 1921. However, he was hopeful that this situation would be corrected by a stricter law, one with teeth in it, recently passed by the General Assembly. Henceforth all children between the ages of eight and fourteen would be required to attend school. He expressed the view that the new County Unit School Law of 1922 would greatly improve general administration as

[12] See A. L. Bennett, "Schools: An Economic and Social Survey of Albemarle County," *University of Virginia Record, Extension Series 7* (Oct. 1922):52–66. This issue, consisting of 111 pages, is a comprehensive survey of living conditions in Albemarle County in the years immediately after World War I.

[13] Ibid., p. 57.

well. Instead of an eighteen-member board with little power made up of three members from each magisterial district and meeting only three times each year, now Albemarle would have a smaller, compact body running its schools, with one representative from each district. Under this new law, the original members, who assumed all powers of the former regional and county boards, were Dr. Joseph P. Blair, W. R. Duke, C. M. Garnett, Charles T. O'Neill, Mrs. Annie R. Page, and B. I. Wood.

Superintendent Bennett credited one of his predecessors, M. M. McManaway, with initiating a core of supervisors who helped hard-pressed teachers from day to day, especially those in small, one-room schools. He also singled out agricultural work at the new Meriwether Lewis School (white) and Union Ridge (black) for special praise. In 1920 Albemarle County had accredited four-year high schools in Scottsville, Red Hill, Crozet, Greenwood, Earlysville, and, on the outskirts of Charlottesville, Meriwether Lewis. Junior highs at Cismont, Stony Point, Alberene, Mountain View, and Midway had achieved similar status. Concerning black education, which lagged far behind and would continue to do so for many years, Bennett observed:

The greatest need of our Negro schools is trained teachers. Many of the boys and girls of the county are not able to go away for high school work, which none of the schools were providing a few years ago. Now we cooperate with the General Education Board and the Jeans and Slater Funds in providing two years of high school work at the Albemarle Training School, but the work done here is not of the academic type. The boys and girls are taught that manual labor is honorable. They learn to cook, sew, weave, cain [sic] chairs, make brooms, build furniture and other useful trades. The graduates are given a second grade certificate.[14] Many of these graduates go into the schools as teachers. Recent competitive examinations have shown that this is one of the finest training schools in the state.[15]

Although only by inference, Bennett pointed to yet another factor thwarting all efforts to improve education: the deplorable state of county roads. True, Virginia, generally considered to have the worst highways on the eastern seaboard, was beginning to dig its way out of the mud; but until Harry Byrd's engineers and construction crews did their work, school consolidation would remain pretty much a dream. In the early twenties Albemarle had only two trucks hauling

[14] "Second grade" was the state classification for high schools offering three-year courses.
[15] Bennett, pp. 58–59.

white children. "Various school boards," Bennett noted, "have used wagons on the dirt roads in past years, but these were not practical because of the deep mud." [16]

Community leagues of that era composed of concerned citizens and parents—Albemarle County had the second largest number in the entire state—were doing much to improve school morale by raising money and backing efforts to erect badly needed buildings. And, as in Charlottesville, athletics had become an important part of the educational scene. Each year a countywide field day was held at Lambeth Field, and baseball teams from various high schools held a championship tourney. No world series, Bennett commented, would "attract as much attention as these games do." [17]

The county superintendent concluded his penetrating analysis of public education with a comparison of Albemarle's schools in 1910 and 1920. The data shown in table 11 reveal both strengths and weaknesses. Again, as fifteen years before, it is apparent that in 1920 a substantial number of white and black county youngsters were not attending school, although by that date white children were enrolling in somewhat greater numbers.

During these years three men had much to do with guiding the development of Charlottesville's public schools. They were James W. Lane, long principal of the high school and also superintendent (1905–9), Benjamin E. Tonsler, principal of Jefferson School at Commerce and Fourth streets from 1895 to 1918, and James G. Johnson, who succeeded Lane as superintendent and served in that capacity until he retired in 1945. Throughout most of the first two decades of this century all local white youngsters were enrolled at Midway School; black students, at Jefferson. In 1911 the 8–4 plan at Midway was cut back to 7–4, and in that same year, because of serious overcrowding, the first three grades were placed on half-day sessions. At that time nearly 1,500 students were attending classes at the top of Vinegar Hill. As superintendent, Johnson began a campaign for construction of a separate grade school, culminating in the dedication of McGuffey School in September 1916. The first principal was Carrie C. Burnley, who presided over that institution for nearly three decades, retiring in June 1944. Within a few years Johnson was actively seeking a second primary school, and in 1925 Venable, honoring yet another distinguished university professor, Charles Scott Venable, opened under the direction of Sarepta A. Moran. Three years later Johnson proposed a third school, but not until 1931 did

[16] Ibid., p. 57.   [17] Ibid., p. 59.

Table 11. Albemarle County schools, 1910–20

	1910	1920
White school population	5,729	5,870
Negro school population	3,833	3,173
Total school population	9,562	9,043
White teachers employed	110	137
Negro teachers employed	51	61
Total teachers employed	161	198
Term in days, white schools	134	146
Term in days, Negro schools	108	116
Total term in days	127	136
White pupils enrolled	3,368	4,072
Negro pupils enrolled	1,916	1,921
Total pupils enrolled	5,286	5,993
Average daily attendance, white	2,143	2,555
Average daily attendance, Negro	1,371	1,243
Total average daily attendance	3,514	3,798
Amount of school funds	$59,990.73	$134,733.05
Average salary per teacher	$211.86	$410.00
Number of two-room schools	10	27
Number of one-room schools	108	62

SOURCE: *University of Virginia Record, Extension Series 7* (Oct. 1922):62.

George Rogers Clark open its doors to serve white youngsters in the southern end of the city. The first principal of Clark School was Florence Buford.

Although all of this construction for grades 1–5 was commendable and apparently necessary, facilities for both black and white students in grades 6–11 changed little. Despite some agitation from time to time, Negroes continued to attend Jefferson, and whites crammed into old Midway. By 1920 the city was spending nearly $100,000 per year on its education system. The high school then had twenty teachers; the grammar school (grades 6 and 7), fourteen; McGuffey, eighteen; and Jefferson, twelve. High school classes, encompassing only standard college preparatory and business subjects, lasted from 9 A.M. to 2:30 P.M. each day. In that year the city high school had 495 students, with 2,091 enrolled in lower grades at Midway and McGuffey.

Jefferson School, now under Principal Margaret Louise Terry, consisted of eight grades. Some 250 students were enrolled, but because of crowded conditions most classes were on half-day schedules. Several teachers were responsible for two grades, and two young women were giving instruction in domestic science to girls. Until

1926, when this school was enlarged and added high school work, black youngsters seeking advanced courses after grade 8 had to continue their education outside of Charlottesville, often in Washington, D.C.

As noted earlier, Albemarle's private schools, many of them very small operations, experienced rather rough going as public education flourished. During a decade or so, from 1897 to 1909, no less than five well-established institutions closed their doors: Edgehill School, Piedmont Female Institute, Pantops Academy, Albemarle Female Institute (Rawlings Institute after 1897), and Major Jones's Charlottesville Institute. In an attempt to remain afloat, some added kindergartens and summer classes or even became coed; but in the face of rising costs and better and better public classrooms offering an increasing range of attractive social and athletic activities, as well as reasonably sound instruction, nothing seemed to work. Only one school of any appreciable size designed to serve children from well-to-do homes, St. Anne's, an offshoot of Rawlings Institute, was able to grow and prosper. As early as 1885 preparatory schools began holding annual field days, and by 1897 these gatherings included track events, potato sack and wheelbarrow races, throwing baseballs, and a tug-of-war. Also, by that date, Major Jones's boys were playing regularly scheduled baseball and football games with rival schools and regional independent teams.

Of course, private instruction did not cease with the demise of these venerable schools. Various teachers took over classrooms and tried their hand at running their own institutes and academies with indifferent success. Two schools of more than passing importance emerged during these years, one for boys and the other for girls. In 1904 E. Reinhold Rogers established the Jefferson School for Boys, which had a thirteen-year career at various locations—the Rixey House at Fry's Spring, a building at the corner of Second and Jefferson streets, Levy's old Opera House, and the quarters of the defunct Piedmont Female Institute at Seventh and Market streets. These perambulations seem to have been dictated by burgeoning classes, since Rogers soon had some seventy-five students and a staff of eight, most of whom were doing graduate work at the university. However, like Pantops before it, in June 1917, seemingly enjoying great success, Jefferson School suddenly closed, and Rogers accepted a position as director of the Boys' Home in Covington. According to Harold Mopsik, the reason was simple enough: Rogers had gotten into financial difficulties.[18]

[18] Mopsik, pp. 121–25.

The birth and growth of St. Anne's School, now St. Anne's-Belfield, presents a much happier tale. Its origins lie in Albemarle Female Institute, a Baptist school established in 1857, although these denominational ties were soon shed. During the late nineteenth century this institute was owned and operated by three men who also directed the school, John Hart (1860–74) and R. H. Rawlings and W. P. Dickinson (1875–94). After the retirement of Rawlings and the death of Dickinson, several individuals headed the school, the most notable being Rev. H. W. Tribble (1897–1908), under whose management it became Rawlings Institute.

Regulations issued in 1895 indicate this was an efficient, well-run operation and no parent needed to fear for the welfare of a daughter entrusted to its care.[19] Students had to have written permission from parent or guardian "in each instance" before receiving "attentions or visits from young gentlemen." Correspondence of young ladies, with all but their own family, was "subject to such restrictions as their best interests may require." Teachers accompanied them when they left the grounds and personally made purchases for them on shopping tours of city emporiums. Bills at local stores were "positively prohibited." All express packages received had to be prepaid, teachers and pupils did not make or receive calls on the Sabbath, and each young lady was summarily dispatched home at the close of a session. Every student was expected "to deport herself, at all times, as a refined and cultivated young lady," and the "honors of the school" were awarded only to those who did so.

Upon Tribble's resignation, or soon thereafter, the school ceased to function, but Rev. H. B. Lee, rector of Christ Church, was convinced that need for a private girls school still existed. He formed a joint-stock company which was able to purchase the rather substantial holdings of the old institute and reopen it as St. Anne's School, named for the parish established in colonial days. The first principal was Mary Hyde Du Val, and in 1920 the school was acquired by the Episcopal Diocese of Virginia as part of its emerging educational system. At the outset St. Anne's was not a college preparatory school per se, but it very shortly adapted its program to meet admission requirements of higher institutions. Also, for many years its kindergarten and first three grades were open to both girls and boys.

While most institutes and academies for the rich were experiencing difficult days, Albemarle's largest private school, thanks to the

[19] Ibid., pp. 70–71.

money of Samuel Miller, continued to prosper, at least for a few decades. In the 1890s, under the direction of C. E. Vawter, the Miller Manuel Labor School added a gymnasium, physical laboratory, and drawing room and instituted postgraduate study. Enrollment remained constant at about 250. That figure could have been much larger if accommodations had been available for more students. Ironically, while institutions such as Edgehill, Piedmont, and Major Jones's passed into oblivion, largely because of dwindling enrollments, Miller School usually had twice as many applicants as it could accept. By 1895 the school consisted of eight separate divisions or departments: (1) Primary, consisting of three grades; (2) Academic, the next five grades, offering arithmetic, algebra, geometry, trigonometry, conics, English, French, German, chemistry, biology, botany, and mechanics; (3) Practical Mechanics—wood, foundry, and iron work; (4) Drawing for boys; (5) Drawing and Design for girls; (6) Mechanical and Electrical Engineering; (7) Domestic Science and Art; (8) Physical Culture. And, as in other schools throughout Albemarle County, organized sports were increasingly important, among them baseball, football, and lawn tennis.[20]

By the first decade of the twentieth century, although annual graduating classes remained rather small, only fifteen or twenty individuals per year, more than a thousand young people had gone forth from Miller School, enriched by the generosity of Samuel Miller even if they departed without diploma in hand. In 1907 Walter Whately, a local resident, published a handbook designed to lure settlers which, in convoluted language, assured those contemplating residence in Albemarle that even if they failed to find gold in the foothills of the Blue Ridge, they need not fear for the education of their children: "Albemarle has probably less need than other counties of the State for such an institution [Miller School], but it is an inestimable boon to the county to have the education of even its poorest children provided for in so munificent a way; whereas the rich and well-to-do citizens of the county may take comfort that no financial adversity can deprive their children of educational facilities of the best kind." [21]

Perhaps this assertion was true, but in the early 1920s Miller School had only 110 students, less than half of its peak enrollment of previous years. County Superintendent Bennett blamed the current

[20] See "Miller School at the Turn of the Century: A Pictorial," *MACH* 29 (1971):82–89.

[21] Whately, *A Handbook Descriptive of Albemarle County, including the City of Charlottesville* (Charlottesville [?], 1907), p. 33.

"business depression" for this decline; yet in light of Whately's reassuring words, one would expect the student body to have increased,
not decreased, amid adverse economic conditions. The explanation
undoubtedly lies in the growth of public classrooms. Despite the excellent facilities provided at Batesville, Albemarle's youngsters seem
to have preferred, if at all possible, to remain in their own communities among those they knew rather than face the regimen of boarding
school life. Miller School, free books, free food, free clothes, and free
housing notwithstanding, somehow seemed less attractive than the
freedom and excitement of those little one- and two-room schools appearing in their own neighborhoods.

The reverberations of Albemarle's educational revolution, though
Alderman, Bennett, and others found it less pervasive than they had
hoped, were real indeed. The University of Virginia had become
deeply involved in the community surrounding its handsome Lawn
and classic columns, and a growing system of free public education,
complete with athletic teams, social events, and community leagues
was stirring a new spirit among both young and old throughout
Charlottesville and Albemarle. If in the process the "old" university
shed some of its traditions, and private schools, even the one created
by the will of Samuel Miller for poor children, suffered somewhat,
gains far outweighed losses; for only with the aid of an alert, literate
citizenry could Mr. Jefferson's "academical village" ever hope to become the capstone of Virginia education.

Chapter 16

Tom Martin's Albemarle

BORN in Scottsville in 1842, Thomas Staples Martin ruled Virginia political life with a firm, quiet hand for nearly a quarter of a century and bestowed upon his native county a certain regional prestige long absent. His machine, based upon close ties with corporations, especially railroads, was both new and not so new. What was different about this U.S. senator was his relatively humble origins, an abhorrence of oratory, and the path he followed to political power. On the other hand, once firmly enthroned, his well-oiled organization functioned much like those that came before and after. A Baltimore reporter, despairing of any response concerning issues of the day from Senator Martin, once called him "the clam in Virginia politics," a somewhat unkind characterization but one which probably amused more than it ruffled Albemarle's imperturbable son.

A small, sturdy man, Martin attended the Virginia Military Institute and the University of Virginia during the 1860s, had a brief brush with warfare as a cadet, and then returned to Scottsville where he began to build a solid reputation as a careful, conscientious lawyer. By the early 1880s Martin was recognized as a forceful courtroom performer, despite his admitted reluctance to speak in flowery phrases so beloved by late Victorians, and respected as an arbiter who, if at all possible, tried to settle litigation between parties within the confines of his office. He also had become local counsel for the Chesapeake and Ohio Railroad in the counties of Albemarle, Fluvanna, and Buckingham and the city of Charlottesville; yet until elected to the U.S. Senate in 1893, Martin shunned political office and declined the offer of a seat on the state court of appeals. True, his practice was a lucrative one, but it is almost as if Tom Martin knew what he wanted from the moment he hung out his shingle on the banks of the James. Always active in politics as a behind-the-scenes organizer, he engineered the election of John Warwick Daniel to the U.S. Senate in 1885, overwhelming the troops of aristocratic John Barbour, who subsequently managed to become the Old Dominion's other member of that august national body. This coup was, in fact, nothing but a dress rehearsal for Martin's own victory eight years later. He was, in the words of his biographer, James A. Bear, Jr., "a struggling young lawyer in 1876, an unknown politician in 1883, an unwanted senator in 1893, and Senate majority leader in 1912." [1] Barbour's death in 1892 precipitated another political confrontation. Elderly General Eppa Hunton of Fauquier County was named to serve in Barbour's place until the legislature convened, but already the political drums were beating; and after the tumultuous national election of 1892 with its Populist overtones, the fight for Hunton's seat began in earnest. Senators then were chosen by the state legislature, and by December 1893 the struggle had narrowed down to two men: Tom Martin and former governor Fitzhugh Lee, nephew of "Marse" Robert. Both men had a carefully controlled, cohesive band of supporters, including scores of backers who button-holed legislators and passed out cigars and, according to Bear and others, a substantial number of dollar bills as well. Hunton easily won confirmation for the short term, the remainder of Barbour's six years, and then Virginia's solons turned their attention to the main event, the full term beginning in 1895. On the sixth ballot Martin won out, precipitating a sea of champagne at his jubilant headquarters (although the senator-elect himself did not drink) and a storm of controversy and outrage.

To say that Albemarle's Tom Martin was an "unwanted senator" is perhaps too mild. The Richmond newspapers fumed against corruption in high places ("Can our legislators be bought and sold?"), and Lee, vain and bitter, fed the fires of resentment by blaming railroad money for his defeat; however, an immediate investigation of fraud charges failed to prove any irregularities, and on December 19 Martin was confirmed as U.S. senator to take office two years hence. Nevertheless, the press continued its assault, claiming the railroad lawyer was "unknown," and for some weeks cheers greeted Lee wherever he went. Of course, Tom Martin was far from being unknown, either in Albemarle or among the ranks of politicians and railroad executives throughout the state. He had recruited a strong legion of faithful followers, waged a skillful campaign, and won a deserved, if somewhat unexpected victory—at least unexpected by the public at large.

An arch conservative, Martin had to battle so-called progressives at each election except that of 1915. Possessing neither the silver tongue of John Warwick Daniel nor the acid wit of Carter Glass, his Washington career was marked by no brilliant floor debate or popu-

---

[1] Bear, "Thomas Staples Martin: A Study in Virginia Politics, 1883–1896" (M.A. thesis, University of Virginia, 1952), p. 42.

lar legislative programs. Martin, says Bear, was "the business type senator who carried his great abilities into the conference and committee rooms." [2] He was an indefatigable worker who believed, like Andrew Jackson, that victors should dispense patronage and spoils only to those of proved loyalty. In the fall of 1919, overwhelmed by his duties as Senate majority leader and World War I and its aftermath, his health began to fail. In November of that year he entered the University of Virginia Hospital for treatment of a minor respiratory condition, but complications developed, and Martin died a few days later. He was buried in the university cemetery in the presence of many state and national dignitaries, as well as hundreds of local residents, Tom's neighbors and friends in both Scottsville and Charlottesville.

One ironic twist in this man's career was that those who deplored his ostensibly "astonishing" victory in 1893 soon clasped Martin to their bosom as their very own. And, in time, they were making political pilgrimages to his home, first Fairview and Scotlands near Scottsville and later Montesano (subsequently known as Old Ivy Inn) on the outskirts of Charlottesville. For many years Martin also maintained a law office at the county seat close by Court Square. That little brick structure was once the home of Johnny Yeargan, the murdered miser. Yeargan, a recluse from Pennsylvania who made money selling whiskey to wagoners of the early nineteenth century, was killed by an unknown assailant in 1834; some $13,000 later was dug up in his yard and cellar. Today the building houses the museum of the Albemarle County Historical Society.

The lone note of discreet flamboyancy in Martin's life was his wooing of Lucy Chamblis Day, daughter of a Smithfield politician. This victory, close on the heels of his election triumph of 1893, was viewed by many of his associates as the greater feat. Almost abnormally shy, a strange liability for one aspiring to national political office, Tom met Lucy at his brother's wedding in 1890. They apparently were attracted to each other, but much of the courting that ensued was done by Lucy and her family, not the prospective suitor. Upon his election, Lucy quickly dispatched a congratulatory telegram, which, contrary to his usual practice, Martin answered and followed up with two dozen American beauty roses. In October 1894, forty-two years of age, the senator-elect was married to this stunning Southside girl who had spurned scores of younger men.

The years of Martin's political power were a time of substantial

[2] Ibid., p. 209.

change in American life and in Albemarle as well. The automobile, suburban development, advancements in education, two wars, Prohibition, and the emancipation of women all had their impact upon his native county; yet serene and secure, Tom Martin seemed either above or apart from most of the controversy involved. In 1896, for example, he embraced free silver rather late in the day and only when no other course was possible. His elevation to the U.S. Senate naturally was greeted with great enthusiasm by local residents, and an elaborate reception was staged in his honor complete with fireworks and speechmaking. However, even in Albemarle some resentment smouldered as a result of the licking administered to Fitz Lee. Several prominent politicians ignored requests from the crowd that they too speak to those assembled.[3]

The first McKinley-Bryan battle shattered Democratic unity in the city and county for a time. Some conservatives, appalled by free silver, deserted to a splinter Gold Bug party. Numerous leading citizens, among them Professors James Garnett and Richard Heath Dabney, joined the antisilver ranks, but on election day both city and county went solidly for William Jennings Bryan. The vote in the city was 219 to 68; in the county, 2,628 to 1,878. Despite all of the furor, John M. Palmer, the Gold Bug nominee, received only 6 votes in Charlottesville, 51 in Albemarle.

The following year, in what must have been the social event of the season, the defeated "Boy Orator of the Platte" was greeted by some twenty thousand enthusiastic Virginians when he visited Charlottesville and the university to give an address appropriately entitled "Jefferson Still Lives." Actually, the invitation by the Washington and Jefferson Literary Societies caused some concern. After a controversial address on emancipation in 1832, the university had decreed that no oration touching upon national or state policies or theological debates could be delivered there. When told this, Bryan, understandably confused, asked for local guidance and agreed to abide by the rules, although under the guise of eulogizing Albemarle's most famous son he managed occasional remarks concerning "the money question."

This address was given on the Lawn before the largest assemblage Charlottesville had ever seen.[4] By wagon and train thousands came from Scottsville, Lynchburg, Staunton, and Orange, and they were not disappointed. It was a truly festive June day, warm and bright.

[3] Unless otherwise indicated, *Daily Progress* files are the source of most of the material found in the remainder of this chapter.

[4] See Anna Barringer, pp. 63–83, for a description of Bryan's visit.

47. R. T. W. Duke, Jr

48. Thomas Staples Martin

49. Hollis Rinehart

50. John Armstrong Chaloner

Impromptu lunch counters lined the walks from the university post office to East Range, and their owners did such a thriving trade that the *Daily Progress* predicted they "will now retire from business." Following his address and luncheon with the faculty, Bryan attended a late afternoon reception at Piedmont, the home of Mr. and Mrs. Jesse Maury, parents of Ellen Maury Slayden, wife of a Democratic congressman from Texas. Guests included many local politicians, but not Tom Martin. He chose to "rusticate" at his new home near Scottsville. One of the younger Maurys later remembered this event, not because of distinguished personages present, but because Bryan ate so much and it was the first time she had ever seen brick ice cream.

Later the idol of the hour went to the Tuesday german at Fayerweather Gymnasium before retiring to the home of Dr. Paul Barringer on East Range. The next day Bryan met with local political leaders, lunched once more at the university, and then departed for Sperryville to visit the home of his ancestors. That evening Dr. Barringer announced to tremendous applause that Bryan had donated $250 to the university, the interest to be used to buy an annual medal to be given to the writer of the best essay on the principles of civil government. Although he had shunned, for the most part, discussion of political matters, it was quite apparent that this man never forgot for one moment that he was campaigning for the White House. According to Anna Barringer, Bryan startled the family at breakfast by asking her mother if she would like to have his autograph. Soon he was signing duplicate slips of paper for all of the Barringer children.

Ironically, during Bryan's two-day whirlwind visit with university students, the Barringers, and thousands of well-wishers, William McKinley passed through Albemarle en route from Asheville to Washington. The *Progress* on June 15 said some two hundred people greeted the chief executive "in mute indifference" when his train stopped briefly in Charlottesville. After all, McKinley perhaps was cast unwittingly in the role of an intruder. Charlottesville was getting ready to welcome William Jennings Bryan, and who shows up but the man who had beaten him!

Six years later during another commencement season, Albemarle was host to the ebullient Teddy Roosevelt, who addressed the university's alumni association. The president, the first distinguished speaker to appear in new Cabell Hall, was honored at a luncheon in Fayerweather Gymnasium gotten up by "a real caterer" and, like Bryan, was guest of the Barringers.[5] Although Teddy did not remain

[5] Ibid., pp. 87–103.

overnight, he was accompanied by Mrs. Roosevelt, a band of secret service agents, and assorted politicians and diplomats, giving the six-hour visit an aura of considerable excitement. While this entourage was making its way up Main Street from the railway station, an elderly woman, widow of Judge John Cochran, startled everyone (especially Edith Roosevelt) by sending a bouquet of flowers to the first lady. She dispatched a friend, Harry Compton, out to the line of carriages to deliver them; but unable to get near the procession, Harry simply hurled the posies, bomblike, into Mrs. Roosevelt's lap, a direct hit. Although somewhat shaken by this display of affection, she later gamely wore the flowers at a luncheon for ladies of the party given by Mrs. Barringer.

Meanwhile, Teddy delivered his speech imploring graduates to support their university and heaping praise upon Edgar Allan Poe; both of Virginia's U.S. senators; Thomas Nelson Page, who was also present; and the surgeon general of the U.S. Navy, Presley M. Rixey, a native of Culpeper and a university alumnus. Then the honored guests and members of the association gathered for a lavish repast featuring filet of beef, cold asparagus, and spring chicken washed down with local wine, some of which happy waiters sold out of side windows to equally happy students. Teddy pronounced the products of the Monticello Wine Company superb (perhaps even "bully"), whereupon the management graciously dispatched cases of claret and burgundy northward to the White House.

Following unscheduled chats with a former Rough Rider and a relative of Matthew Fontaine Maury, ninety-three-year-old Jesse Maury, who as a boy had known Jefferson and remembered Lafayette, the Roosevelts rode off on horseback to call on the Levys at Monticello. Teddy's intent was to tour the historic mansion more or less in private, but the Levys, unaware of protocol, had invited scores of guests who eventually were ushered out on to the lawn so that the presidential inspection could proceed.

Two years later, perhaps as a result of this pleasant visit to Albemarle, Edith Roosevelt bought a hunting lodge for her husband near Scottsville. Pine Knot, originally consisting of fifteen acres and once part of Plain Dealing, later was enlarged to seventy-five acres. It had a simple cottage filled with rather crude furniture but provided a quiet retreat for Teddy during his years as president and later. Roosevelt usually traveled from the North Garden or Red Hill depots by buckboard whenever he visited for a few days of hunting and occasionally spent holidays there as well. In December 1905, for example, the president, his wife, and two of their children celebrated

Christmas at Pine Knot. According to Virginia Moore, Teddy's famous grin often was seen in and around Scottsville as he attended church or stopped to chat with local residents.[6] On one occasion, disgusted with his pack of hunting dogs, Roosevelt tried in vain to borrow those belonging to a black man named George Monroe. Sensing that perhaps Monroe did not know him, Teddy explained that he was the president of the United States. "I don't give a damn if you're Booker T. Washington," Monroe replied. "You can't borrow my dogs!"

Though residents of Albemarle certainly liked the effervescent Teddy (it was hard not to) and turned out in unprecedented numbers to see and hear William Jennings Bryan, it was Woodrow Wilson whom they really loved. He was, after all, almost a native son, an alumnus of the university, and a Democrat. Early in the century he was invited to become president of the institution he attended for two and one-half semesters in 1879–80, but then at Princeton and destined to head that university, Wilson declined the honor, noting that in his opinion Virginia's faculty at that time really did not want a president. Woodrow Wilson continued to maintain close ties with several professors, especially Richard H. Dabney, his old friend of student days. In November 1911, as governor of New Jersey aspiring to yet another presidency, Wilson spoke at the University of Virginia; but despite an expressed desire to visit Albemarle, he did not do so in an official capacity while in the White House. Nevertheless, both students and townspeople rallied to his support with enthusiasm in November 1912, and when the president-elect passed through a month later en route to Staunton, he was greeted with a flashing electric sign, bands, and hundreds of admirers. Wilson won easy endorsement for reelection in 1916, and his death in 1924 was marked by a special memorial service in Cabell Hall. Also, in that same year, President Alderman delivered a eulogy before a joint session of the U.S. Congress.

Social life of Tom Martin's Albemarle County rarely was marked by visits of presidents and would-be presidents. Instead, church groups, various clubs, annual fairs, athletic events at the university, horse shows, political campaigns, and hunting, fishing, and camping trips to recesses of the Blue Ridge such as Sugar Hollow continued to provide recreation and enjoyment for thousands. However, improvements in transportation and education had perceptible impact during these years. Outings to Fry's Spring by trolley were extremely

[6] Pp. 114–16.

popular, vaudeville and commercial theatrical productions, as well as moving pictures, became increasingly common, and community life centered more and more about the new public schools, whether located in city or mountain hamlet.

During the late nineteenth century religious life was characterized by numerous revivals and evangelical campaigns, usually conducted for three or four weeks each year in Charlottesville. Perhaps the best known of these itinerant preachers was Dwight L. Moody, who, in company with his famous singing partner, Ira Sankey, visited Albemarle in April 1886. The *Jeffersonian Republican* waxed eloquent over the famous pair, and Willie Minor noted in his diary that "while Moody makes no pretensions to oratory or fine language, his evident earnestness is most impressive and Sankey's singing is glorious." [7] During the 1890s Charlottesville's Methodists, Presbyterians, and Episcopalians dedicated impressive new structures, although Christ Episcopal Church was hardly completed when a wall of the edifice collapsed on Christmas Eve of 1895, precipitating a prolonged court battle with Newcombe and Kell, the contractors. In September 1910 St. Paul's Memorial University Church opened under the direction of Rev. Hugh M. McIlhany, Jr., long associated with the YMCA. When McIlhany died of blood poisoning a few weeks later, he was succeeded by Beverley D. Tucker, Jr.

The Albemarle County Sunday School Association held a two-day convention each summer at a rural church during the first decades of the new century, and evangelical crusades, often spearheaded by devout Baptists, continued to be waged every autumn. Dr. Henry W. Battle, for many years Charlottesville's leading Baptist clergyman and a dedicated prohibitionist, usually led this annual assault upon sin; but on some occasions outsiders such as British-born Gypsy Smith, Jr., tilted with the devil. In September 1916 Smith regaled crowds at the armory for some six weeks, holding in succession "Baptist Night," "Methodist Night," "Colored Night," "Young Men's Night," "Railroad Night," and so on as various groups vied with each other to attract larger and larger audiences. At other times Seventh-Day Adventists and members of the Christian Church led local revivals, often aided by special trains from points throughout Albemarle and surrounding counties.

According to a federal census of religious bodies taken in 1916, the county had 11,793 church members; the city, 6,925, with the Baptists carrying off top honors in both areas (see table 12). Ap-

[7] Webb, p. 273.

Table 12. Local religious membership, 1916

	Charlottesville	Albemarle County
Baptists	3,602	7,237
Methodists	1,719	2,735
Episcopalians	442	750
Presbyterians	614	482
Mormons		249
Disciples of Christ	300	157
United Brethren in Christ		50
Roman Catholics	157	21
Jews	25	
Others	66	22

SOURCE: *University of Virginia Record, Extension Series 7* (Oct. 1922):38–39.

proximately 75 percent of all citizens over ten years of age said they were church members, compared to 61 percent of the state's population as a whole.

An individual who did much to promote religious life during these years, especially among those living in the hills and coves of western Albemarle, was Frederick William Neve, a British-born clergyman, who became rector of St. Paul's Episcopal Church, Ivy, in 1888, a post he held for thirty-five years.[8] At one time archdeacon of the Blue Ridge and also rector of Greenwood Parish, Neve labored for decades in the Ragged Mountains and other remote regions setting up missions, chapels, and schools, one of which became the Blue Ridge Industrial School at Bacon Hollow. This institution by 1940 had thirty-five buildings and 700 acres of land, property worth $175,-000. A vigorous, dedicated worker, an accomplished writer, and founder of the Order of the Thousandfold, Neve died in 1948, a month short of his ninety-fourth birthday. Because of his heritage and prominence in the community, this man, long a friend of Lady Astor, became the leader of a small colony of expatriate Englishmen in the Ivy-Greenwood area. In July 1911 Neve celebrated a special coronation service at Ivy honoring King George V which was followed by a basket lunch under the trees and a toast to President Taft. In August 1918 as talk of a coordinate female college near the university surfaced once more, he led a short-lived movement to establish Meriwether Lewis College for Women at Ivy. Despite the masculine

[8] See "Autobiography of Frederick William Neve" and Dennis Whittle, "Archdeacon Neve's Later Life," *MACH* 26 (1968):5–79.

name, this proposal won the endorsement of Mrs. Charles Dana Gibson, Mrs. Woodrow Wilson, and (not surprisingly) many Lewis heirs.

During the last years of the nineteenth century, perhaps in reaction to a new, industrialized South which seemed to be forgetting its heritage and the deeds and valor of the "boys in gray" as they grew older and fewer in number, various groups dedicated to honoring and caring for Confederate veterans appeared. In 1889 the John Bowie Strange Camp was organized with Micajah Woods as commander. This unit soon affiliated with a statewide association. Four years later a Charlottesville chapter of the Sons of Confederate Veterans was established, named in honor of Colonel R. T. W. Duke. When the local Ladies Memorial Association refused to become an auxiliary of the new John Bowie Strange Camp, Mrs. James M. Garnett formed what later became a local chapter of the Daughters of the Confederacy. This group, which soon had over one hundred members, elected to name their association for its founder, who claimed that the Charlottesville body predated the national UDC by some five months.

In June 1893 and again in June 1895 Confederate flags waved triumphantly throughout Charlottesville as that young city was host to vast crowds doing homage to southern war dead. The first occasion was the unveiling of the monument towering over the university cemetery. General Fitzhugh Lee on a gray charger led the line of march, followed by various military groups and hundreds of veterans. Lee and Colonel Charles S. Venable both spoke briefly at the cemetery, but Major Robert Stiles was the principal orator of the day. Soldier, lawyer, author, this Confederate hero, although born in Kentucky, grew up in New York City; but when war came, fresh out of Yale and studying law at Columbia University, he immediately set out for Richmond to enlist. After Appomattox he completed his studies at the University of Virginia and began a very successful legal career in Richmond. In 1903, two years before his death, Stiles published *Four Years under Marse Robert*, an account of his wartime experiences.

Upon the conclusion of his address, Sallie Baker, daughter of a local veteran, was led to the flag-draped shaft by Colonel Duke. Cannon roared, musketry rattled, bands struck up the stirring strains of "Dixie"; and when the uproar subsided, there stood the now familiar figure of a young warrior atop a tall pedestal bearing the names of those who died between 1861 and 1865 and were buried nearby. The second event was the eighth annual reunion of the

Grand Camp of Confederate Veterans. This time Fitz Lee was principal orator, Micajah Woods serving as parade marshal. Delegates from more than forty camps attended, spending much of their time reminiscing and pondering two pressing problems: creation of a national park at Appomattox and how to get fair treatment of the southern cause in national textbooks.

On or about April 17 of each year, the anniversary of being mustered into service in 1861, old Monticello guardsmen gathered for an informal dinner and recollections of their wartime exploits. Younger members continued to hold target practice each July 4, often at Fry's Spring before adoring friends and relatives. In 1895 these men rushed to Berryville to assist in thwarting a lynching; two years later they were called to Fairfax where authorities feared a similar outburst of violence. In the early 1900s the guard was called to duty when strikes occurred in Bluefield, Richmond, and Roanoke, and Lynchburg was the scene of yet another lynching threat. In May 1898, when war erupted with Spain, the local unit was ordered to Camp Lee in Richmond, later moving to Camp Alger near Washington. Although they were scheduled to see action in Puerto Rico, that conflict ended so abruptly that the men returned home early in September and were mustered out of national service two months later. Late in April 1916 the guard left for duty on the Mexican border, returning in January 1917. A few weeks later, in mid-April, guardsmen encircled the local jail as hundreds gathered, bent upon lynching two blacks charged with killing a city policeman. However, the pair was found guilty and sentenced to death, and the fury of the mob subsided. Three months later the Monticello Guard departed for Anniston, Alabama, en route to France, Château-Thierry, and World War I.

Next to patriotic and military activities, horse racing and hunting probably provided the strongest motives for organizing clubs in the late nineteenth century. Among the most active were the Charlottesville Jockey Club, Albemarle Jockey Club, Albemarle Racing Association, Garth's Fox Hunting Club, and the Armistead, Blue Ridge, and Keswick hunt clubs. In May 1886 the *Weekly Chronicle* noted that the crowd was large at races staged by the Charlottesville Jockey Club, although the best horses were "principally the stock of English gentlemen in attendance." The annual meet of the Albemarle Jockey Club usually took place on William Garth's Ivy Creek track. In 1895 one unusual event was a trotting match between a horse and a steer, the horse being required to circle the track twice, while his rival was attempting one circuit. Garth, who, it was said, trained more winners in 1906 than any other man in America, lived at Ingleside where he maintained a band of outstanding mares and Masterman, a Belmont Stakes champion. Another famous stud farm, owned by the Pitts and Dorrier families of Scottsville, was ruled by Imperialist, a brilliant steeplechase performer.[9] Organized in 1897, the Albemarle Racing Association staged its meets on the Belmont track just south of Charlottesville. Garth's fox hunt often had as many as thirty riders, some of them women, among them his daughter Berta (Mrs. J. P. Jones).

The famous Armistead Hunt continued to go to its Augusta County preserve each year, Edward Coles, Peyton S. Coles, Walter Durrett, F. P. Farish, C. L. Fowler, George Goodyear, F. Berger Moran, F. W. Robinson, W. W. Waddell, and Norris Watson made the journey in the fall of 1896. After its appearance in 1893, the rival Blue Ridge Hunt held annual outings on grounds near Gravel Hill in Buckingham County. In 1896 members left with forty dogs and four wagons loaded with ample provisions and returned with nine deer, ten foxes, and three wild turkeys. The Keswick Hunt Club, born the following year, almost died a premature death but during its second year secured a charter, erected a clubhouse, and began to grow. According to its charter, the club's goals were many—"to promote the interests of bicycling, riding, golf, tennis, polo, and shooting."[10] In time, this group also staged plays, musical performances, and dances for its members and their guests.

Although several riding groups, notably that in Keswick and the new Albemarle Hunt Club, continued to prosper, during the opening years of the twentieth century many local residents discovered a powerful and very compelling reason for organizing still more clubs: Prohibition. In 1905 Charlottesville had sixteen saloons, four of them combined with grocery stores, a rather impressive number for a community of 6,500 souls. By law these establishments had to be open to the street; that is, no curtains or stained glass hid your face from wife or neighbor as you drank. Saloons could remain open from 5 A.M. to 10 P.M. each day (11 P.M. on Saturday) but were closed on Sunday.

On June 4, 1907, following a hectic campaign, the "drys," led by various clergymen and aided by some businessmen who thought this reform might attract industry to their city, won by forty votes. The Methodists immediately held a service of rejoicing; and according to the *Daily Progress* (strongly antiliquor), "children wept and a

[9] Whatley, p. 24.   [10] Webb, p. 268.

woman dropped to her knees to pray in full view of the curious throng about the Court Square." As September 2, deadline for the beginning of this two-year experiment approached, dealers held sales and announced plans to move to the borders of Albemarle. A dispensary existed near Scottsville for some years, and scores of mail-order ads soon exhorted local residents to have liquor shipped to them from Staunton and Washington. In September 1909 the "drys" prevailed by an even greater margin. The leading local Baptist and Methodist clergymen, Dr. Henry W. Battle and Dr. C. G. Kelly, led the victors; George E. Walker, a well-known lawyer, the vanquished. A year later Charlottesville's best-known saloon, the Log Cabin Bar at 419 East Market, once owned by R. E. Carter and L. S. Via, was razed to make way for a two-story office building.

In September 1914 Virginia approved Prohibition statewide, although Albemarle County dragged its feet hard, refusing to endorse Bishop James Cannon, Jr.'s movement by a vote of 865 to 787. Communities where "wets" remained in command included Free Union (122 to 20), Stony Point (95 to 37), and Blackwells (44 to 5). The city backed Prohibition 349 to 196. Shortly before the Old Dominion became officially "dry" on November 1, 1916, several local entrepreneurs applied for soft-drink licenses, and soon the Jessup Bottling Works was distributing Reif's Special, a brown bottle mixture of cereal, hops, and distilled water said to be nonalcoholic. One also could drink Pablo (made by Pabst), Bevo (Anheuser-Busch), and Famo (Schlitz), all reputed to be free of intoxicants; and, within a few years, both Coca-Cola and Pepsi-Cola opened local bottling establishments. The Monticello Wine Company, of course, had to close its facilities and go out of business.

The club movement precipitated by Prohibition is almost as bewildering as the proliferation of real estate and land development schemes of the 1890s. Two groups, the Elks (1897) and the Redland Club (1905), were not created by the "dry" victory but benefited from it after 1907. The latter, dubbed "the swell and aristocratic club of Charlottesville" by a magazine writer in 1906, allowed no dogs or gambling, and members had to wear coats in the sitting room. Of more importance were several country clubs, in at least one instance part of a growing suburban development. In August 1913 the Redland Corporation, a subsidiary of the trolley company, announced plans to build an eighteen-hole course at Preston Heights. In April of the following year, Eugene Bradbury, William E. Echols, Samuel H. Marshall, T. J. Michie, W. Allan Perkins, E. D. Tayloe, Dr. Charles C. Tennant, F. C. Todd, and George E. Walker organized the Charlottesville Country Club to be situated in the same area. Although a clubhouse soon appeared and there was talk of extending trolley tracks out Rugby Road to its doors, no fairways were built until 1919 when the owners of Meadowbrook Hills subdivision agreed to construct a course. However, a few months later wrestler Bobby Mainfort ("professor" of physiological culture) turned that facility into the White Pine Health Resort, and the golf links subsequently became house lots.

Charlottesville's second country club seems to have been an outgrowth of both the Redland Club and the YMCA. In May 1914 T. B. Benson, president of the Albemarle Golf and Tennis Club, said his group had forty-eight members and soon would build a golf course and tennis courts. Until these were completed, they planned to use greens located near Rose Hill farm or those at the university, neither of which appear ever to have had a clubhouse. Within a year a golf course, now remembered only by Fairway Avenue, was in operation near East Market and Meade Avenue. The members, also interested in baseball and boating on the Rivanna, leased a nearby home but said they did not intend to erect any clubhouse as such. This was, they insisted, not a social group, but a true sports club. In time, however, these men acquired more property and erected a clubhouse which apparently became a prime social center until 1927 when the new development at Farmington absorbed this pioneer group. An unexpected result of this upsurge in golfing was complaints of "lurid language" on various greens. In February 1916 Professor R. H. Dabney developed a lexicon of Latin phrases which, he thought, would fill the needs of most frustrated sportsmen. Swearing, he conceded, was simply part of the game.

Other groups which flourished included the Rivanna Club, originally a fishing association, which leased quarters at Third and High streets. Early in 1915 three hundred members and guests celebrated the opening of that facility with a grand feast of roast shoat, possum, and groundhog. The Fat Man's Club at Fourth and Market, apparently little more than a bottle club with uncertain membership, frequently was in trouble with the law, and soon the term *speakeasy* (replacing the *blind tiger* of earlier decades) became an integral part of local language.

Soon after World War I a new type of urban civic organization appeared. In February 1921 Charlottesville got its first Rotary Club and, a year later, a Kiwanis Club. In 1922 D. Van Wagenen was president of Rotary; Norman T. Shumate, president of the Farmers and Merchants National Bank, headed the Kiwanis. Like the Young

51. World War I parade

52. Negro Odd Fellows march up Main Street, 1915.

Men's Business Club organized in 1920, these groups were dedicated to community service, fostering fellowship, and, at the same time, strengthening professional ties which could be mutually beneficial. The last-named organization, headed by Guy Via, took special pride in contributions to the local Children's Home and the electric lights that members had installed on the Union Station Bridge. By 1920 a pioneer Red Cross chapter, stimulated by the recent war, also was in existence. This body, in effect a clearinghouse for veterans' affairs and emergency relief, had a full-time secretary and quarters in the National Bank Building.

Throughout these years booster groups such as the Chamber of Commerce, Rotary, Kiwanis, and the Young Men's Business Club overlooked no opportunity to extol the virtues of Charlottesville and Albemarle, with the *Daily Progress* joining this chorus of praise. This enthusiasm was, of course, all part of the new urban tradition of twentieth-century America, spurred on by an eight-story bank building, news that Charlottesville had risen from 136th to 106th among southern cities between 1910 and 1920, and real estate ads such as this one:

PRESTON PLACE
Reasonable
Elevated
Salable
Tempting
Ornamental
New

Popular
Large
Attractive
Convenient
Enhancing

Local leaders seem to have taken booming Atlanta as their ideal, and in July 1913 the Chamber offered a $10 prize for the best municipal slogan, boasting that the city soon would have a convention center seating five thousand people and occasionally hinting its population should be five times that number. The slogan contest, extended for months past the original deadline, generated little interest but eventually produced this rather involved salutation: "The Charlottesville Spirit—It's the clean memory of yesterday, a true look of today, a certainty of conquest tomorrow!" The next year following a very successful Chautauqua Week appearance by Dr. Russell H. Conwell, the Chamber proposed erection of a large electric sign near the railway junction: "CHARLOTTESVILLE—ACRES OF DIAMONDS." Still other slogans surfaced, such as "Heart of the Homeland of the Nation," "The Switzerland of America," and "Good enough for Jefferson — why not you?" In November 1920 the Chamber even produced a "city oath": "We will never disgrace this, our City, by any act of cowardice or dishonesty. We will fight for the Ideals and Sacred Things of the City both alone and with many. We will revere and obey the City's laws. . . ."

Charlottesville's theatergoers witnessed substantial change during these decades; in fact, the years from 1890 to 1920 virtually encompass the heyday of vaudeville. The Levy Opera House and Jefferson Auditorium played host to scores of famous names, although the Levy was much too small and the Jefferson's career was terminated by fire in 1907. In October 1912 F. W. Twyman opened the Jefferson Theatre seating 1,000, a "combination house" which could accommodate both touring shows and moving pictures. According to Richard Waddell, the Levy was the community's principal theater until the Jefferson Auditorium opened in 1896; then, after that structure went up in smoke, the Levy resumed its former prominence until it closed with the appearance of Twyman's Main Street entertainment palace.[11] In addition to drama and comedy, Waddell's impressive list of productions at both theaters from 1889 to 1912 includes numerous musical evenings: "Around the World in a Chariot of Song," an illuminated concert with Philip Phillips, the Singing Pilgrim; Goodyear, Cook and Dillon's Refined Minstrels; the Johns Hopkins Banjo and Glee Club; the Boston Symphony Orchestra Club; the University of Virginia's Glee Club (which held its first regular concert in 1893 and a year later incorporated banjos and mandolins and, in time, guitars as well); an old-time fiddlers' contest; the Imperial Russian Ballet; the Mexican Cavalry Band; and John Philip Sousa with his stirring marches. Patrons also had an opportunity to watch Professor D. P. Hurburt's trained animals, the University of Virginia's amateur circus, an illustrated lecture on the Spanish-American War, and a wrestling match between Billy Garth and George Burlingame. Political rallies and private school commencements often were staged at both theaters, as well as numerous local plays, operettas, and benefits.

A handful of these homegrown productions featured Charlottesville blacks; for example, they presented a cakewalk and concert at the Jefferson in November 1889 and a musical evening at the Levy in April 1912 to raise funds for district nurses. Negro social life,

[11] Waddell, pp. 18–22.

rarely noted by the *Daily Progress* during years dominated by a Jim Crow mentality, on occasions included Sunday "colored excursion" trains from Washington to Charlottesville. On August 14, 1911, several hundred blacks came to town for a ball game, a dance at Wayland's Pavilion, and undoubtedly much impromptu revelry among friends and relatives.

Scattered throughout Waddell's "Theatre in Charlottesville, 1886–1912" with its impressive compendium of presentations of comedy, music, athletics, and oratory is one harbinger of things to come. On February 10, 1897, Jefferson Auditorium patrons witnessed a display of Edison's Vitascope and, a month later, his Projectoscope. In April 1899 patrons could enjoy an evening of biograph pictures featuring Pope Leo XII in the Vatican gardens. Within five years moving pictures were appearing with more and more frequency, and by 1910 three small downtown theaters—the Rex (309–11 East Main), the Art (216–18 West Main), and the Lyric (213 East Main)—were showing films on a more or less regular basis, although the Lyric continued to book vaudeville acts.[12] Also, in 1910 Charlottesville's irrepressible John S. Mosby appeared in *All's Fair in Love and War*, and two years later the Edison Moving Picture Company filmed a spectacular based on Jack Jouett's famous ride. In 1915 the university was the scene of *A Virginian's Honor* starring Francis X. Bushman, Beverly Bayne, and Helen Dunbar.

After a fire swept its main auditorium in 1915, seating capacity of the new Jefferson was increased to 1,200 and better ventilation and acoustic facilities were added. This theater booked high-quality Keith attractions. Its season lasted from September to April, and the opening each fall was a social event attended by hundreds from Albemarle and surrounding counties. Prices ranged from seventy-five cents to $2.50, depending upon the reputation of the performers. In January 1921 the Kendler-Zimmerman Company which owned the Jefferson opened yet another modern theater, the Lafayette. Decorated in subdued French gray and gold, the Lafayette cost $150,000, could seat 1,000, and had a $15,000 pipe organ which replaced the singer and orchestra accompanying most silent films of those years. The new theater was principally a movie house with a daily change of features. Prices were still rather low, ranging from ten to thirty cents.

Sometimes these new entertainment centers were rocked by con-

[12] Lilyan Sydenham, "Reflections of National Dramatic Trends in Charlottesville, 1900–1935," *MACH* 13 (1953):46–53.

troversy. In February 1914 Evelyn Nesbit Thaw, estranged wife of Harry K. Thaw who had shot and killed architect Stanford White, was scheduled to appear in *Mariette* at the Jefferson.[13] However, Baptists and Methodists expressed fears that the performance would "work serious harm to the morals of the community," and after a mass meeting attended by men only, Dr. H. W. Battle, M. C. Thomas, and Hollis Rinehart drafted a formal protest to Mayor A. V. Conway. Conway, citing section 29 of the city charter, informed Twyman that Evelyn ("the girl in the velvet swing") could not dance at the Jefferson, although she appeared in other Virginia cities without causing any perceptible havoc and in November 1917 was seen at the same theater- in a photoplay appropriately named *Redemption*. When ministers, mayor, and civic leaders talked of morality, they perhaps were more concerned with loyalty—loyalty to the memory of Stanford White, who had restored the Rotunda, created the buildings enclosing the south end of the Lawn, and designed the president's mansion atop Carr's Hill. Three years later during World War I local clergymen again voiced concern over community morals when some townspeople suggested opening theaters on Sundays for the entertainment of student-soldiers at the university. Once more the ministers prevailed, and theaters remained closed.

That conflict, although American involvement lasted only twenty months, created considerable patriotic furor in the community, especially at the university, which was under virtual military rule throughout much of 1918. Of course, by its very nature, World War I was not so pervasive as either the Civil War or the holocaust of the 1940s, but hundreds of local men and women donned uniforms, home front activity flourished, and the Monticello Guard once more answered a call to action. Yet, one gets the impression that just about the time all this effort reached high gear late in 1918, the fighting ended. Even before the United States entered the struggle, several university alumni, among them R. K. Gooch and Colgate Darden, Jr., were driving ambulances in France. However, the university's most acclaimed hero was James R. McConnell, a colorful Chicago native of Carolina stock now immortalized in bronze near Alderman Library. McConnell, editor of *Corks and Curls*, had a remarkable undergraduate career in 1907–10 which included teas he held for his friends, bagpipe performances, and an attempt to arrange a wrestling match between a two-hundred-pound fraternity

[13] John H. Moore, "When Evelyn Danced in Virginia," *Commonwealth* 33 (Feb. 1966):32–36.

brother and a trained bear. Since McConnell was a founder of the college Aero Club, it comes as no surprise that in 1916 he was flying with the Lafayette Escadrille against the Germans. Late in March 1917, just as Charlottesville and Albemarle were preparing for war, word of his death reached the university community. During commencement two years later Gutzon Borglum's warrior poised in flight was unveiled as a memorial to this intrepid spirit, "soaring like an eagle into new heavens of valor and devotion."

On April 7, 1917, over six hundred undergraduates enrolled in military science courses were promised guns immediately and told uniforms would arrive later. Dr. H. W. Battle was spearheading a drive to create emergency vegetable gardens throughout the city, and although university students celebrated Easter's Week in the usual fashion, the finals ceremony was canceled as scores of young men left for camp. Others joined a back-to-the-farm movement to aid the war effort, and all intercollegiate athletic contests were suspended for the duration of the conflict. In June 1,038 city residents and 1,895 county youths between twenty-one and thirty-one registered for the draft. The first local man called was Andrew Knight, a white county youth who lived on Monticello Road and held number 258. A month later Lieutenant Colonel J. A. Cole was named to head the university's Reserve Office Training Corps (ROTC). At the same time the Monticello Guard prepared to leave for Alabama, and Base Hospital Unit No. 41 was formed at the University Hospital under the leadership of Dr. William H. Goodwin. Both groups would see action in France, the guard becoming part of the 116th Infantry and the 110th Machine Gun Battalion of the 29th Division and the Base Hospital Unit serving at Saint-Denis near Paris. The community's first white draftees reported to Camp Lee in September 1917, and in October the first group of black youths left for the same destination. The latter, some sixty men in all, were honored with a parade and rally at the First Baptist Church (colored). Among those addressing them were Mayor E. G. Haden, Judge R. T. W. Duke, Jr., and Colonel Cole. Refreshments were supplied by the Charlottesville Creamery.

During the winter of 1917–18, one of the coldest on record, city lights were extinguished in order to save fuel, all theaters and amusements places were closed on Mondays, and for five weeks groceries and drugstores closed their doors at noon each day. In the fall of 1918, as these economy measures continued, some university students complained because the library was shut tight at night; others found the darkened grounds even more oppressive.

Fears were expressed that the University of Virginia might close, but establishment of a motor school by the War Department to train auto mechanics and repairmen and creation of the Student Army Training Corps (SATC), including both army and navy units, meant classes would be held more or less as usual, although enrollment declined somewhat. In all, more than eighteen hundred men were trained at the motor camp located on the site of what is now Scott Stadium. Home guard units were formed in Charlottesville, Crozet, and Greenwood to replace the absent national guard, Liberty Loan and bond rallies were held, the university's ROTC went off to Plattsburg, New York, for advanced training, and a Red Cross canteen opened at the railway junction. However, as noted earlier, much of this activity came late in 1918 and by modern standards was poorly organized. With peace, university officials conceded that the SATC program was thoroughly unsatisfactory and, with the armistice, brought weeks of "academic chaos."

A lone dissenting voice in the midst of war was quickly silenced. Professor Leonidas Rutledge Whipple, a recent appointee as professor of journalism, took a stern antiwar stance in an address at Sweet Briar College in November 1917. Whipple, a native of Saint Louis, was no stranger to the Old Dominion. He had been an instructor of English and journalism at the university in 1906–9 and then worked on various newspapers in Washington, Richmond, and Charlottesville before returning to teaching once more. In the uproar that ensued, both Sweet Briar and the University of Virginia disavowed all responsibility for Whipple's pacifism, and within a week he was summarily removed by the board of visitors and his post was declared vacant. Whipple later admitted he was a Socialist and had voted for Eugene Debs in 1912.

When peace came on November 11, 1918, Charlottesville exploded in spontaneous revelry. The morning hours were marked by impromptu demonstrations, a special issue of the *Daily Progress*, and relaxation of the city's speed limits by Mayor Haden. In the afternoon, Haden, other dignitaries, the Albemarle Rifles (the local home guard), fire engines, and the university's SATC unit moved majestically down Main Street accompanied by several bands.

Twenty-nine veterans from Charlottesville (both men and women) received thirty-seven distinguished medals, most of them from a grateful French government. Three of those honored won Distinguished Service Medals for their exploits: Richard Hildreth, Philip Bradley Peyton, and James D. Fife. Nine county men received seventeen honorary medals. On July 4, 1919, a pageant and "welcome home" parade honoring both races culminated with speechmaking at the Rotunda. The ceremonies over, some two thousand blacks continued the celebration at Lambeth Field, while whites picnicked under the trees at the university.

Late in 1919 some of these returning soldiers organized the Charlottesville-Albemarle American Legion Post No. 74, which at first met at the Elks Hall but in 1924 secured quarters on the third floor of the Lafayette Theatre building. Even before that date the legion's annual military ball each spring and a memorial Armistice Night supper had become standard events in the local social calendar. In April 1922, a grim reminder of what had happened overseas, the body of Sergeant Aubrey B. Thatcher, the first Charlottesville youth killed in France, arrived home for burial in his native soil. In years which followed many remembered the winters of 1917 and 1918, not because of the war, but for the influenza epidemic that killed hundreds in Charlottesville and Albemarle. In October 1918 the Old Dominion recorded 6,000 deaths from the dreaded disease. Theaters were closed during that month and drugstores were forbidden to dispense drinks. Timberlake's Pharmacy advertised "Kill-..-Kold" during these weeks, guaranteed to knock out flu germs; and in January 1919 all children exposed to flu at home were told not to attend school. However, by that date the worst was over.

The Albemarle agricultural scene changed little during the decades from 1890 to 1920. After the turmoil and hard times of the nineties these generally prosperous years. In 1920 county farms did not lead the state in any category but held high rank in several areas. Tenancy, which had declined slightly since the turn of the century, was not a pressing problem; only 464 of 3,165 farms were tilled by tenants, less than one-fourth of them black. Fruit production continued important, with apples, peaches, and grapes (despite Prohibition) the most popular crops. The county ranked third in orchard crops and oats, fifth in production of hay and forage, and sixth in total value of all farm property ($28,189,780).

What those studying Albemarle's farmlands found most distressing was the steady decline in rural population, an increase in idle, unproductive fields, and the seeming inability of local farmers to meet local needs. Odie Mayhew noted that in 1919 the county and city produced food and feed worth $6.1 million but consumed similar products valued at $7.3 million, a comparison which did not include luxuries, only basic staples. "From August 1, 1919, to August 1, 1920, one railroad going through our county unloaded at Charlottesville the following foodstuffs which we can and should grow in part: 192 car loads of feed, 26 car loads of Irish potatoes, 41 car loads of oats, 256 car loads of hay, 19 car loads of cabbages, 6 car loads of straw, 2 car loads of shucks, and 40 car loads of corn." [14] Mayhew blamed the 122,611 untilled acres for this deplorable situation and urged Albemarle to seek out new settlers at once. He also pointed to outmoded farming practices such as inept use of fertilizer and failure to rotate crops properly, a livestock population only about one-third that which the county could support, and poor marketing practices. Fruit growers, he noted, had been forced to grade and pack their produce in order to sell it; but farmers growing corn, potatoes, and hay made no effort to standardize what they offered for sale. Wilson Gee, summarizing the research of Mayhew and others, emphasized that the county easily could support 1,634 additional farm families and stated: "There are few as inviting counties anywhere as Albemarle. Its wonderfully responsive soil under proper treatment, its great diversity of crops, the beautiful scenic character of its landscapes, its splendid schools, its stretches of good roads, all make it a most desirable section in which to locate for farming." [15]

Gee's words, all too reminiscent of those found in promotional booklets of the 1890s, actually were flying in the face of reality. No one could deny Albemarle had lovely scenery, but in 1920 its schools, roads, and even the day-to-day life on the farms left much to be desired, at least when contrasted with the pleasures of communities such as Charlottesville. The 1920 census had revealed that for the first time, more Americans lived in urban areas than rural ones; and although the county population still was much greater than city (26,005 compared to 10,688), the national trend was evident even in Albemarle. Simply put, no amount of optimistic rhetoric could disguise the hard fact that until some of the conveniences enjoyed by city dwellers were available in Warren, Cross Roads, Doylesville, and Boonesville, the drift of people from farm to town would continue, and Albemarle's idle lands would increase in number. As always, it cost money to improve worn-out lands, inaugurate new modes of cultivation, and replenish herds of livestock—the same improvements sought by the Agricultural Society of Albemarle a century before.

Yet efforts were being made to aid local farmers. The university held a Rural Life Week each summer between 1910 and 1920, and

[14] *University of Virginia Record, Extension Series* 7 (Oct. 1922):75–76.
[15] Ibid., p. 106.

fairs, both white and colored, brought scores of farm families together each autumn as they displayed produce and studied exhibits of machinery and prize stock. "Farmers' Trains" sponsored by VPI occasionally traveled through the county while professors discussed agricultural techniques and how to apply them. As a result of the federal Smith-Lever Act of 1916, programs were being implemented to interest young people in agricultural careers and assist their parents too. Going forth under the banner, "Make Two Blades of Grass Grow Where One Previously Grew," county agents, most of them trained at Blacksburg, tried to instill better farming methods. Boys' agricultural clubs were an integral part of these efforts. Home Demonstration classes, pioneered in Albemarle by Bessie Dunn, primarily for girls and housewives but including some young men, were being conducted in canning, sewing, poultry, gardening, room improvement, cooking, and bread making. These activities were aided immeasurably by $5,000 given by Paul Goodloe McIntire, a local-boy-made-good, who, in all, lavished nearly $2,000,000 on his native city and county during these years. Miss Dunn, by the way, rose to prominence in 1910 when she won a trip to Bermuda in a contest sponsored by the *Daily Progress*, one of many that daily launched to increase subscriptions. Not surprisingly, the story of her travels soon was being featured by her benefactor. However, although that newspaper lobbied hard for better county roads and paid some attention to the annual fruit harvest, for the most part its columns were monopolized by the Charlottesville business community.

Social life during the decade or so before World War I was dictated largely by how far one could walk or drive by carriage and the condition of Albemarle's roads. The seasons had a certain rhythm. The year opened with a magnificent reception at Birdwood hosted by the Hollis Rineharts and a holiday dance at the Elks Club. In February the Elks held their minstrel show, and in the spring and summer there was baseball, not only at the university but among teams sponsored by the Eagles, Elks, and YMCA. For a brief time the semipro Virginia Mountain League pitted Charlottesville against Covington, Clifton Forge, and Staunton. Each May, Jefferson Park opened once more, and the Fourth of July was a holiday of some consequence, especially during World War I, but was soon eclipsed by the Albemarle Horse Show which opened a few weeks later. In those days this event was dominated by Mrs. Allen Potts, a superb horsewoman, who rode off with scores of blue ribbons. In September the Chautauqua tent appeared on Main street near the Southern

Railway station, and shortly after that the revivals commenced. Then in the fall the hunting season opened, both for those chasing the fox and those seeking bigger, edible game.

Anna Barringer, a girl during those years, recalls weekly at homes held by various hostesses, teas, lawn tennis, and parties at Farmington presided over by Mrs. Warner Wood or similar outings at the Murray Boococks' Castalia and the Coleses' Old Woodville.[16] "These visits were two-hour pilgrimages in your best big hat and fluffiest dress and you were lucky to get home without a thunderstorm." In time a country club appeared off Rugby Road near the fairgrounds providing a swimming pool, clay tennis courts, and more tea. One could always spend a few pleasant hours strolling down Main Street, an afternoon promenade shared with students, faculty wives, and townspeople. Usually, according to Miss Barringer, everyone went down the left side to the C. & O. Depot, perhaps had a chocolate soda at Pence and Sterling's drugstore, and returned by the same route; the right side of the street was "given to vagaries." Toward dusk, "ladies of the evening," probably from Aunt Mat's near the C. & O. station, "heavily painted, ornately coiffured, no hats, and conspicuously though not brazenly clothed," would sally forth. They always had special seats at the theater. In the gallery the left-hand side and center were reserved for whites; the right-hand side, for blacks. Aunt Mat's girls filled seats at the head of the stairs. Miss Barringer notes that her seamstress characterized these painted damsels in this fashion: "They's mostly little country girls, not very bright, that don't want to work, and very fond of diamonds."

For those associated with the university there were lectures, concerts (sometimes sponsored by the DAR), and Easters, which began with Sunday church services ushering in several days of revelry — baseball games, Tilka and Eli Banana dances, Phi Delta Phi initiations, and sumptuous dinners, although classes were supposed to be resumed by Wednesday or Thursday. The university played its first basketball game in January 1906, beating Washington and Lee, 22 to 6, but baseball and football were the major attractions. Before 1910 football was extremely rough and resulted in numerous injuries and even deaths. In 1897 a Georgia player was fatally injured during the Georgia-Virginia game in Atlanta, and in 1909 Archer Christian, Virginia's halfback, died after being hurt in the Georgetown contest. Georgia banned the sport for a time, and Georgetown also gave up football for a year or so. Virginia did not. In 1913 the Lam-

[16] Anna Barringer, pp. 41–48.

beth Field stadium seating 2,500 was completed; however, seven years later more than 6,000 thronged around that gridiron to watch the Cavaliers beat the North Carolina Tarheels, 14 to 0.

One unusual social group of these years was the Hog and Hominy Club, ostensibly as association of Albemarle farmers, but a far cry from any agricultural group the community had seen before that time. Formed in 1912 by seventeen affluent residents, this rather exclusive assemblage held monthly meetings at various estates, gatherings sometimes attended by prominent guests. These evenings, dominated by wine, liquor, ribald jokes, and fine food, were strictly male. Wives often cooked for days in preparation for these feasts and then, together with servants, gathered in the pantry to eavesdrop on the revelry provided by P. H. Faulconer, W. H. Langhorne, Randolph Ortman, W. Allan Perkins, Hollis Rinehart, E. D. Tayloe, and others. Russell Bradford was the group's only secretary, and with his death in 1930 the members decided to disband. Three years later his minutes (if one can so term them) covering the years from 1915 to 1925 were privately printed.

Of course, there was always gossip, largely about events at the university, who was going to marry whom, who had been or was going to Washington, New York, or Richmond for a visit. Several individuals tended to dominate such conversations during these years, notably the beautiful Langhorne sisters, former mayor Sam McCue who killed his wife in 1904, and eccentric (some would say downright crazy) John Armstrong Chaloner. The Langhorne girls, Nancy, Irene, and Phyllis—and there were five other children in the family—were the daughters of Chiswell Dabney Langhorne and Nancy Witcher Keene. "Chilly," a youthful Civil War veteran, tried his hand at several trades in the 1860s and 1870s before becoming interested in tobacco and railroad contracting. His skills brought him substantial prosperity, and in 1894 he decided to move to Albemarle and purchased the gracious country home named Mirador near Greenwood. Two years before his death in 1919 Langhorne established a trust fund of $1.1 million for his heirs. However, as handsome and as successful as he was, most Americans were much more interested in his daughters Irene, who as bride of artist Charles Dana Gibson became the famed "Gibson Girl," symbol of beauty to an era, and Nancy (Lady Astor), an outspoken, controversial wit, who became the first woman to sit in the British House of Commons.

At the turn of the century Irene faced a formidable rival for her throne, a dazzling Albemarle beauty who, after a moment of prominence, died a tragic death. Sometime in the late 1890s a New York

photographer took a picture of Maude Woods, daughter of Commonwealth's Attorney Micajah Woods, which in 1898 appeared on
the cover of a volume entitled *Miss America*. This brought overnight
fame, and two years later she was selected as a model for the seal
of an exposition to be held in Buffalo, New York; however, shortly
after this honor was disclosed, Miss Woods succumbed to typhoid
fever while visiting her mother's relatives in Hanover County.

On a hot Sunday evening, September 4, 1904, J. Samuel McCue—
well-to-do, respected, several times mayor of Charlottesville—and his
wife, Fanny, returned from evening church services, nodded to neighbors as they walked to their gracious Park Street home, and then
apparently retired for the night. A short time later Sam emerged,
rumpled and distraught, shouting that someone had killed Fanny.
Although McCue blamed an unknown assailant, within seventy-two
hours he was arrested and charged with the crime. The motive was
simple enough: the former mayor wanted to marry another woman.

R. T. W. Duke, Jr., a neighbor whom McCue unsuccessfully
sought as his attorney, was one of the first persons summoned, and
on the evening of the crime he noted in his diary that the situation
looked "ugly." The victim presented a "fearful, gruesome sight," and
her husband seemed unable to give any "distinct account" of what
had occurred. The following day the city council held a special meeting, crowds of curious spectators surged into Charlottesville, and a
detective hired by McCue already suspected his employer was guilty,
according to Duke, "and I think justly so." Two days later, soon
after McCue was arrested, twenty men were detailed to guard the
jail to thwart any lynching. Perhaps Duke was influenced most of
all by what one of his daughters told him. She, too, had been at
church that Sunday evening and had walked home behind the
McCues. As they strolled along and greeted friends and neighbors,
she reported, they also were engaged in a rather heated exchange of
words.

The trial which ensued was one of the most sensational ever staged
in Charlottesville. McCue hired a galaxy of legal talent and fought
the prosecution every step of the way; nevertheless, the jury needed
only twenty minutes to reach a verdict of guilty. The *Daily Progress*
sold hundreds of copies each day and later reprinted the whole tale
in book form. Newsboy Marshall Fletcher, who would one day command the Monticello Guard, later recalled that he made a juvenile
fortune during those exciting weeks, the first real money he ever had
to call his own. McCue and his lawyers appealed to higher courts,
but in vain, and the former mayor paid the penalty for murder and

was hanged . . . at least that is the official story. However, according to some old-timers the sentence never was carried out. Mc-Cue, they say, was spirited away from Albemarle forever.

John Armstrong Chaloner, born Chanler, certainly must take top honors for eccentricity in a county which has been home to many individuals of similar bent. For nearly four decades his antics, crusades, and courtroom appearances delighted and confounded both admirers and detractors.[17] Chanler, an Astor heir born to wealth and prestige, first came to Albemarle County from New York as the betrothed of Amélie Rives of Castle Hill. Publication in 1888 of her most famous work, *The Quick or the Dead?*, disrupted their wedding plans temporarily. The hero obviously was Chanler, and his family objected strenuously to some of the sexual allusions expressed by the young writer. Nevertheless, they got married, but soon parted. Then, after Amélie's marriage to a Russian portrait painter, Prince Pierre Troubetzkoy, Chanler bought Merrie Mills near Cobham, and the three became close friends.

Sometime after he settled there, Chanler, whose flights through fantasy land and interest in the occult worried his relatives, was visited by architect Stanford White, then working at the University of Virginia. White proposed a trip to New York; Chanler agreed and soon found himself committed to an asylum. Several years later he escaped, returned to Albemarle where he got himself certified as legally sane (although he remained insane outside of the Old Dominion for a decade or so), and changed his name to Chaloner. In March 1909 Chaloner shot and killed John Gillard, a drunken, English-born neighbor whose wife, fearing a beating, had fled to Merrie Mills. During a scuffle in the dining room Gillard fell, mortally wounded, the exact spot later marked by a bronze star and the walls decorated with photos and news clippings describing what had happened. When the police arrived, Chaloner, garbed in leather pajamas, munched on his customary breakfast of duck and vanilla ice cream and described how he had spent the night with Gillard's lifeless body "to test his nerve." He paid for the funeral and wanted to put a marker over the grave inscribed "HE DIED GAMELY," but cooler heads persuaded him not to. A few years later Chaloner went on the lecture circuit describing this affair. Other speaking tours included "on-the-spot" descriptions of hell, a campaign to reform lunacy

[17] See J. Bryan III, "Johnny Jackanapes, the Merry-Andrew of Merrie Mills: A Brief Biography of John Armstrong Chaloner," *Virginia Magazine of History and Biography* 73 (1965):3–21.

laws, and a spirited defense of buzzards which, he feared, faced extermination.

Irascible, unpredictable, garrulous, proud of a physical resemblance to Napoleon, Chaloner sometimes used his cane to smash windows of autos that came too close to him as he strolled Richmond's streets. On other occasions he waited with horse and buggy at the entrance to his estate and forced any auto driver to dismount and lead his steed past the vehicle. In later years he succumbed to the motorcar, bought a Pierce Arrow complete with field kitchen and bed, and fought insomnia by having his chauffeur drive him through the sleeping towns of northern Virginia. On one of these routine outings Chaloner was stopped and his vehicle searched for whiskey. Police were certain that the big car cruising night after night must belong to a bootlegger. Although he wore a wishing ring which allegedly enabled him to approach any busy intersection and stride through unscathed without looking right or left, apparently that ring did not fend off the law.

Chaloner was a writer of sorts, publishing numerous plays and sonnets, and for a brief time edited *The Confederacy and the Solid South*, a journal printed in Roanoke Rapids, North Carolina. In the Keswick-Cismont-Cobham community "the General," as he was called, was popular indeed. He was a generous man who liked to play the role of the seigneur, lending money, paying rents and doctors' bills, and every Fourth of July held a lavish open house. He was especially interested in visual education and gave substantial sums to various states and educational institutions to promote the use of films. Chaloner also was an advocate of community centers and in 1920 set up a free movie theater on his estate. This facility, which could seat some three hundred people, soon became a mecca for scores of farm families in eastern Albemarle and neighboring Orange and Fluvanna counties. There they saw not only comedies and news but educational films as well. On one occasion the theater was the setting of perhaps the most startling interview in Albemarle's long history. Chaloner let it be known that he was interested in funding a proposed University of Virginia expedition to Norway to view an eclipse of the sun. A professor went to Merrie Mills to discuss the matter, but for thirty-six long hours Chaloner kept him prisoner in the theater as he impersonated great figures of history. His audience of one did not dare leave since two vicious dogs were circling the area on a small trolley. As for the Norwegian venture, Chaloner never mentioned it; and needless to add, the professor never returned to ask why. However, in November 1926 the board of visitors announced that Chaloner in-

53. Tom Martin's law office at 220 Court Square, Charlottesville

deed had honored the university with a "generous gift" which would be used to pay costs of the expedition.

Chaloner died at the University Hospital in June 1935, age seventy-three, a mere shadow of the tempestuous figure he once had been. In his last weeks he became reconciled with his brothers and sisters and asked that he be buried near the swimming pool at Merrie Mills, halfway between the men's and women's bathhouses. They chose instead to inter him in Grace Episcopal churchyard, not far from the final resting place of John Gillard. Chaloner's simple tombstone, topped by a small white cross, bears this inscription: "Blessed is the man who considereth the poor and needy." His funeral, attended by hundreds of his neighbors, was marked by a touching tribute from black friends who sang "Swing Low, Sweet Chariot." For, whenever he showed movies, held a gala Fourth of July fete, or hosted a Christmas party, local Negroes filled one-fourth of the seats and received a similar amount of whatever goodies were dispensed.

In many ways, this age of Tom Martin, 1890–1920, simple enough on the surface, was a complex time indeed. The horse was fighting for survival against the upstart auto, a leisurely agricultural South was battling an industrial, factory-mad New South, and in practically every realm of local and national life past and future seemed locked in combat. Though eager for settlers, Charlottesville, for example, still harbored some resentment against outsiders. At the turn of the century a highly respected local businessman, both Yankee and Catholic, bought a Main Street lot at public auction only to be told that he might rent but not own such prestigious property. The lot was subsequently handed over to the next highest bidder.

If there was a consistent thread throughout these years, it was the influence and power of railroads and their stepchild, the trolley. The latter changed the face of Charlottesville; the former created Tom Martin and elevated him to national prominence. Railroads also bestowed wealth and economic well-being upon men such as "Chilly" Langhorne, Thomas Lafayette Rosser, and Hollis Rinehart. Although, as noted, Langhorne is best remembered for his progeny, his financial success was built upon railroad construction, and the same can be said of Rosser and Rinehart. Rosser, born in Campbell County, a distinguished Civil War campaigner and chief engineer of the Northern Pacific Railroad, purchased Rugby as a summer home in 1883, then part of an extensive farm on the outskirts of Charlottesville.[18] Thwarted in politics, in 1900 he became a Republican and in 1905 was named postmaster of Charlottesville, a post he held until his death five years later despite a stroke which left him speechless in 1906.

At about the time of Rosser's demise, Rinehart, born in Botetourt County in 1871, son of a successful railroad builder and partner in the construction firm of Rinehart and Dennis, moved to Charlottesville and purchased Birdwood Farm just west of the city. Within a short time he became a local power reminiscent of multifaceted eighteenth-century figures such as Thomas Walker. Soon he was active in banking, real estate, local politics, and community and educational affairs. A member of the university's board of visitors, Rotary, the Chamber of Commerce, the Baptist church, the Albemarle Hunt Club, and the Albemarle Auto Club, Rinehart was a true child of the new, booster-minded South. His construction firm reputedly made a considerable sum helping to build Camp Lee near Petersburg during World War I, fulfilling contracts worth nearly $11 million; and when Rinehart later erected several mansions across the road from Birdwood for his sons, local wags dubbed this private development "Camp Lee." However, Hollis Rinehart, creator of the Charlottesville National Bank and Trust Company, was undoubtedly best known in his own day as father of the eight-story skyscraper that housed his financial empire, a bright jewel in the crown of the South's 106th largest city.

[18] See Thomas O. Beane, "Thomas Lafayette Rosser: Soldier, Railroad Builder, Politician, Businessman, 1836–1910" (M.A. thesis, University of Virginia, 1957).

Rinehart's most formidable rival, at least in banking and community development, was George R. B. Michie, president of People's National Bank from 1913 to 1938. Michie was born across the mountains in Staunton in 1870. During the 1880s his father became editor of the *Charlottesville Chronicle*, and after two years of study at the University of Virginia, young Michie followed in his footsteps and worked on newspapers in Charlottesville and Staunton. In the late 1890s he decided to enter book publishing, a move undoubtedly prompted by the appearance of the rival *Daily Progress*. With his brother, Thomas, he founded the Michie Publishing Company, destined to become a nationally known producer of law texts and city and state codes. Although the careers of Rinehart and Michie possess many similarities—both were born outside of Albemarle, both became local business and political powers, both headed important banks and often served on the same boards and committees—the latter, in essence, became prime spokesman for those who deplored what they considered too rapid change, multistoried office buildings and huge hotels, for example.

Rinehart, of course, arrived well-heeled a decade or so after Michie had become an established figure on the local scene and challenged things as they were. It is difficult to say how much he influenced area growth, but in the 1920s Charlottesville's population surged past 15,000, and at the end of that decade the county recorded an increase of 1,000 or so. But, beyond the twenties lay the sobering, even tragic thirties, an era which left an angry scar upon a generation and made much of the boosterism of the previous four decades appear hollow and fatuous.

Chapter 17

Roaring Twenties, Troubled Thirties

THE life of the Charlottesville-Albemarle community from 1920 to 1940 does not fit neatly into ten-year categories; instead, there were seven rather good years followed by seven lean ones and then a period of recovery aided by federal and state spending and economic activity stimulated by World War II. To some extent what was occurring in the foothills of the Blue Ridge mirrors trends evident in the nation as a whole. The seven good years were dominated by lavish pageantry and public spectacles, unabashed civic boosterism, mounting concern over bootlegging and gunplay in the western fringes of Albemarle County, and growing realization of potential benefits accruing from tourism. The lean or bad years were a time of belt tightening for everyone, although both city and county seem to have weathered the Great Depression amazingly well. Pageantry ceased abruptly, the county fair and Albemarle Horse Show disappeared, and several lavish undertakings such as a huge $500,000 country club at Covesville and a similar operation at Swannanoa became part of the debris littering an economic wasteland. The King Lumber Company, largely because of the suicide of its owner, the Bank of Crozet, and the soapstone enterprise at Alberene closed their doors, although the last subsequently was revived by John S. Graves. However, the new country club at Farmington, formed in 1927 with a beautiful eighteenth-century mansion as its nucleus, and the Citizens Bank and Trust Company, which opened four years later with R. T. Minor, Jr., as president, both prospered. University enrollment remained steady, actually increasing a bit, and even in the depths of the depression there was enough construction to provide hundreds of jobs. This included Scott Stadium, Bayly Art Museum, a new engineering school, dormitories, and additions to the University Hospital, as well as Skyline Drive and various school and highway projects (notably Route 29 North) aided by state and federal money. The Blue Ridge Sanatorium, opened in 1920 near Monticello Mountain, also expanded its facilities during these years.

The most unexpected development was a sudden about-face by bankers and local businessmen on the question of industrial growth. After years spent trying to lure factories to Albemarle, they began to sing a different tune. Why? Three factors help to explain what happened. Dedication of Monticello as a public shrine in 1924, transformation of Farmington into a handsome, very profitable club three years later, and John D. Rockefeller, Jr.'s restoration of Williamsburg aroused considerable interest in both tourism and the economic potential of the county's historic past. Over drinks (Prohibition notwithstanding) rich men who had fled the smokestacks and grime of northern industrial centers undoubtedly pressed home their conviction that Charlottesville and its lovely countryside were indeed fortunate to have escaped such a fate. And, lastly, as huge industrial complexes in other communities shut their gates, throwing thousands out of work, Albemarle's leaders quickly revised long-cherished views and concluded that a well-balanced economy, a little of this and that, but no dependence upon any single enterprise, was to be preferred. Also, it is possible that ebullient New South boosterism was wearing rather thin by 1930, and a new generation of would-be business tycoons, realizing that forty years of pro-factory hoopla had done little for Charlottesville and Albemarle, appraised the situation with a shrewd eye, joined hands with the powerful real estate fraternity, to which many of them already belonged, and set new goals for their community. These were, of course, stable, controlled growth, a balanced economy, no dirty industry, and considerable deference to the needs and wishes of the well-to-do who were buying and selling Albemarle's acres in ever-increasing numbers.

In the early 1920s many city-county residents seem to have gone "pageant mad." Construction of the university's McIntire Amphitheatre provided an ideal setting for such events, and soon almost any excuse was sufficient cause for hundreds to don togas, medieval armor, or colonial garb and parade before their friends and neighbors. In 1921 university finals belatedly commemorated that institution's centennial, a year later five thousand gathered for a gigantic homecoming celebration, and during succeeding years the amphitheatre was the scene of still more extravaganzas. The centennial pageant, entitled *Shadow of the Builder*, was filmed and shown at the Lafayette Theatre, where it broke a previous record held by Charlie Chaplin, over four thousand attending in a single day. The homecoming fete on November 1–4, 1922, included yet another pageant, torchlight parades, pilgrimages to Monticello, a fancy dress ball, and a football game with Washington and Lee which Virginia appropriately won, 22 to 6. Water Street, transformed into a "land of mirth," became the scene of a riot on the eve of that contest when university students, having finished their torchlight march down Main Street, stormed the carnival in an effort to gain entrance without paying admission. Rebuffed, they attacked the Jefferson Theatre with torches and eggs and tried to force their way into a colonial ball in progress at the armory. The mayor and President Alderman addressed the mob and eventually order was restored.

Meanwhile, John Armstrong Chaloner was staging even more spectacular gatherings at Merrie Mills. The largest of these, sometimes attracting as many as ten thousand persons, usually occurred on the Fourth of July and was truly a community affair complete with movies, food, games, bands, fireworks, perhaps a performing aviator or two, and speeches, one always by the host himself. These festivities often were managed by extensive committees composed of prominent citizens. Chaloner's celebrations on Labor Day and at Christmas were somewhat smaller but still lured hundreds to his Cobham estate.

Other public spectacles, unlike both the pageants at the university and the merriment at Merrie Mills, were provided by the revived Ku Klux Klan. In February 1922 mourners attending the funeral of C. M. Thomas, county sheriff killed in a Richmond hotel fire, were startled as four white-robed figures advanced and placed a wreath upon the grave. This was evidently the first appearance of the "new" Klan in Albemarle.[1] A month later members posted a warning to university students who had written bad checks to straighten out their financial affairs at once. By the end of that year at least two local units (Nos. 9 and 5) were in existence, although the latter was experiencing differences with the national headquarters in Atlanta and severed relations for a time. In May 1924 flaming crosses appeared in several rural areas, and on June 9 a national lecturer from Saint Louis spoke at the county courthouse on "Americanism." "The speech," said the *Daily Progress*, "was well received and a rising vote indicated that practically every one of his hearers endorsed the statements he made." A short time later crosses were burned at Mechum's River and a few bombs exploded near Negro homes in that region. In September 1924 handbills announced that a speech would be given at the YMCA on the role of women in the KKK; however, "Y" officials said their facilities could not be used, and the meeting, attracting hundreds, convened at the Albemarle County Courthouse instead. Two months

---

[1] In April 1921 the KKK contributed $1,000 to the university's centennial drive to raise $3,000,000; however, this money undoubtedly came from state or national, not local sources. Unless otherwise indicated, most of the material in this chapter comes from files of the *Daily Progress*.

later and again in August 1925 huge Saturday night crowds lined Charlottesville's Main Street to watch parades featuring mounted Klansmen, decorated autos filled with their ladies, and colorful floats dedicated to law and order, education, democracy, and Protestantism. The *Progress*, at first rather scornful of hoods and crosses, now had been won over completely. The 1924 parade was, it said, "one of the most impressive ever witnessed," and the 1925 spectacle, which included over five hundred marchers and units from Fredericksburg, Mineral, and other nearby communities, was "a big success."

During August 1925 a local KKK delegation participated in a gigantic national demonstration held in Washington. A year later, in June 1926, to the strains of "Onward Christian Soldiers," over two hundred robed Klansmen marched to reserved seats at a Hinton Avenue Methodist Church revival. Properly in place, they and several thousand others listened as Rev. Ed Caldwell preached a rousing sermon: "Show Thyself a Man." A few days later E. B. White, another evangelist, spoke to Klansmen at Fife Chapel on "Christian Patriotism." "To be a Klansman," he avowed, "means to be a Christian Patriot and nothing else." Yet by that date the national organization was in deep trouble and local units of the invisible empire soon disbanded.

Even before Monticello became the property of the Thomas Jefferson Memorial Foundation in 1923, that landmark was the setting of scores of speeches and patriotic programs, many of them organized by local DAR chapters whose members subsequently served as that shrine's first hostesses to the public. These events usually were held on April 13, Jefferson's birthday, but July 4, the anniversary of Jack Jouett's ride, or the presence of a national celebrity also could stir plans for such gatherings. Interestingly, in 1923 Chaloner's Fourth of July tournament attracted so much attention that the foundation decided to move its festivities from Monticello to Merrie Mills. There, with proceeds earmarked for charity, Jefferson was properly eulogized and Sarah Belle McCue was crowned Queen of Albemarle, Chaloner viewing the entire proceedings astride a handsome Virginia thoroughbred.

In addition to the master of Merrie Mills, during these years one other local resident often provided the impetus for parades and speechmaking. He was Paul Goodloe McIntire, born in Charlottesville in May 1860, son of a successful merchant.[2] McIntire attended the university briefly, worked as a messenger-clerk for the C. & O.

---

[2] For a summary of McIntire's life, see the *Daily Progress* (Dec. 30, 1960).

Railroad, and then departed for Chicago and New York where he made a fortune in stocks and bonds. Returning to his birthplace in 1918, McIntire began distributing his wealth to local public schools, the University of Virginia, and his native city and county. In all, his bequests totaled $1,199,250; about one-half of this amount went to the university to promote cancer research and improve hospital facilities, establish a department of commerce and finance which bears his name, and build the handsome amphitheatre also named in his honor.

McIntire gave the city of Charlottesville its public library and several parks and playgrounds, some adorned with impressive monuments to Lee, Jackson, and Lewis and Clark. The unveiling of these memorials, often watched by feeble veterans, provided still more patriotic spectacles. The Jackson statue was dedicated during a Confederate reunion held in October 1922, the Lewis and Clark group a few weeks later, and the figure of Lee at another reunion in May 1924. McIntire, cast somewhat in the Horatio Alger mold, appears to have been a rather quiet, reserved, perhaps unhappy individual, very unlike the flamboyant, unpredictable Chaloner. Yet both were true sons of their age. The latter, a bit crazy at times, was a public benefactor no less than McIntire. While parents pointed to Paul Goodloe McIntire, a sturdy, hometown-boy-made-good as the man to emulate, sons who attended these Merrie Mills frolics undoubtedly dreamed of someday becoming John Armstrong Chaloner. After all, he owned the community's first real swimming pool, also its first airfield, one approved by the United States government for planes going from Dayton, Ohio, to Langley Field, provided free movies for thousands in his own theater, and gave glorious parties. What more could one wish for? McIntire lived his last years in New York City, where he died in July 1952, ninety-two years of age.

Civic boosterism of the early 1920s was, of course, aided by the efforts of both McIntire and Chaloner, as well as numerous conventions held by state fraternal and business groups. From time to time the presence of captains of industry such as Henry Ford and John D. Rockefeller, Jr., created rumors they might invest in Albemarle's future. In February 1922 Dr. Robert M. Bird, a chemistry professor at the University of Virginia, addressed the local Rotary Club and ticked off advantages that Charlottesville offered for manufacturing: good climate; people "fit to live with, mostly English, few foreign trouble-makers"; "nearly unlimited" raw materials; proximity to markets, ports, railroads, hydroelectric power, and coal; and scientific expertise at the university. Why, then, was Charlottesville not a true industrial center? The answer, according to Bird, lay in poor local

54. Paul Goodloe McIntire receives French Legion of Honor.

leadership. Two months later speakers at a Chamber of Commerce
dinner advocated two immediate steps to improve this situation: get
chain gangs off Main Street, to avoid making an unfortunate impression upon visitors, and build a new hotel, one the city could be
proud of.

Sobered by census returns of 1920 revealing little increase in area
population during the preceding decade, Charlottesville's business
leaders began a campaign to woo county residents to their side. The
city band, organized in 1922 under the baton of Harry Lowe and with
the financial assistance of Sol Kaufman, soon was giving concerts in
White Hall, Free Union, and various other villages; groups such as
the Young Men's Business Club held meetings in rural communities;
and scores of speakers went forth extolling the virtues of city-county
cooperation. The only tangible results were formation of a joint
health department which continues to the present day and some
cooperation among welfare agencies. The culmination of this campaign was a special eighty-two-page "National Publicity Section"
produced by the *Daily Progress* on June 1, 1923, overflowing with
pictures of the city and especially those of the county. This unusual
edition also included a "Creed and Covenant" composed by the secretary of the Chamber of Commerce and dedicated to Jefferson's Al-

bemarle. Laudatory paragraphs, beginning with the words "I believe in Albemarle County," praised the region as "a land of clear and fathomless skies . . . land of mountains that inspire a sense of intimacy and affection . . . land of peaceful, wholesome and progressive Americans . . . land of purest American stock . . . land of both old and new." This litany of superlatives concluded with a personal pledge to Albemarle County, "to her service, brain, heart and hand—THE GARDEN SPOT OF VIRGINIA!"

How many individuals subscribed to this creed is not known, but buy stock in a new hotel they did. This drive, headed by Fred W. Twyman, succeeded in raising over $500,000 and assured construction of the Monticello Hotel, "a place of beauty and a shrine of hospitality," which opened in April 1926. This imposing structure, built by the Jefferson Park Hotel Corporation, experienced several name changes before registering its first guest. Following a local contest it was first christened the Albemarle, but the corporation decided it would be the Hotel James Monroe. Early in 1925 the emerging skyscraper assumed its more familiar name. In March 1927 the Virginia Public Service Company installed a giant searchlight (1.2 billion candlepower) on the hotel roof, said to be visible for three hundred miles, although people as far away as Spartanburg, South Carolina, swore they could see its beams piercing their skies. When formally dedicated in August 1927, it was supposed to be the world's largest searchlight. For several months of each year from 8 to 11 P.M. it symbolically swept the heavens from Jefferson's mountain home to his university.

Shortly after Monticello became a tourist attraction, an old Buck Mountain Road structure dating from the Revolutionary period was moved from the Earlysville area to Monticello Mountain. When the Michie Tavern opened to the public in January 1928, the *Daily Progress* added another hundred years to its past, hailing it as a "Building of 17th Century, With Marvelous Collection of Furniture." At that time the only notable former guest cited by the *Progress* was Lafayette, who, it was said, once was put up there by Jefferson so he could enjoy a few days of hunting. Within a decade, however, the tavern became the community's oldest landmark, the boyhood home of Patrick Henry, and a haunt of James Monroe, James Madison, Andrew Jackson, and Thomas Jefferson.

By the mid-1920s Charlottesville was staging an annual auto show in the armory, developing bus lines to Cismont, Crozet, and other rural towns, and talking of the need for additional zoning within the corporate limits and construction of a municipal airport. A *Daily*

Progress survey revealed that some citizens thought their city should have a Community Chest campaign, an improved Main Street, better sewers, more dormitories at the university, and electric traffic signals. Dr. H. S. Hedges, when asked, answered succinctly: "The greatest need for Charlottesville is for children to mind their parents." Electric traffic signals and expanded university housing both appeared shortly; whether children began heeding their parents with renewed zeal is anyone's guess.

There also was spasmodic interest in a radio station, something, like a big modern hotel, which any ambitious, growing community had to have. In April 1922 the board of visitors approved creation of transmitting facilities for the university, Pence and Sterling and other stores encouraged customers to "entertain with radio," and by the mid-1920s the *Daily Progress* was printing broadcast schedules of pioneer outlets in Pittsburgh, New York, Philadelphia, and Washington. In 1926 some of the festivities at the local fair were heard over Richmond's WRVA, and in May 1927 the *Progress* sponsored a week of local radio (Station WKBG) from the stage of the Jefferson Theatre. Anyone with talent, black or white, could appear simply by filling out a coupon and describing what they could do. For the most part, programs consisted of various musical selections, hymns, and prayers. The community did not have a real functioning radio station of its own until November 1932 when WCHV, formerly located at Emory and Henry College, began operation.

In 1929 the Dixie Flying Service opened an airport and flying school about six miles northwest of the city, at the Garth Road site that later became the home of Grover Vandevender's famed riding school. On August 21 of that year C. C. Wells, owner of a downtown bookstore, became the first passenger to leave Charlottesville by air when he departed for New York, several weeks before the new facility was christened Wood Field in honor of Robert ("Buck") Wood, a local aviator who died in France in 1918. In May 1930 General Billy Mitchell officially opened the airport, the creation of Ed Sturhahn, a former university student, and his pilot, J. Hamilton Brown. By the end of 1931 the Dixie Flying Service had carried 1,052 passengers to Hot Springs, White Sulphur Springs, Washington, Richmond, and Danville, flown 108,339 miles, and recorded only two forced landings. But within twenty-four months Wood Field was quiet and the Dixie Flying Service no more, casualties of the depression years.

Charlottesville's most ambitious scheme for national recognition, perhaps the crest of local boosterism, was a semiserious proposal in 1927 to host the national Democratic convention to be held the following year. According to the *Daily Progress* of April 8, 1927, several Washington officials had proposed Jefferson's birthplace as an ideal site for reaffirming faith in his beloved party. In succeeding weeks some individuals suggested that Lambeth Field covered with a huge tent could become a convention hall, and Thomas Fortune Ryan offered to raise funds needed to erect a new 500-room hotel which, together with the Monticello Hotel, would provide adequate quarters for delegates and their guests. Ryan, born near Lovingston in Nelson County, was a controversial Manhattan financial wizard who left a fortune of $200 million when he died the following year. Senator Thaddeus Horatio Carraway of Arkansas, for one, lent his support; but in time community leaders acknowledged the plan was much too ambitious, although late in 1927 a local committee apparently pressed Charlottesville's case before national party officials. Some months later the Democrats met in Houston and Franklin D. Roosevelt nominated the "Happy Warrior," Al Smith of New York, to be the party's standard-bearer.

Prohibition had effects both anticipated and unforeseen upon Albemarle's daily life between 1920 and 1933. As noted, it created unprecedented interest in country clubs where the well-to-do could drink, at times heightened tensions between government officials and undergraduates at the university, and produced an upsurge in bootlegging of native "corn licker," a not surprising development since a majority of county residents had opposed Prohibition from the outset. By the mid-1920s raids on suspected purveyors of illicit liquor and arraignment of those supplying them were becoming routine. What few had been prepared for was the increase in bloodshed accompanying this traffic. Headlines such as "Another Killing in the Foothills of the Blue Ridge," "Many Liquor Cases in Circuit Court," and "Over 29 Gallons of Christmas Cheer Poured into Sewer at Police Station" became standard fare for readers of the *Progress*. That daily saluted Bacon Hollow as "moonshine heaven," told of the iron rule of Bose Shifflett, "King of the Blue Ridge," and made no secret of its hopes that the proposed Skyline Drive would clean up bootlegging in western Albemarle or at least turn the perplexing problem over to federal authorities. Local spokesmen also welcomed news of the national park because it would attract travelers. No one seems to have given much thought to conservation. According to the *Daily Progress*, an end to moonshine murders, more tourist dollars, and, in time, jobs that its construction might provide were the principal reasons for supporting this ambitious undertaking approved by President Coolidge in May 1926, a decision preceded by several com-

munity rallies and purchase of some of the property in the park area
by Albemarle businessmen eager to aid this project.

In 1925 three university professors resigned when indicted for
transporting liquor in Hanover County; however, the administration
found a way out of this dilemma by merely suspending one individual
for a year and reinstating those subsequently acquitted. Football
games, especially the Thanksgiving Day contest with North Carolina, always were attended by scores of state Prohibition agents, and
fraternity men clashed frequently with the law amid denials of any
illegal activity at their houses. In 1931 two students, both prominent
campus leaders, crossed swords with two agents. In this incident,
typical of many, the undergraduates charged their adversaries with
gross misconduct and swearing at their dates, alleging they feared
a holdup was in progress. The agents were fined for profanity and
the students convicted of reckless driving, a compromise verdict
greeted with hisses and protests from a crowded courtroom. It would
appear that one legacy of the Roaring Twenties was the University
of Virginia's reputation as a hard-drinking, hell-raising school, an
image which persisted despite the fine work being done in many
departments. In fact, a *Life* article of the late 1930s describing the
university scene provoked an official letter of protest from President
John L. Newcomb.

Eventually local authorities conceded convictions for drunkenness
in the city and county were increasing year by year and they were
virtually powerless to act. As more and more national spokesmen
branded the "noble experiment" a failure, pressure mounted for repeal of Prohibition laws. In April 1933, when it became apparent
that beer might soon flow again legally, Dettor, Edwards and Morris,
Charlottesville wholesale merchants, became the proud owners of the
Old Dominion's first permit to dispense such beverages. Three
months later, on July 10, 3.2 beer was sold openly in local restaurants
for fifteen cents a bottle for the first time in decades; however, about
forty-eight hours later the mayor concluded the status of such sales
was unclear and the city became dry once more. Finally, on Monday,
September 4, the red tape was unsnarled and twenty-nine retailers
received licenses to sell beer. Within ten days their number had
nearly doubled.

In October city and county endorsed controlled liquor sales by
wide margins, and on July 7, 1934, a new state dispensary opened at
421 East Main Street with $30,000 worth of scotch, gin, bourbon,
and wines on its shelves. Proceeds during the first year returned over
$6,000 to the city and $10,000 to the county, an unexpected windfall

which nipped in the bud a campaign by local wine interests to have their products sold by the state at cost. In May 1936 a brandy plant, producing Laird's Apple Jack, opened in North Garden. Most important of all, the appearance of legal beer and state liquor stores cut deeply into the bootleg trade. Though this illicit traffic did not cease completely, deaths, arrests, and Saturday night confrontations between lawmen and those involved in illegal operations declined considerably, aided to some extent by the opening of the Skyline Drive, which cut through some of the best moonshine territory in the entire nation.

Developments in public education and agriculture flowed in familiar channels, influenced to some degree by gyrations of the stock market and the local economy. Three structures were built within the city during these years: a new Jefferson School for Negroes which opened in 1926 and gradually added high school classes, ending the need for blacks to seek such education elsewhere, and two badly needed white elementary schools, Venable (1926) and George Rogers Clark (1931). By 1928, 3,344 students were enrolled in the city system, 930 of them black, creating crowded conditions at old Midway, sometimes called Lane High School, and increasing demands for expanded facilities; however, despite a rise in urban population from 10,688 in 1920 to 15,245 in 1930, a new white high school did not appear until 1940.

County education was marked by somewhat more rigid attention to attendance laws and increased consolidation as highways improved. Since Albemarle's population grew by only 984 in the 1920s, the percentage of blacks dropped from 29 to 23 percent, and nearly six hundred white students were attending classes in Charlottesville and Schuyler, county classrooms rarely were crowded. During that decade six two-room and nine one-room schools closed, and by 1928 Albemarle had accredited white high schools at Crozet, Earlysville, Stony Point, Greenwood, Red Hill, Scottsville, and Meriwether Lewis School near Ivy. Unaccredited high school work was being offered at Cismont, Alberene, Esmont, and Damon.[3] The only black high school, Albemarle Training School, also known as Union Ridge, located four miles west of Charlottesville, now was a four-year institution.

Despite improvements—longer terms, better facilities, transporta-

[3] See Bacon Page Pettus, "The Consolidation of Rural High Schools in Virginia, with Special References to Albemarle County" (M.A. thesis, University of Virginia, 1929), pp. 79–121.

tion of some whites by truck, and a somewhat better rating by the state board of education (59th among Virginia counties in 1920; 36th in 1928) — Albemarle's public school system still presented many problems. About half of all white students in both elementary and high school grades were too old for the level they were attending, only 60 percent of the potential school population was actually enrolled, despite Superintendent Bennett's pledge to enforce attendance laws, and of those who began classes during the 1927–28 session, 13 percent dropped out during the term.

Of course, what was happening in these classrooms cannot be divorced from what was occurring on the farms themselves. After a flurry of prosperity generated by World War I, conditions throughout rural America became increasingly depressed; and long before the nation as a whole faced economic chaos, farmers and their families knew times were indeed hard. Thus many of Albemarle's young people, whatever their personal inclinations, simply could not afford to attend public school. Three successive bad seasons wreaked havoc in the rich Crozet orchard area, drastically curtailing peach and apple production. In 1929 trees were attacked by worms and insects. The following year was one of the driest and hottest ever, 81.2° being the mean temperature for the month of July, and a severe drought hit all county farmers equally hard. Then in May 1931 tornadoes and hail lashed the slopes of the Blue Ridge, ripping through orchards and piling disaster upon disaster.

Perhaps the following statistics alone are sufficient to reveal what was happening. In 1920 all Albemarle farm property was valued at $25 million. Five years later this figure increased to $26.2 million, but in 1930 slipped to $24.1 million, and in 1935 plunged to $16.2 million. The total number of farms reached a peak of 3,379 in 1924, declined to 2,527 in 1930, and then edged upward to 3,197 by 1935, reflecting some back-to-the-land movement during the worst years of the depression era; between 1930 and 1935 about 400 white and 250 black families took up residence in rural communities. Production changed little, with corn, hay, fruit, dairy products, and beef cattle predominating. These were hardly times for radical experimentation. One merely grew enough to feed his family, perhaps eked out an occasional profit if lucky, and prayed for good weather.

The University of Virginia also found these years, not a time of experimentation and innovation, but a period of limited expansion along familiar lines. State appropriations increased, the hospital grew bigger, dormitories arose to house a hundred or so more students who arrived each September, and the summer school enrollment nearly equaled that of the regular session. Rector Frederic W. Scott provided $300,000 for a new stadium, whose dedication on October 15, 1931, was unfortunately spoiled by an 18 to 3 loss to VMI. Scott also was fighting a losing battle to keep the Blue Ridge Parkway off his Royal Orchard estate at this time. William A. Clark, a Montana capitalist and an alumnus, gave the university a handsome new law building, and John B. Cobb, a North Carolina–born tobacco magnate, funds to enlarge the chemistry laboratory. Though this is hardly a picture of retrenchment, one gets the impression that the old school was, perhaps like its president, a bit tired. A huge bequest in 1928 by Philip Francis du Pont of $6 million, one of the largest ever received by an institution of higher learning up to that time, failed to stimulate much immediate activity, although in subsequent decades the funds bequeathed by this alumnus became the foundation of an ambitious and productive scholarship program.[4]

On at least two occasions the university found itself arrayed in public battles to maintain the status quo. In 1921 a movement developed in the General Assembly to consolidate all medical education at Richmond. Alumni eventually won their fight against this proposal and no one in Albemarle backed it, although at the time, just as unification of small high schools brought economy in administration and management, a single medical system made some sense. A decade later the question of a coordinate woman's college arose once more, and the university faced considerable local opposition to its hard-nosed anticoed stand, including the barbed tongue of Lady Astor. Charlottesville residents, as well as those of Lynchburg and several other communities, clearly wanted the school. The Redland Land Corporation offered two free sites, one near Jefferson Park, the other on Monticello Mountain, and a citizens group proposed to donate 150 acres adjoining Rugby Road. However, once more alumni in the legislature prevailed, and late in 1931 a state teachers' institution in Fredericksburg, a safe seventy miles from the Rotunda, was designated as the university's school for women and renamed Mary Washington College. But Governor Pollard vetoed this scheme, and not until 1944 did that institution finally come under the wing of the university's board of visitors.

President Alderman, plagued by ill health, had to spend more and more time defending undergraduates against charges of riotous living, drinking, and excessive spending, assertions which had basis in

[4] See L. Moody Simms, Jr., "Philip Francis du Pont and the University of Virginia," *MACH* 31 (1973):53–75.

fact and hardly endeared the state university to thousands of Virginians facing hard times. Even the du Pont millions were a mixed blessing since many wondered if a university so rich really needed tax dollars. During the debate over coeducation the Alderman era came to a close when "Tony," aged sixty-nine, died on April 29, 1931, after suffering a stroke while traveling on a train through Pennsylvania. He was succeeded by the engineering dean, John L. Newcomb, who for more than a decade had been, in effect, his assistant. Newcomb soon discovered he was only acting president and remained in academic limbo for nearly two and one-half years while the visitors, for reasons known only to them, refused to make a decision. When classes opened in September 1933, alumni, faculty, and students issued formal protests, and the board at last confirmed Newcomb as Alderman's successor. Whether prompt action would have revived the spirit of reform that Alderman had promoted earlier is unlikely, for the early thirties were grim years, but this unconscionable delay caused widespread concern and launched the administration of the university's second president in an air of uncertainty and confusion.

Although Alderman's educational revolution, once so full of spirit and enterprise, seems to have gone conservative, there were bright spots. Not only did the physical plant and enrollment continue to increase; the *Virginia Quarterly Review*, established in 1925, gained a national, even international audience, and the Institute of Public Affairs, inaugurated two years later, brought scores of prominent Americans to Charlottesville. Nearly 17,500 people attended the first series of summer lectures on current problems, and in succeeding years local residents heard views aired by Carter Glass, Norman Thomas, Raymond Moley, Tom Connally, Will Durant, and others. The 1931 session, a study of law enforcement and economic planning, was highlighted by the appearance of New York's dynamic governor, Franklin D. Roosevelt, who received a "great ovation" following a blistering attack upon "excessive costs" of local government.

Some of the best and most provocative work being done at the university came from the Extension Service, under the direction of Charles G. Maphis, also dean of the summer school, and from the Department of Economics, notably studies pioneered by Dr. Wilson Gee, South Carolina–born professor of rural economics and rural sociology. With the aid of the Phelps-Stokes fellowships for the study of the Negro established in 1912, Gee and his students turned out scores of monographs on race relations, crime, education, and other aspects of community life. Charlottesville and Albemarle became their laboratory for instant research, and had residents read more carefully what they said, they could have discerned much of what would occur in their community during coming decades. It is significant, of course, that each of these undertakings—a learned journal, extension work, summer sessions, public lectures, analysis of community life—often had very little to do with classrooms per se and carried on Alderman's original campaign to make the University of Virginia meaningful to many who never would enroll and become students.

One reason Governor Roosevelt, then emerging as a national figure, received the "great ovation" when he attacked excessive spending at the local level was because of hard times. Although the *Daily Progress* maintained an optimistic stance until February 1930, saying very little about unemployment, each year the list of delinquent county taxpayers was becoming longer and longer. And there was another reason why local citizens applauded loudly: the city already had changed to a manager form of government, and within a few years the county would also. In March 1918 H. A. Stecker became temporary city manager, the first man to hold that post. Two years later the municipal government was altered slightly under a bicameral arrangement with a common council and a board of aldermen, really five commissioners. Then in the spring of 1922 a reform movement developed known as the Committee of 56, which included representatives from the Chamber of Commerce, Rotary, Young Men's Business Club, League of Women Voters, and other civic organizations, both white and black. In June of that year their so-called First Ticket swept the city and elected three commissioners (John R. Morris, E. A. Joachim, and J. Y. Brown) to replace the council and aldermen. Some years later their number was increased to five. Boyd A. Bennett, Charlottesville's first city manager with real power, served under the new body from 1922 to 1925. The highlights of his term were stricter enforcement of traffic laws and approval of bonds to construct a reservoir on Moorman's River to assure a good supply of water.

Although numerous reasons motivated civic leaders to advocate change in 1922, resentment against the power of real estate interests seems to have been most important. E. G. Haden, mayor from 1908 to 1912 and again from 1916 to 1920, was followed by B. E. Wheeler; both men controlled considerable property within the city. Wheeler even obtained a court order and tried to prevent the new commissioners from taking over, but eventually gave in. Within a week the

Chamber of Commerce came out strongly in favor of zoning, evidently an area of basic disagreement.

The county's shift to managerial government evolved in somewhat the same fashion and for similar reasons. In December 1928 Seth Burnley was named county manager, although in reality his duties dealt almost exclusively with roads and highways. Early in 1933, inspired perhaps by lectures given at the Institute of Public Affairs, but certainly by a desire to cut operating expenses, the example set by the city, and changes in state law, a group of county residents organized a Citizens League to work for reform.[5] The basic issue was that a small group of officeholders, long in power and rarely facing opposition at the polls, had become rather lax and inefficient, especially in collection of delinquent taxes, which were a serious matter even before the full force of the depression hit. In addition, those already served by good roads were fighting efforts to extend similar facilities to all parts of the county. In the opinion of Edward Overman, had the "courthouse ring" not fought back in 1933, reform never would have been successful. Only one longtime functionary, A. L. Bennett, superintendent of schools, joined the new Citizens League, but even he soon found himself out of office.

The fight against managerial government was led by Bernard Chamberlain, then a candidate for the state legislature, and the *Daily Progress*. Both conceded the old system had flaws but were uncertain the proposed remedy would help. As the day of decision approached, tempers flared, and the struggle became a bitter debate between the "ins" and the "outs," despite frequent assertions by reformers such as E. Nelson Beck, C. M. Garnett, J. B. Kegley, C. Purcell McCue, John Morris, Hollis Rinehart, Professor G. W. Spicer, and E. M. Wayland that they were attacking, not personalities, but "the system." Those in power and their lawyer friends tried to remain in the background and let subordinates distribute handbills and drum up support, but even an attempt to label manager government a Hoover reform failed to help much. On May 2, by a vote of 1,395 to 710, Albemarle approved the change, only eight of twenty-four precincts being opposed. In general, residents of the southern and northwestern parts of the county voted against managerial government, but huge majorities in Alberene (33 to 1), Batesville (81 to 8), Covesville (89 to 0), Crozet (171 to 12), Hillsboro (166 to 10), and

---

[5] See Edward S. Overman, *Manager Government in Albemarle County, Virginia* (Charlottesville, 1940), pp. 19–40.

North Garden (82 to 8) assured victory. Stony Point, possibly because of the personal power of Treasurer G. S. Hamm who lived there, opposed reform, 108 to 48.

Basically the new system meant that matters such as health, public welfare, and schools came under the direct control of the board of supervisors, not the circuit court or the governor as before, and a director of finance replaced the treasurer and commissioner of revenue. All these functions were directed by a county executive or manager chosen by the supervisors. The duties of Commonwealth's attorney, clerk, and sheriff remained essentially the same, and they, like the supervisors, continued to be elected by the voters; other officeholders were appointed by the supervisors. The most obvious improvements came in the collection of back taxes and in savings realized in finance offices, for costs under the county executive were about one-third what they had been before 1933. Despite very hard times delinquent taxes were cut in half, from 20.5 percent in 1932 to 10.5 percent in 1936.

Like Mayor Wheeler before him, County Treasurer G. S. Hamm fought hard to remain in power, adamantly refusing to leave office until ordered to do so by state courts late in February 1934. Meanwhile, Seth Burnley, who became city manager in March 1932, was chosen to be Albemarle's first county executive, but he eventually decided to remain at his new post. As a result, the supervisors hired Henry Haden, who assumed his duties on January 1, 1934. The following year, in a decision unthinkable a decade earlier, the Charlottesville city council declined to annex 1,500 acres of county land. City fathers noted that revenue for five years from parts of Belmont, Fry's Spring, and the university section would amount to only $18,000, while expenses would total $31,000. Boosterism, at least for the moment, was on the wane.

In national elections both city and county remained solidly Democratic. In 1924 local residents followed the campaign of John W. Davis with special interest since he had been a student at Pantops Academy in the late 1880s and had many friends in Albemarle. His successful opponent, Calvin Coolidge, spent Thanksgiving at Swannanoa in 1928 and journeyed to Charlottesville for the Virginia–North Carolina contest. The Coolidges attended services at the First Baptist Church and lunched with President Alderman; then, together with Mrs. Woodrow Wilson and governors of both states, they took special seats at Lambeth Field where the Tarheels won, 24 to 20. Apparently Cal was not much of a fan, or, despite the score, it was a dull affair. The *Daily Progress* said the chief executive and his party only watched the game for about fifteen minutes. A few weeks before, his successor, Herbert Hoover, garnered some support in the national election when he carried the White Hall precinct and lost to Smith by only 994 to 708 in Charlottesville. Distressed by Republican successes in the rest of the Old Dominion, university students draped Jefferson's statue in black and added this sign: "To the memory of Jeffersonian Democracy and Religious Freedom in Virginia—died November 6, 1928."

Four years later, shortly after Franklin Roosevelt's rousing victory at the polls, the Cavaliers ended five years of defeat in the traditional series by upending North Carolina, 14 to 7. Among the spectators were Lord and Lady Astor, who, unlike Coolidge, watched the entire contest. The president-elect's choice of Stephen T. Early, a Crozet native, to be his "front office" or press secretary pleased many who knew him. Early, a member of the staff of *Stars and Stripes* during World War I, had traveled with Roosevelt during his vice-presidential campaign of 1920 and then worked for Paramount News in Washington. In 1936 the Republican vote in Charlottesville slipped to 19 percent, but in the county it rose to 25.7 percent, beginning a trend of growing strength in national elections. By 1948 the Republican nominee enjoyed the support of 40 percent of city-county voters, and four years later both areas joined the Eisenhower landslide.[6]

Disenchantment with Roosevelt and Democratic policies, which after a brief honeymoon increased sharply among conservatives, burst forth at the ninth annual Institute of Public Affairs held in 1935. Over five thousand people crowded into McIntire Amphitheatre on the evening of July 12 as Congressmen James Wadsworth of New York, a prominent member of the American Liberty League, and General Hugh Johnson, a high-ranking member of FDR's first-term team, met head-on.[7] Their words, carried nationwide by radio, focused momentary attention upon Charlottesville. Unwittingly the institute had become a battleground between those assailing Roosevelt and his equally determined defenders, and despite or because of appeals to emotionalism, the league, the plaything of a few upperclass businessmen, soon passed into oblivion. Yet, as the growing Republican strength demonstrated, some of the views the league held concerning

[6] Robert Preston Steed, "Minority Party Organization and Leadership: The Case of the Republican Party in Charlottesville and Albemarle County, Virginia" (M.A. thesis, University of Virginia, 1967), p. 34.

[7] See Robert L. Semes: "Confrontation at Charlottesville: The American Liberty League and Its Critics, 1935," *MACH* 29 (1971):33–48.

federal power and constitutional rights were shared by local residents as well.

Charlottesville's business life, at least until the depths of the depression, was marked by the appearance of more national chain stores, both expansion and merger of banks, and increasing attention to tourism. In 1920 Skill Craft Clothes opened a local store, and the following year a Piggly Wiggly grocery was built at Second and Main. Piggly Wiggly, forerunner of the modern supermarket, sold lemons at 38¢ a dozen, sugar, 6¢ a pound, coffee, 24¢ a pound, and canned corned beef for 19¢. In 1922 a modern Woolworth's opened, and seven years later N. W. Pugh unveiled what was said to be the city's largest department store, successor to Antrim, Leterman, and others. In January 1923 People's Bank announced plans for a branch bank at the university, Guy L. Via, manager, and three years later Farmers and Merchants merged with Hollis Rinehart's National Bank. The year 1924 was an impressive period for construction in the city ($830,304), telephone wires were buried along Main Street as part of an effort to create a "great white way," and the first taxis with meters (Black and White) appeared. Also in April of that year a retail merchants' association was formed. This body was instrumental in helping to maintain a rest room established at 216 East Main for farm families who came to town to shop. Mrs. Ora Landis, matron, said in November 1931 that some twenty-five hundred persons used the facilities each year. A small souvenir shop opened at Monticello in February 1926, and four months later, with appropriate ceremony, Thomas Jefferson's gig set out for Philadelphia, Albemarle's contribution to the sesquicentennial. Mrs. Murray Boocock, soon to emerge as a prominent Republican leader, entered fully into the spirit of the occasion, donning colonial costume and waving gaily as the procession passed her Keswick estate. During that same year Sam Jessup moved the offices of his Virginia Stage Lines, originally a series of local buses between Culpeper and Richmond, to Charlottesville. Eleven years later the system became part of National Trailways.

James A. Patterson in 1927 loaned $100,000 to Martha Jefferson Hospital, organized in 1904 by a group of doctors. Patterson and others later made substantial bequests which enabled the hospital to grow and establish a school of nursing. In 1928 Frank Ix and Son announced plans to build a silk mill, and the *Daily Progress* told of the glorious, completely modern five-story apartment complex which would rise at Altamont Circle. Shortly, however, an air of apprehension is evident in the columns of the *Progress*, somewhat smaller than in previous years as advertising revenues declined. N. T. Shumate, president of the National Bank, predicted neither boom nor depression, but expressed some concern for agriculture. "Overproduction," the local county agent warned, was becoming a serious farm problem, and more and more construction projects experienced trouble, among them a $300,000 theater-playhouse near the university which never materialized and a huge Baptist church in the same area which did.

Early in 1930 various welfare groups began considering relief for "suffering among the poor and unemployed" and urged creation of an unemployment bureau. Students in April of that year stormed the Jefferson Theatre in an angry protest against seventy-five cent tickets. Several were hospitalized before police and President Alderman could quell the uproar, but the outburst succeeded in rolling prices back to fifty cents. During August 1930 the local jail was filled with vagrants, and at the year's end the city was offering work two days a week to all bona fide residents with dependents. Between 1927 and 1930 the number of "free lodgers" in the city lockup increased fourfold, from 239 to 988; about one-third of these individuals were black. Early in 1931 they became so numerous, 486 whites and 202 Negroes by the end of March, that authorities ceased keeping records.[8] Both city and county officials called for economy in all departments in 1931, and the following year Charlottesville was reluctant host to several hundred bonus marchers. Mayor Fred L. Watson agreed that they could camp briefly near Fry's Spring and said that the city would provide them with one free meal "and only one!" His Honor's advice was that they forget their grievances and return home at once. These months were marked by a sudden rise in burglaries and holdups, usually blamed on "outsiders," and repeated theft of coal from county schools. By March 1933 250 "underfed" children were being aided by the Mothers Clubs of Charlottesville, and local welfare agencies were distributing nearly a thousand bags of flour per month to the needy. A few weeks later 200 youths applied for 70 jobs at a new Civilian Conservation Corps camp to be established near White Hall, the first concrete benefit on the local scene of FDR's New Deal.

For several months the federal government maintained a "transient bureau" near city hall to care for hungry men. Yet, for the most part, the depression seems to have been relatively mild in Charlottesville and Albemarle, at least when compared to some communities

[8] Robert Mitchell Lightfoot, Jr., *Negro Crime in a Small Urban Community* (Charlottesville, 1934), p. 42.

throughout the nation. Federal money, state expenditures on roads and university buildings, and over two thousand regular students and almost as many in summer school generated considerable economic activity. Both city and county teachers continued to receive their paychecks, although whenever possible single, not married, women were hired. In February 1935 the *Daily Progress* boasted that *Collier's Magazine* had cited Charlottesville as an ideal community where one could live comfortably on $100 per month. Actually, what the *Progress* was referring to was an insurance ad appearing in that well-known weekly which indeed did say just that. During that same month, after much bickering, the Virginia Public Service Company and Charlottesville signed an agreement whereby the utility would spend $40,000 for new lights on Main Street and make additional improvements throughout the corporate area. In return, the city dropped claims for some $30,000 alleged due under the 1901 franchise. A short time later the community was seized by a twenty-four hour chain telegram craze, a weird outburst of the depression years. More than a thousand messages were sent in one day, but few realized any return on their investment. In July the city abolished an ordinance passed twelve years earlier requiring autos parked on streets after midnight to be lighted front and rear. The original intent was to discourage overnight parking, but complaints from tourists who received tickets made the law a nuisance. And the summer of 1935 witnessed an outbreak of infantile paralysis in the city-county area, virtually an epidemic. Local schools and the university both delayed opening for some weeks, although deaths and permanent paralysis were rare.

During these lean years social life continued apace, at times seeming to defy the realities of the economic world. On May 15, 1929, Farmington County Club marked its second anniversary with a brilliant reception and dance. Among those present were the following founders and charter members: J. B. Belk, Murray Boocock, P. H. Faulconer, Henry L. Fonda (owner of Birdwood since 1920), J. S. Galban, H. A. George, George Gilmer, John S. Graves, B. O. Hall, Graham Harris, Mrs. D. W. Langhorne, J. H. Lindsay, L. S. Macon, Mrs. Sue W. Massie, Robert L. McIlroy, Dr. J. H. Neff, Randolph Ortman (master of a large estate near Greenwood), E. L. Perkins, W. Allan Perkins, George A. Randolph, Hollis Rinehart, Jack Rinehart, Roger Rinehart, W. A. Rinehart, J. M. Rothwell, W. B. Saxon, John E. Shepherd, Gordon Smith, Donald S. Stevens, Dr. Charles C. Tennant, M. C. Thomas, J. Dean Tilman, F. W. Twyman, Dr. Will Walter, Mrs. Will Walter, Dr. H. W. Watts,

Marshall Wells, and Dr. Fletcher Woodward, all local residents, plus Charles A. Stone and Whitney Stone of New York City and Robert A. Stranahan of Toledo, Ohio.

The Farmington Hunt, an outgrowth of the country club, was organized a few months later and soon became a formidable rival of the well-established Keswick Hunt, which continued to flourish. Norris Watson and Jack Rinehart, first joint masters of the new group, Randolph Ortman, Dr. J. P. Jones, and Grover Vandevender, for many years huntsman, were among the leaders in forming this organization. During these years Mrs. Elliewood Page Keith, an able successor to Mrs. Allen Potts, was participating in various hunts and horse shows accompanied by her daughter, young Elliewood, who in time also became an accomplished equestrienne. In October 1922, by the way, Mrs. Keith distinguished herself at the wheel of a Fordson tractor, winning driving contests held at the local fair and in Washington.

However, with the demise of that fair and the crash on Wall Street, community life changed somewhat. Activities centered about church, home, and various clubs continued, perhaps in restricted form, and the 1930s saw the emergence of several one-night festivals. Each June the American Legion staged a Mardi Gras on Courthouse Square. This event, complete with shows, rides, contests, dancing, awards to leading citizens, and prizes (often including an automobile), attracted some two thousand citizens, both white and black. In 1934 Charlottesville's first Halloween parade was held, a holiday celebration conceived largely by Mrs. Robert L. Currier, who served as Charlottesville's first director of recreation in 1933–35. This festival, again for both races, culminated with dancing and the crowning of a queen, Helen Yowell. Also, annual gatherings such as a celebration sponsored by the Crozet Fire Department each Fourth and a community fair at Greenwood tended to replace more lavish displays once staged at Merrie Mills or in Charlottesville. Several local churches celebrated their centennials during this decade, and revivals continued, veteran Gypsy Smith returning once more in 1934 to exhort area residents to repent their sins. For those so inclined, there were Saturday night town-gown brawls, usually staged in or near the Kitch Inn, an all-night eatery at the Corner which on a few occasions was the scene of gunplay as well.

Two sporting events, one very informal, became an integral part of the social scene. This was the heyday of boxing at the university, a phenomenon engineered largely by Johnny La Rowe, an ex-Marine who never fought professionally. La Rowe, a local businessman who was recruited to help coach the sport in 1922, took command four years later and displayed an uncanny ability to mold champions out of raw material. For nearly a decade Johnny's boys dominated Southern Conference tourneys and drew record crowds to the university's gymnasium. "Ivy hockey," a rough-and-tumble affair with some, but not all, of the thrills of boxing, was begun in 1902 by expatriate Englishmen living a few miles west of Charlottesville but in time was played by scores of native-born residents as well.[9] Rules, equipment, and play of this very loose form of field hockey were subject for the most part to individual whim. The season was from Thanksgiving to late spring, and the final game each year pitted Ivy against "the world," that is, natives versus everyone else who dared to participate. All ages and people from all walks of life joined in— small children, country folk, women, professors, former football players, some expert, some woefully inept. Enthusiasm, an ability to run in the brisk open air, and a willingness to take hard knocks seem to have been the only requirements as two teams of indeterminate size battled over an old baseball with bent sticks, walking canes, and well-worn brooms.

For the less active there were the theaters. In 1931 the Paramount, seating 1,300 and featuring a separate entrance and special balcony for blacks, opened its doors. To keep going the management offered special stage shows at no extra charge, but within four years such shows had disappeared from all local movie palaces. This void was filled, in part, by the appearance of the Virginia Players at the university, who finally got suitable quarters when Minor Hall was remodeled in 1935. During these same years efforts to found a local drama company, a community little-theater group, foundered despite some assistance from WPA funds.

In spite of or because of the depression, readers of the *Daily Progress* seem to have been obsessed by what those with money were doing. The shenanigans of underworld characters, royalty, café society, and the great of Hollywood were followed avidly. Presentation at the Court of St. James's of a Virginia debutante with the most obscure local ties, perhaps an uncle living at Farmington or a grandmother in Greenwood, merited widespread attention, and a kidnapping or murder anywhere in the world received considerable coverage. It was almost as if one was able to endure his own plight

[9] See Elizabeth B. Mulholland: "Random Recollections of Ivy Hockey," *MACH* 21 (1963):55–64.

a bit better when compared with that of others less fortunate despite wealth and power.

Thanks to better hotels, a new armory, growth of tourist facilities, the presence of the university, and efforts of the local Chamber of Commerce, Charlottesville was fast becoming a regional convention center of considerable importance. For the most part groups gathering at Albemarle's county seat for a few days of business and revelry were statewide organizations—war veterans, civic clubs (both white and black), professional men and women, and religious bodies, but on occasions the nation's governors and select national organizations also convened in the shadow of Monticello. In October 1931 two hundred leading newspaper editors met at Jefferson's home to dedicate a room to "freedom of the press." Colonel Robert McCormick presided and introduced biographer Claude Bowers, the principal speaker. Each individual present signed a pledge of faith to freedom. These later were picked up in dramatic fashion by an auto-gyro which landed on the lawn of Monticello and flew them to President Hoover at the White House. Each spring annual Garden Week tours of historic estates also brought hundreds of tourists to Albemarle.

In 1938 over eighty thousand people visited Thomas Jefferson's home, university enrollment soared past 2,800, and Dumas Malone, director of the Harvard University Press who as a history teacher had pioneered with the use of films in his classes at the University of Virginia in the 1920s, helped dedicate Alderman Library, a valuable and much-needed structure. The city at last began building a municipal golf course at McIntire Park, and controversy flared over annexation and location of an airport and a new high school. Charlottesville sought to bring some twenty-two hundred county residents living in western suburbs and Belmont under its wing and eventually succeeded. Proposals to create a student flying field at Milton aroused the ire of Keswick citizens, but state authorities agreed that the site could be used by university undergraduates temporarily. At the same time, for a "trial period" only, parking meters designed to relieve downtown congestion were installed on Charlottesville's Main Street, five cents for sixty minutes. Debate over where to build Lane High School involved use of the old Midway location or property on Preston Avenue; the latter was finally selected. With the aid of $339,735 in bonds and federal funds, city fathers commenced construction, earmarking $100,000 for an annex to Jefferson School. In November 1938 Sunset Lodge with accommodations for twenty-six tourists opened one mile west of Ivy, Albemarle's first modern motel.

During that same year both Sears Roebuck and Company and Leggett's established branch stores on Charlottesville's Main Street.

The annexation proceedings, precursor of much more heated words two decades later, reflect the growing importance of the university community, which now had a new post office, a shopping center of sorts, its own movie theater, and several very imposing churches, among them those of the Episcopalians, Baptists, and Presbyterians. Yet, despite growth of the University of Virginia and its environs, an improving economic picture (nearly a million dollars in local construction in 1939), and disagreements over school sites, airfields, and municipal boundaries, Albemarle's citizens were becoming more and more concerned with international, not local, affairs. At first, debate over peace and war was almost exclusively an undergraduate matter; but like a pebble dropped into a pool, the ripples spread, aided by civil strife in Spain and aggressive moves by both Germany and Japan. In April 1935, much to the distress of the American Legion which blamed Communist infiltrators, university students staged an antiwar day. J. B. Mathews was the principal speaker at Cabell Hall, and President Newcomb chose to suspend classes rather than stir unrest. A few days later educator John Dewey, speaking from the same platform, vowed that the legion and the DAR presented much greater threats to American liberty than any Red. In May student hecklers, later rebuked by the administration, forced Clarence Hathaway, editor of the *Daily Worker*, to leave Cabell Hall and complete his address in another building. In November of that year classes were shut down once more so five hundred students could attend a giant peace rally at Cabell Hall.

Spasmodic outbursts concerning war, peace, and rearmament continued, and soon the debate was no longer merely theoretical. In September 1939 World War II began in Europe, and many matters once so very important—annexation, where to put an airfield or a high school, who was curtsying before the king of England, whether Charlottesville had factories, a big hotel, and an ever-increasing population—seemed trivial indeed. Again, as in 1776 and 1861, the people of Jefferson's Albemarle found themselves caught up in a great struggle for survival. Though the war solved the economic problems which had dominated the 1930s, it brought in its wake considerable turmoil and heartbreak, and the return to an uncertain peace in 1945 marked yet another turning point in the history of both city and county.

Chapter 18

Albemarle in World War II

N O CONFLICT in American history, not even the Civil War, affected the people of Albemarle and Charlottesville so profoundly as World War II. Battlefields were further away than in the 1860s, but home front activity was much more highly organized. No household, whether its sons and daughters were in uniform or not, could escape the pervasive power of federal, state, and local agencies geared up to cope with shortages, increase production, and bring victory over the Axis powers. Approximately 5,450 local citizens were in uniform, and of these, 199 men and women died, either in combat or from disease and service-related accidents. One hundred and sixteen were from Charlottesville; 83, from the county. In marked contrast to nearly every other community in the nation, hardly had the dust of war settled when Albemarle went to work composing a permanent record of those exciting, hard, often tragic years. The 429-page volume which resulted, *Pursuits of War: the People of Charlottesville and Albemarle County, Virginia, in the Second World War*, published in 1948 by the Albemarle County Historical Society, is a unique tribute to those who fought, those who died, and thousands at home who did what they could to aid their nation in its hour of need. Edited by W. Edwin Hemphill and Gertrude Dana Parlier and aided by generous assistance from the People's National Bank, it details how one American community waged war, from selling war bonds (with the assistance of various celebrities such as Charlottesville's own Marine hero, Lieutenant General Alexander Archer Vandergrift) to instituting selective service and rationing tires, gas, and some foodstuffs.[1]

Although the United States did not become an active participant until December 7, 1941, the winds of war were sweeping through Albemarle for many months before that "day of infamy." From the outset of hostilities in September 1939 and certainly after June 1940, as Great Britain doggedly fought on alone, local sympathies, heightened by strong ties to the English people, were clearly anti-Hitler. On June 10, 1940, as disaster was overwhelming French and British

[1] Virtually all of the material in this chapter comes from *Pursuits of War*.

armies, the attention of much of the world was riveted upon Charlottesville. Here President Franklin Delano Roosevelt, addressing the
graduating class at the University of Virginia, after a brief comparison of the current crisis to that of the 1860s, turned his scorn upon
Italy, which hyena-like, had joined Germany in crushing a bewildered
French populace, and then announced new departures in American
foreign policy:

On this tenth day of June, 1940, the hand that held the dagger has
struck it into the back of its neighbor.

On this tenth day of June, 1940, in this University founded by the first
great teacher of democracy, we send forth our prayers and our hopes to
those beyond the seas who are maintaining with magnificent valor their
battle for freedom.

In our American unity, we will pursue two obvious and simultaneous
courses; we will extend to the opponents of force the material resources
of this nation; and, at the same time, we will harness and speed up the
use of those resources in order that we ourselves in the Americas may
have equipment and training equal to the task of any emergency and
every defense.

All roads leading to the accomplishment of these objectives must be
kept clear of obstructions. We will not slow down or detour. Signs and
signals call for speed—full speed ahead.

It is right that each new generation should ask questions. But in
recent months the principal question has been somewhat simplified. Once
more the future of the nation and of the American people is at stake.

We need not and will not, in any way, abandon our continuing work
within our borders. We will insist on the need for vast improvements in
our own social and economic life.

But that is a component part of national defense itself.

The program unfolds swiftly and into that program will fit the responsibility and the opportunity of every man and woman in the land to
preserve his and her heritage in days of peril.

I call for effort, courage, sacrifice, devotion. Granting the love of
freedom, all of these are possible.

And the love of freedom is still fierce and steady in the nation today.[2]

The rolling Piedmont landscape which echoed to those stirring
words on that bright June day was still a land at peace, but its
people were disturbed, even alarmed by the events Roosevelt so
eloquently described. In that year Albemarle had a population of
24,652, of whom 18,990 were white and 5,660, black. The city, cover-

---

[2] *Papers and Public Addresses of Franklin Delano Roosevelt* (13 vols.; New
York, 1938–45), 9:263–64.

ing approximately six square miles, had 19,400 residents—15,246 white, 4,154 black. Nearly half of the county's labor force (48.6 percent, 3,839 persons) was involved in some form of agriculture, with 1,068 in business or professional services, 584 in manufacturing, 539 in wholesale and retail trade, 427 in construction, and 92 in mining. Within Charlottesville, 2,432 individuals were engaged in business and professional services, 1,763 in wholesale and retail trade, 1,194 in manufacturing, 618 in transportation, communication, and other utilities, and 530 in construction. Of 2,591 farms in Albemarle, 15.9 percent were operated by tenants, and that year more than half of all farms yielded produce worth less than $400, although the average value of county farms was $8,165. The total value of farm products sold, traded, or used by rural households was $2,323,000, 35.1 percent derived from livestock and livestock products, 33.8 percent from crops. A five-man council governed Charlottesville, headed by Dr. W. D. Haden, chosen as mayor by other council members. Seth Burnley was still city manager, and Henry A. Haden, Albemarle's county executive.

No one, not even Roosevelt, knew what lay ahead, but local Red Cross members already were supplying clothing to war-torn Europe, and the Monticello Guard was preparing for summer maneuvers at Fort Meade, Maryland. The fall of France a few weeks later and the ensuing Battle of Britain increased widespread fears that German might could not be stopped. During the remaining months of an uneasy peace Albemarle's concern was expressed on four fronts: aid to war-ravaged peoples overseas, implementation of the nation's first peacetime draft, mobilization of the Monticello Guard, and organization of a home defense force.

The Red Cross chapter, led throughout most of the war years by Mrs. James Gordon Smith of Greenwood, possessed a cadre of experienced, devoted workers, many of whom had helped organize a special volunteer service during the depression. By May 1940 these ladies had shipped 2,151 garments and 201 layettes overseas and later that same year, upon request of national headquarters, turned their attention to producing surgical dressings for the wounded. According to Mrs. Smith, the first order for 17,000 bandages seemed "staggering," yet four years later the chapter was producing 179,000 in a single month. By that date, all Red Cross activity was coordinated in the old Midway Building, that group's wartime home after January 1942. Although these workers soon would be involved in scores of undertakings—canteens, first-aid classes, a motor corps, blood donor programs, even recruitment of nurses for the armed forces, they could take special pride in those original 17,000 bandages. Albemarle's chapter was among the first in the nation to fill its quota, and late in 1940 a visitor to Manhattan reported, somewhat incredulously, seeing signs reading "Help New York Beat Charlottesville and Boston—Make Surgical Dressings."

With enactment of a selective service law in September 1940, Albemarle commenced registration of men aged twenty-one to thirty-five; this age group would expand after war came. On October 16 young men from all walks of life gathered at schoolhouses and polling places to record their names and receive a selective service card. Oddly enough, exactly the same number, 2,845, were enrolled in both city and county, 1,172 of the latter being University of Virginia students. Also, by coincidence, on the day that approximately one-fifth of the community's male population began to prepare for the struggle to protect American freedom, final payment was made on Monticello, making that shrine debt-free. Meanwhile, draft boards appointed by both city and county assigned a number to each registrant in anticipation of a national lottery on October 29. Lists of names and numbers then were posted in the county office building and city armory. Later they were published and, according to Newton B. Jones, included a surprising number of "Woodrow Wilsons" and "Pershings," namesakes reminiscent of the so-called Great War, but there also was one "Goldenlocks" and a "John the Baptist."[3] However, none of these individuals had number 158, the first drawn in Washington. It belonged to Marion Jerome Wood in the county and Wilson Warner Cropp of Charlottesville. This meant, unless deferred, they faced induction, but those eager to volunteer for one year's service actually were the first to go. The county's first volunteer was Laurie K. Sandridge, Jr., of Crozet, who later would see action as a lieutenant in Normandy. But Sandridge was deferred because of a recent injury to his hand, and the county's first inductee was William Cornelius Knipscher of North Garden. On November 28 Knipscher and Henry Cecil Childress, the city's first soldier under selective service, were given a grand send-off as they departed for Fort Meade. The first Negro inductees, also volunteers, were Frank Sampson from the city and Rayfield Willer Taylor from the county.

Efforts to implement military training at Lane High School were not successful, although Miller School did so late in 1942. While young men were being mobilized, all local aliens were required to register at the Charlottesville Post Office. By the end of 1940, 174

[3] Jones in *Pursuits of War*, p. 187.

persons had recorded their names; by far the greatest number were citizens of Great Britain, with natives of Greece ranking second.

Early in 1941 the Monticello Guard, commanded by Captain Marshall P. Fletcher, was formally inducted into federal service for a year's training. On January 31 some three hundred citizens honored that historic unit at a lavish banquet held in the armory. Among the speakers was Judge A. D. Dabney, who told the men: "You have a great heritage to live up to. Never in my experience in courts has a member of the Monticello Guard been before me for any delinquency. So long as a Monticello stands as a sentinel of freedom, just so long will there be a Guard ready to defend that heritage of freedom." Speechmaking was followed by a gala ball, but during the next two weeks all was business. The men lived a soldier's life, sleeping in the armory and drilling each day on the East End parking lot, watched by scores of interested spectators crowding the Chesapeake and Ohio viaduct. On February 20 three officers and eighty-eight men, slightly less than full strength, boarded a train bound for Fort Meade. They were led by Captain Fletcher and Lieutenant John A. Martin; two lieutenants and two enlisted men had departed earlier. Of that group, soon to become Company K, 116th Infantry, eleven would die in battle, and nearly all would experience bloody trials at Omaha Beach and throughout the months of warfare that followed the invasion of the European continent. After the first flurry of excitement, the business of converting civilians into soldiers became more or less routine. Another registration of men who had become twenty-one was held in July 1941, and more and more local youths volunteered as war crept closer to America's shores.

Home defense actually was a twofold operation in 1940–41: creation of military units to replace the national guard and various programs designed to protect civilians in case of enemy attack. In February 1941 Governor James H. Price established the Virginia Protective Force, which assumed national guard responsibilities and, in time, was supplemented by the Virginia Reserve Militia and the Civil Air Patrol. Fifty-three members of the Charlottesville VPF unit, Company 103, were mustered into service on March 3, 1941, with Captain Edward V. Walker as commander. Like the national guard, these men were not strictly a "home" defense force but subject to duty throughout the Old Dominion. Their original uniforms consisted of blue-gray outfits with mackinaws furnished by the city and county. In April 1942 the state provided summer khakis and a shoulder patch bearing the Virginia seal and the words "Protective

Force." Two years later this group was officially designated as the Virginia State Guard.

As organizational efforts mounted, Charlottesville became headquarters of the Tenth Battalion, composed of VPF companies in Charlottesville, Fredericksburg, Harrisonburg, and Staunton. Walker, now a colonel, was assisted by Captain Walter E. Fowler, Jr., as adjutant, and Sergeant Major Louis H. Matacia. Under their direction men drilled each week, attended summer camp near Free Union, and prepared for any emergency which might overwhelm their community. In December 1941, within hours after Pearl Harbor, details were guarding the armory, Rouss Hall at the university where (unknown to but a few) atomic energy research was in progress, and strategic bridges within the battalion's command.

The fall of France in June 1940 sparked creation of an eleven-man Home Defense Council in Charlottesville, but this group seems to have done little other than vow to cooperate with similar bodies, if organized, point to the danger facing America, and predict Adolf Hitler someday would meet his Waterloo. Nearly a year later, in May 1941, Governor Price appointed a more formal organization known as the Northern Virginia Regional Defense Council, which consisted of nineteen men from an area comprising twelve counties and several independent cities. Local members were Seth Burnley, Dr. W. D. Haden, and Edward V. Walker of Charlottesville and E. L. Bradley, A. G. Fray, and Dr. L. G. Roberts of Albemarle County. Dr. Haden and Randolph H. Perry became director and assistant director, respectively, of the local defense council. Mary Stamps White of Ivy served as executive secretary of this group. Under its direction advisory committees were established, and by December 1941 more than two thousand county and thirteen hundred city residents had volunteered their services. Two months earlier Charles P. Nash, Jr., and Bernard P. Chamberlain were named cochairmen of a Civilian Defense Corps for the city-county area.

During these same months, with the aid of University Hospital personnel, local citizens set up one of the most effective emergency medical units in the state and also formed a very active aircraft warning service headed by C. Venable Minor. In time, more than thirteen hundred spotters spent long hours scanning Albemarle's skies, an undertaking designed to set into motion the wheels of other defense machinery should enemy aircraft appear. Although some individuals undoubtedly viewed all this activity—men drilling in impromptu uniforms, councils and boards crowding each other for public attention, and constant evocation of patriotic spirit—as a bit unnecessary and perhaps even farcical, with December 7 no one doubted the true worth of this organizational groundwork, for America and Albemarle were now at war.

The first six months of 1942 will always rank among the darkest days in our nation's history. Patriotic slogans did little to hide awesome defeats suffered at the hands of the triumphant Japanese at Pearl Harbor, in the Philippines, and throughout the western Pacific. At the same time, thwarted by stubborn defense of the British homeland, Hitler turned his attention to the sands of North Africa and the plains of Russia. Soon his legions were cutting deep in Egypt, threatening the Suez Canal, and closing in on three strategic Russian cities: Leningrad, Moscow, and Stalingrad. By the end of the year, however, the tide was beginning to turn, and Allied forces were on the offensive throughout the world. At first, invasion landings were small affairs, island-hopping in the Pacific and pecking away at the perimeter of Hitler's empire in Africa and Europe; but, in time, momentum accelerated hand in hand with experience, and three years later victory was achieved worldwide.

As such strange names as Guadalcanal, Casablanca, El Alamein, and Tarawa, once only insignificant bits in geography lessons, became part of everyday conversation, home front activity increased by leaps and bounds. This was war on a scale never before experienced by American civilians. Registration of local males continued, eventually including all those between the ages of eighteen and sixty-five, although only younger age groups actually were called into service. From January 1942 to March 1943 Charlottesville was the induction center for northwestern Virginia. In March 1942 the university's medical faculty formed the Eighth Evacuation Hospital composed of thirty-five doctors and twenty-two nurses. The personnel, largely of local origin, was under the direction of Dr. Staige D. Blackford and Dr. E. Cato Drash. Both were commissioned lieutenant colonels; Blackford was in command and also in charge of the medical unit, and Drash headed the surgical staff. The Reverend William H. Laird, rector of St. Paul's Episcopal Church, became chaplain; and among the nurses were Helen Berkeley and Dorothy D. Sandridge.

After several months of training in South Carolina and Georgia, these doctors and nurses passed secretly through Charlottesville en route to an embarkation port. Although forbidden to communicate with friends and relatives, a nurse dropped a note from a train window which told a few individuals what was up. In November 1942, now at full strength with 417 members, the hospital sailed from Staten Island with the first support convoy bound for North Africa.

Nearly a year later staff and enlisted personnel moved on to Salerno, and then followed the fighting up the Italian boot. When dissolved in September 1945, the hospital was at Rivoltèlla on the southern shore of Lake Garda. During the war this unit admitted 45,585 patients, 10,419 of them suffering from battle wounds. A total of 11,398 were operated on, but there were only 129 postoperative deaths. Nine patients succumbed to disease. In addition to those admitted to wards for attention and care, 24,483 individuals were treated as outpatients.[4]

Charlottesville's peacetime recruiting office became the local induction center and for some months also handled enlistments of both men and women. In September 1942 Virginia Pond of Monticello Road became the community's first WAAC, and a year later Mrs. Marshall Wood, a descendant of Chief Justice John Marshall, and her seventeen-year-old son, Claude, volunteered on the same day. Mrs. Wood became an officer candidate; Claude, a naval aviation cadet. By March 1947 the two local selective service boards had processed 2,181 white and 592 black registrants from the city and 1,760 whites and 540 blacks from the county, figures which do not include many who donned uniform without registering. As a result of the deferment of essential farm workers, Charlottesville, with a smaller population, actually furnished more manpower than the county.

Although most men went willingly, like all communities the city-county area had its small share of draft dodgers, deserters, and AWOLs. In August 1943 a soldier won $200 in a drawing held at a dance; however, once the winner's name became known, he was apprehended by police and returned to the base from which he had deserted. In January 1945 a scandal erupted when a large bottle of aspirin was found on a bus transporting inductees to Richmond for physical examinations. Presumably aspirin could cause an artificial heart condition, and according to the *Daily Progress*, others resorted to subterfuges such as putting pepper in their eyes.

Five families had five sons in uniform: Mrs. Eula Gleason, Mr. and Mrs. Frank E. Hartman, and Mr. and Mrs. G. F. Nimmo, all of Charlottesville, Mr. and Mrs. J. E. Pollard of Scottsville, and Mr. and Mrs. J. L. Shaver of Proffit. Three had six children in the

---

[4] Statistical reports (transcripts) of this hospital can be found in the University of Virginia Library; also, see a "Brief History of the Eighth Evacuation Hospital," *Bulletin of the University Medical School and Hospital* 3 (Spring, 1946):12–15, and Byrd Stuart Leavell, *The 8th Evac.: A History of the University of Virginia Hospital Unit in World War II* (Richmond, 1970).

55. Black choir massed in V-for-Victory formation on Rotunda steps during war loan drive

56. Veterans' housing on Copeley Hill

service: Mr. and Mrs. William H. Stoneburner of Charlottesville (a daughter in the marines, a son in the army, and four sons in the navy), Mrs. Thomas M. Estes of the county, and Mr. and Mrs. O. A. Trice of Howardsville. Top honors went to a Negro widow, Mrs. Fanny Estes of Proffit, with nine sons in the armed forces, one of them, Horace O. Estes, an infantry lieutenant.

Why did these young people, nearly all of them willingly, give up home, family, and careers and go to war? Some simply because they had to; others out of patriotism or lured by the glamour of a uniform and adventure and repelled by the dullness of wartime existence as they watched friends depart. In a letter written to his wife from England, Lieutenant James E. Harlow, a flyer from Charlottesville, expressed the thoughts of many. "I was one of these thousands who felt that, though we had everything to gain by remaining out of the Army, this war was destroying everything that could and should exist. We could be happy, yes, but for how long? Even now, instead of being here in combat, I could be home with my wife and thousands of others could be home also. However, it is harder to see something beautiful you've built destroyed than to destroy its possible enemy in the beginning." [5] Lieutenant Harlow eloquently answered the question posed: there was a job to be done, and the farther done from the hills of Albemarle the better.

On the home front, not only did civilian defense, Red Cross, and home guard activities accelerate, but special efforts were made to conserve precious materials, salvage others, produce food and forest products, and provide facilities to meet the needs of both serviceman and civilian. With the outbreak of hostilities, the community began a partial blackout at night and held several air raid drills. Blackouts appear to have been more brown than black. Banks complained that insurance regulations compelled them to maintain lights near their vaults, a few citizens adamantly refused to cooperate, and lights in the attic of the Elks Home, offices of the local newspaper, and county office building blazed brightly throughout what was supposed to have been a complete blackout on the evening of March 20, 1942.

After the installation of air raid warning signals during that same month atop the Monticello Hotel and in the Rugby Circle and Fry's Spring areas, Charlottesville held a daylight test of its defenses in May 1942. Results were even more disappointing than in March. Traffic continued to move freely, and instead of taking cover, many civilians lined streets and watched planes in mock attack. On the

[5] *Pursuits of War*, p. 199.

other hand, "injured" and "dead" Girl Scouts carried out their roles
with enthusiasm. One, when asked by a news photographer to turn
her head, refused. "I can't," she replied. "My back is broken." By
the end of the year, although less urgency for such precautions
existed, tests proved more successful. Nevertheless, during the first
two years of war, aircraft spotters continued to man some twelve to
fifteen posts on a twenty-four-hour basis. Late in 1944, fearful that
V-2 rockets might be launched from enemy vessels, Governor Colgate W. Darden, Jr., alerted local defense officials for the last time.
No enemy planes ever appeared over Albemarle, although a stray
aircraft from a nearby county once caused some concern, and one
spotter was stirred into action by what proved to be motor-driven
lawn mowers at the university.

Red Cross workers, who participated in all these drills, greatly
increased their activities between 1942 and 1945, including disaster
preparedness, blood donor programs, and aid to servicemen and their
families. All told, 6,404 pints of blood were collected. In October
1942, overcoming some opposition from national headquarters, railway officials, and local restaurateurs, the chapter set up a canteen
at the C&O station which, before it closed in February 1946, served
light refreshments to 307,592 service personnel. On September 26,
1943, when a train bearing German prisoners of war was wrecked
near Shadwell, resulting in several fatalities and numerous injuries,
Red Cross ambulances, stretchers, and canteen personnel rushed to
the scene and helped care for the wounded. However, perhaps the
most impressive fact concerning Red Cross work in Albemarle during World War II is that everything was accomplished under the
direction of a five-member staff aided by some three thousand volunteers. These devoted individuals provided direct assistance to more
than ten thousand servicemen, made 5,687,000 surgical dressings at
seventeen workrooms throughout the city and county, and raised
over $200,000 in special war fund drives.

With the outbreak of war Company 103 of the VPF became deeply
involved in all defense planning. In July 1942 members exchanged
1917 Enfield rifles for modern equipment and a month later used
their fifty-seven shotguns and three submachine guns to guard the
wreckage of an army bomber which crashed near Keswick. In
October they were joined by seventy men of the new Virginia Reserve Militia. Popularly known as Minute Men, VRM personnel were
required to furnish their own guns and uniforms but, unlike the
Virginia Protective Force (or State Guard), were not subject to
duty outside of the county. Edwin V. Copenhaver helped organize

the first company, No. 2, and another, No. 404, was established in 1943. For the most part, these men held musters in the colonial tradition, drilled, conducted mock operations, and stood ready to fill the shoes of the absent national guard on the local scene if called upon to do so. As Governor Darden noted in 1945, this was not exciting duty; but as chief executive of the state, he emphasized it was reassuring to know he could call upon such men in the event of an enemy attack or any outbreak of public disorder. The ardor of these impromptu forces admittedly waned as victory drew near. The Minute Men were demobilized soon after V-J Day, but the VPF remained on semiactive status until April 1947, when the Monticello Guard was officially released from federal duty.

During the war years these volunteers were aided by a group sometimes dubbed the "flying fathers." They were part-time aviators, members of the Charlottesville and Albemarle Civil Air Patrol Squadron, organized in March 1942 under the guidance of W. R. Franke, a professional with over two thousand hours of flying time. The primary task of this group was to stand ready to fly doctors and nurses to disaster areas, locate downed aircraft, and train youngsters eager to become pilots themselves. Membership was not limited to flyers but included anyone interested in aviation. The CAP used the University Airport near Milton as its base and had at its disposal eighteen aircraft, some privately owned. Less than two weeks after the initial meeting, members took part in a mock air raid over Charlottesville, the first time civilian aircraft were employed in this fashion in the nation. Four CAP pilots dropped forty weighted streamers carrying messages telling how much damage each "bomb" had done. Four days later local defense headquarters issued a special appeal to all citizens, whether souvenir hunters or merely forgetful, to please return those streamers. Although the CAP participated in numerous defense programs, its most important function proved to be training high school students interested in aviation. During the summer of 1944 approximately forty-five boys and girls, most of them from Lane High School, were enrolled. Attention to lessons in Morse code, map reading, and other requisite skills was keen, since those with highest marks received two hours of free flight instruction. By that date the group had become known as the Lewis Squadron in honor of C. B. "Pat" Lewis, who died in 1943. However, squadron ranks were far from stable as both instructors and students went off to war, and in June 1945 the CAP disbanded.

Although the work of the Red Cross, civilian defense workers, the State Guard, Minute Men, and the CAP was important and occasionally spectacular, most of it was of a precautionary nature designed to protect Albemarle if disaster struck. The community's most vital contribution to the national war effort, aside from manpower, came from its farms, factories, and forests. The beginning of the war found most Albemarle farmers practicing general agriculture, cultivating orchards and raising grain, hay, and other crops for dairy herds, beef cattle, horses, poultry, and sheep. Fruit growers produced a substantial portion of the rural income, leading the state in peach production. The basic problem faced by local farmers between 1942 and 1945 was how to grow and harvest larger crops with less labor. In 1942 some fruit men imported temporary help from Georgia and North Carolina, but in general they relied upon local assistance, schoolchildren, housewives, and various volunteers, some of them recruited by business and social clubs of Charlottesville. During 1944, a bumper year, they welcomed "anyone and everyone" who would lend a hand.

On the seventh of August 260 German prisoners arrived in Crozet. Approximately 240 of them picked peaches and apples, filled silos, harvested hay, shucked corn, cut pulpwood, and sawed logs. D. B. Owen, manager of the Crozet Fruit Growers Cooperative, was active in organizing their work, which, he observed, was satisfactory on the whole. Occasional peaches branded with a swastika or the initials PW were taken from the conveyor belts in packing houses. "It's exactly the same thing as a 15-year-old thumbing his nose at you," said Chesley Haden. "These Germans are some of the crack troops of the North African campaign—fine physical specimens—and they're a little rebellious at times. We have noted a mixed reaction to their work; some growers say they're all right, and others say they're worthless." Though not all of their employers were satisfied with their production, the overall statistical record of their work belied any merely prejudicial contention that the German prisoners were worthless as farm laborers. At the end of four months they had picked 29,803 bushels of peaches, 133,858 bushels of apples, stacked 370,962 board feet of lumber, shucked 906 barrels of corn, cut 74,113 board feet of saw logs and 105 cords of pulpwood, pruned 450 peach trees, and done 22,794 hours of general farm work.[6]

Some 285 Negroes from the Bahamas also joined the harvest, their British accent, bright dress, and zoot suits adding still more international flavor to the rural scene. In addition to German prisoners and island laborers, seventy-five Woman's Land Army volunteers—college students, teachers, businesswomen, and others—went into the

[6] Gertrude Parlier and Elizabeth Dabney Coleman in *Pursuits of War*, p. 103.

orchards and packing sheds that year. Although the volunteers were inexperienced and few in number, many growers found these young women willing workers.

Despite labor difficulties, fruit men posted a fine record during the war years, increasing apple production by 50 percent (up from 583,580 bushels in 1940 to 828,952 in 1945) and peach production by more than 100 percent, 229,026 to 534,067 bushels. Other farmers, although faced with similar labor shortages, rationing of farm machinery, marketing difficulties, and complicated price regulations, also increased their output of foodstuffs. Acreage in pastureland doubled during the war years (from 43,436 to 86,906 acres), and the number of cattle and calves grew from 16,779 to 22,576. Production of dairy and poultry products rose somewhat, and a small increase in sheep and hogs was evident. Pigs within the city, long a source of controversy, enjoyed a brief respite from city hall harassment. As City Health Director T. S. Englar noted, "After all, there are swine in some sections already and, conditions remaining the same, a pig on Rugby Road is no different from his cousin in Belmont." City fathers eventually agreed early in 1942 that hogs could be kept if pens were more than 250 feet from the nearest dwelling and their location was approved by the chief of police. At that time there were sixty-seven hog owners in Charlottesville. Since few others had both property expansive enough and an urge to keep porkers, it is doubtful if many more enjoyed wartime bacon "grown on the place."

One of the most intriguing aspects of war on the local scene was the appearance of innumerable Victory gardens, a phenomenon by no means limited to the county. Spurred on by such slogans as "Food Fights for Freedom" and "You can Shorten the War with Food," as well as soaring prices, hundreds learned how to plant and care for tomato plants and rows of corn, string beans, cabbages, and potatoes. By 1944 96 percent of the county's residents were raising at least part of the food they consumed. Maxine Lamb, president of the Albemarle County 4-H Council, in that year won a $25 war bond for food production on the farm of her parents on Route 2, Charlottesville. Miss Lamb and two other 4-H members, Dan Maupin of White Hall and Anne Carpenter of Scottsville, later described their work on a national radio program sponsored by the U.S. Department of Agriculture. Negro 4-H Club youths also did their part, and in 1945, 99 of them completed 120 gardening projects which netted a profit of $2,100.

Yet city gardens, which sprang up in backyards and vacant lots as if by magic, undoubtedly attracted more attention than those found in the county. Charlottesville's Victory Garden Committee, headed by Louis Chauvenet, was extremely active. Two of his assistants, Mrs. Theodore Hough and Mrs. Leroy Snow, both accomplished horticulturalists, aided scores of amateurs. Mrs. Hough not only visited garden plots but also held a weekly forum at the courthouse, broadcast a program over WCHV, and published a column in the *Daily Progress*, all designed to provide advice and help. In the spring of 1942 a Children's Victory Garden Club was formed, the first in the state, and various Boy Scout troops began growing vegetables. Troop 1, sponsored by the Charlottesville Presbyterian Church, created and tended some twenty-two gardens. In 1943 the city held its first Victory Garden Fair at the old armory, and a year later another display of vegetables, canned goods, and flowers was staged at the First Methodist Church. (Flowers, though inedible, presumably boosted morale.) Of course, much of this produce had to be canned, and within a short time Home Demonstration agents and various club leaders were giving special instruction in how to preserve what had been harvested. In April 1943 a canning center opened in the basement of the new armory, and another appeared in Scottsville the following year. By the end of the war the Charlottesville facility had processed 55,000 cans of food, charging a few cents for each can. The Scottsville operation, which continued long after V-J Day and served the neighboring counties of Buckingham and Fluvanna as well, turned out 43,930 cans of food in 1947. Some of this produce found its way overseas during the war years, and at least part of the Christmas dinner enjoyed by the Eighth Evacuation Hospital in Italy in 1944 came from the soil of Albemarle.

Although the number of farms changed little (2,591 in 1940, 2,599 in 1945), World War II did have its effects. Submarginal operations were abandoned as men departed for the service or took better-paying defense jobs, farm ownership increased somewhat, and tenancy declined. The most striking changes in rural households were more general use of electricity (838 farms had such service in 1940 compared to 1,192 in 1945) and prosperity of sorts after a decade or more of poverty, even deprivation. The total value of Albemarle's annual harvest rose from $1,880,619 in 1940 to $5,504,494 in 1945; however, costs in wages and machinery and wartime inflation cut deeply into profits, and the average value of farmland rose only slightly, from $56.29 per acre in 1940 to $58.83 five years later.

Months before Pearl Harbor the Charlottesville-Albemarle business community began to feel the effects of the defense boom. In 1941 local corporations had their best year since 1929. Many declared

extra dividends, announced expansion plans, or refunded outstanding
bonds. Early in 1942, fearful that government contracts might pass
Charlottesville by, business leaders created an advisory planning
board composed of both city and county residents. This body was
strengthened in October 1942 when Leonard H. Peterson became
executive secretary of the Charlottesville-Albemarle Chamber of
Commerce, a post vacant for several months. In May 1943 Peterson
described what had been happening on the local scene.

For the past year, and in some cases longer, local manufacturing enterprises, with few exceptions, have been working at full capacity to produce
goods for use by the Army, Navy, and Merchant Marine. Both labor and
management have been working long hours and at top speed in order to
complete large contracts on or before the time specified. Some of these
firms have had to make enormous changes in order to convert to production of items entirely foreign to their normal operations and as a result
have given employment to hundreds of persons. Industrial employment at
present is at the highest point in the city's history.

A partial list of the goods now being produced includes such items as
mechanical parts for merchant ships, wood, metal and electrical parts for
naval vessels, cloth for parachutes and flare chutes, uniform cloth for
the Navy, parts for anti-aircraft shells, braids for uniforms, lumber and
pre-fabricated buildings and other building materials, mattresses and
clothing.

Local transportation facilities are moving large numbers of service men
and huge quantities of war materials at all hours of the day and night.
Local utilities are adequately meeting unprecedented demands in a most
efficient manner.

It is estimated that approximately 2,000 people are employed locally in
work directly related to the war effort and that monthly payrolls for this
group amount to nearly $250,000.[7]

By the end of 1943 this effort reached its peak. In that year fifteen
leading industries employing 2,400 persons produced goods worth
$13,250,000, 80 percent of them war materials. Like county farmers,
stores and businesses scrambled to find workers. Laundries, especially
hard hit, often could not return a finished shirt for three weeks; and
on four occasions the Home Laundry simply ceased collections until
soiled clothes on hand were clean. The *Daily Progress*, confronted
with a newsprint shortage, cut the number of its pages, and Saturday editions shrank to tabloid size devoid of advertising. In the spring
of 1944 the labor shortage became so acute that employers launched,
with little success, a "Charlottesville Go-to-Work" campaign, fol-

[7] Marvin Schlegel in *Pursuits of War*, pp. 77–78.

lowed by a house-to-house canvass by city schoolteachers under the direction of Mrs. J. Tevis Michie. They found only 208 unemployed individuals willing to work. The bottom of the manpower barrel had been scraped clean, and the only way to meet production schedules and maintain business operations was to abandon the forty-hour week. Nearly all employees became accustomed to time and a half or even double time for work done after regular hours and on weekends and holidays. Some were attracted by the extra money, as well as being stirred by patriotism.

Radio Station WCHV, which devoted one-third of its air time to the community war effort, promised listeners a special service as D-Day aproached: if they would submit their names and phone numbers, they would receive a personal call telling them when a second front opened in Europe. By the morning of June 6, 1944, 300 residents had done so; and at 3 A.M., when news of the invasion was confirmed, WCHV was on the air. Within an hour and a half Charles Barham, Jr., the station's owner, and his manager, Randolph Bean, placed calls to 175 advertisers and 125 families with sons in the service.

Three traditional industries, textiles, lumber, and quarrying, and three new ones, welding, rubber processing, and frozen foods, provided the bulk of local war output. The looms of Frank Ix and Sons turned out hundreds of silk and nylon parachutes, some designed to carry aviators to safety, others to drop bombs and supplies. The Ix staff nearly doubled during the war years, from 370 to 650, women assumed jobs once handled by men, and supervisors implemented both share-the-ride programs and a special bus to bring employees in from the county. Ix also purchased or built houses for some workers. The Virginia Braid Company produced parachute cords as well as those used for tents, cargo covers, and uniforms. The Charlottesville Woolen Mills turned out 15,000 yards of uniform cloth a month, most of it going to the navy, a regular customer since 1935. Three smaller plants—Henderson and Ervin, the Monticello Shirt Company (Knothe Brothers), and the Albemarle Weaving Company—produced shirts and shorts, although the last was unable to secure equipment needed to convert completely to wartime requirements.

In the fall of 1944, as demand for wood fiber mounted and the labor situation worsened, power-driven saws were introduced into Albemarle's forests and soon some two thousand cords of pulpwood were being shipped to processing plants each month. Twenty-four Scottsville High School boys joined fire-fighting crews protecting these woodlands. Several lumber companies, among them Barnes

Lumber, Charlottesville Lumber, and L. H. Wiebel, turned out special wood products for the army and navy. Barnes filled government orders worth nearly $2 million and Charlottesville Lumber manufactured crates, prefabricated barracks, and radar huts.

Although the Alberene Stone Corporation had no direct government contracts, soapstone valued at $3 million was used in hospitals, at air bases, and even on aircraft carriers. Like all industries, quarries had labor problems and had to do battle with price regulations and various government controls. John S. Graves, Alberene's president, in 1944 succinctly summed up his difficulties: "Too many agencies—too much red tape—too many conflicting reports." To add to these woes faced by all businessmen, in September of that year a devastating flood swept through his plant and disrupted rail service for over two months. The Blue Ridge Slate Company, somewhat more fortunate, was able to continue producing all of its peacetime lines except roofing slate. Although new machinery doubled output in 1941, production declined somewhat during the war; nevertheless, 80 percent of some 14,500 to 18,000 tons of slate processed annually went indirectly to the war effort.

One of the community's leading producers of implements of war was the Southern Welding and Machine Company. This concern, a true rags-to-riches success story, was founded in the 1930s by two partners, R. R. Harmon and J. Tevis Michie, both long on enterprise and ingenuity but short on capital. Their first order, it is said, brought them twenty-five cents. By 1939 this company had twenty-five employees and was doing an annual business of $50,000. A year later Michie and Harmon received their first defense contract, a request from the Coast Guard to build tubes conducting electric cables through bulkheads (partitions) on ships. Success brought more orders, including gas purification equipment utilizing some of Harmon's patents. Southern Welding's greatest achievement was the creation of aircraft deck cables to snag and slow down planes as they landed. By 1943 no less than forty-five carriers were using cables produced in Charlottesville. This firm also manufactured crash barriers designed to stop planes if they failed to connect with the deck cables and four-wheeled mobile jacks which helped park planes in carrier holds and on crowded decks. Not neglecting the army, its employees built numerous bomb parts and carriers and platforms for guns.

Sales rose from $67,000 in 1940 to over $1,000,000 in 1943, and the plant itself tripled in size. Much of the material used for expansion came from dismantled sections of Manhattan's old Sixth Avenue elevated railway. Despite labor problems, Southern Welding, like the

57. Alexander Archer Vandergrift   58. John S. Battle, Sr.

59. Mary Rawlings

Ix Mills, received a coveted army-navy E pennant for excellence of production. Another local firm, N. W. Martin and Brothers, turned out roofing and sheet metal for army needs and plastic noses for "Black Widow" bombers. The latter enterprise, a highly guarded wartime secret, was a new departure for the Martins but proved to be an extremely successful undertaking. By the war's end, over two thousand nose cones had been shipped from Charlottesville.

Rubber processing and quick freezing of foods, new on the local scene, undoubtedly had the greatest impact of all wartime innovations. Both industries continued to thrive long after fighting ended, and in time each became prime factors in the economies of two county towns, Scottsville and Crozet. Early in 1944 the federal government, with the aid of the U.S. Rubber Company, decided to build a plant in Scottsville. Opened in October of that year, the installation was a model of twentieth-century automation. Within weeks it had several hundred workers and almost overnight had transformed that rural village into an industrial town. Soon after V-J Day federal authorities announced intentions to release the plant to private hands; despite keen bidding, the U.S. Rubber Company, which was already managing the facility, carried off the prize for $1,837,500. The Crozet Cold Storage Corporation founded in 1929 actually was merely a warehouse for Albemarle's annual fruit harvest until 1941 when, fortuitously, the company added quick-freezing equipment. With war, operations expanded enormously; soon not only fruit but vegetables, poultry, meat, eggs, and lard were being stored there or prepared for shipment overseas.

Although the Charlottesville-Albemarle community remained essentially nonindustrial, the demands of war resulted in the manufacture of an amazing variety of goods. Some, such as frozen foods, lumber, slate, fountain pens, and textiles, were merely a continuation of peacetime operations; but others, notably rubber and aircraft parts, were entirely new enterprises. In 1944 the city-county had 1,936 industrial workers, compared to 1,711 in 1940. Business leaders estimated that with the war's end, 300 more might be employed. The region nevertheless remained closely tied to its rural, service-oriented heritage. War brought temporary change, but neither huge defense installations nor sprawling factories appeared. Unlike many American communities, Albemarle did not have to adjust to any large influx of new citizens between 1941 and 1945 and, with victory, did not face the traumatic experience of converting gigantic wartime operations to peacetime needs.

For most residents war meant buying war bonds, getting along with less, and doing whatever they could to help those in uniform. Purchases of defense and war bonds, actually a form of savings which decreased demand for goods in short supply, became an integral part of daily life. Parades, minstrel shows, Gilbert and Sullivan operettas, exhortation of interschool rivalries, and appearances by movie stars and local war heroes all were part of extensive campaigns to boost sales. Celebrities at area rallies included movie star Greer Garson; Secretary of the Treasury Henry Morgenthau; war correspondent Ernie Pyle; Mrs. Demas T. Craw, widow of Colonel "Nick" Craw, the first American to die in North Africa; Willis Henderson, a black employee at Monticello whose family had lived there since the days of Jefferson; and Lieutenant General Vandergrift, Marine Corps commandant. Lane High School students on one occasion purchased enough bonds and stamps to buy forty-seven jeeps, one-fourth of the quota originally set for schools throughout the entire state, and later topped that achievement with the purchase of a PBY Catalina bomber (value $172,000), the first high school in Virginia to do so. Not only students but Boy Scouts, townspeople, everyone took part in eight bond drives which netted $42,229,293, nearly double the goal established for the city-county area.

Getting along with less meant both salvaging scarce materials and living under regulations of the Office of Price Administration. Wastepaper, scrap iron, rubber, copper, rags, and aluminum were among goods collected for reprocessing. Paper drives, usually led by Boy Scout troops, 4-H clubs, and schoolchildren, rounded up thousands of pounds of used material; and at the same time, customers frequently carried purchases home unwrapped. Metal, the second most important item on the salvage list, was assembled in great piles made up of everything from razor blades to junk iron. The old streetcar tracks at the Rugby Road turning went off to war, as did gas fixtures, kettles, an iron fence from the Old Ladies Home, a cannon fired on the Lawn of the university to herald secession in 1861, and scores of outmoded cars and trucks. However, three helmets (American, French, and German) contributed to the city firemen's collection did not make it out of Charlottesville; a nocturnal souvenir hunter apparently could not suppress an urge to add these items to his trophies.

Salvage of tin cans, although some 12,000 to 20,000 pounds were gathered in the community during some months of 1944, proved rather disappointing. Apparently only half of Charlottesville's households cooperated. Efforts to salvage rubber in 1942–43 were somewhat more successful, possibly because the drives lasted little more than a year until synthetic substitutes became available. Under the direction of Mrs. Lyttelton Waddell, scores of city children became temporary "commandos" during the summer of 1942 and piled up so much old rubber that gas stations and oil companies were swamped with tires and similar products. Local authorities had set a 400,000-pound quota which was easily surpassed, and a few months later city and county together collected 250.5 tons of used rubber. Gathering of kitchen fats, which could provide glycerine for antiaircraft ammunition, like attempts to salvage tin, met only limited response. Charlottesville's salvage committee estimated the community would yield about 6,000 pounds per month, but despite house-to-house canvasses by Girl Scouts, Camp Fire Girls, and PTA members, less than one-fourth of that amount usually was realized. Even payment of four cents per pound and extra ration stamps to be used when purchasing meat failed to stir much interest.

Other material accumulated for war purposes from time to time included rags, aluminum pots and pans, license plates, silk stockings, and phonograph records, which could yield small quantities of shellac. On occasions the Paramount Theatre accepted records as admission to movies. County 4-H members gathered forty-five bags of milkweed pods in 1944, enough to fill twenty-two life preservers. Fur for lining some military uniforms was collected by the Shadwell DAR chapter. It is apparent that residents posted a creditable, if not spectacular, salvage record. Local custom perhaps explains lack of success with tin cans and fats. Many households still relied upon foods stored in glass jars, and nearly all cooks made widespread use of fats for seasoning and gravies, certainly more than their counterparts to the north and west. However, the so-called experts should have realized these facts before setting unattainable goals. Also, to be effective, salvage of kitchen items demanded constant, day-to-day attention by those individuals actually preparing food. Drives for wastepaper, iron, rubber, and clothing, by their very nature, aided by scores of enthusiastic young people, could easily be promoted by appeals to team spirit and rivalry.

Shortages of gasoline, heating oil, kerosene, tires, cigarettes, shoes, coffee, liquor, dried fruits, sugar, lard, meat, and various other foodstuffs resulted in the rationing of most of these items under OPA. In general, limitations on travel, drinking, and smoking caused the greatest outcry. Americans always had plenty of food during World War II, although they might not have been able to get precisely what they wanted to eat at every meal. Boards were established in both city and county to regulate prices and ration goods. Tires were the first commodity to be rationed officially, followed shortly by gasoline. In May 1942 all citizens with autos went to local schoolhouses to register for fuel allotments. Under the original plan each owner received an A card entitling him to three gallons a week. Those with greater needs got B cards (nine gallons per week), and a lucky few—only 328 out of 3,639 individuals in Charlottesville—received X cards granting unlimited supplies. The last group included doctors, ministers, government officials, and certain essential workers. This system soon collapsed, partly because service station attendants often failed to punch cards. In July 1942 an A, B, C scheme of gas ration books appeared. Those with A books could use certain stamps during a specified period, but the value of each stamp varied in relation to available supplies. The B and C holders got somewhat more liberal treatment, again based upon occupational needs. Hand in hand with these new ration books came a lower state speed limit of forty miles per hour (later cut to thirty-five) and exhortations to join car pools.

On December 18, 1942, sale of all gasoline except for emergency use suddenly was suspended because of black market profiteering and circulation of a substantial number of counterfeit stamps. Three days later the *Daily Progress* commented, "This morning the gasoline situation returned to normal, or rather to the state of abnormality which has existed for many months." Early in 1943 the OPA simply banned all nonessential driving: "If it's fun, it's out." At first, local residents generally accepted this stern dictum as a wartime necessity. On January 16 police found eleven cars parked near Memorial Gymnasium during a Virginia-VPI boxing match, but investigation revealed all but one driver had stopped off en route home from work, allowable under OPA regulations. Citizens soon discovered how to get around, even within the wording of these rules, if not quite according to their intent. Ivy hockey players, for example, arranged to pick up laundry before or after a match, thus giving them a valid reason for a trip to the playing field. In March the OPA threw in the sponge, at the same time slashing the value of A stamps and urging voluntary compliance with the pleasure-driving ban.

After 1943 the gas crunch eased somewhat with advent of serially marked coupons that were virtually counterfeit-proof. Any dealer turning in bogus stamps had them charged against his allotment. This action curbed illicit operations but prompted several individuals to break into local ration headquarters in September 1944 and steal legitimate stamps.

The German U-boat campaign in the Atlantic early in 1942 caused severe shortages of bananas and sugar, resulting in distribution of War Ration Book No. 1 in May of that year. This flimsy little folder given to all citizens contained stamps granting each individual half a pound of sugar per week and included blank coupons which, come November, were used when purchasing coffee. The coffee allotment, one pound every five weeks, was extremely niggardly, providing devoted drinkers with perhaps one cup per day. The sugar allowance, on the other hand, was adequate for normal household needs; however, for abnormal pastimes such as bootlegging it was not. Simultaneous shortages of both sugar and moonshine customers (many of them away in uniform) created an unprecedented situation at the Albemarle County Jail on May 24, 1942. For the first time in the memory of Sheriff J. Mason Smith, a lawman for four decades, his jail had no prisoners. Usually host to twenty or thirty inmates, it was completely empty! At about the time that coffee was rationed, liquor purchases were limited to one quart per day. In January 1943 bourbon, gin, scotch, and similar potions joined the ration list; and during succeeding months, local residents often found that even if they had valid stamps, state stores had no liquor. Cigarettes, though never rationed, became extremely scarce during the winter of 1944–45. Brands once ridiculed were immediately snatched up by nervous smokers, many of whom, with indifferent success, resorted to rolling their own.

In February 1943 city and county residents signed up for War Ration Book No. 2, a more substantial volume than its predecessor. This book introduced a point system assigning certain foods a value which fluctuated according to supply. When signing up for Book No. 2, each family had to state how many pounds of coffee and how many cans of food they had at home. One household declared 2,167 cans; another family of two, 975. Most reported no great hoard of supplies, despite occasional glances from skeptical neighbors. A lady declaring only 4 pounds of coffee and 10 cans of food, for example, was found to possess 48 pounds of coffee and 510 cans of food. In general, certain items on grocery shelves required so many points when purchased, and a group of stamps (perhaps worth 48 points) became valid each month. The task facing a housewife with four mouths to feed was to weigh choices carefully, decide how to spend her 192 points during a thirty-day period, and, whenever possible, round out meals with items requiring few or no points at all.

Books 3 and 4 followed later in 1943, and in 1944 the system was simplified by assigning each stamp a uniform value of ten points and issuing red and blue tokens worth one point. As Allied fortunes soared in Europe, food supplies increased substantially; but with the Ardennes Forest offensive by the supposedly beaten Germans, lard, shortening, oils, and fruit juices were rationed once more. Victory brought an end to most food shortages except meat and butter, which remained scarce because price controls discouraged production. When OPA regulations expired temporarily on June 30, 1946, meat suddenly became plentiful, but at high prices. Restoration of price ceilings in September drove almost all meat from local markets, resulting in the worst shortage of these years. About a month later controls on meat were removed, and in June 1947 those on sugar also disappeared as wartime rationing ended.

Control of rental costs was another important aspect of local life, especially during the first years of peace as university enrollment soared. During the war, despite inauguration of the School of Military Government at the University of Virginia, bringing scores of families to the area, housing remained relatively adequate, and no government rent ceilings were imposed. However, in the fall of 1945, as students crammed into basements and garrets, Charlottesville's mayor, Roscoe S. Adams, became alarmed. One property owner increased rents 25 percent on September 1, just in time for the opening of classes. In a surprise move OPA on January 3, 1946, announced that all city-county rents would be rolled back to the level of October 1, 1944. Bernard Chamberlain, formerly a rationing executive with the Richmond OPA office, was named local rent director, a thankless task since landlords were very unhappy with this turn of events. When OPA expired six months later, so did rent control, only to be reinstated on June 26, 1946, and continued in modified form throughout much of 1947. The most tangible results of this campaign were some restraints on soaring rents, considerable red tape, a hundred trailers on Copeley Hill to house married students, and more and more families sharing living accommodations, either because no rental units could be found or in an effort to cut costs.

Numerous volunteer groups provided for the needs of servicemen between 1941 and 1945, but efforts to establish a United Service Organizations facility in Charlottesville were stymied for some months after Pearl Harbor. Only one member agency, the Salvation Army, was active locally, and the absence of huge encampments or naval installations seemed to make any lounge or club unnecessary. However, various church and civic groups were host to both visiting servicemen and local inductees. The most important reception center in 1942 was in the Annex Building of the Charlottesville Presbyterian

Church, First and Market streets, under the direction of Nan Crow. From July to December of that year some seven thousand black and white men used the lounge, and during those months a handful of British sailors also visited the community on leave.

Stiff gas rationing and inauguration of several service-connected schools at the university convinced many that Charlottesville needed a full-fledged facility, and in February 1943 the old armory, rejuvenated with donated furniture and bright paint, opened with a gala ball as the community's USO. This operation, at the outset supported entirely by local citizens, received merely official blessing and good wishes, not money, from the national headquarters. Soon a full program of activities developed, and accommodations for overnight guests were added. On occasions the USO even took entertainment to those who could not come to Charlottesville. Guards at a German prisoner of war camp at White Hall, for example, were given a radio, furniture, reading material, and Christmas gifts. Before it closed down in June 1946, over a thousand junior and senior hostesses assisted some thirty thousand servicemen, many of them transients, others home on leave or stationed at the university.

Not all local relief efforts were directed toward the welfare of men in uniform. "Bundles for Britain," aided by a benefit reception for movie star Madeleine Carroll at Farmington Country Club in August 1940, appeals from Lady Astor and author John Wheeler-Bennett, and an auction featuring an undergarment once owned by Queen Victoria, was an extremely active organization in 1939–41. With Pearl Harbor and intensification of the war, the desire to aid Greeks, Dutch, Russians, Chinese, and even fellow Americans and German civilians after April 1945 limited this group's activities somewhat, although British relief by no means ceased. In a moment of generosity a group of citizens donated a bed to Queen Charlotte Hospital, London. Some years later the mayor received a letter from a mother whose "bonny boy" had been born in the "Charlottesville" bed. She wanted to convey thanks to the donors, but neither His Honor nor local newsmen could recall who was responsible.

A somewhat different type of relief operation occurred at Alderman Library. There in 1942, as part of a national campaign, some three thousand books were collected for distribution to service personnel. The university's library also served in a secret capacity as custodian for nearly three years of many treasures from the Library of Congress, including the papers of numerous presidents. According to Francis L. Berkeley, Jr., then curator of manuscripts, he had "the devil of a time" getting these materials moved to Charlottesville during the Christmas season of 1941. Berkeley also recalls that he and President Newcomb had an equally difficult time getting the U.S. Army to withdraw its personnel from Alderman Library and the physics lab and replace them with local guards, thus maintaining some degree of secrecy.

The purpose, of course, of all this activity—production of food and matériel, salvage drives, rationing, and so on—was to increase support of men on far-flung fronts and bring victory over the enemy as quickly as possible. Boys from Charlottesville and Albemarle were found throughout the world, and the name "Charlottesville" went into battle on a bomber piloted by Captain Charles W. Lucas and was borne by a Coast Guard frigate launched in Wisconsin in July 1943. The U.S.S. *Charlottesville*, christened by Mrs. J. Emmett Gleason, wife of the current mayor, was 306 feet long and carried a crew of 208. When the vessel put into Norfolk a year later, five sailors were honored guests in Charlottesville for a day.

Three local residents were awarded the Medal of Honor. In 1942 Colonel Demas T. Craw, a youthful World War I veteran, was trying to deliver a message to the French commander at Port Lyautey, French Morocco, when he was shot and killed instantly, becoming the first man to die in the invasion of North Africa. An airfield near the port was named in his memory. Sergeant Frank Peregory, a former Barnes Lumber Company employee and member of the Monticello Guard since 1931, was honored for heroic action on the Normandy coast; he died a week later while leading his platoon near Saint-Lô. The third recipient, Major General Vandergrift, received his medal at the White House from President Roosevelt in February 1943 in recognition of his leadership in the Solomons. Vandergrift later became commandant of the Marine Corps and its first full general.

At seven o'clock on the evening of August 14, 1945, radio listeners throughout the city-county area learned that Japan had capitulated and World War II was over. The next day *Daily Progress* headlines told of national rejoicing, the immediate end of rationing of gasoline, canned fruits and vegetables, heating oil, and oil stoves, and plans to release seven million Americans from the armed services at once. Few issues of that paper were received so enthusiastically or read so carefully. Nearly four years of fighting were at an end, the boys were coming home, and rationing was a thing of the past . . . well, almost so. Barely noticed by most readers was a small eagle pin reproduced in the upper right-hand corner of page one—the lapel button signifying honorable discharge from the service. Men and women wearing this emblem, as students, teachers, businessmen, bankers, real estate agents, farmers, and laborers, would shape the future of Albemarle. Amid the rejoicing there was a tendency to believe one could pick up life where war had interrupted it, but, of course, that was not to be. Although gunfire and battle touched neither America nor Albemarle between 1941 and 1945, World War II affected every citizen, some more than others, and in succeeding decades the full impact of that conflict, even at the local level, became apparent to all.

Part IV
An Urban City–County, 1945–1976

THE hallmark of local life during the past three decades quite clearly is change, but change is in the eye of the beholder and dates merely from the moment he or she first saw the hills of Albemarle. For most individuals this phenomenon entails new shopping centers, apartment houses, superhighways, expansion of the university, and hundreds of newcomers; yet these trends are not unique. Since World War II nearly all American communities of comparable size have witnessed similar developments. Even growth of the university and an influx of people are not new. Pioneers who resented the presence of enemy prisoners in the 1770s and their descendants who watched the University of Virginia grow through the years and were disturbed from time to time by town-gown brawls undoubtedly expressed views not unlike those voiced in recent decades. One gracious lady, native-born and wise and perceptive as a result of eighty summers spent in Charlottesville, says the greatest change is not physical expansion but the absence today of mud. In her childhood each of Charlottesville's major intersections was delineated by large stepping stones carefully placed so that pedestrians could walk from board sidewalks on one side of the street to the other and wagons and carriages could pass between them. These stones, her father often remarked, gave local matrons an excellent opportunity to advertise trim ankles and perhaps a bit of leg as they lifted their skirts to attempt a crossing. Small fry, on the other hand, often were transported to a neighbor's yard on the backs of older brothers who ignored the conventional pathway and sloshed ankle-deep to the other side.

For many residents, especially the region's black minority, the most profound development of recent years has been the dramatic turnabout in race relations. No longer do their children attend separate schools, nor do they eat at segregated restaurants or in the dingy anterooms of white facilities. Not all barriers have fallen, of course, since economic realities still consign most Negroes to areas of poor housing and low-paying jobs. Nevertheless, after the uproar of the 1950s and early 1960s which now seems ancient history, a handful of very able black leaders have forged to positions of considerable prominence in Charlottesville's public life. In 1970 Charles J. Barbour, a black Democrat who faced strong opposition within his own party, won a seat on the city council. Four years later Barbour, a chief cardiac technician at the University Hospital, was chosen mayor for a two-year term, the first Negro ever to hold that post. In 1968 Raymond L. Bell, graduate of Boston University, a World War II veteran, and the first black to serve on Charlottesville's school board, chose not to be reappointed and was succeeded by another leading Negro citizen, Rev. Henry B. Mitchell, pastor of Trinity Episcopal Church. Mitchell is now chairman of the board, and thus he and Barbour hold two of the most influential positions in municipal government.

The political life of Charlottesville-Albemarle has changed markedly during the past quarter century, influenced largely by racial matters and a struggle between conservative and liberal ideologies. After decades of Democratic dominance, voters frequently have crossed into the Republican column in national elections, although traditional party ties have remained somewhat stronger at the state and local levels. The upshot of this interplay, regardless of labels which often have become meaningless, is that the city-county area now has a healthy two-party system not unlike that evident before the Civil War when Whigs and Democrats scrambled for power. In the late 1960s Republicans even dominated the Charlottesville City Council for a brief time.

Looking beyond Interstate 64, Route 250 Bypass, Barracks Road Shopping Center, a burgeoning university, once muddy streets, race relations, and politics, the most far-reaching change in Charlottesville-Albemarle since 1945 has been the manner in which thousands of citizens make a living. What was at one time a community serving, for the most part, as an outlet for agricultural produce and a trading center for those raising wheat, corn, apples, and peaches, has become an urban industrial-technical complex. A few hundred working farms remain, but they provide jobs for less than a thousand full-time employees. Field after field which once grew crops or produced fruit has become residential property or pastureland for cattle, and over half of Albemarle's farm owners are semiretired or commercial folk with only limited interest in the fertility of the soil they live on.

The decline of rural life has made Thomas Walker's county a land of commuters. Hundreds, even thousands of individuals drive to work each day in Charlottesville, Scottsville, Waynesboro, Earlysville, and other centers to sit behind a desk, clerk in a store, or work in a hospital or laboratory. In 1970 approximately 5 percent of the area's work force, 1,340 persons, were commuting to communities outside of Albemarle, but this outflow was more than offset by 5,700 individuals traveling into the region from Orange, Nelson, Fluvanna, and Greene counties. This commuting, of course, is what urban living means, and such seems to be Albemarle's fate, as well as that of numerous towns and villages lying outside of its borders. Yet this is a destiny not without redeeming features since tourism and those eager to perpetuate a gracious way of life of former decades have done much to ease the transition from an agricultural to a commercial-industrial world which has blighted less fortunate areas.

The key to Albemarle County's good luck through the centuries has been a mix of relative isolation; the presence of a coterie of well-to-do, educated leaders; superb, even beguiling scenery; and, above all else, the growth of a university in its midst. The University of Virginia, established near Charlottesville in 1819, is now a major employer and serves as a magnet for small industries that can utilize its expertise. The region certainly heard the siren song of the New South and tried for some four decades, 1890 to 1930, to lure smokestacks to its soil, but there always were those who marched to a different drum and wanted their community to remain much as it was. Their wishes have not been respected at all times, especially since 1950; yet today Charlottesville-Albemarle seems to have the best of all possible worlds. It has kept its treasured past, created a stable economy where other rural communities have failed, and remains, despite substantial change, a good place to live, perhaps the highest accolade that can be paid to any region as our nation greets its third century.

Chapter 19

Race Relations, Annexation, and Rural Change

URING decades of "peace" complicated by wars half a world away in Korea and Vietnam, Jefferson's county experienced many of the problems found in hundreds of American communities. These included housing shortages, traffic congestion, inflation, a declining agricultural economy, and a growing awareness of pollution and unsightly roadside waste in a region boasting of its beauty. Yet two issues tended to dominate local life throughout the 1950s and 1960s: segregation, especially in public schools, and annexation of still more county land by the city of Charlottesville. In a sense these battles possessed certain similarities, although one was pushed forward relentlessly by civil rights activity far beyond Albemarle's boundaries. Each was an attempt, at least in the eyes of some observers, to unify the community. The struggle to end legal separation of the races, highly emotional at times, entailed much more rhetoric and endless legal maneuvering. Charlottesville's efforts to control suburban development, almost exclusively a local problem, although many regions faced the same dilemma caused by rapid urbanization, also were designed to bring together divergent but similar elements of city-county life. This is how some proponents of a greater Charlottesville viewed the situation, although the heady prospect of added tax revenue flowing into municipal coffers also certainly had substantial influence.

The roots of the race relations issue, of course, are buried deep in slavery, politics, decades of Reconstruction and Jim Crow, experiences that soldiers of both races had in World Wars I and II, the new vitality evident among colonial peoples throughout the world, and attitudes reinforced by religious teaching and everyday life. Also, discrimination practiced by America's enemies in 1941–45 proved highly embarrassing at times. Without becoming apologetic or maudlin, at least on the surface, the community's record in racial matters appears to have been quite admirable, that is, until the 1950s, when local conservatives were buttressed by adamant state politicians who chose to defy decisions handed down by federal courts. White and black lived, for the most part, in separate worlds, usually meeting as servant and master as they had for generations; however, this did not preclude close bonds of personal friendship and interdependence, nor did it prevent the rise of considerable bitterness and even hatred long before segregation laws were effectively challenged.

Negroes often held their own fairs and revivals but generally were welcome at any communitywide event such as Chaloner's movie shows and his Fourth of July extravaganzas, the American Legion's Mardi Gras, and Halloween festivities. Young people of both races were honored by city fathers when they departed for or returned from war. Groups such as the State Colored Dental Association and Negro Elks held conventions in Charlottesville in the 1920s, and the latter staged a huge parade, a dance at the city armory, and a baseball game at Lambeth Field. Vaudeville and movie houses always reserved seats at reduced prices for blacks and sometimes featured benefits produced by local Negroes. As public education developed, the city appears to have made some effort in behalf of black students, although it delayed setting up a high school for them as long as possible. On the other hand, although county authorities established a full program of black classrooms much earlier, these facilities, even at mid-century, often were woefully inadequate, sometimes primitive. Throughout these decades the proportion of blacks in city and county was declining as their educational level rose. Thus, numerically the Negro presented little threat to local whites; yet the new knowledge they were acquiring in scores of classrooms created desire for social equality and greater opportunities.

On July 23, 1923, at the very moment that the Ku Klux Klan was becoming more active, the John Boaz family of Covesville held a lavish party for their veteran cook, Judy Piper, who had been with them for thirty years. Supper for Judy and her guests was prepared and served by Mrs. Boaz and her children, and music for dancing was provided by a black orchestra. While a turnabout of this sort was rare indeed, such things could happen. During these years, as noted, Charlottesville's Negroes often used city and university facilities, held conventions, marched down Main Street, and participated in many community affairs, including the drive in 1922 to institute managerial government. County blacks undoubtedly flocked to town for any parade, convention, or festival and had just as much fun as their city cousins, perhaps more. Also, because of strong local roots, a sense of belonging to the soil of Albemarle, and firm faith in the power of education, proportionally their children attended public schools in greater numbers than either county whites or city blacks.

An intriguing study of Negro land ownership in Albemarle by Samuel T. Bitting, published in 1915, reveals that 1,554 blacks living in the county were taxpayers, more than two-thirds of them residents of Scottsville and Ivy districts.[1] Few then were tenants; in fact, white farm tenants outnumbered blacks 463 to 44. Negro farms were small but often well cared for, and many owners actually were part-time farmers, frequently working also as railroad hands, day laborers, and at various trades. Sanitary conditions, in Bitting's view, were much better than those found in urban areas. Homes were bigger, sometimes painted, less crowded, and well maintained. He found that thirty-four households subscribed to at least one newspaper; the *Charlottesville Messenger*, a black publication, was the most popular, but others read the *Daily Progress*, *Toledo Blade*, *New York World*, *Kansas City Star*, and *Washington Post*. Of 487 families interviewed, virtually all were Republican and Baptist, although one man admitted he had been expelled from the church for "getting drunk" and two others said they did not "care for preaching." Bitting noted that while the total Negro population was declining during the years just before World War I, the number of black farmers in Albemarle remained stable, and these individuals, more so than their white counterparts, tended to stay on the land and not join the drift to urban areas.

Fourteen years later, in another inquiry aided by the Phelps-Stokes Fund, Marjorie Felice Irwin examined various aspects of Negro life in Charlottesville and Albemarle.[2] She found that most black communities in the county were somewhat apart from white settlements, often "a bit off the main road." The village of Proffit, she observed, was entirely black during the years immediately after the Civil War and called first Egypt, then Bethel. When the railroad was built, the settlement took the name of the man, Proffit, who purchased the right of way and gradually whites moved into the area. There were, in the late 1920s, about fifteen to twenty Negro families in Proffit. Most of them had small truck farms and supplemented their income by working in Charlottesville.

Within the city an irregular north-south band of black settlement cut through the heart of the corporate area, stretching from Old Scottsville Road (South Sixth Street) across Main Street and Vinegar Hill to Preston Avenue. This district, although haphazardly developed, possessed certain advantages. Admittedly it included un-

---

[1] Bitting, *Rural Land Ownership among Negroes of Virginia, with Special Reference to Albemarle County* (Charlottesville, 1915), p. 61.

[2] See Irwin, *The Negro in Charlottesville and Albemarle* (Charlottesville, 1929).

desirable, cheap housing sites close to railroad tracks and in low-lying areas subject to frequent flooding; yet it gave residents easy access to the university community to the west and business and residential areas to the east where they worked. The poorest Negroes lived in the Sixth Street section, once a red light haven, in two- or three-room shacks, with no conveniences, rented from white landlords for perhaps as little as five dollars a month. (In later decades, thanks to pressure from municipal authorities, long rows of outside privies with plumbing would appear.) Poverty, dirt, mud, vice, and unpaved streets were the earmarks of this slum. Between Ridge and First streets was Happy Hollow, which, despite its name, presented a similar air of disordered decay.

North of Main Street and behind Vinegar Hill was another great natural bowl known as the "gas house district." It was filled with homes of every description, some perched precariously on steep slopes, but usually clean with fenced-in yards, and the occupants appeared somewhat more energetic than residents of the slums to the south.

This is the district of the washerwoman and cook, though the homes of those who perform such services are by no means confined to this area. There is not that atmosphere of hopelessness about the gas-house district that seems to hover over the Scottsville Road district. There is, however, a stream which leaves the gas-house, carrying away the refuse from it, and making the entire bowl smell of gas. It is an unsightly and unsavory stream, and the houses are built close beside it, so that at times it over-flows into the yards and even floods the first floors of the houses. This stream runs along Williams Street and is lost under Preston Avenue. The houses in this area are nearly all rented. There is here, also, some evasion of the law and of moral precepts, but the region can hardly be called a vice area.[3]

To the north and west housing along Preston Avenue was markedly better, most of it owned by the occupants, and here were located three of Charlottesville's black Baptist churches; however, the Negro "four hundred," as their own people called them, lived south of Main in the Ridge Street area.

These houses are of good quality, some of them unusually nice looking. They are lighted with electricity, heated with heatrolas, good stoves, or even with electricity, have bathrooms, separate dining rooms and kitchens, and comfortable furniture. Parlors are frequently furnished with over-stuffed suites. The mistresses of the houses are not uncomfortable in the

[3] Ibid., p. 18.

presence of white callers and can converse intelligently and pleasantly. If there are children the parents are planning to send them to college, provided they wish to go, and for this purpose both parents usually do some kind of work to help earn the necessary income. In this area and in the one described above, live preachers, doctors, dentists, insurance agents, teachers, the well-to-do of all trades and professions. Vice is not smiled upon or ignored in these regions. They are areas of high respectability and high morality.[4]

There were also several outlying areas of fine Negro homes, some of which had been owned by the same families for several generations. These included Lankford Avenue, the south end of Ridge Street, "old" Barracks Road, and Gospel Hill, a triangular section carved out by the Southern and Chesapeake and Ohio railroads. Despite Miss Irwin's assertion that the Negro elite, the "four hundred," lived south of Main Street, local blacks indicate today that the homes of leading citizens of that era were widely dispersed throughout the community. For the most part these people were businessmen, ministers, teachers, and contractors, although their ranks also included a barber, doctor, cobbler, and undertaker. They bore names such as Bell, Brown, Buckner, Burley, Coles, Ferguson, Gibbons, Goodloe, Inge, Jackson, Tonsler, and West. George Pinckney Inge, for example, born a slave in Southside Virginia but given substantial aid by his white father, graduated from Hampton Institute and taught school in Charlottesville for a time. Discouraged by low wages, on July 1, 1891, he opened a grocery store at 330 West Main Street which is still operated by his son, Thomas. Active in local politics and chairman of the city's Republican party in 1900, George Inge was a classmate at Hampton of Booker T. Washington, a frequent guest at the Inge home during his travels.

By far the most successful Negro of his day, the "first" of the "four hundred," was John West, a barber by trade who, when he died in 1927, left a huge estate. His wife, a stately woman, ran a boardinghouse and occasionally displayed her diamonds at church. West, the adopted son of Jane West, Charlottesville's richest free black in 1860, inherited a house, lot, and $3,200 when his benefactor passed on in 1869. At the time of his death John West left his heirs cash bequests totaling $23,600, Liberty Bonds worth $25,800, twenty houses, twenty unimproved lots, two tenements, two warehouses, and some 2,000 acres of farmland scattered from Barboursville to Gilbert to Augusta County. This property included a substantial expanse of

[4] Ibid., pp. 19–20.

land along Grady and Preston avenues where the Monticello Dairy now stands and eleven lots in Preston Heights. West also gave his cook life tenancy of a house and bestowed $500 upon the local Colored Ladies Home.

Some (but by no means all) members of the "four hundred" were virtually white, and their sons and grandsons now can laugh at experiences which, during the height of the Jim Crow years, must have caused considerable frustration and pain. The father of one local Negro was unable to buy the usual half-price tickets to athletic events at the University of Virginia and had to ask his "black" friends to get them for him. The aunt of another once returned from the train station in high dudgeon, furious because the local agent could not tell whether she was black or white. Disgusted with his indecision, she picked up her bags and stalked out, proclaiming for all to hear that if he knew he was a much better detective than she was. In addition to skin pigmentation and money, one other factor separated Charlottesville's "four hundred" from many of their black brothers: they knew where they came from. Distinctions between those of "free born" ancestry and those "shot free" (slaves released by war) were real indeed, and many households could pinpoint their roots with considerable accuracy.

Miss Irwin and Helen Camp de Corse, who analyzed black life in Charlottesville in 1933,[5] agreed that, on the whole, the business and professional Negro appeared "fairly well educated." Many had worked their way through school and held various service jobs before becoming teachers, undertakers, and shopkeepers. One, a great admirer of Paul Robeson and a collector of his operatic and classical records, observed: "The colored man is making a place for himself in America and I'd rather be an American than anything else. I fought in World War I." These folk lived a middle-class existence, played bridge according to Culbertson, and were the core of an Episcopal mission and six Baptist churches—First Baptist, Mt. Zion, Ebenezer, Bethel Institutional, Zion Union, and Shiloh. They also provided the leadership for thirteen art, literary, and social clubs for women and seven for men. Most of the ladies' groups were associated with the State Federation of Colored Women's Clubs, whose motto was: "Lifting As We Climb." The oldest and most prominent was the Taylor Art and Literary Club. The Progressive Club's twenty male members included two dentists, two doctors, an undertaker,

[5] See de Corse, *Charlottesville—A Study of Negro Life and Personality* (Charlottesville, 1933).

several merchants, and the superintendent of the Southern Aid Insurance Company.

The principal black business area was Vinegar Hill, a section of Main Street once the site of tanneries which, from their odor, probably gave the region its distinctive name. The Hill, now swept bare by an urban renewal scheme which seems to have faltered, then had forty-one buildings on the north side of the street and sixteen on the south.

Of the latter only one is occupied by Negroes—the Paramount Inn catering to transients. On the north side there are both white and colored establishments. Here are barber shops, pool-rooms, stores for furniture, food and clothing, shoe repair shops, cleaning establishments, drug stores, fish markets, beauty shops, insurance companies, tailors, restaurants, etc. Much of this property is owned by Negroes. The largest building on the Hill, the Coles Building, is owned by Charles Coles, a Negro building contractor, and occupied by a haberdashery, and a ladies clothing shop, a dentist, a physician, a life insuance company, a beauty parlor and a cafe. A number of other buildings are occupied by two or more businesses. Only one white establishment, a lunch room, is patronized by whites only, while one Negro business, a barber shop, is patronized by whites only. All other white businesses are patronized by both races or by Negroes only. Some of the Negro businesses are patronized by both races and some by Negroes only.

Vinegar Hill is never entirely deserted. Although the street is mostly deserted at night, the poolrooms and restaurants are always occupied. In the daytime there is constant movement on the Hill. Very few white people are seen on the north side; Negro loiterers standing in groups, sitting in the shops built flush with the sidewalks and lolling in cars of all makes and conditions are seen from morning until late at night. Few Negro women are seen until dark when the street becomes literally engorged with the influx of Negroes from their places of work. They are mostly a well dressed group. One Negro boy of nineteen, who works for a group of University students during the day and in the poolroom on Vinegar Hill at night, told me that he had ten tailor-made suits given him by students with ties, shirts and socks to match. He added that most of his friends worked in some capacity for students and all were "swell dressers, jest like the students." This boy drives a fairly good car and works in the poolroom for gasoline money. He pays his mother board and "don't run with women—they gets you in trouble and take your time." He finished high school.

Negroes from all classes consider certain establishments on Vinegar Hill a menace to the Negroes of Charlottesville. Some of the places sell liquor to school children, permit them to gamble and loiter in the poolrooms, shops and restaurants. Arrests are frequent on "the Hill" for loitering, fighting and drunkenness. Several shop owners act as informers in detecting suspects and law-breakers for the police. Sooner or later they appear or word is dropped where they can be found and the police are tipped off. Conditions are well known to the Negroes of Charlottesville and much bitterness is felt. One old woman, who was born just after the war and is devoted to several white families, recounts the following. She found her drunken grandson, aged twelve years, in the alley back of a restaurant where he had been sold liquor. "Gawd won't punish me for wicked thoughts, but I wish the Hill would burn down and be destroyed and all the white folks what is responsible along wid de black folks what is making my Bubbie (her grandson) bad." [6]

Vinegar Hill did not burn down nor did all the "bad folks" disappear when that sordid but colorful jumble of buildings was razed. Center of bootleg activity and vice it was, but the hill most assuredly was much more vibrant and alive in its former guise than it is today, now merely an expanse of bare ground stretching like a no-man's-land, perhaps to be the site of the downtown business district's last stand should the upstart shopping centers mushrooming a few miles to the west ever launch an all-out attack.

Other Negro businesses of the early 1930s included a pressing and cleaning establishment near the university, five transfer and trucking concerns, three taxi companies (one of which served both races), a coal and wood business, six beauty parlors, two undertaking establishments, several grocery stores, and a blacksmith's shop. The owner of the latter boasted, "I shoes most of de horses what's shoed in de city—I stays right smart busy." Hairdressers, however, were feeling the pinch of depression, one commenting that do-it-yourself straightening was much in vogue. "They buy Sterno heat and a comb from the Five and Ten and fix their own hair," a beautician commented. Yet, Miss de Corse indicates most black businesses in both city and county were doing rather well, despite hard times. Depression had stymied the flow of blacks north and west, and others had returned, creating a solid nucleus of customers. Also, some blacks, thanks to an unprecedented demand for labor during World War I and the years immediately after, had moved into jobs which, a decade or so earlier, would have been closed to them.

In addition to the social life provided by Vinegar Hill, club activities, and parties in private homes, Negroes of that era also gathered at the Blue Goose Inn near Keswick, the Press Inn at Union Ridge, and the Odd Fellows Hall. The city high school had, in the opinion

[6] Ibid., pp. 12–13.

of Miss de Corse, an "excellent" glee club and the grade school, an active PTA. The Progressive Club was trying to organize a Boy Scout troop, and the men's athletic associations, each with about fifteen members, staged games at Washington Park during the summer months, using the proceeds to beautify the grounds.

Miss Irwin talks much of the "old" and "new" Negro. The former, still possessing some of the attitudes of pre–Civil War days, was willing to continue his dependence upon whites, "go on just as things are." The latter believed in the essential equality of all races, felt the stirrings of race consciousness and race pride, appreciated the advantages of education, and thought the black man would have to work out his own destiny. "He lives a life of variety and increasing intellectual activity," she wrote. "He is not merely an imitator, he is a thinker. And he seeks recognition of that fact." [7] In her view all classes of the black community were becoming conscious of a need for solidarity and, as "old" Negroes passed on, tended to reject white guidance. The poorest blacks, in her opinion, sometimes hated whites as a group, the middle class (who had the most association with them) were rather indifferent, and the elite, bitter.[8]

William L. Leap's exhaustive analysis of the Red Hill community, a Phelps-Stokes study published in 1933, discloses that though segregation certainly existed in rural Albemarle, it was merely an accepted pattern of daily life common to much of the nation during those years.[9] Whites lived in clearly defined neighborhoods with their own stores; blacks, in other areas with similar facilities. Leap found only twelve Negro families with automobiles, a fact which had considerable influence upon local society. Negro religious services began rather late each Sunday morning (11 A.M.) to accommodate many who had to walk to church. For most black youngsters education ceased with elementary school since few could get to the county's only black high school at Union Ridge, and many were migrating to towns and cities both to work and continue their training. However, lack of mobility had advantages. Black churches and especially lodges and fraternal groups exhibited somewhat more vigor than those of whites living in the Red Hill area. Whites, in fact, were unable to keep any lodge alive, most individuals preferring to associate with various organizations in Batesville and Charlottesville. Blacks, on the other hand, had three healthy lodges: St. Luke's, the Shepherds, and

[7] Irwin, p. 30.   [8] Ibid., p. 109.
[9] Leap, *Red Hill—Neighborhood Life and Race Relations in a Rural Section* (Charlottesville, 1933).

Odd Fellows, all in effect benefit insurance companies. St. Luke's had membership groups at South Garden, Cross Roads, and Hickory Hill, and several bodies, usually with about thirty-five members, had their own halls. About 40 percent of Red Hill's whites and 71 percent of its blacks attended regularly the meetings of some fraternal or agricultural group, exclusive of those involved with church and school activities.

One of the first times that racial matters far from Albemarle exerted local influence was in March 1933, when blacks and whites gathered at Mt. Zion Church in Charlottesville to form a committee to raise funds to aid the Scottsboro boys, nine Alabama black youths charged with raping two white women. Five prominent local Negroes and two University of Virginia students spearheaded this drive. A few days later when County Superintendent A. L. Bennett mentioned this sensational case while speaking to the local ministerial association, the leading white Baptist minister, Rev. H. W. Battle, for one, was furious. It was, in his opinion, something which should not be discussed. Two years later, in August 1935, a young black woman from Richmond, Alice C. Jackson, age twenty-two, applied for graduate study in French at the University of Virginia. A graduate of Virginia Union and once a student at Smith College, Miss Jackson appears to have been well qualified, but the board of visitors summarily turned down her application, noting simply that enrollment of Negroes was contrary to established policy. Within a year the visitors had to deal with thirty more applicants who received similar treatment. However, in 1950 Gregory Swanson, the first of his race to be so honored, was admitted to the law school.

Quite obviously, in the intervening years, 1936–50, much had occurred. Federal programs during the depression years and after, World War II, and both increasing demands by blacks and rising educational levels creating new expectations all had their effects; nevertheless, as with the Scottsboro boys and Miss Jackson's pioneer effort to enroll at the university, national and even international events, not local, were shaping the future of race relations in both Charlottesville and Albemarle. South Carolina's Strom Thurmond, speaking as a staunch states' rights candidate, drew the largest crowd seen in Charlottesville during the 1948 presidential campaign. The following year the city and county agreed to build a huge joint high school for Negroes (Jackson P. Burley School), and black golfers were permitted to use the municipal course at McIntire Park one day each week. Blacks continued to cheer the Cavaliers from the end zone at Scott Stadium, and whites, if they chose to watch the Burley Bears (probably the most exciting local eleven of those years), sat in the shadows of the goalposts, but the days of segregation as a way of life clearly were numbered.

During the 1940s, quietly and almost unnoticed, the Charlottesville Inter-Racial Commission came into being. This group of some thirty citizens, about equally divided between white and black, met for the first time in December 1942, with Rev. Benjamin F. Bunn, pastor of the First Colored Baptist Church, as chairman. Other prominent members include Lambert Molyneaux and Jack Dalton of the university community, Rabbi Leonard Kasle, and Dr. Dwight M. Chalmers. In general, this association was composed of black professional people (ministers, social workers, and teachers), white clergymen, and a scattering of University of Virginia faculty. They usually met in facilities provided by the Catholic and Presbyterian churches or in the county office building, and their initial concern was not integration per se but nursery schools and better housing and working conditions for local blacks. By 1949 this organization, which later became the local chapter of the Virginia Council on Human Relations, could report that the Carver Inn, the only Negro hotel in Charlottesville, was serving various racially mixed groups without incident. Yet at that first meeting during the dark days of World War II, members of this interracial body were listed separately in the minutes by race; however, this rather incongrous practice was soon abandoned.

In 1949 John S. Battle, a distinguished attorney with two decades of experience in the state legislature and son of the Baptist clergyman who winced at mere mention of the Scottsboro case, became governor of Virginia, the first local resident to live in the chief executive's mansion in over a century. Battle, a protégé of the Byrd machine, had to fight off a remarkable challenge from liberal elements within his Democratic party and apparently beat Francis Pickens Miller only with the aid of Republican votes.[10] Colonel Miller, once a member of the General Assembly from Fairfax, was also a local resident, having moved to Albemarle after service during World War II which included duty on the staff of General Dwight D. Eisenhower. For the most part, Battle enjoyed four rather peaceful and fruitful years since confrontation over education policies did not develop until after his term ended. Ironically, his most trying moments came as a

[10] For a thorough analysis of Battle's career as governor, see Peter R. Henriques, "John S. Battle and Virginia Politics, 1948–1953" (Ph.D. diss., University of Virginia, 1971).

result of a lurid rape in Martinsville, a case reminiscent of what happened in Alabama in the 1930s, although in this instance little doubt existed as to the guilt of most of the seven black youths involved. Eventually, after many legal appeals, all were executed. Battle had good rapport with the General Assembly, and the main thrust of his legislative program was the creation of truly equal public schools for both races throughout the state. He projected expenditures on education totaling $75 million, and in March 1950 Albemarle County unveiled a seven-year school improvement package costing $3.4 million. These plans included consolidation of all white high schools, nine new buildings, and extensive alteration of numerous existing structures. Battle, a segregationist, said these classrooms must be built and properly equipped because it was the "right" thing to do, but it was apparent that he and other southern leaders were putting their houses in order for the struggle they knew was coming. Even as Battle's term ended, the local NAACP was registering strong protests with the Charlottesville City Council. In January 1954 members complained that facilities at Burley, only three years old, were inferior to those found at Lane and expressed alarm when the councilors tried to divert $70,000 earmarked for Burley to Jefferson. After leaving office Battle became attorney for the city school board and for several years tilted with federal judges in a doomed attempt to maintain the status quo. By the late 1950s his son, John S. Battle, Jr., then Charlottesville's city attorney, stepped into the breach and became legal spokesman for the board.

The ensuing fifteen-year struggle, centered largely in Charlottesville, Norfolk, and Arlington, with the outcome destined to establish trends throughout Albemarle County and other communities of the Old Dominion, can be divided into three phases.[11] From May 17, 1954, when the Supreme Court spoke, to September 8, 1959, when a dozen black students enrolled peacefully at Lane High School and Venable Elementary School, local residents were subjected to emotional appeals, threats, and predictions of dire consequences representing all points of view concerning segregation. The second period, following very limited token integration and covering the years to August 31, 1965, was marked by efforts to establish private white schools with tuition grants to parents and the birth of intricate pupil

---

[11] Much has already been written on this subject. For a review, first at the local and then the state levels, see Dallas R. Crowe, "Desegregation of Charlottesville, Virginia, Public Schools, 1954–1969: A Case Study" (Ph.D. diss., University of Virginia, 1971), and Virginius Dabney, *Virginia: The New Dominion,* pp. 528–47.

placement schemes. Lyndon Johnson's far-reaching Civil Rights Act of July 2, 1964, and continuing defeat in federal courts took the steam out of this campaign to maintain separate facilities, not only in schools but in restaurants and other realms of local life as well. (Segregation of Charlottesville's buses and trains, by the way, ended quietly in January 1956 with removal of all signs requiring separation of the races.) Beginning in September 1965, the city school board, which after much agitation had its first Negro member, funeral home director Raymond L. Bell, bowed to the inevitable and effectively desegregated the entire system. Two years earlier Albemarle's supervisors fired county school board members who placed a ban on all interschool athletics if one school was integrated, replacing them with individuals who rescinded that order and also, in time, began desegregation of county classrooms. Meanwhile, Charlottesville's police force enrolled its first black employees, James W. Jones and Mrs. Rosetta Louise Whitlock.

The third phase, extending perhaps to 1969, was characterized by racial friction in some schools, notably Lane, but little actual violence. In fact, just as state authorities strengthened the forces of resistance in the mid-1950s, federal action during these years emboldened those advocating compliance. There is little doubt that the great majority of Charlottesville and Albemarle citizens preferred segregated schools, but if their maintenance meant an end to public education, then, admittedly with much reluctance, they would accept integration. This view, that the continued existence of public schools was all-important, was propounded forcefully by Colgate Darden, former governer and president of the University of Virginia from 1947 to 1959, from the outset of this battle. The business community, fearful that industry and investment would pass Virginia by and go elsewhere, concurred; however, evolution of this general consensus was slow and tortuous. In a sense, perhaps delay possessed advantages. Every conceivable view was aired fully, and when Governor Lindsay Almond closed both Lane and Venable in September 1958 to prevent court-ordered integration, the community realized the full implications of Senator Harry Byrd's so-called massive resistance. On the other hand, this futile struggle cost thousands of tax dollars in legal fees, disrupted classrooms and learning, split the city into warring factions, raised false hopes among those fighting change, and, in the end, contributed directly to the demise of the political machine that had guided Virginia's destiny for decades.

In the beginning it appeared that state officials would acquiesce to the Supreme Court ruling of 1954. Governor Thomas Stanley,

Battle's successor, named a commission to study the matter, but it soon became apparent that Senator Byrd and politicians from rural Southside counties intended to wage an all-out fight against any form of integration. To a large degree, this struggle pitted age against youth, rural against urban dwellers, with Virginia's blacks, a distinct minority and the pawns in the fray, watching more or less from the sidelines. Ultimately the General Assembly took over control of all schools, suspended attendance laws, and outlined a complex pupil placement plan, all moves designed to thwart integration. The state gubernatorial race of 1957 provides some insight into how Charlottesville voters viewed these events. A predominately black ward backed Republican Ted Dalton, while Democrat Lindsay Almond, the winner, received small majorities in two wards and substantial support in another.

In 1958, a crucial year in this unfolding drama, Darden continued his fight to save public classrooms, now aided by Chester Babcock, editor of the *Daily Progress*, an increasingly active Council on Human Relations chapter, and, more importantly, a newly organized Committee for Public Education. With the closing of Lane and Venable by Almond, Mayor Thomas Michie added his voice in support, asking simply that the Old Dominion "accept the degree of integration accepted by every state which borders Virginia." [12] In January 1959, after adverse rulings on massive resistance in both state and federal courts, Almond made one last wild assertion of defiance, "We have just begun to fight," and then capitulated. A few days later Lane and Venable reopened on a segregated basis for the remainder of the school year. Meanwhile, segregationists set up several private schools, two of which managed, despite many difficulties, to remain in operation, Rock Hill Academy and Robert E. Lee Elementary School. The former soon had 345 students; Lee, 190. Under the tuition grant scheme existing until 1969, parents received some $234 a year from city and state to help meet costs.

Construction and location of public school buildings, naturally enough, became part of this entire controversy. Just before the Supreme Court decision the county opened a new white high school serving all communities except Scottsville, and in January 1955 the city unveiled two white elementary schools, Burnley-Moran on Long Street and Johnson on Cherry Avenue. Then, for a time, city and county ceased to build, but by the late 1950s, forced by population pressures, both were contemplating new structures. At first city authorities planned to erect two more elementary schools for whites and

[12] Crowe, pp. 114–15.

make further addition to Jefferson Elementary; however, when the smoke cleared, both Jefferson and Burley had been closed, their pupils transferred elsewhere, and the proposed elementary classrooms transformed into integrated junior high schools, Buford on Cherry Avenue and Walker on Dairy Road.

Gerrymandering of school districts and freedom of choice schemes tried during the second phase, 1959–65, satisfied few and resulted in serious overcrowding in some classrooms. And, after passage of the Civil Rights Act of 1964 and repeated rebuffs in federal courts, it became clear to many that true integration was the only answer. Judge John Paul, who dealt the local school board several setbacks during these eventful years, poured out his frustrations in a letter to a friend written on September 12, 1958. Paul, a cautious, thoughtful man, felt, on one hand, that the Supreme Court had to be obeyed; on the other, he would have been content if that obedience were merely procedural, not substantive. Paul was especially distressed by the hard-nosed defiance of the Byrd machine and the silence of those who, he thought, should speak out in behalf of public education. He frequently told associates that he was unable to understand the attitude of the state government and was distressed by the failure of editors, religious leaders, and professional men and women to make their views known. If Judge Paul, the man at the vortex of this local debate, was disturbed by both action and inaction of various forces within the Old Dominion, then perhaps one can appreciate the bafflement and confusion experienced by parents and children, white and black, of Charlottesville and Albemarle during these traumatic years.

The second great confrontation of these decades concerned annexation, an issue which split the community no less than the integration fight but along different lines. On two occasions, in 1963 and 1968, the city waged successful court battles to annex county property on its borders (see table 13). The first assault, encompassing 2,514 acres and increasing the corporate limits by 61 percent, proved to be a hell-for-leather affair which aroused considerable acrimony, perhaps because, to that date, this was the largest bite yet taken by the city. The second, involving only 51 acres, stirred few to action. Then, in March 1970, in what turned out to be a premature move, a group of community leaders (including some county officials) engineered a referendum on merger of Charlottesville and Albemarle. In the eyes of opponents this was nothing less than "massive" annexation, and arguments that merger would cost less in the long run than endless legal wrangling to keep up with mushrooming suburbs swayed few. Pleas that consolidation would result in greater efficiency also

Table 13. Growth of Charlottesville by annexation

Year	Acres annexed	Total acreage	Percentage increase
1765		38	
1818	18	56	47
1860	118	174	211
1875	44	218	25
1888	564	782	259
1916	1,676	2,458	214
1938	1,660	4,118	68
1963	2,514	6,632	61
1968	51	6,683	.007

SOURCE: Map, Charlottesville City Planning Commission (1968).

fell upon deaf ears as cries against an "isolated bureaucracy," high taxes, and a school system manipulated by city educators became more and more common.

Most county residents feared, frankly, that several well-established land developers, with the acquiescence and perhaps even the cooperation of Albemarle's officialdom, were embarking upon massive, planned, forced urbanization. Property owners, especially those with a small farm or a home and a few acres of land, were alarmed that they would be taxed heavily to support schools, water systems, and sewage facilities for an urban complex not unlike that found in Virginia counties near Washington. They realized that these increased costs might force them to sell out and move elsewhere.

Voters rejected this proposal by an overwhelming margin, four to one in the county, two to one in the city. Only two precincts, both in Charlottesville, backed the proposition. Considering this trend of events — recurring annexation fights and now debates over merger — one can be excused from wondering if perhaps, just perhaps, separation of city and county in 1888 was a serious mistake. For, as Albemarle grows more and more urban, city-county interests and problems are becoming increasingly similar, and merger, even if not accomplished in a legal sense, clearly is occurring to some degree. The views of those dedicated to preserving the character and charm of quiet little rural communities some fifteen or twenty miles from Charlottesville's sprawl can be appreciated. The city, on its part, has a duty to try to exert some control over development on its borders — homes, supermarkets, apartments, factories, research facilities built on land which may soon be within its corporate limits and whose owners, despite their present denials, will no doubt eventually request numerous municipal services. Nevertheless, the hard fact remains that as proposed construction mounted in Albemarle to unprecedented heights ($13.6 million in 1962 alone) and dwindled within Charlottesville, city fathers, some of them still imbued with the spirit of boosterism, and ambitious developers viewed that economic upsurge with covetous eyes.

The heart of the matter was Barracks Road Shopping Center: "Shop in Ease and Comfort in Our Arcade Connected Shops—Acres of Free Parking." This ever-increasing complex, carved out of woodlands bordering Route 29 North by the Rinehart interests, opened in October 1959. One corner of it displaced a famous tavern which for a generation or so was an oasis for thousands of thirsty university students, Carroll's Tea Room, often said to possess neither tea nor room. The result is a bleak stretch of concrete and asphalt, taking no advantage of the natural environment from which it was bulldozed. Though this shopping center served the needs of the university section and new suburbs such as Hessian Hills and Greenbrier, it also created many problems. It has provided impetus for even greater suburban development and still more stores and supermarkets in the region, severely taxed highways and roads in the immediate area (despite "acres of free parking"), and stymied economic life in downtown Charlottesville. Retail sales at Barracks Road reportedly grew by as much as 14 percent a year in 1962–66, while increasing only 3 percent in the traditional shopping area and, in fact, declining slightly in 1966. One must remember, however, that cumulative growth at a new, expanding facility always will be statistically impressive and that, in contrast to the downtown section, Barracks Road is the home of several high-volume grocery outlets.

Nevertheless, ironies abound. In 1919 Hollis Rinehart built a proud eight-story tower in the heart of the city; forty years later his heirs erected a complex several miles away which, for all practical purposes, has left his monument aloof and alone. City fathers for decades gave voice to countless appeals designed to generate population growth and economic activity, only to discover that both were occurring, not within their corporate limits, but just outside their borders.

The solution, of course, was annexation, and soon after the first customer appeared at Barracks Road a battle began to add four and one-half square miles of county land to the city. During the two years which followed, even the city's bicentennial celebration and the Cavaliers' first football victory after twenty-eight consecutive defeats were overshadowed somewhat by this bitter debate. Municipal authorities eventually convinced the courts that their view was correct, that the shopping center and several nearby communities were essentially urban and should become part of Charlottesville. However, in the final weeks before annexation became effective on January 1, 1963, the county, much to the distress of the city, issued construction permits totaling more than $5 million, most of them for apartments and commercial buildings on land shortly to be annexed. The most controversial proposal was a 104-apartment, twelve-story complex to be built in the Rutledge area. As soon as annexation was accomplished, the city immediately ordered work stopped, precipitating still more legal confrontations. In time, though, it became apparent that many of the eleventh-hour permits issued by the county were merely speculative and most of the contemplated structures never appeared, among them the huge apartment tower which would have loomed over the city (and county) skyline.

The turmoil of both annexation and attempted merger has had very dramatic results, exacerbating city-county relations and creating considerable resentment among many Albemarle residents against their county officials. In 1974 a special grand jury probe headed by Robert Merrill of Greenwood castigated some of these individuals for inept administrative practices, favoritism toward certain land developers, and failure to enforce county ordinances. In Merrill's view, one key problem is concentration of the assessment, collection, and expenditure of taxes in a single office. He believes the county should consider a commission form of government with elected revenue officials, one man to assess taxes, another to collect them.

This debate has given rise to new attitudes toward zoning and land taxes within the county. Until 1974 all land was assessed according to its potential value; but, beginning in October of that year, a land use tax was instituted. The board of supervisors agreed to set values for acres used for agriculture, horticulture, open space, and forest substantially lower than those of land destined for residential use or commercial development. Upon application, an owner received an exemption based upon soil quality, forestation, and type of use, perhaps 50 to 75 percent less than what fair market value might be. As long as his land retains that specific status, he continues to pay lower taxes; should he sell to a developer or decide to alter that special status, then he is liable for back taxes and interest equal to fair market value. The aim of this voluntary program is, of course, twofold: to relieve farmers and rural folk of inordinate tax burdens and to preserve some of Albemarle's open country. County leaders also are considering a cluster approach toward future development; that is, urbanization would occur only in certain established regions possessing adequate facilities. However, those living in such areas often view clusters with as much alarm as annexation or merger since, as far as they are concerned, the results would be similar.

Charlottesville itself has not been free from controversy. Again, to some extent, Barracks Road Shopping Center and other shopping areas being constructed just outside of the present city limits have provided the seeds of this discontent. Late in 1974, as part of the bicentennial celebration, Charlottesville began building a downtown pedestrian mall costing $3.5 million. Several blocks of Main Street in the heart of the city were swept clear of traffic, cars and trucks diverted to Water and Market streets, and a brick plaza created where wagons, carriages, street cars, buses, trucks, and autos once reigned supreme. Part of the cost, $500,000, was borne by merchants themselves, some of whom had considerable misgiving concerning the wisdom of what they consider an unorthodox venture at best. Yet both storekeepers and city fathers have a large stake in the downtown area. The former must remain truly competitive to stay in business; if they do not, expanded county shopping centers could siphon off more and more sales tax revenue from municipal coffers in the future. To some the plaza is little more than a subsidy of tax dollars aiding downtown merchants; to others, blatant interference with private enterprise; and to still others, a very necessary innovation which had to be implemented to save Charlottesville's traditional business district. Nevertheless, one cannot help wondering what an early nineteenth-century wagoner from the Valley or a prosperous merchant prince of the 1890s might say if he came down Vinegar Hill, now denuded of buildings, to be greeted by a brick-paved Main Street decorated with trees and kiosks.

At the eastern end of this expanse stands Charlottesville's new City Hall. Built at a cost of $1.2 million and officially opened by Miss America, Miss Virginia, and Mayor G. A. Vogt in March 1969, it replaced a comfortable, rambling, but inadequate Fifth Street structure which had served as the center of municipal life for three-quarters of a century.

It is apparent to everyone that Thomas Jefferson's county is becoming less and less agricultural, especially within a radius of ten miles or so of Charlottesville. Apartment complexes, sprawling outward instead of toward the heavens, have eaten up hundreds of acres of land which once grew tobacco, corn, and hay. In the 1960s two censuses of rural life were taken by the federal government, the first in 1964, the second in 1969. In those five years alone the number of farms decreased from 964 to 706, although their average size grew from 252 to 275.6 acres. This average size is substantially larger than the 114.1 acres of 1935, but the total number of farm units has shrunk from that year's peak of 3,197. Of course, Albemarle farms come in all shapes and sizes, but most are between 10 to 49 acres (125 farms) and 280 to 499 acres (137 farms). Only five encompass more than 2,000 acres. The majority of the larger units have 30 to 100 acres of cropland; only two have more than 500 acres, and none over 1,000. In 1969 there were thirty-four tenant farmers, an increase of twelve since 1964; only one of these individuals was black. Twenty-four Negroes owned and operated farms in 1969. The total value in that year of all land and buildings was $83.2 million, and the market value of agricultural products, $7.9 million, up from $5 million five years earlier. More than half of all farms, 399, were owned by part-time or retired operators, a statistic which should surprise no one.

Few farmers now have sheep or lambs, and none harvests tobacco, the county's "first love." Cattle and hog populations, 34,000 and 5,000 respectively, remain essentially unchanged despite a decline in the number of individual farms. Production of broiler chickens, encouraged by expansion of Morton's processing plant which opened in Crozet in 1953, has increased somewhat in recent years, while laying pullet flocks have become smaller. Horse raising continues important, nearly a third of all farms reporting horses (and ponies) in 1969. Peach and apple production is decreasing rapidly. Only fifteen farms sold peaches commercially in that year, while nineteen marketed apples. One vineyard, relic of what was once an important industry begun by William Hotopp in 1866, still was producing grapes. Actually, Albemarle's share of the Old Dominion's fruit crop began to decline during the previous decade. In 1956 the county, long the state's leading peach-growing area, slipped to second place behind Frederick County and was no longer among the top five counties in apple production, a development which cast a dark shadow upon Charlottesville's annual Apple Harvest Festival begun six years before. Even as that hoopla got underway in October 1950, the fruit industry was in deep trouble. William S. Wolfe, who studied the orchards of Crozet during that year, noted that 90 percent of the apple trees were over thirty years of age and 75 percent of the peach trees were more than ten years old.[13] According to Wolfe, many

[13] Wolfe, "A Geographical Study of the Orchards of the Crozet District, Albemarle County, Virginia" (M.A. thesis, University of Virginia, 1950), pp. 45–46.

growers, especially small producers, were not renewing their orchards; instead, because of rising costs, trees were being uprooted
and fields converted to pasturage for beef cattle.

Ray Y. Gildea, Jr., surveyed Albemarle's cattle in 1950 and found
that Hereford and Angus were the most popular breeds in these expanding beef herds and Guernseys held top rank among dairy cattle.[14]
They were concentrated in several distinct regions: within a few
miles of Scottsville and Carter's Bridge; near North Garden, Ivy,
Crozet, and Greenwood; and along Route 22 between Shadwell and
Cobham. Yet livestock and poultry populations do not tell the full
story since their numbers can fluctuate dramatically from year to
year depending upon market conditions. More importantly, in 1950
about one-third of Albemarle's labor force was employed in agriculture. Ten years later 14 percent were directly involved with farming,
and in 1970 only 847 individuals over the age of sixteen, out of a total
county labor force of 14,208, were full-time agricultural workers. In
short, over 90 percent of Albemarle's residents technically were "rural
non-farm" folk working at food-processing and rubber plants in
Crozet and Scottsville, perhaps commuting to Charlottesville,
Waynesboro, and even Lovingston to work in offices, stores, and
small factories, or employed in a professional capacity at numerous
research facilities, many of them drawn to the region by advantages
offered by the University of Virginia.

The impact of these changes, more subtle than any emotion-
charged struggle over education or annexation, is profound indeed.
Not only those of school age and individuals living on the outskirts of
Charlottesville are affected, but all citizens of Albemarle from Gibson
Mountain to the banks of the James. Driving many miles to and from
work is becoming a way of life for family after family, many of whom
have moved to the community from other parts of the nation, and
gone is the rhythm dictated by the seasons—planting, cultivation, and
harvest time—which dominated Albemarle's daily existence for over
two centuries. Although sentimentalists may deplore these trends,
and with good reason, there are inherent advantages for the community as a whole and for individuals involved. The divisions between urban and rural worlds that characterized city-county relations
for decades are being mitigated considerably, or at least blurred, and
annual income, once subject to the caprice of weather and national
and international markets, is much more stable. Those most dis-

[14] Gildea, "Geographical Aspects of Cattle Production in Albemarle County,
Virginia" (M.A. thesis, University of Virginia, 1950), pp. 118–20.

tressed by the change undoubtedly never watched a windstorm uproot their orchards or prayed for rain as crops withered and died. Albemarle is indeed fortunate that unlike some regions, its fields and woodlands are not being abandoned; instead, green meadows, neat fences, and well-tended lawns surround hundreds of homes, both great and small. Yet the occupants rarely have much rapport with the land they live on other than perhaps cruising their acres on the seats of power-driven mowers. Their "farm" is an investment, a place to live, perhaps a comfortable tax deduction, but not a means of making a living; and the demise of agriculture, long the base of the local economy, is sad to contemplate, for with its passing the yeoman farmer, so revered by Albemarle's first citizen, is no more.

Chapter 20

Bill Hildreth's Charlottesville

W ILLIAM SOBIESKI HILDRETH, orchardist, storekeeper, financial wizard, community leader, avid bridge player, and dedicated sports fan, was, like both of the Old Dominion's spokesmen in the U.S. Senate at mid-century, a product of West Virginia. He was born in Wheeling in 1893, eldest child of a successful doctor with family ties to Albemarle who suddenly terminated his medical career and moved his large brood first to Charles Town and then to Key West on the Stony Point Road. Young Bill, stocky, aggressive, quick-spoken, and self-assured, accumulated high honors at Shenandoah Academy and enrolled briefly at the University of Virginia, 1910–11, but completed his undergraduate days at the University of Wisconsin, where he was a member of the track team and joined Phi Gamma Delta fraternity. Hildreth also studied fruit culture at Ohio State and served in France during World War I as a first lieutenant in the field artillery. Upon returning to Albemarle he managed the family's orchards for several years and was co-owner of a small grocery store at the Corner near the university. According to family tradition, his mother was intent upon raising peacocks and bees, but her son, of more practical bent, quickly turned the Stony Point property into a successful general farm. In 1926 he became assistant to the president of People's National Bank, George R. B. Michie, his father-in-law, and began his rise to regional, even national financial prominence, becoming head of that institution in May 1938. When young Hildreth joined People's, it had assets of $6 million; when he retired as chairman of the board in December 1963 and was given a small second-floor office where, he said, his only callers were pigeons on the window sill, thanks to shrewd management, mergers, and considerable personal drive, that bank's assets had swelled to over $400 million.

Twice married, father of two daughters and one son, this man was a gregarious, engaging, somewhat unpolished, down-to-earth personality who did much during his lifetime to mold present-day Charlottesville and Albemarle. As a member and sometimes president of various groups such as the Chamber of Commerce, Redland Club, Farmington Country Club, and the Thomas Jefferson Memorial

Foundation and spokesman on the boards of numerous corporations, he wielded great power. Unlike Thomas Walker and Senator Martin, his interests centered almost exclusively upon his city and county. Although he possessed political clout, Hildreth never sought political office; instead he labored mightily to build a balanced economy based upon local trade, the university, tourism, and "clean industry," two words which, in his vocabulary, were virtually inseparable. Also, it was his task to preside over the decline of agriculture, a role which must have caused him some pain in view of his great interest in apples and peaches.

For all practical purposes, as head of People's National Bank during the expansive years following World War II, Hildreth became the crown prince of "neo-boosterism." This view of community growth, less blatant and much more realistic than the hoopla of the 1920s, attempted to accommodate conflicting interests for the good of the entire region, urban and rural. In part, Hildreth may have inherited this attitude from his predecessor at People's, who wanted Charlottesville to remain essentially a university community. George Michie, who often introduced his protégé in a jocular way as "my son-in-law Bill, the butcher," was adamantly opposed to construction of the Monticello Hotel and would have preferred a rambling inn rather than a skyscraper with searchlight. However, in his day Bill Hildreth had to grapple with stern economic realities that had not troubled his father-in-law. To provide jobs as farming became less profitable he envisioned an influx of small, light industries, many of them profiting from research facilities at the University of Virginia. None of these, of course, were to be allowed to erect belching smokestacks or import hordes of unskilled workers, developments which would have aroused the ire of the well-to-do in such communities as Keswick, Ivy, and Greenwood, as well as hundreds of Charlottesville residents, nor should any of these establishments upset the prevailing wage scale, rather low by both state and national standards. Since a prime goal was to furnish jobs for local citizens, any business planning to bring a substantial staff to Albemarle received little encouragement. Naturally enough, if clean industry employing largely clerical and white-collar workers came to the community, then both management and workers would need housing, much of it above average in price and quality, creating an ever-expanding market which appealed to developers and real estate agents. And builders and homeowners, in turn, would need bank loans. This formula for controlled growth has worked well indeed, but not without some protest, for scores of local residents, rich and poor, old and new, view

60. William S. Hildreth

61. George R. B. Michie

any alteration in the status quo with considerable abhorrence, an attitude born of a love of tradition and an admirable reverence for old
things and old ways. Yet the other choice, the economic stagnation
and widespread unemployment which can be seen on every hand in
once prosperous counties of eastern Virginia, is sad to contemplate.

Although agent of substantial change, William S. Hildreth was
among those most conscious of Albemarle's historic past. He labored
tirelessly in behalf of Monticello, for example, while permitting himself occasional flights of personal fantasy into realms of history far
beyond the foothills of the Blue Ridge. Like many small of stature
men filled with ambition, he was a great admirer of Napoleon, collecting memorabilia of that eminent Corsican turned dictator and
sometimes dressing up in his image for fancy balls held at Farmington. As a youth, Hildreth also dreamed of becoming an Indian
fighter, and one of his heroes was Jonathan Zane, an ancestor, whose
name his only son bears. Zane, with two brothers, Ebenezer and
Silas, sons of a Pennsylvania farmer who became a non-Quaker by
marrying outside of the fold, in 1769 founded Zanesburg, later called
Wheeling. This trio of trailblazers, Revolutionary fighters, and
swashbuckling land-grabbers was part of the cutting edge of settlement that soon won control of much of what is now West Virginia
and Ohio. Hildreth had a life-size portrait painted of Jonathan Zane
and placed in his office at the bank. Since no one knew what that
eighteenth-century frontiersman looked like, the result was a com-
posite of Hildreth features staring out defiantly, not at a buckskin
world, but into the urbane milieu of twentieth-century finance and
commerce. Perhaps, as he dreamed, if Napoleon, then Albemarle
was his empire; if Zane, then those eager to desecrate that lovely land
with factories were the Indians.

But Bill Hildreth was rarely a dreamer for long. He was a prag-
matic, tough-minded builder who saw the basic needs of his city and
county more clearly than most and tried to steer a compromising,
constructive course between rapid change and agricultural decline,
both of which could have endangered the well-being of all citizens. In
1963, when he retired after thirty-seven years with People's Bank, he
could look back upon a remarkable career, a job well done. Three
years later William S. Hildreth died at the age of seventy-three.
Thus he witnessed the acrimonious annexation fight of the early
1960s but did not live long enough to experience the unpopular merger
referendum of 1970, both the fruits of policies he designed and pursued with characteristic vigor.

The greatest changes in Charlottesville and Albemarle during the quarter century or so which one might call the Hildreth years, 1945 to 1970, were growth in population and in the manner in which people made a living.[1] Yet this population increase was not phenomenal by either state or national standards, nor was it quite as spectacular as federal census figures might indicate (see table 14). Annexation placed more and more citizens within city boundaries, and the 1970 tabulation for the first time in recent decades included university students by local residence, city or county, thus blurring somewhat the total picture. In fact, Chamber of Commerce officials believe that Charlottesville's population may now be declining a bit. During these same years the area's nonwhite population has increased, but at a slower rate than that of the white sector. In 1950 the community was about 18 percent nonwhite; in 1970, 14.6 percent, with slightly more of those individuals living in the city than in the county, 15.5 percent compared to 13.6 percent respectively; but,

Table 14. Population growth, 1950–70

	Charlottesville	Albemarle	Total
1950	25,969	26,662	52,631
1960	29,427	30,969	60,396
1970	38,880	37,780	76,660

SOURCE: *U.S. Census of Population* (Washington, D.C., 1961), 1, Pt. 48A: 12; *1970 Census of Population* (Washington, D.C., 1973), 1, Pt. 48: 13, 15.

again including some 13,000 university students, nearly all of them white, tends to distort any current racial analysis.

In 1970 there were 26,003 year-round dwellings in the city and county, 17,234 of them single-unit structures. Despite a seeming proliferation of rental complexes in the county, the city had many more apartments and mobile homes, 6,147 compared to 2,622 in Albemarle. The area's poorest housing still was near Charlottesville's business district, where 337 units, 25 percent of them without plumbing, rented for an average of $62 per month. And the people of Charlottesville-Albemarle continued to be overwhelmingly of American birth, only 1,200 citizens being foreign born, about equally di-

[1] Much of the information in this chapter comes from material supplied by the Charlottesville-Albemarle Chamber of Commerce and the files of the *Daily Progress*. See especially an excellent review of the 1960s by Alan Bruns which appeared in that daily, Feb. 22–March 3, 1970.

vided between city and county. Of 76,660 residents, 50,539 were natives of the old Dominion.

The most important and cohesive foreign colony, if one can call it that since many members now are American-born, is Charlottesville's Greek community.[2] Consisting of some fifty or sixty families, these people have fulfilled the immigrant dream of success in the New World almost unnoticed by their neighbors. Nearly all came to America nearly penniless, somehow found their way to Albemarle, and set up fruit stands, restaurants, and confectionaries. Their descendants, especially since World War II, often have eschewed these trades for careers in construction, real estate, investment, and education. As a rule, those of Greek heritage are well-to-do, have fine homes, and take special pride in the handsome Greek Orthodox Church built on Perry Drive near Lane High School in 1954. This modern structure, really a community center with meeting hall, classrooms, kitchen, and stage, aroused the ire of a traditional bishop who wanted something more Byzantine; but since local Greeks received no financial aid from the national church, they chose to build what they wanted. Within twenty-four months, with typical Greek abhorrence of debt, the $100,000 complex was paid for in full. Two years later, when Lane and Venable were closed by disputes over integration, this center became an impromptu school ministering to the needs of local students of all faiths.

The decline of agriculture and changes in travel habits, railroad tracks giving way to superhighways, have had a very perceptible impact upon the region; yet as Bill Stevens, a veteran real estate man, is fond of emphasizing, what has happened on Albemarle's land must be seen in perspective. Farms and farm workers are fewer, but maintaining estates, large and small, creates considerable economic activity. Though these acres produce smaller crops and much less income in the traditional sense, feeding and care of cattle and horses (which probably are increasing in number), construction of fences, paddocks, and buildings, money paid in taxes, and all of the many subsidiary needs that rural living entails put millions of dollars into local pockets each year.

If the influence of county life defies absolute analysis, tourism does not. It is big business and source of substantial area income. Some 322 firms in Charlottesville employing 1,929 individuals cater to travelers, both local and out-of-state, and in the county 84 major

[2] See Gloria Galban Smith, "The American Greek Community of Charlottesville, Virginia, 1903–1960" (M.A. thesis, University of Virginia, 1961).

outlets with 757 workers serve tourists in one way or another. In 1973, according to a federal survey of what is called "Virginia's Billion Dollar Industry," sales of these concerns amounted to $36,288,000 in the city and $5,682,000 in the county. In each instance about 17 percent of these dollars represent service to area residents. The region has twenty-one motels with 1,260 rooms, some of them with swimming pools, meeting facilities, and banquet halls, a far cry from the modest accommodations provided by Sunset Lodge when it opened its doors in 1938.

Though the great mass of tourists arrive by car, the community's air and bus facilities improved greatly during these postwar years. In July 1951 city and county agreed, with the aid of federal funds, to build an airport near Earlysville about eight miles north of Charlottesville. This modern establishment opened on August 17, 1954, and during the first four and one-half months Piedmont Airlines, the major carrier, served 3,540 boarding passengers. By 1973 some 47,765 persons were boarding Piedmont planes to points in Virginia, West Virginia, North Carolina, Washington, D.C., Maryland, and New York, and about the same number were arriving at the local airport. Regional charter service also is available. On two occasions area air travel has been marred by tragedy. Late in October 1950 three West Virginia football fans en route to an interstate contest were killed when their small craft hit WCHV's radio tower, and nine years later almost to the day, a Piedmont plane crashed on Buck's Elbow, killing twenty-six people. The sole survivor, Ernest P. Bradley, a union representative from Clifton Forge, was thrown clear but spent seven weeks in the University Hospital recovering from his injuries.

Area bus travel, an outgrowth of the Virginia Stage Lines organized by Sam Jessup in the mid-1920s, was enhanced considerably in December 1963 when Continental Trailways opened a new bus station on West Main Street close by what was once the headquarters of Charlottesville's street railway system. Technically, Charlottesville is an in-between stop on a north-south route from New England to the Deep South, but Trailways also provides service for scores of communities within Albemarle on daily runs to Richmond, Fredericksburg, Waynesboro, and Staunton. Municipal bus service, furnished by the Yellow Transit Company owned by J. T. Graves, was subsidized by annual appropriations ($55,000 in 1974) until acquired by the city in 1975. That company operated ten vehicles for the general public and owned seventeen school buses. Since September 1972 the university has maintained a fleet of blue and orange buses which transport students and personnel from dorms to classrooms. It now has fifteen buses, two of them used for charter purposes. Though rail travel is far less popular than only a decade or so ago, the Southern Railway has three passenger trains departing north for Washington and three more to Lynchburg and points south each day. The Chesapeake and Ohio has four passenger trains leaving its station daily, two of these being Amtrak's James Whitcomb Riley running from Newport News to Chicago.

The area no longer has a first-class commercial hotel in the traditional sense. The Monticello, greeted with so much fanfare in 1926, is now a condominium, and public houses in Afton, Greenwood, and Scottsville have long since closed their doors, victims of the decline of train travel and the rise of the auto and motel. For a decade or so the Thomas Jefferson Inn, creation of the same individuals who built the Barracks Road Shopping complex nearby, catered to the traveling public, but in 1968 that structure was leased to the federal government as an executive training center. In 1963, resplendent with a lavish helping of what passes for Old English charm and overtones of Williamsburg, the Boar's Head Inn and Sports Club opened near Farmington; unlike the country club on the other side of Route 250, it frequently is host to conventions and business meetings and actively encourages this trade. For a time Farmington had a cross-town rival at Keswick when a group of developers purchased the Villa Crawford in 1947 and turned it into a similar operation complete with golf course, pool, clubhouse, and house lots. However, success never smiled upon this venture, and after numerous reorganizations and recurring financial crises, the club finally closed in the early 1970s.

.Whether visitors sleep at Farmington, in motels, or at private homes, they often are drawn to Albemarle by Monticello, Ash Lawn, Michie Tavern, and similar historic landmarks or perhaps come during Garden Week to tour sprawling estates in their springtime splendor. In 1973, for example, 525,032 persons visited Jefferson's mountaintop home; admittedly, many of them came to the area principally to see his university or perhaps sons (and now daughters) studying there. Athletic contests and cultural events, increasingly important since the opening of University Hall and a new university theater, also attract thousands to Charlottesville each year. In 1972 university officials estimated that such visitors were spending $1.6 million in the community annually. Of much greater importance were vast sums spent by the University of Virginia and its students and personnel. In that year nearly 6,000 faculty and staff members received $53 million in wages and students spent $19.1 million locally. Overall, visitors, students, and the institution itself expended $88.4 million, $63.3 million of that sum in direct expenditures and $25.1 million in an indirect fashion which, nonetheless, aided the local economy greatly.

Although the University of Virginia has been a vital factor on the local scene for many decades, the small, clean industries sought by Bill Hildreth and other community leaders are becoming increasingly important (see table 15). They now have a combined annual payroll of over $75 million, somewhat more than the university pumps directly into the Charlottesville-Albemarle area. The venerable woolen mills experienced considerable difficulty in the 1950s, showing a profit during only one year of that decade. In 1959 the firm was purchased by a Pennsylvania manufacturer, but five years later it closed its doors for good and the facilities were sold to a moving and storage company. Management apparently relied too heavily upon traditional fabrics and was unable to adapt the plant to new synthetic materials. The Ix mills, on the other hand, have grappled with changing conditions and continue to prosper. The local textile scene also has been enhanced by creation in 1944 of the Institute of Textile Technology, a small, highly specialized graduate center established at Boxwood, a former Rinehart estate. This operation, located just west of Charlottesville and essentially a training school for management, was perhaps the first research facility to see distinct advantages in a site near the university; however, it did not arrive without protest. The same Keswick residents who bristled when a carpet factory considered settling in their midst and sent it packing to Buena Vista were extremely skeptical of anything incorporating the word *textile* and tried to thwart the institute's plans, even if it was to be located several miles across town and far from the gates of their estates. In addition to the woolen mills, the soapstone quarries in southwestern Albemarle's Esmont-Alberene area have cut operations drastically after a checkered career which saw production vacillate to and from Schuyler in Nelson County from time to time.

In March 1972 approximately 7,540 persons were employed in manufacturing, most of them producing either electrical and electronic equipment or food products. Between 1950 and 1972 this working force nearly tripled, but at a very uneven rate, much of the upsurge occurring in the 1950s. Another 3,850 individuals were engaged in education and research; development of this sector of the economy basically paralleled enrollment gains at the university. And

Table 15. Major manufacturing firms in the Charlottesville-Albemarle area, 1972

Firm	Location	Established	Principal product	Approximate number of employees
Established before 1950				
Monticello Dairy	Charlottesville	pre-1950	dairy products	120
Coca-Cola Bottling Company	Charlottesville	pre-1950	soft drinks	20–40
Pepsi-Cola Bottling Company	Charlottesville	pre-1950	soft drinks	100–150
Frank Ix and Sons	Charlottesville	pre-1950	broad woven fabrics	460
Uniroyal, Inc.	Scottsville	pre-1950	tire cord and fabrics	450
Barnes Lumber Corporation	Albemarle	pre-1950	wood products	50–100
Blue Ridge Veneer & Plywood	Albemarle	pre-1950	veneer and plywood	70
Charlottesville Newspapers	Charlottesville	pre-1950	newspapers	120
Michie Company	Charlottesville	pre-1950	book publishers	210
Jarman Printing Company	Charlottesville	pre-1950	commercial printing	20–40
H. T. Perron Company	Charlottesville	pre-1950	concrete products	40
Established 1950–59				
Acme Visible Records	Crozet	1950	metal office furniture	720
Teledyne Avionics [a]	Earlysville	1951	industrial measuring and control instruments	160
King Lindsay Printing Corp.	Charlottesville	1953	commercial printing	20
Morton Frozen Foods, Division of ITT Contintental Baking	Crozet	1953	frozen foods	1,510
Smith Land and Lumber Company	North Garden	1953	rough lumber	20–40

Table 15 (*cont.*)

Firm	Location	Established	Principal product	Approximate number of employees
Stromberg-Carlson Corporation [b]	Albemarle	1954	telephone equipment	1,020
Sperry-Rand Corporation [c]	Albemarle	1956	radio-telephone transmission equipment	660
Ovenaire [d]	Charlottesville	1957	oscillators, electronic ovens, megaphones	150
Allied Concrete Company	Charlottesville	1959	concrete products	60
Established 1960–72				
R. A. Yancey Lumber Corp.	Albemarle	1960	sawmill and planer	30
Murray Division of Arrow-Hart [e]	Earlysville	1962	electrical equipment	610
A. T. O., Inc.	Albemarle	1964	nonelectrical machinery	30–60
Automated Structures	Proffit	1964	prefab wooden buildings	90
Chemetron Welding Products	Albemarle	1964	welding equipment	180
General Electric Company	Charlottesville	1966	industrial controls	180
Walter Kiddie and Company	Charlottesville	1966	firefighting equipment, aerospace accessories	100–150
Ridge Electronics Corporation	Charlottesville	1968	electronics components	20
Systems, Technology, Inc.	Albemarle	1968	radio-television transmission equipment	20–40

Table 15 (*cont.*)

Firm	Location	Established	Principal product	Approximate number of employees
Coyne and Delany Company	Charlottesville	1969	plumbing fixture fittings	30
Mr. Hank Enterprises, Ltd.	Charlottesville	1971	women's apparel	20–40

SOURCE: *Projections and Economic Base Analysis: The Albemarle County–Charlottesville City Area* (Richmond, 1973), p. 29.

[a] This company is an outgrowth of Specialties, Inc., an aircraft instrument plant established in conjunction with creation of the Charlottesville-Albemarle Airport.

[b] Originally U.S. Instruments, that company merged with Stromberg-Carlson in January 1965.

[c] Ironically, when the local Sperry-Piedmont branch opened, no one seems to have remembered that the famed Monticello Hotel searchlight was a Sperry product.

[d] Ovenaire was omitted from this survey.

[e] Originally Panorama, that company is now a division of Murray-Hart.

some 2,130 persons were employed by medical services, notably at the University of Virginia Hospital (1,700) and Blue Ridge Sanatorium (240).

Financial services (banks and insurance companies) provided employment for another 1,400 people, the largest concentration being the eastern regional offices of State Farm Mutual Insurance Company, which opened its Emmet Street quarters in 1952. Charlottesville's two largest banks, People's and National, erected numerous branches during the decades after World War II in an effort to keep pace with suburban growth. Eventually they were permitted to acquire smaller banks in nearby counties, and in 1963 Bill Hildreth's People's consolidated with the National Bank of Commerce in Norfolk to form Virginia National Bank, at that time the second largest financial institution in the Old Dominion. This merger, conceived and cemented by Hildreth, reflects his deep-seated antipathy toward Richmond financial circles, which he considered rather stodgy and uninspired.

In 1961 the federal government established a regional office of the new Department of Health, Education, and Welfare in Charlottesville. Employing some four hundred persons, these quarters served five mid-South states, the District of Columbia, Puerto Rico, and the Virgin Islands. In 1969 this facility moved to Philadelphia, but the imposing structure near historic Court Square later become the home of the U.S. Army's Foreign Science Technology Center, which now provides jobs for approximately the same number of civilian workers as before. Some military personnel also are employed in the area's recruiting offices and in the ROTC program and the army's Judge Advocate General's School at the University of Virginia. The state government, which operates the university, its hospital, Blue Ridge Sanatorium, and various smaller facilities (the Virginia Division of Forestry, Division of Mineral Resources, Department of Vocational Rehabilitation, Virginia Commission for the Visually Handicapped, and so on) is by far the region's largest single employer.

As it has for decades, Charlottesville continues to be a major trading center and retail outlet for Albemarle and several surrounding counties. In 1956, bucking the trend to suburban shopping, Miller and Rhoads of Richmond opened a six-story department store at Fourth and Main, and the following year Sears Roebuck split the difference and erected new quarters on West Main Street which were neither downtown nor in the suburbs. The only other commercial centers of any consequence within Albemarle, Scottsville and Crozet, have changed somewhat during recent years. The latter, profiting from business activity generated by Acme Visible Records and Morton Frozen Foods, now has new suburbs and its own shopping center, and in 1970 that community's population soared past the 1,000 mark for the first time in history. Scottsville, Albemarle's only incorporated town and nearly as large as Crozet although it has less than 300 inhabitants within its official boundaries, also has a shopping mall; but construction of this collection of stores on high ground away from the waters of the James was prompted, not by any upsurge in population, but by recurring floods which have ravaged the area for generations. It is ironic that the river, long that town's lifeblood, is in some measure its undoing. A devastating storm in August 1969, the last gasp of a hurricane with the genteel name of Camille, proved to be a crippling blow. That disaster, which arrived before dawn without warning, turned Nelson County into a living hell and killed some 125 persons, most of them engulfed by landslides. Southern Albemarle was more fortunate, but nonetheless damage to property in the Scottsville community was awesome. Three years later Agnes caused even more havoc, water rising in the business district to record heights and submerging signs commemorating what had happened only a

62. Morton Frozen Foods, Crozet

short time before. Agnes was followed four months later by what residents call affectionately an "old-timey" flood, just a few feet of water, a nuisance they have learned to cope with through the years. Reluctantly and with considerable sadness, some local businessmen, but by no means all, concluded that a new, safe commercial center had to be developed.

In addition to floods, Albemarle has been hit from time to time by tornadoes, especially along a line from Charlottesville west to the mountains. In August 1922, a spectacular blast, said to have been "the worst storm in over thirty years," touched down briefly at Crozet and then whirled through Ivy leveling trees, ruining crops, tearing off roofs, and smashing small outbuildings and barns. On one farm alone, that of H. W. Vandevender, over a thousand trees were flattened to the ground. The prolific Lewis family, then encamped at Forest Hill for an annual reunion, saw their tents, cots, and belongings scattered over the surrounding countryside. Incredibly, no one was killed. In October 1959 another tornado struck Ivy, this time wreaking similar havoc and claiming eleven lives.

Two other venerable river towns of southern Albemarle, Warren and Howardsville, also were hard hit by the storms of 1969 and 1972. Warren's ferry no longer plies the waters of the James, the little community is littered with abandoned vehicles and rusting railroad equipment, and its railway station, windows broken and doors sagging, stands deserted, the dreary scene relieved only by a chalk-scrawled message in what once was the baggage shed: "Pollard is the Man— Nov., 1929." Howardsville still has a general store which doubles as a post office, a charming old Methodist church, several fine homes, and what is reputed to be the second oldest Masonic lodge home in Virginia, a historic structure moved many years ago from Warminster, a village which has disappeared completely. In addition to general agriculture, pulpwood continues to be an important element in the economy of this region, as it is in southeastern Albemarle as well.

Other little communities south of Routes 250 and 64, which divide the county roughly in half, have suffered similar fates. Covesville, still an important fruit-packing center, has all but been obliterated by the four-laning of Route 29. Esmont, created by quarries and a rail line, the Nelson and Albemarle Railway which ended passenger service in 1950 and closed down completely in January 1963, stands bleak and quiet, nearly all of its store windows vacant and festooned with cobwebs. Old Dominion consists of one store and a group of small homes, and only in Alberene does quarrying of soapstone continue in a very limited fashion, a crew of six men being employed there in mid-1974. This industry, once a major enterprise and a source of jobs for southwestern Albemarle and much of Nelson County, has suffered both from shifts in market demands and capricious management. In 1956 the surviving company, which proudly supplied window ledges for Rockefeller Center and material for scores of other prestigious landmarks, was sold to Georgia Marble. Stone taken from Alberene today is finished either in Schuyler or Georgia, most of it becoming building facing or bathroom walls. Only Batesville, a pleasant collection of comfortable, neatly painted old homes, exhibits much vigor. It has two charming churches and a busy general store, Page's, established in 1913 and now air-conditioned, which also serves as the local post office.

In the northern half of Albemarle, Proffit and Burnleys no longer reveal any commercial activity, although the latter still has a distinctive one-lane bridge which arches dramatically over the Southern trains passing underneath, not stopping as they once did. Nortonsville, Boonesville, Brown's Cove, and Free Union each have a grocery and a few homes. The post office villages of Mount Fair and Doylesville have shrunk to a few modest homes and small farms—victims of RFD service, mail-order catalogues, school consolidation, and better highways. White Hall, somewhat more prosperous, has two stores and a showgrounds where annual celebrations are held each Labor Day. Ivy and Earlysville, closer to Charlottesville and profiting somewhat from suburban and industrial growth, appear to be thriving little centers. Several crossroads communities of regional importance when Peyton drew his map of Albemarle County in 1875 and others which developed as railroad stops have virtually disappeared, among them the old tobacco center at Milton, Stony Point, Owensville, and South Garden. Hillsboro, big enough to supply a company of its own in Civil War days, has now become Yancey's Mills, and only a proud little church retains the former name. On the first slopes of the Blue Ridge above Crozet stands a cluster of Negro homes called New Town, reminiscent of many such enclaves once scattered throughout the countryside. However, the general picture is all too clear: changes in travel and work habits have exacted a heavy toll. For every rural business establishment operating outside of Charlottesville, Crozet, and Scottsville, at least two more stand stark and abandoned, gas pumps rusting and once jaunty signs advertising Coca-Cola and various brands of cigarettes and chewing tobacco obscured by dust.

One of the less attractive aspects of the Charlottesville-Albemarle scene during recent decades has been a substantial increase in roadside litter. Expanded highways, throwaway containers, food-to-go outlets, tourists, students, and thoughtless local residents have all contributed to this desecration of the landscape. At times, those who often preach ecology and praise Albemarle scenery seem to be among the region's worst enemies.

Urbanization and a decline in agriculture have had considerable impact upon rural churches, especially those of Methodists and Baptists, and rare is the congregation which can support a full-time minister. In 1936, even before the full force of urbanization and better highways was felt, the Baptists, for example, were supporting, in some fashion, seventeen rural churches, twelve of them in open country, five in the villages of Alberene, Covesville, Crozet, Hillsboro, and Scottsville. Joseph H. Cosby, who conducted a survey of these congregations, found that over a quarter of the members were nonresidents driving out from Charlottesville occasionally to attend services.[3] He concluded there were far too many churches in some parts of the county and strongly urged consolidation, which, of course, has since taken place. When Charlottesville celebrated its bicentennial in 1962 it had some forty churches, and several major faiths had established active student centers near the university to

[3] See Cosby, "A Survey of Rural Baptist Churches in Albemarle County" (M.A. thesis, University of Virginia, 1937).

care for the spiritual and social needs of undergraduates, graduates, and faculty. Although membership totals are not available, today the majority of local churchgoers undoubtedly are Baptists, Methodists, Episcopalians, and Presbyterians, as they have been for two centuries or more, with Roman Catholics increasing substantially in recent decades as more and more out-of-state residents move into the region.

Under the aggressive leadership of two very able presidents, one a former governor who drove an ambulance and was a Marine Corps aviator during World War I, the other a young professor of English, the University of Virginia grew by leaps and bounds during the quarter century following World War II. To some extent this upsurge was inevitable owing to a baby boom and unprecedented expenditure of state and federal funds. However, both Colgate Darden (1947–58) and Edgar Shannon (1959–74) stressed quality at all times; and unlike some institutions which gloried in more buildings, more students, and more gridiron triumphs, the university at their direction not only regained much of its former prominence but forged ahead in new, uncharted areas. Well-known and respected scholars were enticed to join the faculty in such fields as physics, history, English, mathematics, medicine, and law, and the admissions office set out to get the best students possible. These included many top graduates of the Old Dominion's public high schools, for Darden, more so than any of his predecessors, was determined that the University of Virginia would fulfill the dream of Thomas Jefferson and become the capstone of Virginia education, a true state university. This view caused some animosity among alumni, and even his appointment as president was hailed with unofficial mourning by many undergraduates who donned black ties to deplore the beginning of the Darden administration. The former governor probably encountered greatest resistance during the early years of his tenure, but gradually, through tact, persuasion, and, above all, results that anyone could see, he prevailed; and as he stepped down in 1959, the full impact of his career as a builder was evident to all. Until his administration, for example, each department usually had only a central office, no private cubicles or rooms for individual professors, and duplicating of exams and other materials was arranged at the Corner by the instructors themselves. Except for a stormy confrontation over student power and United States involvement in Vietnam and Cambodia which ripped many campuses apart in the late 1960s, Shannon enjoyed a quiet, constructive administration, characterized by remarkable energy and understanding of the timely opportunities open to the university.

63. University of Virginia installs fifth president. *From left to right:* Joseph C. Smiddy, Clinch Valley College chancellor; Edgar F. Shannon, Jr.; Frank L. Hereford, Jr.; and Colgate W. Darden, Jr.

In 1974 he was succeeded by Frank Hereford, a Louisiana-born alumnus and a well-known physics professor, who had held various administrative posts under both of his predecessors. Hereford, the university's fifth president, coordinated efforts in 1965 to obtain a major National Science Foundation grant ($3.8 million) used to establish an Institute for Advanced Study which attracted a number of eminent scholars to Charlottesville. Then dean of the Graduate School of Arts and Sciences, Hereford helped to build up a graduate faculty with federal funds which, as enrollment stabilized, could infuse new life into undergraduate study as well. Imaginative and energetic, he had held the highest administrative post in the university next to Shannon, that of provost and vice president in charge of academic affairs. His selection as president was recognition of the constructive achievements he shared with Shannon in the university's recent development.

Both Darden and Shannon represented a substantial breakthrough in the development of the university, much more conspicuous than that engineered by Barringer and Alderman at the turn of the century. Darden was the first president who convinced Old Dominion legislators to support the institution, often their alma mater, with a massive outlay of tax dollars. Shannon, with state backing assured and a physical plant rapidly taking shape, gave free rein to departments, deans, and students to propose imaginative programs, frequently supported by federal, not state, funds. Yet each man, not surprisingly, was a captive of his own times. Darden, a product of the Byrd machine and a politician, not an educator by trade, seemed to harbor some suspicion of federal schemes and of professors who advocated them. In short, he secured state support for his university, but at a price: increased dependence upon the General Assembly. Shannon, a younger, perhaps more resilient man whose personal ties were to the academic world of Virginia, Harvard, and Oxford, not the political realm of Richmond, favored the alliance carefully constructed by his predecessor, but his horizons were broader because, thanks to the work of Colgate Darden, they could be. And this rather freewheeling stance served him well when the Kent State tragedy threatened to close classes in May 1970. He chose a middle-of-the-road course which, like all such paths, pleased few yet, in retrospect, proved to work. Shannon was able to defuse a very explosive situation, and a month later the University of Virginia held finals as usual.

Despite student unrest and greater emphasis upon nonstate money, this man was a builder no less than Darden, and in the final years of his administration fourteen projects worth $34.5 million were added to the Charlottesville scene. During his first decade, enrollment at five major centers—the University of Virginia, George Mason, Mary Washington, Clinch Valley, and the School of General Studies—rose from 17,110 to 48,387. In those same years faculty salaries, a problem which plagued Alderman, Newcomb, and Darden in turn, nearly doubled and became truly competitive with those throughout the nation.

Under Shannon's leadership qualified women and blacks became more and more a part of the university scene. Traditional raids by competing institutions upon the university's promising scholars were stopped, not only by higher salaries but also through creation of better research facilities. In fact, the situation was reversed as the University of Virginia attracted scores of young and established teachers to Charlottesville from rival seats of learning. At the outset of the Shannon era there were only a handful of endowed faculty positions. When the former president stepped down in 1974 and returned to classroom teaching, the university had over one hundred endowed chairs. Edgar Shannon also developed local facilities for editing and publishing the papers of two of the founding fathers, George Washington and James Madison.

Physical changes under Darden and Shannon are almost too numerous to mention, among them a huge annex to the University Hospital, an addition to Alderman Library nearly doubling its size, new quarters for the law school and a flourishing graduate business school, a student union named for President Newcomb, University Hall, a theater complex, and scores of classrooms and dormitories. Though numbers alone mean little, full-time enrollment at Charlottesville totaled about 5,000 when Darden took over. A quarter of a century later as Hereford moved into Pavilion VIII there were some 14,000 students in residence, 463 of them black and 4,524 of them women; for, beginning in the fall of 1970, after decades of foot-dragging, resort to various forms of subterfuge, and a tongue-lashing from Lady Astor who once turned her barbed wit upon an institution which could honor her but denigrate all other women, the board of visitors at last agreed to admit the fair sex on the same basis as men.

In the early 1970s Piedmont Community College, a two-year school similar to others appearing throughout the state, was built on a high plateau overlooking Interstate 64 and the famous old road leading to Scottsville, but not in that community as many residents of southern Albemarle had hoped. This nonresident institution, which opened classes at its present site in 1973 and now has 1,500 students, serves Albemarle, Fluvanna, Greene, and Nelson counties and provides training in numerous technical fields, as well as a liberal arts program for those planning to complete their education at a four-year college. Also, in 1972, George Mason and Mary Washington became independent schools with their own governing boards, although Clinch Valley remained under the wing of the University of Virginia.

Charlottesville's public school scene, littered with heated words and tensions created by the integration confrontation of the 1950s and 1960s, continued to be a vortex of controversy in the early 1970s. At issue was the decision to build a huge, central four-year high school. Every aspect of this undertaking—site, cost, even the name of this new institution—was hotly debated, but in the fall of 1974 some two thousand students began classes in Charlottesville High School, a $9 million complex located near McIntire Park. This institution effectively ended the last vestiges of racial segregation at the high school level but left Lane and Burley, both constructed at considerable cost within the past three decades, dark, deserted, and unused, their fate uncertain.

64. Medical School complex. Jefferson's Rotunda and University Hall in
   background

The social and cultural life of Albemarle County mirrored trends
throughout the nation during the Hildreth years with more and
more activity centered in Charlottesville, not rural towns and villages.
Clubs and organizations abound, from traditional social, religious,
and fraternal groups to those catering to everything from stamp
collecting to bird watching and spelunking. The columns of the
University of Virginia's *Cavalier Daily* attest to the great variety to
be found on every hand. One association of more than passing importance is the League of Women Voters of Charlottesville and Albemarle County, organized in 1946 under the dynamic leadership of
Mary Stamps White, a Red Cross worker in Europe during World
War II. In the past quarter century members have focused attention
upon such key community matters as schools, housing, recreation,
mental health, and, of course, voter registration. Yet perhaps the
league's best-known service is publication of a guide to the local
government of Charlottesville and Albemarle designed to assist both
native-born and newcomer.

In 1972, evidence of the increasing role of women in local public life, Jill T. Rinehart became the first woman to be elected to the Charlottesville City Council. Mrs. Rinehart, founder of the Charlottesville-Albemarle Democratic Women's Club and long active in politics, previously had coordinated the successful campaigns of several area politicians for state offices.

Travelers and local residents can dine in atmospheres inspired by Japan, Italy, and eighteenth-century England, as well as America, and, since 5 P.M., December 29, 1968, they no longer have to carry their own bottle in a brown bag but can order mixed drinks at licensed restaurants. According to *This Week*, a local publication for travelers, those so inclined can enjoy everything from jazz to country music with their food and drink and top off the evening with a massage or a sauna at a health salon operated by an all-girl staff.

Also, since World War II, two University of Virginia groups, the Tuesday Evening Concert Series and the Artist Series of the University Union, have brought a galaxy of world-famous performers to Albemarle. Audiences have enjoyed, among other things, the music of the London and Boston symphonies, evenings with Birgit Nilsson and Andre Watts, and the pantomimes of Marcel Marceau.

For a decade or so after the advent of television Charlottesville had no station of its own and was served instead by cable connections and facilities in Harrisonburg, Richmond, Petersburg, Lynchburg, and Washington. One program of special interest to area residents is Bernard Chamberlain's "Community History," a series of thirty-minute broadcasts highlighting aspects of Albemarle's past. In 1973 WVIR-TV, an NBC affiliate, began operating in Charlottesville. This is a commercial UHF channel, the community's first such station. The ubiquitous "tube" has closed virtually all of the lavish downtown vaudeville-movie palaces of former days, their place being taken by small suburban movie houses, drive-ins, an occasional dinner theater, and live productions at the university.

Riding to the hounds continues important and, with an influx of well-to-do, self-made squires, probably is increasing in popularity each year. The Keswick and Farmington hunts provide the nucleus of a round of social gatherings each fall and winter, augmented by a Tri-County Riding Club organized in 1952 which now has its own quarters near Keene and some 130 members. This group, serving for the most part southern Albemarle and not a true hunt in the traditional sense, stages a horse show each October.

University athletics, especially football (despite a rather lackluster record overall) and basketball, which has enjoyed somewhat more success, attract thousands to Charlottesville each season. Lacrosse and polo also have won many converts during the postwar years. The Apple Harvest Festival, plagued by rain and a declining apple crop, in 1958 was converted into a Dogwood Festival held in April, presumably on the premise that weather conditions would be more propitious and dogwood blooms a more reliable commodity than apples. Charlottesville's recreation program, an outgrowth of Paul McIntire's generosity and pioneer efforts during the 1930s of the Mothers Clubs and a Negro recreation league, has developed into a full-scale, year-round operation. In 1974 the city had fourteen parks and playgrounds, an excellent golf course, scores of tennis courts, picnic grounds, a swimming pool, and a ball park. Several rural villages, notably Greenwood, as a result of the work of Rev. Lee Marston and the beneficence of Mrs. William Massie, her daughter, Mrs. James Gordon Smith, and others, have created very active community centers which serve as focal points for athletics, club meetings, and a variety of social gatherings.

Within recent decades Albemarle's journalistic world has witnessed substantial change. The black weekly of the 1920s, the *Charlottesville Messenger*, edited by J. G. Shelton and bearing the slogan "Progress, Racial Unity, and Education," was supplanted in 1954 by the *Charlottesville-Albemarle Tribune*, also a weekly publication. And, on September 15, 1968, an augmented *Daily Progress* staff produced its first Sunday edition. Symbolically, this venerable newspaper bore a new masthead design. Monticello, the university, and agriculture still received recognition, but gone were the factory smokestacks and in their place stood a modern office building, an innovation which reflects the demise of the woolen mills and the arrival of hundreds of white-collar workers in plants operated by the Michie Company, Sperry Rand, State Farm, and others. Twenty-seven months later, in January 1971, the Lindsay family, after over three-quarters of a century of control, sold the *Progress* to the Worrell Newspapers, Inc. In May 1971 Thomas E. Worrell, Jr., president, transferred the headquarters of his publishing empire from Bristol to Charlottesville.

The region's literary life, sparked by publications from the pen of Virginia Moore and Nancy Hale and highlighted by Douglas Day's prizewinning biography of Malcolm Lowry and Elizabeth Langhorne's work on Lady Astor, was rejuvenated in the late 1950s by the presence of one of the nation's most distinguished writers, William Faulkner. In 1963 the University Press of Virginia was formed to serve the entire state as a publisher of scholarly works. Also, both creation of the Virginia Center for the Creative Arts, a MacDowell-

65. John-Boy Walton on the Hatton Ferry

like retreat for writers, sculptors, artists, and composers which was located at Wavertree Farm, Greenwood, for several years before moving to Louisa County, and the addition of more and more well-known scholars to the university faculty had perceptible effects. Among these individuals is Dumas Malone, who in his retirement (if one can call it that) is completing his monumental six-volume work, *Jefferson and His Times*. In 1975 he received the Pulitzer Prize for history.

The writer who in recent years has brought Charlottesville and its environs into millions of homes throughout the nation, Earl Hamner, Jr., has only peripheral ties to Albemarle, for he grew up in Schuyler in neighboring Nelson County. But both *Spencer's Mountain*, published in 1961, and the very successful television series based upon that book, "The Waltons," mention Charlottesville often, and the Charlottesville-Albemarle Chamber of Commerce has scores of calls from tourists who want to visit "Walton's Mountain."

Late in November 1972 Charlottesville won national attention for a far different reason when an excavation at 303 Fifth Street, S.E., uncovered hundreds, even thousands of dollars in long-buried bills and coins. This property was the site of the city's most respected twentieth-century bordello, Marguerite's or Marguiretta's, which closed in 1948. A few years later, after Marguerite's death, the contents of this fancy establishment, said to have been furnished with numerous antique pieces, were auctioned off, and many a mirror, chair, and table found a new home at Farmington and other equally prestigious addresses. Apparently the rich soil yielded up some $17,000 in treasure, one of those rare occasions when prostitution has bestowed dividends upon a subsequent generation which had no ties to either the participants or the activity.

Charlottesville-Albemarle is a very different community from that which Bill Hildreth returned to as a young ex-serviceman in 1919, just as it differs from what men and women who served in World War II, Korea, and Vietnam found when they came home. Everything somehow seems bigger, the pace of life faster; yet, stroll about the Corner and across the university grounds on a quiet Sunday morning or drive down any country road a few miles outside of Charlottesville on almost any day of the week, especially the byways of southern Albemarle, and one will begin to wonder how great the change actually has been. But stand at the doors of a university classroom as males and females, whites and blacks, emerge; drive out Route 29 North with its motels, industrial plants, shopping centers, and hamburger or fried chicken dispensaries; or glide along Interstate 64 with one eye on the broad highway and the other on Charlottesville's sprawling suburbs and it is apparent that much indeed has happened. Many sections of Albemarle have lost their rural flavor, and much of their rural poverty as well. At the same time, though the region is more national in outlook, less southern, and more urban, interest in preserving elements of its historic past and unique regional quality never was greater.

At the moment (mid-1975), under the direction of Michael Gleason, the Charlottesville-Albemarle Bicentennial Commission is busy with plans for the nation's two-hundredth birthday. In all, the commission has some thirty-two programs, most of them in the fields of history, cultural life, and education. Two of the most ambitious projects are a documentary film depicting life in eighteenth-century Albemarle and an extensive information center to be constructed near the Monticello exit of Interstate 64. This facility, one of three to be built within the Old Dominion, will highlight the colonial and Revolutionary world of western Virginia.

This ground swell of concern for the past has been aided from time to time by similar celebrations such as the university's centennial and sesquicentennial observances and anniversaries marking the creation of both county and city. It had its beginning in the 1920s with efforts of Professor A. K. Davis, Jr., to rescue mountain ballads from oblivion as the Blue Ridge Parkway cut through pockets of settlement which time had forgotten, creation of the Thomas Jefferson Memorial Foundation to make Monticello a national shrine, and research by Mary Rawlings into Charlottesville's history. During the harsh 1930s scores of WPA employees dug through local records, interviewed old-timers, and copied words engraved on vine-covered tombstones. Nurtured by the DAR and UDC, the birth of the Albemarle County Historical Society, and the research of university graduate students in such fields as history, rural sociology, drama, geography, and political science, this work has continued. Bank presidents and real estate men, individuals who often pay only lip service to the heritage of their community, have joined, at times even led, this campaign. William S. Hildreth and Bill Stevens, author of a volume on local homes which is a charming mix of historical research and salesmanship, are outstanding examples. With luck, a hallmark of the Charlottesville-Albemarle scene no less than change, this valiant attempt to blend old and new may well succeed.

66. A Bicentennial event: stairways in restored Rotunda.

Chapter 21

Albemarle—The Lucky County

A LBEMARLE is indeed a fortunate land on which both the Almighty and Dame Fortune seem to have smiled for nearly two and a half centuries. Its scenery remains strikingly beautiful, even if Charlottesville's immediate environs are marred by displays of neon tubing as garish as any found in New Jersey and other highly industrialized areas. Route 29 North, now four lanes and sometimes six, is bordered by a carnival-like midway of giant motel signs and quick-eat joints with similar beacons designed to ensnare both traveler and local resident. The weather is attractive and mild, the average year-round temperature being 57°. Tornadoes and other freaks of nature are rare, although most summers bring several spells of stifling humidity, an occasional winter snowfall snarls traffic while delighting children and a growing army of skiers, and floodwaters are all too common in some areas.

Wars have swirled around Albemarle's hills and valleys but seldom touched them. No conflict with Indians disturbed the county's early years, and even though the enemy appeared briefly in the 1780s and again in the 1860s, he did little physical damage. True, Phil Sheridan's men wrecked the James River Canal in March 1865, but its fate already was sealed by the growth of railroads. In fact, each major confrontation—the Revolution, Civil War, and World Wars I and II—has brought substantial economic benefit, not devastation. The Hessians and British prisoners from Saratoga and hospital patients and refugees some eighty years later created widespread demand for local goods and products, as did the wars of this century.

This land has been the home, either by choice or by birth, of some extremely able leaders, men and women of great talent. Towering over all others, of course, is the gentleman from Monticello who, among many achievements, took greatest pride in his role as author of the Declaration of Independence, promulgator of religious freedom, and father of the University of Virginia. No other president and few other Americans have made such an enduring imprint upon an area as Jefferson upon Albemarle. Consigned to relative obscurity for several decades after his death in 1826, his words and ideas have

67. Tally-ho!

proved to be perhaps as powerful in our own time as in his. If nothing else, Thomas Jefferson and his beautiful home have become the county's trump cards in the battle for tourist dollars, for in 1973 alone his mountaintop estate was host to over 525,000 people, roughly twenty-six times the population of Albemarle in Jefferson's day.

His trusted lieutenant, James Madison, rector of the University of Virginia following his death, and James Monroe, the last member of the brilliant dynasty which ruled the United States during its formative years, also were closely associated with Albemarle. Those who blazed western trails during that same era included two distinguished native sons, George Rogers Clark and Meriwether Lewis. Some of these men, but by no means all of them, were the product of a wave of well-to-do settlement which engulfed the area in the 1760s. Wealthy Tidewater families, the Carters, for one, saw opportunity in lands drained by the James, Rivanna, and Rockfish and their tributaries, especially with the creation of new counties which multiplied local offices several fold, positions which, in turn, could lead to seats in the House of Burgesses at Williamsburg and the chance to obtain still more land in the west. Some individuals, much more interested in opportunity than scenery, did not tarry long in the foothills of the Blue Ridge, pushing on to what is now West

Virginia, Tennessee, and Kentucky. Others, such as Thomas Walker who laid out the little village of Charlottesville, thought of following in their footsteps but, for reasons best known to them, did not. Several factors undoubtedly influenced their decision to remain, among them war, independence, and the emergence of Albemarle as a center of unusual political prominence in the new nation. Some of these restless folk, like the legendary princes of Serendip, may have lost sight of their true goals, but they did not emerge empty-handed. They came to the Piedmont seeking new lands, especially for tobacco crops and as a basis for accumulated wealth; but diverted by the events of several tumultuous decades, they found themselves possessed of reasonably good farms and estates amid very pleasant surroundings. Somehow the frontier world, once so beguiling, seemed much less attractive. Yet thousands of younger brothers, sons, daughters, and cousins did go south and west, and, in time, even north, especially during the ensuing six decades, 1820-88, which were no golden age, at least not for the great mass of Albemarle's citizens.

Nevertheless, through good times and bad, this nucleus of wealthy residents, either from the Tidewater originally or augmented by shrewd immigrants who pushed their way upward and won grudging but sometimes relatively easy acceptance, has continued to be a crucial factor in local life, perhaps the most important single element. Its members built proud estates, homes of enduring beauty—Castle Hill, Monticello, Estouteville, Blenheim, Enniscorthy, Farmington, Edgemont, Old Woodville, and others—establishing a social pattern which persisted throughout the harsh years of the nineteenth century and has done much to attract both tourists and modern immigrants to Albemarle today. These folk and their progeny provided astute, educated leadership in local, state, and national affairs, and they never became a select caste nor hesitated to recruit able new blood from time to time. Their presence, perhaps as much as anything else, led to establishment of a university on the outskirts of the little village of Charlottesville in 1819. Though Jefferson was the prime mover in this drama, he did not act alone. Knowing the benefits of higher education firsthand, they realized the great influence the University of Virginia could have upon Charlottesville, Albemarle, and surrounding counties. What they failed to foresee, of course, was that the little institution someday would be of such great economic importance, replacing in large measure income then derived from fields of tobacco, corn, and wheat.

Luck was with Albemarle even during the hard decades of the nineteenth century. Not a rail center of any consequence, it was spared the horrors of the Civil War; and possessing no cities, the county was largely ignored by those seeking to reshape the defeated South in the image of the North during the decade that followed. Also, overwhelmingly rural and given over to general agriculture, Albemarle knew few of the excesses of the so-called Gilded and Industrial Ages. Brooks Museum, Miller School, and perhaps the university's chapel and Nydrie are what many people consider to be the only reminders of architectural horrors perpetrated throughout much of the nation during the late 1800s, although today their uniqueness enables them to exude a sort of exuberant charm. Even destruction of the Rotunda with its ungainly Annex in the great fire of 1895 is now viewed as a blessing. Failure during the first thirty years of this century to attract factories and heavy industry can be seen in a similar light, for an Albemarle scarred with smoke and grime in the image of Pittsburgh or Wheeling could conjure up few visions of its historic past for either tourist or prospective homeowner.

The decline of agriculture has been more than offset by growth of the university with its innumerable subsidiary activities and arrival of some twenty or thirty small, light industries. Though most of these newcomers are concentrated near Charlottesville, three of them, Acme, Morton, and Uniroyal, are the prime employers in two smaller communities, Crozet and Scottsville. So, in an age of economic change which has wreaked havoc in other parts of rural America, Albemarle's good fortune has held firm. In 1970 the median family income in Charlottesville was $9,231, in Albemarle $8,949, and throughout the Old Dominion as a whole $9,076. The average male worker in Charlottesville received $6,155 that year; the average female worker, $3,859. County salaries were somewhat lower, $5,755 and $3,854 respectively. According to a U.S. Department of Commerce survey conducted a year later, overall per capita income in the Charlottesville-Albemarle area was $3,636, approximately 93 percent of the state average.[1] Census figures indicate that although local salaries have risen dramatically since mid-century, they lag behind those in some nearby communities, a fact which must bring smiles to the faces of employers, both old and new. In 1970, for example, the average male worker in Staunton and Waynesboro was receiving nearly $1,000 more than his Charlottesville counterpart. What all

[1] *Projections and Economic Base Analysis: The Albemarle County–Charlottesville City Area* (Richmond, 1973), p. 16. To some extent, including university students as local residents tends to lower any regional statistics concerning income and wages.

this clearly means is that hundreds of individuals see distinct advantages in living in Charlottesville-Albemarle and will take somewhat less in their pay envelopes in order to do so. Also, since the region has many affluent, even rich citizens and the per capita income does not yet equal that of all Virginians, it is apparent that considerable poverty is hidden in the back streets of Charlottesville, decaying little rural villages, and the recesses of the Blue Ridge. The annual budgets of both city and county surged past the million-dollar mark soon after World War II, and today Albemarle is spending over $18 million each year on schools, roads, and a variety of services, and Charlottesville, nearly $27 million.

For some, the key element in this tale is a good land filled with streams, rivers, valleys, rolling hills, and beautiful mountains. But without people and especially people with a keen appreciation for that land and the wherewithal to develop and preserve it (and the latter, preserving the land, is extremely important), the rest of the story would not have unfolded. That indefinable thing called luck enters Albemarle's history early and persists throughout. If the American Revolution had not occurred when it did, that coterie of very able, well-to-do settlers, realizing what tobacco does to the soil (even that of Albemarle), undoubtedly would have moved on. With independence, if Jefferson, Madison, and Monroe had not dominated national political life for a quarter of a century, still more would have pushed westward or departed for new lands in Alabama and Mississippi. During the difficult times that followed, the county's most able minds created an agricultural society which ministered as best it could to a troubled economy, and a little university began to flourish, foreshadowing its importance in decades to come. Luck seems to be involved even in Albemarle's disappointments, for example, its failure for many years to become a true rail center and inability to attract huge factories.

If Lady Luck has been kind and Albemarle, for the most part, has been able to retain its distinctive identity, this is not to say it is a land without problems. Its most precious commodities today are a historic heritage, a lovely land with breathtaking vistas, and a very healthy economy based upon the university, small industries, tourism, and retail-wholesale trade. However, growth means change which endangers the physical remains of the past and the scenery which is so much a part of that heritage. Apartment complexes and housing developments already cover hundreds of acres west and north of Charlottesville which only a decade ago were open fields and woodlands. Mobile homes, with even less life expectancy than apartments, are springing up in mountain coves and along various highways throughout the breadth of the county. Unlike Williamsburg, which has the omnipotent hand of a wealthy foundation to mold its future (for better or worse), Richmond and Norfolk, clearly metropolitan centers, and Alexandria-Arlington-Fairfax, merely the bedrooms of Washington interspersed with shopping malls and ribbons of concrete, Charlottesville is still a relatively small community, and much of the surrounding countryside, especially southern Albemarle, remains wooded, rural, and tranquil. In fact, in 1969 over half of the county's 472,000 acres could be classified as commercial forestland, and in that year hardwood growth exceeded the number of board feet harvested.

Nevertheless, many individuals fear that current population growth, about 2 percent annually and roughly equal to worldwide trends, endangers the way of life they know and love. Albemarle's citizens, despite frequent reassurance from both city and county officials, fear that a large industry will appear unannounced on the borders of their estate or farm. Also, alarmed by annexation and attempted merger, they watch carefully any move which might make them municipal residents subject (in their opinion) to higher taxes, centralized government, and bureaucratic control. This wary mood, naturally enough, permeates all city-county relations, at least as far as the average rural household is concerned. And, if nothing else, recent change has bestowed upon the Charlottesville area traffic congestion far in excess of what its population would seem to warrant, even if one makes allowance for out-of-state drivers. In 1971 there were only 17,361 cars, trucks, and motorcycles in the city and slightly fewer in the county (16,875); yet during many a midweek afternoon, it seems that nearly half of these vehicles are waiting for lights to change on city streets and highways while the rest move slowly past.

Thus the community's greatest problem is how to regulate growth so as to retain the flavor of years gone by, a very valuable travel commodity and a factor influencing nearly everyone who enters the offices of the region's prosperous real estate agencies, and, at the same time, not throttle the industrial, university, and commercial activity which is the area's lifeblood. To some extent, industrial expansion is limited by sewerage facilities, local ordinances and state laws, and the hard fact that low unemployment (now 1 or 2 percent) may make it difficult for any newcomer to recruit workers, unless, of course, he chooses to buck the prevailing wage scale. The University of Virginia already has entered an era of relative stability.

68. "All my wishes end, where I hope my days will end, at Monticello."

Neither enrollment nor employment rolls will expand in the foreseeable future as they did during the 1950s and early 1960s. The college-bound age group is becoming smaller, and as a result, both state and federal governments are less lavish with their expenditures on higher education. Even commercial growth may be approaching natural limits, since a slowly increasing population, estimated to reach 94,000 in 1980, up from 76,660 in 1970, can support only so many shopping centers, theaters, and stores. Barring further annexation or merger, this growth is expected to see Charlottesville's population expand from 38,880 to 40,000, Albemarle's from 37,780 to 54,000. Perhaps the community's greatest safeguard, as it has been for decades, is the reverence and love its citizens have for their soil. Any banker, developer, industrialist, or university official contemplating radical innovation must weigh carefully the full effects of his proposal, but even Charlottesville-Albemarle's most pressing dilemma, how to control growth, has a silver lining, for it is a problem many less fortunate regions would dearly love to grapple with.

Frontier settlement carved out of virgin forest and meadow,

troubled agricultural community during much of the nineteenth century, would-be industrial center in decades dominated by blatant boosterism which swept much of America, and an urban, educational, white-collar complex in the late twentieth century, Albemarle's story is hardly one of constant growth and unrivaled success. Like the life of any individual citizen, it contains both hard knocks and disappointment; and what has been a boon to one part of the county often proved disastrous to other regions only a few miles away. Water transport, early turnpikes, railroads, and superhighways have, in turn, both given birth to and smashed the dreams of thousands. One community, because it became the seat of county government early in the drama and enjoyed a central location, has managed to weather all these vicissitudes of change.

There is a tale, perhaps apocryphal, that as he lay dying on a cold January evening in 1870 a well-known Charlottesville resident was told by his physician that he had to prepare for the inevitable journey to meet his maker in heaven. William M. Keblinger, merchant, pioneer alderman, postmaster, and railroad agent, reflected for a moment and replied softly that if it was all right with the Almighty, he would prefer to compromise and remain in Charlottesville. Today some eighty thousand Virginians feel much the same way, although they might choose Crozet, Scottsville, Red Hill, White Hall, or some bit of rolling county landscape which has become, as far as they are concerned, their heaven. In 1796 Isaac Weld wrote of Albemarle that "many persons . . . even consider it to be the garden of the United States." Nearly two centuries later, despite substantial change on every hand, those words of praise seem as enduring and as true as when first written.

Appendixes

Sources for Charlottesville-Albemarle History

Index

Illustration Credits

Appendix A

Albemarle Soldiers of the Revolutionary War

From Edgar Woods, *Albemarle County in Virginia* (Charlottesville, 1901), pp. 367–71.

Officers

David Anderson, Ensign, 9th Va.
Nathaniel Anderson, Lieut., 3rd Va.
John Beck, Ensign, 9th Va.
Samuel Bell, Ensign, Grayson's Reg.
Thomas Bell, Captain, Gist's Reg.
Bezaleel Brown, Captain, State troops at Yorktown.
Henry Burke, Captain, State militia.
John Burke, Captain, State militia.
May Button, Captain, State militia.
Peter Davie, Quartermaster, 14th Va.
Samuel Eddins, Captain, 1st Cont. Artillery.
Edward Garland, Captain, 14th Va.
Peter Garland, Captain, 6th Va.
Nathaniel Garland, Lieut., State militia.
William Gooch, Lieut., State militia.
William Grayson, Captain, State militia.
John Hargis, Ensign, 13th Va.
Benjamin Harris, Captain, State militia.
Robert Harris, Captain, State militia.
Reuben Hawkins, Captain, State militia.
William Henderson, Captain, 9th Va.
Reuben Herndon, Lieut., 7th Va.
Joseph Holt, Lieut., 4th Va.
Samuel Hopkins, Lt. Col., 10th Va., captured at Charleston, S.C.
Charles Hudson, Quartermaster, 14th Va.
John Hudson, Captain, State militia.
Isaac Israel, Captain, 8th Va.
John Jameson, Lt. Col., Dragoons.
Matthew Jouett, Captain.

Robert Jouett, Captain, 7th Va.
John Key, Ensign, 8th Va.
Mask Leake, Captain, State militia.
Charles Lewis, Colonel, 14th Va.
Nicholas Lewis, Captain, State militia.
William Lewis, Lieut., Cont. Line.
Reuben Lindsay, Col., State militia.
Richard Lindsay, Col., Gen. Lawson's Brigade.
Bernard Lipscomb, Captain, State militia.
Col. Mallory.
John Marks, Captain, 14th Va.
Hudson Martin, Lieut., 9th Va.
John Martin, Captain, State militia.
Abraham Maury, Adjutant, 14th Va.
David Meriwether, 14th Va., captured at Charleston.
James Meriwether, Adj., State militia.
Thomas Meriwether, Major, State militia.
Peter Minor, Captain, 5th Va.
Archelaus Moon, Lieut., 14th Va.
Jacob Moon, Paymaster, 14th Va.
George Nicholas, Lt. Col., 11th Va.
John Nicholas, Lieut., 9th Va.
Wilson C. Nicholas, Com., Washington's Guards.
Lipscomb Norvell, Lieut., 5th Va.
John Piper, Lieut., State militia.
James Quarles, Captain, State militia.
Robert Rodes, Captain, captured at Charleston.
Clough Shelton, Captain, 10th Va., captured at Charleston.
William Simms, Captain, 6th Va.
Larkin Smith, Captain, 4th Dragoons.
George Thompson, Lieut., State militia.
John Thompson, Lieut., 7th Va.
Leonard Thompson, Lieut., State militia.
Roger Thompson, Captain, 2nd Va.
Thomas Walker Jr., Captain, 9th Va.
Captain Warr, probably Marr.
Daniel White, Captain, State militia.
Tarleton Woodson, Sergeant, State militia.

Privates

John Burton, disabled and pensioned.
John Buster, died 1820, served against Indians, and in Revolution.

Nathan Clausby, Grenadier, 1st Partisan Legion.

James Craddock, died in the service.

Charles Davis, 1st Light Dragoons, wounded and pensioned.

David Epperson, died in the service.

John Fagg Sr., died 1829, aged 92.

Simpson Foster, died in the service.

John Gillaspy, 9th Va., killed at Germantown.

Charles Goolsby, Corporal, 9th Va., captured at Germantown, and died in the service.

James Goolsby, 9th Va., captured at Germantown, and died in the service.

John Goolsby, 9th Va., died in the service.

John Greening, 2nd Va.

William Hardin, killed at Ninety-Six.

Bartlett Hawkins, pensioned.

Ambrose Howard, 9th Va.

Richard Marshall, pensioned by Act of Assembly.

Peter Massie, 5th Va.

Thomas Mitchell, Sergeant, Cont. army, died in the service.

James Old, died 1821, in battles of Quebec and Long Island.

William Smith, died 1823, aged 95, served against Indians, and in Revolution.

John Snead, in Cont. army.

Kenneth Southerlin, State militia.

Daniel Tilman, died 1820, served at 16 against Indians, and in Revolution.

Applying for pensions under Act of Congress passed in 1818.

Enlisted in Albemarle

William Bailey, in Capt. Thomas Walker's Co., 9th Va., in battles of Brunswick and Saratoga, discharged in Pa.

Joseph Brockman, in Capt. Lindman's Co., Col. Davies's Reg., in no battle, discharged at Powhatan.

William Eastin, in Capt. Reuben Taylor's Co., Col. Moses Hazen's Reg., in battles of Staten Island, Brandywine and Germantown, discharged at Morristown, N.J.

Nehemiah Greening, in Capt. Stribling's Co., Buford's Reg., at Fort Motte, Ninety-Six and Eutaw Springs, discharged at Salisbury, N.C.

Edward Hughes, in Capt. John Mark's Co., 1st Va., in battles of Brandywine, Germantown and Guilford C.H.

Thomas Johnson, in Capt. Roger Thompson's Co., 2nd Va., in no battles, discharged at Long Island, Holston River.

John Jones, in Capt. Winston's Co., Col. Charles Lewis's Reg., in battles of Brandywine, Germantown, and Monmouth, discharged at Middlebrook, N.J.

Sabrit King, in Capt. Robert Jouett's Co., 7th Va., in battle of Monmouth.

Martin Mooney, in Capt. Fontaine's Co., 14th Va., and Capt. Wm. Lewis's Co., Col. Cleveland's Reg., in battles of Long Bridge, King's Mountain and Ninety-Six.

Richard Mooney, in Capt. John Mark's Co., 1st Va., in battles of Guilford C.H., Camden, Ninety-Six and Eutaw Springs, discharged at Salisbury, N.C.

Samuel Munday, in Capt. Wm. Simm's Co., Col. Green's Reg., at Guilford C.H., Camden, Ninety-Six and Eutaw Springs, discharged at Salisbury, N.C.

Enlisted in other places, but residents of Albemarle after the war.

Humphrey Beckett, in Frederick County, Capt. Porterfield's Co., 11th Va., in battles of Somerset, Amboy and Monmouth, discharged in Frederick.

Thomas Burton, in Hanover County, Capt. Hurd's Co., Buford's Reg., in no battle, discharged in Fluvanna.

Youen Carden, in Cumberland County, under Lt. Benj. Garrett, Capt. Baylor's Cavalry, and twenty months under Col. Washington, discharged at Charleston, S.C.

John Grinstead, in Hanover County, Capt. Woodson's Co., Col. Posey's Reg., at Savannah and Yorktown, discharged in Cumberland County.

Sabrit Hoy, in Culpeper County, Capt. Harrison's Co., 2nd Va., at Cowpens, Guilford C.H., Camden, Ninety-Six and Eutaw Springs, discharged at Salisbury, N.C.

William Kirby, in Hanover County, Capt. Stribling's Co., Buford's Reg., at Guilford C.H., Camden, Ninety-Six, and Eutaw Springs, discharged at Salisbury, N.C.

Isaac Milliway, at Dover, Del., Capt. McCannon's Co., Col. Vaughan's Reg., at Guilford C.H., Camden, Eutaw Springs, where he was severely wounded, discharged at Dover.

George Norvell, in Capt. Richard C. Anderson's Co., 5th Va., at Brandywine, Germantown and Yorktown, discharged at West Point.

Joseph Shepherd, at Fredericksburg, in Capt. John Wallace's Co., 3rd Va.

Cephas Shickett, in Capt. John Stuart's Co., 1st Maryland, at Brandywine and Germantown, discharged at Annapolis.

John Wm. Shube, in Philadelphia, in Pulaski's Corps, at Savannah, Camden, Mount Scoota, and James Island, discharged at Smithfield, Va.

John Smith, in Pennsylvania Artillery, Capt. Proctor, at Trenton, with Gen. Clark down the Ohio in 1781, and one year with Gen. Harmar, discharged at Fort Pitt.

William Turner, in Capt. Francis Taylor's Co., 2nd Va., at Germantown and Stony Point.

John Williams, in Brunswick County, Capt. John Overton's Co., 10th Va., at Guilford C.H., Eutaw Springs, and Yorktown, discharged at Williamsburg.

Privates in State Militia

Samuel Barksdale	Adam Keblinger
Micajah Bowen	Samuel McCord
William Boyd	Cornelius Maupin
Gideon Carr	Daniel Maupin
Meekins Carr	William Maupin
John Collins	Jonathan Munday, at Yorktown
Major Dowell	Ephriam Seamonds
James Dunn	Richard Snow, at Yorktown
George Gentry	Richard Spinner
James Gentry	John Spradling
Sharod Going	David Strange, at Yorktown
John Hall	John Taylor
Nathan Hall	Nathaniel Thacker
George Hardin	Absalom Thomas
William Harris	John Thomas
Richard Hill	Roger Thompson, at Yorktown
Charles Huckstep	Micajah Wheeler
Richard Johnson	John Wood.
William Jordan	

Appendix B

Telephone Subscribers in Charlottesville and Albemarle County, 1901

From *A Directory of Representative Business and Professional Men of Albemarle County and Charlottesville* ([Charlottesville], 1901), pp. 122–33.

From *A Directory of Representative Business and Professional Men of Albemarle County and Charlottesville* ([Charlottesville], 1901), pp. 122–33.

CHARLOTTESVILLE'S BUSINESS PHONES

137	Adams & Co.	477	Chancellor, S. C.
90	Albemarle Hotel.	68	Charlottesville Bargain House.
48	Allegree, A. T. & Co.		
236	Allen, C. W.	108	Charlottesville Fire Department
479	Anderson Bros.		
226	Andrews, J. B.	222	Charlottesville Hardware Co.
35	Armstrong Knitting Co.	86	Charlottesville Lumber Co.
14	Aronhime, E.	54	Charlottesville Post Office.
196	Aronhime, S.	355	Charlottesville Undertaking Co.
92	Bank of Albemarle.		
132	Bucher, Mrs. C. E.	106	Charlottesville Woolen Mills.
361	Bishop, G. W.	36	City Gas Works.
310	Bowman, L. M.	9	City Hall.
333	Breechin, A. C. & Son.	374	City Pumping Co.
7	Brown, L. A.	56	City Transfer Office.
135	Browning, Dr. J. H.	388	Clermont Hotel.
308	Bruce, G. S. & Co.	122	Coles, C. M.
398	Bunch, H. D.	11	Colvin & Barksdale.
195	Burgess Restaurant.	255	Conlon, T. C.
28	Burnley & Smith.	205	County Clerk's Office.
112	Burnley, Smith & Burnley.	25	Covington & Peyton.
85	Car Sheds.	70	C. & O. Freight Office.
131	Carter, C. D.	161	Davis, A. J.
287	Carter House.	419	Defenbaugh, Frank.
88	Carter, R. L.	123	Dickeson & Richardson.
158	Carver, T. P.	261	Dinwiddie, Walter.
417	Chairman's Office.	167	Duke & Duke.

110	Early, Dr. J. E.	298	Leterman Co.
67	Edmonds, W. H.	140	Lewis & Cochran.
80	Eiseman, Mrs. J. B.	94	Link, C. R.
251	Ellington, J. P.	189	Macon, L. S. & Co.
21	Elliott & Carter.	379	Macon, Dr. W. D.
186	Elliott, J. F.	97	Magruder, Dr. E. M.
412	Family Supply Co.	141	Maphis Drug Store.
104	Farrar, J. S.	27	Marchant, H. C.
115	Farrar, W. P.	272	Marwood, E. M.
312	Fishburne, J. W.	100	Martin, W. T.
248	Fitzhugh & Flewellyn.	183	Masonic Temple.
150	Gentry & Irving.	159	Mathews, J. C.
111	Gleason & Bailey.	147	Michie, E. D. & Co.
51	Gleason Hotel.	266	Michie Printing Co.
52	Gleason, J. E.	197	Midway Meat Market.
118	Gleason, M. S.	292	Midway School.
343	Gilmore, Frank.	250	Model Steam Laundry.
283	Goodyear & Robertson.	249	Monticello Cigar Co.
452	Gordon & King.	156	Monticello Wine Co.
323	Greaver, J. A.	245	Moon, J. B.
153	Greaver, W. H. & Bros.	277	Moore, Mrs. L. J.
367	Haden, E. G.	165	McCue, E. O.
89	Hall, R. W.	55	McCue, J. S.
181	Harlen, J. F.	366	McCue, Dr. F. C.
126	Harman, Dan.	40	McKennie, J. C.
16	Harris, R. F. & Son.	199	Nelson, Dr. H. T.
383	Hartman, J. D.	138	Newman, R. J.
105	Hartnagle, H. A. W.	13	Noel, L. W.
173	Hawkins, Bros. & Co.	485	Noreck, H., "Shop."
33	Hedges, Dr. H. S.	211	Norman & Smith.
206	Holsinger, R. W.	200	Norris, J. B.
130	Home Steam Laundry.	471–3	Observatory.
32	Huyett, F. M.	473	Olivier's Bookstore.
82	Inge, G. P.	65	O. K. Bakery.
12	Irvine & Stevens.	10	Pantops Academy.
221	Irving & Spitzer.	305	Paoli News Co.
166	Johnson & Hildebrand.	42	Payne & Co.
416	Johnson, I. C. & Co.	154	Payne, G. D.
81	Kaufman Sons.	176	Payne's Livery.
264	Keller & George.	174	Payne, W. C.
43	Keller, W. J. & Co.	3	People's National Bank.
1	Kelley, J. Frank.	377	Perkins, Geo.
185	Key, R. P.	145	Perley, Jos. & Son.
182	King, Chas. & Son.	324	Phelps, C. W. C.
340	King Lumber Co.	203	Philpott's Restaurant.
194	Lawman & Hankins.	20	Poindexter, C. W.

24	Porter, H. P.	444	University Meat Market.
50	Portner Brewing Co.	499	Post Office.
57	Power Plant Office.	291	Utz, J. J.
439	Proctor's Office.	128	Valentine, R. P.
190	Progress Publishing Co.	31	Via, J. D.
87	Prout, the Printer.	353	Walker, Geo. E.
134	Randolph, Dr. W. C. N.	300	Ward, E. J.
262	Rawlings Institute.	172	Watkins, W. S. & Co.
151	Rhodes, W. P.	171	Watson, J. D.
164	Robertson, Dr. R. L.	243	Western Union Telegraph
372	Rogers, Dr. W. G.		Co.
179	Schwaner, Conrad.	155	Wheeler, J. B. & Co.
458	Scott, W. C.	114	White & Long.
390	Sieburg & Co.	29	Williamson, H. M.
23	Shackelford, Z. N.	193	Wills Drug Co.
136	Southern Freight Office.	17	Wills, F. C. & Co.
209	Southern Railway Baggage	113	Wills, T. J. & Co.
	Room.	6	Wood, C. M.
75	Thomas, R. L.	121	Wood, J. B. & W. H.
61	Thomas, T. Waddell.	107	Wood, J. H.
146	Thomason, J. H.	381	Wood & Massie.
263	Tilman & Carroll.	168	Wood, O. M.
387	Turner, Eldridge & Co.	184	Wood, Vest & Co.
139	Tyson, W. J.	247	Woods, Micajah.
422	University Boiler House.	260	Woods, Samuel B.
494	University Dispensary.	306	Zimmerman, Miss L. C.
448	University Infirmary.		

COUNTY TELEPHONE LINES

Line 601—Miller School and
Batesville.

Miller School.
Crozet Depot.
Garth, B. G.
Tillman, John T.
Barksdale, W. I.
Page, W. G. & Bro.
Joseph, C. S.
Goodwin, J. A.

Line 605—Keswick.

Jackson & Company.
Bowcock, C. S.

Shepherd, H. C., (Keswick.)
Shepherd, H. C., (Boyd's Tavern.)
Thurman, Dr. F. L.
Keswick Depot.
Magruder, H. E.
Hopkins, H. C.
Reed, W. C.

Line 606—Stony Point.

Goss, J. W.
Kase, Alvan.
Nelson, P. W.
Crittenbarger, W. A.
Shackelford, W. C.
Ferguson, J. R.

Line 607—Reservoir.

Miller, H. M.
City Reservoir.
Payne, J. F.
Nelson, Maj. William.
Spring, Joseph.

Line 608—Birdwood.

Humbert, James.
Chamberlain, W. C.
Lea, J. T., (Bloomfield.)
Lea, J. T., (Bloomfield, Mgr.
  House.)

Line 609—Red Hill.

Lindsay, J. H.
White, J. G.
Woods, S. B.
Anderson, Mrs. R. D.
Bruner, J. D.

Line 610—Covesville No. 1.

Birch, S. A.
Williams, Dr. J. W.
Harris, W. H.
Johnson, L. B.

Line 612—Brown & Bolton.

Bolton, Maj. C. M.
Brown University School.

Line 613—Esmont.

Line No. 702
  Powell & Coles.
  Dr. John E. Coles.
  Dr. B. L. Dillard, residence.
  Dr. B. L. Dillard.
  Alberene Soapstone Works.
  White & Sutherland.
  North Garden.
Line No. 703
  E. C. Butler & Co.
  Beal Bros.

Gault, S. R.
Pereira, J. V.
Line No. 704
  Bell, A. G., residence.
  Pitts & Dorrier.
Line No. 705
  Laird, Rev. H. W., residence.
  Omohundro, T. T., residence.
  Merrick, W. G., residence.
  Wilmer, W. M., residence.
  Leckie, S. M.
Line No. 706
  Way, C. T.
  Thomas, P. P.
  Beasley, T. H.

711   Peyton S. & Dr. John E.
         Coles, residence.
712   Waters, W. D., residence.
713   Shaw, Miss Jane, residence.
714   Coles, Miss Sallie, residence.
715   Crobarger, J. C.
716   Lane, J. E., residence.
717   Lane, H. L., residence.
718   Shaw, Lieut. C. P., resi-
         dence.
719   Jones, J. T.
720   Bennett, C. S., residence.
721   Bugg, L. W.
722   Hopkins, J. G., residence.

Line 614—Cismont.

Powers & Stevens.
Whitten, R. Q.
Randolph, F. M.
Shackelford, Dr. R. B.
Lindenkohl, G. S.
Boocock, Murray.
Ingersol, C. J.

Line 615—Rio.

Hughes, G. A.
Moon, John B.

Line 616—Hotopp.

Smith, A.
Hotopp, Henry.

Line 617—Ivy.

Rhodes, Layton.
Hall, W. E.
Hinks, J. C.
Baptist, Dr. H. L.
Greaves, John.
Higginson, J. M.

Line 618—Eastham.

Minor, John B.
Eastham Post Office.

Minor, John.
Cheape, J. A.
Magruder, F. M.

Line 619—Edge Hill.

Randolph, Miss Carrie.
Taylor, Miss Cornelia J.
Shadwell.
Chittenden, Mrs. C. A.

Line 620—Martin & Boaz.

Martin, H. S.
Martin, H. G.
Boaz, W. H.
Boaz, J. J.
Maury, M. F.

Appendix C

Albemarle County Newspapers

Unless otherwise indicated, these are weekly, semiweekly, or bi-weekly publications. No copies remain of some of these newspapers and journals and there are only random files of others. Researchers may wish to consult a similar list compiled by Glenn Curtis Smith and published in the *MACH* 1 (1940–41):36–37. The most complete files found in the University of Virginia Library (some of them on microfilm) are those of the *Daily Progress*.

Place published	Title	Date	
Charlottesville	*Central Gazette*	1820–27	
Charlottesville	*Virginia Advocate*	1827–60	
Scottsville	*Scottsville Aurora*	1829–32	?
Charlottesville	*Charlottesville Chronicle*	1832–33	?
Charlottesville	*Jeffersonian Republican*	1835–62	
Scottsville	*Times*	184?–48	?
Charlottesville	*Union Christian Intelligencer*	1844–58	?
Charlottesville	*Jeffersonian*	1847	
Scottsville	*Independent*	1850–	?
Charlottesville	*Era*	1858–	?
Scottsville	*Scottsville Register*	1859–72	
Charlottesville	*Charlottesville Advocate*	1860–61	?
Charlottesville	*Review*	1860–61	?
Charlottesville	*May-Flower*	1860–	?
Charlottesville	*Charlottesville Chronicle* (w, sw, d)	1863–1925	
Charlottesville	*Third Division Cavalry Chronicle*	1865	
Charlottesville	*Charlottesville Intelligencer*	1869–73	?
Scottsville	*Scottsville Courier*	1872–1906	
Charlottesville	*Jeffersonian Republican*	1873–94	
Charlottesville	*Virginia's Advocate*	1880–81	?
Crozet	*Miller School Monthly*	1884–	?
Charlottesville	*College Topics*	1890–1948	
Charlottesville	*Advance*	1890–96	
Charlottesville	*Daily Progress* (d)	1892–	
Charlottesville	*Morning News* (d)	1905–6	
Charlottesville	*Old Dominion News*	1907	
Scottsville	*Scottsville Enterprise*	1907–20	
Charlottesville	*Summer School News*	1908–41	

Charlottesville	*Virginia Headlight*	1908–13	?
Charlottesville	*Messenger*	1909–28	?
Charlottesville	*Militant Maid*	1913	
Charlottesville	*Big Tent*	1914	
Scottsville	*Scottsville News*	1920–46	
Charlottesville	*Community Interests* (m)	1921	
Charlottesville	*Midway Student*	1921–41	
Charlottesville	*Extension Topics*	1926–31	
Charlottesville	*Charlottesville Shopper's Guide*	1931	
Charlottesville	*Charlottesville Guide*	1931–32	
Charlottesville	*Albemarle News*	1931–36	
Charlottesville	*Engineering News*	1932–40	
Charlottesville	*Rotunda* (m)	1933	
Charlottesville	*Bulletin*	1935	
Crozet	*Crozette* (sm)	1935–40	
Charlottesville	*Charlottesville Radio News*	1936–	?
Charlottesville	*Charlottesville Movie News*	1937–39	
Charlottesville	*Jeffersonian* (m)	1937–43	
Charlottesville	*Albemarle Courier*	1939–40	
Charlottesville	*Election Extra*	1940–42	
Scottsville	*Scottsville News and Albemarle Courier*	1940–	?
Charlottesville	*Lanetime*	1941–60	
Charlottesville	*College Topics* (summer series)	1942–58	
Charlottesville	*Rotunda Topics*	1947–48	
Charlottesville	*"Y" News*	1947–53	
Charlottesville	*The Cavalier Daily*	1948–	
Charlottesville	*Charlottesville Tribune*	1950–51	
Charlottesville	*The Easterner*	1952–61	
Charlottesville	*Virginia Gazette and Journal*	1954	
Charlottesville	*Charlottesville-Albemarle Tribune*	1955–	
Scottsville	*Scottsville Sun*	1955–69	
Charlottesville	*The Communicator* (bm)	1956–60	
Charlottesville	*Summer Session Bulletin*	1959–	
Charlottesville	*Jefferson Journal*	1971–73	
Charlottesville	*This Week*	1971–	
Charlottesville	*The Declaration*	1973–	

Sources for Charlottesville–Albemarle History

This work is based, in large measure, upon interviews with numerous local residents, files of Charlottesville's *Daily Progress*, U.S. Census reports, various published materials found in books and journals, and studies by several graduate students at the University of Virginia who have delved deeply into area life. Individuals wishing to launch their own research into Charlottesville-Albemarle history should begin with *Albemarle County in Virginia* (1901) by Rev. Edgar Woods; *Jefferson's Albemarle* (1941), a WPA guide to Charlottesville and Albemarle; and the writings of Mary Rawlings, *The Albemarle of Other Days* (1925), *Ante-Bellum Albemarle* (1935), *Early Charlottesville: Recollections of James Alexander, 1828–1874* (1942), and *Historical Guide to Old Charlottesville* (1958). Woods's *Albemarle*, a highly personal effort, is often frustrating since he rarely, if ever, gives sources; but nearly two-thirds of the book is devoted to family history, an obvious boon to genealogists. Miss Rawlings's books stress life in Charlottesville and on the great estates throughout the county, although the Alexander *Recollections*, which she edited for publication, tell the story of the county seat's growth from mere village to a town of some consequence as seen through the eyes of a veteran newspaper editor. A rather rare and less well known work, Emily E. St. Claire's *Beautiful and Historic Albemarle* (1932), is a good general guide to the county's history.

Three doctoral dissertations and two master's theses produced at the University of Virginia provide invaluable insights: William Minor Dabney's "Jefferson's Albemarle, 1727–1819," Newton Bond Jones's "Charlottesville and Albemarle County, 1819–1860," William Edward Webb's "Charlottesville and Albemarle County, 1865–1900," Charles Wilder Watts's "Colonial Albemarle, 1727–1775," and Joseph Carroll Vance's "The Negro in the Reconstruction of Albemarle County." The trio of dissertations, written in the years immediately after World War II and sponsored in part by the People's National Bank, were conceived by that institution's president, William S. Hildreth, and Professor Thomas Perkins Abernethy, then head of the university's Corcoran Department of History, as the nucleus of a proposed history of Albemarle County. At length their hopes have been realized.

In all there are some sixty-five master's theses and perhaps half as many doctoral dissertations by University of Virginia graduate students in such fields as history, rural sociology, geography, political science, drama, and education which shed light upon Albemarle's past. These items, nearly all of them unpublished, can be found at the University Library. The authors have studied a great variety of subjects, and anyone intrigued by local life in any era should consult this mass of graduate research to see if his or her special interest has been explored. In addition to writing biographies of distinguished citizens such as John E. Massey, John Harvie, William C. Rives, Joshua Fry, Thomas Lafayette Rosser, John S. Battle, and Thomas Walker Gilmer, students have analyzed—to pick a few subjects at random—rural high schools, race relations, Charlottesville's gasworks, the Albemarle Livestock Market, Crozet's orchards, the woolen mills, public housing, Charlottesville's Greek community, juvenile delinquency in the city and county, local welfare programs, the rise of the Republican party since 1945, and the politics of community action. Of special interest are two recent theses and one dissertation: Ann Lenore Stauffenberg, "Albemarle County, Virginia, 1850–1870: An Economic Survey Based on the U.S. Census," Karl Hess, "Four Decades of Social Change: Scottsville, Virginia, 1820–1860," and Dallas R. Crowe, "Desegregation of Charlottesville, Virginia, Public Schools, 1954–1969: A Case Study."

Files of the *Daily Progress*, which began publication in 1892 and added a Sunday edition in 1968, are available, either on microfilm (regrettably of poor quality) or in bound form since 1908. It is an indispensable guide to the twentieth century, though no index exists, and researchers may wish to consult these special issues which often explore local history and summarize conditions existing in the community: *Daily Progress, Illustrated Edition* (a promotional magazine produced in 1906), a so-called "National Publicity Section" (June 1, 1923), the Monticello Hotel edition (April 8, 1926), a bicentennial issue (April 13, 1962), a University of Virginia sesquicentennial issue (April 13, 1969), and an undated magazine describing the effects of Camille produced in September 1969. Genealogists will find these biographical series, portraits of contemporary citizens appearing in the *Progress*, very helpful: February 1919, February–March 1936, and January–April 1937. Those interested in current history should consult a detailed review of the 1960s by Alan Bruns, February 22–March 3, 1970. Sometimes, but by no means always, the *Daily*

Progress has summarized events of the preceding year in an early January issue.

U.S. Census reports—dry, unemotional, specific—are extremely revealing, especially those of the mid-nineteenth century, 1850–70, giving estimates of personal wealth. Yet, since each director seems intent upon altering categories and methods of classifying data collected every ten years, comparison of these materials throughout succeeding decades can prove baffling indeed. The original census rolls, available on microfilm at the National Archives, Washington, D.C., are now open for inspection through 1900. A handful of articles in the *William and Mary Quarterly*, *Virginia Magazine of History and Biography*, and *Virginia Cavalcade* contain information relating to the local scene. More pertinent, of course, is the *Magazine of Albemarle County History*. Begun in 1941 and originally called *Papers*, this annual is produced by the Albemarle County Historical Society and is an unusually rich repository of local lore and regional information.

The writings of Jefferson scholars such as Dumas Malone, Merrill D. Peterson, Bernard Mayo, and Nathan Schachner tell us something about Albemarle and Charlottesville; but since their hero often traveled far afield and usually in select circles, they can shed only limited light upon events and developments on the local scene. Philip Alexander Bruce's five-volume history of the University of Virginia published in 1920–22 gives very intimate details of that institution's first one hundred years, yet somehow fails to develop a coherent story. Rare is the alumnus who actually has read this work page by page. Much more enlightening is Thomas Perkins Abernethy's brief *Historical Sketch of the University of Virginia* (1948). Publications such as the *University Record, College Topics, Cavalier Daily*, and *Corks and Curls* contain a wealth of information concerning the University of Virginia in this century. Also, some departments such as the hospital and law school have produced their own newspapers and quarterly journals.

The Manuscripts Department of the University of Virginia Library has a substantial number of letters, diaries, pamphlets, photographs, and reminiscences relating to Albemarle and Charlottesville, augmented by the Albemarle County Historical Society's collection which is housed there. Outstanding among filmed materials is the diary of Rev. Robert Rose, first rector of St. Anne's Parish, written circa 1750. And, of course, one should not overlook official records— wills, deeds, reports of meetings, etc.—held by county and municipal authorities. There are two historical museums within the region.

One, that of the Albemarle County Historical Society, is at 220 Court Square, Charlottesville; the other is the Scottsville Museum, a former church.

In a very real sense the volume of published material on Charlottesville and Albemarle parallels the rise, eclipse, and reemergence of Thomas Jefferson as an American hero figure and, in recent decades, the growth of the University of Virginia. The presence of enemy prisoners in 1779–80 and Jefferson's role as a politician, elder statesman, and lavish host from 1790 to 1826 produced a wealth of travel accounts during those years, among them the writings of Isaac Weld, Banastre Tarleton, Thomas Anburey, the marquis de Chastellux, and Baroness von Riedesel, to name a few. Nevertheless, numerous broad topics, especially in this century, remain nearly untouched. We know all too little about changes occurring in the local black community since 1865, the frustrated campaign to lure heavy industry, Charlottesville's suburban growth, the advent of small, clean industrial plants, the role played by the real estate fraternity in local life, the ups and downs of the soapstone quarries through the years, the story of Albemarle's wine industry, recent and far-reaching changes in agriculture, the rise of the region as a major tourist center, the complexities of local politics, and city-county rivalries. Perhaps most ironic of all, even the University of Virginia's last half century is largely an untold saga.

Index

Abernethy, Thomas P., 141, 144, 145
Abolition, 105, 118, 121
Accommodation Mail Line, 183
Acme Visible Records, 457, 474
Adams, Charles Francis, 174
Adams, John Quincy, 159
Adams, Robert, 20
Adams, Roscoe S., 415
Advance, 299
African Church (Carter's Bridge), 233
Afton, 13, 243, 245, 293, 452
Agnes, 457-58
Agriculture, 124, 420, 450; importance of, 31; reforms in, 88-92; in 19th century, 165-70, 249-55; in 20th century, 355-57; statistics on, 377, 393, 441-42, 443; in World War II, 403-4, 405; decline of, 441-44
Airplanes, 295-96, 373, 451
Airport, city-county, 451
Albemarle, William Anne Keppel, earl of, 15
Albemarle Academy, 93, 129
Albemarle Aero Club, 364
Albemarle, Agricultural Society of, 90, 165-66, 170, 180, 267, 356
Albemarle Auxiliary Colonization Society, 118
Albemarle Bible Society, 156
Albemarle Colportage and Sunday School Association, 268
Albemarle County: settlement of, 1-2, 8, 16-30 *passim;* creation of, 9, 21-23; boundaries of, 9, 10, 22; geographical features of, 9-10; place-names of, 12-15; origin of name, 15; division of, 29, 30, 43; resolutions of 1774, 46-47; declaration of 1779, 53; attractions of, 108-9; migration from, 170; creed of, 371-72
Albemarle County Handbook, 252
Albemarle County Historical Society, 217, 335, 391, 470
Albemarle Female Institute, 147-48, 160, 209, 258, 329, 330
Albemarle Golf and Tennis Club, 347
Albemarle Horse Show, 281, 357, 366
Albemarle Hotel (ca. 1820), 98
Albemarle Hotel (Main Street), 266
Albemarle Hotel (Fry's Spring), 278, 299
Albemarle Hunt Club, 364
Albemarle Insurance Company, 172, 264
Albemarle Iron Works, 40
Albemarle Jockey Club, 267, 344
Albemarle Lafayette Guards, 158
Albemarle Literary Society, 156
Albemarle Military Academy, 197
Albemarle pippins, 153-54, 250
Albemarle Ploughing Society, 267
Albemarle Racing Association, 344, 345
Albemarle Rifles, 195, 354
Albemarle Sunday School Association, 341
Albemarle Telephone and Telegraph Company, 248
Albemarle Telephone Company, 248-49
Albemarle Training School, 376. *See also* Union Ridge
Albemarle Volunteers, 49, 55
Albemarle Weaving Company, 407
Alberene, 262, 283, 284, 303n, 326, 366, 376, 381, 459, 460
Alberene Railway Company, 284
Alberene Soapstone Company, 297
Alberene Stone Corporation, 408

Alderman, Edwin A., 295, 304, 308, 309, 340, 378-79, 382, 390, 462, 463; career, 313-19; quells student riots, 368, 385
Alderman Library, 352, 389, 416-17, 464
Alexander, F. M., 316
Alexander, James, 125-26, 219
Alexandria, 171, 177, 183, 286, 476
Aliens, registration of, 394-95
Allen, David, 49
Allen, Lewis F., 252
Almond, Lindsay, 435, 436
Alpha Tau Omega, 304
Altamont Circle, 384
Ambroselli, C. L., 262
American Legion, 355, 387
American Liberty League, 383
Amherst County, 9, 30, 53, 55, 182, 183, 196
Anburey, Thomas, 61, 62-64, 67, 76
Anderson, M. L., 148
Andrews, J. S., 266
Anglicans, 53, 78. See also Episcopalians
Anne, Queen, 12
Annexation, 275, 382, 389, 437-40
Antietam, 197, 200
Antislavery, 114
Antrim, E. M., 262, 299, 384
Apple, Charles S., 290, 292
Apple Harvest Festival, 442, 467. See also Dogwood Festival
Appleberry's Mountain, 12
Apples, 153-54, 250, 442
Appomattox County, 9
Appomattox Courthouse, 211
Appomattox River, 22
Arlington County, 434, 476
Armistead Hunting Club, 344, 345. See also Camp Armistead Hunting Club
Armstrong, James A., 296-97
Arrowhead, 287
Art (theater), 351
Artist Series, 466
Arundale, Nellie, 320
Ash Lawn, 452. See also Highland Tract

Association for the Preservation of the Traditions of the University of Virginia, 317
Astor, Nancy Langhorne, Lady, 311, 342, 359, 378, 383, 416, 467
Astor, Lord, 383
Atlanta, Ga., 286
Augusta County, 9, 92, 228, 255, 345, 427
Aunt Mat, 358
Automobile Blue Book, 293-95
Automobiles, 289, 290, 293
Austin, Arthur W., 260
Austin, Mary, 260
Ayres, S. Edward, 21, 34, 41, 43

B. H. Brennan and Company, 263-64
Babcock, Chester, 436
Bacon, Allan, 218
Bacon Hollow, 342, 374
Bailey, T. W., 269
Bain, Robert, 56
Baker, Sallie, 343
Baldwin, C. P., 160
Ballenger's Church, 78
Ballenger's Creek, 13, 32
Ballou, S. P., 182
Ballou, Thomas, 22, 23, 26
Balthis and Keller (jewelers), 262
Baltimore, Md., 100, 171, 172, 243, 250, 296
Bank of Albemarle, 263, 299
Bank of Crozet, 366
Bankhead, Anne, 104
Bankhead, Charles L., 103-5
Banks, 172, 263-64, 299-300, 384, 456
Baptists, 36, 53, 77, 79, 80, 147, 155, 215-16, 267, 341, 346, 352, 364, 428, 460-61
Barbour, Charles J., 419-20
Barbour, James, 90
Barbour, John, 333, 334
Barboursville, 427
Barboursville Road, 14, 28, 98
Barclay, James, 253
Barclay, Thomas, 133
Barham, Charles, Jr., 407
Barksdale, I. R., 323
Barley, 35
Barnes, C. H., 269

Barnes Lumber Company, 407-8, 417
Barnett, David, 54
Barnett, S., 119
Barnwell, R. W., Jr., 204
Barracks, the, 55-56, 57-60, 61-62, 64
Barracks Road, 427
Barracks Road Shopping Center, 439, 441, 452
Barringer, Anna, 311, 338, 358
Barringer, Paul B., 308-11, 338, 462
Barringer, Mrs. Paul B., 339
Base Hospital Unit No. 41, 353
Basic City, 293, 299
Batesville, 14, 102, 163, 193, 232, 249, 259, 332, 381, 431, 459
Bath County, 244
Battersby, William, 39
Battle, Henry W., 341, 346, 352, 353, 432
Battle, John S., 433-34, 436
Battle, John S., Jr., 434
Battle(s) family, 119
Battles, Shadrack, 54, 55, 67
Bayley Art Museum, 366
Bayne, Beverly, 351
Bean, Randolph, 407
Bear, James A., Jr., 333, 334, 335
Bear Cornfield, 14
Bear Creek, 14
Bear Spring, 14
Beaver Creek, 13
Beaverdams, 13, 14
Beck, E. Nelson, 381
Beck's Hill, 217, 218, 290-92
Beleu, S. P., 182
Belk, J. B., 386
Bell, A. J., 188
Bell, John, 172, 192-93
Bell, Raymond L., 420, 435
Bell family, 427
Belle View, 109
Belmont: Harvie home, 72; Ficklin home, 72n, 167, 252, 345; city ward, 277, 304, 345, 382, 389
Belmont Club, 267
Belt Line, 278, 279
Belvoir, 42, 78
Benefit insurance companies, 431-32
Benner, Edward, 172

Bennett, A. L., 325, 326-28, 331-32, 377, 381, 432
Bennett, Boyd A., 380
Benson, C. P., 276
Benson, T. B., 347
Berkeley, Francis L., Jr., 416-17
Berkeley, Helen, 397
Berryville, 344
Bethel Institutional Baptist Church, 428
Bicentennial, celebration of, 469
Bird, Robert M., 370
Birdwood, 167, 357, 364, 386
Birdwood Jockey Club, 155
Biscuit Run, 13
Bishop, Joseph, 95, 96, 103
Bitting, Samuel, 424-25
Black, Samuel, 78, 82
Black and White taxis, 384
Blackford, Staige D., 397
Blacks: free, 41, 83, 94, 113, 114, 115, 118, 119-20; in Revolutionary War, 54; social life of, 118, 350-51; ordinances regarding, 126-27; taxes on, 163-64; in Civil War, 199; in politics, 224-30, 420; in General Assembly, 242; population of, 275; at John A. Chaloner's funeral, 363; living conditions of, 423-31; hold conventions, 424; "shot free," 428; "born free," 428; at University of Virginia, 463. See also Slaves
Blacksburg, 309, 357
Blackwell's, 163, 346
Blaetterman, George, 133, 139
Blair, Joseph P., 326
Blalock, Richard, 42
Bland, Richard, 50
Blenheim, 60, 88, 473
Bloomfield Academy, 146
Blue Goose Inn, 431
Blue Ledge: See Blue Ridge Mountains
Blue Ridge Hunt Club, 344, 345
Blue Ridge Industrial School, 342
Blue Ridge Mountains, 9-10, 12, 14, 17-18, 29, 61. See also Great Mountain
Blue Ridge Parkway, 378, 469

Blue Ridge Railway Company, 188
Blue Ridge Sanatorium, 366, 456, 457
Blue Ridge Slate Company, 408
Bluefield, 344
Board of Trade, 264
Boar's Head Inn, 452
Boaz, John, 424
Boiling Springs, 78
Bolton, Channing M., 282
Bonnycastle, Charles, 133
Bonus March, 385
Boocock, Murray, 272, 358, 386
Boocock, Mrs. Murray, 384
Boone, Daniel, 65
Boonesville, 356, 459
Boonsboro, Md., 197, 200
Boosterism, 272, 349, 364, 367, 370-
    74, 382, 439. *See also* Neo-
    boosterism
Booth, John Wilkes, 219
Bootlegging, 374-75, 414, 430
Borglum, Gutzon, 353
Boston, Mass., 47
Boston University, 420
Botetourt County, 364
Bowen, William, 112
Bowers, Claude, 389
Bowles, Stephen, 54
Boxing, 76, 387-88
Boxwood (estate), 453
Boy Scouts, 405, 411, 431
Boyden, Ebenezer, 125
Boyd's Tavern, 158, 181, 182, 232, 295
Bradbury, Eugene, 346
Bradford, Russell, 359
Bradley, E. L., 396
Braham, John, 42
Brand, 293
Breckenridge, John C., 192, 193
Bremo, 131
Brennan, B. H., and Company, 263-
    64
Brennan family, 217, 302
Bridges, 99, 179, 293
Bristol, 212, 467
Brock, Henry C., 320
Brockman, Mrs. Ann, 163
Brookhill School, 146
Brookland School, 146
Brooks, Lewis, 260

Brook's Mill, 22
Brooks Museum, 260, 262, 474
Brooksville, 208
Broun, W. LeRoy, 146
Brown, Andrew J., 164
Brown, Benjamin, 14
Brown, Benjamin, Jr., 42
Brown, Benjamin, Sr., 42
Brown, Bezaleel, 14
Brown, Brightberry, 94
Brown, Elijah, 96
Brown, J. Hamilton, 373
Brown, J. Y., 380
Brown, Thomas Harris, 204
Brown, Wallace, 56
Brown, William, 98
Brown, William H., 217
Brown family, 83, 427
Brown's Cove, 12, 204, 232, 459
Brown's Gap, 12, 177, 205
Brown's Gap Turnpike, 98, 206n
Brownsville, 294
Brownton, 14
Brunswick County, 8
Bryan, William Jennings, 336-38, 340
Buchanan, James, 192
Buchanan, 185, 186
Buck Island Branch, 13
Buck Island Creek, 13, 36
Buck Mountain, 12, 14
Buck Mountain Creek, 12, 13, 14, 42
Buck Mountain Road, 40, 78, 102,
    372
Buckeyeland, 268
Buckingham County, 9, 30, 53, 333,
    345, 405
Buckingham Courthouse, 316
Buckner family, 427
Buck's Elbow, 451
Buck's Elbow Mountain, 12
Buena Vista, 453
Buffalo Meadow, 14
Buford, Florence, 328
Buford School, 437
Bull, Ole, 160
Bunch, Rebecca, 42
Bundles for Britain, 416
Bunn, Benjamin F., 433
Burke Archer and Company, 171
Burley family, 427

Burley School, 432, 434, 437, 464
Burlingame, George, 350
Burnley, Carrie C., 327
Burnley, Nathaniel, 98
Burnley, Seth (ca. 1828), 166
Burnley, Seth (county manager),
    381, 382, 393, 396
Burnley, W. R., 262
Burnley-Moran School, 436
Burnleys, 287, 459
Burrus, William, 42
Buses, 372, 384, 435, 451
Bushman, Francis X., 351
Bushnell, David I., Jr., 6
Butler, Edward, 74
Butler-Norris House, 74
Byrd, Harry F., 326, 435, 436

Cabell, Joseph C., 90, 129
Cabell, Nicholas, 82
Cabell, William, 22, 25-30 passim,
    38-41 passim
Cabell Hall, 315, 316, 338, 340, 390
Caffry, Charles, 20
Calathump, 141, 231
Caldwell, Annie, 321
Caldwell, Ed, 369
Cameron, William E., 242, 257
Camille, 457
Camp Armistead Hunting Club, 267.
    See also Armistead Hunting
    Club
Camp Fire Girls, 412
Camp Lee, 364
Camp Strange, 197
Campbell County, 9, 364
Camping Creek, 13
Canals, 98, 242
Cannon, James, Jr., 346
Cannon, John, 20
Carleton, 104
Carpenter, Ann, 404
Carr, Dabney, 46, 82
Carr, Mrs. Frank, 166
Carr, George, 102
Carr, Thomas, 19
Carr, William, 42
Carr family, 83, 115
Carraway, Thaddeus Horatio, 374
Carriages, 96, 262

Carroll, E. L., 282
Carroll, Madeleine, 416
Carroll's Creek, 13
Carroll's Tea Room, 439
Carr's Hill, 295, 315, 352
Carter, Edward, 40, 43, 53, 60, 84
Carter, John, 19, 43
Carter, R. E., 346
Carter, Robert, 19, 118
Carter, Mrs. Robert, 124
Carter, Robert Hill, 133
Carter family, 88, 124, 170, 472
Carter's Bridge, 78, 118, 232, 233,
    252, 443
Carter's Mountain, 12
Cartersburg, 14
Carver Inn, 433
Cary, Archibald, 49
Case, R. R., 282
Cash, Howard, 20
Caskie, Philenae, 233
Castalia, 358
Castle Hill, 65, 68-69, 72, 150-53 pas-
    sim, 174, 194, 276, 361, 473
Castle Rock, 12
Catton, Bruce, 194
Cavalier Daily, 465
Central College, 93, 100, 128, 129
Central Gazette, 95, 96, 97, 103, 122,
    123, 158, 161, 162, 163, 180
Central Hotel, 97, 158, 159, 263, 267
Centreville, 197, 199
Chalk Mountain, 12
Chalmers, Dwight M., 433
Chaloner, John Armstrong, 272, 359,
    361-63, 368, 369, 370
Chamber of Commerce, 300-301, 349,
    364, 371, 380, 381, 389, 406,
    445, 449, 468
Chamberlain, Bernard, 381, 396, 415,
    466
Chanler, John Armstrong. See Chal-
    oner
Chaplin, Charlie, 367
Charles II, 15
Charles Town, W.Va., 208, 445
Charlotte Sophia of Mecklenberg-
    Stretilz, 29
Charlottesville: creation of, 29-30;
    state government in, 64-65; Tar-

Charlottesville (*cont.*)
leton's raid on, 65; merchants in, 99, 170-72, 262-64, 299, 384, 429-30, 441, 457; ordinances of, 126-27, 162, 386; chosen as site for University of Virginia, 129; conducts lottery, 156; town government of, 162-64, 215; streets of, 164-65, 246, 287; internal improvements convention at, 182; railroads reach, 188-89; effects of Civil War on, 201-11; freedmen's schools in, 231-32, 233; becomes a city, 239, 268-69; railroad facilities in, 243-44; growth of, 271-73, 275-76; slogans for, 349; recreation department, 387; police department, 435; new city hall, 441; Mall, 441

Charlottesville Academy, 102

Charlottesville-Albemarle Tribune, 467

Charlottesville and Albemarle Railway Company, 282-84, 302

Charlottesville and Rapidan Railway Company, 243, 286

Charlottesville and University Gas Light Company, 246

Charlottesville and University of Virginia Electric and Gas Light Company, 305

Charlottesville and University Railway Company, 276-77, 278

Charlottesville Chronicle, 214, 217, 220, 226-232 *passim*, 263, 297-99, 302, 344, 365

Charlottesville City and Suburban Railway Company, 278-79, 282

Charlottesville City Code: on motor vehicles, 290

Charlottesville Cornet Band, 160, 199

Charlottesville Country Club, 281, 347, 358

Charlottesville Creamery, 353

Charlottesville Daily Progress. See *Daily Progress*

Charlottesville Debating Society, 156

Charlottesville Factory, 173

Charlottesville Female Academy, 102, 103

Charlottesville General Hospital, 202-5

Charlottesville Hardware Company, 249, 292

Charlottesville High School, 320, 464

Charlottesville Hook, Hose, and Ladder Company, 247-48, 305

Charlottesville Industrial and Land Improvement Company, 296, 302

Charlottesville Institute, 258, 259, 329. *See also* Major Jones's School

Charlottesville Inter-Racial Commission, 433

Charlottesville Jockey Club, 344

Charlottesville Land Company, 296, 302-4

Charlottesville Lumber Company, 301-2, 408

Charlottesville Messenger, 425, 467

Charlottesville Milling and Manufacturing Company, 262, 297

Charlottesville National Bank, 263

Charlottesville National Bank and Trust Company. *See* National Bank and Trust Company

Charlottesville Presbyterian Church, 405, 415-16

Charlottesville Thespian Society, 156

Charlottesville Woolen Mills, 173, 248, 261-62, 297, 301, 407, 453, 467

Chastellux, marquis de, 67, 76

Chauvenet, Louis, 405

Cherry Avenue, 277-78

Chesapeake and Ohio Railroad, 173, 188, 217, 218, 243-48 *passim*, 263, 277, 282-94 *passim*, 302, 333, 358, 369-70, 401, 427, 452. *See also* Virginia Central Railroad

Chester Station, 200

Chestnut Mountains, 19. *See also* Southwest Mountains

Chewning's Mill, 297

Chicago, Ill., 452

Children's Home, 147, 349

Childress, Henry Cecil, 394

Chinard, Gilbert, 87
Chisolm, Hugh, 123
Christ Episcopal Church, 147, 155, 218, 330, 341
Christian, Archer, 358
Christian Church, 216, 268, 341
Church of England. *See* Episcopalians
Circuses, 266
Cismont, 42, 125, 326, 362, 372, 376
Citizens Bank and Trust Company, 366
Citizens Ice and Manufacturing Company, 299
Citizens League, 381
Citizens National Bank, 263
Civil Air Patrol, 395, 402
Civil defense, in World War II, 395-97, 400-403
Civil Rights Act of 1964, 435, 437
Civil War, effects of, 216
Civilian Conservation Corps, 385
Clark, Christopher, 20
Clark, George Rogers, 67, 88, 472
Clark, Jefferson, 156
Clark, Margaret Fowler, 74
Clark, William, 88, 175, 370
Clark, William A., 378
Clarke, James, 166
Clarke, Mrs. James, 166
Clay, Charles, 46, 77-78
Clay, Henry, 78, 150
Cleveland, Grover, 237
Cliffside, 211
Clifton Forge, 186, 287, 357, 451
Clinch Valley College, 463, 464
Clubs, 267, 346-49, 428, 431-32, 465
Cobb, John B., 378
Cobb Chemical Laboratory, 319
Cobham, 148, 188, 232, 288, 361, 362, 368, 443
Coca-Cola, 346
Cochran, Howe P., 320
Cochran, John L., 245, 269, 320
Cochran, Mrs. John L., 339
Cochran's Mill, 264
Cocke, John Hartwell, 90, 131
Cocke, Philip St. George, 197
Cockfighting, 76, 141, 155, 253

Coeducation, at University of Virginia, 312, 313, 318, 342-43, 378, 463, 464
Coffee (University of Virginia workman), 130
Cogan, Thomas, 171
Cole, J. A., 353
Coles, Charles, 429
Coles, Edward (1786-1868), 88, 120-21, 153
Coles, Edward (ca. 1896), 345
Coles, Isaac, 88
Coles, John, 48, 51, 84, 124
Coles, John Carter, 170
Coles, John S., 216
Coles, Peyton S., 167, 216, 345
Coles, T. S., 216
Coles, Tucker, 124, 151
Coles, Tucker, Jr., 151
Coles family, 5, 75n, 151, 152, 216, 276, 358, 427
Coles Building, 429
Colgan, George, 281
Colle, 36, 60, 62
College Topics, 278, 282
Colman, Benjamin, 90
Colonial Hotel, 294
Colonnade Club, 317
Colored Ladies Home, 428
Columbia, 181, 211
Columbia College (University of South Carolina), 128
Committee of Correspondence, 46
Committee of 56, 380
Committee of Safety, 52
Committee on Public Education, 436
Community Chest, 373
Community Leagues, 327
Commuting, 420-21, 443
Compton, Harry, 339
Concord, N.C., 309
Confederate veterans, 264-66, 343-44
Congressional Reconstruction, 221, 224-36
Connally, Tom, 379
Conscription: in Revolutionary War, 55; in World War I, 353; in World War II, 394, 397, 398
Conservatives, 227-30, 240

Consolidated Ice and Electric Company, 282
Constitution of 1787, 88, 194
Constitution of 1902, 237
Continental Association, 48, 49
Continental Congress, 47, 48
Continental Trailways, 451. *See also* National Trailways
Conventions, 389, 424
Conway, A. V., 352
Conwell, Russell H., 349
Cool Spring Barbecue Club, 267
Coolidge, Calvin, 374, 382, 383
Cooper, Thomas, 128
Cooperative Drug Company, 299
Copeley Hill, 415
Copenhaver, Edwin V., 401
Corcoran, W. W., 260
Corcoran Department of History, 311
Corks and Curls, 195, 313, 352
Corn, 35
Corner (at University of Virginia), 277, 387, 445, 461, 469
Cornwallis, Charles, 60, 65, 66
Cosby, Joseph H., 461
Council on Human Relations, 436
Country clubs, 346-47
County court, 160-62, 163
County Unit School Law, 325-26
Coursey, William, 20
Courthouse (precinct), 163
Cove Church, 78
Covesville, 78, 163, 232, 245, 287, 288, 295, 366, 381, 424, 459, 461
Covington, 185, 329, 357
Cow Branch, 13
Cox, L. W., 262
Craddock, William, 20
Craven, Andrew J., 218
Craven, Avery, 34
Craven, John H., 94, 124, 166, 180
Craven, S. E., 302
Craw, Demas T., 411, 417
Craw, Mrs. Demas T., 411
Crop rotation, 89
Cropp, Wilson Warner, 394
Cross Keys, 206
Cross Roads, 163, 182, 356, 432
Crow, Nan, 416

Crozet, Claudius, 177, 181, 183, 189, 254
Crozet, 9, 249, 254, 267, 271, 294, 300, 326, 354, 372, 376, 377, 381, 383, 387, 394, 403, 410, 442, 443, 457, 458, 460, 461, 474, 478
Crozet Cold Storage Corporation, 410
Crozet Fruit Growers' Cooperative, 403
Cuckoo Tavern, 65
Culbertson, Ely, 428
Culin, J. C., 264
Culpeper, 153, 166, 203, 206, 339, 384
Cumberland, Md., 23
Currant's Mountain, 12
Currier, Mrs. Robert L., 387
Curry Memorial School of Education, 315
Curtis, Christopher, 42
Custer, George A., 206-11, 262

D. S. Church, 78
Dabney, A. D., 395
Dabney, Richard Heath, 256-57, 317, 336, 340, 347
Dabney, Virginius, 194
Dabney, William Minor, 89, 92
Daily Progress, 264, 279, 287-88, 299, 305-7, 321, 338, 345-46, 349, 351, 354, 357, 360, 365-88 *passim*, 398, 405, 406, 413, 417, 425, 436, 467
Dalton, Jack, 433
Dalton, Ted, 436
Dalton, Timothy, 20
Damon, 376
Dancing, 32, 159
Daniel, James, 22
Daniel, John Warwick, 333, 334
Danville, 286
Darden, Colgate, Jr., 352, 401, 402, 435, 436, 461-64 *passim*
Daughters of the American Revolution, 358, 369, 412, 470
Davenport, Jesse, 97
Davidson College, 309
Davies, Isaac, 48
Davis, A. K., Jr., 469

Davis, Eugene, 164
Davis, Isaac, 14
Davis, Jefferson, 211
Davis, John A. G., 133, 138-39
Davis, John Staige, 142
Davis, John W., 269
Davis, John W. (politician, b. 1873), 382
Dawson, Martin, 181
Dawson's Mill, 14
Dawson's Row, 144, 181, 195, 279
Day, Douglas, 467
Day, Lucy Chamblis, 335
Dayton, William Lewis, 174
Debt controversy, 240
De Corso, Helen Camp, 428-31
Deems, J. M., 160
Deer Hunting Club, 267
Defoe, James, 20, 26, 28
Defaux, James, 20
Delevan House, 173, 203. *See also* Mudwall
Delevan Hospital, 223, 226, 232
Delta Kappa Epsilon, 141
Democratic party, 192-93, 237, 242, 373, 466
Depression, 385-86, 430
Desegregation, 434-37
Desoin (Designs), Daniel, 20
Dettor, G. Russell, 281
Dettor, Edwards, and Morris (wholesale grocers), 375
Dewey, John, 390
Dickerson, John, 94
Dickey, John, 42
Dickinson, W. P., 330
Diet, in early Albemarle County, 70-71
Dinsmore, James, 100
Dinwiddie, William, 146
Dissenters, 53, 78n
Divers, George, 53, 151, 170
Dixie Flying Service, 373
Doctors, 38
Dodd, John B., 164
Dogwood Festival, 467. *See also* Apple Harvest Festival
Dohorty, Hugh, 20
Dolin, J. W., 109
Dollins, John, 250

Donner, J. W., 321
Dorrier family, 345
Douglas, Stephen A., 192, 193
Doyle, Dennis, 42
Doylesville, 356, 459
Drash, Cato, 397
Dudley, S. J., 269
Dudley's Mountain, 12, 182
Duels, 103-5, 134
Duke, James, 96, 166
Duke, R. W., 269
Duke, R. T. W., 164, 264, 267, 343
Duke, R. T. W., Jr., 155, 193, 195, 204, 208, 229, 268, 269, 353, 360
Duke, Richard, 96
Duke, Thomas H., 171
Duke, W. R., 326
Dummy Line, 278
Dunbar, Helen, 351
Dunglison, Robley, 133, 136
Dunkards, 69
Dunmore, John Murray, earl of, 47, 49, 50, 56
Dunn, Bessie, 357
Du Pont, Philip Francis, 378, 379
Durant, Will, 379
Durrett, Bartholomew, 20
Durrett, Walter, 345
Du Val, Mary Hyde, 330
Dyer's Mill, 14
Dyke, 141

Eagle Hotel, 159
Eagle Tavern, 97, 158, 166, 173
Eagles (lodge), 357
Eakins and Hillbish (laundry), 297-99
Early, James T., 167-68
Early, Jubal, 206, 208
Early, Stephen T., 383
Earlysville, 163, 192, 206, 207, 232, 316, 326, 372, 376, 420, 451, 459-60
Ebeling, Christopher Daniel, 93-94
Ebenezer Baptist Church, 428
Echols, W. H., 317
Echols, William E., 346
Edgehill, 2, 90, 220
Edgehill School, 148, 258, 329
Edgehill Memorial Chapel, 258

Edgemont, 2, 473
Edge's Creek, 13
Ednam Hall, 294
Education: private, 81-83, 102-4, 145-49, 258-61, 329-32, 436; public, 129, 215, 230-32, 316, 319-29, 376-77, 434-37, 464. *See also* Virginia, University of
Edwards, H. P., 262-63
Eighth Evacuation Hospital, 397-98, 405
Eisenhower, Dwight D., 383, 433
Eisenmann's Saloon, 263
Elections: of 1840, 138; precincts of 1851, 163; of 1856 and 1859, 192; of 1860, 172, 192-93, 195; of 1869, 229-30; of 1872 and 1876, 236; of 1880 and 1888, 237; of 1896, 336; of 1924-52, 382-83; of 1948, 432; of 1957, 436
Electric lights, 261, 305-7
Electric Railway Journal, 281
Elk Run. *See* Buck Mountain Creek
Elks Club, 346, 357, 400
Ellerslie, 252
Ellington, J. P., 289, 292
Emancipation, 111
Emmet, John Patton, 133
Emmet Street, 456
Emory and Henry College, 373
Englar, T. S., 404
English settlers, 17
English migrants, 249
Enniscorthy, 121, 151, 472
Episcopalians, 53, 77, 78, 155, 216, 267, 341, 461
Epperson's Mountain. *See* Yellow Mountain
Eppes, Francis, 19
Eppes, Francis (Thomas Jefferson's grandson), 128
Eppes Creek, 13
Esmont, 300, 376, 453, 459
Estes, C. T., 262
Estes, Mrs. Fanny, 400
Estes, Horace O., 400
Estes, Rebecca, 103
Estes, Mrs. Thomas M., 400
Eston Updike Brickyard, 302
Estouteville, 151, 473

Everett, C. D., 216
Everettsville, 163
Excelsior Shops, 263

Fairfax County, 344, 433, 476
Fairs, 166-67, 266
Fairview, 292, 335
Fairway Avenue, 347
Fan's Mountain, 12
Farish, A. J., 269
Farish, F. P., 345
Farish, Thomas L., 211, 216, 217
Farish, William P., 152, 182
Farish family, 302
Farish, Ficklin and Company, 182
Farish House, 173, 263
Farm (Farish home), 211
Farmers, defined, 33
Farmers' Alliance, 244, 255
Farmers and Merchants Bank, 263, 347, 384
Farmers' Bank of Virginia, 172
Farmers' Trains, 357
Farmington (estate), 56, 150, 151, 170, 216, 304, 358, 473
Farmington Country Club, 347, 366, 367, 386-87, 416, 445, 452, 469
Farmington Hunt Club, 466
Farmville, 243, 286
Fat Man's Club, 347
Faulconer, P. H., 359, 386
Faulkner, William, 467
Fauquier County, 152, 255, 334
Fayerweather Hall, 312, 338
Federal agencies in area, 456-57
Federalists, 88
Ferguson, Mabel P., 320
Ferguson family, 427
Ficklin, Slaughter W., 167-68, 182, 217, 250-52, 267
Ficklin family, 72n, 302
Field, James G., 255, 264
Fife, James D., 354
Fife, Robert Herndon, 109, 210, 252
Fife family, 217-18, 302
Fife Chapel, 369
Fifeville, 218, 304
Firemen, 164, 247-48, 305, 387
First Colored Baptist Church, 216, 353, 428, 433

First Street, 217
Fischerz, A. von, 147
Fishburne, C. D., 218, 269, 276
Fisherville, 293
Fitch, William D., 98
Flannagan, B. C., 262, 263, 264, 300
Flannagan, Mrs. B. C., 217
Fletcher, Marshall P., 360, 395
Floods, 457-58
Fluvanna County, 9, 10, 66-67, 78, 120, 180, 333, 362, 405, 421, 464
Fluvanna River, 12-13. See also South Fork
Fonda, Henry L., 386
Ford, Henry, 370
Forest (community), 323
Forest Hill, 458
Forge Church, 78
Fort Frederick, Md., 64
Fort Meade, Md., 393, 394, 395
4-H clubs, 404, 411, 412
Fourth of July, 156-58, 368, 369, 387
Fowler, Christopher L., 208, 211, 246, 345
Fowler, Walter E., Jr., 396
Fox's Mountain, 12
Frank Ix and Sons, 407, 410, 453
Franke, W. R., 402
Franklin, Benjamin, 121
Franklin, James, 55
Fraternities, 304
Fray, A. G., 396
Frazier, Flavy, 49
Frederick County, 442
Fredericksburg, 32, 35, 65, 68, 243, 369, 378, 396, 451
Fredericksburg Female Academy, 103
Fredericksville Parish, 9, 29, 61, 77, 78, 95, 95n, 145-46, 151
"Free born" blacks, 428
Free Bridge, 13, 181, 268
Free State (Dunlora), 115
Free Union, 14, 163, 232, 346, 371, 396, 459
Freedmen's Bureau, 220, 221, 222, 234
Fretwell, William, 266
Frey, Charles T., 147, 160
Frizell (groceries), 262

Fry, Henry, 43
Fry, John, 84
Fry, Joshua, 22-30 passim, 38, 72, 269
Fry, W. O., 269
Fry-Jefferson map, 23
Fry's Spring, 278-84 passim, 299, 304, 329, 340, 344, 382, 385, 400
Fruit, 442
Funders, 236
Funding Act of 1871, 240, 242

Gabriel Plot, 112
Gaines, Martha, 72
Gaines Mill, 200
Galban, J. S., 386
Galt, Alexander, 310
Gamble, Robert, 89
Gantt, Henry, 156, 197
Garden Church, 78
Garden Week, 389, 452
Gardner, Ann, 80
Gardner, Anna, 231-32, 233-34, 236
Garland, Edward, 49
Garland's, 177, 232
Garlick, Samuel, 42
Garnett, C. M., 326, 381
Garnett, James M., 336, 343
Garrett, Alexander, 129
Garrett, John Bolling, 133-34
Garrett Street, 320, 321
Garrison, William Lloyd, 231
Garson, Greer, 411
Garth, Billy, 350
Garth, David, 53
Garth, Eugene, 125-26
Garth, Garland, 166
Garth, Thomas, 53
Garth, William (ca. 1850), 167
Garth, William (horse trainer), 344-45
Garth Road, 373
Garth's Fox Hunting Club, 344
Gas House District, 426
Gaslights, 171, 246, 305-7
Gault, Samuel, 292-93
Gay's Mountain, 12
Gee, Wilson, 356, 379-80
Geiger's Drugstore, 263
Gentry family, 83

George I, 15, 40
George II, 15
George III, 22, 29, 53
George, Harry Alexander, 299, 386
George, Mrs. M. P., 103
George Mason University, 463, 464
George Rogers Clark School, 328, 376
Georgia Marble Corporation, 459
Gemmill, Chalmers, 203, 204, 205
General Assembly, 29, 30, 64, 65
Germans: as settlers, 17, 61, 190, 249; as prisoners of war, 58-62, 401, 403. *See also* Hessians
Gettysburg, 200
Gianniny family, 36
Gianniny, Anthony, 36
Gibbons family, 427
Gibson, Charles Dana, 359
Gibson, Mrs. Charles Dana, 359
Gibson Mountain, 443
Gilbert, 287, 427
Gildea, Ray Y., Jr., 443
Gillard, John, 361, 363
Gillespie, W. G., 262
Gilmer, Francis Walker, 128, 132, 133
Gilmer, George (Williamsburg doctor), 68
Gilmer, George (patriot), 48-57 *passim*, 67, 84-85, 107, 133, 159
Gilmer, George (ca. 1930), 386
Gilmer, Thomas Walker, 182
Gilmer, William W., 125, 167-68
Ginseng, 35
Girl Scouts, 401, 412
Glass, Carter, 334, 379
Glass, E. C., 321
Gleason, Mrs. Eula, 398
Gleason, H. M., 320
Gleason, Mrs. J. Emmet, 417
Gleason, M. S., 299
Gleason, Michael, 469
Gleason Hotel, 294, 299
Glendower, 14, 109, 234
Glenmore, 90
Glenn's Store, 14
Godwin, Nettie M., 320
Goings, Henderson, 168
Goings, Sherard, 54, 55, 120

Goings, Susannah, 55, 120
Goings family, 119
Gooch, R. K., 352
Gooch, William, 8-9
Goochland County, 9, 21-22, 23, 25, 80
Goochland Courthouse, 28, 295
Good Roads Association, 287, 289
Goodloe family, 427
Goodman, David, 222
Goodwin, William H., 353
Goodyear, George, 345
Goolsby family, 54
Gordonsville, 158, 177, 188, 189, 207, 224, 243, 255, 267, 287, 295
Gospel Hill, 427
Gosport, 56
Goss, David, 42
Goss, James W., 148
Grace Episcopal Church, 125, 363
Grady, Henry, 108, 272
Grady Avenue, 428
Grange, 244, 255
Grant, Ulysses S., 200, 211, 213, 229, 236
Gravel Hill, 345
Graves, J. T., 451
Graves, John S., 366, 386, 408
Graves, L. W., 302
Gray, Edmund, 22, 39
Gray, William Farley, 134
Great Mountain, 12, 42. *See also* Blue Ridge Mountains
Greaver, Maurice F., 284
Greeks, 450
Greeley, Horace, 236
Green, Forest, 20
Green Mountain, 12, 151, 177, 272, 275
Greenbrier, 439
Greene County, 9, 421, 464
Greenwood, 146, 208, 237, 250, 272, 275, 311, 326, 342, 354, 359, 376, 386, 387, 393, 440, 443, 446, 452, 467, 468
Greetham, Miles L., 134
Guano, 168, 169

H. E. Young and Company, 302
Haden, Chesley, 403

Haden, E. G., 353, 354
Haden, Henry, 382, 393
Haden, W. D., 393, 396
Hale, Nancy, 467
Hall, B. O., 386
Hamilton, John, 82
Hamm, G. S., 382
Hammack, Richard, 71
Hammack's Gap, 71, 72
Hammer (Hamner) family, 83
Hamner, Earl, Jr., 468
Hampden-Sydney College, 81
Hampton Institute, 427
Hampton Roads, 238
Hancock, R. J., 252, 297
Hanckel, Louis T., 269, 282
Hanover County, 275, 360, 375
Hanover Courthouse, 65
Happy Hollow, 426
Harden, Benjamin, 98
Hardware River, 10, 12, 13, 46, 78,
    99, 287, 297
Harlan, J. F., 248-49
Harlow, James E., 400
Harmer, Robert, 168
Harmon, R. R., 408
Harper, Carleton, 22
Harper, J., 166
Harper, Mary A., 216
Harper's Ferry, 196, 199
Harper's Weekly, 206-7
Harris, Charles P., 297
Harris, Graham, 294, 386
Harris, J. A., 267
Harris, John, 124
Harris, John O., 252
Harris, R. F., 269, 297
Harris, Robert, 42
Harris, W. H., 269
Harris family, 83
Harrison, Benjamin, 237
Harrison, Edward, 134
Harrison, Gessner, 134, 138, 140,
    144, 146
Harrison, William Henry, 138
Harrisonburg, 134, 396, 466
Hart, John, 148, 330
Hartman, Frank E., 398
Hartnagle, Fred, 171-72
Harvard University, 132, 137, 144

Harvie, John (1706-67), 21, 29, 39,
    72, 82
Harvie, John (1742-1807), 57, 64
Hathaway, Cecil, 390
Hats, 96
Havens, Beckwith, 295-96
Hawkins, John, 60, 85
Hayes, Rutherford B., 236-37
Hayes, Mrs. Rutherford B., 237
Headquarters, 204, 205
Health, Education, and Welfare,
    U.S. Department of, 456-57
Heard's Mountain, 12
Heck, William Henry, 315
Hedges, H. S., 373
Heller, M. B., 262
Hemp, 35
Hemphill, W. Edwin, 391
Henderson, James, 124
Henderson, John, 49
Henderson, John, Jr., 48
Henderson, Willis, 411
Henderson and Ervin (manufactur-
    ers), 407
Henderson's Branch, 13
Henderson's Warehouse, 64
Hendren, Samuel O., 159
Hening, William Waller, 120
Henrico County, 9, 152
Henry, Patrick, 48, 49, 58, 66, 372
Hercules Company, 299
Hereford, Frank, 462, 464
Hessian Hills, 439
Hessians, 60-61. See also Germans
Hickin, Patricia, 114
Hickman, Edwin, 22
Hickory Hill, 432
Higginbotham, Joseph A., 197
Higgs, A. F., 220
High Street, 217, 218, 304
High Top Mountain, 12
Highland Tract, 240. See also Ash
    Lawn
Highways: creation of, 26, 27-28,
    98-99, 177-82, 183-84; improve-
    ment of, 245-46, 287, 288-89;
    condition of, 326
Hildreth, Richard, 354
Hildreth, William Sobieski, 445-48,
    453, 456, 469, 470

Hill, J. C., 266
Hillsboro, 163, 196, 271, 294, 381, 460, 461. *See also* Yancey's Mill
Hillside plow, 90
Hinton Avenue Methodist Church, 369
Hoffman, J. H., 159
Hog and Hominy Club, 359
Hole and Corner Club No. 1, 167, 168, 170
Holkham, 167
Holland, Charlton G., Jr., 6
Holly Fork, 125
Home Defense Council, 396
Home front, in World War II, 400-417
Home Laundry, 406
Homer, 315
Honor code at University of Virginia, 139-40
Hoomes, George, Jr., 19
Hoover, Herbert, 383, 389
Hope, M. L., 320
Hopkins, Arthur, 20
Hopkins, James, 48
Horowitz, Dr. (teacher), 103
Horse racing, 76, 155-56, 267, 344-45
Horse shows, 387
Hotels, 97-98, 173, 263, 299, 372, 374, 452
Hotopp, William, 249-50, 260, 261, 442
Hotopp's Wine Cellar, 297
Hough, Mrs. Theodore, 405
House of Burgesses, 25, 43, 46, 47, 50, 472
Howard, Allen, 19, 22, 25, 27, 43
Howard family, 98
Howardsville, 10, 25, 108, 163, 172, 193, 196, 212, 243, 323, 400, 458-59
Howardsville Grays, 197
Howland, Patrick, 20
Hudson, Charles, 19
Huff, J., 171
Humphreys, Mrs. Susanna, 96
Hundley, George A., 199
Hunter's Hill, 294
Hunting, 344-45
Huntington, William, 100

Hunton, Eppa, 334
Ice plants, 297-99
Imboden, John D., 196
Income, statistics on, 474-75
Indians, 5-6, 14-15
Infantile paralysis, 386
Influenza epidemic, 355
Inge, George Pinckney, 427
Inge, Thomas, 427
Inge family, 427
Ingleside, 345
Institute of Public Affairs, 379, 381, 383
Institute of Textile Technology, 453
Insurance companies, 456
Interstate Route 64, 459, 464, 469
Irish, 188, 189-90
Iron, manufacture of, 40
"Iron clad" oath, 229
Irvin, William, 78
Irving, Charles, 81
Irving-Way-Hill Funeral Home, 292
Irwin, Marjorie Felice, 425-28
Isaac, David, 81, 100
Isaac, Isaiah, 81
Isaacs, Nancy, 119
Isaacs, Tucker, 119
Israel, Michael, 81
Israel's Gap, 81
Israel's Mountain, 81
Italians, 36, 131-32
Ivy, 14, 78, 146, 272, 275, 294, 323, 342, 376, 388, 389, 396, 443, 446, 458, 459-60. *See also* Woodville
Ivy Creek, 13, 42, 57, 102, 181, 294, 323, 344
Ivy District, 425
Ivy hockey, 388
Ix, Frank, and Sons, 407, 410, 453

Jackson, Alice C., 432
Jackson, Andrew, 335, 372
Jackson, Stonewall, 191, 202n, 205, 212, 370
Jackson family, 427
Jacob's Run, 13
James, Thomas, 20

James River, 6-12 *passim*, 17, 22-28
    passim, 32, 33, 93, 98, 108, 181,
    182, 293, 443, 457, 472
James River and Kanawha Canal, 98,
    169, 183-88 *passim*, 243, 245,
    284, 471
James River Migration Society, 109
James River Valley Fair, 266
Jameson, John, 42. *See also* Jemir-
    son
Jameson family, 8
Jameson's Gap. *See* Turk's Gap
Jameson's Mountain. *See* Pigeon Top
    Mountain
Jamestown, 6
Jarman, J. E., 262
Jarman's Gap, 12, 28, 177. *See also*
    Woods's Gap
Jarman's Mill, 14
Jarratt, Devereux, 75, 82
Jeans Fund, 326
Jefferies, B. E., 262
Jefferson, Martha, 82, 99, 253
Jefferson, Peter, 19, 20, 21, 22, 26,
    27, 36, 38, 39, 69, 72, 107, 209;
    career, 23-25
Jefferson, Peter Field, 74
Jefferson, Thomas, 2, 10, 17, 29, 35,
    36, 46, 48-49, 52, 62, 64, 67,
    82, 84, 89, 90, 92, 94, 100, 102,
    104, 105, 109, 111, 112, 121,
    122, 124, 134, 136, 137-38, 149,
    150-51, 158, 175, 188, 231, 260,
    272, 315, 339, 372, 384, 461,
    473, 475; on Indians, 5; as a law-
    yer, 39; on wheat, 44; on trea-
    son by slaves, 54*n;* opposes
    conscription, 55; on Barracks,
    58; eludes Tarleton, 65; em-
    barrassed by Tarleton's raid,
    66; influence of, 87-88, 471-72;
    on balloon travel, 99; on slavery,
    112-13; frees five slaves, 113; on
    abolition, 128; on public educa-
    tion, 129; plans University of
    Virginia, 129-30; problems with
    workmen, 130-32; description of,
    152
Jefferson Auditorium, 266, 350, 351
Jefferson Hotel, 159

Jefferson Land Company, 278, 279,
    304
Jefferson National Bank, 300
Jefferson Park, 357, 378
Jefferson Park Company, 282
Jefferson Park Hotel, 278, 281
Jefferson Park Hotel Corporation,
    372
Jefferson School, 232, 233, 320-21,
    323, 327, 328-29, 376, 389, 434,
    437
Jefferson School for Boys, 266, 329
Jefferson Society, 141, 159, 195, 256,
    336
Jefferson Theatre, 350, 351, 352,
    368, 373, 385
Jeffersonian Republican, 125-26, 229,
    243-48 *passim*, 263, 276, 277,
    299, 341
Jemirson, John, 42. *See also* Jameson
Jerdone, Francis, 56
Jessup, Sam, 384, 451
Jessup Bottling Works, 346
Jews, 81, 268
Jim Crow laws, 424, 428
Jitneys, 283
Joachim, E. A., 380
John Bowie Strange Camp, 343
Johnson, Hugh, 383
Johnson, James G., 327
Johnson, Lyndon B., 435
Johnson, Ossian, 226, 227
Johnson, Sarah, 80
Johnson, Thomas Cary, 15
Johnson, William, 49
Johnson and Cator (merchants), 299
Johnson School, 436
Jones, Horace W., 258
Jones, J. P., 387
Jones, Mrs. J. P. (Berta Garth), 345
Jones, James W., 435
Jones, Joseph, 204-5
Jones, Meredith W. D., 98
Jones, Newton Bond, 123, 167, 394
Jones, W. T., 269
Jones and Wiant (merchants), 171
Joplin, Thomas, 42
Jordan, Charles, 20
Jordan, Winthrop, 111-12, 113
Jouett, Jack, 65, 66, 351, 369

Jouett, John, 64, 65
Joyes, Lt. (Freedmen's Bureau official), 223, 224, 232
Judge Advocate General's School, 415, 457
Justices (magistrates), 27, 160-61, 163

Kasle, Leonard, 433
Kasson, John Adams, 118-19, 170
Kaufman, Moses, 262, 320
Kaufman, Sol, 371
Kean, Robert G. H., 219-20
Kean family, 253
Keblinger, William M., 164, 478
Keelona, 118, 170
Keene, Nancy Witcher, 359
Keene, 177, 466
Kegley, J. B., 381
Keith, Elliewood, 387
Keith, Mrs. Elliewood Page, 387
Keller, John, 158
Keller, Samuel, 299
Keller, W. J., 300
Keller and George (jewelers), 262, 299
Kelley, T. Frank, 248
Kelly, Aleck, 227
Kelly, C. G., 346
Kelly, John, 74
Kennie (Kenny) family, 11
Keswick, 232, 272, 275, 295, 362, 384, 389, 401, 430, 446, 453
Keswick Club, 267
Keswick Country Club, 452
Keswick Hunt Club, 344, 345, 387, 466
Key, Thomas Hewitt, 133
Key West, 445
Key's Mill Creek. See Red Bud Creek
King, W. W., 301
King Lumber Company, 301, 366
Kinkead, David, 42
Kinkead, William, 139
Kinkead family, 8
Kinsolving, G. W., 97
Kitch Inn, 387
Kiwanis Club, 347, 349
Knight, Andrew, 353
Knights of the Golden Horseshoe, 8

Knipscher, William Cornelius, 394
Knothe Brothers. See Monticello Shirt Company
Ku Klux Klan, 368-69, 424

L. H. Wiebel Company, 408
La Baume, F. E., 301
Lafayette, marquis de, 120, 158-59, 295, 339, 372
Lafayette Theatre, 351, 355, 367
Laird, William H., 397
Laird's Apple Jack, 376
Lamb, Maxine, 404
Lambeth, William A., 304, 312
Lambeth Field, 282, 295-96, 312, 327, 355, 359, 374, 382, 423
Land, ownership of, 41, 43
Land patents, 8n, 19-20, 42
Land use tax, 440
Landis, Mrs. Ora, 384
Lane, James W., 321, 327
Lane High School, 376, 389, 394, 402, 411, 434, 435, 450, 460
Langhorne, Chiswell Dabney, 294, 359, 364
Langhorne, Mrs. D. W., 386
Langhorne, Elizabeth, 467
Langhorne, Irene (Mrs. Charles Dana Gibson), 359
Langhorne, Phyllis, 359
Langhorne, W. H., 359
Langhorne family, 276, 359
Langley, William, 123
Lankford, Thomas, 42
Lankford, W. A., 248
Lankford Avenue, 427
Lanza, G., 147
La Rowe, Johnny, 387-88
Laundries, 297-99
Lawyers, 39
League of Women Voters, 380, 465
Leake, Samuel, 78
Leake, Shelton, 192
Leap, William L., 431-32
Leaton, Ann, 147
Leaton, Jane, 147
Leckie, R. J., 269
Lee, Fitzhugh, 334, 336, 343, 344
Lee, H. B., 330
Lee, Robert E., 211, 212, 213, 370

Lee, Robert E., Jr., 201
Leftwich, E. H., 263
Leftwich, E. M., 263
Leggett's, 390
Leitch, James, 100
Lemon Hill, 14
Leterman, Ben, 299
Leterman, Jake, 299
Leterman, Moses, 269, 299, 300
Leterman, Philip, 299
Leterman, Simon, 262, 299, 384
Leterman family, 279
Levy, Jefferson Monroe, 253-54, 266, 339
Levy, Uriah P., 253, 254
Levy Opera House, 266, 329, 350. See also Town Hall
Lewis, Betty, 147
Lewis, C. B., 402
Lewis, Charles, 19, 48, 49
Lewis, Charles B. J., 84
Lewis, Charles L., 49
Lewis, David, Jr., 39
Lewis, H. M., 282
Lewis, James H., 148
Lewis, Jesse, 180
Lewis, Meriwether, 88, 175, 370, 472
Lewis, Nicholas, 29, 48
Lewis, Robert, 29, 39, 42
Lewis, Warner, 162
Lewis, William T., 49
Lewis family, 53, 54, 343, 458
Lewis County (now West Virginia), 170
Lewis Meeting House, 79
Lewis Mountain, 13
Lewis's Ferry. See Moore's Ford
Lexington, 129
Lick Run, 14
Lile, W. M., 304
Limestone Creek, 13
Lincoln, Abraham, 152, 174, 192-95 passim, 219, 229
Lincoln School, 233
Lindsay, J. H., 299, 386
Lindsay, Reuben, 49
Lindsay family, 467
Lindsay's Turnout, 163
Lipop, J. W., 172, 218
Literature, 467-68

Little, William, 42
Little Mountain, 12
Little River. See Rivanna River
Little York, 179-80. See also New York
Lively's Mountain, 12
Livers, J. L., 282-83
Livestock, 166-70 passim, 250-52, 442-43
Local government, 22-23, 26-27, 162, 163-64, 215, 268-69, 380-81, 440
Locust Grove, 217
Locust Valley Academy, 146
Log Cabin Bar, 346
Logon, 255
Lomax, John Tayloe, 133
Long, George, 133
Lotteries, 155-56
Loudon County, 255
Louis Philippe, 153
Louisa County, 9, 10, 22, 28, 61, 181, 228, 288, 468
Louisa Courthouse, 65, 295
Louisa Railroad Company. See Virginia Central Railroad
Lovingston, 374, 443
Lowe, Harry, 371
Lowry, John, 49
Lowry, Malcolm, 467
Loyal Land Company, 69
Lucas, Charles W., 417
Lutherans, 216, 268
Lynch, Charles, 21, 22, 26, 28, 43
Lynchburg, 21, 99, 103, 172, 177, 182, 183, 184, 189, 259, 286, 288, 310, 321, 336, 344, 378, 452, 466
Lynchburg Republican, 202, 207-8
Lynchburg Road, 212
Lynchings, 268, 344
Lynch's Ferry, 28
Lynch's River, 13
Lyric (theater), 351

McClellan, George B., 206
McConnell, James R., 352-53
McCord, William, 42
McCormick, Leander, Jr., 260
McCormick, Robert, 389
McCrory's, 299
McCue, C. Purcell, 381

McCue, Fanny, 360
McCue, Samuel, 359, 360-61
McCue, Sarah Belle, 369
McDowell, 206
McGhee, N. C., 269
McGhee's Old Field, 14
McGuffey, William Holmes, 142, 201
McGuffey School, 327, 328
McGuire, Murray M., 312
McIlhany, Hugh M., Jr., 341
McIlroy, Robert L., 386
McIntire, Paul Goodloe, 212, 357, 369-70, 467
McIntire family, 218
McIntire Ampitheatre, 367, 383
McIntire Park, 389, 432, 464
McKee, Andrew, 96
McKennie, C. P., 96
McKennie, J. H., 96
Mackilligott, Alexander, 20
McKinley, William, 338
Mackneely, Robert, 42
McMannaway, M. M., 326
Macon, L. S., 386
McPhearson, Christopher, 120
Madison, Dolley, 153
Madison, James, 82, 88, 111, 121, 128, 134, 137, 152, 158, 182, 464, 472, 475
Madison, 206
Madison County, 180, 209
Madison Hall, 282, 315, 317
Magisterial districts, replace parishes, 214-15
Magistrates. See Justices
Magruder, Benjamin H., 191, 244
Magruder, Edward May, 311
Magruder, Henry M., 269
Mails, complaints concerning, 99
Main Street (Charlottesville), 165, 218, 288, 371, 373; street cars on, 277-78; parades, 367-68; improvements, 384, 386; parking meters, 389; Mall, 441
Mainfort, Bobby, 347
Major Jones's School, 258, 329. See also Charlottesville Institute
Mahone, William, 240, 242
Mall, 441

Malone, Dumas, 23, 313, 314, 318, 389; wins Pulitzer Prize, 468
Managerial government, origins of, 380-82
Manassas, 109, 195-203 passim
Manassas Gap Railroad, 196
Manchester, 35
Mannoni, Andrew, 172
Mannoni, John, 218, 263
Manufacturing, 40, 173, 261-62, 301-3, 453; in 1820, 94-98; efforts to attract, 296-97; rejection of, 366-67; in World War II, 406-10
Manumission, 113
Maphis, Charles S., 316, 379
Marchant, Henry Clay, 173, 261, 282
Marchant, John Adams, 173
Marguerite's, 468-69
Marks, John, 48, 49
Marr, Gideon, 39
Marr, John, 77n
Marshall (merchant), 262
Marshall, John, 182, 398
Marshall, Samuel H., 346
Marston, Lee, 467
Martha Jefferson Hospital, 311, 384
Martin, Goulay, 295
Martin, John (ca. 1775), 49
Martin, John (brother of Thomas S.), 293
Martin, John A., 395
Martin, Key, 84
Martin, N. W., and Brothers, 410
Martin, Thomas, Jr., 49
Martin, Thomas S., 292, 296, 333-36, 338, 364, 446
Martinsville Seven, 434
Mary Washington College, 378, 463, 464
Maryland, 190, 214, 249
Mason, R. P., 266
Massey, John, 240-42, 255
Massie, Frank A., 282, 296, 320, 323, 324
Massie, John O., 268
Massie, Mrs. Sue W., 386
Massie, Mrs. William, 467
Massive Resistance, end of, 435, 436
Matacia, Louis H., 396

Mathews, J. B., 390
Matthews (confectioner), 262
Maupin, Addison, 142
Maupin, Daniel (ca. 1750), 42
Maupin, Daniel (ca. 1945), 404
Maupin, Socrates, 201, 208
Maupin, William, 14
Maupin(e) family, 54, 83
Maupin's Tavern, 14
Maury, James, 78, 82
Maury, Jesse, 338, 339
Maury, Matthew Fontaine, 211, 339
Maury, Nannie, 211
Maury, Thomas J., 158
Maury family, 154
Maury's Mills, 305
Mayfield, John, 42
Mayhew, Odie, 355-56
Mazzei, Philip, 36, 53, 60, 89, 249
Meade, R. K., 147
Meadow Creek, 13
Meadowbrook Hills, 304, 347
Mechum, George, 13
Mechum's Depot, 14
Mechum's River, 12, 13, 82, 177, 180, 188, 205, 206, 232-33, 294, 368
Mechunk Creek, 13
Merchants, 39, 99, 170-72, 262-64, 299, 384, 429-30, 441, 457
Meredith, James, 39
Merger, city-county voters reject, 440
Meriwether, Jane, 42
Meriwether, John, 29
Meriwether, Margarett, 84
Meriwether, Mildred, 82
Meriwether, Mildred Thornton, 68
Meriwether, Nicholas, 19, 29, 42, 68
Meriwether, Nicholas, Jr., 20, 81
Meriwether, Peter, 167
Meriwether, Mrs. T. W., 166
Meriwether, Thomas, 19, 29, 39
Meriwether, William H., 134, 179
Meriwether family, 54
Meriwether Lewis College for Women, 342-43
Meriwether Lewis School, 326, 376
Merrick, W. G., 109, 266
Merrie Mills, 361-70 passim, 387
Merrill, Robert, 440
Merrill, Thomas, 31

Methodists, 53, 79-81 passim, 155, 215-18 passim, 267, 341-52 passim, 460-61
Michie, George R. B., 365, 445, 446
Michie, J. Tevis, 408
Michie, Mrs. J. Tevis, 407
Michie, James, 240
Michie, John A., 102
Michie, L. A., 323
Michie, T. J., 346
Michie, Thomas (co-founder, Michie Publishing Company), 365
Michie, Thomas (mayor, ca. 1958), 436
Michie, William, 40
Michie Publishing Company, 302, 365, 467
Michie Tavern, 40, 98, 102, 372, 452
Middle Church, 78
Midway (Garth home), 167
Midway Building, 393. See also Midway School
Midway Hospital, 204
Midway Hotel, 159
Midway House, 203, 320
Midway School, 203, 284, 320-28 passim, 376
Miller, Mrs. (milliner), 99-100
Miller, Francis Pickens, 433
Miller, James R., 134
Miller, John, 259
Miller, Samuel, 259-61, 312, 331-32
Miller, Thomas, 134
Miller and Rhoads, 457
Miller School, 249, 250, 257, 259-61, 268, 294, 296, 330-32, 393, 474
Miller's Branch, 13
Miller's Tavern, 14
Millet, 90-92
Millington, 233
Mills, David, 42
Mills, Mathew, 20
Mills, 36, 58, 94-97, 102, 173, 261-62, 297, 384, 407, 453
Milton, 10, 13, 28, 32, 64, 89-98 passim, 108, 163, 179, 187, 271, 389, 402, 460
Mineral, 369
Minor, C. Venable, 396
Minor, Charles, 146

Minor, Dabney, 90, 124
Minor, James, 188
Minor, John, 20
Minor, John Barbee, 142, 201, 208, 209, 230, 234, 257
Minor, Peter, 90
Minor, R. T., Jr., 366
Minor, William, 342
Minor family, 124
Minor Hall, 315, 388
Minute Men, 52
Mirador, 276, 294, 359
Mitchell, Billy, 373
Mitchell, Henry B., 420
Moley, Raymond, 379
Molyneaux, Lambert, 433
Monacans, 5-6
Monasukapanough, 5, 6
Monck, George, 15
Monroe, George, 340
Monroe, James, 128, 158, 159, 372, 472, 475
Monroe, 286
Montesano, 335
Montgomery, Ala., 308
Monticello, 2, 65, 76, 85, 86n, 90, 94, 99, 100, 104, 137, 151, 152, 158, 252-54, 266, 339, 367, 369, 384, 389, 394, 411, 448, 452, 467, 471, 473
Monticello Association, 253
Monticello Bank, 172
Monticello Cigar Company, 262
Monticello Dairy, 428
Monticello Guard, 195, 264, 268, 344, 352, 353, 393, 395, 402, 417
Monticello Hotel, 263, 372, 374, 400, 446, 452
Monticello House, 163, 173, 203. See also Old Stone Tavern
Monticello Mountain, 12, 366, 372, 378
Monticello Shirt Company, 407
Monticello Wine Company, 250, 297, 339, 346
Moody, Dwight L., 341
Moon, J. B., 282
Moon, Jacob, 53, 75
Moon, Samuel, 216
Moore, James O., 206

Moore, James T., 242, 257
Moore, Shepherd, 168
Moore, Virginia, 211, 340, 467
Moore's Creek, 13, 137, 179, 181
Moore's Ford, 13, 95, 98, 181
Moorman, Marcellus N., 206, 207
Moorman, Thomas, 13
Moorman's River, 12, 13, 233, 380
Mopsik, Harold, 258-59, 329
Moran, Charles E., Jr., 292
Moran, F. Berger, 345
Moran, John, 42
Moran, Sarepta A., 327
Morea, 204, 205
Moreman, Charles, 20
Morgenthau, Henry, 411
Morrill, Caroline, 154
Morris, John, 381
Morris, John R., 380
Morris, William, 42
Morse, Jedidiah, 92-93
Morton's Frozen Foods, 442, 457, 474
Morven, 2
Mosby, John S., 212-13, 351
Moser, Emma, 321
Mosley, Willard, 295
Moss, W. W., 290
Motels, 389, 451
Mothers Clubs, 385, 467
Motor vehicles, plethora of, 476
Mount Ed, 102
Mount Fair, 271, 459
Mt. Moriah Methodist Church, 80
Mount Pleasant, 234
Mount Walla, 72-74
Mt. Zion Baptist Church, 428, 432
"Mountain Chappel," 78
Mountain Falls Creek, 13
Mountain Plains, 78
Mountain Ridge Road, 28. See also Three Notched Road
Mountain View, 326
Movies, 279, 350-52
Mudwall, 216, 227, 231, 232. See also Delevan House
Mullins, John, 42
Mullins, Mathew, 42
Munford, Mary Cooke Branch, 318
Murphy, J. M., 276

Musgrove, R. A., 232
Music, 159, 160

N. W. Martin and Brothers, 410
NAACP, 434
Napier, Patrick, 22
Napier, Thomas, 48
Napoleon III, 153
Nash, Charles P., Jr., 396
National Bank and Trust Company, 300, 364, 384, 385, 456
National Bank of Commerce (Norfolk), 456
National Public Service Company, 284
National Science Foundation, 462
National Trailways, 384. See also Continental Trailways
Native Reconstruction, 221-24
Neff, J. H., 386
Negroes. See Blacks
Nelson, H. T., 276
Nelson, Hugh, 124, 166, 182
Nelson, Mrs. Hugh, 150
Nelson, Hugh T., Jr., 290
Nelson, P. W., 323
Nelson, Robert, 84
Nelson, Thomas, 40
Nelson, Thomas H., 134
Nelson, William, 40
Nelson family, 151
Nelson and Albemarle Railway, 459
Nelson County, 9, 10, 25, 180-83 passim, 196, 303n, 374, 421, 453, 459, 464, 468
Neo-boosterism, 446-48. See also Boosterism
Neve, Frederick William, 342
New Deal, 385
New Light: religious movement, 75; readjusterism, 240
New Orleans, La., 286
New South, 108, 272
New Town, 460
New York (Albemarle County), 89, 93. See also Little York
New York (state), 190, 214, 249
New York City, 387
New York Times, 244
Newcomb, John L., 375, 379, 390, 417, 463

Newcomb Hall, 464
Newcombe and Kell (contractors), 341
Newcomb's Mountain, 247
Newport News, 243, 452
Newspapers, 263, 299, 467
Nicholas, George, 19
Nicholas, George (younger), 85, 88
Nicholas, John, 88
Nicholas, Robert Carter, 84
Nicholas, Wilson Cary, 88, 89, 98
Nicholas family, 54, 85
Nimmo, G. F., 398
Nineteenth Virginia Regiment, in Civil War, 195-201
Nixville. See Free Union
Norfolk, 56, 103, 177, 193, 229, 287, 289, 417, 434, 456, 476
Norfolk and Western Railroad, 287
Norfolk County, 152
Norris, Opie, 74, 182
Norris family, 193
North Carolina, University of, 314, 375, 382, 383
North Fork, 12. See also Rivanna River
North Garden, 42, 78, 156, 177, 192, 245, 262, 286, 339, 376, 382, 394, 443
North Milton, 33
Northern Neck, 19
Northern Pacific Railroad, 364
Northern Virginia Regional Defense Council, 396
Nortonsville, 245, 271, 459
Nydrie, 474

Oak Lawn, 210
Oakland, 294
Observatory Mountain, 211
Odd Fellows, 432
Odd Fellows Hall, 430
Office of Price Administration, 411, 412-15
Ohio State University, 445
Old Dominion (village), 459
Old Ivy Inn, 335
Old Scottsville Road, 425, 426
Old Stone Tavern, 203. See also Monticello House

Old Woodville, 2, 151, 358, 473
Oliver's Store. *See* Batesville
O'Neal, John L., 96
O'Neill, Charles T., 326
Orange, 200, 243, 281, 287, 336
Orange and Alexandria Railroad, 189, 195, 243, 286. *See also* Southern Railway
Orange County, 9, 28, 61, 180, 362, 421
Order of the Thousandfold, 342
Ordinances, of Charlottesville, 126-27, 162, 279, 386
Ordinaries, 26, 27, 39. *See also* Taverns
Ortman, Randolph, 359, 386, 389
Overman, Edward, 381
Owen, D. B., 403
Owensville, 233, 460
Owsley, Frederick, 293
Oxford University, 23, 463

Page, Annie R., 326
Page, James, 263
Page, James M., 317
Page, Jane Walker, 150, 151
Page, Mann, 124, 150
Page, R. C. M., 195
Page, Thomas Nelson, 339
Page family, 151
Pageants, 367-68
Page's Store, 459
Palmer, John M., 336
Pamunkey River, 32
Pantops Academy, 259, 329, 382
Paramount Theatre, 388, 412, 429
Parent-Teacher Association, 412, 431
Park Street, 218, 219, 304, 360
Parking meters, 389
Parlier, Gertrude Dana, 391
Parrott, C. H., 269
Parrott, W. J., 263
Pasture Fence Mountain, 12
Patterson, John C., 262
Patterson, Camm, 313
Patterson, James A., 384
Patti, Adelina, 160
Patton, Alexander, 42
Paul, John, 437
Payne, A. D., 276, 290, 292, 299

Payne, Bruce R., 315, 316
Payne, W. C., 269
Payne and Massie (real estate dealers), 109
Peabody Fund, 321
Peabody Hall, 315
Peabody Teachers College, 316
Peace conventions, 194
Peach brandy, 60, 70, 86
Peaches, 86, 250, 403, 442
Peagram, Colonel (mill executive), 248
Peebles and Carpenter (architects), 321
Pen Park, 85, 133, 166, 249
Pence and Sterling's Drugstore, 358, 373
Pennsylvania, 190, 214, 249
People's National Bank, 263, 281, 299-300, 365, 384, 391, 445, 465
Pepsi-Cola, 346
Percival (University of Virginia workman), 130
Peregory, Frank, 417
Perkins, E. L., 386
Perkins, George, 276
Perkins, W. Allan, 346, 359, 386
Perley, James, 262
Perry, Calvin L., 134
Perry, John M., 100, 122
Perry, Randolph H., 396
Perry, W. D., 172
Peter's Mountain, 12
Petersburg (Albemarle County), 14
Petersburg, 56, 99, 200, 227, 242, 364, 466
Peterson, Leonard H., 406
Petrie, George, 268
Peyton, Charles, 134
Peyton, Green, 126, 192, 254, 460
Peyton, Philip Bradley, 354
Phelps-Stokes Fund, 379, 425, 431
Phi Gamma Delta, 445
Philadelphia, Pa., 100, 171
Phillips, Joseph, 42
Phillips, William, 60
Pi Kappa Alpha, 304
Piedmont (Maury home), 154, 211, 338
Piedmont Airlines, 451

Piedmont Candy Company, 218
Piedmont Community College, 464
Piedmont Female Academy, 148
Piedmont Female Institute, 147, 148, 160, 258, 329
Piedmont Hospital, 310
Piedmont (*Charlottesville*) *Intelligencer*, 263
Pigeon Top Mountain, 12
Piggly Wiggly grocery, 384
Pigs, in Charlottesville, 269, 404
Pine Knot, 339-40
Piney Grove, 323
Piney Mountain, 13, 21
Piney Run, 13
Piper, Judy, 424
Pitcher, William, 248
Pitts, John L., 293
Pitts family, 345
Plain Dealing, 339
Planters, defined, 33
Pleasants, Mrs. J. W., 233
Pleasants, Richard, 168
Plum Orchard Branch, 13
Plum Tree Branch, 13
Poe, Edgar Allan, 339
Poindexter's Mountain. *See* Piney Mountain
Point of Fork, 10, 22, 64, 66, 181
Politics, 192-94, 226-30, 236-37, 420
Pollard, J. E., 398
Pollard, John Garland, 378, 459
Pond, Virginia, 398
Population, 83, 94, 105, 108, 115, 119, 123, 152, 159, 189-90, 214-15, 237-38, 249, 271, 275-76, 324-25, 356, 392-93, 449, 457, 477
Populists, 237, 244, 255
Port Republic, 203, 206
Porter, H. D., 276
Porter, J. W., 250
Porter, Belden and Company, 182
Porter's, 163, 192, 271
Portsmouth, 56
Portsmouth Navy Yard, 196
Potts, Allen, 312
Potts, Mrs. Allen, 357, 387
Poultry, 442, 443
Pouncey, Anthony, 20

Powers, D. P., 234-35, 269, 323
Powhatan County, 197, 212
Presbyterian Manse, 218
Presbyterians, 53, 77-80 *passim*, 155, 216, 267, 268, 341, 433, 461
Press Inn, 430
Preston, John B., 162
Preston, T. L., 218
Preston, William B., 159
Preston family, 302
Preston Avenue, 218, 425-28 *passim*
Preston Heights, 218, 283, 346, 428
Preston Place, 349-50
Pretty's Creek, 36. *See also* Priddy's Creek
Price, James H., 395, 396
Price, John, 94
Priddy's Creek, 13, 14, 36
Princeton University, 81, 128, 256, 340
Prisoners of war, 55-62 *passim*, 403
Proffit, 286, 398, 400, 425, 459
Progressive Club, 428, 429, 431
Prohibition, 345-46, 374-75
Pugh, N. W., 384
Purdie, Alexander, 48
Pursuits of War, 391
Pyle, Ernie, 411

Quakers, 75n, 77, 79
Quarles, James, 48, 49
Quinn, Patrick, 180

Rabies, 163
Race relations, 120, 221, 222, 419-20
Radicals, 226-30, 240, 262
Radio, 373, 407
Ragged Mountains, 10, 12, 142, 247, 342
Raggi, Giacomo, 131-32
Raggi, Michele, 131
Railroads, 452; plans for, 187; effects of, 189, 364; growth of, 242-45, 284-89; desegregation of, 435
Raleigh Tavern, 47
Ramsay, John, 77
Randall, John Witt, 311
Randall Hall, 311
Randolph, Benjamin F., 134
Randolph, George A., 386

Randolph, James, 134
Randolph, Jane, 23
Randolph, Jane Nicholas, 104, 148, 258
Randolph, Richard, 19, 29
Randolph, Thomas Jefferson, 103-5, 123, 124, 148, 166
Randolph, Thomas Jefferson, Jr., 216, 226
Randolph, Thomas Mann, 32-33, 84, 89-90, 154
Randolph, W. C. N., 266
Randolph, William, 78
Randolph family, 154, 253, 258
Rappahannock River, 8, 28, 32, 223
Rapidan River, 207
Rationing, in World War II, 412-15
Rawlings, Mary, 26, 470
Rawlings, R. H., 330
Rawlings Institute, 258, 329, 330. See also Albemarle Female Institute; St. Anne's-Belfield School
Readjusters, 236, 240-42, 257
Real estate, development of, 302-4
Reconstruction, 219-36
Recreation facilities, 387, 467
Red Bear Hollow, 14
Red Bud Creek, 13
Red Cross, 309, 349, 354, 393-94, 400-401, 465
Red Hill, 286, 326, 339, 376, 431-32
Redland Club, 346, 347, 445
Redland Land Corporation, 304, 346, 378. See also Redland Power Corporation
Redland Power Corporation, 283. See also Redland Land Corporation
Redlands, 170
Reed, Clement, 39
Rees, Miss (teacher), 147
Reg, Daniel, 168
Reierson, Oscar, 250, 262
Religion, 29, 53, 77-81, 141-42, 155, 215-16, 341-42, 267-68, 428, 460-61. See also Dissenters; Vestry
Rent control, 415
Republican party, 193, 237, 240, 242, 383, 427
Reserve Officers Training Corps, 353, 354, 457

Reservoir Creek, 305
Resolutions of 1774, 46-47
Review, 125, 126, 142, 146, 148, 160, 165, 171, 172-73, 192, 193
Revivals, 341, 357-58, 387
Revolutionary War, causes of, 45
Rex (theater), 351
Reynolds, David, 161
Reynolds, William C., 168
Rhodes, John, 124
Rhodes, Leroy, 268
Rhodes family, 268
Rich Cove, 14
Richard Woods Road, 14
Richmond, Nicholas, 227
Richmond, 8, 9, 10, 23, 25, 28, 30, 48, 57, 85, 92, 93, 99, 103, 108, 137, 150, 160, 166, 171, 174, 177, 182-96 passim, 200, 202, 206, 209, 211, 220, 227-29 passim, 242-44 passim, 264, 277, 287-89 passim, 293, 295, 310, 343, 344, 362, 373, 384, 398, 432, 451, 456, 457, 466, 476
Richmond and Allegheny Railroad, 243, 284
Richmond and Danville Railroad, 286
Richmond and West Point Terminal Company, 286
Richmond Examiner, 203
Richmond-Parkersburg Pike, 294
Ridge Street, 217, 218, 278, 304, 427
Riedesel, Baron von, 58-62 passim
Riedesel, Baroness von, 61, 62
Rinehart, Hollis, 300, 352, 357, 359, 381, 384, 386, 439; career, 364-65
Rinehart, Jack, 386, 387
Rinehart, Jill T., 466
Rinehart, Roger, 386
Rinehart, W. A., 386
Rinehart family, 439, 453
Rinehart and Dennis (contractors), 364
Rio, 287
Rio Bridge, 14
Rio Hill, battle of, 206-8
Rio Mills, 262, 297
Riots, at University of Virginia, 137-38

Rivanna River, 5, 6, 12-14 *passim*, 21, 30-33 *passim*, 64, 77, 93, 177, 179, 183, 206, 242, 294, 347, 472; influence of, 10, 27-28. *See also* North Fork
Rivanna and Rockfish Gap Turnpike Company, 179-80
Rivanna Canal, 98, 180
Rivanna Club, 347
Rivanna Mills, 96-97
Rivanna Navigation Company, 181, 187, 188, 245
Rivanna Water Gap, 28, 29, 94
River Road, 28, 98
Rives, Alexander, 227, 228
Rives, Alfred, 174
Rives, Amélie (writer), 361
Rives, Amélie Louise, 153
Rives, George, 118-19, 151
Rives, Judith Walker, 150-53, 165, 170, 174-75, 190
Rives, William Cabell, 107, 150-52 *passim*, 158, 166-67, 174, 211; career, 153; on secession, 193-94
Rives family, 151, 152, 276
Rixey, Persley M., 339
Rixey House, 329
Roanoke, 344
Roanoke Rapids, N.C., 362
Robert E. Lee Elementary School, 436
Roberts, L. G., 396
Robertson, William, 42
Robertson, William J., 212, 216
Robeson, Paul, 428
Robinson, F. W., 345
Robinson, Morgan Poitiaux, 316-17
Rock Hill Academy, 436
Rock Springs, 181
Rockefeller, John D., Jr., 367, 370
Rockfish Gap, 12, 14, 89, 93, 130, 177, 208, 293
Rockfish Gap Commission, 129
Rockfish Gap Turnpike, 98, 99, 177-80, 181, 183
Rockfish Mountain, 93
Rockfish River, 9-14 *passim*, 25, 28, 69, 181, 472
Rocky Creek, 13
Rodes, David, 48, 51
Rodes, Jim, 268

Rogers, E. Reinhold, 329
Rogers, John, 42
Rogers and Wyatt (teachers), 103-4
Roman Catholics, 216, 268, 433, 461
Rood (arrested for subversion), 190
Roosevelt, Franklin Delano, 374, 380, 383, 417; speaks in Charlottesville, 379, 392
Roosevelt, Theodore, 338-40
Roosevelt, Mrs. Theodore, 339
Rose, Robert, 31-32, 33, 69, 75-78 *passim*
Rose Hill, 218, 297, 302, 347
Roseisle, 33
Ross, Charles H., 268
Rosser, Thomas Lafayette, 364
Rosser family, 302, 304
Rotary Club, 347, 349, 364, 370, 380
Rothwell, J. M., 386
Rotunda, 131-32, 136, 141, 203-5 *passim*, 212, 278, 315, 317; Annex to, 144; banquets at, 158-59; Confederate flag on, 195; burns, 301, 310, 474; restored, 310
Round Top Mountain, 13-14, 247
Rouss, Charles B., 311
Rouss, Peter, 311
Rouss Hall, 315, 396
Route 20, 177
Route 22, 443
Route 29, 6, 182, 288, 366, 439, 469, 471
Route 250, 98, 177, 288, 452, 459
Royal College of Surgeons, 25
Royal Orchard, 153-54, 378
Ruffner, William H., 234
Rugby (estate), 364
Rugby Circle, 400
Rugby Hills, 304
Rugby Road, 283, 304, 347, 358, 378; turntable on, 282, 284, 411
Runalds, Henry, 20
Rural Free Delivery, 271, 459
Rural Life Week, 356-57
Rutledge, 440
Ryan, Thomas Fortune, 374
Rye, 35

St. Anne's Parish, 29, 30, 31, 46, 61, 77-78, 95n, 145-46, 151

St. Anne's-Belfield School, 258, 329-
    30. *See also* Rawlings Institute
St. Luke's (lodge), 431, 432
St. Paul's Episcopal Church, 342
St. Paul's Memorial University
    Church, 341, 397
Salvage drives, in World War II,
    411-12
Salvation Army, 415
Sampson, Frank, 394
Sampson, John R., 259
Samuel Miller District, 42
Sandridge, Dorothy D., 397
Sandridge, Laurie K., Jr., 394
Sankey, Ira, 341
Saponi, 6
Saunders, John, 218, 263
Saunders House, 218
Savage, Thomas W., 164, 193, 228-29
Saxe-Weimar-Eisenach, Bernard Karl,
    duke of, 136, 182
Saxon, W. B., 386
Sayler's Creek, 201
Scales Creek, 13
Schenck's Branch, 246
Schuyler, 303*n*, 376, 453, 459, 468
Scotch, 39
Scotch-Irish, 78
Scotlands, 335
Scott, Daniel, 27, 40
Scott, Daniel (ca. 1850), 151
Scott, Mrs. Edward, 22, 269
Scott, Frederic, 378
Scott, John, 72-74, 84
Scott, Samuel, 27
Scott family, 90, 119, 153-54, 217
Scott Stadium, 354, 366, 378, 432
Scott's Landing, 64
Scott's Mill, 14
Scottsboro Boys, 432
Scottsville, 10, 14, 22, 72, 89, 95-99
    passim, 103, 108, 115, 156, 159,
    163, 169-80 *passim*, 187-96
    passim, 205, 209, 211, 233-35
    passim, 243, 245, 266, 267, 271,
    273, 286, 292-93, 300, 323, 326,
    333-40 *passim*, 345, 346, 376,
    398, 404, 405, 410, 420, 436, 443,
    452, 457-64 *passim*, 474, 478;

effects of canal on, 184-86; eco-
    nomic growth of, 183-86
Scottsville Courier, 263
Scottsville District, 425
Scottsville High School, 407
Scottsville Register, 263
Scottsville Road, 288
Sea Food Grill, 218
Sears Roebuck and Company, 271,
    390, 457
Secession, 192-94
Secretary's Ford, 28, 77, 177
Selden, Charles, 162
Semmes, Joseph E., 139
Seven Oaks, 294
Seven Pines, 200
Seventh Day Adventists, 341
Seward, William, 174
Sewerage system of Charlottesville,
    305
Shackleford family, 253
Shadwell, 109, 187, 202, 294, 401,
    412, 443; example of plantation
    economy, 36-38
Shallows, 10
Shannon, Edgar, 461-64 *passim*
Sharecropping, 221
Shaver, J. L., 398
Shelton, Clough, 55
Shelton, J. G., 467
Shenandoah Academy, 445
Shenandoah Valley, 1, 8, 61, 191, 192;
    influence of, 17-18, 92
Shepherd, John E., 304, 386
Shepherds (lodge), 431
Shepherd's Store, 295
Sheridan, Philip, 187, 192, 201, 208,
    211, 224, 252, 471
Shiflett, Bose, 374
Shiflett, Thomas, 61
Shiflett family, 61, 83
Shiloh Baptist Church, 428
Short, William, 113*n*
"Shot free" blacks, 428
Shryock, Richard H., 17-18
Shumate, Norman T., 347, 385
Shumate's Tavern, 14
Sieburg and Company (beverages),
    301
Sims, Richard D., 166

Sims, William, 48
Sinclair family, 217, 302
Sioux, 6
Skill Craft Clothes, 384
Skinner, John S., 90
Skyline Drive, 272, 366, 374, 376
Slater Fund, 326
Slavery, 107, 111-12
Slaves: ownership of, 34, 41, 42-43, 79, 84, 123-24, 142, 151-52, 167-68; price of, 36; treasonable acts by, 54n; number of, 83; attitudes toward, 114; runaway, 122-23; sale of, 123; treatment of, 124-27. See also Blacks
Slayden, Ellen Maury, 338
Smith, Alfred E., 374, 383
Smith, Ambrose Joshua, 20, 29
Smith, Daniel, 161-62
Smith, Francis H., 261
Smith, Gordon, 386
Smith, Gypsy, Jr., 341, 387
Smith, J. Mason, 414
Smith, J. Massie, 109
Smith, Mrs. James Gordon, 272, 393, 467
Smith, John, 5
Smith, Johnson, 54
Smith, Lindsay, 233
Smith College, 432
Smithfield, 335
Smith's Central Hotel, 173
Smith's Pasture Mountain. See Pasture Fence Mountain
Snead, L. R., 300
Snow, John, 42
Snow, Mrs. Leroy, 405
Soapstone, 262, 297, 303n, 366, 408, 453, 459
Social life, 75-76, 155-60, 264-66, 340-41, 345-49, 357-59, 386-87, 424, 464-66
Sons of Confederate Veterans, 343
Sons of Liberty, 195
South Anna River, 28
South Carolina, 249, 372
South Fork, 12-13, 181. See also Fluvanna River
South Garden, 40, 42, 233, 432, 460
Southall, James C., 126, 192, 232, 236

Southall, William H., 216, 228
Southern Aid Insurance Company, 429
Southern Guards, 195
Southern Planter, 125, 169, 184, 245
Southern Railway, 14, 203, 218, 243, 277, 286-87, 357-58, 427, 452, 459. See also Orange and Alexandria Railroad
Southern Welding and Machine Company, 408-10
Southside Club, 267
Southwest Mountains, 9, 12, 13, 19, 28, 29, 71, 72, 82, 94
Spanish-American War, 344
Sparks, Henry B., 289-94 passim
Spartanburg, S.C., 372
Spencer, Mrs. (teacher), 103, 159
Sperry Rand Corporation, 467
Sperryville, 338
Spicer, G. W., 381
Sports, 75-77, 141, 155, 266-67, 312, 327, 329, 344-45, 357-59 passim, 382-88 passim, 413, 432-33, 439, 466-67
Spotswood, Alexander, 6-8, 77
Spotsylvania County, 8, 201
Spottswood, William A. W., 134
Sprouse family, 83
Stack, Gerard E., 102, 103
Stampp, Kenneth, 119-20
Stanardsville, 206, 207, 243
Stanley, Thomas, 435-36
State agencies in Albemarle County, 457
State Farm Insurance Company, 456, 467
State Federation of Colored Women's Clubs, 428
State Highway Commission, 289
State Literary Fund, 102, 131
Stauffenberg, Ann Lenore, 169, 216-17
Staunton, 61, 65, 66, 103, 129, 181-89 passim, 196, 205-6, 229, 243, 267, 281, 288, 293, 295, 310, 336, 340, 346, 357, 365, 396, 451, 474
Staunton-Rockfish Gap Turnpike, 177-80. See also Rockfish Gap Turnpike

Stagecoaches, 182-83
Stecker, H. A., 380
Stevens, Bill, 450, 470
Stevens, Donald S., 386
Stevenson, Andrew, 151, 153
Stevenson, Sally Coles, 153-54
Stiles, Robert, 343
Stinson, L. R., 293
Stith, William, 19
Stockton, David, 42, 78n
Stockton Fork Cross Road, 294
Stockton's Creek, 13
Stockton's Mill Creek, 13
Stone, Charles A., 387
Stone, Whitney, 387
Stoneburner, William H., 400
Stony Point, 14, 98, 148, 163, 196,
    326, 346, 376, 382, 445, 460
Stranahan, Robert A., 387
Strange, John Bowie, 197-200 passim,
    212
Strasburg, 196
Stratton, Franklin A., 219
Strawberries, 250
Streetcars, 276-84, 364
Strickler, Sarah Anne, 209-10
Stuart, Alexander H. H., 221, 229,
    230
Stuart, J. E. B., 206
Stuart, James, 19
Student Army Training Corps, 354
Sturhahn, Ed, 373
Subversion, fears of, 190
Sugar Hollow, 340
Sugar Loaf Mountain, 12
Summer Hill. See West Cote
Sunnyside, 267
Sunset Lodge, 389, 451
Supervisors, board of: origins of, 215
Surber-Arundale Company, 302
Surry County, 75
Surveyors, 38
Swamp Creek. See Red Bud Creek
Swan Creek, 38
Swan Tavern, 64, 97, 98, 156
Swannanoa, 366, 382
Swanson, Gregory, 432
Sweet Briar College, 354
Syme, Milly, 82
Syme, Sally, 82

Tailors, 99
Talley, Mable Apple, 281, 290
Tallwood, 2, 5, 151
Tarleton, Banastre, 65-66
Tate, Thad, 56
Taverns, 40, 97, 98. See also Ordi-
    naries
Taxes, 83-84, 163-64
Tayloe, E. D., 346, 359
Taylor, Bennett, 266
Taylor, Fairfax, 227
Taylor, James, 227-28
Taylor, John (of Caroline), 82
Taylor, Rayfield Willer, 394
Taylor family, 253
Taylor Art and Literary Club, 428
Television, 466
Telegraph, criticism of, 172-73
Telephone, 248-49
Temperance Society, 141
Temple Beth-Israel, 268
Tennant, Charles C., 290, 346, 386
Terrell, Joel, 40, 42
Terry, Margaret Louise, 328
Test oath, 226
Tetlow, E., 160
Tetlow, G. A., 199
Thacker, William, 297
Thatcher, Aubrey B., 355
Thaw, Evelyn Nesbit, 352
Thaw, Harry K., 352
Thayer, James L., 266
Theaters, 156, 350-51, 362, 388, 466
This Week, 466
Thom, John, 166
Thomas (confectioner), 262
Thomas, Athanasius, 80
Thomas, C. M., 368
Thomas, Charles, 134
Thomas, Herbert, 200
Thomas, M. C., 300, 352, 386
Thomas, Norman, 379
Thomas, Robert W., 134
Thomas family, 83
Thomas Jefferson Inn, 452
Thomas Jefferson Memorial Founda-
    tion, 254, 369, 445-46, 470
Thomas Jefferson Memorial Fund,
    314-15
Thompson, C. L., 171, 228

Thompson, George, 199
Thompson, Joseph, 22, 23
Thompson, Roger, 20
Thompson, Roger, Jr., 20
Thompson family, 54
Thonton, William M., 289
Three Chopt Road, 28, 295. *See also*
Three Notched Road
Three Notched Road, 28, 40, 77, 78,
98, 177-81 *passim*, 188, 288, 293.
See also Three Chopt Road
Thurman, Benjamin, 19
Thurmond, Strom, 432
Tidball, William, 220-24 *passim*,
231-35 *passim*
Tidderdale, John, 56
Tilden, Samuel J., 236
Tilman, J. Dean, 386
Timberlake, E. J., 188
Timberlake, Walker, 217
Timberlake's Pharmacy, 355
Tinsley, J. W., 320
Tiverton, 293
Tobacco: influence of, 1-2, 16-17; cul-
tivation of, 31-32, 33-34, 168-69;
transport of, 32-33; manufacture
of, 94, 95-96; decline of, 44, 88-
89; appeal of, 171
Todd, F. C., 346
Toledo, Ohio, 387
Toll gates, 177-80 *passim*
Tonsler, Benjamin E., 327
Tonsler family, 427
Tories, 56
Tornadoes, 458
Totier, 22
Totier Creek, 19
Tourism, 389, 450-52 *passim*, 466,
472-76 *passim*
Town, Lt. (Freedmen's Bureau offi-
cial), 220
Town Hall, 160, 193, 195, 203, 216,
228, 248, 266. *See also* Levy
Opera House
Townshend Acts, 46
Treiber, M. (merchant), 262
Trent, Alexander, 40
Tribble, H. W., 330
Trice, O. A., 400
Tri-County Riding Club, 466

Trinity Episcopal Church, 420
Troubetzkoy, Prince Pierre, 361
Troy, T. O., 277, 278
Tubbs, W. Willoughby, 146
Tucker, Beverley D., Jr., 341
Tucker, George, 133
Tucker, Henry St. George, 139
Tudor Grove, 212
Tuesday Evening Concert Series, 466
Tufton, 104
Tulane University, 309, 314
Tullock, Thomas, 20
Turkey Run, 13
Turk's Gap, 12, 177
Turk's Gap Turnpike, 98
Turner, Eldridge, 323
Turpin, George R., 212
Turpin, Thomas, 38
Twyman, Fred W., 350, 372, 386
Tye River, 33, 69, 77
Tyler, John, 194
Tyree family, 119

Union College, 144
Union Ridge, 326, 376, 431. *See
also* Albemarle Training School
Union Run, 13
Uniroyal. *See* U.S. Rubber Company
United Daughters of the Confederacy,
343, 470
United Service Organizations, 415-16
U.S. Army's Foreign Service Tech-
nology Center, 457
U.S. Military Academy, 197, 261
U.S. Rubber Company, 410, 474
U.S.S. *Charlottesville*, 417
Universalists, 155
University Book Store, 141
University Hall, 452, 464
University of Virginia. *See* Virginia,
University of
University of Virginia Airport, 389,
402
University of Virginia Cemetery,
212, 343
University of Virginia Chapel, 257,
262, 474
University of Virginia Glee Club,
350
University of Virginia Hospital, 310-

University of Virginia Hospital
(*cont.*)
11, 353, 363, 366, 396, 420, 451,
456
University of Virginia Medical
School, 378. *See also* University
of Virginia Hospital
University of Virginia Record, 288,
302, 325-26
University Place, 304
University Press of Virginia, 467
University Virginia Magazine, 256,
257

Valentine, R. P., 276, 278, 282
Valley Turnpike, 183, 186, 288
Van Doren, M. L., 266
Van Wagenen, D., 347
Vance, Joseph C., 154, 219-22 *passim*, 226, 230, 234
Vanderbilt, William H., 260
Vandergrift, Alexander Archer, 391,
411, 417
Vandergrift, R. C., 269
Vandergrift and Son (contractors),
321
Vandevender, Grover, 373, 387
Vandevender, H. W., 458
Vaudeville, 350-51
Vaughan, Thomas W., 159
Vawter, C. E., 331
Vegetables, 35-36
Venable, Abraham, 29
Venable, Charles Scott, 327, 343
Venable School, 327, 376, 434-36 *passim*, 450
Verdeman, William, 20
Vestry, duties of, 29, 79
Via, Guy L., 349, 384
Via, Mrs. J. D., 301
Via, L. S., 346
Via family, 83
Victoria, Queen, 153-54, 416
Victory gardens, 353, 404-5
Viewmont, 124
Villa Crawford, 452
Vinegar Hill, 96, 103, 165, 218, 277,
290, 320, 327, 425, 426, 441;
conditions on, 429-30
Viniculture, 36, 86*n*, 249-50, 442

Virgin Spring Branch, 13
Virginia, University of, 14, 87, 93,
100, 212, 218, 221, 227, 234,
245, 294, 308-19 *passim*, 333,
358-70 *passim*, 377-80, 392, 394,
396, 419, 421, 428-33 *passim*,
443-46 *passim*, 451-56 *passim*,
461-64, 466, 470, 473, 476-77;
workmen at, 130-32; first students, 133-34, 141; first faculty,
133; begins classes, 133; student
rules, 134, 138; organization of,
134, 144-45; riots at, 137-38;
uniforms at, 138, 140; honor
code at, 139-40; student life at,
141; enrollment at, 142-44, 310,
315, 464; influence of, 145, 452-
56 *passim;* reaction to secession
at, 195; effects of Civil War on,
201-2, 255-56; bequests to, 259-
60, 311, 378; in World War I,
353-54; reputation of, 375; in
World War II, 415-17 *passim;*
Institute for Advanced Study at,
462
Virginia Advocate, 118
Virginia Braid Company, 407
Virginia Center for Creative Arts,
467-68
Virginia Central Railroad, 148, 188,
189, 205, 242-43. *See also* Chesapeake and Ohio Railroad
Virginia Council on Human Relations, 433
Virginia Gazette, 48
Virginia Loan and Trust Company,
263
Virginia Midland Railroad, 284-86,
299
Virginia Military Institute, 197, 333,
378
Virginia National Bank, 456
Virginia Piedmont Real Estate
Agency, 109
Virginia Players, 388
Virginia Polytechnic Institute, 309,
357
Virginia Protective Force, 395, 401,
402. *See also* Virginia State
Guard

Virginia Public Service Company, 284, 307, 372, 386
Virginia Quarterly Review, 379
Virginia Reserve Militia, 395, 401, 402
Virginia Stage Lines, 384, 451
Virginia State Agricultural Society, 166-67
Virginia State Guard, 396. *See also* Virginia Protective Force
Virginia Union University, 432
Virginia-Western Power Company, 284
Vogt, G. A., 441

Waddell, Mrs. Lyttelton, 412
Waddell, Richard E., 266, 350, 351
Waddell, W. W., 217-18, 237, 238, 245, 345
Wadsworth, James, 383
Walker, C. H., 282
Walker, Edward V., 395, 396
Walker, George E., 346
Walker, Gilbert C., 229, 230
Walker, John, 29, 46, 47, 48, 84
Walker, Lucy, 48
Walker, Thomas, 27, 29, 35-40 *passim*, 48, 65, 72, 82-86 *passim*, 107, 150, 151, 175, 239, 273, 364, 420, 446, 473; career, 68-69
Walker School, 437
Walker's Mill, 14
Wallace, William, 20
Wallace family, 8
Waller, Benjamin, 49
Waller, John, Jr., 20
Walter, Will, 386
Walter, Mrs. Will, 386
Walters, J. L., 269
"Waltons," 468
War bond drives, in World War II, 410-11
Ware, John, 48
Ware, Richard, 100
Ware, T. A., 266
Warminster, 25, 92, 129, 459
Warren, James, 42
Warren, 10, 19, 89-98 *passim*, 163, 233, 283, 284, 356, 458
Warrenton, 213, 281

Wars, effects of, 471
Washington, Booker T., 308-9, 340, 427
Washington, George, 23, 49, 152, 180, 315; birthday of, 156-58; Papers of, 464
Washington, D.C., 93, 99, 183, 191-94 *passim*, 213, 244, 286, 287, 329, 344, 346, 369, 387, 452, 466, 476
Washington and Lee University, 129, 358, 367
Washington City, Virginia Midland, and Great Southern Railroad, 286. *See also* Virginia Midland Railroad
Washington Monument, 158
Washington Park, 431
Washington Society, 141, 195, 336-38
Water Street, 218
Water supply, of Charlottesville, 247, 257, 304-5, 380
Watkins, Thomas G., 90
Watson (assaults British officer), 61
Watson, Fred L., 385
Watson, Norris, 345, 387
Watson, W. O., 247, 276
Watson, William, 100
Watts, Charles Wilder, 10, 42, 81; on land patents, 20, 21; on plantation economy, 36, 38; on colonial life, 70-72
Watts, David, 20
Watts, H. W., 386
Watts, Lucian M., 269
Watts, 287
Waud, Alfred R., 206-7
Wavertree Farm, 468
Wayland, E. M., 381
Wayland, J. F., 250
Wayland's, 254. *See also* Crozet
Wayland's Pavilion, 351
Waynesboro, 208, 209, 293, 420, 443, 451, 474
WCHV, 373, 405, 407, 451
Wealthy residents, influence of, 271-72, 275-76
Webb, William E., 219
Webb family, 14
Webb's Mountain, 12

Webster, Daniel, 150
Weld, Isaac, 76-77, 85-86, 478
Wells, C. C., 373
Wells, H. H., 229, 330
Wells, Marshall, 387
Wertenbaker, C. C., 226, 262
Wertenbaker, William, 134, 141
West, Jane, 119, 427
West, John, 427-28
West family, 427
West Cote, 25
West Indies, 35
West Virginia, 170, 287
Whateley, Walter, 331-32
Wheat, 44, 88-89, 92
Wheeler, B. E., 380, 382
Wheeler-Bennett, John, 416
Wheeling, W.Va., 445, 448
Whig party, 192-93
Whipple, Leonidas Rutledge, 354
Whiskey, 96, 97
White, E. B., 369
White, Isaac, 118, 170
White, Jeremiah, 42
White, John M., 269, 296, 300
White, Mary, 224
White, Mary Stamps, 396, 465
White, Preston, 224
White, Stanford, 310, 315, 352, 361
White Hall, 9, 14, 80, 163, 371, 383,
    385, 404, 416, 459, 478
White Hall District, 42
White Pine Health Resort, 347
Whiteside, William, 42
Whitlock, Rosetta Louise, 435
Whitmore, C. F., 302
Wiebel, L. H., Company, 408
Wilkerson, John, 40
Wilkerson, William L., 102
William and Mary, College of, 23,
    32, 81, 128, 129, 318
William of Orange, 15
William the Conqueror, 15
Williamsburg, 6, 8, 17-25 passim, 30,
    43-56 passim, 68, 109, 200, 367,
    472, 476
Wills, Fred William, 49
Wills, Frederick M., 171, 262
Wills, T. J., 300
Wills's Ice Pond, 165, 218

Wilmington, N.C., 313
Wilson, Joseph R., 314
Wilson, Woodrow, 256-57, 314, 340
Wilson, Mrs. Woodrow, 343, 382
Winchester, 183
Wingfield family, 83
Wingfield and Utz (carriage mak-
    ers), 262
Wingfield's, 163, 193
Winn, John, 99
Wirt, William, 133, 159
Wisconsin, University of, 445
Wolf Pit, 13
Wolf Trap, 13
Wolfe, William S., 442
Wolfe and Raphael (merchants),
    100
Woman's Land Army, 403-4
Wonderland, 279
Wood, Archibald, 20
Wood, B. I., 326
Wood, Claude, 398
Wood, Drury, 164
Wood, Isaac, 49
Wood, J. Edwin, 248-49, 300
Wood, J. Snowden, 269
Wood, John, Jr., 180
Wood, Lew, 263
Wood, Marion Jerome, 394
Wood, Marshall, 398
Wood, Robert, 373
Wood, Mrs. Warner, 358
Wood, William, 49
Wood family, 8, 42, 83. See also
    Woods family
Wood Field, 373
Woodbridge, 14
Woodfork, Richard, 80
Woods, Edgar, 36-42 passim, 49, 54,
    78n, 166, 170, 180, 187, 190, 259;
    on local place names, 10-15; on
    Reconstruction, 219, 230
Woods, J. B., 262
Woods, John R., 148, 167
Woods, Maude, 360
Woods, Micajah, 218, 264, 269, 296,
    323, 343, 344, 360
Woods, Michael, 19-20
Woods, Richard (pioneer), 39
Woods, Richard (teacher), 102

Woods, S. B., 269
Woods, Samuel, 74
Woods, T. T., 262
Woods family, 8, 42, 83. *See also*
    Wood family
Wood's Crossing, 211
Woods Station, 294
Woods's Gap, 12, 20, 28. *See also*
    Jarman's Gap
Woodville, 14, 163, 188. *See also* Ivy
Woodward, Fletcher, 387
Woody, John, 26, 28
Woolworth's, 384
Worrell, Thomas E., Jr., 467
Worrell Newspapers, Inc., 467
World War I, 284, 287, 344, 352-55
WPA, 388, 470
Wright, Willard Huntington (S. S.
    Van Dine), 278
WVIR-TV, 466

Xaupi, J. A., 159

Yager, Bessie, 320
Yancey, William L., 192
Yancey's Mill, 233, 460. *See also*
    Hillsboro
Yeargan, Johnny, 335
Yellow Mountain, 12
Yellow Transit Company, 451
YMCA, 141-42, 268, 341, 347, 357,
    368
Young Men's Business Club, 347, 349,
    371, 380
York River, 17, 50
Yorktown, 66, 150, 200
Young, H. E., and Company, 302
Yowell, Helen, 387

Zane, Jonathan, 448
Zion Union Baptist Church, 428
Zoning, in Charlottesville, 381

Illustration Credits

1: photo by Ralph R. Thompson, Charlottesville

2: portrait in Albemarle County Courthouse

3: from Mary Rawlings, ed., "The Albemarle.County Order Book, 1744–45—1745–46," *Papers of Albemarle County Historical Society* 5(1944–45): opp. p. 16

5: Merritt Todd Cooke Collection, University of Virginia Library

6, 7, 9, 11, 12, 15, 17, 20, 25, 27, 29, 31, 32, 33, 34, 36, 42, 43, 44, 45, 46, 50, 52, 53, 54, 56: Manuscripts Department, University of Virginia Library

8: from *Captain Jack Jouett, Junior, American Revolutionary War Hero, 1754–1822* (n.p.: Jack Jouett Chapter, National Society, Daughters of the American Revolution, 1966)

10, 68: Thomas Jefferson Memorial Foundation

13: Virginia State Library, Richmond

14: portrait in Gilmer Hall, University of Virginia

16: courtesy of Mrs. Theodore Murphy, Charlottesville

18: portrait owned by Mrs. Don-Michael Bird

19: from Virginia Moore, *Scottsville on the James* (Charlottesville: Jarman Press, 1969)

21: courtesy of Miss Anne Freudenberg, Charlottesville

22: from John R. Brown, "The Battle of Rio Hill," *MACH* 22 (1963–64): opp. p. 33

23: drawing by Henderson Heyward, from Mary Rawlings, *Antebellum Albemarle* (Charlottesville, 1935)

24: *The Daily Progress* (Charlottesville)

26: from *Autobiography of John E. Massey*, ed. Elizabeth H. Hancock (New York and Washington, D.C.: Neale Publishing Company, 1909)

28: from Henry E. Poindexter, "Henry Clay Marchant and the Foundations of the Charlottesville Woolen Mills, 1865–1882," *MACH* 14 (1954–55): opp. p. 34

30: courtesy of Misses Anne, Lucretia, and Maria Woods

35, 37, 38, 39, 40, 41, 51: Holsinger Studio Collection, University of Virginia Library

47, 48: courtesy of Miss Helen Duke, Charlottesville

49: from *The National Cyclopedia of American Biography*, vol. 40 (Clifton, N.J.: The James T. White & Company, 1955)

55, 57: from Gertrude Dana Parlier and others, *Pursuits of War* (Charlottesville: Albemarle County Historical Society, 1948)

58: photo by Morton & Roland, Arlington, Virginia
59: courtesy of Mrs. J. Rawlings Thomson
60, 61: Virginia National Bank
62, 65, 67: Charlottesville-Albemarle Chamber of Commerce
63: University of Virginia Information Services
64: Department of Graphics, University of Virginia
66: Daniel Grogan

915.5   Moore, John Hammond (B)
Cop. 12

Albemarle,
   Jefferson's county,
   1727-1976

DATE			